Early Modern Japan

A

Philip E. Lilienthal

Book

The Philip E. Lilienthal imprint
honors special books
in commemoration of a man whose work
at the University of California Press from 1954 to 1979
was marked by dedication to young authors
and to high standards in the field of Asian Studies.
Friends, family, authors, and foundations have together
endowed the Lilienthal Fund, which enables the Press
to publish under this imprint selected books
in a way that reflects the taste and judgment
of a great and beloved editor.

Early Modern Japan

Conrad Totman

UNIVERSITY OF CALIFORNIA PRESS
Berkeley · *Los Angeles* · *London*

University of California Press
Berkeley and Los Angeles, California

University of California Press, Ltd.
London, England

© 1993 by
The Regents of the University of California

First Paperback Printing 1995

Library of Congress Cataloging-in-Publication Data

Totman, Conrad D.
   Early modern Japan / Conrad Totman.
      p.   cm.
   "A Philip E. Lilienthal book."
   Includes bibliographical references and index.
   ISBN:13 978-0-520-20356-3
   ISBN 0-520-20356-9 (pbk. : alk. paper)
   1. Japan—History—To 1868. I. Title.
DS850.T68   1993
952'025—dc20   92-22617
                             CIP

Printed in the United States of America
09 08 07 06

9 8 7 6 5

*Dedicated to T. O. and Edie, Jean, Helen, Maida,
and my other lifelong friends in Amherst*

Contents

Illustrations

Abbreviations for Journal Titles

The following abbreviations are used in the footnotes and bibliographical essay.

AA   *Acta Asiatica*

Dower   John W. Dower, *Japanese History & Culture From Ancient to Modern Times: Seven Basic Bibliographies* (New York: Markus Wiener, 1986)

HJAS   *Harvard Journal of Asiatic Studies*

JAS   *Journal of Asian Studies*

JJS   *Journal of Japanese Studies*

MN   *Monumenta Nipponica*

TASJ   *Transactions of the Asiatic Society of Japan*

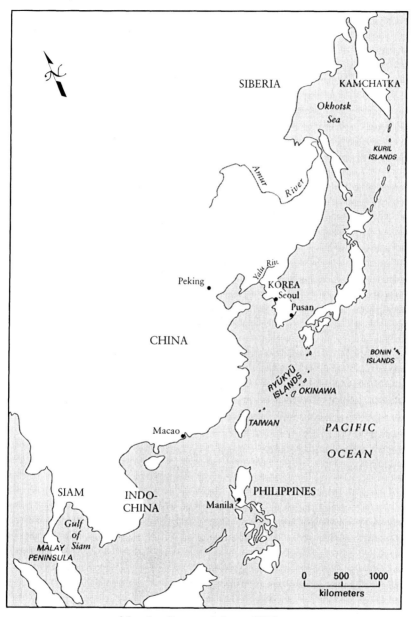

Map 1. Eastern Asia ca. 1800.

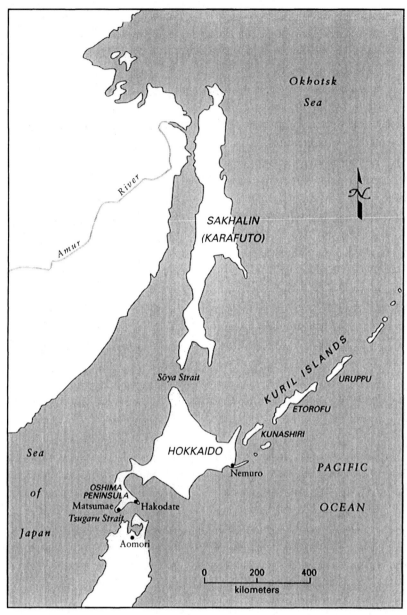

Map 2.   Ezo.

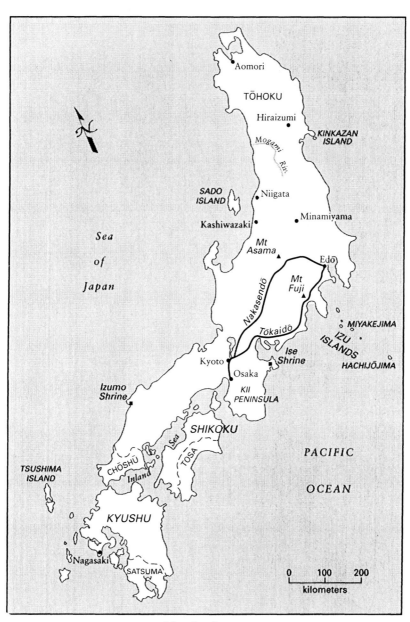

Map 3. Japan.

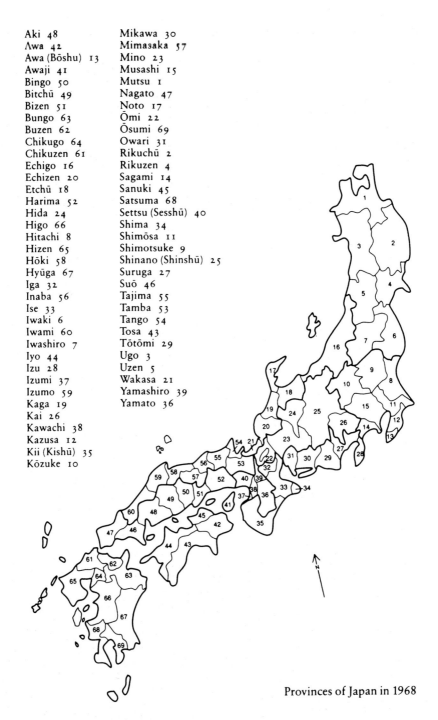

Aki 48	Mikawa 30
Awa 42	Mimasaka 57
Awa (Bōshu) 13	Mino 23
Awaji 41	Musashi 15
Bingo 50	Mutsu 1
Bitchū 49	Nagato 47
Bizen 51	Noto 17
Bungo 63	Ōmi 22
Buzen 62	Ōsumi 69
Chikugo 64	Owari 31
Chikuzen 61	Rikuchū 2
Echigo 16	Rikuzen 4
Echizen 20	Sagami 14
Etchū 18	Sanuki 45
Harima 52	Satsuma 68
Hida 24	Settsu (Sesshū) 40
Higo 66	Shima 34
Hitachi 8	Shimōsa 11
Hizen 65	Shimotsuke 9
Hōki 58	Shinano (Shinshū) 25
Hyūga 67	Suruga 27
Iga 32	Suō 46
Inaba 56	Tajima 55
Ise 33	Tamba 53
Iwaki 6	Tango 54
Iwami 60	Tosa 43
Iwashiro 7	Tōtōmi 29
Iyo 44	Ugo 3
Izu 28	Uzen 5
Izumi 37	Wakasa 21
Izumo 59	Yamashiro 39
Kaga 19	Yamato 36
Kai 26	
Kawachi 38	
Kazusa 12	
Kii (Kishū) 35	
Kōzuke 10	

Provinces of Japan in 1968

Map 4.   Provinces of Tokugawa Japan.

Map 5.   Castle Towns Mentioned in the Text.

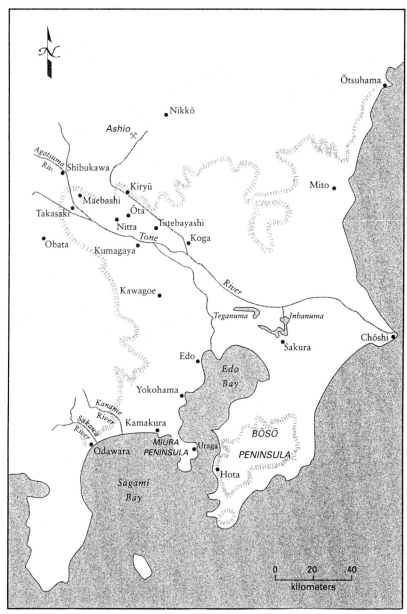

Map 6.   Kantō Plain.

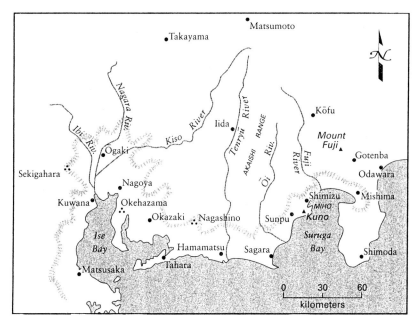

Map 7.   Tōkai Region.

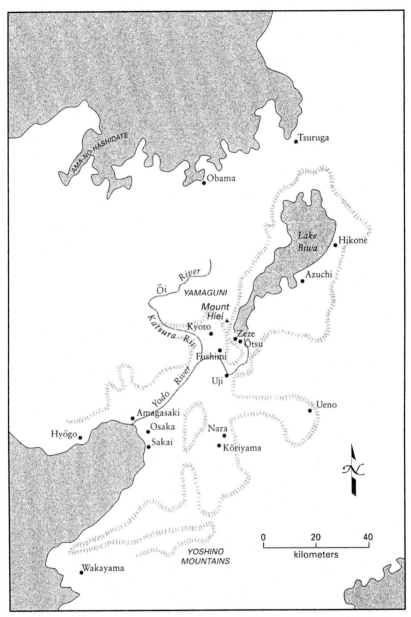

Map 8.   Kinai Basin.

Map 9. Kyushu.

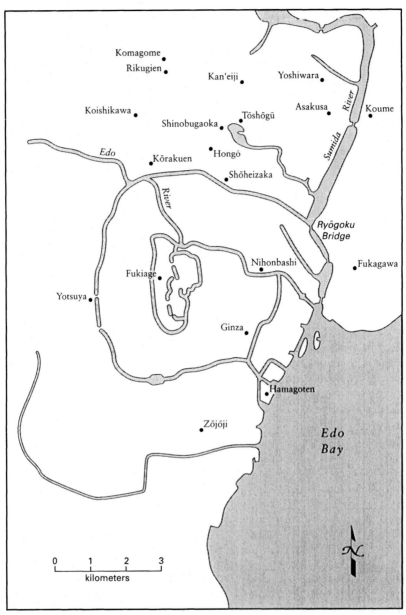

Map 10.   Edo.

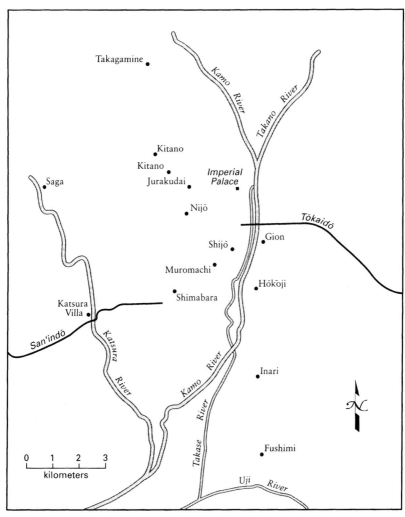

Map 11. Kyoto.

Introduction

In 1568 the powerful regional baron Oda Nobunaga marched his army from a castle near modern-day Nagoya into the ancient imperial capital city of Kyoto. There he compelled the powerless emperor Ōgimachi to recognize the hapless thirty-year-old Ashikaga Yoshiaki as fifteenth—and last—shogun, or military dictator, of the Ashikaga lineage.[1] Just three centuries later, in 1868, Kyoto was seized again, this time by leaders of powerful baronial armies from Satsuma and Chōshū in southwest Japan. They compelled the boy emperor Meiji to designate their forces imperial armies with the duty of crushing the hapless thirty-year-old Tokugawa Yoshinobu, fifteenth—and final—shogun of the Tokugawa lineage.

Between those two moments of imperial puppetry the people of Japan left a 300-year record of agonies and accomplishments that is instructive even today. Commonly called Japan's early modern period, these three centuries divide, in largest terms, into a century and a half of extraordinary growth and a century and a half of equally extraordinary stasis. The ingredients of that growth strike us as familiar because they generally conform to our notions of "progress," "development,"

---

1. Japanese names are given in the usual order, surname first, in the text of this book. Some individuals are subsequently identified by surname but many by given name, especially when the surname is common. In the footnotes and Suggestions for Further Reading in English, Japanese authors' names are given as they appear in the works cited, sometimes surname and sometimes given name first. Birth and death dates of Japanese historical figures appear in the index.

or "social growth": the polity was elaborated, scholarly and other higher cultural production flourished, the human population grew, cities and towns proliferated, economic output and material consumption rose, and exploitation of the ecosystem intensified enough to make all that possible.

The ingredients of stasis are more complex. In some sectors, they constituted near-absence of growth, but mostly they involved processes of displacement and transfer, with "more" in one area being offset by "less" in another. Overall, Japan's human population almost ceased to grow after about 1720, but in regional terms a near-balance was achieved, which involved population reduction in some regions, particularly the northeast, that offset continuing growth elsewhere, mostly in the southwest. Artistic and literary creativity continued, with an array of new genres developing, while others atrophied. The increased affluence of some social strata was offset by losses in others. To characterize the latter half of the early modern era in terms of stasis is not, moreover, to deny areas and eras of absolute growth, and one of our tasks will be to explore the types, timing, and logic of such growth.

These large-scale rhythms of growth and stasis reflected human rhythms of polity, economy, society, and culture, but they involved far more than just people. They also entailed a ceaseless interplay of people and their environmental context, which fundamentally determined the scope and nature of early modern Japan's growth and the necessity and shape of its stasis. To explain the dynamics of this history requires, therefore, much more than an examination of the human record. It also requires scrutiny of farmlands, forests, wetlands, and the sea, and of the creatures living therein. Unfortunately, it is impossible at present to study this broader history satisfactorily because much of the story, particularly that of the nonhuman players, is barely recorded. And where the record does exist, most of it is only beginning to be explored by historians, whether writing in Japanese or in foreign languages such as English. The reconstruction of this ecological experience attempted here thus inevitably has its gaps, which are bridged by suggestion and deduction when possible, but are as often as not left for others to explore and fill in coming years.

Even the human story has been told unevenly.[2] The era of growth

2. Footnotes identify the sources of quotations, as well as supplying data not commonly available and some opinion. They are also intended to guide readers to additional works, recent scholarship in particular. Considerable factual material also derives from

long received the lion's share of attention, especially in foreign languages.[3] The customary interest in political history encouraged that focus because it enabled one to concentrate on the drama of the early modern order's formation while sketching lightly the tedium of its later stability and deterioration. The study of intellectual and cultural history similarly focused on seventeenth-century thinkers and creative artists, who were seen as delineating an ideological order and creating cultural precedents that persisted thereafter.

During recent decades, however, more and more scholarship has focused on the latter half of the early modern period, and that monographic work makes it possible to treat the era of stasis more fully than do earlier historical overviews. Indeed, the present study gives considerably more attention to the latter half of the period than to the former.

This shift in temporal emphasis reflects a shift in interpretive premises. Today our society's belief in the limitless linear process commonly called progress is increasingly being challenged by rising awareness of the constraints a finite ecosystem imposes on human choice. As a result, the vision of history as a story of progress and the view that the historian's task is to construct narratives of that progress—images of polities becoming more structured and rational, economies becoming more commercialized, standards of living rising, literacy spreading, life spans lengthening, populations growing, cities burgeoning, intellectual life becoming more rational, political consciousness more widespread and informed—this sense of the historian's task seems less and less adequate.

Rather, we wonder how human social systems have functioned in their environmental contexts, how sustainable particular arrangements have been, and how the costs and benefits of those arrangements have been distributed among both the human and the nonhuman participants in the system. The present study endeavors to incorporate both

---

Japanese reference works, of which the following were particularly helpful: *Daijinmei jiten* [Biographical encyclopedia] (Tokyo: Heibonsha, 1958), 10 vols.; *Nihon rekishi daijiten* [Encyclopedia of Japanese history] (Tokyo: Kawade shobō shinsha, 1961), 22 vols., including *Nihonshi nenpyō* [Chronology of Japanese history] and *Nihon rekishi chizu* [Atlas of Japanese history]; *Nihon annai bunken chizu* [Atlas of Japan] (Tokyo: Shogakkan, 1965); and *Konsaisu chimei jiten: Nihon hen* [Concise geographical dictionary: Volume on Japan] (Tokyo: Sanseido, 1975).

3. The standard treatment in English is volume 3 of George Sansom's monumental *History of Japan* (Stanford: Stanford University Press, 1963), covering the years 1615–1867, in which Sansom devotes 150 pages to the century between 1615 and 1715 and 90 pages to the following 150 years. The 1560–1615 period is covered in 135 pages in volume 2.

the older perception of history as progress and the newer one of history as equilibria that form, fail, and form anew into an understanding, albeit incomplete, of Japan's early modern history.

In one specific sense the current state of scholarship encourages greater emphasis on the later Tokugawa period. Much of the early English-language work on Japanese history concentrated on diplomatic relations, leaving domestic developments badly underreported. During the past half-century, however, that imbalance has been redressed; indeed, scholarship of the recent past has tended to slight diplomacy in favor of internal affairs. Accordingly, the later chapters of this study devote substantial space to the impact of foreigners during the nineteenth century.

In a broader sense, too, the times invite a sharper focus on the diplomacy of those years. The two former "superpowers," having squandered their resources on their arms race and the comforts of the socially advantaged, now seem less and less able to enforce the post-1945 global distribution of power and privilege. One potential casualty of this changed situation is the fixedness of Japan's territorial boundaries, notably those of the far northeast. For years the Japanese government has, to no great effect, claimed sovereignty over a number of islands east of Hokkaido, including the two large and economically significant islands of Kunashiri and Etorofu, which were seized by military forces of the Soviet Union at the end of World War II.[4] That northern boundary may now be subject to renegotiation, and this book devotes several pages to tracing the early history of Russo-Japanese relations in the northerly region once known as Ezo.

This study's shift in temporal emphasis from early to later Tokugawa history does not, however, overcome all problems of imbalance and omission. Quite apart from the tentativeness of the environmental history, readers will find some aspects of the human story inadequately covered, despite the book's attempt to view its subject broadly. Perhaps the most disturbing lacuna relates to women, but family history as a topic, the truly poor, and pariahs as a group are also scarcely noted, and children, the elderly, and the handicapped escape almost untouched. Some facets of human culture—for example, music, folk dance, gō, shogi, sumō, flower arranging, attire—are untreated, and the Oki-

---

4. Kunashiri and Etorofu are Japanese pronunciations. Kunashiri is 577 square miles in area; Etorofu, 1,207. For comparison's sake, Oahu island (with Honolulu) has 598 square miles; Luxembourg, 999; Rhode Island, 1,067; Corsica, 3,367. Fisheries are an important part of the islands' economic value.

nawan and Ainu peoples and Japanese-Korean relations receive only cursory comment.

Finally, acknowledgements are due. Yale University granted me a year's respite from teaching to complete the manuscript. Even with time to write, however, the book simply would not have taken shape without the dedicated and careful monographic work of scores of scholars. Wherever possible I have relied on English-language works, citing some 350 of them in footnotes so that readers may explore topics further. In selected areas, such as fisheries and river policy, foreign scholarship scarcely exists, and I have accordingly relied on the work of Japanese scholars. I hope this volume will make scholarly accomplishments in both languages more widely known and inspire future scholars to enrich the corpus. The University of California Press has been generously cooperative and the comments and corrections of press readers wonderfully helpful.

PART ONE

Background

Like all human history, that of early modern Japan emerged from the interaction of accumulated historical precedent, conditions of the moment, and geographical context. Put differently, that history was the product of what was within the minds of human actors at any given moment, the social context that impinged on those actors, and the larger ecological context within which those internal and external factors interacted.

Part I begins with a concise review of the environmental context and a somewhat longer examination of those elements in Japan's pre-1568 history that seem most relevant to the early modern experience. The overview that completes this background foreshadows the chapters that follow by identifying basic aspects of the history that early modern Japanese shared and that seem particularly significant to readers today.

ONE

Geography and Climate

Aspects of Geography
Aspects of Climate and Ocean Currents
The Environmental Setting in 1600

The fundamental rhythm of Japan's early modern history sprang from the interaction of the human populace and its environmental surroundings. The lay of the land, the climate, and the flora and fauna that flourished there gave shape and limits to that human experience. They influenced not only the temporal sequence of growth and stasis but also the regional relationships of center and periphery and, later in the Tokugawa period, tension between southwest and northeast.

ASPECTS OF GEOGRAPHY

Since ancient times the heartland of Japanese civilization has been the Inland Sea region, particularly the rich Kinai basin at its eastern end. The Inland Sea permitted convenient, reasonably safe transportation and was lined with small but productive and comfortable sedimentary basins, supported by richly wooded hinterlands. As society grew during the centuries before 1600, the heartland was extended eastward along Honshu's southern littoral to the Kantō plain, the largest area of flat land in the country. This elongated strip of coastal plain retained its role as heartland because the Kinai, Nobi, and Kantō plains, all of which were attractive climatically, provided agricultural foundations large enough to support political organizations that ambitious leaders could employ to conquer outlying populations to the south and north.

During the early modern period, Japan consisted essentially of the

3

three major islands of Honshu, Kyushu, and Shikoku, with a gross land area of about 295,000 square kilometers (113,500 square miles), making it about the size of Arizona or Italy.[1] The three islands lie along the eastern edge of the Eurasian continent, extending from about 31° north latitude at the southern end of Kyushu to 42° at the northern tip of Honshu. The climate ranges from subtropical to cold temperate, roughly akin to the range between Georgia and New Hampshire on the east coast of North America. Natural forest vegetation ranges similarly from evergreen broadleaf in the south through deciduous broadleaf to coniferous boreal forest in the north and in higher mountain areas of central Honshu.

Japan's topography betrays its geologic youth. Mountain building in the region accelerated about 5 million years ago, becoming especially intense during the past 2 million years, so the archipelago's mountains are exceptionally young. As a corollary, they thrust skyward with exceeding abruptness, a characteristic unmodified by glacial activity, because Japan experienced little glaciation during the Pleistocene ice ages. Instead, the archipelago's mountains still culminate in sharp peaks and ridges, which are subject to uncommonly rapid erosion. Debris-laden streams and rivers rush precipitously down to the lowlands, where the detritus settles out to form alluvial fans and sedimentary flood plains.

The thrust-and-fold activity that formed the ranges proper has been supplemented by vulcanism, which has dotted the islands with volcanoes, lava and ash surfaces, and regions of continuing geothermal activity. Indeed, Japan's sixty-odd active volcanoes constitute about 10 percent of the total number of currently active volcanoes worldwide.[2]

The bedrock mountains produced by this tectonic activity constitute about 80 percent of Japan's modern land surface. The other 20 percent is sedimentary terrain of very recent provenance, situated in small basins, mostly fronting the sea and mostly giving way abruptly at their inland borders to acutely tilted mountain slopes. This means that easily manipulable surfaces are modest in scope and inelastic: when one reaches the edge of flatland, there is, except for fans and terrace deposits, very little in the way of gradually rising plains or hill country that can with somewhat more labor be turned to human use. Compared to most re-

---

1. As will be apparent in chapter 13, the island of Hokkaido, which was mostly populated by Ainu or other northern peoples, was a borderland, only its southern tip being subject to a sustained Japanese presence before the nineteenth century.
2. Yutaka Sakaguchi, "Characteristics of the Physical Nature of Japan with Special Reference to Landform," in Association of Japanese Geographers, ed., Geography of Japan (Tokyo: Teikoku-Shoin, 1980), p. 17.

gions of dense preindustrial population, this topography has helped make the transition from ampleness of land to ecological overload an exceptionally abrupt one.

On the other hand, because Japan was not subject to significant glaciation, its lowlands contain little glacial residue and their natural drainage systems have remained more regular in configuration and hydrologic behavior than in areas where glaciation has occurred. This more orderly lowland topography has fostered uniformity and regularity in land-use patterns—notably irrigated rice culture—and in the social arrangements that accompany them.

Pleistocene glacial cycles also shaped Japan's natural environment in another way that was consequential to early modern history. By dropping ocean levels substantially, the several epochs of glaciation periodically transformed Japan from an island chain into a mountainous northeastward extension of a vast coastal lowland that reached southward to Vietnam and westward to interior China. These events sustained Japan's association with the East Asian biome, enabling the archipelago to share in East Asia's extraordinary vegetational wealth. Whereas western Europe records about 80 species of indigenous trees and North America about 250, for example, East Asia, including Japan, numbers some 500.[3]

This richness of floral diversity has given the archipelago an extremely adaptable biosystem, which has offered humans a variety of resources and could make many responses to human encroachment. Unquestionably that biological diversity helped the island chain cope with the widespread deforestation, land reclamation, and population growth that marked the seventeenth century.

ASPECTS OF CLIMATE AND OCEAN CURRENTS

Situated in the Earth's northern temperate zone, Japan experiences a regular seasonal pattern that assures the islands of ample precipitation, averaging 180 centimeters annually, ranging from more than 400 in the southwest to about 100 in the northeast. This moisture enables the island chain to convert its rich floral potential into uncommonly lush

3. Franz Heske, *German Forestry* (New Haven: Yale University Press, 1938), p. 52. Heske attributes Europe's silvic poverty to the region's east-west running mountains, which stymied Pleistocene plant migration. More recently, I. G. Simmons, *Biogeography: Natural and Cultural* (North Scituate, Mass.: Duxbury Press, 1979), p. 114, has reported the maximum number of plant species at forty per hectare in North America and eight per hectare in Europe, a disproportion somewhat greater than Heske's.

forest cover. However, the combination of steep slopes and heavy rainfall gives the archipelago one of the world's highest rates of natural erosion, and that condition, which is sporadically intensified by the natural shocks of earthquake and vulcanism, can also be exacerbated by human activity, as we shall see. Climate thus complicates hillside tillage and reinforces the abruptness of transition from potentially arable to nonarable terrain.

The island chain's mountainous backbone and its 1,500 kilometer length from northern Honshu to southern Kyushu give Japan's climate important regional variations. On the Sea of Japan littoral, cold, snowy winters have discouraged human settlement, whereas generally sunny winters along the Pacific seaboard have made habitation comparatively pleasant. Although annual precipitation is high along the Sea of Japan, furthermore, the bulk of it comes as snow and rushes to the sea as spring runoff, providing relatively little value for cropping. In the southwest, by comparison, most precipitation comes as rain, and the growing season is long enough to permit widespread double cropping.

Agriculture in northern Honshu, especially along the Sea of Japan, has been discouraged by summer weather as well as winter, because the area is subject to the *yamase* effect, in which cool air from the Sea of Okhotsk irregularly prevails throughout the summer, sharply lowering temperatures and damaging agricultural production.[4] The impact of the yamase effect has been especially serious for rice culture because the type of rice grown in Japan (*Oryza sativa japonica*) requires a mean summer temperature of 20° centigrade or higher to flourish.[5] A drop of 2–3° can lead to a 30–50 percent drop in rice yield. The yamase influence can produce an even greater drop than that and appears to have played an important role in crop failure and famine of the later Tokugawa period.

Annual rhythms of climate have thus shaped Japan's agricultural capacity and sharpened regional differences. In the longer term, as well, fluctuations in temperature have affected human affairs. Most significant for this study, there is a close correlation between unusually low summer temperatures during the 1780s and 1830s and crop failures that led to two exceptionally severe periods of famine in northern Ja-

---

4. Ikuo Maejima, "Seasonal and Regional Aspects of Japan's Weather and Climate," in Association of Japanese Geographers, ed., *Geography of Japan,* p. 67.

5. H. Arakawa, "Three Great Famines in Japan," *Weather* (publ. by the Royal Meteorological Society, London) 12 (1957): 211–12. Strictly speaking, there are several varieties of *japonica* rice, with modest variations in climatic tolerance among them.

pan. The timing of those disasters may reflect a longer-term "Little Ice Age" in the later Tokugawa period.[6] Or it may indicate that human activity had altered the landscape, particularly in the northeast, in ways that made crops more vulnerable to cold summers than during earlier centuries. Or it may simply reveal that inequities in the distribution of yield had become so pronounced by then that the poor succumbed in time of stress. In any case, the situation surely added to the regional tensions between northeast and southwest.

In short, the climate in general and patterns of precipitation in particular have historically encouraged the Japanese to cluster their settlements along the southern littoral, most densely along the sheltered Inland Sea, and it is only more recently that they have reluctantly moved into the northeast and the coastal plains facing the Sea of Japan. In the latter areas, the limits that topography imposes on production are drawn tighter by climate, with the result that agricultural output has been more modest and less reliable, making it easier to fall short of the margin needed for survival once the human population reached the limits of a given locality's carrying capacity.

This general climatological bias in favor of the south has long been reinforced by the flow of offshore ocean currents. The southern coast is warmed by the *kuroshio,* or Japan Current, which carries equatorial water from east of the Philippines northward through the Ryūkyūs, eastward along the coast south of the Kantō plain, and on into the Pacific. North of the Kantō, by contrast, the *oyashio,* or Chishima Current, brings arctic water down along the Kurils, past Hokkaido, to the east coast of northern Honshu, depressing ambient temperature and shortening the growing season, thereby exacerbating the north-south distinction.

These warm and cold currents also exerted other influences on early modern Japan. They helped give the archipelago rich and varied sources of fish, shellfish, seaweed, and other marine products. The rich fisheries

6. Arakawa, "Three Great Famines," pp. 212–17. Sources do not fully agree on whether the century or two before 1850 were generally colder than earlier ones. Most notably, see Takeo Yamamoto, "On the Nature of the Japanese Climate in So-called 'Little Ice Age' between 1750 and 1850," *Geophysical Magazine* 35-2 (Jan. 1971): 165–85, and the following essays by Arakawa: "Twelve Centuries of Blooming Dates of the Cherry Blossoms at the City of Kyoto and Its Own Vicinity," and "Remarkable Winters in Japan from the Seventh Century," both in *Geofisca pura e applicata* 30 (Jan. 1955): 144–46, 147–50; "Fujiwhara on Five Centuries of Freezing Dates of Lake Suwa in the [*sic*] Central Japan," *Archiv für Meteorologie, Geophysik und Bioklimatologie,* ser. B, 6 (1955): 152–66; "Climatic Change as Revealed by the Data from the Far East," *Weather* 12 (1957): 46–51; and "Dates of First or Earliest Snow Covering for Tokyo since 1632," *Quarterly Journal of the Royal Meteorological Society* 82 (1956): 222–26.

off the coast of northeast Honshu, for example, provided many villagers with employment during the later Tokugawa period, when
wholesale harvesting of marine life became economically feasible owing
to a rise in demand for fish-meal fertilizer. This growth in maritime
exploitation added a new dimension to the economic relationship between the northeast and the metropolitan region around Edo—today's
Tokyo. Within a few decades, however, those same fisheries became
targets of American and European whalers, whose appearance on the
scene promoted a transformation in Japan's external relations that culminated in destruction of the Tokugawa order.

THE ENVIRONMENTAL SETTING IN 1600

To the people of sixteenth-century Japan, the geography and climate of
their realm were too commonplace for comment. For travelers from
afar, however, they were distinctive and received considerable mention,
so visitors' observations give us a look at the land. The foreigners did
not, of course, see with unprejudiced, all-knowing eyes. An observer
carrying in his mind recollections of the lush, rolling hills of Kent surely
saw Japan differently from one making a silent comparison with the
arid plateaus of Iberia. The traveler to southern Kyushu could not thereby
know Tōhoku. The year-long sojourner could observe more than the
springtime visitor. The commentator moved by aesthetics did not report
in the same way as one looking for crops of value. Despite the idiosyn-
cracy of every observer, however, we can still glean from these reports
a partial picture of this island realm in the years around 1600.[7]

The richness of the archipelago's biological inheritance impressed one
of the earliest European visitors, Jorge Alvares, a Portuguese merchant
who described the lush vegetation he had seen in the vicinity of Kagoshima in 1546:

> It is a beautiful and pleasing country, and has an abundance of trees, such
> as the pine, cedar, plum, cherry, peach, laurel, chestnut, walnut, oak (which
> yields many acorns) and elder. . . . There is also much fruit not to be found
> in our country; they grow the vegetables which we have in Portugal, except
> lettuces, cabbages, dills, corianders, and even mint; all the rest they have.
> They also cultivate roses, carnations and many other scented flowers, as well

7. The quotations that follow can be found in Michael Cooper, *They Came to Japan:
An Anthology of European Reports on Japan, 1543–1640* (Berkeley and Los Angeles:
University of California Press, 1965), pp. 6–7 (Jorge Alvares), 10–11 (João Rodrigues),
7–8 (Arthur Hatch), and 10 (Bernardino de Avila Girón).

as both sweet and bitter oranges, citrons (though I did not see any lemons), pomegranates and pears.

The land is intensely cultivated and each year three crops are laid down in the following manner. In November they sow wheat, barley, turnips, radishes and other vegetables, such as beet, which they eat; in March they sow Indian corn, maize, mangoes, chick-peas, beans, artichokes, cucumbers and melons; in July they sow rice, yams, garlic and onions. The land is fertilised each time with horse manure and dug with a spade, and then left fallow for a year. They use small, tough horses when working the land because they have but few cows, although in some places they use cows.

There are no pigs, goats or sheep, and only a very few stringy hens. They hunt and eat deer, rabbits, pheasants, quails, doves and other birds. They hunt deer and rabbits with bows and arrows, and catch birds with nets. The nobles employ splendid hawks and falcons and I was told that they also hunted with royal eagles, but only the great lords were allowed to keep these birds for their amusement.

João Rodrigues, a Portuguese Jesuit who lived several years in Japan, commented on the scarcity of arable land and the comparative absence of contagious disease:

Although in various regions of the kingdom of Japan there are broad and ample plains, cultivated or otherwise, the country is in general very mountainous with great lofty ranges and dense forests of trees. Some mountains are so high that their peaks pierce the very clouds, which in some places remain far below the summit. As Japan is so mountainous the country is more barren than fruitful, and hence they must diligently dung the land in order to raise crops every year.

The air is extremely wholesome and temperate and thus there are no prevailing maladies, such as the plague, in the kingdom. As a result the common people, who are not given to luxuries, usually lead a long life, and the old folk are well disposed, strong and healthy.

Arthur Hatch, an Englishman who visited Hirado in 1620 also noted the mountainous character of the country, its dearth of flatlands, and its comparative freedom from epidemic disease, as well as its disruptive storms and earthquakes:

The Countrey of Japan is very large and spacious, consisting of several Ilands and pettie Provinces; it is Mountainous and craggie, full of Rockes and stonie places, so that the third part of this Empire is not inhabited or manured; neither indeed doth it affoord that accomodation for Inhabitants which is needfull, or that fatnesse and conveniencie for the growth of Corne, Fruit, and small grayne as is requisite; which causeth the people to select the choysest and plainest parts and places of the land both to till and dwell in. The Climate is temperate and healthie not much pestred with infectious or obnoxious ayres, but very subject to fierce windes, tempestuous stormes, and terrible Earthquakes, insomuch that both Ships in the harbour have been over-set, and driven ashore by the furie of the one, and Houses on the land disjoynted and shaken to pieces by the fearefull trembling of the other.

Finally, Bernardino de Avila Girón, a Spanish merchant who spent some years in Japan, commented on mineral resources and weather in 1619,

There are many gold and silver mines in this realm, and at the present day only the king still works them. But there are mines everywhere and the metal is of high quality; the gold ore is so rich that they obtain ten *taels* of gold from every spadeful. In the same way there is a great deal of copper and iron which they extract very easily. There is also quicksilver and lead.

The land for the most part is barren with many mountains and high ranges. It is exceedingly cold with much snow and the cold weather often lasts from October to April, in which last month it sometimes snows. And the hot weather lasts from July to the middle of September, the pestilential and unbearable dog-days beginning on the sixth day of July. But there is no regularity in this either and it varies from year to year.

In sum, these voyagers found Japan a mountainous land, its plains few but—by European standards—vigorously tilled. Despite its volcanoes and earthquakes, it seemed an agreeable place to dwell. Particularly to Iberian eyes, it was a lush realm, well peopled, and fruitful. And it had been so for centuries.

TWO

The Human Legacy

Village Japan
The Superordinate Few
  The Political Legacy
  The Religious Legacy
  The Commercial Legacy
The Urban Tradition

By 1568 Japan was one of the world's largest civilizations, with over 10 million people living on the three main islands of Honshu, Kyushu, and Shikoku and the countless islets that dot their coastal waters. They inherited a rich historical legacy, which exercised a commanding influence on the three centuries of early modern history.[1] The legacy was imbedded in towns and villages scattered all across the archipelago, but its most visible aspects appear in the record of the superordinate few: the rulers, religious leaders, and others who constituted the social elite.

VILLAGE JAPAN

Most sixteenth-century Japanese lived in villages whose size—generally numbering from a few to scores of dwellings—depended on the productive capacity of the locality. Villages usually were larger on the broader plains, smaller in mountain valleys. Their occupants survived primarily on local agricultural output, but many supplemented that with specialized production for market.

Agricultural production consisted mainly of wet-field rice, dry-field grains, and other dry-field crops. Meat and milk production was nil; there were no sheep or goats, and cattle and horses ordinarily were used only to carry and haul. In upland areas, some dry-field crops were grown

1. For more information on Japanese history before 1568, see Suggestions for Further Reading in English.

through slash-and-burn techniques, but most fields, like the thatch-roofed settlements themselves, were permanent. Some rural production was for home consumption, but some was for barter, some for sale, and perhaps a third or more went to the superordinate few in the form of rent and tax payments.

Depending on its location, a village's market goods included fish, salt, seaweed, other marine products, timber, firewood, charcoal, other forest products, vegetable oils, reeds for mats, pottery, roof tile, and diverse handicraft goods. They also included the grains themselves, although much grain, rice in particular, left villages as rent and tax payments. The use of money was so widespread that tax collectors commonly defined the taxable value of land in terms of the anticipated cash value of its production. In central Honshu, at least, creditors and debtors calculated their obligations in money terms, and money expedited commercial transactions throughout the islands.

The technology of production was reasonably specialized. To produce field crops, villagers prepared the soil with iron spades and hoes and iron-pointed plows pulled by draft animals. They harvested with knives, sickles, and flails. For wet rice production, they maintained stream- and pond-fed irrigation systems, whose complexity varied with local topography. They used boats, nets, and lines in fishing, and in forest work they employed hatchets, axes, wedges, and winches, as well as various tools for measuring, sawing, and shaping wood. Where appropriate, they knew how to operate such manufacturing devices as forges, kilns, potters' wheels, oil presses, spinning and weaving frames, fermenting vats, evaporating pans, and drying racks. Finally, they employed raised storage sheds to preserve the harvest from rot and infestation.

Village life embodied a mix of hierarchical and egalitarian relationships. An inherent tension existed between the tendency of some villagers to dominate their fellows and the need for villagers as a group to collaborate in the face of a hostile world. The tension could deteriorate into absconding, harassment, legal disputes, or even violent confrontation, but it was commonly kept within manageable limits by development of procedures and attitudes that acknowledged the special place of the locally powerful while they accommodated the needs of fellow villagers.

Both the hierarchical and egalitarian qualities of village life sprang from the ecological realities of rural existence in late medieval Japan. Villages were organized in household units, and in most villages some households controlled disproportionate amounts of land and labor, which gave them a preponderant role in village affairs. These preeminent families might retain their status from generation to generation, and often they functioned as local political and even military leaders. They might enjoy some formal association with regional power holders, which could bring recognition of them as a legitimate military, or samurai, family.

Whether regarded as heads of samurai households or not, these local men of power commonly supervised the agricultural activity of nearby households. They organized land-clearing projects, developed irrigation works, oversaw planting and harvest, managed tax collection and transport, provided largesse and leadership in times of crop failure or other crisis, and probably played a key role in arranging marriages and mediating village disputes. As quid pro quo, they received rent in goods and services, secured extra labor as needed for their land, and enjoyed bigger houses, more luxuries, and more esteem than their neighbors. Villagers understood their hierarchical relationship to be one of "asymmetrical mutual reciprocity," in which local leaders were to command and nurture their subordinates while the latter served and obeyed them, the relationship being viewed in terms of father and child, main and branch household, or leader and follower.

Villages also utilized egalitarian arrangements, particularly in the larger rice-growing plains of central Honshu, because all villagers had a vested interest in maintaining irrigation works, deciding how water was to be allocated, and regulating the use of common land. This last ordinarily was forest or brush land that provided fodder, fuel wood, green fertilizer, construction timber, and emergency foodstuffs. Where higher political authority was fragmented and armies were on the loose—as was the case in much of Japan during the century up to 1568—residents had a shared interest in defending themselves against outsiders.

These shared interests brought neighbors together in assemblies or other communal organizations that drew up and enforced regulations for their villages. Village codes dealt with such matters as how strangers and migrants were to be treated, where houses might be built, how common land was to be used, how community entertainments were to be funded, what things were forbidden, how offenses were to be defined, and what punishments would be meted out to offenders.

Egalitarian practices such as dividing the yield from common lands equitably or assembling as equals to discuss and decide village matters were justified in diverse ways. In some instances, villagers claimed that every honorable person had a basic right to survive, and hence to be heard in village affairs. In others, they contended that they, unlike outsiders and newcomers, had a right to be heard and heeded because of their long-established presence in the village. In yet others, they asserted a more limited right as members of the local temple or shrine, whose parishioners stood as equals before their deity.

As this last observation suggests, Buddhist temples and Shintō shrines were widely scattered through the countryside. Sites dedicated to specific deities, whose formal religious identity or affiliation might be quite unknown to local people, were innumerable, some marked by nothing more than a heap of stones or a small statue. In larger villages, more substantial shrines and temples existed, often supported by tithes, volunteer labor, or the yield from village land dedicated to their support. Many were branches of major sects, such as Ikkō or Hokke Buddhism. Those sects consisted of a central temple in or near Kyoto and branch and local temples scattered through the countryside. In vigorous sects, local temples might become the political centers of village life, even forming regional confederations, with priests deploying villagers for military action against rival temples or outside military leaders.

The role of religion in village life entailed far more than politics, needless to say. Temples and shrines provided sites for handling community business as well as the sacred routines of prayer and communion with the gods. Religious events, both those common to society at large and those peculiar to specific localities, offered occasions for recreation, served to mark the seasons and years, and helped tame the terrors of life's passage. A rich array of deities, spirits, and forces filled the lives of villagers, helping them explain the inexplicable and providing both beneficent powers to be thanked and unpredictable or downright nasty powers to be avoided, appeased, bullied, or berated, whichever seemed most helpful.

This pattern of village life—of large, permanent villages set among permanently cultivated fields and organized internally for purposes of local management and participation in the broader economy—was a recent development, accompanying the rise of a more intensive agriculture from around the thirteenth century. By 1560, the regimen of moderately intensive agriculture had helped transform villagers in much of central Japan into players on the local political scene. Whether organized around temples, local samurai, or their own most vigorous members, some villagers lived in defensible, moated communities, devised their own villagewide command structures, and maintained the capacity to fend off attackers. To an extent unprecedented in Japanese history, the superordinate few had to take peasants into account when pursuing their ambitions. Only by doing so could they stop the insurgencies that continually thwarted attempts to repacify a realm that had been convulsed by a century of endemic warfare.

THE SUPERORDINATE FEW

The superordinate few in any society can be viewed as a tripartite elite: those whose privileges are sustained by the force of their ideas, those who rely on politico-military might, and those who use economic power. All three groups can use their particular strength as carrot or stick, to entice or threaten. The three strengths may, of course, be found in a single person or group, but if viewed separately, they constitute the religio-intellectual, politico-military, and economic or commercial elites. In historical practice, the three are habitually entwined: myth, muscle, and money work as one, or social order weakens.

In Japan these political, ideological, and economic aspects of elite status have been linked from prehistoric times. When the linkages have decayed, there has been a clear connection between their dissolution and the more general dissolution of social order. Most pertinently, during the fifteenth century, a political system anchored in reasonably unified military arrangements, durable methods of taxation, and a supportive ideology fell apart when the claimants to political authority lost control of empowering ideas and essential income. The result was a century of endemic warfare that lasted from 1467 until the 1560s. In the decades after 1568, the construction of new linkages between ideology, armament, and the economy was a central theme of Japanese history. The linkages that took shape—and that made possible early modern Japan's era of dynamic growth—derived much inspiration from the social elite's political, religious, and economic legacies.

THE POLITICAL LEGACY

The political legacy of late-sixteenth-century Japan contained three main components, each a product of a different epoch. The first was the legacy of the *tennō*, or emperor, which formed in the seventh and eighth centuries. The second was that of the shogun, or hegemonial military leader, which emerged during the twelfth and thirteenth. The third was that of the daimyo (literally, "great name"), or regional baron, which took shape during the fourteenth to sixteenth centuries. This third component proved to be the fountainhead of the repacified realm, but those who imposed order on late-sixteenth-century Japan employed all three legacies, and all survived as elements in early modern governance.

Before the seventh century, a lineage group (*uji*) known as the Yamato uji exercised a dominant role in the Kinai region. Its dominance was based on a claim to special religious authority derived from the gods (*kami*), an array of political alliances based on hereditary kinship associations, and a tribute base anchored in village production. As Yamato leaders extended their sway eastward and westward, they encountered more complex domestic political problems and became entangled in diplomatic difficulties with the new and mighty T'ang dynasty in China. To cope, they undertook political reforms that incorporated T'ang legitimizing principles and bureaucratic practices. These included the Confucian concept of the emperor as sole ruler, bureaucratic organs of central, provincial, and local government, a military system based on conscription, and an elaborate tax system tied closely to the productive capacity of land.

By skillful maneuver and successful warfare, Yamato uji chiefs, now calling themselves emperors, reformed their political system, discredited rival claimants to the throne, established direct control over much tax land, and extended administrative authority into most settled areas from the Kantō plain westward. During the eighth century, they enhanced the awesomeness of their regime by building a grand palace and fine mansions in a durable capital city, Nara in 710 and Heian in 794. They deepened their government's sacred character by linking it closely to Buddhism. The monastery that gave physical expression to the ideal of church-state symbiosis was the Tōdaiji, whose Buddha hall was reputedly the largest wooden structure ever erected, which Emperor Shōmu ordered built in Nara during the 740s. Its beneficent powers were extended into the hinterland through the construction of provincial monasteries, or *kokubunji*.

This centralized imperial bureaucracy constituted the government of Japan for the next four centuries. It gradually lost effectiveness, however, as its leaders assigned more and more productive land to monasteries and hereditary aristocratic families, the *kuge,* as part of a "pork-barrel politics" that emperors and senior officials used to shore up their political alliances of the moment. The strategy gradually reduced officialdom's control over rural production, and defiance of imperial authority increased in both frequency and scale, with religious leaders, landed aristocrats, and local men of power repeatedly using their muscle to extract further concessions in return for momentary peace. By 1200 the cumulative effect was to convert about half of all imperial tax land into chartered corporate estates (*shōen*) controlled by semi-autonomous religious institutions and aristocratic households.

Even as tax land was alienated, the government also lost control of its military forces. The conscript system disintegrated during the eighth and ninth centuries, and thereafter government leaders relied increasingly on professional military men, or samurai (*bushi*), who hired out their services, together with those of their followers. Government leaders used these men in a number of ways, most notably to keep the peace in Heian and to conduct border wars. These latter gradually extended imperial authority into the northeast, despite resistance from the local population, a people known as the Ezo or Emishi. For decades these mercenary samurai performed their peacekeeping duties reasonably satisfactorily, and more and more of their leaders rose to eminent positions in the Heian government. As time passed, however, they became ambitious and dissatisfied, and insurrections became more frequent and more serious. From the eleventh century on, the imperial regime found itself losing control of both army and income and saw its pretensions to govern ever more widely questioned.

By the 1150s, commanders of samurai bands were, in fact, the most powerful men in Japan. During the next three decades, leaders of major military coalitions maneuvered and fought for supremacy, until Minamoto no Yoritomo emerged victorious, defeating a coalition of bushi led primarily by members of the sprawling Taira family. Probably because his home territory lay in the Kantō, Yoritomo established a military headquarters (*bakufu*) at Kamakura. He and leaders in Heian then worked out a division of control, in which he received more estate lands, specific rights to tax income, and authority to enforce tax collection and military deployments. In return he recognized Heian authority in most judicial matters and agreed to uphold most existing tax and administrative arrangements on shōen and imperial tax lands.

The title *seii taishōgun*, handsomely translated as "barbarian-subduing generalissimo," was one of several Yoritomo received from the emperor. He and his successors held on to power long enough to give their shogunal authority the legitimacy of custom, and the Kamakura regime became the first of three successive shogunal governments, or bakufu, that dominated Japan's political history until 1868. Like its

successors, it was an overtly military regime that claimed to be keeping
the peace at imperial behest. In fact, it kept the peace on behalf of its
own members through the maintenance of superior standing forces,
consisting of the shogun's administrative subordinates and vassals
(*gokenin*) and their retainers, who were financed by combinations of
stipend and yield from assigned lands.

In terms of the money-muscle-myth nexus, it should be noted that
Yoritomo's shogunate reconsolidated the three in a way that divided
them between his new regime and the old imperial one, leaving considerable legal authority and wealth, as well as some armed power, in the
latter's hands. Bakufu leaders justified the power they did exercise by
claiming that they had restored order to the realm, that they respected
imperial authority and existing elite claims to land and income, and that
they were performing their "familial" task of nurturing the personal
followers of the Minamoto family head. From the outset, then, the ideology of shogunal rule linked its own legitimacy to preservation of imperial and elite privilege. It did not purport to stand alone, much less to
stand society on its head; instead, it divided control of the realm with
cooperative others. Kamakura's claim to a monopoly over arms, income, and ideology was thus qualified, not absolute.

Initially, these arrangements sufficed to keep the peace. As decades
passed, however, changes in rural society enabled the countryside to
support ever-larger numbers of people who had not been socialized to
the ideology of the regime and who were unable to share in its largesse.
Proliferating bands of local warriors became more and more contemp-
tuous of the urban elite and more defiant of both shogunal and imperial
authority. This was especially true after they repelled at great cost two
massive Mongol invasions during 1274 and 1281, for which service
they received little thanks and even less recompense. So they encroached
on shōen and imperial tax lands, generating legal disputes and armed
clashes.

Under this assault by the aggrieved and ambitious, the division of
privilege originally worked out by Yoritomo and Heian leaders eroded.
That process both fostered and reflected the disintegration of imperial
and shogunal legitimacy, which trend culminated during the 1330s in a
flurry of rebellions against Kamakura. Emperor Godaigo made an un-
successful attempt to restore imperial power, but Ashikaga Takauji, an
erstwhile lieutenant of Kamakura's and the head of a military coalition,
finally seized control. He caused a puppet emperor to award him the

title of shogun and used his power to establish a new bakufu in the Muromachi district of Kyoto, as Heian had come to be called.

Takauji strove to demonstrate the legitimacy of his regime. He claimed imperial sanction and Minamoto ancestry and used Kamakura nomenclature for his organs of government. In fact, however, whereas the Kamakura regime was anchored in Yoritomo's band of followers, Takauji's came to rely on the support of a coalition of regional barons, who backed the Ashikaga opportunistically in return for titles and taxable grants of land. The greatest of these barons, or daimyo, acquired authority over so much land that their autonomous power rivaled that of the Ashikaga, whose own estates were sufficiently modest that the regime's treasury depended less on land taxes than on tariff income from foreign and domestic trade.

This second bakufu, even more than the first, was thus from its inception a qualified rather than an absolute dictatorship. Where the Kamakura regime had divided its control of muscle, money, and myth with the imperial government in Heian, the Muromachi bakufu acknowledged only a nominal imperial government, while functionally dividing muscle and money with daimyo, recognizing their right to exist as highly autonomous agents as long as they rendered nominal obedience and some real service to the shogun.

Weak from the outset, Ashikaga leaders soon found themselves trying to govern a realm that was growing at an accelerating rate, and neither bakufu nor barons devised means to control that growth. Instead, local men of power (kokujin), whether originally commoners, samurai, or priests, became the dominant figures in villages and valleys across much of Japan. Exploiting their local bases of power, they seized the remnants of imperial tax lands, laid claim to the shōen of temples, kuge, and even daimyo, and repeatedly tried to grasp neighboring areas. In the process, they came into conflict with both rival kokujin and superiors who were trying to prevent their rise to prominence.

The inability of bakufu and barons to pacify the countryside led them to try and strengthen their hand at one another's expense. But that strategy only poisoned the political atmosphere in Kyoto, precipitating battles between the armies of scheming daimyo. In 1467 the fragile political order dissolved when the greatest barons went to war in the city. They reduced much of it to ashes and then retreated to their domains. There they continued fighting sporadically for a decade, whereupon Japan slid into a state of endemic civil war commonly called gekokujō, "those below toppling those above." Local warriors battled one another incessantly, repeatedly overthrew their superiors, and rose in the world, only to be overthrown in turn.

By the early sixteenth century, local power holders controlled so much of the country that some of them had essentially become daimyo themselves, and the imperial court, ever alert for political allies, awarded them titles that helped give them legitimacy. Having built their power from the ground up through processes of battle, land seizure, and imposition of control, these *sengoku,* or "warring states," daimyo were more capable than early Muromachi barons of expanding their domains without losing control of them. They based their power more fully on personally reliable vassals and claimed only territories they could actually control. They also kept fuller records of both their own and their vassals' men and lands, which helped them organize and sustain larger armies without losing control of their commanders. And they placed a firmer grip on agricultural and commercial production, encouraged mercantile activity, and devised ways to make increases in output reinforce their own positions. In other words, they strengthened the links between military and economic power, in the process discovering how to make social growth work for rather than against them.

Finally, most sengoku daimyo avoided entanglement in destructive struggles over the empty symbols of traditional central authority, thereby escaping the sort of pointless quarrels and conflicts that had harmed their erstwhile superiors. Their combination of local control and skepticism of traditional authority made these lords key figures in the politics of the day. By 1568 a number of them were demonstrating a capacity to govern that surpassed anything Japan had seen in a century or more.

In the decades that followed, the power of the most successful sengoku lords grew with dramatic speed. As they came to realize that they might yet dominate the entire realm, they began thinking about how to do it. Addressing that issue compelled them to confront the shogunal and imperial legacies and to consider their possible roles in such a venture. The process of pacifying Japan thus became a task, not simply of figuring out how in fact to control land and people, but also of how to control ideology by placing one's claims of authority in a larger historical context to make them persuasive to others. Only by succeeding in that task could a would-be ruler establish a legitimate successor regime to the imperial and shogunal governments of the past. Otherwise he would remain a mere usurper, who fully deserved to be challenged by any who dared.

THE RELIGIOUS LEGACY

The dominant position enjoyed by the superordinate few was based in part on the secular authority of government, with its administrative and military organization and its legitimation in Confucian principles and the ideals of imperial and shogunal rule. Their position was also buttressed by belief in the kami of Shintō and the Buddhas of Buddhism. Besides giving direct ideological support to government, pre-seventh-century Shintō myths and the Buddhism of later times also undergirded powerful religious institutions—Shintō shrines and Buddhist monasteries—whose ties to the ruling elite were so close that when church and state collaborated, both flourished, and when they quarreled, both suffered.

Shintō, which presumably was the folk religion of pre-seventh-century Japan, had by the 1500s developed into a set of elaborate religious institutions and traditions. Some shrines, notably the great ones at Ise and Izumo, were associated with the imperial family as part of "high culture," while some Shintō practice constituted autonomous sectarian movements, and some remained imbedded in the religious customs of the general populace, often in the form of idiosyncratic rituals directed to specific local deities.

The role of Shintō in legitimizing the social elite is evident in one of its oldest documents, the *Kojiki,* a version of the creation myths and subsequent genealogy of the Yamato uji, recorded at imperial behest in the year 712 to strengthen the recently self-proclaimed emperors by demonstrating their incomparable links to the highest godly ancestors. The sacred ties were perpetuated thereafter by religious ceremonies conducted regularly at the Ise Shrine and other sites dedicated to the imperial ancestors. They were given new visibility in the 1330s, when Godaigo's fruitless attempt to rebuild imperial power inspired sympathizers to produce essays supportive of imperial pretensions. Most notably, the scholar Kitabatake Chikafusa's polemic *Jinnō shōtōki* (1339) sought to demonstrate that if governing authority resided with the emperor, all would be well with Japan.

Long before Kitabatake's time, Shintō had developed into a much more elaborate set of religious practices than those employed by the

Yamato uji. During the centuries when the imperial authorities ruled from Heian, Shintō became entangled with Buddhism and other continental religious traditions. Kami became identified with Buddhas, and many shrines and monasteries were inter-built, with small shrines erected in monastery compounds and Buddha images installed in shrine precincts, each serving as spiritual protector of the other. Later religious thinkers tried to sort out the jumbled traditions, and by the sixteenth century, they had established separate Shintō sects, such as Yuiitsu Shintō, which had their own shrines, lands, priesthoods, tables of organization, and formalized religious practices.

Buddhism likewise evolved through the years, and sixteenth-century Japan contained a large, variegated, and dynamic Buddhist establishment. Introduced from the continent a millennium earlier, Buddhism was adopted by members of the Yamato elite for its promised political efficacy. They built monasteries and nunneries, endowed them with land, and employed priests and nuns to perform the desired rituals. During the seventh and eighth centuries, landed monasteries entrenched themselves in the vicinity of Nara, and during the ninth, Japanese scholars introduced two additional sects from China, Tendai and Shingon. The two quickly won political favor and rapidly acquired estates, branch monasteries, and an extensive hierarchy of prelates. Doctrines and practices that reinforced the belief among kuge that they were especially blessed with religious virtue and hence deserved their hereditary privilege were one source of their appeal.

By the latter half of the Heian period, however, with agricultural production showing only meager growth, attempts to continue expanding ecclesiastical power and glory pitted the great monasteries against imperial rulers, kuge, and rising bushi in struggles for control of the realm and its usufruct. Those struggles helped fracture the alliance of muscle, money, and myth, undermining the coherence of the elite and leading to considerable soul-searching and disillusionment within the monastic orders.

Out of these difficulties emerged a radical new religious development as proponents of select Buddhist teachings directed their ministries to the general public. New sectarian movements arose in the thirteenth century, most notably those espousing Jōdo, Zen, and Hokke (Nichiren) doctrines, and these rapidly gained adherents among both the proliferating bushi and the general public. The Rinzai branch of Zen did, it is true, develop close links to the Kamakura and Muromachi shogunal regimes and became the wealthiest and politically most influential sect of Buddhism, but the main thrust of this medieval religious development was to remove Buddhism from its earlier role as legitimizer of elite privilege.

By the sixteenth century, followers of Hokke teachings and members of Ikkō congregations (who followed a particular Jōdo interpretation) had developed into militant local religious groups. Whereas the older sects had consisted of monks who pursued expert religious practices in monasteries, the new sects were operated by priests whose temples were open to congregations of lay believers. These priests ministered to the faithful and ran their parish affairs, and as civil strife spread, more and more of them cooperated with fellow adherents at other temples in the pursuit of common military objectives both defensive and offensive.

By 1568, then, Japan's religious legacy no longer shored up the superordinate few. To the contrary, it had developed into a large, internally discordant institutional and intellectual tradition whose constituent temples and shrines pursued their own interests, often at one another's expense. Moreover, that religious legacy, particularly in its Buddhist aspect, had gone far toward empowering broad segments of the general public by justifying villagers' defiance of their betters and participating in their attempts to organize and run their own affairs.

THE COMMERCIAL LEGACY

Sixteenth-century Japan did not have a burgeoning bourgeoisie. But it did have a commercial legacy, a growing part of which was entrepreneurial. From earliest times, however, most of the country's commercial activity had been handled through institutions of the political and religious elite.

As early as the sixth century, a major portion of both agricultural and handicraft production was taken as tribute by the leaders of uji. Later the imperial government collected goods from tax lands, and kuge, monasteries, and shrines obtained them from their shōen. Those arrangements decayed during the medieval centuries, and bushi assumed more and more of the extractive role by obtaining produce as tribute from the lands they controlled. From the beginning, some of that yield was consumed directly by the tribute takers. But much was bartered or sold, finally to be marketed in the capital cities of Nara and Heian and during later centuries in Kamakura, Kyoto, and the many smaller towns that sprang up throughout Japan.

Even during the Nara period, some commerce was handled apart from these elite institutions. Villagers near the capital brought charcoal and firewood to sell in city markets. Others brought pottery, timber, pelts, antlers, and bamboo products. Some of the purveyors were producers; others were entrepreneurial agents. Not until the rural economy began to achieve sustained growth in the thirteenth century, however, did entrepreneurial activity really begin to blossom. Especially during the fourteenth century, some flourished in conjunction with overseas commercial ventures, when successive Ashikaga shogun and various daimyo and monasteries developed a brisk trade with China. In that trade, venture capitalists helped outfit and man ships, sending them to the continent in hopes they would return safely some months later with goods enough to yield an appropriately high profit.

Other entrepreneurs went into domestic commerce. Some were essentially artisans who produced and marketed valued items such as metal tools, swords, armor, lacquerware, elegant storage chests, or commodities of daily use. Others concentrated on transporting and selling foodstuffs, vegetable oils, cloth, pots, pans, and other handicraft items in the cities and, increasingly, in the market towns that sprang up. Many of these towns appeared initially as intermittent trading posts, later developing into settled commercial nodes at ports, river fords, highway junctions, or other points where people met and tarried.

As the realm slipped into deepening political disorder, merchants found it useful to acquire patrons who would help them monopolize areas of trade in return for license fees, highway tolls, or other forms of tribute. By the sixteenth century, such merchants had not only acquired a significant role in the economy but some were trying their hand at politics. A few, such as the oil seller Saitō Dōsan, managed to transform themselves into domanial lords. Others, notably merchants in the port of Sakai, gained control of their town, governing it through a council of peers independent of any shogun or daimyo. For most, however, collaboration with the political authorities seemed a surer way to succeed, and many merchants served lords as provisioners, advisors, and administrators.

The value of such collaboration was not limited to merchants. It was also crucial to daimyo. With so much commercial activity handled by merchants, the reconstitution of an orderly society—the linking again of ideology, muscle, and wealth—required the reintegration of economic and political activity just as surely as it required the reconsolidation of religion and polity.

THE URBAN TRADITION

Early in Japan's history, the superordinate few became an urban elite, and higher culture, an urban culture. Japan never developed a sustained tradition of high-status rural gentry, feudal barons, or country gentlemen who resided from choice on their own large and durable estates or fiefs. Rather, the fortunate few preferred to assemble in the headquarters of their leaders, where they could pursue higher cultural activities. Only when political exigency prevented urban residence did they settle in the countryside, and when that happened, they did their best to bring urban amenities and cultural pretensions to their rural location.

This urban tradition traces back at least to the construction of Nara in 710. Within decades, Nara and, subsequently, Heian grew into great cities of from one to two hundred thousand souls, which number included the several thousand kuge, uncounted Buddhist and Shintō clerics, and a vast array of lesser people. Some of these lived with their kuge employers in rambling wooden mansions, while others occupied the primitive bark-and-wattle dwellings that lined the city's narrow back alleys. The kuge themselves were so city-oriented that when posted to the provinces, most longed to return to the capital, and some resigned or declined their posts or despatched substitutes so as to escape the lonely privation of exile in the hinterland.

The higher culture that arose during those centuries embraced not only the literate routines of government and elegant rituals of Buddhism but also a wide array of arts and entertainments. Most notable was poetry, the 31-syllable *waka* in particular, which became deeply imbedded in both daily life and the arts, and which was saved for posterity in such great anthologies as the *Man'yōshū*, *Kokinshū*, and *Shinkokinshū* (see Glossary for English titles). Closely tied to poetry was narrative prose fiction, which included poetic tales such as the *Ise monogatari* and culminated in the famous *Genji monogatari*. Composed by the court lady Murasaki Shikibu around A.D. 1000, the *Genji* dwelt on the elegant lives and sensibilities of the fictional Prince Genji and his acquaintances.

Following Chinese precedents, the rulers of Nara-Heian Japan created official histories to record governmental performance. They did so on the Confucian premise that the merits and demerits of a regime would and should be revealed by its annals, which could then guide future generations of leaders. The *Kojiki* and *Nihon shoki* (also called *Ni-*

hongi) were the first of several works to record that history, those two purporting to tell the story from the beginning, when kami in the Plain of High Heaven created the world, down to the seventh century, by which point the recorded information had become largely credible. Later histories carried the story from there.

Architecture also flourished, establishing a tradition of stone-based, tile-roofed, wood-framed, mortise-and-tenon construction that survived intact until the late nineteenth century. Sculpture, painting, music, dance, and elegant "parlor games" (making incense, matching colors, and making and identifying perfumes or literary allusions) also flourished in Nara and Heian, adding to the luster of the courtly elite and establishing standards and precedents for future reference.

The decay of imperial rule did not end Heian's cultural role, even after warrior leaders established their bakufu at Kamakura. During Kamakura's century of vitality, both it and Heian (known increasingly as Kyoto) nurtured cultural production, with the great Zen monasteries in both cities promoting architecture, sculpture, painting, and religious study. Aristocrats in Kyoto continued to make music, write poetry and essays, and practice their courtly games. Scholars wrote more histories such as the *Azuma kagami,* which recorded the founding of the Kamakura bakufu, and other narrative war tales (*gunki monogatari*) that celebrated samurai heroics.

When Ashikaga Takauji and other rebellious lieutenants destroyed the Kamakura regime in the 1330s, they situated their own government in Kyoto, a choice determined in great part by the fact that the city had survived as a major metropolitan center. Under Takauji and his successors, Kyoto again became the undisputed center of higher culture. Supported by income from domestic and foreign trade as well as land taxes, the urban elite flourished, building more mansions and monasteries and adorning them with exquisite landscape gardens and precious paintings and ceramics. Architectural innovations, most notably the decorative alcove (*tokonoma*) and the utilization of tatami mats and sliding doors throughout, made mansions more flexible, comfortable, and attractive.

In their mansions, the elite raised the drinking of tea to an art form (*chanoyu*), which eventually came to be practiced in specially designed tea huts. They developed poetry composition into an erudite party game of linked verse (*renga*) controlled by strict rules of procedure. Older forms of popular entertainment and religious dance evolved into the *nō* drama, its principles most thoroughly articulated around 1400 by the playwright Zeami Motokiyo. The China trade, which helped pay for this elegance, also brought new cultural influences. One such was an ink-line style of painting (*sumi-e*) that challenged the artistic dominance of the established *Yamato-e* style, with its bright colors and clearly delineated perspective. Others were continental ceramics, a deeper interest in Zen Buddhism, and a renewed interest in Confucian scholarship, particularly that having to do with governance, or "the arts of peace and war" (*bunbu*).

Ashikaga weakness vis-à-vis regional barons facilitated the spread of urban culture by allowing major daimyo to hire artisans, scholars, prelates, and poetasters, who brought the arts and pretensions of Kyoto to regional bastions such as Odawara and Yamaguchi. That trend, which seemed to be generating a baronial pattern of regional gentrification, was perennially weakened, however, by the proclivity of daimyo to prefer life in Kyoto. Moreover, the cultural life of regional centers was repeatedly vitiated by warfare.

At a lower social level, on the other hand, the diffusion of higher culture went on apace. Itinerant musicians, tale tellers, and religious mendicants brought rural people songs and stories of mystery, humor, and warrior heroics and messages of suffering and salvation. In doing so, they revealed to the general public intellectual and aesthetic vistas that had previously been closed to all but the literate few.

With the proliferation of temples, trading posts, wealthy village leaders, and resident samurai, literacy itself, a skill once monopolized by the urban few, began to spread through the hinterland. Its diffusion further opened doors to higher culture. It introduced those with disposable income to new ways of using their wealth and exposed their neighbors to new experiences, possibly awakening in them new wants and even new expectations. One effect of these trends and their companion trends of growing village size, production, and organization was to facilitate new claims of privilege. By their nature any such claims must collide with the claims of those who would rule, making more difficult any attempts to reconsolidate force, fisc, and philosophy into a new governing system.

By 1568, then, centuries of change had created in the islands of Japan a large, complex, and expanding society. It had produced rich political and cultural traditions and an economy experiencing considerable growth. Japan was in that same year completing a century of nearly incessant and widespread warfare that had produced large armies of battle-hardened soldiers and ruthless leaders. Those leaders were only gradually devising ways to reimpose peace on the country at large by combining new forms of organization with older elements of the political and cultural legacies. Within a half-century of 1568, however, their efforts would give rise to a political structure of unprecedented magnitude and coercive power.

THREE

Early Modern Japan

An Overview

The Period of Growth, 1560–1710
The Period of Stasis, 1710–1850

In general terms, as suggested in the Introduction, early modern Japan experienced a phase of social expansion that gave way in the early eighteenth century to a phase of overall stasis. On closer examination, of course, one is dealing with diverse phenomena that do not fit together nicely. Few of the changes involved were abrupt or decisive. Most were gradual and entailed much backing and filling, and some worked quite against one another. Lest one lose sight of the forest for the trees, however, it seems worthwhile to examine the overall rhythm of this history before scrutinizing its parts more closely.

THE PERIOD OF GROWTH, 1560–1710

Mid-sixteenth-century Japan embodied both profound disorder and re-markable potential for change. On the surface, its political legacy was a shambles, which brought widespread suffering to many, both high and low, and distinct, though risky, opportunity to the fortunate. Below the surface, as noted in chapter 2, dynamic processes of more fundamental significance were at work. Fueled by pervasive changes at the village level, population and production were rising, economic activity was spreading, urban centers were proliferating, local groups were gaining greater control over their affairs, and literacy and learning were spreading across the realm.

These conditions set the stage for early modern Japan's period of growth. Extending from around 1560 to 1710, these 150 years commenced with an era of pacification that led to the Tokugawa regime's heyday. Pacification proceeded initially through a military stage in which political violence attained unprecedented levels as armies numbering scores of thousands pounded one another in ruthless sieges and bloody open-field battles. After 1590, however, pacification entered a largely nonviolent phase of political manipulation and management that by 1640 produced an elaborately organized and highly routinized system of government.

During these same decades, Japan carried on extensive trading activity with East and Southeast Asia and even engaged in cultural and economic dealings with the handful of Europeans who reached the islands during the age of Iberian empire. Tragically, during the 1590s, Japan's military dictator, Toyotomi Hideyoshi, launched two devastatingly sanguinary invasions of Korea that were supposed to result in conquest of "the known world," essentially meaning China.

Hideyoshi's failed invasions proved to be the high water mark of Japan's overseas activity, even though foreign trade flourished for a century thereafter. The embitterment and distrust they produced, together with changes in the East Asian economy, political upheaval on the continent, and recurrent difficulties with Europeans, fostered among Japan's leaders the belief that poorly regulated foreign connections were fraught with unacceptable risk. Consequently, as the seventeenth century advanced, they reduced and carefully regulated foreign contacts, in the process establishing a highly restrictive diplomatic orientation that persisted until the 1850s.

The measures controlling foreign relations were an integral part of an overall political culture of regulation and restraint that came to blanket the realm. By carefully allocating goods and privileges on the basis of hereditary social status, this political culture sought to eliminate disruptive competitive relationships among the general populace, thereby minimizing the risk of disorder and protecting the perquisites of the elite. The result was a regulatory regime that reached from the lowliest hamlet to the most lordly household.

Rigorous control of foreign connections made life difficult for some people, most cruelly for the followers of Iberian missionaries. But neither it nor the broader policy of regulation stopped economic expansion. Rather, within the context of peace, domestic growth continued. Especially during the early decades of the century, economic activity spurted ahead, propelled by rapid growth in rural production and shaped by a burst of urban expansion. This early phase of growth was predominantly regional, involving castle towns and their hinterlands, but as overall growth slowed late in the century, what expansion did continue was centered on the great cities of Osaka and Edo. By 1700 it was creating in Japan a substantially integrated, metropolitan-centered national economy.

This long period of sustained growth provided goods enough to support the burgeoning population and, in addition, enough employment opportunities to accommodate most of the fighting men driven onto the job market by the coming of peace. Most did not mean all, however, and eruptions involving unemployed soldiers and hard-pressed civilians punctuated the century, giving it some of its most visible and moving moments.

The increases in production generated wealth that enabled rulers and affluent urban commoners to support an outpouring of cultural production: elegant architecture, arts, letters, philosophy, music, drama, and diverse forms of meretricious entertainment. The character of this cultural output changed as the century passed. The initial ruler-inspired activity, known as Azuchi-Momoyama culture, had many facets but was most notable for gigantic and highly ornamented buildings. By midcentury, philosophy, mainly political thought, was the field of samurai-dominated cultural production that remained most creative, and in that field intellectuals cranked out an impressive volume of commentary that helped legitimize the existing social order by undergirding it with elegant theory.

In other areas, notably art, drama, and fiction, dynamism derived mostly from outside the samurai class. Kyoto enjoyed a century of vibrant cultural production thanks to cross-fertilization among kuge, cultured samurai, and wealthy merchants. Their efforts yielded a splendid heritage of antiquarian publications, pictorial art, crafts, and architectural monuments. In cities and towns in general, however, commoners were the dominant cultural force by century's end. They gave recreational and aesthetic production a distinctive character and content, that of *ukiyo,* the "floating world" of Genroku culture, so-called after the year-period 1688–1704.

As the seventeenth century advanced, economic expansion slowed, and as it drew to a close, a careful observer could see signs that the good times might not endure, the liveliness of Genroku notwithstanding. Governments were bankrupt and policy disagreements were growing rancorous. Price fluctuations were sharp, and entrepreneurs were becoming more frenetic in their pleas for government protection. The maintenance of cities was proving difficult, and from the early eighteenth century on, village hardship started becoming acute. Despite the pervasiveness of regulations on status and consumption, they were only partly successful in defining social relationships, rationing goods, and controlling rates of consumption, and as a result some natural resources were being taxed to the limit. Proposals and demands for reform were becoming more extreme and more insistent, and a sense of pessimism about the future was appearing in the writings of social commentators. Unencumbered by a later generation's hindsight, a thoughtful observer might well have suspected in the early years of the eighteenth century that the existing order was on its last legs.

THE PERIOD OF STASIS, 1710–1850

Despite the deepening shadows of the late 1600s, the first half of early modern Japan's history is essentially a grand story of dramatic developments, heroic in dimension and gratifying in character. With some tragic exceptions, even the underdogs may have fared better than they usually do in life.

By contrast, the latter half of that history seems dominated by fundamental and deeply frustrating problems, repeated and largely unsatisfactory attempts to resolve them, and consequent tensions and hardships. To paint the era in darkest hues, it pitted villagers against one another even as they struggled to address their problems communally. It pitted whole villages against one another. It pitted village against town and town against city. It pitted daimyo domains against one another and against the bakufu, even as they sought conjointly to govern the realm and preserve elite privilege. It pitted upper-class samurai against lower-class samurai, even though the latter sustained the former. It pitted samurai against merchants, and merchants against one another. It pitted intellectuals against the regime even when they were trying to save the regime. And insofar as urban marriage, death, and family survival rates are indicative, it probably pitted the urban well-to-do against the urban poor.

To some extent, nearly all these statements also apply to the seventeenth century, but the difference in degree of applicability seems striking. Moreover, since there are winners as well as losers in most situations of conflict, signs of social disorder can never be construed as signs of universal disadvantage. Still, the signs of pain became uncommonly visible after Genroku, especially during the eighteenth century.

The later Tokugawa period was not unchanging, however. Just as the earlier period of growth embraced an era of pacification followed by one of order, so the period of stasis had its phases. The eighteenth century was a grim time devoted to conscious "systems maintenance," with most political, economic, cultural, and intellectual efforts directed at the preservation, repair, and elaboration of established arrangements. By century's end, however, one can see early signs of a wide-ranging and eclectic quest for new cultural, economic, and political forms, constituting an imaginative but not very successful attempt to solve the problems of the existing order.

None of these temporal segments emerged abruptly, of course, and not all facets of history can be shoehorned into them satisfactorily. But just as the shift from pacification to order can be somewhat arbitrarily dated to the 1630s, so the shift from systems maintenance to exploration can be dated to the 1790s.

Especially during the eighteenth century, the central problem around which all else pivoted was how to allocate the resources of a realm whose material production, given the technology and social organization of the age, no longer reliably met the basic needs of a population that had more than doubled in a century's time. That fundamental ecological issue lay at the heart of politics, both local and countrywide, and was revealed in the Kyōhō reform of the eighth shogun, Tokugawa Yoshimune. The reform was a wide-ranging and remarkably energetic program of the 1720s, and its character and outcome both illuminated and foreshadowed many facets of the later Tokugawa experience.

Central to this later experience were recurrent crop failures and famines, those of the 1730s, 1780s, and 1830s being the most brutal and extensive. With most lowlands opened to agricultural production by the 1720s, reclamation projects became less and less cost-effective and gradually petered out, giving way to the rapid diffusion of techniques of labor- and land-intensive cultivation. Changes in agronomic technique were accompanied by a reorganization of village life that exacerbated disparities between rich and poor. That development, together with the hardship caused by crop failure, fostered changes in the character and scale of rural unrest, with protests altering their form and focus and becoming more extensive, more frequent, and more violent.

In addition to intensified tillage, other measures to enhance basic production began appearing in the eighteenth century and paying social

dividends by the nineteenth. Most notable were the development of a
large fishing industry and aggressive reforestation. Less helpful were
such other means of terrestrial exploitation as utilizing ground coal,
managing large rivers, and gaining access to Hokkaido's vast forests
and other resources.

The onset of endemic ecological stress in the early eighteenth century
was also manifested, as noted in the Introduction, in a fundamental
shift in Japan's demographic trajectory from the seventeenth century's
rapid population growth to an overall stability in numbers. An array
of factors contributed to that shift, some of them leading to spatial
demographic changes that had regional socioeconomic and, eventually,
political ramifications.

The social and political tension of later Tokugawa society was reflected in its intellectual life. Whereas one can speak of the seventeenth
century as an era in which a dominant ideology—that is, a coherent
rationale for the established order—was successfully crafted and disseminated, the eighteenth and nineteenth centuries were marked by a
proliferation of discordant doctrines and interpretations. During the
eighteenth century, the authors of these formulations mostly intended
them to shore up the existing order, but their very proliferation suggests
that for many the dominant ideology was losing whatever persuasiveness it once may have held.

As satisfaction with the existing order waned, the rulers and their
supporters tried to neutralize worrisome lines of thought. Most visibly,
in the 1790s, the bakufu leader Matsudaira Sadanobu attempted to
propagate a self-conscious Confucian "orthodoxy." But iconoclasm
prevailed. Diverse pragmatic analyses of society's ills and writings that
addressed problems of production and distribution began to appear
during the eighteenth century and proliferated during the nineteenth,
along with the pursuit of European studies, vigorous reexamination of
indigenous myths and history, and the rise of unauthorized popular
religions and movements. These developments provoked sporadic acts
of government suppression and created an intellectual milieu increasingly conducive to radical action.

In terms of popular culture, the century and a half after Genroku
saw striking changes in arts and letters, with some aspects of Genroku
culture fading, while others gained greater vitality. From the late eighteenth century on, other new forms of art, literature, and entertainment
also arose, giving popular culture unprecedented diversity and richness.
The above-noted changes in rural society and the overall economy were,

moreover, accompanied by a blossoming of rural cultural life that by the nineteenth century brought to at least some people in the hinterland many of the arts and entertainments enjoyed by city folk.

Finally, during the nineteenth century, domestic problems were complicated by unprecedented foreign pressures, initially from the north and later from the south. In a series of incidents that, from the 1790s on, began breaking like waves over the heads of the rulers, foreigners requested diplomatic and commercial arrangements that by their nature could be accommodated only at great risk to the regime. For half a century, leaders in Edo maneuvered to minimize the danger of foreign contacts and successfully avoided crisis. But, as is obvious in hindsight, essentially they just delayed the day of reckoning.

During the 1850s, that day came. Foreign requests gave way to demands, and the regime's leaders recognized correctly that they could refuse to comply only at the risk of unwinnable war. So they capitulated, which act set in motion developments that rapidly rearranged the political landscape, realigning forces, transforming latent grievances into active complaints, and transmogrifying supportive ideas and groups into criticisms and critics of the established order—or at least of its current leaders. Armies mobilized, a domestic arms race ensued, and bloody battles were fought. In the early days of 1868, Yoshinobu, the fifteenth shogun, aware that his choices were to surrender or throw society into violent, indecisive warfare that might lead to European intervention and occupation, lost heart for the cause, surrendered control of his armies and headquarters at Edo, and thereby ended the era of Tokugawa rule.

That outcome left Japan's fate in the hands of the boy-emperor Meiji and his newly empowered handlers, who swiftly moved Japan into a sharply altered historical trajectory. Drawing upon a mix of domestic ideas that had been developing for a century or more and foreign ideas that were enjoying popularity abroad, they effected a radical restructuring of government, repudiated the early modern diplomatic policy of self-limitation, and moved aggressively to acquire industrial techniques of resource exploitation. With those changes, Japan's early modern era came to a close.

PART TWO

The Era of Pacification, 1570–1630

From a military perspective, early modern Japan's period of growth from around 1560 to 1710 encompassed two very dissimilar phases, a short one of war and a long one of peace. The wars raged on through the 1580s, giving way in the summer of 1590 to a peace that endured thereafter save only for five years of brutal combat in Korea and then brief outbursts of domestic armed struggle in 1600, 1614, and 1637.

One captures the tone of political life better, however, by arguing that until the 1630s, politics was essentially the continuation of war by other means, with the objective unchanged: more thorough consolidation of central power by more complete pacification of the realm. After that decade, by contrast, politics settled down during the heyday of the Tokugawa regime to a more habitual maintenance of the status quo.

Changes in the character of domestic violence after 1590 reveal the pacifiers' progress. The last confrontation to pit the organized forces of allied daimyo against one another occurred in the fall of 1600, when an eastern coalition led by Tokugawa Ieyasu routed a western coalition of lords claiming to act in the name of the recently deceased Toyotomi Hideyoshi. Subsequent military outbursts essentially pitted *rōnin*—samurai who had lost their jobs as peace was restored—against entrenched rulers. In fierce battles at Osaka in 1614–15, ronin found unenthusiastic sponsors in the handful of surviving Toyotomi family loyalists, but their rebellion only resulted in their own slaughter, dissolution of the Toyotomi legacy, and further tightening of Tokugawa control. On the Shimabara peninsula in Kyushu in 1637–38, ronin derived support from commoners who were addressing major grievances of their own, but again the rulers finally and bloodily prevailed. The last attempts by ronin to make space for themselves in the ruling establishment consisted of pitiful, abortive uprisings in the 1650s, in which handfuls of men, lacking either sponsors or collaborators, failed miserably.

By then the realm as a whole was settled into the routines of peace, and most domestic strife had acquired a different character. Contestants were not attempting to renegotiate the settlement of 1600 but, instead, were wrestling with problems produced by the new order. One type of problem, the *oie sōdō,* or "disturbance in the great houses," pitted factions of samurai in a particular daimyo domain against one another. Another type, the peasant protest, essentially pitted the taxpayer against the collector.

As a political process, pacification thus evolved through a violent military phase into a largely nonviolent phase of political manipulation and management. Pacification also had economic dimensions, however. In the last decades of the sixteenth century, political leaders energetically used economic resources to support their military enterprises and in so doing spurred economic expansion. By the early seventeenth century, the resulting economic opportunity was serving the interests of the peacekeepers by providing employment and well-being to people who might otherwise have attempted to improve their condition by resorting to violence.

The flourishing economic activity that accompanied and expedited pacification also underwrote a burst of cultural creativity, which during the last decades of the sixteenth century involved grandiloquent display by the rulers and lively recreation by commoners. In the early seventeenth century, it evolved into a period of elite cultural elaboration that from around 1610 on was accompanied by intensification of government measures to contain and direct the recreational energies of the masses.

FOUR

The Politics of Pacification

Political Reconsolidation, 1568–1598
  Oda Nobunaga
  Toyotomi Hideyoshi
Political Stabilization, 1598–1632
  Tokugawa Ieyasu
  Tokugawa Hidetada
  Daimyo Governance: Tosa and Kaga

Contemporary comments by two Europeans nicely capture the basic political change that Japan experienced during the era of pacification. The Portuguese Jesuit Alessandro Valignano lamented that the Japanese of the 1570s and 1580s were "much addicted to sensual vices and sins." He continued:

> The second defect of this nation is the meagre loyalty which the people show towards their rulers. They rebel against them whenever they have a chance, either usurping them or joining up with their enemies. Then they about-turn and declare themselves friends again, only to rebel once more when the opportunity presents itself; yet this sort of conduct does not discredit them at all. . . . The chief root of the evil is the fact that . . . there was a rebellion against [the emperor] and Japan was divided up among so many usurping barons that there are always wars among them, each one trying to grab for himself as much territory as he can.

Valignano went on to characterize the government of Japan as "far less centralised than that of Europe."[1]

By 1620, however, the English merchant official Richard Cocks saw the situation very differently. He wrote:

1. Michael Cooper, *They Came to Japan: An Anthology of European Reports on Japan, 1543–1640* (Berkeley and Los Angeles: University of California Press, 1965), p. 46. According to Cooper, Valignano also charged the Japanese with "dissimulation and cruelty," balancing his criticism with praise for "their prudence, discretion, bravery and forbearance."

This government of Japan may well be accompted the greatest and powre-
fullest Terrany, that ever was heard of in the world, for all the rest are as
Slaves to the Emperour (or greate commander as they call him), whoe upon
the leaste suspition (or Jelosie) or being angry with any man (be he never soe
greate a man) will cause hym upon the Recepte of his Letter to cutt his bellie,
which if he refuse to doe, not only he, but all the rest of their race shall feele
the smart thereof.[2]

Admittedly a Jesuit and a merchant might well see things dissimi-
larly, but it remains true that in the years between those two reports,
Japan changed dramatically. The later decades of the sixteenth century
were the most violent in Japanese history, with warfare cresting in a
spate of horrific battles, which were followed during the 1590s by a
domestic peace more complete than anyone could have imagined.

By the autumn of 1600, the heavy work of pacifying the realm actually was done, but many more years were to elapse before the samurai
elite acknowledged as much. Instead, they continued to maintain armies, store weapons and munitions, recruit gifted swordsmen, strengthen
home castles, tighten control of domains, keep their eyes peeled, and
bide their time. As the years passed, however, political violence was
contained and government rules and regulations helped routinize the
handling of daily affairs. Old warriors died off, young men outgrew
their wildest dreams, and slowly, surreptitiously, the habits of peace
became entrenched.

POLITICAL RECONSOLIDATION, 1568–1598

The passage from violence to peace signified the reintegration of society's muscle, money, and myth. The form of reintegration was determined by Japan's medieval experience, which produced the shogunal
and baronial institutions. These, together with the older imperial legacy, constituted the three key organizing elements of political reconsolidation, and during the years up to 1598, they were utilized by two
successive aspirants to hegemony, Oda Nobunaga and Toyotomi Hideyoshi.

ODA NOBUNAGA

The interaction among these three elements of the political legacy was
nicely demonstrated by Nobunaga, the dynamic young daimyo who

2. Ibid., pp. 57–58.

dominated the Nobi plain from his castle near present-day Nagoya. In 1568, as earlier noted, the 34-year-old Nobunaga took Ashikaga Yoshiaki under his wing and arranged to have Emperor Ōgimachi install him as shogun. Yoshiaki chafed under his benefactor, however, and indulged in some hostile scheming, which prompted Nobunaga, after annihilating rivals in the Kyoto vicinity, to run the imprudent shogun out of town. In the process, he unwittingly ended the Ashikaga shogunate.

Neither emperor nor shogun intimidated Nobunaga, but, political triumph notwithstanding, he chose to claim neither shogunal nor imperial title. He did accept high court titles as his due but really based his claim to primacy on the evidence that his armies could pound rivals into submission and that once he had "pacified" an area, it stayed that way. Nobunaga was announcing, in effect, that he had the right to rule because he had displayed more competence than other daimyo and was, therefore, more qualified than they to govern the realm (*tenka*). He was thus properly engaged in the honorable task of handling public affairs (*kōgi*), rather than the selfish task of advancing Oda family interests.[3]

An essential aspect of Nobunaga's success was his military skill. One incident that suggests the violence of the times also illustrates the qualities that led to his triumph. In the spring of 1560, Imagawa Yoshimoto, who dominated the Tōkai region from a great castle at Sunpu, marched his army of twenty-five thousand westward, intending to overrun Owari province and annihilate the much smaller force of the impertinent young Nobunaga. The armies deployed for battle near Okehazama in southeast Owari, only to be caught in a heavy downpour. Knowing he would lose in a set-piece battle, Nobunaga quickly ordered his men to mount a surprise assault in the pouring rain. Leaping from their brushy concealment and racing across the sodden fields, his troops caught the enemy hunkered down against the elements and slashed their way through forward units into Yoshimoto's headquarters. By the time the battle ended that afternoon, Yoshimoto lay dead and his routed army was streaming eastward in disarray. They left behind some 3,100 fallen comrades, nearly 600 of them samurai, the rest foot soldiers.

Nobunaga brought to his civil projects the same raw will to succeed. His forcefulness is evinced in this Jesuit description of him supervising

3. The fullest English-language study of Nobunaga is Neil McMullin, *Buddhism and the State in Seventeenth-Century Japan* (Princeton: Princeton University Press, 1984), which focuses on Nobunaga's policies toward politicized Buddhist temples. Also see Herman Ooms, *Tokugawa Ideology* (Princeton: Princeton University Press, 1985), pp. 26–28 and passim, for discussion of Nobunaga's ideology.

the construction of a castle in Kyoto in 1569, the year after he installed Yoshiaki as puppet shogun:

> Nobunaga built a castle there, the like of which has never been seen before in Japan. First of all he gave orders for [two] temples to be razed and then commandeered the site, measuring four streets long and four wide. All the princes and nobles of Japan came to help in the building operations; usually there were from 15,000 to 25,000 men at work, all dressed in cloth breeches and short jackets made of skins. When he went around supervising the operations, he carried his sword in his hand or rested it on his shoulder, or else he carried a baton in his hand. He decided to build the castle completely of stone—something, as I have said, quite unknown in Japan. As there was no stone available for the work, he ordered many stone idols to be pulled down, and the men tied ropes around the necks of these and dragged them to the site. . . . Other men went off to work in quarries, others carted away earth, others cut down timber in the hills.
>
> He always strode around girded about with a tiger skin on which to sit and wearing rough and coarse clothing; following his example everyone wore skins and no-one dared to appear before him in court dress while the building was still in progress. . . . The most marvellous thing about the whole operation was the incredible speed with which the work was carried out. It looked as if four or five years would be needed to complete the masonry work, yet he had it finished within 70 days.[4]

The following years brought Nobunaga more military triumphs. Some were victories over rival lords, but others constituted a more basic victory over two forms of political organization that challenged his own "warring states" (*sengoku*) daimyo style of rule. The two were sectarian and communal organization. As adumbrated in chapter 2, the former dated back to the Heian period; the latter became established in villages during the fifteenth and sixteenth centuries. When the two were combined in village-based, religiously inspired, temple-led political movements, they presented formidable threats to the likes of Nobunaga.

Particularly in central Japan—where agronomic development was most advanced, pressure on the biosystem most severe, and the need for management of communal resources most acute—village regulation of local affairs was well developed by the 1560s, with temples frequently serving as the organizing mechanism. As lords such as Nobunaga tried to strengthen their positions by extending control over adjacent localities, they found their efforts resisted with particular effectiveness by villagers, who took to the field flying Ikkō, Hokke, or other religious ban-

4. Cooper, *They Came to Japan*, pp. 93–94. The Jesuit was Luis Frois.

ners. When necessary, moreover, the villagers forged alliances with like-minded groups or even with sengoku lords opposed to their enemy of the moment.

Whereas sengoku lords organized their forces in traditional samurai patterns of hierarchical lord-vassal relations, these villagers organized as congregational groups acting communally in their own defense. When Ikkō groups became very large, they of necessity acquired the hierarchical command structures of old, established sects, but they still used villages as their organizational units. By retaining the ideal of a communal movement, they sustained enough enthusiasm among followers to be extremely difficult for lords to control. Consequently, during the 1560s and 1570s, warfare frequently pitted lordly armies against local, temple-led forces, and those conflicts became especially brutal as lords concluded that the enemy would never really submit and must be destroyed. Better armed and more dedicated to warfare, samurai crushed most of these rival forces by the 1580s. With their defeat, the sectarian and communal principles of organization lost influence on the larger political scene, and the lord-vassal ideal of the shogunal and daimyo legacies prevailed.

Two examples, both involving Nobunaga, illustrate the brutality of these contests and suggest how the outcomes eliminated domestic sectarian power. The better-known incident occurred two years after he built his grand castle in Kyoto. Enryakuji, the venerable Tendai monastic community that overlooked the city from Mount Hiei, had for centuries engaged in politico-military intrigue, and in 1570 its leaders made the grievous mistake of allying with Nobunaga's enemies. The following fall, after defeating some of those enemies, Nobunaga turned his wrath on Hiei. He deployed thirty thousand men at the foot of the hill and had them work their way methodically to the summit. They did as ordered, burning all Enryakuji buildings, some three hundred of them, including libraries, residences, and historic treasures, and slaughtering the survivors, some three thousand men, women, and children.

Less well known, but more representative of samurai-sectarian struggles, was a campaign Nobunaga mounted three years later during the late summer and fall of 1574. Harassed on his southern flank by Ikkō groups that refused to submit, he ordered troops out to pacify the area. They drove the Ikkō members back into two bastions near the upper end of Ise Bay and then mounted a series of assaults that forced the twenty thousand defenders deeper into their fortresses. When their food supplies had given out and they were weakened from hunger, he torched their stockades, burning the defenders within and slaying those who tried to escape.

Ruthlessness paid off, and Nobunaga's triumphs continued. By way of demonstrating his right to hegemonial power, during the years 1576–79 he built at Azuchi, on a hillock overlooking Lake Biwa, the greatest castle Japan had ever seen. It consisted of a sprawling array of barracks, warehouses, and other buildings situated in courtyards encircled by moats and stone ramparts surmounted by wood and plaster gates and parapets. The layout centered on a 138-foot high, tile-roofed, wood and plaster keep that towered seven stories in the air and was decorated more lavishly than any mansion or palace in the country's history. It attested to a simple truth: its builder enjoyed unprecedented power.

TOYOTOMI HIDEYOSHI

For all his energy, prowess, savagery, and display, in the end Nobunaga's pretensions came to nought. In 1582 he was murdered by an ungrateful vassal, and another of his men, the brilliant general Toyotomi Hideyoshi, outmaneuvered rivals to inherit the Oda domain in central Japan. From his position astride the Kinai and Nobi regions, Hideyoshi mounted relentless political and military offensives against enemy lords and within a decade forced them one by one to accept his leadership. In the process he ended Japan's century of endemic civil strife.

Hideyoshi showed little more interest than Nobunaga in the shogunal title, which had been badly debased by later Ashikaga claimants and instead took other high but inconsequential imperial appointments. He outdid his predecessor in showering marks of esteem on the court, displaying to all the world his intimacy and solicitude for its well-being. Such gestures notwithstanding however, he, like Nobunaga, still regarded the daimyo domain as the basic building block of the polity and governing competence as the basic criterion of political legitimacy.[5]

A pair of examples will illustrate Hideyoshi's respect for competent performance. He dismissed as vacuous the political claims of Nobunaga's heir on the ground that he was a frivolous playboy. But, by way of contrast, he said of Nobunaga's eastern neighbor, Tokugawa Ieyasu, that he "may not be very refined, and he lacks musical skills, but he can govern a realm, is an astute judge of men, and is expert at arms. He is

5. The fullest study of Hideyoshi is Mary Elizabeth Berry, *Hideyoshi* (Cambridge, Mass.: Harvard University Press, 1982).

an impressive man by any standard."[6] Ieyasu, in other words, had the qualities necessary to be a successful daimyo and for that reason deserved respect even though utterly incompetent in the finer arts.

During the decade after Nobunaga's death, Hideyoshi forced all daimyo to accept his leadership. Over the years, he issued edicts regulating their behavior, but he destroyed very few lords, allowing them to survive as essentially autonomous regional leaders with their own lands and vassals. In part he did so because he found them useful: daimyo did most of his dirty work. But one suspects that he also left able lords in control of domains out of the conviction that competent performance was what counted and that those capable of governing a domain should be allowed to do so as long as they obeyed him. He adhered to that policy until 1598, when he died in bed at the age of sixty-two.

To some degree, no doubt, Hideyoshi was less ruthless toward daimyo than Nobunaga because the latter's uncompromising performance had instilled the fear of God into them, making them more responsive to enticement. Similarly, Nobunaga's savage handling of religious groups allowed Hideyoshi to deal with them more gently. There, too, instead of destroying, he left establishments intact and issued regulations to guide them.

In his treatment of villagers, however, Hideyoshi fully shared Nobunaga's resolve to deny villages and local temples the right of political autonomy that he extended to lords and major fanes. Rather, he insisted that they be incorporated into daimyo domains as peaceful, productive elements. But whereas Nobunaga had used armed force to subjugate militant villagers, Hideyoshi was able to employ other mechanisms, notably ordinances issued during the late 1580s and 1590s that guaranteed villagers security of place while denying them the capacity to revolt and assured tax collectors of access to their production.

Most famously, after subjugating the Shimazu, the last holdouts in Kyushu, he issued an edict in 1588 that called on all villagers to surrender any bows, swords, spears, firearms, or other weapons they might have, and he ordered officials to ensure the edict's implementation. Three years later, in conjunction with a military campaign in the northeast, he ordered censuses taken in all villages to prevent military men from taking refuge in them. He also decreed that henceforth no peasant could become a samurai and no samurai could settle secretly as a peasant. In 1598, in culmination of a practice that had been growing for several

6. Quoted in Conrad Totman, *Tokugawa Ieyasu, Shogun* (South San Francisco: Heian International, 1983), p. 68.

years, he ordered cadastral surveys made throughout the realm to measure land, determine its productivity, and clarify how taxes from such land would be assessed and collected.[7]

In some matters, notably his own succession and two issues relating to foreigners, Hideyoshi failed to make satisfactory arrangements. As a result of earlier rash decisions, when he died his heir was a five-year-old son, Hideyori, whom he left in the hands of a group of mutually distrustful daimyo. He charged them with keeping the peace on the lad's behalf, but within months of his death, factional politics disintegrated into preparation for battle, which willy-nilly precipitated the very war that Hideyoshi had feared would destroy his family fortunes.

The two foreign problems, one pertaining to Europeans and the other to East Asians, require fuller comment. The European presence in Japan began unpropitiously when three Portuguese aboard an ocean-going junk were shipwrecked on Tanegashima, a small island just south of Kyushu, in the autumn of 1543. They happened to be carrying arquebuses, and military commanders quickly recognized the battlefield utility of those horrendous, metal-hurling, explosive iron tubes, which the Japanese soon dubbed Tanegashima. Blacksmiths shortly began reproducing them, and by the 1560s, lords such as Nobunaga were using them to tactical advantage.

A few years after the shipwreck of 1543, Portuguese merchantmen began arriving in Kyushu, their captains seeking trade, while accompanying Jesuit missionaries sought converts. Daimyo welcomed the trade, which included guns, and in following decades trade and missionary activity grew apace, primarily around Nagasaki and the other Kyushu ports where foreign vessels usually anchored. By the mid 1580s, there may have been as many as two hundred thousand converts to the new creed, mostly in the poorer regions of the island. They included several daimyo, whose devotion produced numerous conversions among prudent retainers and subject peoples.

In 1587, while in Kyushu overseeing subjugation of the Shimazu, Hideyoshi evidently became fearful that the missionaries were creating circumstances dangerous to his emerging supremacy. They already controlled Nagasaki and its environs and were aggressively proselytizing among daimyo and their retainers.[8] Accordingly, he took direct control

7. These documents, along with others, are given in translation in David John Lu, *Sources of Japanese History* (New York: McGraw-Hill, 1974), 1: 186ff.
8. On the missionary role in Nagasaki's early years, see Diego Pacheco, "The Founding of the Port of Nagasaki and its Cession to the Society of Jesus," *MN* 35-3/4 (1970): 303–23.

of the Nagasaki vicinity and issued a pair of edicts designed to manage the situation. "Japan is the country of the gods, " he asserted, adopting a high-toned, tolerant stance. "Whether one desires to become a follower of the padre is up to that person's own conscience."[9] The two edicts went on to make clear that what troubled him was the reported behavior of daimyo and lesser military leaders. Some, he charged, were compelling their retainers and subject peoples to follow them in conversion, which he likened to Ikkō behavior. And some were granting land to the missionaries, who, he said, converted people and then allowed them to desecrate Buddhist temples and Shintō shrines. To prevent such misconduct, which he saw as dangerous to social order, he forbade lords to become Christian without his permission or to compel followers to convert. He also ordered the padres to leave Japan, but added that trade was a separate matter and he wished it to continue.

In following months, other issues occupied Hideyoshi's mind, and both Portuguese trade and missionary work continued to flourish. During the 1590s, however, Spaniards arrived and began competing with the Portuguese for trade and influence. Franciscan missionaries, who arrived aboard the Spanish ships, challenged the Jesuit claim of a sole right to proselytize in Japan, and the rivals began maligning one another to Japan's rulers. That conduct only compounded the distrust that Hideyoshi and other leaders, as well as proponents of Buddhist doctrine, already felt toward the foreign prelates. In 1596, when other affairs were going poorly for Hideyoshi, a Spanish ship's officer allegedly boasted that missionaries were merely the vanguard of Iberian conquest. A report of that comment led Hideyoshi to order a harsh crackdown, and twenty-six priests and converts were executed. The larger goal of expelling the missionaries and halting the spread of Christian sectarianism was not effectively pursued, however, in great part because the rulers' interest in trade undermined the effort. As a result, at the time of Hideyoshi's death, the situation was still unresolved.[10]

One of the affairs going poorly for Hideyoshi in 1596 was his grand policy toward China. Even before subduing the Shimazu back in 1587, he had dreamed of conquering China and standing astride the known world. No one knows whether he was inspired by conquest legends of the *Kojiki,* the past exploits of Mongols, the example of globe-girdling

9. Lu, *Sources,* 1: 191–92. See also George Elison, *Deus Destroyed: The Image of Christianity in Early Modern Japan* (Cambridge, Mass.: Harvard University Press, 1973), pp. 115–18.

10. C. R. Boxer, *The Christian Century in Japan, 1549–1650* (Berkeley and Los Angeles: University of California Press, 1951), treats these matters in great detail.

Europeans, some inner messenger whom he alone could hear, or by a wish to exhaust daimyo armies in further warfare. But whatever moved him, in 1591, upon learning that the last major daimyo was about to submit, and before the momentum of triumph could dissipate, he began preparing his conquest. He ordered lords in western Japan to construct hundreds of ships to carry men and supplies across the strait to Pusan. From there his army was to march northward through Korea and proceed overland to Peking. Once the fighting was done, Hideyoshi proposed, he would sail to China in his gigantic new flagship, the *Nihonmaru*, to establish his headquarters in Peking. From there he would rule all civilization.

His reach exceeded his grasp. In 1592 a vast armada transported his forces to landing points in the Pusan area, from where they started driving northward.[11] After several weeks of success, they began encountering intensified Korean guerrilla resistance, brilliant counterattacks by the naval commander Yi Sun-sin, and a massive Chinese counterthrust across the Yalu River. After months of costly and fruitless stalemate, Hideyoshi and Chinese leaders commenced negotiating a settlement. He finally agreed to pull his troops back to the Pusan region, where he established a defensive perimeter while talks continued. The negotiations eventually broke down in bitter recriminations, and he renewed the war in 1596. It was still dragging on when he died, leaving to key advisors the task of liquidating the whole tragic misadventure and reconstructing diplomatic relations with China and Korea.

At his death, then, Hideyoshi left a realm that had known eight years of uninterrupted domestic peace. In a sense the violence had merely been exported to the Korean peninsula, where its human toll was appalling. For Japan, however, the political landscape of 1598, with all lords subject to a central authority that could extract even the most costly service from them, stood in dramatic contrast to the endemic warfare that Alessandro Valignano had observed just a few years earlier.

To say that a central authority could extract service from even the greatest lords is not, however, to say that Hideyoshi had forged a centralized state. That he had not done. As this brief narrative has suggested, of the three legacies of emperor, shogun, and daimyo, the last

---

11. A fine new examination of this matter appears in Jurgis Elisonas [George Elison], "The Inseparable Trinity: Japan's Relations with China and Korea," in *The Cambridge History of Japan*, vol. 4, *Early Modern Japan*, ed. John W. Hall (Cambridge: Cambridge University Press, 1991), pp. 235–300.

and most recent was the predominant element in the reconsolidation of political order. The imperial institution was fulsomely revered and thoroughly disempowered. The shogunal title was disdained by both Nobunaga and Hideyoshi, not to be resurrected until 1603, when Hideyoshi's successor, Tokugawa Ieyasu, finally accepted it amid great pomp and circumstance, only to hand it on to his son two years later.

Clearly, it was the legacy of the daimyo, specifically that of sengoku daimyo, that proved central to political reconsolidation. Unusual competence as a lord had become in itself the basis for claiming a right to rule. Only in the final stages of pacification, when triumphant daimyo could no longer ignore the task of justifying their de facto power, did they turn to the legacies of emperor and shogun for help in converting domanial power and authority into a countrywide right to rule. But by then they had already participated in the creation of a "feudal" or "federal" political structure that assigned enduring power and essentially autonomous administrative authority to daimyo.[12]

The particulars of Hideyoshi's political arrangements were unique, of course, but the basic pattern of qualified territorial autonomy was not. Ross Hassig, in describing basic characteristics of Aztec and Roman governance, has identified the key attributes of Hideyoshi's order. Hassig writes that Aztec and Roman rule shared these characteristics:

> (1) expansion of political dominance without direct territorial control, (2) a focus on the internal security of the empire by exercising influence on a limited range of activities within the client states, and (3) the achievement of such influence by generally retaining rather than replacing local officials. Because their imperial concerns were limited, maintenance of the empire was achieved with great economy of force, local resources being relied on for local security and order.[13]

In later years, Tokugawa rulers elaborated rules and regulations to guide daimyo—their "client states"—but they adhered to the basic principle of qualified territorial autonomy. So the distribution of real power that Hideyoshi had recognized survived the coming of peace and remained largely intact until the 1860s.

12. The word *feudal* is habitually and haphazardly applied to Japan's political arrangements from the Kamakura to Tokugawa periods. That the term *federal* could usefully be applied to the early Tokugawa regime was suggested in 1967 in Conrad Totman, *Politics in the Tokugawa Bakufu, 1600–1843* (Cambridge, Mass.: Harvard University Press, 1967), p. 242. And Berry, *Hideyoshi,* has thoroughly explored its application to Hideyoshi's regime.
13. Ross Hassig, *Trade, Tribute, and Transportation: The Sixteenth-Century Political Economy of the Valley of Mexico* (Norman: University of Oklahoma Press, 1985), p. 93.

POLITICAL STABILIZATION, 1598–1632

Hideyoshi died in 1598 after a rule that spanned eight years of nearly continuous domestic warfare and eight of domestic peace. In the course of those years, he had defined a workable relationship between daimyo and court, but at the time of his death he still had not found a proper place for the shogunal legacy. That task fell to his successor.

TOKUGAWA IEYASU

After Hideyoshi's death, rivalries among his lieutenants quickly got out of hand. As tensions escalated, Tokugawa Ieyasu, the greatest among them, combined the resources of his sprawling domain in the Kantō plain with those of several allied lords to field an army of some eighty thousand, which defeated a rival coalition near Sekigahara in the autumn of 1600. He then acknowledged the baronial rights of all daimyo who accepted his leadership, letting them retain their castles, armies, and administrative autonomy. He rewarded allies in proportion to their service with lands taken from the losers in proportion to their mistakes. He also made elaborate displays of respect for the imperial court and ensured its fiscal well-being even while insisting that it conform to his wishes.

By 1603 much of the political rearranging was complete, and Ieyasu agreed to let a docile Emperor Goyōzei award him a number of titles, one of which was *seii taishōgun*. Two years later he had the titles transferred to his son, Hidetada, much as Nobunaga, shortly after receiving similarly fine imperial titles, had resigned them and instructed the court to award them to his heir. Ieyasu retained the signifiers that really mattered: titles associated with his status as head of the Tokugawa family and leader of the realm's predominant military domain.

With those moves, Ieyasu had in fact defined the basic relationship of emperor, shogun, and daimyo as it would remain for the next 250 years. All honor was shown to the court, but it was nearly powerless. All governing authority rested in the hands of a hereditary Tokugawa shogun, a man who might rule or might be under the control of his father or some other person or group. The title of shogun was pragmatically accepted as one of several that denoted imperial sanction of Tokugawa pretensions and legitimized Tokugawa regulation of the daimyo. But the hard base of those pretensions, the muscle that enforced regulations and kept daimyo in line, was the Tokugawa family head's tightly organized army of fighting men and the domain that supported it. In short, the accoutrements of real power remained in the hands of daimyo, of whom the greatest, the head of the Tokugawa domain centered on Edo, was expected to control all the others.

For ten years after shifting the title of shogun to Hidetada, Ieyasu continued to dominate the realm. To strengthen his family position, he enlarged his castles at Edo and Sunpu and built new ones at Nagoya and at Nijō in Kyoto, hard by the imperial palace. He relocated several daimyo to expand his own domain and strengthen its borders, took charge of Japan's foreign trade and major bullion mines, seized its best timberlands, and fostered production of agricultural and commercial goods in his lands and cities. He also consolidated the settlement by strengthening his political alliances and by addressing immediate problems as they arose, disposing of them in a pragmatic, piecemeal fashion.

Ieyasu labored at strengthening his position because, his title of shogun notwithstanding, the Tokugawa remained only the greatest of barons, *primus inter pares*. The others were as concerned as he to protect their own positions, and the result was a poorly concealed arms race. For example, Ikeda Terumasa, a key supporter of Ieyasu's at Sekigahara, was rewarded with a great domain headquartered at Himeji. After moving in, he expanded the existing castle into one of Japan's finest, the White Heron Castle, which stands intact today, serving as a movie set and tourist attraction. Terumasa strove to equip his fortress properly, and, when he died in 1613, he bequeathed to his successor "75 naval ships, 36,984 pounds of gunpowder, 1212 muskets, 513 bags of shot each containing 260 pellets, 56,378 pounds of lead, 14,772 pounds of saltpeter, 3702 pounds of sulfur, 1123 bows, 1640 arrows, 122 suits of armor, 400 pieces of gold, 100 *kan* of silver, numerous famous swords, and art objects." [14]

Ieyasu tried to discourage the widespread military preparations. He punished a number of daimyo for suspicious activity and "allowed" others to make ceremonial visits and send hostages to his headquarters. He forbade certain types of military construction and sought to reduce the capacity of lords to arm themselves by making them pay for much of his own castle building. However, given his understanding of politics and reliance on supportive lords, he never tried to abolish daimyo au-

14. John Whitney Hall, *Government and Local Power in Japan* (Princeton: Princeton University Press, 1966), p. 387.

tonomy itself. Rather, he chose to encourage lords—as well as priests and Kyoto aristocrats—to handle their affairs in an orderly and acceptable fashion.

To this end, he enacted one civil administrative measure after another. Within months of Sekigahara, he began issuing regulations, and as the years passed, he repeatedly revised them, making them more specific and more inclusive.[15] Even in their later forms, however, his edicts were basically hortatory, serving more as guidelines than explicit prohibitions. Thus in his most well-known code, the Laws for Military Households (*Buke shohatto*) of 1615, Ieyasu admonished daimyo to cultivate civilian skills, report any trouble or troublemakers, stay out of mischief, refrain from unauthorized castle construction or marriage arrangements, visit him at his headquarters, live frugally, and appoint officials who would govern wisely. Although he did not say as much, lords knew that if they were convicted of breaking any of those rules, he could strip them of their domains, which would not only leave them homeless but also reduce their entire vassal force to unemployed status as ronin. It was a powerful threat, one that disposed more and more vassals to urge caution upon their lords.

In one matter, Ieyasu's attempts at peaceful routinization failed disastrously. Back in 1598, Hideyoshi had been succeeded by his child-heir, Hideyori, and Ieyasu's enemies at Sekigahara claimed to be acting on the lad's behalf. Ieyasu knew better, of course—he was making the same claims for himself—and after the battle he allowed Hideyori, his mother, and a modest force of Toyotomi vassals to stay on at their gigantic Osaka castle. For over a decade all went tolerably well, but for reasons that had little to do with either Hideyori or the Toyotomi legacy, relations between Ieyasu and the young man disintegrated during 1614.[16] Large numbers of ronin began streaming to Osaka to take service with Hideyori in opposition to the Tokugawa, and as that happened, their grievances and goals began to determine Toyotomi actions.

This development, together with other problems of the moment, persuaded Ieyasu that the peace was coming undone. He failed to obtain a negotiated settlement so tried intimidation, deploying an army numbering one hundred thousand to crush the ronin, whose presence gave Hideyori a force estimated at ninety thousand. Under pressure from the

---

15. Lu gives translations of key documents in his *Sources*, 1: 201ff. Ieyasu's regulatory policies are discussed in Totman, *Tokugawa Ieyasu.*
16. Totman, *Tokugawa Ieyasu*, p. 130, suggests factors shaping Ieyasu's conduct in 1614.

ronin, Hideyori rejected Ieyasu's order that he dismiss them, abandon his castle, and either move to Edo or settle in the provinces, presumably as a "guest" of some lord. Intimidation, too, had failed, so Ieyasu's men attacked. They invested the castle and laboriously bombarded, burned, bargained, battered, and butchered their way in, finally subduing its defenders after Hideyori committed suicide.

Lest the lesson be missed, Ieyasu ordered the heads of dead ronin posted along the highway to Fushimi, creating one of the grimmest displays of authoritarian power in Japanese history. In following months, he presented rewards for loyal service and issued more regulations, most notably the *Buke shohatto*. Finally, in what surely was the most painful decision of all, he moved to prevent any future revival of Toyotomi pretensions by ordering Hideyori's son executed and his daughter placed in a nunnery. The youngsters were Ieyasu's own great-grandchildren by Hidetada's daughter, Senhime, who had been Hideyori's wife for twelve years. Senhime herself survived the catastrophe, living on to become a topic of popular legend, less for her role in the Osaka tragedy itself than for marital troubles of later years, which gave rise to gossipy stories of romantic entanglements.[17] One suspects that she had become emblematic of the many people, particularly the many women of samurai families, who were victims of the ruthless politics of pacification.

For all its savagery, the Osaka struggle did not really alter the character of the Tokugawa settlement. It eradicated a large population of ronin, eliminated a potential rallying point for the disaffected, and brought into Tokugawa hands a great castle, its bustling port and town, and its accompanying land. But when Ieyasu died in 1616, the central polity still consisted of a physically comfortable, ritually honored, firmly controlled and powerless imperial court in Kyoto, an immense shogunal headquarters in Edo, a string of auxiliary Tokugawa castles situated along the highway from Mito to Osaka, and a domanial base—about a fourth of the country—to support this central axis of military power.

In some 190 other castle towns scattered across the remaining three-fourths of Japan, daimyo continued to administer domains equipped with their own armies, tax systems, administrative staffs, and regulatory codes. To control those lords, the Tokugawa insisted they abide by a short list of regulations, expected them to make frequent pilgrimages to the Tokugawa headquarters, nurtured marriage alliances with them,

17. Richard Lane, *Images from the Floating World* (New York: G. P. Putnam's Sons, 1978), p. 17, reproduces one of the early *ukiyo* screens depicting Senhime and a lover identified as Honda Heihachirō.

and punished any who appeared overly ambitious or unable to keep their domains at peace.

TOKUGAWA HIDETADA

Hidetada, Ieyasu's heir and successor, made very few changes. Like his father, he relied on close retainers known as *toshiyori* (elders) to staff top supervisory posts. They were the most trusted of the Tokugawa family's hereditary vassals (*fudai*). The heads of some fudai families had at one time been independent lords who took service with Ieyasu or his ancestors, while others rose from lesser positions. Thanks to decades of useful assistance, at Sekigahara in particular, several dozen of these fudai had been rewarded with modest castles, situated on domains of sufficient size for them to become known as daimyo—fudai daimyo.

Of the ninety-one fudai daimyo of 1615, the half dozen or so who served as toshiyori oversaw all subordinate bakufu officials. These officials commanded the Tokugawa legions, governed Edo, Kyoto, and other towns under shogunal control, administered Tokugawa lands, supervised foreign trade, oversaw construction projects, operated bullion mines and mints, managed the regime's tax warehouses, and dealt with the imperial court, daimyo, foreign visitors, high-ranking prelates, and wealthy merchants. In 1623, Hidetada transferred the shogunal title to his son Iemitsu, but he and his toshiyori continued to supervise affairs until his death nine years later.

In foreign affairs, Hidetada continued promoting trade, even though it sometimes led to diplomatic incidents. By then numerous ronin and others had traveled to ports of call throughout East and Southeast Asia, taking employment as seamen, traders, and rough-service shore police. A hard lot, they repeatedly got into scuffles and riots with local people and other foreigners, in the process creating ill will toward Japan. In the most serious incident since Hideyoshi's invasion of Korea, a Japanese merchant-adventurer fitted out thirteen junks, loaded them with fighting men, and despatched them to conquer Taiwan in 1616. They bungled their attempt at entrepreneurial imperialism and turned to freebooting along the China coast, in the process causing hardship and resentment.[18] On other occasions, men of other nationalities caused the trouble, but whoever precipitated the incidents, they eroded the appeal of overseas trade.

18. Boxer, *Christian Century*, p. 298.

Nevertheless, Hidetada continued to encourage foreign trade. He did, however, try to eliminate one domestic product of European contact, the Christian communities created by Iberian missionaries. His predecessors had crushed the analogous, domestically inspired communities of Ikkō and Hokke Buddhists but had not suppressed those of European inspiration. Ieyasu continued Hideyoshi's policy of sporadic, half-hearted harassment, but for years he was constrained by his wish for trade. And doubtless the relatively marginal nature of the issue kept pushing it out of mind.

By 1613, however, Ieyasu had Dutchmen and Englishmen to trade with, so the following year as scandals erupted and domestic affairs worsened, he decided to sever the Iberian connection. He reissued his earlier order expelling missionaries, outlawed the practice of Christianity, and ordered places of worship torn down. Whereas he earlier had tried to preserve trade links, moreover, this time he simply ordered the Iberians to go. Henceforth, it appeared, his European commerce would be handled through the Dutch and English.

Within weeks, the problem of Hideyori's ronin took center stage and the expulsion order fell into desuetude. Ieyasu died without reviving it, perhaps because he hoped the outcome at Osaka had solved the missionary problem as well as that of ronin. Osaka defenders had flown Christian banners, and two Jesuits and three Franciscans had been found among the defeated. Ieyasu may have felt that his ruthless suppression of the insurgency had eliminated enough followers of the padres to suffice, at least for the moment. In any case, it was left to Hidetada to deal with the issue, and when he did, he took his father's last directives of 1614 as the guide to policy.

Hidetada reiterated his father's proscription late in 1616 and urged daimyo to arrest missionaries and break up Christian communities. The following year, renewed missionary activism and feuding among apostate merchants in Nagasaki (including the sponsor of the Taiwan expedition) led him to order more thorough application of the 1614 edicts. For several years, he and his daimyo worked to stamp out missionary activity and eliminate Christian communities, which may have numbered three hundred thousand people at the time, mostly in far western Japan. By 1630 the brutal business of extracting apostasies was largely complete. Most villagers had recanted or feigned as much; many had fled or gone into hiding; many more had been forcibly relocated to other villages where they lived, in effect, as hostages. And large numbers—perhaps as many as four or five thousand, of whom fewer than

seventy were Europeans—had been executed, martyrs to their faith.[19]
With that suppression the last overt form of unauthorized communal
political organization had been crushed. What survived was hidden.

DAIMYO GOVERNANCE: TOSA AND KAGA

Leaders at Edo were not alone in pursuing political stabilization after
1600. Daimyo all over Japan established routines of peaceful governance even while readying for war. For many the task was complicated
by transfers to new domains. They went essentially as "carpetbaggers,"
outsiders unfamiliar with their new territories and most likely unwelcome to the inhabitants, especially to local warriors who had served the
previous lord.

To cite an illustrative case, Ieyasu assigned the domain of Tosa on
Shikoku to an ally, Yamanouchi Kazutoyo, who moved there in 1601.[20]
He inherited a large population of Tosa farmer-warriors who were
thoroughly hostile to his coming. But he must placate them, he knew,
lest Ieyasu punish his failure by taking away his new domain, his rank
and income, or very possibly his life. He faced the task of moving his
own retainers to Tosa and getting them properly settled and the even
more delicate task of installing an adequate tax system. That system
would have to yield enough income to support his officials and troops,
build a headquarters castle appropriate to his status, and pay the other
costs of rulership, including Ieyasu's sporadic levies. And it would have
to do so without provoking a widespread tax revolt.

Realizing that war could erupt again at any moment, Kazutoyo
promptly identified a castle site and assigned officials to handle construction. By 1603 he had erected a satisfactory defensive bastion at
Kōchi. Meanwhile his officials carried out a land survey that identified
tax sources and delineated fiefs for assignment to senior retainers. And
he cajoled and confronted local warriors, suppressing the last diehards
by the time his castle was built.

The new Yamanouchi land surveys and corvée labor demands caused
many villagers to abscond, even though anyone convicted of doing so
was subject to severe punishment. For several years, a major task for

19. Ibid., pp. 332–34, 358, 361. Boxer estimates 5,000–6,000 martyrs for the period
1614–1640, which I have simply modified to 4,000–5,000 for the years up to 1630.
20. This material on Tosa is drawn from Marius B. Jansen, "Tosa in the Seventeenth
Century: The Establishment of Yamauchi Rule" in John W. Hall and Marius B. Jansen,
eds., *Studies in the Institutional History of Early Modern Japan* (Princeton: Princeton
University Press, 1968), pp. 115–29.

Kazutoyo and his successors was persuading the able-bodied to stay in their villages and produce crops. Regulations of 1612 sought to promote resettlement by forbidding Tosa officials to punish villagers who fled to other places in the domain and by stopping the worst of the extortion that some retainers used to extract income from villagers on their fiefs. By 1630, it appears, basic consolidation had been achieved, and the Yamanouchi administration subsequently turned to longer-term programs of economic development.

Even daimyo not assigned to new domains faced analogous problems. Maeda, the lord of Kanazawa, had sided with Ieyasu in 1600 and received a bit of contiguous territory as reward for his help, but basically he retained his pre-Sekigahara domain.[21] Like Yamanouchi he felt compelled to prepare for the next war and devoted much energy to expanding his castle. He also enlarged his castle town by laying out new residential areas and ordering retainers to build and settle there. As they did so, he developed regulations to prevent his horde of underemployed young men from getting into trouble or engaging in seditious activity should their ambitions outreach their prospects. He issued such regulations in 1601, again in 1605, and a third time in 1610, with additions in 1613. He also set up chains of command to enforce the rules.

As Maeda's retainers left the countryside, he replaced them with a hierarchy of administrators who collected taxes, resolved civil disputes, and handled criminal cases. His finance officials supervised intendants, who were samurai assigned to administrative offices spotted about the domain. They oversaw village officials, who usually were larger landholders and not of samurai rank, although in many instances they or their ancestors had once been fighting men.[22]

The influx of retainers to Kanazawa was accompanied by an inflow of commoners who developed their own neighborhoods, provided myriad services to the samurai, and in turn required the service of others. By 1614 these processes had given Maeda a large castle town, so he established a hierarchy of administrators for urban commoners that paralleled the one supervising samurai. Whereas the command structure of his military units provided the hierarchy for samurai, however,

---

21. This material on Kanazawa is drawn from James L. McClain, *Kanazawa: A Seventeenth-Century Japanese Castle Town* (New Haven: Yale University Press, 1982), pp. 27–31, 56–63.
22. The fullest study in English of the early decades of Maeda administration in Kanazawa is Philip Carlton Brown, *Domain Formation in Early Modern Japan: The Development of Rural Administration and the Land Tax System in Kaga Han, 1581–1631* (in press).

he appointed merchants or other well-regarded townsmen to manage the sections of town occupied by commoners.

Throughout Japan, daimyo addressed problems of governance, and gradually a countrywide system took shape, in which most samurai dwelt in castle towns under the supervision of officials, who handled affairs on the basis of regulations drafted by their lord and his advisors. Townsmen managed urban commoners in accord with regulations issued by the lord's government; in the countryside, villagers administered their affairs subject to surveillance by higher authorities, who enforced regulations to keep the peace and collect taxes.

In Edo, the toshiyori and lesser officials of the Tokugawa bakufu ran their own domain in much the same way. Doing so probably consumed the bulk of their time, but in addition, as noted above, bakufu leaders exercised the functions associated with shogunal authority. As of 1632 then, the newly pacified realm was still in the hands of a rough-hewn class of fighting men, who governed through simple, hierarchical structures of authoritarian control. Their system, which had grown out of sengoku daimyo arrangements, was organized, was stable, did function, and kept the peace.

The Economics of Pacification

During the decades 1570–1630, Japan experienced economic growth as striking as its political change. Initially, the growth, which was tied to the activity of warring daimyo, seemed to accelerate in tandem with the violence, but the end of warfare did not halt it. Rather, the economic vigor persisted, mainly because governments promoted agriculture, mining, construction, and foreign trade. Entrepreneurial initiatives, especially those of villagers, were crucial to the expansion of agricultural production, but not until the mid seventeenth century did entrepreneurs displace government as the key element sustaining growth in the economy as a whole.

The prosperity resulting from this economic growth was crucial to the peace. It deprived malcontents of a broad base of support by providing career opportunities for the ambitious and, one suspects, a basic sense of well-being for the general public. Only a portion of the career opportunities were in government, so most of the ambitious had to turn elsewhere, either to commerce, which many did, or to cultural production, which also flourished. In the countryside, a historically less visible arena than the towns, energies could be devoted to increased production, because there remained land to open, trees to fell, ore to mine, and seafood to gather.

Crime, protest, rowdyism, and sedition were alternatives, of course, and they were present. Except for the fierce battles at Osaka in 1614–15 and at Shimabara in 1637–38, however, most incidents did not escalate into major crises, because few found themselves so squeezed by circumstances that defiance seemed to be life's most promising or least disagreeable alternative.

Certainly, the rulers' power reinforced that reticence: shogun and daimyo exacted a high price, whether loss of job, status, or life, from those charged with misconduct. As the law became regularized, moreover, it held accountable not only the accused but their kin and community. In response to pursuit of this peacekeeping strategy from above, communities tried to police their own below. The stick of social discipline was generally effective, however, only because the carrot of social opportunity provided most people with adequate peaceable alternatives to rebellion. Such alternatives existed because the ecosystem's production generally satisfied society's essential needs, despite inefficiencies and inequities in the distribution system. In later centuries, as we shall note subsequently, those same sticks, absent those same carrots, no longer sufficed.

DOMESTIC ECONOMIC EXPANSION

The economic growth of the years 1570–1630 was grounded in basic expansion of rural output, but it was most visible in an unprecedented surge of urban construction. The growth was sustained by increased exploitation of natural resources and gains in efficiency of exploitation. The increases in exploitation included opening more land to tillage and expanding mining and forest-product extraction. The improvements in efficiency mainly related to the use of land and labor, transportation, storage, and exchange.

RURAL ECONOMIC GROWTH

Several developments of the decades 1570–1630 enabled villagers to expand rural production. The expansion was inextricably linked to a rapid rise in gross population, most of which was rural and hence available to work the land. Many other changes also contributed to the expansion, and government initiatives underlay a number of them. In essence, governments established conditions more favorable to agricultural expansion at the village level and then facilitated it by regularizing official involvement in village life, producing, in effect, an agreement between rulers and villagers that the former would leave the latter to handle their own affairs and the latter would pay taxes as required and stay out of trouble.

Several government policies encouraged rural output. Most directly, daimyo and hegemons promoted reclamation projects and facilitated land clearance through logging activity. Less directly, a number of policies fostered production by increasing the rural labor supply. The suppression of Ikkō and other communal military activities, Hideyoshi's "sword hunt" of 1588, and other measures that disarmed villagers all reduced their choices in life, thereby increasing the hours they had available for work. The demobilizing of armies from the 1590s on returned thousands upon thousands of able-bodied men to the countryside. The cessation of hostilities curtailed emergency corvée levies, and while lords continued to requisition vast amounts of peacetime labor, they generally tried to do so in ways that minimized interruptions of farm work.

Those policies made more workers available; other policies gave them more reason to engage in farm work. Most obviously, the end of warfare reduced the destruction, disruptions, and enervating fears that accompanied armies in action, giving villagers more reason to believe that tilling and planting now could be expected to yield a harvest later. Not so obviously, daimyo ordered samurai living in villages, who frequently extracted tribute heavily and arbitrarily, to move into castle towns, thereby relieving many villagers of onerous and unpredictable exactions. As the decades advanced, moreover, daimyo transfers occurred less frequently and disruptively. Where lords vacating an area had once attempted to take with them all the wealth they could grab, by 1630 the bakufu was trying to establish the principle that normal tax levies must be shared by departing and incoming lords. Not all lords obeyed, but the magnitude of the problem diminished with time.

The rulers still taxed, of course, and they taxed assiduously, but they did so in a manner that would not stifle production. In place of erratic and arbitrary exactions, daimyo and hegemons implemented censuses and land surveys to establish a basis for orderly and durable taxation.[1] The inquests, which became more precise over the years, identified landholders by name, age, and household composition and their fields by location, size, and soil quality. They helped to delineate boundaries

---

1. The finest description of such land surveying in English is Philip C. Brown, "The Mismeasure of Land: Land Surveying in the Tokugawa Period," *MN* 42-2 (Summer 1987): 115–55.

and social relationships, thus eliminating some areas of dispute, and they let tillers know which plots of land they would be accountable for at tax time.

Diverse types of production were taxed, but collectors were mainly interested in the rice crop. In the tax procedure that became most common from the 1590s on, officials visited every village annually to sample the rice harvest, estimate the yield, and assign that year's tax obligation, using as a base the village's arable acreage as indicated by the official land survey.[2] Officials could make adjustments downward in response to poor harvests. Where they found new fields, they could temporarily assign reduced taxes to take into account the costs of improvement and the relatively poor yield of new plots of land, later adjusting the rate upward to a level they deemed appropriate to the type and quality of field.

The inspectors then departed, leaving it to village officials to assure that the village as a unit fulfilled its tax obligations. In most villages, a headman (commonly known as *shōya*) and his fellow officials (*hyaku-shōdai* and *kumi gashira*) constituted the village leadership. They were charged with assuring that the village tax was delivered, but they also were expected to keep the village peaceful. Insofar as they could, they doubtless preferred to shift the tax burden onto their poorer neighbors, but they were constrained by the survey documents, which identified the lands for which they were responsible, by the fact that excessive abuse of position could lead to damaging unrest, and by a web of asymmetrical interdependency that bound them to their neighbors. These constraints made it difficult for village officials to develop into capricious local strongmen comparable to the recently departed samurai.

This regularized system of taxation eliminated many forms of tax abuse, even while it steered tax yield into the hands of daimyo and bakufu. It permitted villagers to anticipate their crop needs and prospects and to allocate energies accordingly. Moreover, since tax regulations often granted special concessions to newly opened land, they made reclamation work seem particularly advantageous. In consequence, villagers devoted time to opening and upgrading land and engaging in other pursuits that yielded the goods necessary to sustain not only the rapidly rising population but also the growing cities and booming monumental construction.

2. Philip C. Brown has also penned a helpful essay on early Tokugawa land taxation, "Practical Constraints on Early Tokugawa Land Taxation: Annual versus Fixed Assessments in Kaga Domain," *JJS* 14-2 (Summer 1988): 369–401.

URBAN CONSTRUCTION

Changes in medieval warfare, including the use of cannon late in the sixteenth century, led to ever-larger defensive bastions. Around these citadels, regional lords created castle towns (*jōkamachi*) by assembling their vassals and a supporting population of merchants, artisans, and service personnel. During the years of Nobunaga and Hideyoshi, small castle towns sprang up like toadstools, along with a variety of port and highway towns—some ninety new towns appearing between 1572 and 1590 alone[3]—and after 1600 most of them continued to grow.

The economic impact of castle and town construction should not be underestimated. To mention only its main aspects, construction required the assembling, equipping, feeding, housing, and supervising of armies of ill-paid corvée labor and innumerable technical specialists. The workers toiled for weeks and months, digging and moving soil; hauling, shaping, and installing stonework; felling, transporting, shaping, and placing the lumber that framed buildings; gathering, carrying, and installing the thatch and wattle of ordinary housing; constructing and operating the kilns that baked clay into roof tiles and produced charcoal for smelting metal; and mining the ore and working the forges that yielded the diverse metal items of urban construction.

Most laborers came from the countryside. Daimyo conscripted them from villages in their domains; Hideyoshi and Ieyasu compelled lords all over the country to furnish workmen and matériel. In 1591, for example, Hideyoshi requisitioned over sixty-two thousand men from throughout Japan to work on the Hōkōji, a gigantic new temple he was building in Kyoto, and three years later he reputedly had lords despatch a quarter of a million workers to build his sprawling castle at Fushimi.[4] Later, Ieyasu was even more demanding.

Around the castles grew towns, as vassals and service people settled. Lords often designed samurai neighborhoods as a first line of defense, and they encouraged commoners to move into adjacent areas, luring

3. Conrad Totman, *The Green Archipelago: Forestry in Preindustrial Japan* (Berkeley and Los Angeles: University of California Press, 1989), p. 53. On this urban growth, see, too, Nakai Nobuhiko and James L. McClain, "Commercial Change and Urban Growth in Early Modern Japan," in *The Cambridge History of Japan*, vol. 4, *Early Modern Japan*, ed. John W. Hall (Cambridge: Cambridge University Press, 1991), pp. 519–95.

4. Mary Elizabeth Berry, *Hideyoshi* (Cambridge, Mass.: Harvard University Press, 1982), pp. 198, 229. The burden that Hidetada imposed on daimyo for Osaka castle construction during the 1620s is reported in William Hauser, "Osaka Castle and Tokugawa Authority in Western Japan," in Jeffrey P. Mass and Hauser, *The Bakufu in Japanese History* (Stanford: Stanford University Press, 1985), pp. 159–72.

1.   Kumamoto Castle. One of Japan's largest castles, this was the headquarters of the Hosokawa domain in central Kyushu. The photograph, taken from within an outer enceinte, shows the castle's central wood-and-plaster tower directly ahead, a second tower to the left, and the primary approach to the central keep uphill to the right and through a fortified gate. Courtesy of the Study and Documentation Centre for Photography, University of Leiden, Collection Bauduin, Neg. No. C7.

them with promises of free trade and land on which to erect houses and mercantile facilities. At lordly behest, labor gangs laid out streets, dredged canals, constructed bridges, built wharfs and warehouses, erected fire-lookout towers, and equipped them with alarm bells. Settlers built houses and storefronts and commenced fabricating products, selling their wares, and providing myriad forms of service to samurai and commoner neighbors alike.

    The organizational requirements of urban construction were similar to those for equipping and deploying armies, and lords commonly turned to the same men when undertaking both tasks. During the later sixteenth century, men with demonstrated skill in project management and mercantile ventures served many daimyo as quartermasters and civil administrators, managing finances, handling commissariat tasks, supervising transport operations, and even administering assigned territories.[5] Ieyasu, for example, employed the wealthy merchant Suminokura Ryōi for many tasks: capitalizing overseas trade, dredging rivers, and managing other engineering projects and provisioning duties. Similarly, Maeda of Kanazawa hired Kanaya Hikoshirō, son of a minor samurai, to supply him with gunpowder and lamp oil. At Maeda's urging, Hikoshirō settled in Kanazawa, and from 1604 on, the daimyo exempted him and his fleet of ten ships from city and port taxes in return for continued handling of official shipping and participation in Maeda's fiscal administration.[6] Needless to say, some of these merchants enriched themselves handsomely while serving their lords.

Some daimyo levies, especially those made hurriedly in time of war, diverted labor from farmwork. Generally, however, lords tried to arrange construction and corvée duty in ways that minimized disruption of field work. They scheduled projects for slack seasons or spread duty broadly enough so that a particular individual would not be kept overlong from his regular tasks. In essence, the strategy improved the efficiency of a lord's labor supply by directing to his use hours and days that villagers might have devoted to sleep, leisure, religious practice, troublemaking, or other "uneconomic" activities.

Kanazawa and Edo will illustrate the growth of castle towns, though most other jōkamachi between Hirosaki and Hitoyoshi would do as well. When the powerful daimyo Maeda Toshiie took it as his headquarters in 1583, Kanazawa was a small temple town of a few thousand people.[7] He promptly set labor gangs to work building a castle and added more moats and walls during the 1590s. In 1599 a military showdown seemed imminent, and Toshiie and his advisors feverishly prepared for it by assembling huge labor gangs to move vast quantities of soil and stone to create new enceintes, walls, and moats. Within the new revetments, they put crews of carpenters to work erecting houses for Toshiie's chief vassals.

Toshiie died that spring, but after Ieyasu's victory at Sekigahara in 1600, his successor, still cautious, had labor gangs build yet another ring of moats and walls. When war did not resume, his vassals began

5. A concise introduction to merchant quartermasters is E. S. Crawcour, "Changes in Japanese Commerce in the Tokugawa Period," *JAS* 22-4 (Aug. 1963), which is reprinted in John W. Hall and Marius B. Jansen, eds., *Studies in the Institutional History of Early Modern Japan* (Princeton: Princeton University Press, 1968), pp. 189–202.

6. James C. McClain, *Kanazawa* (New Haven: Yale University Press, 1982), p. 49. McClain describes a number of other merchants and their relationship to Maeda.

7. This summary is based on McClain, *Kanazawa*.

moving out of the castle to more spacious locations, but their houses were arranged to form additional defense works. Maeda lords subsequently dug other canals—some fifteen kilometers of them—to enhance castle security and provide drinking water. And as they settled more vassals around the castle, they did so in ways that further secured their bastion. Maeda ordered dozens of temples and shrines relocated to improve city organization and castle defense. He also designated areas for occupancy by merchants and other commoners. The many projects not only generated poorly remunerated by-employment for unskilled corvée laborers but also work for loggers, carpenters, roofers, tatami makers, masons, and a host of other artisans.

When Kanazawa's urban sprawl reached nearby agricultural villages, Maeda ordered them relocated. When the bed of a nearby stream hampered growth, he had the stream rechanneled and the braided river bed filled in to form new areas for townsmen. He ordered roads straightened and canals improved to facilitate transport and storage. Other commoners, seeing job opportunities, settled along the roads approaching town, gradually creating residential strips that straggled out into the countryside on all sides of the castle. By 1614 Kanazawa numbered some thirty to forty thousand residents in samurai households, and by 1630 it housed an equal number of commoners.[8]

The archetypal castle town was Edo. Despite its unique status as shogunal headquarters it differed from other castle towns not so much in timing or pattern of development as in scale. In the summer of 1590, Ieyasu assisted his lord, Hideyoshi, in crushing the Hōjō, who controlled the Kantō plain from their huge seaside castle at Odawara. In the settlement that followed, Hideyoshi claimed Ieyasu's domain in the Tōkai region for himself and awarded Ieyasu the Kantō. Rather than moving into Odawara, whose vulnerability to blockade had just been demonstrated, Ieyasu looked for a more defensible headquarters. He chose a small, derelict, earthen-walled fortification on a coastal bluff nearly encircled by two creeks. The creeks emptied into a brackish swamp at the head of a broad bay that penetrated to the heart of the fertile Kantō plain. Both the castle town and bay eventually came to be known as Edo, from the village of some 100–200 residents that lay just below the bluff along the Edo River, as the more northerly of the two creeks was called.

For the rest of his life, Ieyasu labored to transform his little fortress

8. McClain, *Kanazawa*, pp. 30–46.

site into a castle town, and his successors continued the task. In spurts of work that went on from the early 1590s until the 1630s, and sporadically thereafter, crews cleared forest, leveled hillocks to fill in the swamp, laid out streets, rerouted rivers, dredged creeks and canals, pounded in miles of pilings, spanned the waterways with bridges, laid up the castle's huge rock walls, constructed scores of wooden castle buildings, and erected the shrines, temples, mansions, warehouses, storefronts, row houses, and common dwellings of what by 1600 was a town of some five thousand dwellings, and by 1610, reportedly a clean, well-organized city of a hundred and fifty thousand people.[9]

Projects of this sort went on all over the country during these decades, constituting in totality a massive exercise in capital investment. Through uncountable hours of effort, two generations of poorly paid and harshly driven laborers transformed forests into cities and monuments that future generations were able to utilize, even while directing most of their own energies to other tasks.

From the 1620s on, the pace of construction slackened perceptibly. In Edo, Hidetada slowed it sharply, in part, no doubt, because much of the desired castle and mansion work had already been accomplished, but in part because the work bore heavily on daimyo and generated more discontent than it seemed to warrant. Daimyo, likewise, cut back, because the bakufu discouraged castle building, because they themselves saw less and less reason to pursue it, and because their exchequers were already in such poor condition that they were eager to economize. Some projects were initiated in later years, but by 1630 the great age of urban construction had passed.

NATURAL RESOURCE EXPLOITATION

The countrywide surge of urban construction had wide ramifications. It generated productive activity throughout the countryside, causing a sharp increase in the exploitation of natural resources.

One aspect of the work on Edo Castle will illustrate how the fingers of urban construction reached into the hinterland. Ieyasu ordered Satsuma to build three hundred vessels to haul stone for use in the castle. The shipbuilding consumed Kyushu timber and created work for loggers, transporters, and shipwrights in Satsuma. When put into service

9. Michael Cooper, *They Came to Japan: An Anthology of European Reports on Japan, 1543–1640* (Berkeley and Los Angeles: University of California Press, 1965), p. 284, quoting Vivero y Velasco for 1610. Totman, *Green Archipelago*, p. 57 for 1600.

the vessels hauled rock from the Izu peninsula to the castle site, providing work for merchant seamen and their provisioners throughout the Izu-Edo area. Getting out and shaping the rock employed stonecutters in both Izu and Edo. The masons used iron drills and wedges produced by smiths. The smiths used charcoal, which created work for charcoal makers, who went into the woods, cut up trees, hauled sticks to the charring site, racked them, covered them with soil, and then started the smoldering fire whose heat generated the anaerobic combustion that converted wood fiber to charcoal. Then someone bagged the charcoal and hauled it to the forge. The smiths also required pig iron, which was smelted from ore extracted by miners. Someone furnished the miners with mine timbers, and someone collected wood to fire the furnaces that smelted the ore. And yet further back in the supply chain, all these workers required food, salt, clothing, and diverse other goods, many of which they could not provide for themselves.

Castle stone work thus created jobs at many places. Wood was the other major raw material of urban construction, and the economic effects of its provisioning were felt even more widely. Wood frequently came from forests some distance from the construction site, and moving it required great quantities of unskilled labor. Most lumber traveled by river, sea, or ocean, and timber provisioning involved the cooperation of villages not only near the felling site but along the transportation routes. Villagers cleared rivers of debris, and when wood was floated out of the mountains, they lined riverbanks to keep sticks from jamming or beaching, to dislodge those that did, and to ensure that nobody stole any.[10]

Besides creating activities that linked castle town to hinterland, timber use abetted agricultural expansion by removing the large trees that constituted a major obstacle to cultivation of old-growth ("virgin") woodland. Because villagers found such trees too difficult to fell and remove, they generally killed them by girdling or fire and then had to wait years while the hulks decayed before the site became fully open to cultivation. When logging crews cut out timber, they simplified and speeded up the conversion of woodland to arable.

During the decades of pacification, however, only a portion of Japan's reclamation work converted old-growth forest to arable. Much of it simply restored to tillage land previously used for cropping or pas-

10. For a description of early modern lumber transport, see Conrad Totman, "Logging the Unloggable: Timber Transport in Early Modern Japan," *Journal of Forest History* 27-4 (Oct. 1983): 180–91.

ture. During especially violent spasms of warfare, such as those that accompanied the suppression of Ikkō activism, cultivated areas were abandoned, to be resettled and reactivated later. As sengoku daimyo consolidated their realms, they urged tillers to reopen abandoned land, and with the return of general order from the late 1580s, the trend became widespread.

The reclamation of abandoned land phased directly into the opening of new land; the shared interest of ruler and tiller in producing more food promoted both processes. Generally, the reopening of former arable occurred first, because it proceeded more rapidly and easily. Moreover, it usually furnished better, more manageable soil and, for a few years at least, higher production. But when all such land in a vicinity was again under the hoe, areas cleared by loggers became favored for reclamation. It is likely that by 1600 most abandoned land was back in cultivation and that reclamation thereafter largely involved the opening of hitherto untilled sites.

Reclamation was accompanied by measures to upgrade existing arable, most notably by improving and expanding irrigation systems and by converting dry fields to paddy, which yielded much more grain per acre. Gradually, of course, land for reclamation became more difficult to develop and expansion or improvement of irrigation systems harder to achieve, but those problems did not become insistent until later in the century.[11]

Mining was another important area of increased resource utilization. Iron was in great demand for weapons, tools, and construction work. Gold, silver, and copper were sought for gift giving and decorative work, and, especially from the 1590s on, for money. Lords encouraged prospecting, mine development, and the processing of ore, and they employed new techniques that enabled miners to get at hitherto inaccessible veins, work accessible veins more efficiently, and extract metal from inferior ores.[12]

As Hideyoshi consolidated his position, he laid claim to bullion mines throughout Japan, and after Sekigahara, Ieyasu took them over. During

11. One examination of land reclamation, which indicates the nature and limits of relevant data, is Kozo Yamamura, "Returns on Unification: Economic Growth in Japan, 1550–1650," in John Whitney Hall et al., eds., *Japan before Tokugawa* (Princeton: Princeton University Press, 1981), pp. 327–72.

12. On mining technology, see Robert Leroy Innes, *The Door Ajar: Japan's Foreign Trade in the Seventeenth Century* (Ann Arbor: University Microfilms International, 1980), 2: 532–44. And see too Nagahara Keiji and Kozo Yamamura, "Shaping the Process of Unification: Technological Progress in Sixteenth- and Seventeenth-Century Japan," *JJS* 14-1 (Winter 1988): 78–81.

his lifetime, some fifty gold mines and thirty silver mines were brought
into production, and his mines in Iwami, Izu, Kai, Sado, Tajima, and
elsewhere yielded up ore in unprecedented quantities.[13] Production figures are few and scattered, but it appears that gold output peaked during the 1620s. At that time, bakufu silver mines on Sado were yielding
some sixty to ninety thousand kilograms of bullion per year.[14] In following decades, silver production also dropped, but until the 1630s the
yield from mining played a crucial role in both urban construction and
foreign trade.

Mining, like lumbering, had ramifications that reached well beyond
the source of raw material. Large numbers of people found employment
providing wood for mine timbers and smelting fuel, and the yield from
the mining-smelting work employed haulers and craftsmen and furnished tools that improved the efficiency of agricultural and other production and money that expedited commerce.

EXPEDITING COMMERCE

Money's importance to trade lies, of course, in its fungibility and por-
tability. Despite the inherent attractions of money and the long history
of its use in Japan, however, the monetary system of the late sixteenth
century worked poorly. Diverse gold, silver, and copper coins were in
circulation, but they were of uncertain metallic purity, and their relative
values varied inconstantly from region to region. Furthermore, the better coins were mostly of Chinese origin, and their import had been sharply
curtailed from the late fifteenth century on, so good coinage had gradually become scarce and expensive. That undermined its utility as a
medium of exchange by converting it into a commodity of such value
that people hoarded it and tax collectors preferred it to the material
goods that taxpayers actually produced.[15]

Nobunaga and Hideyoshi mainly used their precious metal for foreign trade, political gift giving, and decoration, but they also recognized
the value of coinage as a medium of exchange. Nobunaga tried to stan-
dardize the values of coins in his domain as early as 1569, and Hide-

13. Iwao Seiichi, "Japanese Foreign Trade in the 16th and 17th Centuries," AA 30
(1976): 5.
14. A. Kobata, "The Production and Uses of Gold and Silver in Sixteenth- and
Seventeenth-Century Japan," Economic History Review, 2d ser., 18, no. 1–3 (1965):
248, text and n. 4.
15. Kozo Yamamura, "From Coins to Rice: Hypotheses on the Kandaka and Kokudaka Systems," JJS 14-2 (Summer 1988), pp. 351–52.

yoshi minted coinage for his own use a few years later. Effective coinage reform did not occur, however, until after Hideyoshi's death.[16]

Ieyasu also used precious metals in trade, gift giving, and decoration. But he went much farther than his predecessors in establishing the credibility of money by suppressing inferior coins, setting up regulated mints, and issuing currency and bullion of reliable weight and fineness. In 1601 he commissioned trusted merchants to establish silver, gold, and copper mints (*ginza, kinza,* and *dōza*) in Fushimi and Sunpu (later moved to Kyoto and Edo) and to mint bullion from his mines into coins with specified values based on their metallic content. His new gold and silver coins circulated well, but the output of copper coins was too limited to serve as small-denomination money, and they failed to circulate widely until later in the century.

The use of money to expedite commerce was one aspect of the broader process of improving efficiency of distribution. The process also involved improvements in commercial measurement, storage, and transportation. In the late sixteenth century, different regions of Japan employed different measures for such basic items as grain and timber. The diversity hampered trade by generating misunderstanding and mistrust. It forced merchants to repackage or remeasure materials and recalibrate sale prices to fit local usage, and at times it produced useless goods, such as lumber cut too short for its purpose. Hideyoshi, who requisitioned goods from all over Japan, played a key role in standardizing measurements, the most important of these being the *ken* and *masu,* basic units of linear and bulk measure. After his death, Ieyasu also promoted uniformity, but a few anomalies survived, such as different-sized floor mats, and hence building dimensions, in the Edo and Kyoto regions.

Improvements in storage paralleled those in money and mensuration. As peace returned to the realm, daimyo stabilized domanial administration, assigning district officials to supervise orderly tax collection and erecting storage sheds and warehouses at district offices and castle towns to keep tax grains safe from rodents and rot. Merchants, often working for daimyo, also erected warehouses and timber storage areas, which further reduced the portion of goods lost to spoilage.

Leaders in the late sixteenth century also fostered commerce by improving transportation arrangements. Nobunaga and others, hoping to

16. Berry, *Hideyoshi,* pp. 268–69, n. 79. Kobata, "Production and Uses of Gold and Silver," pp. 245–66, is a helpful introduction to this topic, with particular emphasis on the use of these metals in overseas trade.

steer goods in their own direction, abolished river and highway tolls and other fees that local leaders and representatives of higher authorities had customarily used to tax commerce and travelers. To lure commerce to their castle towns, they also designated the towns as *rakuichi*, meaning that commercial taxes would not be levied on merchants who did business there.

Lords also addressed physical problems of transport, primarily to expedite the movement of produce. Hideyoshi ordered construction of a large fleet of river boats to transport goods and people on the Yodo between Kyoto and the sea. In addition, he invested much effort in widening and rearranging city streets to enhance Kyoto's elegance and facilitate its growth and accessibility to commerce. Ieyasu promoted transportation improvements with especial vigor. By 1600 the decades of logging had already made such inroads into woodland that good timber was becoming difficult to obtain, so he had Suminokura Ryōi and his son Soan (Yoichi) mobilize corvée labor gangs to clear rocks, sandbars, and accumulated debris from the Ōi River northwest of Kyoto and the Tenryū and Fuji rivers in the Tōkai region, thereby securing timber for his great projects. He also improved transit at the city end of the network, creating a maze of canals to facilitate the provisioning of Edo. Better known is the fact that in 1608–11 he allowed Toyotomi Hideyori to have Ryōi dredge a new ten-kilometer canal, the Takasegawa in Kyoto, and, using water diverted from the Kamo River, to haul building material up it from the Uji River for reconstruction of the recently burned Hōkōji. Ieyasu then transported timber on it to erect a new imperial palace, and shippers used it thereafter to bring bulk goods into the city.

Ieyasu also improved highways. He had daimyo deploy labor gangs to broaden and smooth main roads, erect distance markers, plant shade trees, and establish rest stops for travelers. The result was a set of main highways wider and smoother than any found elsewhere in the seventeenth-century world. In 1613 an Englishman described the Tōkaidō, linking Edo and Kyoto, in this fashion:

> The way for the most part is wonderfull even, and where it meeteth with Mountains passage is cut through. This way is the mayne Roade of all this Countrey, and is for the most part sandie and gravell: it is divided into leagues, and at every leagues end are two small hills, viz. on either side of the way one, and upon every one of them a faire Pine-tree trimmed round in fashion of an Arbor. These markes are placed upon the way to the end, that the Hacknie men, and those which let out Horses to hire, should not make men

pay more than their due, which is about three pense a league. The Roade is
exceedingly travelled, full of people.[17]

Daimyo also improved transportation. We noted the case of Maeda
of Kanazawa. To cite one more example, in 1624, Yamanouchi of Tosa
ordered a canal dug and wharf areas constructed at Kōchi to facilitate
the unloading of wood and bamboo. Townsmen worked for three years
to complete the task, and when it was done, Yamanouchi allocated
plots to local merchants and issued regulations to guide them in their
pursuit of the lumber business, which generated income for his treasury.[18]

OVERSEAS TRADE

Most of the ships that anchored in the canals and roadsteads of Edo,
Osaka, and Japan's other coastal cities and towns between 1570 and
1630 were coasting vessels hauling goods and people from elsewhere in
the islands. Some, however, carried cargo from abroad. Foreign trade
had a long history in Japan, but during the half century after the 1560s,
it attained unprecedented magnitude and involved more diverse participants than ever before.

DEVELOPMENTS TO 1600

From early in the Muromachi period, after the Ming dynasty displaced
the Mongols in China, both authorized and covert Sino-Japanese trade
grew to great proportions, providing Muromachi leaders with most of
their coinage. During the sixteenth century, however, that trade declined because of disruptions in both countries.

Japan's domestic turmoil produced a large number of men who turned
to the sea for a living. Known as *wakō*, many traded when they could
but resorted to piracy and even slaving when they could not. Some of
their plundering occurred in Japanese waters, but the more intrepid sailed
on piratical raids to the continent, sometimes in the service of daimyo,
other times on their own, and often in collaboration with Korean and
Chinese seamen. These raids, which occasionally involved thousands of
marauders on dozens of vessels, became so frequent and devastating by

17. Cooper, *They Came to Japan*, p. 283, quoting John Saris.
18. Totman, *Green Archipelago*, p. 66.

midcentury that coastal villages and major estuaries in China and Korea were abandoned and legitimate seagoing activity diminished sharply.[19]

The suffering and disorder caused by pirates led the Ming government to discontinue all formal relations with Japan after 1557, ending what remained of authorized trade between the two countries. Illicit trade by Chinese entrepreneurs continued, but when peaceful ventures failed, it tended to degenerate into wakō-like piracy. In addition, political conflicts within China and predatory activity by nomadic leaders on the northern border began to consume the Ming empire's resources and attention, further reducing its interest in foreign trade. Finally, in the 1590s, Hideyoshi's campaigns of continental conquest utterly ruined Japan's relations with neighboring countries.

While these developments in the late sixteenth century were undermining relations with China and Korea, however, skilled Japanese seafarers were venturing farther and farther south in search of trade and booty. By the 1560s they were working the Philippines and Malay Peninsula, and as peace returned to Japan in the 1580s, commercial opportunities increased. After securing Kyushu in 1587, Hideyoshi suppressed the piracy, freeing legitimate Japanese traders from the worst of the seaborne menace and encouraging them to pursue commerce throughout Southeast Asia. They seized the moment, developing ports of call and trading posts in Indochina and communities of settlers in Manila. The communities initially included ex-pirates as well as people sold abroad as slaves, and during the early seventeenth century, their numbers were augmented with hundreds of ronin and exiled Christians.

The overseas trade was diverse. Imports to Japan included silk, other cloth goods, sugar, various tropical foods, woods, medicines, and saltpeter, which was unavailable in Japan and essential to the manufacture of gunpowder. Exports included silver and other metals, metal products, specialty clothing, umbrellas, fans, and art objects. Despite the diversity, however, silk and silver were far and away the principal items of trade. Japan's new rulers wanted the silk because it was of higher quality than domestic varieties, and foreigners wanted the silver because the plenitude being mined in Japan made it cheaper in the islands than elsewhere, so they could acquire it at low cost and exchange it abroad at a handsome profit.

19. Iwao, "Japanese Foreign Trade," summarizes Japan's trade relations. A fuller examination of *wakō* and Japan's continental relations to about 1640 is Jurgis Elisonas, "The Inseparable Trinity: Japan's Relations with China and Korea," in Hall, ed., *Early Modern Japan*, pp. 235–300.

Europeans were key participants in this silk-for-silver trade. The Portuguese, joined in the 1590s by Spaniards, were especially successful in making it part of a triangular trade system that generated profits at each port of call. Normally, only one Portuguese vessel visited Japan each year, but it was "a large lubberly carrack, often of 1200 or 1600 tons," that left Goa in India in April or May, bound for Macao on the China coast.[20] At Macao it sold cargo in June or July and took on great quantities of silk floss and cloth. Catching the monsoon winds, the carrack rode northeastward to Nagasaki to exchange its load of silk and other goods for silver and sundries. It departed Japan some time after November, propelled southward by wintry continental winds that sent it back to Macao, where it traded the silver for Goa-bound cargo. The Spanish triangle never developed as smoothly, but when it did operate, it took the Manila galleon, as the vessel was known, from Manila to Japan, thence to Mexico, and finally back to Manila.

TRADE AFTER 1600

After Sekigahara, Ieyasu inherited Hideyoshi's authority over foreign trade, including that of the Iberians. His central concern, no doubt, was to assure that he, rather than any daimyo, was the primary beneficiary of the weapons and saltpeter imports, trade profits, and political connections, but like his predecessor, he was uneasy about the political effects of Iberian missionary activity, and he saw control of overseas commerce as a means of addressing that concern.

Ieyasu regulated the trade in several ways. He designated who would receive permits to trade and which Japanese ports traders could use. He controlled most of the silver trade by controlling most mines and mints. In 1604 he tightened his grip on the silk trade by forming the *itowappu*, or yarn guild. This was an association of textile merchants in the major cities who agreed to dispose of all yarn brought by the carrack in return for the right to purchase at a negotiated price any yarn that Ieyasu and his agents did not want. The agreement helped Ieyasu promote trade by assuring potential traders that if they brought yarn to Japan, they would have outlets and should, therefore, be willing to risk venture capital on the trip.

In his attempts to contain Iberian missionary activity without sacrificing foreign trade, Ieyasu went beyond Hideyoshi's policy of sporadic

20. C. R. Boxer, *The Christian Century in Japan, 1549–1650* (Berkeley and Los Angeles: University of California Press, 1951), pp. 122–23.

suppression by actively seeking commercial alternatives to the Portuguese. Most notably, whereas Hideyoshi had only commissioned a
handful of Japanese trading expeditions to Southeast Asia, Ieyasu approved great numbers, issuing sailing permits (*shuinjō*) that authorized
trade both in Japan and at overseas ports. Between 1604 and 1616, he
licensed nearly two hundred trading missions to China and Southeast
Asia, the licenses going to several daimyo, about sixty merchants and
entrepreneurial samurai, and some twenty foreigners then in Japan. He
and his successors issued another one hundred and fifty licenses between 1616 and the 1630s.[21] The trade was so profitable, moreover,
that a good many unlicensed merchantmen sailed from ports in western
Japan. Gradually the composition of the trading fleet changed: whereas
the carrack had been the dominant element before 1600, by 1610 Japanese vessels had taken over much of the trade.

Chinese traders were another mercantile component that emerged
during Ieyasu's day. Although Ming rulers sustained the 1557 prohibition on commerce, Chinese merchants, knowing the profits in silk-
for-silver trade, wished to participate. Initially, they evaded the Ming
prohibition by sending goods to Southeast Asia, the Ryūkyūs, or other
entrepôts, where Japanese or European shippers purchased them with
silver for resale in Japan. By 1610, Chinese navigators were sailing directly to Japan, where Ieyasu welcomed them, and Chinese merchants
soon settled in Nagasaki to handle the trade. By the 1620s, some thirty
to sixty Chinese vessels were arriving annually, and 2,000–3,000 Chinese
reportedly were resident in Nagasaki.[22] As the numbers of Japanese and
Chinese traders grew, moreover, their ships brought more and more silk
cloth, which reduced the market for the carrack's yarn and undermined
the value of the special relationship between Portuguese and itowappu
merchants.

In addition, Ieyasu followed Hideyoshi in sanctioning two other av-
enues of trade with the adjacent mainland. The daimyo of Tsushima
Island, who had traded with Korea before Hideyoshi's invasions, began
seeking renewed agreements with the Korean government almost as soon
as Japanese troops left the peninsula in 1599. Not until 1607, however,
was he able to broker a peace settlement between Edo and Seoul, which
enabled him two years later to complete negotiations with the Korean
government for resuming trade at Pusan. The trade recommenced in

21. Innes, *Door Ajar*, 1: 58, 129. Iwao, "Japanese Foreign Trade," pp. 9–10.
22. Iwao, "Japanese Foreign Trade," p. 11.

1611, and for the rest of the Tokugawa period, Korean-Japanese trade was handled through Tsushima under the daimyo's supervision.[23]

Rather similarly, Shimazu of Satsuma, who had previously carried on a lucrative trade with Ryūkyū islanders and through them with China, obtained Ieyasu's permission to restore his trade role. Instead of using diplomacy, however, after his first communications bore no fruit, he adopted the brutal expedient of despatching an island-hopping invasion force of fifteen hundred samurai, which pushed southward to Okinawa. It overran the headquarters of the Ryūkyūan king in 1609 and compelled him to accept Satsuma's suzereignty and trade arrangements. Shimazu's tactics worked, but they seem to have unsettled Ieyasu: two months after acquiescing in the fait accompli, he ordered daimyo in the southwest to surrender all ocean-going vessels in excess of 500-*koku* capacity and forbade construction of any new ones.

Once the relationships with Korea and the Ryūkyūs had been settled, they were maintained, providing the governments of Tsushima and Satsuma with important sources of income. By sanctioning those arrangements and then asserting authority over the scale of daimyo maritime construction, Ieyasu was able to claim, somewhat disingenuously, that even at the extremities of Japan, trade occurred only with Tokugawa approval.

Other traders also arrived from Europe, and they provided Ieyasu with more alternatives to the Iberians. In the spring of 1600, even as rivalry among the daimyo was lurching out of control, he learned from the famished survivors of a shipwrecked Dutch vessel commanded by Jacob Quaeckernaeck that not all European traders would insist on bringing missionaries along. Preoccupied with domestic affairs, Ieyasu did not pursue the matter. Indeed, he took no action for several years, merely housing Quaeckernaeck and some of his crewmen near Edo pending the day when he might have a use for them.

During 1604–5, while Ieyasu was actively encouraging overseas connections, new reports and rumors of daimyo-missionary troubles came to his ears. Whether in response to those rumors or simply as part of his broader pursuit of trade, in 1605 he sent Quaeckernaeck to Southeast Asia on a Japanese vessel with instructions to encourage Dutch traders to visit Japan. As a result, in 1609 a pair of Dutch ships, having failed in their main purpose of capturing the carrack, went on to Japan

23. Ronald P. Toby, *State and Diplomacy in Early Modern Japan* (Princeton: Princeton University Press, 1984), pp. 25–40.

to establish contacts. Their arrival enabled Ieyasu to initiate a regular trading arrangement with the Netherlands.[24]

Four years later, an English vessel arrived, and Ieyasu agreed to trade with England.[25] By then more rumors, scandals, and clashes had further tarnished the credibility of Iberian merchants, and Ieyasu's attempts to dissuade them from bringing missionaries had failed. So in 1614, as noted in chapter 4, he reissued his earlier decree expelling all missionaries without reiterating his wish to preserve the trading link. Evidently he was satisfied that Dutchmen and Englishmen could handle his European trade.

Of the new Europeans, the Dutch proved the more energetic in pursuit of trade. As an envious Englishman described Dutch activities in 1615:

> The Hollanders go beyond all, not only us but all strangers here of late, by reason of the great quantities of raw silk, tafities, satins, velvets and China wares which they steal from the Chinese, having of late robbed many junks, whereby they sell at such rates that none that cometh truly by their goods can make profit here; . . . their stealing trade supplying them yearly when other fails.[26]

The wakō would have admired that Dutch entrepreneurial spirit.

The Dutch also lobbied fiercely to oust the Portuguese, repeatedly warning Japan's leaders of the danger in religious proselytizing and using their seapower to intercept and seize Portuguese merchantmen as they sailed to and from Japan. They fought their Japanese competitors by warning Tokugawa leaders of the diplomatic complications that might arise because of brawls and conflicts involving Japanese seamen overseas.[27] As a result of their forceful efforts, the Dutch trade gradually expanded while that of the Iberians declined.

Through the first three decades of Tokugawa rule, foreign trade thus continued to grow and prosper. The ocean voyages were risky and not a few ships were lost at sea, but for investors in a Japanese venture, a successful six-month round trip to China could yield profits ranging from 35 to 110 percent, and that prospect was grand enough to attract a motley array of would-be traders, thus maintaining a lively com-

24. Boxer, *Christian Century*, p. 288.
25. Derek Massarella, *A World Elsewhere* (New Haven: Yale University Press, 1990), details the English role in early seventeenth-century Japan.
26. Innes, *Door Ajar*, 1: 97.
27. Iwao, "Japanese Foreign Trade," pp. 14–16.

merce.[28] Satisfactory overall trade figures do not exist.[29] However, by
one estimate traders carried some 130,000–160,000 kilograms of silver
out of Japan during the decade 1615–25, and by the 1620s, annual
imports of silk yarn reached an estimated 300,000 to 400,000 catties in
weight.[30]

Only gradually during the seventeenth century did the silver trade
lose its lure as massive exports of the metal and modest imports of gold
brought their relative values within Japan into line with those abroad.
Until the 1630s, Japanese and foreign merchants continued to profit
from the disequilibrium.[31] By then, however, the carriers of that trade
had changed appreciably. In 1623 the English gave up, unable to show
a profit, and the Spanish left after the bakufu denied their request to
resume trade in 1624. The Portuguese still clung to their posts, but
because of the Japanese, Chinese, and Dutch competition, they were in
fact carrying much less than a few decades earlier. During the 1630s,
both Portuguese and Japanese were forbidden to participate in the trade,
and from then until the 1850s, the commercial fleet carrying Japan's
overseas trade was operated almost exclusively by Chinese, Dutch, and
Korean traders.

28. Conrad Totman, *Tokugawa Ieyasu: Shogun* (South San Francisco: Heian International, 1983), p. 103.

29. Innes, *Door Ajar,* 2: 379–80, lists in table 17 assembled figures for the years 1604–39.

30. Iwao, "Japanese Foreign Trade," pp. 4, 10. One catty = 1.32 lbs. in Japan and slightly different weights in southeast Asian countries. The 130,000–160,000 kilograms equal about 35,000–43,000 *kan* of silver. Innes, *Door Ajar,* 2: 379, gives figures of 12,000 to 25,000 *kan.* Kozo Yamamura and Tetsuo Kamiki, "Silver Mines and Sung Coins—A Monetary History of Medieval and [Early] Modern Japan in International Perspective," in J. F. Richards, ed., *Precious Metals in the Later Medieval and Early Modern Worlds* (Durham: Carolina Academic Press, 1983), p. 352, prefer the figures 40,000–50,000 *kan* and a total of 1.6 to 2.0 million *kan* for the period ca. 1600–1638. The figures seem high, but the authors are emphasizing the global importance of Japan's silver exports for those years.

31. Kobata, "Production and Uses of Gold and Silver," pp. 250–55.

SIX

Culture and Pacification

Cultural Blossoming, 1570–1599

    Decorating Castles and Other Edifices

    Other Facets of Elite Culture

    Popular Arts

Cultural Consolidation, 1600–1639

    Promoting Peaceful Uses of Architecture

    Pacifying Prelates and Courtiers by Other Means

    Establishing Tokugawa Cultural Qualifications to Rule

    Disciplining Popular Culture

The decades of pacification were also decades of vibrant cultural activity. The vibrancy derived in part from the rulers' enthusiasm for conspicuous consumption and their success in expropriating wealth enough to pay for it. Usually known as Azuchi-Momoyama culture, after the sprawling castles of Nobunaga at Azuchi and of Hideyoshi in the low Momoyama hills at Fushimi, this elite culture constituted a bombastic display of power and of the treasure and privilege that power could command. The display continued into the early decades of the seventeenth century, but deepening political and material restraints gradually choked it off by the 1630s.

A less visible dimension of this cultural vigor was a heightened joie de vivre among common people, an affirmation of their right to a place in the world and a celebration of the peace that freed them from chronic fears and oppressive burdens. At this level, too, the culture showed a period of flowering that gave way to stabilization after 1600 as rulers imposed more and more controls on popular cultural activity.

CULTURAL BLOSSOMING, 1570–1599

By the 1570s, daimyo had established a long tradition of introducing urban amenities to their headquarters towns: collecting libraries and works of art and surrounding themselves with artists, scholars, skilled craftsmen, and the poetasters who could appreciate their creations. However, Nobunaga and Hideyoshi pursued cultural pretensions with an energy that dwarfed their predecessors, most visibly in their castle construction, and many contemporaries shared their enthusiasm for the arts.

DECORATING CASTLES AND OTHER EDIFICES

The castles of Nobunaga and Hideyoshi were huge. They were floored with tatami mats or polished wood, equipped with elegant sliding doors, and decorated with rare and expensive woods, pillars coated with lacquer and gold leaf, and immense gold-leafed murals. The preferred artists were of the Kanō school, most notably Kanō Eitoku, who "created the main features of the stirring Momoyama style."[1] Eitoku's art was fitted to the task. He employed bold brush strokes in a grand, flowing manner, and his gigantic screens commonly utilized a large unifying central figure, such as a plum tree, with other elements arranged about it as subordinate parts of an integrated whole.

These grand decorative works were collaborative undertakings. The artist examined the building to be decorated, learned his patron's wishes, prepared sketches, and after the patron approved them, set to work with his crew to produce the finished product. In theory, as the later Kanō Einō explained, the artist was to

> paint landscapes in the *jōdan* [the raised area of a palace room, used by nobles and lords], figures in the *chūdan* [the area between *jōdan* and *gedan*], and flowers and birds in the *gedan* [the lower part of the room, used by vassals]. In the rooms under the eaves, paint animals. In a magnificent palace, the various pictures should be done in rich colors throughout. It is in accordance with the rules to paint what is suitable to the given circumstances and the request of the client.[2]

1. Robert Treat Paine and Alexander Soper, *The Art and Architecture of Japan* (London: Penguin Books, 1974), p. 95. Much of Eitoku's work has been lost, but many artists emulated his style, and many works have been erroneously attributed to him according to Tsuneo Takeda in his richly illustrated *Kanō Eitoku* (Tokyo: Kodansha International, 1977), pp. 43–44.

2. Doi Tsugiyoshi, *Momoyama Decorative Painting* (New York: Weatherhill, 1977), p. 32. Macrons added.

In practice these guidelines were unlikely to be followed to the letter, but the spirit of artist-client collaboration remained basic to the decorative painting tradition.

Surrounded by elegant art, the rulers arranged scholarly lectures on Confucian and Buddhist subjects and Japanese classics, as well as sponsoring other tasteful activities intended to entertain, edify, and impress themselves, their guests, and their followers, such as poetry sessions, tea ceremonies, and nō dramas.

Nobunaga's use of murals was part of a calculated display of wealth and power. It was far more than mere display, however. In a brilliant recreation of the great keep at Azuchi Castle, Carolyn Wheelwright has captured the tone and intent of this warlord taste, as well as the artistic range of Eitoku, describing the interiors of the seven floors.[3] The first floor was a service area; public space began with the second. There, she reports, the rooms held paintings of pheasants, wild geese, doves, plum trees, and a work titled *Evening Bell from a Distant Temple:*

> This is one of the famous Chinese scenic spots, the *Eight Views of Hsiao and Hsiang,* favored by Japanese landscape painters from the fifteenth century onward, and it provided an appropriate complement to the miniature landscape (*bonsan*) set in front of it. Somewhat dissociated from the other two large *zashiki* [sitting rooms] by its theme was the eight-mat southeast room furnished with ink paintings of Chinese Confucian scholars.

Third-floor rooms were adorned with paintings of horses, legendary Chinese beauties, and other topics esteemed by the ruling warriors. On the fourth floor were paintings of "craggy rocks, dragons and tigers, bamboo, pine, phoenix, hydrangeas, falcon breeding, and Chinese examples of model conduct." The sixth floor was very different, being totally Buddhist in theme. The paintings on walls, ceilings, and columns portrayed flying dragons, hungry ghosts, demons, and other creatures of religious import:

> Inside the octagonal hall, all columns were gold and all paintings were *kinpeki* [strong colors on a gold background]. On the walls were depictions of the *Ten Great Disciples of Buddha* and *Buddha Establishing the Way and Preaching the Law,* and on the coffered ceiling were Buddhist angels. The chapel presented a radiant microcosm of the Buddhist universe, from dragons in the depths of the earth to divine spirits in the heavens.

3. The quotations are from Carolyn Wheelwright, "A Visualization of Eitoku's Lost Paintings at Azuchi Castle," in George Elison and Bardwell L. Smith, *Warlords, Artists, and Commoners* (Honolulu: University of Hawaii Press, 1981), pp. 91, 103, 108, 109. Wheelwright reports (p. 108) that "no paintings were found in the fifth level."

For Nobunaga, however, Buddhist salvation was not the ultimate objective, and therefore,

> surmounting this spiritual realm, another world occupied a position even higher and more exalted than that of the celestial Buddhist angels. The square room on the top story symbolized Nobunaga's aspirations to rule all of Japan. . . . It was painted with Chinese culture-heroes, political models, and sages, its theme being good government as sanctioned by the Chinese concept of the Mandate of Heaven. About twenty-one feet square, the room had an entrance in the middle of each of its four sides communicating with an outer gallery. Such dignified symmetry would reinforce the aura of moral rectitude. The pillars, the beams of the coffered ceiling, the windows lining the encircling gallery, even the floor gleamed with lustrous black lacquer, setting off the brilliant *kinpeki* paintings on the wall panels and ceiling coffers, and creating a stunning contrast to the gold of the castle's exterior at this level.

Clearly, Nobunaga's interest in painting stemmed from more than an impulse to decorate. It was educational in nature and political in intent: a display that showed the world how well he understood the proper hierarchy of things, with wise rulership—one that understood the unity of the arts of peace (*bun*) and war (*bu*)—surpassing all else. Luxury, leisure, learning, and leadership were entwined.

In addition to castles, the builders erected and decorated mansions, temples, and shrines with great abandon. Hideyoshi erected several mansions for court nobles and in 1586–87 built and had Eitoku decorate a huge, fortified, castlelike mansion, Jurakudai, for the use of himself and his first heir. Eight years later, after a tragic falling out with that heir, he tore the mansion down and moved a number of its buildings to other sites, but the memory of Jurakudai's splendor has survived, making the name an undying symbol of luxurious power and glory.

In the provinces, barons built castles and mansions and hired artists to decorate them. Several years before finding himself on the losing side at Sekigahara, Mōri Terumoto, the lord of Hiroshima, hired the painter Unkoku Tōgan and brought him to settle near his castle town. Among the folding screens Tōgan painted for Terumoto was a starkly romantic Chinese landscape, dated 1593, in which he consciously sought to replicate the dramatic style of the great fifteenth-century artist Sesshū.[4]

Temple building was even more widespread than mansion work; hundreds of temples, large and small, were built and rebuilt throughout

---

4. Paine and Soper, *Art and Architecture*, p. 99.

2. Unkoku Tōgan, *Landscape*. One of a pair of six-panel folding screens; ink on paper, 145.7 x 348.4 cm. Grand painted panels like this Chinese-inspired landscape were prized by daimyo and other influential figures for decorating their castles, mansions, palaces, and temples. Courtesy of the Museum of Fine Arts, Boston. Fenollosa-Weld Collection. Acc. #11.4533.

the country. One of the grandest and most ill-fated temple projects was
the earlier-mentioned Hōkōji, a Tendai temple that Hideyoshi began
erecting in Kyoto in 1586. It was to house a wooden, twenty-meter
statue of Buddha that would supplant the ancient image at the Tōdaiji
in Nara as supreme Buddhist protector of the realm. Two years later,
he prepared to construct the Buddha image itself, using nails and fas-
teners made from the weapons collected in his "sword hunt." The Hōkōji was thus to symbolize and sustain the new peace that his armies
had just established with the pacification of Kyushu. He completed the
temple, but earthquake and fire destroyed it in 1596. Six years later, his
child-heir, Hideyori, began rebuilding the Buddha hall, only to lose it
to fire again, and in 1608 construction commenced yet a third time.
That time artisans cast a great bronze statue to replace the wooden
Buddha, erected a covering edifice, and finally completed the project in
1614 at the immense cost of eight hundred thousand gold *ryō*. Their
aesthetically disappointing creation, which surely reflected the faded glory
of its sponsor, survived into the 1980s as one of the least celebrated
tourist sites of Kyoto. After a fire consumed it, the temple authorities
converted the site into a parking lot.

OTHER FACETS OF ELITE CULTURE

Despite the efforts of barons such as Mōri Terumoto, Kyoto remained
the site of most higher cultural production. The city experienced a revival of cultural vigor thanks to Hideyoshi's encouragement of arts and
letters and provision of income to the court and kuge (court nobility).
The kuge viewed themselves as "hereditary custodians of the various
arts and pastimes that had given the court of their Heian period ancestors its stamp of rare aesthetic refinement."[5] Some were specialists in
music, others in poetry, calligraphy, Chinese and Japanese history, Shintō,
Buddhism, Confucian classics, or Chinese calendar-making. Encouraged by the return of peace and prosperity, they began cultivating their
diverse specialities with renewed enthusiasm.

This revival was not restricted to kuge, however. As evidenced by
Nobunaga's art work in Azuchi, cultural production played an important sociopolitical role. Much was participatory activity rather than individual effort or professional presentation to passive elite audiences.
And it cut across status boundaries, bringing kuge, military men, wealthy

5. Herschel Webb, *The Japanese Imperial Institution in the Tokugawa Period* (New
York: Columbia University Press, 1968), p. 94.

townsmen, and professional artists and literary figures together. Thus poetry writing flourished in the form of *renga,* or linked verse, in which each participant composed a segment of the poem in accord with principles of versification that were well articulated by the 1570s. Renga sessions brought diverse people together with professional poets such as Satomura Jōha, who taught poetry to the powerful at his school in Kyoto.

Other cultural activities embodied this socially diverse, participatory quality. Flower viewing, long a staple of aristocratic culture, enjoyed popularity. Stylish picnics and outings complete with music-making and dance took kuge, samurai, and merchant men and women to noted scenic spots to view cherry blossoms in spring and foliage in autumn. Tea masters such as Sen no Rikyū gave lessons in the countrified style known as *wabicha,* or "poverty tea." In a wabicha session, the host, whether Rikyū, Hideyoshi, or a common merchant, might prepare the tea himself, using rough-textured utensils, and serve it directly to his guests in the small, thatch-roofed, coarsely plastered, and undecorated tea room where they were gathered. Even the nō drama was frequently handled as participatory theater rather than spectacle, with lords such as Hideyoshi joining their guests and resident experts in producing nō episodes.

Most of the paintings that decorated mansions, castles, and temples, and that provided backdrop for musicians, calligraphers, and versifiers, were works of the Kanō school. The older, less boldly colorful artistic tradition of *Yamato-e,* which painters of the Tosa school had successfully promoted a few decades earlier, was in eclipse, but the talented Hasegawa Tōhaku did succeed in reviving the ink-line (*sumi-e*) style of the earlier Muromachi period.

Apart from the Kanō school, the most important genre of Momoyama art was the strikingly new one known as *nanban* art. This art of the "southern barbarian" portrayed the Europeans, primarily Portuguese, who reached Japan from Southeast Asia. These exotic foreigners—with their grand ships, grotesque clothes, strange speech, odd physiognomies, unusual foods, peculiar religious notions, quaint ways of eating, clumsy styles of walking and sitting, and curious knickknacks—were grist for the mills of artists whose paintings brought edification and entertainment to the many who could never hope to see these remarkable creatures in the flesh.[6]

6. A splendidly illustrated examination of *nanban* art is Yoshitomo Okamoto, *The Namban Art of Japan* (Tokyo: Weatherhill, 1972). Ronald P. Toby, "Carnival of the

Nanban art was, in turn, part of a material culture introduced or inspired by the Europeans. Besides firearms, it included an array of exotica, such as food, clothing, and articles of daily use, and writings from Europe, about Europe, or by Europeans. An important segment of the corpus was a literature of religious propaganda that missionaries produced on a printing press they brought with them. It, together with one or two locally constructed presses, used metal type initially, shifting to wood later. They were the first European-style movable presses in the country, and for several years the missionaries used them to print in both European and Japanese script. By 1614, however, one had come into Japanese hands, and the others had been removed from the country.

Contemporaneously, Korean-style presses that employed movable metal type were brought to Japan in the wake of Hideyoshi's first invasion of the peninsula. He presented one to Emperor Goyōzei, and the emperor used it, as well as a duplicate that employed wooden type, to reproduce a number of works, mostly Chinese Confucian classics, such as the *Classic of Filial Piety* [*Kobun kōkyō*] and the *Four Books* [*Shisho*].[7]

POPULAR ARTS

The cultural flowering of these decades reached well beyond the fortunate few in Kyoto. By the late sixteenth century, rice planting was commonly a disciplined communal affair, and villagers often relieved the back-breaking tedium of the planting by singing songs (*taue-uta*) whose words celebrated the glorious sights and sounds of the city, the excitement of mounted warriors, and the joys, sorrows, and humor of love and lust.

Some entertainers made a living by traveling from village to village, putting on musical skits (*sarugaku*) for the community. In larger towns, residents participated in religious holidays and festivals (*matsuri*), in-

Aliens: Korean Embassies in Edo-Period Art and Popular Culture," *MN* 41-4 (Winter 1986): 415–56, shows nicely how Japanese fascination with exotica continued, or at least revived during the eighteenth century, in artistic treatments and popular attitudes toward the Korean embassies that periodically visited Edo. In passing he also observes (p. 425) that during the early seventeenth century, commoners were not necessarily able to distinguish Englishmen from Koreans.

7. David Chibbett, *The History of Japanese Printing and Book Illustration* (Tokyo: Kodansha, 1977), p. 69. Chibbett reports that in Korea the presses used bronze or ceramic type. C. R. Boxer, *The Christian Century in Japan, 1549–1650* (Berkeley and Los Angeles: University of California Press, 1951), pp. 189–98, also discusses the European presses.

cluding dance festivals in which musicians accompanied communal round dancing. The best-known matsuri were those of Kyoto, notably the summer Gion Festival in which members of temples, shrines, neighborhoods, and urban associations decorated portable shrines or great wheeled vehicles and pushed and pulled them through crowd-lined streets in long parades.

Storytellers flourished. Some specialized in humor; others recited stories of Buddhist mystery or samurai heroics and tragedy. Many used the lute (*biwa*) for accompaniment, but the *samisen*, a long-necked, three-stringed instrument recently developed from the Ryūkyūan *jamisen*, became immensely popular, perhaps because its loud twanging was audible over a noisy crowd and so made effective accompaniment for both storytellers and dancers. By the 1590s, some entertainers were combining music, dance, and story in skits and dramas that drew enthusiastic crowds of commoners and samurai alike. Some of these storytellers used puppets in dramatizing their stories, a style that proved hugely popular.

The mingling of elite and commoner culture reflected Hideyoshi's own personality in the sense that he was a man of humble origins who had maneuvered and bludgeoned his way to the hegemonial heights. Even when astride the realm, he still participated in Kyoto's Gion Festival and neighborhood dances, and he invited commoners to the nō dramas that he arranged in Osaka and Fushimi. His best-known instance of mixing high and low was the Kitano tea party of 1587. To celebrate the Shimazu family's submission, he invited people from all walks of life to join him for tea on the grounds of Kitano shrine, a few blocks away from his new Jurakudai. Groups gathered to enjoy the ceremony in some fifteen hundred stalls that autumn day, with Hideyoshi's stall reportedly serving tea to some eight hundred people.[8]

CULTURAL CONSOLIDATION, 1600–1639

In terms of higher culture, nothing much changed in the year 1600, but over the following decades it did. Monumental construction was the area of most obvious continuity immediately after Sekigahara, but also the area of most noticeable reorientation and curtailment in later decades. As noted in chapter 5, the urge to build and decorate waned as structures were completed, resources consumed, and political restrictions imposed. In other areas of cultural output, the rulers disciplined

8. Mary Elizabeth Berry, *Hideyoshi* (Cambridge, Mass.: Harvard University Press, 1982), pp. 190–91.

Buddhist thought, channeled kuge energies into arts and learning (*bun*), promoted the Confucian view of samurai government as a balanced mastery of both civilian and military skills (*bun* and *bu*), and tried to control popular culture by suppressing European influence and regulating urban recreation.

PROMOTING PEACEFUL USES OF ARCHITECTURE

The creation of Katsura villa near Kyoto was emblematic of the linkages between upper-class cultural activity and pacification.[9] The villa, one of Japan's finest architectural treasures, was primarily the handiwork of the politically astute Toshihito, a younger brother of Emperor Goyōzei. He had been adopted by Hideyoshi but returned to the imperial family in 1590 when Hideyoshi begot a son of his own. To help make the dismissal palatable, Hideyoshi obtained for the eleven-year-old boy the household name Hachijō, a suitable stipend, and a residence adjacent to the imperial palace. In the following years, Toshihito pursued literature and learning, added buildings to his estate, and maintained discreet contact with the Toyotomi family even after Ieyasu established Tokugawa preeminence.

In 1611, when Goyōzei abdicated in favor of his son, Gomizuno-o, Toshihito became a key advisor to his youthful nephew and was drawn into the thorny politics of court-bakufu relations. A sizable burr under Goyōzei's saddle had been Ieyasu's persistent wish to establish a marriage bond with the imperial family, and given Toshihito's Toyotomi connection, one suspects that he shared his brother's distaste for the prospect of Tokugawa in-laws. But after the destruction of Hideyori in 1615 and Ieyasu's death the following spring, Toshihito seems to have made his peace with Edo. Late in 1616, he wed a daughter of the daimyo Kyōgoku Takatomo, a former Toyotomi vassal who had served Ieyasu ably at Sekigahara and enjoyed Tokugawa goodwill thereafter.[10] And early in 1617 he visited Hidetada at Edo.

One suspects that Toshihito's visit to Edo expedited the marriage

9. This summary of Katsura villa's creation is based on the following works, which are primarily collections of photographs and drawings with architectural commentary: Isozaki Arata, *Katsura Villa: Space and Form* (New York: Rizzoli International, 1987); Walter Gropius et al., *Katsura: Tradition and Creation in Japanese Architecture* (New Haven, Yale University Press, 1960); Akira Naitō, *Katsura: A Princely Retreat* (Tokyo: Kodansha International, 1977); Naomi Okawa, *Edo Architecture: Katsura and Nikko* (New York: Weatherhill, 1975).

10. According to Naitō, *Katsura*, p. 93, in early 1616 Ieyasu considered remarrying Senhime, Hideyori's widow, to Toshihito. But Ieyasu's death ended that scheme.

arrangement that Ieyasu had wanted because Goyōzei, shortly before his death later that year, finally agreed—it is said—to eventual betrothal of Hidetada's ten-year-old daughter Kazuko and Gomizuno-o. And a month after Goyōzei's death, the bakufu affirmed Toshihito's income rights in an area of land embracing five villages in Lower Katsura adjacent to the river. Three years later, Kazuko (who is usually known by her retirement name Tōfukumon'in) entered the imperial court despite continuing kuge objections. She and Gomizuno-o reportedly enjoyed a happy marriage despite it all, and she went on to become a distinguished patroness of the arts and to see her daughter Meishō serve as emperor from 1629 to 1643, the first woman emperor in 850 years.

After Tōfukumon'in entered the court, Toshihito continued participating in ceremonial affairs, but he seems to have shifted his attention from politics to his estate.[11] Over the course of several years, he moved the Old Shoin, the main building of his former residence, to the new site, built a pair of teahouses, and hired master designers and gardeners to lay out a walking garden. A delightful segment of the garden represents Ama no Hashidate, a tree-studded, rocky spit that projects into Miyazu Bay on the Sea of Japan northwest of Kyoto. Toshihito had visited the spot in 1612 and was so impressed that he made it a focal point for his tea garden. The choice was apt. Katsura lay some distance from natural hills, so the designers employed natural vistas to complete the garden, and this "borrowed vista" style was one for which Ama no Hashidate, similarly separated from mountains, was ideally suited.

By 1624, Toshihito had completed his villa, and that summer a priestly guest described it in his diary: "I visited the villa of Prince Hachijō at Lower Katsura. Boats sailed on the pond dug in the garden under the bridges connecting its islands. There is an artificial hill and a summerhouse in the garden. Mountains are seen from this summerhouse beyond the gardens on all four sides: withal the finest view in Japan."[12] Following Toshihito's death in 1629, the unused villa fell into disarray, but his son repaired it during the 1640s, assisted by gifts from the sho-

11. There is reason to think that Toshihito's construction work at Katsura may actually have begun earlier, perhaps as soon as Hidetada confirmed his Katsura site. A panoramic representation of Kyoto produced in 1617 (*Ikedake hon rakuchū-rakugai-zu*), which generally is accurate in its depictions, shows "three small buildings facing the pond and a soan-style pavilion on the opposite shore. The main building with a cypress shingle roof is thought to be the Old Shoin." The Old Shoin was built by Toshihito, presumably at his former residence in the Imadegawa section of Kyoto, in 1615. Isozaki, *Katsura Villa*, pp. 1, 258.

12. Isozaki, *Katsura Villa*, p. 258. The writer was the priest Kinshuku Kentaku of the Shōkokuji.

gun Iemitsu. He added a major segment to the main pavilion, erected another teahouse, hired Kanō artists to decorate interior doors and walls, and landscaped adjacent areas. Except for a few modest changes in later years, that set of additions completed the Katsura villa, giving it the basic character that has persisted to the present.

Toshihito's redirection of energy from politics to culture was symbolic of the process whereby the bakufu eased the imperial court out of active politics and into a role as model practitioner of cultural arts. But while his role in reconciling Kyoto to Tokugawa dominance may have been the service Edo most valued at the time, in the longer term his lasting accomplishment was the villa at Katsura. Rescued from decades of dilapidation during the Meiji period, it stands today not only as a masterpiece of landscape architecture but as perhaps the most influential example of a major Japanese architectural tradition, that of modular composition, or *kiwari*, "which was to adopt a basic module (the length of the span between posts, measured from the center of each post) and to compute from it all proportional relations connecting the beams, the rafters, the lintels, and all other visible parts of the frame." [13]

Ieyasu himself engaged in lavish mansion construction, ordering up a new palace for Gomizuno-o and assisting as well in the renovation of other Kyoto mansions. He built fine shogunal residences in his castles at Edo, Sunpu, and Nijō, and when he turned Edo over to Hidetada and retired to Sunpu in 1607, he built a small mansion, known as *hama goten*, at Shimizu southwest of Mount Fuji. Two years later he built a villa not far away on a spit of land called Miho that gave him a breathtaking view eastward across Suruga Bay to the Izu peninsula, northeastward to Hakone and Mount Fuji, northwestward to the great Akaishi range, with its winter cap of snow, and southwestward to the gentle slopes of nearby Mount Kuno, where he was interred seven years later.

Mansion-building was one thing, castle construction quite another. Even as Ieyasu pursued his own projects, he tried to restrain castle building by daimyo, and after 1615, Hidetada enforced firm restrictions on military construction. With options so limited, daimyo domesticated their castles, installing tatami and painted screens and attaching teahouses and verandas for moon viewing. As the peace held year after year, they began erecting elegant mansions outside their castle walls. Similarly, when they brought wives and heirs to live in Edo as hostages, they erected mansions on their assigned lots. By 1640, no self-respecting dai-

---

13. Kenzo Tange, "Tradition and Creation in Japanese Architecture," in Gropius et al., *Katsura*, p. 32.

myo could do without these appurtenances of power and glory, which enabled them, too, to host parties and sponsor cultural and educational events.

By then building costs were becoming prohibitive: fine timber was more difficult to come by and neither bakufu nor daimyo was as ready to pay for it. Moreover, the canons of architectural decoration had become more gaudy and intricate, which increased the costs of fabrication.[14] So monumental construction tapered off, and by the 1630s it was mostly limited to rebuilding after conflagrations.

The last major efforts in this ornate, decorative style produced monuments to Tokugawa glory. In 1625, Hidetada set daimyo to work on the Kan'eiji in Edo.[15] It was to be a great Tendai headquarters, eastern Japan's equivalent to the venerable Enryakuji on Mount Hiei. A decade later, Iemitsu put the lords to work at Nikkō in the mountains north of Edo. There they disassembled a small Tōshōgū, or memorial shrine to Ieyasu, that had been installed in 1617, transferred it to the village of Nitta (purportedly the Tokugawa ancestral home in the central Kantō), and replaced it with an elaborate collection of buildings set among towering, often mist-shrouded cryptomeria, the Nikkō Tōshōgū of today. One of its most spectacular structures, the Yōmeimon, or Gate of Sunlight, epitomizes the shrine:

> Only of small dimensions, twenty-two feet wide, fifteen feet deep, and thirty-seven feet high, it is a twelve-columned, two-storied structure having hipped-gable ends with cusped gables on four sides. Its extremely rich carved decoration on the ends of rafters consists of dragons' heads or dragons and clouds, all in gold foil, while other beam-ends are carved with lions' heads and dragons' heads painted white. The elaborate brackets supporting the balcony are designed in the form of peonies and lions, with carvings of a Chinese prince, sages, and some immortals between them. The railing of the balcony depicts a group of Chinese children at play. On the ceiling of the porticoes are two beautiful paintings of dragons; the one nearer the entrance, known as the *nobori-ryū* or ascending dragon, is the work of Kanō Tan'yū, 1602–1674; the inner one, the *kudari-ryū* or descending dragon, was executed by Kanō Eishin, 1613–1685.[16]

---

14. The elegance of these Edo mansions of the early seventeenth century is suggested by William H. Coaldrake, "Edo Architecture and Tokugawa Law," *MN* 36-3 (Autumn 1981): 263–69.

15. For a discussion of the ideological implications of Kan'eiji and the Tōshōgū, see Kate Wildman Nakai, *Shogunal Politics* (Cambridge, Mass.: Harvard University Press, 1988), pp. 178, 180.

16. H. Batterson Boger, *The Traditional Arts of Japan* (New York: Bonanza Books, 1964), pp. 136–37.

The shrine complex at Nikkō was by far the most elaborate and ornate Tōshōgū, but it was only one of several erected to honor Ieyasu's memory and consolidate the Tokugawa hegemony. Within five years of Ieyasu's death, Tōshōgū were also erected at Edo, Sunpu, Kawagoe, Hirosaki, Nagoya, Wakayama, and Mito. Between 1624 and 1651, additional ones were built at Maebashi, Sado Island, the village of Nitta, Okazaki, and Nagashino in Mikawa. With the erection of a Tōshōgū at Sendai in 1654, even monumental construction to honor the great founder came to an end.[17]

PACIFYING PRELATES AND COURTIERS BY OTHER MEANS

Bakufu efforts to guide architecture into peacetime channels were paralleled by measures to direct intellectual life in acceptable directions. High-ranking people were the immediate danger to Ieyasu, so he directed his intellectual disciplining mostly at them rather than at commoners.

Disputatious Buddhist prelates were a chronic annoyance, and Ieyasu tried to guide them by issuing rules for their temples. Thus, in 1608 he issued a seven-clause code for the Enryakuji. Its first three clauses stipulated that only those who intended to study religious doctrine could reside there, that any distinguished by special training should be nurtured, but that any who failed to abide by the spirit of the teachings must leave Mount Hiei. In later regulations for Buddhist and Shintō sects, the theme of scholarly dedication remained central. Finally, in 1614, having failed to end sectarian quarrels, he ordered reproduction and distribution to major temples of some hundred copies of the *Daizō ichiranshū*, an assemblage of Buddhist writings that Ming scholars had prepared to clarify Buddhist doctrine, which Ieyasu hoped would resolve disputes by defining correct doctrine and relationships.[18]

Ieyasu similarly urged the court to nurture cultural activities. In 1612

17. *Nihon rekishi daijiten* (Tokyo: Kawade shobō shinsha, 1961), 13: 225. Actually, in 1859 a Tōshōgū was built on Hokkaidō, probably to protect it from foreigners, and in 1881 one was built at Okayama for unknown reasons. Nitta was claimed as the ancestral village of Ieyasu's lineage. Okazaki was his birthplace. Nagashino was the site of a great victory by Nobunaga in which Ieyasu participated. The other locations were castle towns of his relatives, or locations, evidently, that enabled his spirit to blanket the realm: Hirosaki, Sendai, and Sado. Significantly, it appears that no Tōshōgū were built west of Wakayama during the Tokugawa period.

18. Chibbett, *History of Japanese Printing*, pp. 70–72. Conrad Totman, *Tokugawa Ieyasu: Shogun* (South San Francisco: Heian International, 1983), pp. 123, 149, 185–86, 188.

news of disorder in Kyoto prompted him to send a message westward advising kuge to pursue their family traditions of learning, be discreet in conduct, and stop hawking, which, as a samurai sport, was unseemly. Reports of quarrelsome kuge persisted, however, so in 1613 he issued a five-clause code that "admonished the nobles to study assiduously, perform their duties, avoid crowds, troublemakers, gambling halls, and other improper places, and abide by appropriate regulations—or be banished."[19] After Hideyori's destruction two years later, he revised and expanded the code for kuge, and its first article called upon the emperor and his courtiers to devote themselves to scholarship and the arts: "Only through study can one illustrate the ancient Way and one's rule achieve great peace."[20]

Ieyasu also promoted the peaceful arts in Kyoto by encouraging distinguished artisans, thereby demonstrating the virtue of his regime and hence its right to rule. One of the most fruitful products of this policy was the artists' colony at Takagamine, a site overlooking the city just northwest of Kyoto that was ideally suited for artistic detachment. Centuries earlier the poet Ki no Tsurayuki had celebrated its beauty at sunrise, "when mists lie over the valley and a hundred hills rise above the tree-tops, and Kyoto's Nijō and Kujō towers can be seen in the distance across a sea of white."[21]

In 1615, Ieyasu approved a stipend and grant of land at Takagamine for Hon'ami Kōetsu, a versatile artist who, "excelled equally in calligraphy, ceramics, lacquerware, book designing and a dozen other minor arts."[22] For some years, Kōetsu had been publishing new editions of nō texts and such famous Japanese classics as the *Hōjōki, Tsurezuregusa,* and *Ise monogatari.* He collaborated with the decorative artist Tawaraya Sōtatsu and was assisted by Suminokura Soan. Soan operated a movable-type printing press at his headquarters in the village of Saga, just west of Kyoto, and the thirteen titles he printed are known as Saga books (Saga *bon*) from the printing site. The Saga books were praised for their quality and for the caliber of the works reproduced, and they set a standard of excellence for later publishers.

Ieyasu's award of land at Takagamine may have been an act of reli-

19. Totman, *Tokugawa Ieyasu,* p. 144. The quoted passage is a summary paraphrase of the document.

20. Webb, *Japanese Imperial Institution,* p. 60.

21. Bernard Leach, *Kenzan and his Tradition* (London: Faber & Faber, 1966), p. 44. On pp. 47–48, Leach quotes a lengthy description of Takagamine by Hayashi Razan.

22. Richard Lane, *Images from the Floating World* (New York: G. P. Putnam's Sons, 1978), p. 34.

gious management as much as cultural encouragement.[23] In his attempts to quiet doctrinal disputes, he had found priests of the Hokke sect particularly adamant about their convictions, and a number of influential people in Kyoto, including Kōetsu and the Suminokura, were said to be Hokke adherents or sympathizers. Ieyasu was reluctant to move against such a distinguished cultural figure or such an influential—and useful—merchant house, however, so instead of suppressing them, he encouraged them to settle in an isolated site and pursue safely apolitical ventures of artistic value.

Whatever Ieyasu's motivation, Kōetsu accepted the invitation. He had carpenters erect rows of dwellings along two intersecting roads at Takagamine and assembled there a community of artisans that included brushmakers, papermakers, potters, metalworkers, and lacquerers. During his remaining twenty years of life, the group produced diverse craft and art goods, primarily for sale to the powerful who lived in or passed through Kyoto, including Tōfukumon'in. In the process, they gave splendid expression to the ideal of peaceful artistic production.

ESTABLISHING TOKUGAWA CULTURAL QUALIFICATIONS TO RULE

While managing specific elite groups, Ieyasu also took steps to assert a more general claim of Tokugawa qualification to rule. Whereas Nobunaga may have been content to anchor his hegemony in demonstrated competence, Ieyasu tried to forge a more comprehensive base, drawing legitimacy from every usable source. With the help of allies at court, he "proved" that he was properly descended via the Nitta lineage from the Minamoto founders of the original bakufu. Also with court help, he adorned himself with a garland of titles. Having previously risen through the court offices of acting great counselor, captain of the left imperial guards, and inspector of the left imperial stables, he was designated, according to John W. Hall, minister of the right (*udaijin*), barbarian-quelling generalissimo (*seii taishōgun*), chief of the Minamoto (*Genji no chōja*), and rector of the Junna and Shōgaku colleges (*Junna, Shōgaku ryōin bettō*). In addition, he was given, "the second court rank, the genealogical status of *ason*, and the privilege of riding in an ox-drawn carriage."[24]

23. Hiroshi Mizuo, *Edo Painting: Sōtatsu and Kōrin* (New York: Weatherhill, 1972), pp. 50, 65–69.

24. John Whitney Hall, *Government and Local Power in Japan* (Princeton: Princeton University Press, 1966), p. 347.

Besides gathering such titular signifiers of achievement, Ieyasu strove to demonstrate his understanding of righteous governance. In the early days of 1600, even before mobilizing his armies to crush his rivals at Sekigahara, he ordered scholarly advisors to use the Korean printing press in Kyoto to make copies of *Jōgan seiyō*, an eighth-century Confucian text on the art of good government. The preface to the new edition said that Ieyasu wished it reprinted to nurture the people, honor Hideyoshi's memory, and promote loyalty to young Hideyori. Doubtless his choice of a text reputed to express the views of T'ai Tsung, second emperor of the long-lived T'ang dynasty, indicates his view of his family's proper destiny and the way he wished to represent his relationship to Hideyoshi.

On several occasions in the following years, Ieyasu reproduced classics that he deemed politically beneficial. Most tellingly, in 1605 he used the Korean press to reproduce *Azuma kagami,* the record of the Kamakura founding, which he seemed to regard as the basic textbook of shogunal governance. In 1611 he ordered his scholars to begin keeping a complete record of his own decisions and decrees and on his deathbed ordered the material published as *Sunpuki.* Its purpose, presumably, was to record precedents for his successors to follow, in the manner of classic Chinese dynastic annals.

In 1614 the European-style press in Kyoto seems to have come into Ieyasu's hands, enabling scholars to use it to reproduce two major compilations. The first was the fifty-volume *Gunsho chiyō* compiled at the behest of T'ai Tsung. Meant to demonstrate the principles of good government, it praised firm lord-vassal ties, which gave it particular pertinence. The second work was the *Daizō ichiranshū,* which, as noted above, was a compendium of Buddhist tenets.[25]

This publishing work helped Ieyasu give his regime an ideological foundation by demonstrating that he was conducting himself in the manner of a rightful ruler, promoting the literary arts (*bun*) even as he maintained military readiness (*bu*). This quintessential Confucian formulation reflects Ieyasu's education and the view of some advisors. He was not, however, an ideologue, being far less concerned with grand theories of rule or abstract claims to virtue than with finding solutions to immediate issues. In seeking workable answers, he consulted widely with Buddhist monks, Confucian and Shintō scholars, vassals, merchants, and even occasional foreigners. And he did not insist on doc-

25. Chibbett, *History of Japanese Printing,* pp. 70–72. Totman, *Tokugawa Ieyasu,* pp. 13, 123, 185–86, 188.

trinal purity or elegance, as evidenced by his continual tinkering with rules for nobles, prelates, and daimyo.

Ieyasu and his advisors encouraged courtiers, lords, and prelates to pursue scholarship and civil learning, and lords began employing the same strategy in their own domains. Thus the daimyo of Owari, one of Ieyasu's sons, established a Confucian temple in his castle town. And in 1630, when Iemitsu authorized the bakufu scholar-scribe Hayashi Razan to establish a Confucian school in Edo, the Owari lord donated a building so Razan could commence instruction. By the 1630s the basic trajectory of political thought was established; during the Tokugawa heyday it would be elaborated in loving detail.

DISCIPLINING POPULAR CULTURE

Early Tokugawa leaders recognized that the maintenance of social discipline involved more than controlling the elite, and they attempted to guide society more broadly, particularly in terms of public morals. For generations itinerant dancers had performed dances and skits, earning a living as entertainers and prostitutes. In 1603 a woman named Okuni, said to be from Izumo, came to Kyoto and performed what purported to be Izumo shrine dances but were essentially folk dances.[26] Suggestive in style and seductive in purpose, Okuni's dances evidently enjoyed such success that her name became associated with *onna kabuki,* a type of popular dance-drama performed by women's troupes. The stage performance, it appears, was mostly prologue to entertainment backstage, for which the castle town populations of young samurai made a lucrative clientele, and onna kabuki soon began showing up in castle towns all across the country.

In 1608 a women's troupe visited Sunpu, but after a brawl erupted among spectators, Ieyasu ordered the troupe out of town and restricted such performances, as well as the work of other prostitutes, to a nearby location. Within a few years, kabuki developed more elaborate stage productions, but it continued to be associated with the skin trade, and in 1629 the bakufu forbade female actors to perform.

Well before then, the bakufu was also taking measures to regulate prostitution in general. With the coming of peace, many castle towns were disrupted by troublemaking gangs of poorly controlled, underemployed samurai thugs, and regulation of nightlife in general and

26. Donald Keene, *World within Walls* (New York: Grove Press, 1976), p. 232.

prostitution in particular seemed necessary for the control of urban disorder. In 1617 the bakufu followed Ieyasu's Sunpu precedent by compelling brothel operators in Edo to move their businesses to Yoshiwara, a neighborhood newly formed on reedy swampland adjacent to the bay, where carnal activities could be better regulated (later this red-light district was moved northward beyond Asakusa). In 1629 a comparable area was delineated in Osaka, and in 1641 one was created in Kyoto.[27]

In castle towns across the country, rulers subjected urban life to similar discipline. Daimyo issued codes to guide vassals, established urban administrations to control townsmen, and treated cultural regulation as part of the task. In Kanazawa, for example, kabuki performances became occasions for brawls and commotions, which led to a ban on traveling troupes in 1611 and 1612. Within a few years the ban was eased and troupes returned. The trouble reappeared, too, and during the 1620s the daimyo finally shut down the local theater and bathhouses and punished those convicted of egregious wrongdoing. Thereafter kabuki and puppet troupes rarely visited Kanazawa, and prostitution was driven underground. Public bathhouses resigned themselves to providing baths *sans autre,* and city culture settled into an orderly rhythm of annual holidays and festivals.

Like regulation of urban nightlife, Hidetada's suppression of Christianity during the 1620s restricted and shaped cultural activity. Not only did suppression limit religious thought, it also limited the field of artistic endeavor by proscribing Christian iconography and ritual. More broadly, it restricted the range of secular knowledge by discouraging study of European learning, lest one be accused of adherence to the tabooed sect. The repressive cultural effects of anti-Christian measures were reinforced during the 1630s by decisions to forbid Japanese travel abroad and Portuguese visits to Japan. Those measures stifled the introduction of Southeast Asian plants and products, which had been so valued in preceding decades, and led to the gradual disappearance of nanban art, which had become too risky to produce or enjoy.

These moves by early Tokugawa rulers to regulate the cultural life of commoners foreshadowed the approach to social administration that became normative in the following decades. Because the islands were administered as an assemblage of some 250 daimyo domains, the de-

27. Donald H. Shively, "The Social Environment of Tokugawa Kabuki," in James P. Brandon, William P. Malm, and Shively, *Studies in Kabuki: Its Acting, Music, and Historical Context* (Honolulu: University Press of Hawaii, 1978), pp. 5–7.

gree and focus of regulation varied from place to place and decade to decade. However, by the 1630s the process of cultural consolidation had moved Japan from a period of cultural openness and vibrancy to one of general regulation and routinization. That movement marked the passing of the Azuchi-Momoyama period of nearly unfettered cultural creativity.

PART THREE

The Tokugawa Heyday, 1630–1710

The 1630s marked a watershed in Japanese history as the pacifying of a tumultuous realm gave way to maintenance of a stabilized order. The political life of subsequent decades was notable, not for violence, change, or even institution building, which had mostly occurred by 1640, but for the persistent attempts by rulers to solve current problems with minimal conflict and to prevent their reappearance through managerial attentiveness and insistence on the righteousness of the established order.

The rulers' managerial capacity was weakened, however, by a gradual decline in government control of the domestic economy. As they cut back on monumental construction, they lost interest in controlling many forms of production and allowed merchants to handle commercial activities once managed through their own offices and warehouses. And as samurai became ensconced in towns and cities, they left village affairs more fully in the hands of local people, allowing villagers more choice in their use of time and land and merchants a greater role in marketing produce and handicraft goods.

As merchants assumed more control of the commercial economy, they created larger organizations to coordinate personnel and mobilize capital for large ventures and to cope with the intensifying market fluctuations that accompanied the growing use of money and declining role of government. As the century waned, established merchants lobbied government more and more for regulations to protect their market positions. By 1680 the cry for protection was persistent, and the bakufu tacitly agreed to sanction—and in the 1720s officially to authorize—an oligopolistic system of commerce controlled by organizations of merchants.

In terms of abstract models, one might say that the economy evolved from a predominantly command or "feudal" economy (in which rulers used tribute mechanisms to extract goods from producers and control their distribution among consumers) in the direction of an urban-centered entrepreneurial or "capitalist" economy (in which the purchasing power and priorities of consumers, as mediated through commercial channels, guided producers). But in the eighteenth century, as Japan lost an environmental context favorable to laissez-faire economics, entrepreneurialism was incorporated into a state-sanctioned, oligopolistic or "fascist" order (in which government farmed control of the commercial economy to major mercantile interests in return for fiscal and political collaboration).

Within this context of changing ruler-merchant-villager relations, the most striking economic developments of the Tokugawa heyday were matters of degree, not kind. Growth—in population, the amount and diversity of production, the volume and range of transactions, and the urban life sustained by that activity—continued at an exceptional, although slowing, pace. Whether the growth translated into improved standards of living for most people is difficult to say, but clearly it benefited the urban population, or at least its samurai and merchant sectors.

These economic developments helped shape seventeenth-century intellectual life. Changing class relationships and the passage of time, which reduced the exploits of wartime samurai to ever-more-distant memories, eventually raised the question of why samurai had a right to special privilege. As the century advanced, a rich corpus of political writings, mostly by samurai intellectuals, emerged to explain why the Tokugawa order and its hereditary elite existed as they did, why they had the right to do so, and how the rest of the populace fitted into the picture. By the 1680s an elaborate ideology of rule explained why people should be diligent in their tasks and obedient to their superiors. Unsurprisingly, an undercurrent of skepticism was also evident, but during the seventeenth century, the dominant ideology faced minimal challenge.

This intellectual production was only one aspect of seventeenth-century cultural life. The three great cities of Kyoto, Osaka, and Edo, where most of the discretionary wealth accumulated, witnessed a flowering of higher cultural production. Decorative art, drama, poetry, and prose all flourished, giving rise to the vibrant but risqué *ukiyo,* or "floating world," culture that has come to be associated with the Genroku year period, 1688–1704. The creative juices were especially vital in Kyoto, where court nobles, resident samurai, clerics, wealthy *chōnin,* and artists participated as patrons and producers of art, literature, and drama. By transcending the status categories of the social order, the world of arts and letters was able to draw talent from a wide spectrum of the populace, a consideration that was, one suspects, central to the remarkable cultural flowering of the Tokugawa heyday.

The Politics of Order

A new phase in Japan's political history commenced in 1632, when Hidetada, the second Tokugawa shogun, died, and his son Iemitsu succeeded. Hidetada had been cautious and uncreative, generally adhering to the policies of his father, but Iemitsu was different. He moved energetically to consolidate Tokugawa control by commanding obedience, intimidating the recalcitrant, and then subjecting them to sustainable regulation. By 1640 he had attained most of those goals, and in the decades that followed, his domestic and foreign arrangements became fixed in their essentials, defining for two centuries the basic character of both polity at home and policy abroad.

Iemitsu's legacy survived for several reasons. His successor, Ietsuna, was a child, who was guided by his father's surviving lieutenants, and they clung to established policies, fearful lest a misstep bring the regime tumbling down. His domestic policies, notably those vis-à-vis the daimyo, survived because they accommodated the times. Most lords found their fiscal situations growing awkward or worse, which made them receptive to Edo's restrictions on castle construction, armies, and ritual display. Moreover, disorder among their vassals was more troubling for most daimyo than the schemes of rival lords, which gave them reason to accept bakufu calls for tighter social control. Finally, lest his point be missed, Iemitsu punished offenders with an iron hand, and the most rudimentary sense of prudence kept daimyo in line. His successors eased the harshest of his policies, and that seemed to reduce lordly grievances without lowering appreciation of Edo's capacity to punish or reward.

Iemitsu's diplomatic policy endured because no foreign power capable of defying it cared enough to insist. Also, his successors found ample reason to sustain it: turmoil on the continent, which lasted until the Manchus secured China in the 1680s, made foreign relations in general seem risky. Concern over missionary-daimyo connections and Christian communal vitality within Japan sustained government interest in permanent control of European influence. Finally, three economic factors—the decline of domestic mining, changes in the Asian bullion market, and problems of government finance—diminished the attractiveness of overseas trade.

By the time Iemitsu died in the autumn of 1651, the routines of domestic administration and foreign policy were largely in place. They provided precedents that Ietsuna and his successor, Tsunayoshi, used in keeping the peace until 1709. Many daimyo as well, especially those with larger domains (*han*), had developed extensive regulatory regimes to maintain order within their territories, and as the decades passed, rules and regulations of similar intent and character proliferated throughout the country. They commonly did so in response to factional tensions and fiscal troubles that became pervasive within han, displacing both fear of the bakufu and suspicion of one another as the dominant issues in daimyo politics.

Ietsuna was Edo's first child-shogun. Both logic and precedent suggested that the regime was unlikely to survive the break in leadership, and the most noteworthy aspect of his regime may have been the mere fact of bakufu survival. That outcome certainly owed much to Iemitsu's measures of consolidation, but it owed much, as well, to the competence and dedication of Ietsuna's key advisors and to the generally benign conditions of the day. Nevertheless, the leadership's nervousness is evident in the ideological shrillness with which it suppressed individuals and groups suspected of having subversive intentions or influence.

Ideological considerations also weighed heavily in the rule of Tsunayoshi, younger brother and successor to the childless Ietsuna. But where the ideology of Ietsuna's rule derived from his advisors and seemed defensive in character, Tsunayoshi's came from his own heart, was broad in vision, and aggressively constructive in intent. The high visibility of Tsunayoshi's ethical politics notwithstanding, however, he encountered such unprecedented financial difficulties that in the end fiscal policy proved the most significant part of his legacy.

TOKUGAWA IEMITSU

Iemitsu became shogun in 1623 at the age of nineteen, but Hidetada retained control until his death in 1632. When Iemitsu inherited the power that year, he was the first Tokugawa shogun who had never commanded troops in wartime and never known the head of his family to be but one among many barons. Perhaps for those reasons, during his two decades of rule, he showed no interest in the coalition politics employed by his father and grandfather.

The only compelling form of authority he knew was shogunal, but to exercise it, he first had to establish effective control over his own regime, and it was in the hands of his father's lieutenants. They were grizzled old veterans with decades of military and political experience, and they surely had no appetite for a callow youth questioning the policies of giants whose accomplishments made him look like the merest upstart. Nevertheless, he succeeded in gaining control of officialdom by skillful use of appointive power and shrewd administrative manipulation. Moreover, he projected shogunal power outward by engaging in rigorous management at home and carefully regulated contacts abroad.

IEMITSU'S DOMESTIC POLICIES

Within months of his father's death, Iemitsu began improving administrative effectiveness and putting his own men in positions of power. He designated a few special inspectors (*ōmetsuke*) to oversee the performance of officials subordinate to the *toshiyori* (elders, later called *rōjū*, or senior councillors) and to investigate problems relating to daimyo. He formalized *junkenshi,* the teams of officials who periodically visited daimyo domains to ascertain whether all was in order. He set up a records office for the bakufu and issued new codes on criminal adjudication. He formed or reorganized a number of other offices, high and low, civil and military, to improve overall administration, and issued regulations to guide their operation. He brought more mines under Edo's control, restructured the shogunal domain to tighten his finance office's (kanjōsho) control of production, and reformed bakufu warehouse operations to give them more professional supervision.

One of Iemitsu's main goals was to improve bakufu finances. Another, possibly more pressing, task was to tighten control of the cities, especially Edo. By the 1630s it was a burgeoning city full of men with time on their hands. Some were samurai, the most visible being the five thousand or so middling shogunal retainers called hatamoto. Some of them (along with the seventeen thousand lesser shogunal vassals known as gokenin) esteemed themselves overmuch, becoming town bullies and rowdies, swaggering and carousing about in gangs called hatamoto yakko. Other troublemakers were commoners, some of whom also formed gangs, the machi yakko, that gambled, robbed, picked fights with hatamoto yakko, and otherwise disturbed the peace, sometimes in the name of egalitarianism or social leveling.

To cope with these problems, the bakufu issued regulations on dress, hair style, deportment, and the wearing of swords, and both bakufu and daimyo deployed police patrols, set up street barriers, and instituted curfew arrangements. These became permanent features of urban government, but rowdies remained a problem for decades. The passage of time more than the passage of laws gradually brought urban peace, and Tsunayoshi consolidated it in the 1680s by rounding up and banishing or executing members of both samurai and commoner gangs.

More important, in retrospect, than Iemitsu's measures of urban control were his moves to regularize the daimyo hostage practice that had operated haphazardly since Ieyasu's day. During the 1630s he developed it into the intricate sankin kōtai, or "alternate attendance" system, in which lords and large numbers of retainers moved between castle towns and Edo every year, and wives, heirs, and suitable numbers of attendants lived in Edo permanently. Sankin kōtai became the single most important mechanism of daimyo control, remaining intact and little changed until 1862.

To look at the development of sankin kōtai more closely, within months of Sekigahara, tozama daimyō—meaning those lords whom Ieyasu did not regard as relatives (kamon) or hereditary retainers (fudai)—began visiting him, cultivating goodwill and seeking rewards for service. Lordly visits and hostage arrangements were a staple of medieval politics, and as Ieyasu enlarged Edo, he allotted building sites for daimyo use. In the first hint that attendance was to be compulsory, Hidetada in 1609 notified tozama lords that he expected them to stay the winter. In following years daimyo continued making frequent, pro-

3. Exterior of the Hosokawa mansion in Edo. Major daimyo, such as Hosokawa of Kumamoto han, billeted their samurai in barracks such as this. The whitewashed building at center right is a fireproof storehouse. Water buckets for firefighting are in place beside the entrance in the foreground, and the barracks themselves are fireproofed with plaster and tile roofs. Courtesy of the Study and Documentation Centre for Photography, University of Leiden, Collection Bauduin, Neg. No. B2–9.

longed visits, and the practice became more habitual. In 1635 Iemitsu ordered them henceforth to visit in accord with clearly specified schedules. The order, given as an amendment to the *buke shohatto*, stated:

> It is now settled that the [lords] are to serve in turns (*kōtai*) at Edo. They shall proceed hither (*sankin*) every year in summer during the course of the fourth month. Lately the numbers of retainers and servants accompanying them have become excessive. This is not only wasteful to the domains and districts, but also imposes considerable hardship on the people. Hereafter suitable reductions in this respect must be made. [If daimyo] are ordered to go to Kyoto, [they must] follow the instructions given. On official business, however, the number of persons accompanying [them] can be proportionate to the rank of each [lord].[1]

1. David John Lu, *Sources of Japanese History* (New York: McGraw-Hill, 1974), 1: 204.

That order applied to tozama lords, but Iemitsu was also determined to regulate the Tokugawa family's pre-Sekigahara vassal families. During the 1630s he issued regulations to the hatamoto that, among other things, required the greatest of them to follow sankin kōtai schedules. In 1634 he instructed fudai lords to bring their wives and heirs to Edo, and eight years later he ordered them to travel as scheduled. Thereafter nearly all daimyo made the biennial twelve-month sojourns in Edo, about half of them one year and half the next, traveling either in the fourth or in the eighth month, depending on their assigned time slot.

Daimyo retinues commonly numbered in the hundreds, scores of the men being haughty samurai disinclined to tolerate slights to their lord's dignity. To avoid congestion and the risk of clashes should retinues collide en route or compete for rooms at inns along the way, lords had to move as scheduled. Accordingly the bakufu enforced its travel rules rigorously, and failure to make timely progress could subject a lord to house arrest or other serious punishment.

Besides sankin kōtai, Iemitsu employed direct manipulation, intimidation, and bribery to control potential rivals. In 1634 he overawed the court—and gave others an unforgettable display of shogunal power—by visiting Kyoto with an army drawn largely from the daimyo and said to number 309,000. Even as segments of this monstrous retinue were still snaking their way westward toward bivouacs around the city, Iemitsu was distributing largesse to nobles and Kyoto citizens alike.

At Edo he gradually eased out of power those high officials who offended him, and he coopted or coerced his most powerful relatives into collaboration or capitulation. He continued his predecessors' policy of aggressively transferring and attainting daimyo, thereby expanding the portion of central Japan administered by shogunal intendants (*daikan*) and more reliable lords. Those transfers perpetuated the "carpetbagger" quality of much daimyo governance, undercutting lordly power by severing ties to local populations. And because such moves were expensive and disruptive, the threat of transfer helped assure daimyo obedience.

On the other hand, the frequent daimyo transfers surely contributed to Iemitsu's worst domestic crisis, the Kan'ei crop failure and famine, which began in the early 1630s and peaked in 1641–42. The historical record on this first major famine of the Tokugawa period is scattered and thin, but it seems likely that a combination of factors precipitated it. At the time, it appears, northeast Asia as a whole was experiencing unusual irregularity in the weather.[2] From the early 1630s on, cold rainy summers led to a succession of crop failures, especially in northeastern Japan, suggesting the influence of the yamase effect mentioned in chapter 1.

Just when food production was being buffeted, Iemitsu's policies created great new pressures on it. His regularization of sankin kōtai spurred the growth of Edo, and while the city population was ill-situated to obtain its own foodstuffs, it was headed by a military elite still capable of compelling rural areas to yield up food supplies on demand, even if that left local folk hungry. And compel they did, requisitioning from villages the goods and labor needed to build and stock their Edo mansions. In addition, sankin kōtai retinues required porters as they traveled, mostly during months when farmers were cropping their fields, and villagers along the highways had to leave their farm work to provide the service. Moreover, until Edo cracked down on the practice, Iemitsu's aggressive transferring of daimyo worsened affairs by encouraging lords to intensify and speed up tax collection before leaving the old domain and impose emergency levies upon entering the new one.

Finally, mariners had still not mastered the hazards of sailing large cargo junks around the promontories of the Kii and Bōsō peninsulas, so rapid shipment of rice to Edo was difficult. And the recent prohibition of overseas travel by Japanese and imposition of restrictions on the size of vessels may have further hampered the capacity of mariners to convey food supplies from area to area, making urban supply even more difficult.

This combination of factors reducing food output and availability just when demand for it was sharply increasing, especially in Edo, produced hard times.[3] It precipitated peasant protests in 1632, 1633, and 1635, and led to famine conditions in several provinces during 1636. The Shimabara rebellion of 1637–38 was the most dramatic consequence of this worsened situation, but peasant protests occurred contemporaneously in the northeast and continued during the next few

2. William S. Atwell, "Some Observations on the 'Seventeenth-Century Crisis' in China and Japan," *JAS* 45-2 (Feb. 1986): 226. In "A Seventeenth-Century 'General Crisis' in East Asia?" *Modern Asian Studies* 24-4 (Oct. 1990): 661–82, Atwell revises and improves his analysis of these years.

3. This summary of the Kan'ei famine and Edo's reaction to it is based on Nagakura Tamotsu, "Kan'ei no kikin to bakufu no taiō" [The Kan'ei famine and bakufu response], in *Edo jidai no kikin* [Famine in the Edo period] (Tokyo: Yusankaku shuppan, 1982), pp. 75–85. Tōdō of Tsu had substantial land in Iga, which he administered through a branch headquarters at Ueno.

years. Harvests fell especially short during the years 1639–42, and worse
hardship ensued. During 1640 the deaths of large numbers of work
animals (presumably as a result of slaughter, not starvation) were reported, including 6,511 in the Tōdō domain in Iga province. In the
summer of 1642, 15,802 people were reported suffering from hunger
in the Kiso River valley, 45 having starved to death and 179 having
been reduced to begging. By then food prices in Edo had risen sharply,
and people were found starving along the highways.

Over the years, Iemitsu's government had issued numerous regulations on rural affairs, but the crisis of 1642 finally concentrated his
attention. Late in the spring, he assembled officials to discuss the famine
and deployed high-powered investigators across bakufu domains in the
Kantō and Kinai regions. He ordered the disbursement of emergency
food supplies and set officials to work drafting legislation to prevent
recurrence of the trouble. In a summer of intensive effort, bakufu leaders implemented a number of relief measures and produced a body of
regulations that delineated the essential characteristics of the village system they wished to perpetuate.

Their vision looked like this. Each village was to constitute a self-
sustaining collectivity of smallholders clearly separated from merchants. They were to eschew luxuries and work diligently to produce
essential goods on their own lands, while collectively paying taxes and
caring for their village. They were to be responsible for one another's
good behavior, an obligation exercised through *goningumi*, or "five
household units," neighborhood groups modeled on classical Chinese
precedents. Overseeing these collectivities was the hierarchy of village
officials, intendants, and daimyo or Edo officials, all attentive to their
duties, dedicated to preserving the productive vitality and well-being of
the villagers, and effectively controlled by regulations that derived ultimately from Edo.

This communal ideal, which scholars now identify by the term *kyōdōtai*, was articulated not in abstract philosophical terms but in specific
prohibitions and admonitions. Earlier bakufu decrees had forbidden the
buying and selling of people or the maintenance of serflike employment
arrangements, and an edict of 1642 urged villagers to avoid any use of
wage labor. Rather than exploiting others, householders were to work
their own land. Other decrees issued between the summer of 1642 and
the following spring contained clauses urging villagers to maintain village roads and bridges and to ensure that no land in the village went
untilled. Other clauses called upon more fortunate villagers to help the

unlucky by providing irrigation water or other assistance as needed. Specific clauses forbade merchants to settle in villages or villagers to deal with them and listed luxury crops and products that were forbidden. Others prohibited the seizure of any villager's land for reason of negligence or failure to pay taxes, prohibited the buying and selling of arable, and forbade farmers to work land outside their own villages.

Yet other clauses specified the nature and extent of village officials' authority and restrictively defined the amounts of animal and human corvée that daimyo or officials could requisition. And, finally, should higher authorities continue to be abusive, a clause specified that villagers had the right to abscond after they had paid their taxes but not to leave without doing so. Presumably this final limitation aimed at preventing villagers from fleeing without real grievance, while the main clause sought to discourage abuse from above, since no daimyo or official could afford to lose his agricultural labor force or face the public embarrassment of such a rebuke.

By these several administrative and political measures, Iemitsu imposed his own control on officialdom, daimyo, lesser shogunal vassals, and the imperial court. He likewise attempted to restrict the influence of merchants and stabilize village affairs. In brief, he strengthened bakufu control over the domestic polity as a whole. During those same years he also put his stamp on foreign affairs, in the process departing sharply from his predecessors' policy.

IEMITSU'S FOREIGN POLICIES

During the late 1620s, Hidetada's government encountered foreign problems that seemed fraught with danger, but he did not let them alter the basic thrust of his trade and diplomatic policies. On the continent, a Manchu army was attempting to overthrow the Ming dynasty, and in 1627 it invaded Korea after the badly divided government in Seoul adopted a pro-Ming posture. When the rulers in Edo learned of the invasion, they debated sending troops to help the Koreans repel it, thereby forestalling a reprise of the invasions that had followed the Mongol conquest of Korea some 350 years earlier. They despatched a fact-finding mission, but before further action was needed, the problem resolved itself when the Manchus withdrew.

While the question of Korea was hanging fire, problems erupted in the area of foreign trade. Over the years, Edo had received occasional reports of ronin and others colliding with foreigners in ports and on the high seas, and in 1628–30 two such incidents created alarm. In one, the crew of a Spanish galleon plundered a Japanese trading vessel in the Gulf of Siam; in the other, Japanese trader-adventurers in Taiwan clashed with some Dutchmen, in the process kidnapping the senior Dutch authority on the island, raising the specter of a major clash between Edo and the Netherlands. Hidetada dealt with the two incidents by temporarily suspending all overseas trade. He hoped this would prevent escalation of the clashes and discourage future misconduct, thereby helping sustain a stable, long-term trading environment. Since all parties wished the trade to continue, the issues were resolved by 1632 and commerce resumed.

After Hidetada's death, other incidents occurred, and the trade was also marred by domestic disputes among the merchants handling it. To resolve the problems, Iemitsu decided to reverse key parts of established policy. Most important, in regulations of 1633, which were slightly modified over the next few years, he instructed his administrators in Nagasaki to prevent any Japanese, on pain of death, from going overseas or returning from abroad. The regulations also laid out procedures for handling domestic distribution of trade goods. Those measures would eliminate trouble caused by Japanese, and Iemitsu enacted other measures to end problems of foreign origin. Edicts of 1634 and 1635 reduced the number of Portuguese in Japan and restricted their movements, and new regulations specified procedures for enforcing the existing proscription on missionary activity.[4] Concurrently the bakufu converted a strip of mud flat in Nagasaki harbor into an artificial islet, and from 1636 on, it required the Portuguese to reside and conduct all trade there.

A vastly more ambitious scheme involved a proposal by Dutch traders at Hirado seeking to clear the seas of commercial competition. The Dutch advised Edo to attack its problem at the source by mounting assaults on the Portuguese in Macao and the Spaniards in Manila. Bakufu leaders debated the proposal off and on for nearly two years, and late in 1637 Iemitsu reportedly decided to mount the attack on Manila, with the Dutch providing a six-vessel escort for an invasion force of some ten thousand fighting men.

Before the venture could get under way, domestic trouble derailed it. As noted earlier, Hidetada had tried to eradicate the last communities of Christian converts during the 1620s. Secret religious practice contin-

4. Lu, *Sources*, 1: 216–18, offers translations of edicts of 1635 and 1639.

4.   Dejima, ca. 1875. The curving waterfront of Dejima is visible in the center
of this photograph from the early Meiji period. On the islet are visible the
unloading areas, warehouses, and other buildings of the Dutch trading post.
Directly behind Dejima are pine trees in the Nagasaki magistrate's office compound (*bugyōsho*). The buildings in the right foreground are the Chinese trading post and settlement area. Despite their steepness, the hillsides are carefully
terraced and cultivated. Courtesy of the Study and Documentation Centre for
Photography, University of Leiden, Collection Bauduin, Neg. No. K5.

ued, however, mostly in Kyushu, and bitter grievances against government persecution survived. This reservoir of deep disaffection burst in
1637 during the Kan'ei famine, when harsh daimyo rule on the Shimabara peninsula precipitated resistance that snowballed into an insurrection involving some thirty-five thousand people, primarily villagers, but
a number of them ronin.

   The upheaval resulted mainly from local abuses during a difficult
time, but because the insurgents rallied support and sustained their morale by flying Christian banners and appealing to Christian symbols,
thereby giving their enterprise the color of a religiously inspired rebellion in the Ikkō tradition, Edo saw in it far more than local misery or
lordly malfeasance. When the vaunted legions of bakufu and daimyo
proved unable to overrun the little rebel fortress, even with Dutch military assistance, humiliated leaders shifted to the time-proven and less

risky strategy of starving the defenders out. That policy enabled them to overwhelm and destroy their emaciated opponents after about four months, but the affair, so embarrassing for leaders and so tragic for the losers, only reinforced offical resentment of Christianity and fear of foreign influence.

In reaction, the rulers resolved to break up the last Christian enclaves and strengthened organs of surveillance to ensure that such unauthorized communal political organization never reappeared. Iemitsu tightened trading regulations, expelled Portuguese traders, and forbade their return, saying they had ignored earlier prohibitions on admitting missionaries and so were ultimately to blame for the upheaval. With that move he also solved the Dutch problem of Iberian competition, and the Dutch proposal to send expeditions against Macao and Manila was quietly forgotten.

By the late 1630s, Iemitsu had thus brought foreign relations under firmer control. One situation that seemed likely to create diplomatic trouble—clashes between traveling Japanese and local people—was eliminated. A second worrisome situation, that of missionaries in Japan, had been addressed head on, even at the price of losing the Portuguese trade. The Dutch were the only Europeans still active in Japan, and in 1640 they were ordered to move from Hirado to Nagasaki and to handle all their trade at Dejima, the artificial islet built there four years earlier. On Dejima, the scope, content, and procedures of their trade could be—and were—subject to careful surveillance.

These restrictive measures were taken, as noted in chapter 8, without actually reducing the volume of trade. The Dutch took over some of the Japanese and Portuguese business, while Chinese traders at Nagasaki, whose activities were also brought under closer supervision, took over the rest. The outcome gave Iemitsu reason to believe that his trade with southeast Asia could be sustained without foreign relations accidentally getting out of hand.

Meanwhile, affairs on the mainland were begging for attention. As bakufu leaders wrestled with trade issues and debated attacks on Macao and Manila in 1636, the Manchus mounted a second invasion of Korea, crushing all resistance and compelling the Yi dynasty to accept Manchu suzerainty. Already facing a plateful of foreign problems, Iemitsu, unlike Hidetada in 1627, did not consider responding militarily despite the much more serious outcome of the renewed Manchu action.

Once those other issues were dealt with, however, Edo again addressed the rapidly changing cross-channel situation. In 1644 the Manchus drove the Ming out of Peking and established their own regime, but resistance continued in the south of China, and Ming loyalists such as the scholar Chu Shun-shui appealed to Edo for military assistance. From the end of 1645 on, Iemitsu and his advisors debated the requests and considered despatching a Japanese battle force of twenty thousand to China either by sea or via Korea. Discussion continued through the following summer, with senior officials and advisors deeply divided, until reports of major Manchu successes reached Edo near year's end. Those reports, which implied that the time for helpful action had passed, led Iemitsu to scrap the invasion proposal.[5] With that decision, Japan pulled back from the brink of renewed continental involvement, and the foreign policy arrangements of the 1630s survived, eventually becoming fixed as holy writ and acquiring the designation *sakoku,* or "closed country," policy in the mid nineteenth century.

DAIMYO DOMAINS AND THEIR MANAGEMENT

By the time of Iemitsu's death in 1651, few of Japan's leaders could remember the age of war. For veterans in their fifties, Sekigahara meant war stories they had heard as boys. The Osaka battle was a distant memory of youthful heroics, and even the humiliation at Shimabara was thirteen years gone. The world they knew was one of order, routine, and regulation, and in it fiscal issues had become the ones around which most politics turned. Such problems notwithstanding, lords habitually made their well-attended sankin kōtai treks, displaying the symbols and performing the rituals appropriate to their rank. And ranked they were, in several ways and with great care.

DOMAIN TYPES AND TRENDS

By then the basic categories of daimyo, *fudai, shinpan,* and *tozama* were well established. Fudai lords were reputedly descended from Ieyasu's pre-Sekigahara retainers and tozama from other lordly families of 1600. Shinpan were those Tokugawa relatives (*kamon*) who traced their lineage to Ieyasu by way of his several sons.[6] Of them the three greatest,

5. Ronald P. Toby, *State and Diplomacy in Early Modern Japan* (Princeton: Princeton University Press, 1984), pp. 118–30.
6. Other *kamon,* whose ancestry led back to Ieyasu's siblings and uncles of varying remove, were treated by Tokugawa leaders as *fudai* daimyo. Here, as in all categorizations of Tokugawa society, exceptions can be found, which reminds us that the categories to considerable extent are generalizations about a reality that had already arisen in piecemeal fashion.

known as the *sanke,* or "three houses," held the sprawling castles at Mito, Nagoya, and Wakayama.

By 1651 decades of daimyo attainder had increased the numbers of fudai and shinpan lords at the expense of tozama, particularly those on the losing side at Sekigahara. Indeed, descendants of only three of Ieyasu's enemies of 1600—Shimazu, Mōri, and Nabeshima—still held major domains. By one calculation, the bakufu transferred some 3 million *koku* of land from tozama to fudai-shinpan administration between 1616 and 1651, and, "of the twenty-four great outside daimyo, nine had been dispossessed, one reduced, and four transferred."[7] In contrast, the 69 or so vassals of Ieyasu who held daimyo-sized domains in 1601 had increased to 91 in 1616 and 115 by 1690.[8] And shinpan lords, nonexistent in 1600, numbered about 20 a century later. Clearly these groups were the chief beneficiaries of the processes of attainder and transfer that seventeenth-century shogun practiced so energetically. In 1700 Japan's assessed land was distributed as follows:[9]

Category of land	Estimated yield (koku)
Imperial family lands	141,151
Shogunal domain	4,213,171
Hatamoto-gokenin lands	2,606,545
Fudai-shinpan lands	9,325,300
Tozama lands	9,834,700
Temple and shrine lands	316,230

The process of shifting lords about not only weakened the tozama as a group but also reduced the threat of autonomous daimyo action by cutting the number of great domains while increasing the number of small ones.

The influence of great lords was also restricted by their exclusion from roles in the bakufu. In general the senior offices of the bakufu that controlled policy-making were staffed by men selected from the relatively large middle echelon of fudai lords, while lesser posts were held by lesser fudai lords, hatamoto, and gokenin. With few exceptions,

7. John Whitney Hall, *Government and Local Power in Japan, 500–1700* (Princeton: Princeton University Press, 1966), p. 343.
8. Harold Bolitho, *Treasures among Men* (New Haven: Yale University Press, 1974), p. 45.
9. Hall, *Government and Local Power,* p. 343.

shinpan and tozama lords of all ranks were excluded from bakufu posts. Although Edo frequently received advice from the greatest shinpan, their views were rarely welcomed or heeded.

In short, the processes of daimyo transfer and attainder had gradually reduced the size of domains and placed more of them in the hands of lords whose legacy and situation disposed them to support the regime. And the process of recruitment to bakufu office staffed the regime with lords who were comparatively lacking in autonomous power and so had reason to support it as the guarantor of their hereditary privileges.

Nevertheless the greatest domains were still held by shinpan and tozama lords, and each constituted a bastion of autonomous power complete with a legitimate authority figure, ideology of rule, government staff, administrative regulations, armed forces, tax base, producer populace, and defined territories. And all those attributes of petty statehood survived intact until 1868. Ranked by the putative yield (*kokudaka*) of their lands, the ten greatest daimyo domains in 1690 were as follows: [10]

Province	Castle town	Daimyo family	Kokudaka	Daimyo status
Kaga	Kanazawa	Maeda	1,022,700	tozama
Satsuma	Kagoshima	Shimazu	729,000	tozama
Mutsu	Sendai	Date	620,000	tozama
Owari	Nagoya	Tokugawa	619,000	sanke
Kii	Wakayama	Tokugawa	555,000	sanke
Higo	Kumamoto	Hosokawa	545,000	tozama
Chikuzen	Fukuoka	Kuroda	520,000	tozama
Aki	Hiroshima	Asano	426,000	tozama
Chōshū	Yamaguchi	Mōri	369,000	tozama
Ise & Iga	Tsu	Tōdō	363,000	tozama

Most of the greatest lords were thus tozama daimyo, and most were located on the periphery of the realm, in Kyushu, Shikoku, far western

10. Lists of daimyo are numerous. This one, for ca. 1690, derives from Nihon keizaishi kenkyūjo, comp., *Nihon keizaishi jiten* [Encyclopedia of Japanese economic history] (Tokyo: Nihon hyōronsha, 1936), 5: 975–90. A *koku* is a volume measure of about 5 bushels, so *kokudaka* is a figure that purports to represent the production of a domain in terms of rice or goods of equivalent value.

Honshu, and Tōhoku. A good many minor lords held domains located among these great han, but more were situated nearer the center of Japan, where their lands lay among those of the bakufu and its non-daimyo landholding vassals.

ISSUES IN DOMAIN GOVERNANCE

One of the most striking aspects of han was their variation in size, ranging from that of Maeda, with over a million koku—which ideally meant enough productive capacity to sustain a million people—to a large number of petty barons, about a third of the total, with domains too small even to justify a castle.[11] In 1690, to be precise, 91 of the 240 daimyo were minor lords with only 10,000–20,000 koku. They had to maintain daimyo appearances both at home and in Edo on the basis of a domain that embraced only a handful of villages. And while their lands often included scattered parcels, they were unlikely to provide the diversity of yield necessary to protect them from the vagaries of climate that could generate crop failure, human hardship, and severe tax loss.

The bakufu, which expected daimyo to provide military assistance on call, accommodated the great range in han tax bases by establishing a proportionality between the size of a domain and its military liability. In Iemitsu's regulations of 1649, for example, the obligations of two key grades of daimyo were as follows:[12]

Obligation	Domains of 100,000 koku	Domains of 10,000 koku
Horsemen	170	10
Firearms	350	20
Bows	60	10
Spear bearer	150	3
Banner bearer	20	3
Total manpower	2,155	235

A minor lord was thus supposed to field an armed force of 235 samurai

11. A few lords in the 10,000–20,000 koku category had castles, but most did not, and several with larger domains were also spared the cost of a castle. Most of these petty lords were fudai daimyo.

12. Derived from Hall, Government and Local Power, p. 371. The scheduled obligations of lesser shogunal retainers, also revised in 1649, were based on their hereditary family stipends.

(a handful of whom would have a few retainers of their own): 10 fully armored horsemen, 20 foot soldiers carrying muzzleloaders, 10 archers, 3 pikemen, 3 men flying their lord's battle streamers, and the remaining 189 wielding swords. A major lord, by contrast, was expected to deploy thousands, with his senior vassals bringing additional scores of retainers to the fray.

Even with Edo's careful fitting of obligations to resources, lords were hard pressed to meet bakufu requirements because they faced other, more insistent expenses. Domanial output sustained their families, their castles or fortified residences, sankin kōtai travel and ceremonial, their one or more mansions and warehouses in Edo, any offices they had in Osaka or Kyoto, and government offices and operations at home, and paid the basic stipends of all their vassals and the salaries of officials, guards, and attendants. They were also expected to provide aid to commoners in moments of dire need and special contributions to the bakufu on request.

Han leaders thus had to allocate resources among several competing constituencies, and that task underlay most domanial politics. By Ietsuna's day, lords were stretched so thin trying to satisfy the several demands on their income that few could entertain ambitions greater than mere domanial survival, and "politics" was coming to mean not external maneuvering to displace the Tokugawa or otherwise advance one's family on the larger stage but internal maneuvering to keep vassals and producers pacified. Han rule was becoming administration: devising, modifying, and implementing regulations and maintaining a command structure to enforce them. The timing of this political routinization varied from han to han, in part because bakufu transfers delayed the process, but in general it was most evident during the mid seventeenth century.

Administrative manipulation was aimed primarily at solving fiscal problems. As noted in chapter 5, rulers used cadastral surveys to identify taxable rural output. By tightening survey methods and surveying repeatedly, the rulers increased their income substantially, but by midcentury they had recorded most of Japan's arable land, and thereafter resurveying was less and less fruitful. Bakufu records indicate that for the country as a whole, the reported output of rice and other grains rose only 5.4 percent in the 52-year period 1645–97. Given the rate of continuing population increase, the figure suggests that a growing portion of total rural production was escaping the tax collector's eye.[13]

13. Susan B. Hanley and Kozo Yamamura, *Economic and Demographic Change in Preindustrial Japan, 1600–1868* (Princeton: Princeton University Press, 1977), p. 71. The

Fiscal need spurred han leaders to seek new income, manage its distribution better, and contain expenses. Other measures tightened control over vassals and commoners, in part for fiscal reasons and in part to reduce the threat of unrest, which was exacerbated at times by steps taken to improve finances. In toto, these policies surely contributed to the peacefulness of seventeenth-century Japan by assuring vassals of acceptable living conditions. Not all daimyo governance went smoothly, however, and internal difficulties often pitted factions of vassals against one another. The most severe of these factional disorders were known as *oie sōdō*, or "household disturbances."

Sōdō affected many han, some as early as Hideyoshi's day, others as late as the mid nineteenth century. However, most occurred during the seventeenth century, notably the Kuroda (1623–33), Aizu (1638–43), Ikoma and Ikeda (both in 1640), Date (1660–71), and Echigo sōdō (1679–81).[14] Sōdō proliferated then because they were a quintessential reflection of the age. The coming of peace produced "losers" not only in the form of ronin but also in the form of retainers who could no longer aspire to great deeds or even appreciable career advancement because high positions were few and those that existed were closed to men of lower rank. Within daimyo households as well, tensions rose because only one family member could be daimyo at a time, and an heir might find himself long in the tooth before his revered parent at last went to his final reward. Factions formed as ambitious men colluded to advance their interests against rival groups. Later generations of samurai became more habituated to the stabilized status order, but in the seventeenth century, that order was still being consolidated, and oie sōdō were another measure of consolidation's cost.

Factional unrest was not, however, merely an expression of mindless ambition. Governing involved serious decision making, and failures of honest policy, abuses of power, and sheer incompetence all gave someone reason to seek changes in leadership. Heated charges of corruption,

increase is from 24,553,757 *koku* in 1645 to 25,876,392 *koku* by 1697. This figure for 1697 may understate actual yield, but how seriously is unclear. Insofar as the two figures do indicate total grain output, they suggest that it was not growing as fast as population, which may help explain the contemporary proliferation of sumptuary regulations designed to restrain consumption. Of course, the rates of population growth may be overstated, and it is likely that improvements in transportation and storage reduced rates of food loss to rot, rodents, and leakage.

14. Concise information on these several disturbances is given in *Nihon rekishi daijiten* [Encyclopedia of Japanese history] (Tokyo: Kawade Shobō shinsha, 1961), 20 vols. For a description of the Date *sōdō* in Sendai, see George Sansom, *A History of Japan*, vol. 3, *1615–1867* (Stanford: Stanford University Press, 1963), pp. 64–67.

mismanagement, and abuse of power were a common characteristic of sōdō, and their settlement involved punishments and changes of governing personnel. The intensity of feeling notwithstanding, it was in everyone's interest not to let rivalries get out of hand, lest, in the worst scenario, they provoke Edo to dissolve the domain and thus reduce an entire vassal force to ronin status. The combination of compelling reason to struggle for power and equally compelling reason to keep the struggle within bounds bred conflicts that sometimes simmered on and on, occasionally erupting in bursts of anger and even violence, but commonly persisting for years, controlled but unresolved.

Daimyo administrations aspired to do better than simply keep the lid on, however. Rivalry among vassals was important in prodding lords to improve administrative control, clarify criminal procedures and principles, and foster Confucian, Shintō, and other learning as means of inculcating such virtues as diligence, frugality, and deference toward superiors. The decline in frequency of sōdō after 1700, even in the face of growing samurai hardship, suggests that their efforts enjoyed some success.

THREE EXAMPLES: KAGA, TOSA, BIZEN

Three examples of han government—those of Maeda of Kaga, who settled permanently at Kanazawa in the 1580s, Yamanouchi of Tosa, who settled at Kōchi in 1601, and Ikeda of Bizen, who did so at Okayama in 1632—will illustrate the process of administrative development of major domains during the Tokugawa heyday.

Kaga, with a putative yield of 1,195,000 koku around 1690, was not only the largest han but also one of the most entrenched. By 1630, as noted in chapter 4, it possessed in Kanazawa a large and bustling castle town. Its treasury was badly strained, however, by fires that roared through the town in 1631 and 1635, leading Maeda to impose special dues on merchants and enabling the han to rearrange the housing of vassals and townsmen, imposing more order on their lives and social relationships. Legal codes issued in 1637 and 1642 defined crimes and punishments for urban commoners, laying a firmer foundation for city administration. From about the middle of the century, Maeda promoted land opening, and during the 1650s he carried out a major reform of rural administration, placing vassals' fiefs under direct han control to improve tax collection. He also tightened overall governmental structure, clarifying procedures and areas of authority in both town and hinterland. In a spate of new regulations issued in 1659–61, he tried to deepen government control of castle town life, most notably by issuing a host of sumptuary regulations and addressing problems caused by indebtedness to merchants.[15] In later years, administrative tinkering continued, but the basic configuration of Kaga rule was settled.

Tosa han, with some 222,000 koku in 1690, came under the control of Yamanouchi's senior advisor, Nonaka Kenzan, in 1631. During three decades of leadership, Nonaka strove to remedy Tosa's serious and worsening fiscal shortfall by pursuing political tightening, commercial management, and stimulation of production. He enlarged Tosa's claim to income from lands assigned to vassals and improved tax collection on the han's own tax land. He mobilized labor to expand irrigation facilities and rewarded those who opened large areas to cultivation. He regulated prices and market activities and encouraged production of raw materials and handicrafts. Finally, he cultivated a Confucian ideology to strengthen Yamanouchi's legitimacy.[16]

Bizen han, headquartered in Okayama, was assessed at 310,000 koku around 1690. Iemitsu assigned the domain to Ikeda Mitsumasa in 1632, and during the 1640s Mitsumasa engaged in a flurry of codification. He issued regulations on taxation, fiscal management, fire control, and other aspects of village and domain administration, and he set up new procedures and positions to enforce the regulations. Moreover, he established a domain school where his retainers could study and hired Kumazawa Banzan, a gifted Confucian scholar, to serve as his advisor. In 1654, after torrential rains caused flooding that ravaged his castle and destroyed some 1,400 houses in Okayama and another 2,200 in rural areas, Mitsumasa tightened control of his domain and pushed a vigorous program of reconstruction.

During the 1660s, following the discovery of Christian communities north of Nagoya, Mitsumasa shifted his focus to ideological strengthening. He appointed inspectors to examine the general populace of Bizen for hidden Christians, promoted Confucian doctrine and its use in education, ordered everyone to register at Shintō shrines, and tore down about half the Buddhist temples in his domain. When Mitsumasa retired in 1672, his son took over, and for the rest of the century Bizen's

15. James L. McClain, *Kanazawa* (New Haven: Yale University Press, 1982), pp. 70–101. The fullest study of Maeda's early rural administration is Brown, *Domain Formation in Early Modern Japan* (in press; see ch. 4, n. 22, above).
16. Marius B. Jansen, "Tosa in the Seventeenth Century: The Establishment of Yamauchi Rule," in John W. Hall and Jansen, eds., *Studies in the Institutional History of Early Modern Japan* (Princeton: Princeton University Press, 1968), pp. 122–27.

policy focused more closely on expanding domain production, especially through land reclamation and riparian work. The han also improved port facilities to enhance access to the broader market and reorganized administration to strengthen control of commoners' activities.[17]

By century's end, domains across the country had implemented a wide array of policies to improve finances and tighten control of vassals and the general public, thereby keeping the peace and preserving the advantages of the ruling elite. In so doing, these "client states" were functioning, as leaders in Edo intended, as the local organs of the broader Tokugawa political structure, or *bakuhan taisei,* as scholars call it.

TOKUGAWA IETSUNA

Iemitsu was succeeded in 1651 by his ten-year-old son, Ietsuna, who held the shogunal title until his death in the late spring of 1680. His rule presents a curiously contradictory appearance. On the surface, his years (together with those of his successor, Tsunayoshi) seem the most tranquil and prosperous of the 265-year Tokugawa rule. Beneath the surface, however, one finds hints that for Japan's leaders the 1650s and 1660s were fraught with uncommonly intense fears and suspicions.

Looking first at the evidence of tranquillity in foreign relations, incidents involving Japanese abroad ceased during the 1630s. The last ones to involve Portuguese occurred in 1642–43, when two missionary groups attempted to infiltrate and were quickly captured, tortured, and recanted or died, and four years later, when a Portuguese ship was turned away at Nagasaki. After Iemitsu's decision in 1647 to stay clear of the Ming-Manchu struggle, Edo declined all invitations to intervene and refused most requests for military assistance. Some anti-Manchu forces did obtain weapons from Japan, but none received official support until 1676, when Edo formally permitted, almost as a token gesture, the export of some munitions to insurgents in south China. Even that incident led to no further entanglement.

Domestically, the tranquillity reflected the stabilized bakufu-daimyo relationship. Before Iemitsu's death, daimyo had become habituated to the routines of sankin kōtai and the basic political restrictions imposed by Edo. A reduction in daimyo transfers and attainders after 1651 eased han fiscal and political stress, which facilitated continuing lordly partic-

---

17. Hall, *Government and Local Power,* pp. 404–9.

ipation in sankin kōtai. And the other routines of regulated political life also remained intact or were elaborated by both bakufu and han.

Within this picture of tranquillity, the most dramatic and destructive event of Ietsuna's years was the Meireki fire that ravaged Edo in 1657. It killed an estimated hundred thousand people, making it one of history's great urban tragedies, and was also a political event because, in the course of ravaging the city, the fire consumed most parts of the castle, destroying documents and causing a massive disruption of political and administrative processes. In terms of architecture, it devoured a vast number of handsome buildings, and even though bakufu and han drained their treasuries to rebuild the city, Edo never again enjoyed its pre-Meireki level of elegant structures.

Beneath the surface of Ietsuna's years, one sees signs of a nervous and divided leadership wrestling with fears that stemmed from the unprecedented dilemma Edo faced after 1651. For the first time in its history, the bakufu lacked a mature leader with the authority and strength of personality to command obedience from officials and daimyo. Ietsuna the boy did grow up, but Ietsuna the man never took charge. Instead, a mixed group of senior officials and advisors, none of whom enjoyed a clearly superior status with well-defined authority, attempted to work together to keep the ship of state afloat.

Their collective nervousness evinced itself in a severely defensive ideological posture that was sharply at variance with the boldly assertive pragmatism of preceding decades and the devout and forceful advocacy of Confucianism that marked Tsunayoshi's rule. During Ietsuna's time the control of ideas, mostly by suppression of feared alternatives, acquired an importance that far exceeded that of both earlier and later years. "The air," as Herman Ooms has put it, "was thick with ideological concerns."[18] Ronin were feared and suppressed, as were Christian communities. And methodical procedures for registering the entire population in local temples or shrines were extended and enforced. The radically autonomous Fujufuse sect of Hokke Buddhism was eradicated, and Buddhism more broadly was subjected to attack. Shintō came under more intense management, and intellectuals were disciplined as never before.

This story of uneasy leadership began legitimately enough with Edo's response to a ronin plot to topple the regime just a few months after Ietsuna took office. The ronin problem stemmed from Edo's policies of

18. Herman Ooms, *Tokugawa Ideology* (Princeton: Princeton University Press, 1985), p. 198.

attainting and transferring daimyo, which had been major mechanisms for reducing wartime armies to peacetime size in the half-century up to 1650. They drove tens of thousands of men out of military service, most being absorbed into the civilian economy. Some failed to make the adjustment, however, and thousands of embittered and poorly employed ronin lived in Edo and elsewhere. A few groups of them plotted insurrection, the most well-known band being organized in 1651 by Yui Shōsetsu, an ambitious teacher of military arts.[19] As chance would have it, the schemes of Yui and others were nipped in the bud during 1651–52, but to deter other malcontents, the leaders in Edo were ruthless in punishing the conspirators and their families.

When, following the Shōsetsu incident, Edo officials finally addressed the broader question of what to do about ronin in general, they decided to slow the production of masterless samurai and find stable employment for those already needing it. One result was a sharp reduction in the rate of daimyo attainder; another was the employment of ronin in such tasks as city administration and patrol. These policies, together with continuing economic growth, gradually shrank the population of alienated ex-samurai, and ronin unrest did not reappear as a major issue until the 1860s.

Long before those policies yielded results, however, the ronin issue became entangled with diverse others, including fear of Christianity, Confucian doctrinal disagreements, clashing scholarly ambitions, and the Manchu conquest of China. The convergence of these issues produced one of the period's most celebrated victims, Kumazawa Banzan, the scholarly advisor to Mitsumasa of Okayama.

The threads of the story are not entirely clear, but in the interrogation that followed arrest of Yui Shōsetsu's followers, the plotters denied the suggestion that they were Christians. Some claimed, instead, to be followers of Banzan, who advocated the idealist Confucian teachings of the Ming dynasty scholar Wang Yang-ming (Ōyōmei in Japanese). Banzan, who was thirty-two in 1651, was a popular teacher and through Mitsumasa had friends in high places. However, his philosophical position and his popularity as a teacher made him a rival of Hayashi Razan, an aged shogunal scribe and advisor who propounded Ch'eng-Chu Confucianism (Shushigaku; also called Neo-Confucianism), the Confucian formulations of the scholarly Sung-dynasty brothers Ch'eng Hao and Ch'eng I and their successor Chu Hsi. Razan was highly critical of

19. Sansom, *History of Japan*, vol. 3, *1615–1867*, pp. 54–57, examines the Yui Shōsetsu incident.

Ōyōmei thought, and he saw Banzan as a threat to the survival of his
school, which he hoped to see perpetuated by his son Gahō, who was a
year older than Banzan.

When Razan learned that Banzan had been linked with the ronin, he
seized the occasion to attack both Banzan and Ōyōmei thought, asserting in a letter to a friend that, "Almost all of this gang were followers
of that heterodox school and accepted its false teachings. . . . These are
proxies for the Jesuits and represent their transformation." He specifically denounced Banzan, not merely on the grounds that his teachings
fostered insurrection, but because he "uses witchcraft to delude the deaf
and blind, and those who hear him go astray and cannot be enlightened.
. . . At bottom this is but Jesuitry transformed. . . . These bandits all
listened to Kumazawa's monstrous words."[20]

One suspects that Razan also made his case to officialdom. Officials,
mindful of Hideyori's ronin in 1614 and Shimabara in 1637, already
feared a link between the ronin and Christianity, but Razan's attempt
to tie the two to Ōyōmei Confucianism and thus to Banzan was less
compelling. It may have prompted the efforts by bakufu officials in 1652
and 1654 to persuade Mitsumasa to shift his support from Ōyōmei to
Ch'eng-Chu, but it was not enough to undermine his trust in Banzan.
However, Banzan's affection for Ming dynasty philosophy made him
hostile to the current Manchu conquest, and at about this time he seems
to have offended bakufu leaders by offering unsolicited advice on foreign policy, warning that a Manchu invasion was imminent and decry-
ing the lack of defense preparations.[21]

In one way or another, Banzan generated bakufu displeasure, and in
1654, during a stop in Kyoto while en route back to Okayama, he was
advised by a resident bakufu official to stay away from Edo for his own
safety.[22] Banzan heeded the advice and did not thereafter accompany
his lord on his biennial treks to the shogunal headquarters. Despite his
prudence, however, he became embroiled in such severe political dis-

20. George Elison, *Deus Destroyed: The Image of Christianity in Early Modern Ja-*
pan (Cambridge, Mass.: Harvard University Press, 1973), p. 236.
21. Ian James McMullen, "Kumazawa Banzan and 'Jitsugaku': Toward Pragmatic
Action," in Wm. Theodore de Bary and Irene Bloom, eds., *Principle and Practicality:*
Essays in Neo-Confucianism and Practical Learning (New York: Columbia University
Press, 1979), pp. 339, 368, n. 5.
22. John W. Hall, "Ikeda Mitsumasa and the Bizen Flood of 1654," in Albert M.
Craig and Donald H. Shively, eds., *Personality in Japanese History* (Berkeley and Los
Angeles: University of California Press, 1970), pp. 66, 69. Galen M. Fisher, "Kumazawa
Banzan, His Life and Ideas," *TASJ* 2-16 (May 1938): 238.

putes within Okayama that he resigned his position in 1657 and retired to a quiet life of teaching and writing in Kyoto.

In that same year, long after Edo leaders assumed that all Christian communities had been dispersed, a secret Christian group numbering over six hundred was discovered near Nagasaki. About a hundred recanted, but the rest refused, even under torture. Some died in prison; the survivors were executed a year later. In the 1660s other hidden communities of the faithful were discovered, this time near Kumamoto and north of Nagoya, locations suggesting that the creed was surreptitiously spreading across the country. Again local authorities ordered adherents arrested and forced to recant their faith. Again many refused, and hundreds were slain and hundreds more exiled to other villages.[23] Despite these harsh measures, other believers continued their secret religious practice, but they kept it sufficiently hidden that major incidents of suppression did not recur.

As with the ronin, however, the effectiveness of suppression did not become apparent for years, and fears of the moment prompted rulers to take other measures to tighten overall control of religion. In Hidetada's day, Edo had required villagers on shogunal domains to enroll their family members in the registers of local temples and shrines to demonstrate that they were not Christians. During the 1620s the procedure was tightened, and in 1640 Iemitsu established a board of examiners (shūmon aratame) to assure that the registers were properly maintained. Near the end of 1664, Edo reacted to the evidence of Christianity's apparent spread by ordering all daimyo to establish systems of registration similar to those employed by the bakufu.[24] The policy of strict control that had previously been required only on bakufu lands, and left to daimyo to implement as they chose elsewhere, was henceforth to be applied by everyone.

Christians were not, however, the only objects of bakufu attention. Since Hideyoshi's time, as noted earlier, adherents of Hokke Buddhism had been targets of political suppression, and one branch in particular, the Fujufuse or "no receiving and no giving" sect, had been especially resented because of its inflexible fundamentalism. Suppressed in 1600

23. C. R. Boxer, The Christian Century in Japan, 1549–1650 (Berkeley and Los Angeles: University of California Press, 1951), pp. 395–96.
24. The order of 1664 is translated in Robert J. Smith, "Small Families, Small Households, and Residential Instability: Town and City in 'Pre-Modern' Japan," in Peter Laslett, ed., Household and Family in Past Time (Cambridge: Cambridge University Press, 1972), p. 432.

and again in 1630, Fujufuse had revived yet again, and by the 1660s its advocates were bitterly at odds with the main Hokke sect. In 1663, leaders of the main sect asked Edo to suppress it, but the bakufu took no action until 1665, when it outlawed Fujufuse for a third time. That time the authorities took forceful steps to enforce its suppression, arresting adherents and punishing them severely.[25]

Another aspect of this doctrinal consolidation was the promotion of Shintō as taught in the Yoshida Shintō tradition, which propounded its own interpretation of the *Kojiki* and of the history and meaning of the imperial regalia. In 1665 the bakufu decreed that only those properly certified by priestly scholars of the hereditary Yoshida house in Kyoto would be licensed to operate shrines. During the next few years, major daimyo, including Mitsumasa of Okayama, Hoshina Masayuki of Aizu, and Tokugawa Mitsukuni of Mito, who had recently been key advisors to the bakufu, moved to suppress Buddhism in their han and to consolidate the role of shrines under properly trained Yoshida Shintō priests.

These moves to strengthen Yoshida Shintō, suppress Fujufuse, and weaken Buddhism in general probably reflected the views of Yamazaki Ansai, an influential scholar-teacher in Kyoto. A year older than Banzan and one of the most forceful and dogmatic of Ch'eng-Chu scholars, Ansai took service with Hoshina Masayuki in 1665 and through him shaped policy. Taking up where Hayashi Razan had left off when he died in 1657, Ansai launched attacks against the two most esteemed proponents of rival lines of Confucian thought.

His main scholarly victim in 1666 was Yamaga Sokō, a man four years his junior. A successful teacher of Confucianism and the military arts, Sokō had already been attacked by Razan, his former mentor, who evidently saw him as an academic competitor. From about 1660, Sokō began to argue that one could not understand Confucius by reading works of the Sung period or later, but must read the original ancient texts (*kogaku*). That view put him on a collision course with Ansai, and in 1665, when Sokō spelled out his convictions in the essay *Seikyō yō-roku*, he explicitly charged that two key practices of Ch'eng-Chu thought, "the scholarly study of texts or book-learning, and the practice of quiet-sitting," were impractical for samurai.[26] That argument elicited harsh criticism from Hoshina, who was very likely reflecting Ansai's opinion, and at Hoshina's insistence the bakufu ordered Sokō into exile in Akō,

25. Ooms, *Tokugawa Ideology*, pp. 37, 192, 199.
26. The phrasing is that of Wm. Theodore de Bary, "Sagehood as Secular and Spiritual Ideal," in de Bary and Bloom, eds., *Principle and Practicality*, p. 140.

a small han near Osaka where he had served briefly as scholar-advisor some years earlier.

The other scholarly victim of this ideological crackdown in the mid 1660s was Kumazawa Banzan. Following his move from Okayama to Kyoto in 1657, Banzan acquired followers among the nobility. But he continued to be tarred with charges of Christian taint, and some blamed him for the assault on Buddhism that Mitsumasa implemented in Oka-yama during the 1660s. By then, however, Mitsumasa had shifted his preference from Ōyōmei to Ch'eng-Chu, and he was no longer willing to defend Banzan. With his protector gone, Banzan found himself or-dered into house arrest in Yoshino in 1667, and for much of his re-maining life he lived in one or another form of detention.

Doubtless Banzan and Sokō were attacked by the academic empire-builders Razan and Ansai because they were professional and intellec-tual rivals. For bakufu leaders, however, they posed a different sort of threat. The rulers wanted a peaceful realm, and in terms of *bun* and *bu,* "the civil and military arts," they wished emphasis to be put on *bun* to help domesticate career military men and discourage others disposed to violence. But Sokō was a seminal exponent of *bushidō,* "the way of the warrior," and Banzan was celebrated as a "model samurai." Both gave primacy to *bu,* an intellectual posture that seemed dangerously encour-aging of ronin and other dissidents, as suggested by the Yui Shōsetsu affair fifteen years earlier. And more recently a worrisome sort of ag-gressive machismo had become popular at a broader social level. Even as the prolific and widely read author Asai Ryōi was inveighing against abuses by the privileged, a type of puppet play, *kinpiramono,* whose single-minded hero courageously crushed the villains, enjoyed great popularity.[27] It seems likely, therefore, that the punishment of Banzan and Sokō was intended as a message to others to stop dreaming of heroic military solutions to political discontents.

As the 1660s ended, bakufu leadership became more stable, and this surge of ideological politics seemed to wane. A fudai lord, Sakai Tada-kiyo, established himself as the dominant figure at Edo, and he con-trolled the senior council (*rōjū*) and bakufu policy until Ietsuna's death. The influence of Hoshina, and hence of Ansai, diminished sharply, and lesser officials fell into line under Tadakiyo's guidance. The political atmosphere quieted down for a decade, although Tadakiyo himself was

27. On Asai Ryōi, see chapter 10 below. Masako Nakagawa Graham, "The Consort and the Warrior: *Yōkihi monogatari,*" *MN* 45-1 (Spring 1990): 5, mentions *kinpiramono* briefly.

so harshly smeared following Ietsuna's death that his reputation has been among the worst of all bakufu leaders.

Ietsuna, the first child shogun, was also the first to die childless. Tadakiyo, other senior officials, and Ietsuna's most influential relatives, notably Mitsukuni of Mito, discussed the unprecedented situation and, after considerable infighting, settled on a successor. They chose Ietsuna's younger brother, Tsunayoshi, daimyo of a large domain headquartered at Tatebayashi. Whereas Ietsuna had been a child shogun and later a passive one, Tsunayoshi was mature and chose to govern by his own lights. In the process he gave Edo a decisive, creative, and self-assured—if no wiser—leadership.

TOKUGAWA TSUNAYOSHI

Tsunayoshi's rule is associated with Genroku, the year period (nengō) 1688–1704. The term evokes images of cultural efflorescence and urban opulence, the culmination of the tranquillity evinced in Ietsuna's day. Whereas the irony of Ietsuna's rule was that the tranquil surface masked political insecurities manifested in ideological repression, Genroku concealed no such ideological engagements, because Tsunayoshi boldly made issues of doctrine and morality the public centerpiece of his regime. The irony of his rule lay, rather, in the extent to which the critical issues of the day were fiscal and economic despite the emphasis he gave to ethics. In the end, it was the way his administration addressed those issues, rather than its high-powered rhetoric, that mattered most to later generations.

ETHICS IN GOVERNMENT

Tsunayoshi's decision to rule by his own lights meant, initially, that he had to attack an entrenched, thirty-year-old, political culture of official supremacy and replace it with a culture of shogunal supremacy. To do so he was compelled, much as his father had been, to replace uncooperative office holders with men who would do his bidding. He did so by relying heavily on men who had served him at Tatebayashi and thereby opened the way to new policy departures. The process made his succession one of the most difficult in the Edo period, however, and that, together with policy complications of later years, helped give rise to a body of commentary that has blackened his reputation ever since. To wit:

He is depicted as a tyrant who favored beasts more than men, who meted out cruel and harsh punishments. . . . His palace was the scene of moral depravity. . . . He was driven by superstition, and he was under the influence of a woman. He was extravagant, wasting the substance of the realm on lavish gifts to unworthy favorites and to Buddhist monks. . . . During the final years of his rule, heaven condemned his lack of virtue by causing strange natural phenomena and by visiting disasters on the country.[28]

Truly, as any well-trained Confucian could tell, he had drawn the wrath of heaven down upon himself.

In fact, his record is not nearly so clear-cut, and much of the calumny seems undeserved, but for better or worse, the record is his, not that of some obscure advisor. He governed as he did because he had been reared, not in the classic mold of the warrior, but as a Confucian scholar, and he brought those values and priorities to his job as ruler. He aspired to be a sage-king, and this orientation led him to increase the stipends of the imperial court as a gesture of respectful benevolence, to repair imperial tombs and memorials to Ieyasu as expressions of reverence for the ancestors, to foster the study of Confucianism among officials and samurai in general, and to exhort samurai and commoners alike to proper behavior.

To ensure that his government followed proper Confucian practice, he had Confucian scholars (*jusha*) compile a code of mourning procedures and added Confucian ceremonies to his calendar of annual events. He had his jusha lecture regularly, at least thrice monthly, and between 1693 and 1700 he personally delivered 249 lectures on the *Book of Changes*.[29] His audiences included daimyo, hatamoto, Confucian scholars, monks, Shintō priests, and even envoys from Kyoto.

In the same spirit he issued and enforced regulations to cultivate virtue and a sense of compassion or humaneness. As a contemporary explained his reasoning:

The old practices of the warring states period became the way of the samurai and officials; brutality was regarded as valor, high spirits were considered good conduct, and there were many actions which were not benevolent and which violated the fundamental principles of humanity. . . . [It was essential that Tsunayoshi, therefore] admonish the slightest unbenevolent act in order to try to perfect the benevolent spirit of the common people.[30]

28. Donald Shively, "Tokugawa Tsunayoshi, the Genroku Shogun" in Craig and Shively, eds., *Personality*, pp. 110–11.
29. Kate Wildman Nakai, *Shogunal Politics* (Cambridge, Mass.: Harvard University Press, 1988), p. 31.
30. Shively, "Tokugawa Tsunayoshi," p. 113.

To that end, his government issued numerous decrees to aid the vulnerable. He improved jail conditions because of high mortality among the imprisoned. He erected shelters for the outcast, sick, and homeless, forbade infanticide and child abandonment, and ordered that needy families be aided.

He also tried to cultivate a general sense of compassion by focusing public attention on animal suffering. Perhaps because flourishing trade had led to chronic overloading of packhorses, he issued a number of regulations on their usage. Other creatures of land and sea also received attention, but the most notable "acts of compassion" related to dogs. Edo, with its highly transient samurai population, was beset with pet and guard dogs abandoned by masters leaving town on sankin kōtai return trips, and Tsunayoshi's laws seem only to have exacerbated the canine crisis. So in 1695 he ordered the establishment of dog pounds, sustained by a new tax on property holders, and in two years they held some forty thousand dogs.[31]

While thus attempting to succor the powerless, Tsunayoshi demanded that the powerful measure up to his own standards of virtuous performance. And he punished those who failed. He stripped thirty-three daimyo of their domains, reduced the holdings of thirteen others, and deprived "more than one hundred hatamoto and countless go-kenin" of their fiefs or stipends.[32] His reasons ranged from a lord's failure to administer his fief satisfactorily or an official's failure to perform his duties properly to such personal errors as carelessly visiting the licensed quarters set aside for prostitutes or otherwise offending the shogun's sense of propriety.

Tsunayoshi's commitment to Confucian learning had a practical cast, which prompted him to take umbrage at failures of performance rather than flaws of logic. Errant intellectuals felt the bite of his displeasure for criticizing government policy, not because of particular views on abstract doctrine, as Kumazawa Banzan discovered in the twilight of his life, when he managed once again to provoke Edo's ire.

For nearly twenty years after being exiled to Yoshino in 1667, Banzan continued writing from the shelter of a benign house arrest, addressing substantive issues of state and adhering to his convictions even when it put him at odds with the authorities. When some lords, including Hoshina of Aizu and Mitsumasa of Okayama, attempted to replace

31. Ibid., p. 95; Beatrice Bodart Bailey, "The Laws of Compassion," MN 40-2 (Summer 1985): 171–73, 178.
32. Shively, "Tokugawa Tsunayoshi," p. 93.

the Buddhist burial practice of cremation with the Confucian use of coffins and graves, for example, Banzan criticized the policy on the grounds that the poor could not afford the cost of burial, cemetery space would become inadequate, and the custom would exhaust the country's timber supply. Elsewhere he contrasted his own practicality with the bookishness of Ch'eng-Chu proponents such as Yamazaki Ansai's followers. "Master Chu has the fault of too extensive a reliance on texts," he wrote, and among Ch'eng-Chu scholars nowadays, "exploration of principle is conducted from books and consists of lectures on texts or empty discussions."[33]

Banzan's critics denounced him as a Taoist, a follower of Ōyōmei, or even a Christian. Had Tsunayoshi wished to hound him for deviant views, he could have found ample pretext in his writings, but instead, during the early 1680s, bakufu leaders began to solicit his opinions. In 1687, however, with the Manchu conquest of China newly completed and Edo facing an abrupt and unwelcome expansion in the Nagasaki trade, Banzan submitted a lengthy memorial he had drafted the preceding year. The memorial presumably was the treatise *Daigaku wakumon*, a 22-part essay that purported to expound on a classic Confucian text but actually was an encyclopedic series of rhetorical questions and answers on issues of the day.[34] In it, Banzan adopted positions implicitly critical of current bakufu practice. He advocated "benevolent government," appointment of "humble men" of talent, attentiveness by rulers to both the advice and needs of such men, a major reduction of daimyo obligations to perform sankin kōtai, fiscal relief for daimyo and samurai, and conversion of samurai into samurai-farmers. He offered unsolicited advice on eradicating Christianity and rectifying Buddhism, which he considered corrupt, and sprinkled his essay with suggestions for regulating rice prices, easing social hardship, conserving resources, and enhancing production.

His decision to submit such an outspoken document to Edo evidently was prompted by renewed fear of a Manchu invasion.[35] He equated Manchus, as "Northern Barbarians," with Mongols and seems to have

33. The quotations in this paragraph come from McMullen, "Kumazawa Banzan and 'Jitsugaku,' " p. 354.

34. A translation of *Daigaku wakumon* by Galen M. Fisher is available in *TASJ* 2-16 (May 1938): 263–356.

35. Fisher uses the term "Mongol," while McMullen uses "Tartar." It is clear in either case that Banzan was uninterested in fine ethnic distinctions and saw the current threat by "Northern Barbarians" as a reprise of the Mongol invasions of the thirteenth century.

assumed that once they secured China, they would turn on Japan, the
one surviving holdout, the more surely since Japan's leaders clearly
sympathized with the fallen Ming dynasty and the Confucian civilization it represented. In his memorial, Banzan made his arguments in terms
both of their general value and of their specific utility in the event of a
Manchu invasion. In 1686, when he mentioned his proposed memorial
in a letter to a friend, he wrote, "I think it likely that the Tartars will
come next year or the year after. . . . [They] will come suddenly and
without warning. There is not the slightest evidence of the necessary
military preparedness."[36]

For his temerity in offering advice on a wide range of issues, thereby
suggesting that officials were being derelict in their duty, Banzan was
summoned east and put into firmer house arrest in the castle town of
Koga north of Edo. It was hardly the harshest of punishments: he was
not ordered to commit suicide, was not executed or jailed, or placed in
handcuffs for an extended period, as were scholarly victims of earlier
and later rulers, but this newest decree did put an end to the old man's
intellectual life. He fell silent on public affairs and died four years later
at the age of seventy-two.

The utilitarian purposefulness of Tsunayoshi's ideological politics was
also evinced in sumptuary regulation. Edicts limiting consumption began appearing when Ieyasu was alive, but they proliferated under Iemitsu and turned into a flood under Tsunayoshi.[37] In 1683 alone at
least seven laws specified what forms of clothing urban people might
wear. Thus, a law issued at year's end specified that thin silk crepe,
embroidery, and dappled tie-dye were prohibited in women's clothing,
that "unusual weaving and dyeing must not be done," and that "one
length of outer material for a padded robe may not be bought or sold
for a higher price than 200 *me* of silver."

Rules about clothing may have been most common, but others sought
to control the foods people ate, the size of houses and other buildings,
the construction materials used in them, the scale of entertainments,
weddings, funerals, and other ritual occasions, and a plethora of objects
used in daily life, including, "women's combs and bodkins, . . . tobacco
pouches, purses, incense containers, lacquer sake-cup stands, cake boxes,
and ornamental decorations." Occasionally, Tsunayoshi punished people for ostentation, but the instances seem to have been rare, and it

36. McMullen, "Kumazawa Banzan and 'Jitsugaku,'" p. 337.
37. The quotations are from Donald H. Shively, "Sumptuary Regulation and Status
in Early Tokugawa Japan," *HJAS* 25 (1964–65): 126, 135.

appears that the flood of regulations only irregularly restrained consumption. From powerful daimyo and their wives down to clerks in offices, those who could afford to showed a stubborn willingness to flout the restrictions.

These sumptuary regulations clearly reflected ideology: as Confucian dogma became entrenched, especially during Tsunayoshi's day, rulers became convinced that in a well-ordered society, consumption should be proportional to status, and the rules sought to achieve that end. The regulations also addressed more concrete political, fiscal, and economic concerns. They sought to maintain a visible distinction between rulers and ruled. And they had the fiscal value of providing leaders with a basis for defining precisely appropriate levels of consumption, and hence of stipends, for their vassals. In broader economic terms, sumptuary regulations provided an ideologically based mechanism for controlling the distribution of goods—rationing—which became an increasingly important political task as the population grew and its resource base came under increasing pressure.

FISCAL POLICIES

Despite Tsunayoshi's engagement with moral issues, the bakufu's major problem of substance during his tenure was growing financial strain. By the 1680s, Ieyasu's vast accumulation of reserves was gone and income was failing to cover expenses. To cope, Tsunayoshi tried several strategies, some aimed at increasing income, others at reducing outflow. His whole campaign of sumptuary regulation was essentially an attempt to hold down outflow. Most of his other measures aimed to enhance income.

When Tsunayoshi took office, he moved quickly to tighten fiscal control and accountability by placing trusted retainers in key finance posts and promoting fiscal specialists of recognized expertise, such as Ogiwara Shigehide. He tried to enhance land-tax income by tightening control of his regional administrators, the intendants, or *daikan*. By his day they had entrenched themselves and become negligent about forwarding tax receipts, so during the 1680s he cashiered thirty-six of them, and eight more later on—altogether about three-quarters of the total—replacing many with men from Tatebayashi. By these forceful moves, he reestablished Edo's control over its appointed officialdom.[38]

38. Nakai, *Shogunal Politics*, pp. 10–12, 119.

Tsunayoshi also tried to increase the regime's productive base by seizing additional areas of value. As Arai Hakuseki, one of his most famous critics, later reported, "whenever daimyo or hatamoto had their fiefs transferred, the fertile fields and places blessed with mountains, forests, rivers and marshes were all made Bakufu domain; the remainder was given away as private domain."[39] A striking instance of this policy occurred in 1692, when the timber-starved bakufu seized mountainous Hida province in central Honshu, the last great area of accessible, well-wooded forest south of Ezo, transferring the hapless lord there to a domain in the northeast.

Tsunayoshi also instructed officials to increase the output of bakufu mines. The best ones having been depleted long since, the effort yielded little gain, so the shogun, unable to increase his bullion supply, tried to limit its use. One method, as noted in the next chapter, was to reduce foreign trade, which he and others viewed as impoverishing the realm by robbing it of permanently valuable goods (silver, copper, and gold) while providing in exchange perishables of only transient worth.

Besides saving bullion, Tsunayoshi's administration pursued other sources of income. Even as it curtailed foreign trade, it devised new ways to milk what trade it did allow. In return for permit fees, it began approving supplemental barter arrangements between Chinese traders and Japanese merchants, who mostly exported copper. The arrangement, which lasted until 1715, eventually encompassed about a third of the total China trade. In 1697 the bakufu also began skimming profits from the itowappu trade in silk. Moreover, it raised tariff rates and tightened control over foreign-trade accounts, establishing a bakufu-operated clearing house (Nagasaki kaisho) in 1698 to oversee them.[40]

In another facet of bullion policy, in 1695, Ogiwara Shigehide commenced, with shogunal approval, a series of currency recoinages designed to provide direct fiscal relief. By melting down old coins and sharply reducing the bullion content of the replacement issue—from 80 percent silver content before 1695 to 20 percent by 1711—the bakufu was able to mint a large quantity of coins and put them into circulation at great initial profit. The proliferation of coins created confusion in the marketplace, however, inducing an epidemic of hoarding of higher-grade

---

39. Quoted in Bolitho, *Treasures*, p. 177. Also in Joyce Ackroyd, tr., *Told Round a Brushwood Fire: The Autobiography of Arai Hakuseki* (Princeton: Princeton University Press, 1979), p. 149. Most "private domain" was daimyo domain.

40. Robert LeRoy Innes, *The Door Ajar: Japan's Foreign Trade in the Seventeenth Century* (Ann Arbor: University Microfilms International, 1980), 1: 333–41.

coins. And the magnitude and suddenness of the new issue triggered an abrupt inflation when currency traders discounted its market worth. As that occurred, Tsunayoshi lost the fiscal value of recoinage because the regime and its samurai dependents, being essentially consumers, bore the brunt of the inflation. In the short run, however, the recoinage reportedly netted the bakufu a profit of some five million ryō, with an undisclosed windfall going to the minters and finance officials.[41]

In 1705, Tsunayoshi combined his politics of morality with fiscal expediency in another measure of short-run financial value. He denounced the wealthy Osaka merchant house of Yodoya for ostentation, presumably because its behavior was inappropriate to its position and erosive of public morals. As punishment he dissolved the house and confiscated its wealth, a move said to have yielded the bakufu "fifty pairs of gold screens, three hundred and sixty carpets, innumerable precious stones, mansions, granaries and storehouses . . . , and gold pieces by the hundred thousand."[42] The confiscation brought cash and possessions to the bakufu, and as a bonus Yodoya's dissolution erased the considerable indebtedness that numerous daimyo had accumulated over years of borrowing.

In the outcome, when Tsunayoshi died in 1709 he left his successor a realm that was essentially tranquil, at least on the surface. Decades of attentive administration by daimyo and bakufu leaders had guided society through the transition from turbulence to political stability. The costs—borne mainly by ronin, by those whose aspirations for lives of drama and triumph went unrealized, and by Christians, Fujufuse sectarians, and other adherents of tabooed doctrines—had been met without the new order unraveling. In part, as preceding pages have suggested, the political stabilization can be credited to leaders of the bakuhan order, but in part, perhaps in greater part, the credit accrued to producers, whose industry so expanded the economic base of society that a burgeoning population could obtain sufficient necessities to lead reasonably satisfying lives.

41. Sansom, *History of Japan*, vol. 3, *1615–1867*, p. 134. Nakai, *Shogunal Politics*, pp. 61–63, 98–99, 103–4, passim, carefully discusses these monetary maneuvers. For an expansive interpretation of this recoinage, see Beatrice M. Bodart-Bailey, "A Case of Political and Economic Expropriation: The Monetary Reforms of the Fifth Tokugawa Shogun," *Papers on Far Eastern History* 39 (Mar. 1989): 177–89.
42. G. B. Sansom, *Japan: A Short Cultural History* (New York: Appleton-Century-Crofts, 1943), p. 472.

Economic Growth and Change

Overseas Trade

Trends in Primary Production

Changes in Urban Growth

Changes in Merchant Organization

Japan's economy expanded rapidly during the seventeenth century. The expansion included rapid population growth, a comparable increase in agricultural output, widespread urban development, and the diversification and elaboration of commercial organization. Foreign trade played only a modest role in this larger picture, not because it was forbidden—it was not—but because it was essentially a luxury trade that catered almost solely to the interests of the superordinate few.

Gross population figures provide a striking measure of the century's overall growth. No well-grounded numbers for the early years exist, but a figure of some 12 million is currently considered the best guess for 1600.[1] The population in 1720 is reliably estimated, on the basis of a nationwide census, at about 31 million, which suggests that the population more than doubled during the seventeenth century. That constituted a sharply faster rate of increase than in preceding and following years, expanding demand for food and clothing commensurately and creating a substantial rise in fuel and shelter requirements. If, in addition, there was any general rise in material standard of living, that further raised the demand for goods and services.[2]

1. Akira Hayami, "The Population at the Beginning of the Tokugawa Period—An Introduction to the Historical Demography of Pre-industrial Japan," *Keio Economic Studies* 4 (1966–67): 1–28. Hayami discusses the flaws in the older figure for 1600 of 18 million. The new figure, readers should bear in mind, heightens the contrast between early and later Tokugawa demographic history. If the 18 million figure is ever rehabilitated, this book's images of growth and stasis will have to be tempered.

2. For a general discussion of the material culture of daily life, see Susan B. Hanley, "Tokugawa Society: Material Culture, Standard of Living, and Life-styles," in *The Cam-*

Economic expansion continued throughout the century, but as the decades passed, its character changed. The rate of growth in primary production appears to have slowed, making decisions on the allocation of goods more necessary and more difficult. Commerce, which remained domain-oriented into the early 1600s, became much more integrated at the countrywide level during the latter half of the century. As a corollary, urban growth, which involved most castle towns (*jōka-machi*) during the early decades, was concentrated in Edo and Osaka by century's end. This shift in locus was linked to a marked decline in government's role as promoter of urban growth. And that change, together with other changes in the handling of production and distribution, altered both the economic role of merchants and the nature of mercantile organization itself. Finally, in regard to foreign trade, from the 1630s on, it was subjected to closer regulation and its scale restricted. By the early eighteenth century, this policy of "containment" was giving way to one of reduction.

OVERSEAS TRADE

Until the 1630s, as noted earlier, Japan's foreign trade was carried on vessels flying Japanese, other East and Southeast Asian, and various European flags. During that decade, however, political considerations led Iemitsu to terminate Japanese and Portuguese participation and to regulate more closely the surviving Chinese and Dutch trade at Nagasaki. How those changes actually affected the total volume of trade is not crystal-clear, but Dutch and Chinese trade expanded during the 1630s, taking up much, if not all, of the slack left by the exit of the others.

Diverse goods were traded, but for the century as a whole, silk yarn and cloth were the principal imports and silver and copper the main exports. Despite disruptions caused by the Ming-Manchu struggle, the trade in Dutch and Chinese bottoms remained vigorous, with annual yarn imports through Nagasaki peaking during the 1660s at upwards of half a million catties. By 1700, domestic yarn production was beginning to displace imports, and the trend intensified thereafter. Silver was the primary export for most of the century, but its scarcity led to export restrictions from the 1660s on, and by century's end copper had be-

bridge History of Japan, vol. 4, *Early Modern Japan,* ed. John W. Hall (Cambridge: Cambridge University Press, 1991), pp. 660–705.

come the dominant export, with fifty to sixty thousand piculs (approx. 3,300 metric tons) leaving Nagasaki annually.[3]

In addition to bakufu-controlled trade at Nagasaki, Satsuma handled Chinese trade via the Ryūkyūs, and Tsushima carried on Korean trade through Pusan. From the 1630s on, the bakufu encouraged Satsuma to use its Ryūkyūan connection to obtain Chinese goods, silk in particular, and for half a century the trade flourished. During the 1680s, however, Edo imposed restrictions to limit the silver Satsuma could export. That reduced the trade flow, and it shrank even further after 1695, when currency debasement slashed the purchasing power of the money Satsuma was allowed to use in trade.[4] To some unknown degree, however, declines in the Ryūkyūan trade were offset by smuggling activity that Chinese merchants carried on along the coasts of Satsuma and other areas in Kyushu. In 1710 the Nagasaki magistrate (bugyō), who was supposed to oversee foreign trade in general, complained about the smuggling in this way:

> In recent years the Chinese have licentiously engaged in private trade. Whenever their profits from trade in Japan lessen, even just a little, they increase their volume of imports, thereby maintaining their profit levels. For twenty years this private trade has gone on. Although west country daimyo have been instructed to keep an extremely sharp watch on the coastline and seas of their domains, it is for the most part beyond their power. The reason for this is that the smugglers, both Chinese and Japanese, have become more adept lately. As evening comes the Japanese ride at sea two or three ri away from the Chinese junk. After the sun sets and vision decreases they row to the junk and do their illicit trading.[5]

With Pusan lying completely outside bakufu jurisdiction, Tsushima's foreign trade was less subject to Edo's whim than Satsuma's. The Pusan trade survived the Manchu conquest of 1636, and by Genroku it consisted of a stable official trade and a large and highly profitable entrepreneurial trade, in which imports of Chinese silk and Korean ginseng were bought with silver and copper exports valued at 3,000–4,000 kan of silver per annum, roughly two to four times the authorized level.[6] Edo winked at the private trade because it knew that Tsushima han

3. Robert LeRoy Innes, *The Door Ajar: Japan's Foreign Trade in the Seventeenth Century* (Ann Arbor: University Microfilms International, 1980), 2: 494, 528. A picul = 100 catties. See also chapter 5, n. 30, above.

4. Robert K. Sakai, "The Satsuma-Ryukyu Trade and the Tokugawa Seclusion Policy," *JAS* 23-3 (May 1964): 395–97.

5. Innes, *Door Ajar*, 1: 331.

6. Tashiro Kazui, "Tsushima han's Korean Trade, 1684–1710," *AA* 30 (1976): 91–92.

depended on it for survival. Indeed, after 1695, when the bakufu was debasing its own currency, it allotted Tsushima special high-grade silver coins to preserve its trade.

Edo claimed the right to regulate all foreign commerce, but its control was hardly absolute: quite apart from coastal smuggling, the extent of Ryūkyūan trade was scarcely known to Edo, and Tsushima trade in toto greatly exceeded its authorized limit. At Nagasaki itself, smuggling was restrained—but not eliminated—only by policy concessions and firm insistence, and even then not until the early eighteenth century. Still, the basic trend after midcentury was from promotion to containment of trade. At Nagasaki the problems of bullion scarcity and currency outflow were beginning to shape trade policy by the 1650s, and their influence grew as the century waned. The trade in silk yarn illustrates both the evolution of bakufu policy and the difficulties Edo encountered in pursuing its goals.

In Ieyasu's day the *itowappu* (yarn guild), a guild of merchants subject to bakufu regulation, handled yarn imported by the Portuguese, as noted in chapter 5. Its influence declined as the Portuguese share of trade shrank and cloth imports replaced yarn. But then maritime incidents of the late 1620s disrupted trade and drove up silk prices, prompting Edo to extend itowappu authority to cover the pricing of all silk imports, both cloth and yarn, whether brought in European or Chinese vessels.

Itowappu trade flourished until 1648, when the Ming-Manchu struggle disrupted China's silk exports, again causing price rises in Japan that upset weavers and their customers, most notably the rulers and their retainers. The rises also heightened silver exports and generated denunciations of the itowappu for reaping windfall profits. In hopes of reducing silk prices, the bullion outflow, and the general clamor, Ietsuna's government abolished the itowappu in 1655. In its place, Edo tried market pricing through an open-bid system, but that did not suffice. Prices stayed high, silver kept flowing, and the merchants and administrators of Nagasaki and of the other Kyushu towns that had benefited from the itowappu suffered and complained.

A fire devastated Nagasaki in 1663, eliciting calls for restoration of the itowappu system to aid in urban recovery. Authorities refused to make any basic changes, but they did tinker with trade procedures and "loaned" the city two thousand kan of silver to aid rebuilding. Five years later, however, after a major fire ravaged Edo (which had scarcely been rebuilt since the Meireki holocaust), the bakufu addressed the problems of foreign trade while dealing with scarcities and inflation generated by the fire. To counter inflation, it prohibited the export of silver and issued an unprecedentedly broad-ranging set of sumptuary regulations. At Nagasaki, moreover, it "banned the import of non-medicinal exotic woods, mangrove bark, [and] fine fabrics other than those used in clothing, . . . among other things. The import of woolen cloth was banned from the following year."[7]

In 1670 the authorities tried to plug another loophole by moving against smuggling. They also reorganized purchasing procedures and by 1672 had replaced the open-bid system with a managed market. In the new system, authorized merchants collaborated to set the wholesale prices they would offer, with the bugyō's approval, to foreign traders. Unlike the old yarn guild, the new setup applied to all imports, not just silk.

This arrangement eased the silver outflow in part by the unsatisfactory expedient of replacing it with gold. It appears to have reduced the total value of imports by squeezing foreign traders, but it failed to lower retail prices, which were not subject to the oligopoly's control. Middlemen at Nagasaki were the main beneficiaries, which enriched the city, and its population rose from some thirty thousand in the late 1660s to nearly fifty-three thousand by 1681. The local prosperity also invited indulgence, however, as an informed commentator observed in the early eighteenth century:

> The bugyō also began to conduct themselves like merchants. Bidding was carried out in official offices. The bulk of the profits were hoarded: from the bugyō down to the local functionaries, officials shared in it. . . . Because wild rumors made these excesses sound ten times worse than the reality, Edo heard that a fondness for worthless pomp was developing in Nagasaki while the people went hungry. On the basis of such exaggerated reports, the market system commodity trade was abolished [in 1684] even though it was an effective means of regulating commerce.[8]

The "wild rumors" could hardly have pleased the vigorous new shogun, given his strong commitment to Confucian probity, and his concern was given a more substantive dimension when Edo learned of the Manchu conquest of Taiwan in 1683.

Bakufu leaders realized that with the restoration of peace in China, they could expect an expansion of trade, and given the new Ch'ing

7. Innes, Door Ajar, 1: 305.
8. Ibid., p. 318. Innes is quoting Kiyō gundan, a source attributed to Ōoka Kiyosuke, Nagasaki bugyō from 1711 to 1717.

regime's demonstrated capacity to mount overseas operations, trade disputes could have serious complications. To deal with current problems and forestall worse ones, at the end of 1684 they abolished existing market arrangements and restored the old itowappu system for silk. In a new departure they set a maximum value for all imports by Chinese and Dutch traders. Basing their figures on the volume of imports each had recently been able to cover with exports other than gold and silver, they authorized the Chinese to bring imports worth 6,000 kan of silver, and the Dutch, 3,400 kan's worth.[9]

As officials had feared, Chinese trade escalated as soon as the K'ang-hsi emperor permitted merchants to resume direct trading with Japan. Some 85 junks arrived in 1685, more the following year, and a peak number of 194 in 1688. Those 194 vessels brought goods valued at 19,008 kan (81,280 kg.) of silver.[10] Each year the junk trade proceeded until the limit of 6,000 kan's worth was reached, after which later vessels were turned away. The policy halted most silver exports at Nagasaki, but the limits pushed up import prices, making trade even more lucrative. Some of the rebuffed Chinese merchants marketed their cargo illicitly via Korea or Tsushima, while others turned to smuggling along the Kyushu coast, as noted earlier. They fared well enough one way or another to continue bringing goods to Japan, even though unable to trade at Nagasaki.

In further attempts to avoid trouble with China, the bakufu replaced its first-come-first-served policy with a rationing arrangement that spread the 6,000 kan's worth of legal trade among seventy vessels from the several trading regions of China. To accommodate more trade, it encouraged alternative exports, most notably of copper, which Japan was still mining in quantity and which was in great demand in China, where the Ch'ing were minting a new coinage. To contain smuggling, Edo ordered more coastal patrols, but to no great effect. Smuggling did decline from about 1700 on, but primarily, as noted in chapter 7, because Tsunayoshi's government began allowing supplemental barter trade for fiscal reasons, thereby providing smugglers with a profitable legal alternative.

In the end, these various measures coped with the problems, real and

9. Ibid., p. 319. The Dutch East India Company was allotted imports valued at 3,000 kan of silver, and individual traders were authorized to bring in an additional 400 kan's worth.

10. Iwao Seiichi, "Japanese Foreign Trade in the 16th and 17th Centuries," *AA* 30 (1976): 13.

feared, stemming from the Manchu conquest. If, as Kumazawa Banzan
had warned, there was a risk of Manchu invasion, it had been avoided.
Edo's efforts to contain trade prevented expansion but did little to shrink
it. Insofar as figures can be assembled, the total annual value of imports,
although it fluctuated greatly from year to year, lay in the general range
of 15,000–25,000 kan of silver, with peak volume around 1637, 1660,
and 1698.[11]

To the extent that bullion scarcity was Edo's key concern, the problem persisted, because domestic demand for gold, silver, and copper
grew along with the economy, and copper mines, too, gave out during
the eighteenth century. Tsunayoshi's successors wrestled with the issue
of metal exports, and they ended up replacing the policy of containment
with one of trade reduction, which over several decades effected a gradual, but substantial, shrinkage in Japan's overseas commerce.

As this summary of particulars suggests, although politico-military factors may have determined Edo's trade policy early in the seventeenth
century, monetary factors eventually became decisive. This is not to say
that political factors ceased to operate. The wish to mollify domestic
discontents was ever-apparent, and the old bugaboo of Christian subversion, which had manifested itself again during the 1660s, reappeared
in the 1680s when expanded relations with China seemed in the offing.

To elaborate, in 1684, as Edo prepared for a rush of Chinese traders,
it armed itself against religious infiltration by appointing an official to
serve as *shomotsu aratame yaku* (inspector of books). The appointee
and his assistants were to examine all books brought in by Chinese
traders to ensure, as required by statutes of the 1630s, that they contained no references to Christianity. In the following years, moreover,
Chinese sailors were questioned more closely about their religious affiliation. In 1687 the Dutch warned Edo of Jesuit influence in Peking, and
that warning, which surely heightened Edo's fear of smuggling, was
followed in a few months by a bakufu decision to segregate the Chinese
community in Nagasaki by restricting it to a high-walled compound
with closely controlled egress.

Still, these were residual fears. By the 1680s, monetary concerns were
the driving force in bakufu trade policy. The silk-for-silver trade had
gradually lost attractiveness to participants because by midcentury bul-

11. Innes, *Door Ajar,* 2: 429–31.

lion ratios in Japan were nearly in line with those abroad, which eroded Japanese silver's overseas purchasing power.[12] Moreover, scarcity of gold and silver was beginning to disrupt currency values and commodity prices in the domestic market, so that exports once viewed as a source of material advantage came to seem a source of material harm.

That view was reinforced by thinkers who linked the five basic Confucian categories of fire, water, earth, metal, and wood to the Shintō notion of Japan's uniqueness to argue that the metals found in Japan were an infrangible part of what made Japan special. Thus their mining and export constituted piecemeal destruction of the sacred realm itself. Banzan put it this way in the 1680s:

> What Japan has that is superior to [foreign lands beyond] the Four Seas are the sacred qualities of the national land and the purity of the people's hearts. [But] the reason that in recent years the spirit of the national land has become thinner, and her people have become inferior [to what they once were], is surely that [we have] not preserved the gold, silver, copper, and iron that are the ultimate spirit of the mountains and streams [of our land], but have dug them out and [not only used them domestically but even] shipped them to foreign lands in great quantity, so that our mountains are laid waste, and our rivers become shallow.[13]

Others gave Banzan's ethico-ecological concern a more bluntly economic cast. Miyazaki Antei, an autarchically inclined agrarian improver, argued in the 1690s that instead of exporting specie to pay for imports, prudence called for Japan to eliminate the imports by producing the goods at home. "From old times useless things in Chinese ships have come every year and have been traded," he wrote. "How can we allow our country's wealth to be another country's gain? It is simply because the people of our country do not know the art of planting and misunderstand the principle of the land."[14] The solution he was advocating—import substitution—was beginning to occur, but as noted in a subsequent chapter, it did not become a major part of trade policy until the 1720s.

12. A. Kobata, "The Production and Uses of Gold and Silver in Sixteenth- and Seventeenth-Century Japan," *Economic History Review*, 2d ser., 18–1/3 (1965): 236, 266.

13. Ohba Osamu and Ronald P. Toby, " 'Seek Knowledge throughout the World': International Information and the Formation of Policy in Edo-period Japan and K'ang-hsi Era China," paper presented at the Conference on the International History of Early-Modern East Asia, Kauai, Hawaii, 4–9 Jan. 1988, pp. 39–40, quoting *Shūgi gaisho*.

14. Jeffrey Marti, "Intellectual and Moral Foundations of Empirical Agronomy in Eighteenth Century Japan," in *Select Papers from the Center for Far Eastern Studies* (University of Chicago), no. 2 (1977–78), pp. 41–80, quotation at p. 63.

Seventeenth-century Japan, in sum, was actively engaged in trade with East and Southeast Asia. Trade was the lifeblood of Nagasaki, and as Robert LeRoy Innes has shown, it was important to Kyoto. That city's major industry was the Nishijin silk industry, and as late as the early eighteenth century, it depended on imports for the bulk of its yarn. The trade was also important to Osaka in several ways, most notably because metal works in the city provided much of the export copper.

On the other hand, lest one lose sight of the relative scale of things, foreign trade was a minor activity in terms of the total Japanese economy. Complete trade figures are unavailable, but near century's end, as noted above, imports were generally worth some 15,000 to 25,000 kan annually. By way of comparison, around 1705 the annual income of the daimyo of Shōnai han (140,000 koku), a somewhat larger than average domain, was about 35,900 ryō, which is equivalent to some 2,240 kan of silver. So Japan's annual imports late in the seventeenth century had a value roughly equal to the tax income of ten Shōnai governments. Or, with a koku of rice worth about one-sixteenth of a kan (1 ryō), they had a value comparable to the agricultural output of two or three daimyo domains the size of Shōnai.

Viewed from another angle, if one uses the figure 26,400,000 koku, the official estimate of agricultural output around 1700, as an indicator of the country's annual domestic production, the hypothetical market value of that output in terms of silver may have been some 1,650,000 kan. That figure gives 20,000 kan of foreign trade a value equivalent to less than 1.5 percent of domestic agricultural production.[15] Overseas trade clearly was important to certain groups and localities, but despite the attention foreign trade has received here because of its superior documentation and scholarly treatment, the heart of the seventeenth-century Japanese economy was domestic activity.

TRENDS IN PRIMARY PRODUCTION

As Japan's population grew from 12 to 30 million, the accompanying increase in demand for goods and services was met by increases in pri-

15. John W. Hall, *Government and Local Power in Japan, 500–1700* (Princeton: Princeton University Press, 1966), p. 343, gives the figure of 26,437,097 koku. My kan figure assumes a koku to have a market value of 1 ryō, and 16 gold ryō to be worth 1 kan (1,000 monme) of silver. In fact, market prices varied sharply from year to year, with rice usually ranging between 50 and 80 monme per koku, sometimes higher or lower. The gold ryō was pegged at 60 monme, so at any particular moment a koku of rice might be worth appreciably more or less than a ryō. See Conrad Totman, *Politics in the Tokugawa Bakufu* (Berkeley and Los Angeles: University of California Press, 1988), p. 186, n. 38.

mary production. Reliable statistics on the increases are few, but some generalizations seem possible.

Food production was Japan's preponderant productive activity, and much of the increase in agricultural output resulted from opening up untilled land and converting dry fields to paddy culture. According to one estimate, "paddy acreage increased by more than 70 percent between 1450 and 1600, and by another 140 percent by 1720."[16] This tripling of paddy area provided many of the added calories required by the growing population, doing so even where it simply replaced dry fields with wet. Improvements in irrigation added to the output of arable acreage, particularly along Japan's southern littoral, where it extended double cropping.

Besides lowland reclamation, tillers converted more and more terrace deposits and alluvial fans to dry-field cropping and undertook considerable slash-and-burn cultivation in mountainous areas. The greatest gains in arable acreage occurred before 1650, but new land continued to be brought into production, and fields kept being upgraded from dry to wet use for the rest of the century.[17] In Tosa, for example, reclamation created some 8,100 chō of paddy fields by 1676, adding roughly a third to what the han had in 1600. In Morioka, in the northeast, taxable yield "rose from 205,550 koku in 1634 to 226,580 in 1652 and reached 268,160 koku by 1735."[18] For the country as a whole, by one calculation, arable increased from 1,635,000 chō in 1600 to 3,050,000 by 1720.

In some sectors of primary production, the period of expansion was appreciably shorter. Quarrying fell off as castle work petered out during Hidetada's lifetime. Gold and silver production peaked during the

16. Kozo Yamamura, "Returns on Unification: Economic Growth in Japan, 1550–1650," in John W. Hall et al., eds., *Japan before Tokugawa* (Princeton: Princeton University Press, 1968), p. 334. Whether all of the land embraced by this statement was newly opened or a substantial part the reactivation of abandoned arable is unclear.

17. Nagahara Keiji and Kozo Yamamura, "Shaping the Process of Unification: Technological Progress in Sixteenth- and Seventeenth-Century Japan," *JJS* 14-l (Winter 1988): 87, report that the pace of irrigation system development "increased in the second half of the seventeenth century." They seem to mean that reclamation and conversion of fields from dry to wet required more labor effort or more complex engineering, not that the rate of paddy creation rose, because they indicate (p. 103) that 75 percent of the seventeenth-century increase in paddy land had occurred by 1650.

18. Susan B. Hanley and Kozo Yamamura, *Economic and Demographic Change in Preindustrial Japan, 1600–1868* (Princeton: Princeton University Press, 1977), p. 127. The figures for Tosa come from Marius B. Jansen, "Tosa in the Seventeenth Century: The Establishment of Yamauchi Rule," in John W. Hall and Jansen, eds., *Studies in the Institutional History of Early Modern Japan* (Princeton: Princeton University Press, 1968), p. 124; and for the country from Takeo Yazaki, *Social Change and the City in Japan* (Tokyo: Japan Publications, 1968), p. 247.

1620s, despite improvements in mining. Lumber production was sustained for a while by laborious river clearing and elaborate systems for skidding, rafting, and storing timber, but output probably peaked while Ieyasu was still alive, declining thereafter until late in the eighteenth century. Whereas quarrying faded because demand fell, the declines in mining and logging were mainly determined by changes in supply.

In other areas, growth persisted. Copper mining flourished into the eighteenth century, iron mining into the nineteenth. Throughout the 1600s, salt output expanded along with population.[19] Production of roof tile and other ceramics increased as the population grew and urban centers expanded, but expansion in the tiling industry mostly occurred after 1720, when changes in government policy facilitated the widespread adoption of simpler types of roof tile.[20] The fishing industry developed somewhat during the seventeenth century, but its major growth also occurred later, after agronomic changes created a large and growing demand for fishmeal fertilizer.[21]

Whether the seventeenth century's growth in total production involved an increase or decrease in productivity per capita is difficult to say, but the overall gain in output clearly required an absolute increase in labor, and that requirement was met in a number of ways. The rise in total population was basically an increase in the number of producers, because rulers limited the number who could be samurai. The demobilization of armies, petering out of mines, and halting of overseas travel freed labor for other tasks, and villages absorbed most of those workers. Completion of the giant projects of the Hideyoshi-Ieyasu years released armies of corvée laborers, although the porter and packhorse requirements of sankin kōtai retinues and other official travelers utilized some of their time. Finally, villagers may have worked more hours per day and more days per year than in earlier centuries, when cultivation was less disciplined, the prospects of a harvest less sure because of

19. For a survey of and bibliographical introduction to the early modern salt industry, see Watanabe Noribumi, "Maekindai no seien gijutsu" [The techniques of early modern salt manufacture], in Engyō-gyogyō [The salt and maritime industries], vol. 2 of Kōza Nihon gijutsu no shakaishi [A symposium on the social history of Japanese technology] (Tokyo: Nihon hyōronsha, 1985), pp. 93–131.

20. William H. Coaldrake, "Edo Architecture and Tokugawa Law," MN 36-3 (Autumn 1981): 259–61, discusses the situation in Edo, which influenced trends elsewhere in the country.

21. Amino Yoshihiko, "Kodai-chūsei-kinsei shoki no gyorō to kaisanbutsu no ryūtsū" [Ancient-medieval-initial early modern fisheries and maritime production], p. 271, and Ninohei Tokuo, "Kindai gyogyō gijutsu no seisei" [The creation of modern fisheries technique], in Engyō-gyogyō, p. 275. These two essays are helpful introductions to these topics and to the Japanese scholarly literature on them.

political disorder, and—possibly—the tax collector less insistent on his portion of the yield.

As the century advanced, growth in primary production slowed and problems of distribution became more severe. Fiscal problems became central to politics, as suggested in chapter 7, and governments issued more and more sumptuary regulations, which reserved the choicest products for the highborn and required the low to settle for inferior food, clothing, and housing.[22] In the marketplace, as noted below, merchants increasingly sought government protection as business became more competitive and erratic. In response, government gradually reversed a policy of reducing its involvement in mercantile affairs, instead intervening increasingly in markets in hopes of influencing prices in its own favor.

CHANGES IN URBAN GROWTH

The long-term increases in food production sustained a century of urban growth. Most of that growth occurred in castle towns, even though the coming of peace seemed to deprive them of their raison d'être as military bastions. Castle towns survived by transforming themselves into politico-economic centers. And they were able to continue growing for several decades because their residents devised ways of channeling the necessary rural production into their own hands.

Taxation was the principal channeling device, but direct commercial exchange between town and hinterland also helped, especially from the 1630s on. More and more urban artisans and merchants produced and marketed goods and services, including debt service in the form of usury, throughout daimyo domains and beyond. In Kanazawa, for example, skilled swordmakers found their customers few by the 1630s, and some turned to the production of pots and pans, knives, and other metal goods for general consumption, while others began purveying firewood that they brought to town from the mountains.[23]

Because lords did succeed in increasing their tax take during much of the century, and because urban-based commercial linkages did develop between town and country, urban growth continued despite the

22. Hanley and Yamamura, *Economic and Demographic Change*, p. 89, give examples of sumptuary legislation by daimyo with dates of issue that run from 1668 to 1829.
23. James L. McClain, *Kanazawa* (New Haven: Yale University Press, 1982), pp. 103, 114, 136. McClain shows in lovely detail Kanazawa's evolution from wartime citadel to peacetime city.

coming of peace. However, it gradually slowed, and the locus of growth shifted from castle towns in general to the great cities of Osaka and Edo.

Initially, several factors promoted the growth of castle towns. Following Sekigahara, as noted in chapter 5, it was essentially a by-product of daimyo preparation for the next war. After the fall of Osaka in 1615, Ieyasu reiterated an old edict of Nobunaga's that called on each lord to tear down every castle but one in his domain, and in following years Hidetada's government enforced that order. As lords tore down frontier fortresses and secondary bastions, they reassigned vassals to their jōkamachi, and the number of commoners in those towns rose commensurately.

Then regularization of sankin kōtai and proscription of foreign travel in the 1630s set the rhythms and scope of life for daimyo, their retainers, and the merchants who served them. Within this context, castle towns gradually stopped growing and town life acquired stable routines. As the years passed, and no war erupted, the habits and tastes of peace spread among samurai of all ranks. Lords built comfortable mansions and landscape gardens, and lesser warriors cultivated the arts and letters. Artisans, merchants, entertainers, and others settled around the castles and provided goods and services to satisfy these peacetime wants. In Kanazawa, some fifty craftsmen who earlier had produced saddles, armor, and other military goods for the daimyo were shifting by the 1630s to the fabrication of such peacetime luxury items as lacquer ware, paintings, and nō masks.

By Ietsuna's day, the size of many jōkamachi, particularly those not on transportation routes, was nearly static. Early-seventeenth-century census figures are scattered, few, and of uncertain credibility, but Kanazawa, a town of perhaps 5,000 before 1580, had grown to some 70,000 by 1615, 100,000 by 1667, and 120,000 in 1710. Nagoya grew from a small town to a regional center with 55,000 commoners by 1654, rising to 64,000 by 1692, which was about its limit. The city also included 30,000 residents of samurai status. Hiroshima appears to have had as large a number of commoners in 1619 as in 1633, and a total urban population of 70–80,000, which did not grow much thereafter. Kōfu grew from a small town to 10,000 by the latter half of the century and stayed at that level.[24]

24. The figures for Kanazawa come from McClain, *Kanazawa,* pp. 17, 30; the others from Yazaki, *Social Change,* pp. 130–31, 134.

By midcentury the locus of urban growth was shifting from towns such as these to the great urban centers, Edo and Osaka. Osaka, primarily a commoner city and the major rice market for western and central Japan, appears to have grown gradually from an estimated 200,000 in 1610 to some 360,000 by 1700, and then to have risen by the 1780s to a peak that may have been in the 450,000 to 500,000 range. In part it grew at Kyoto's expense by siphoning off industries like metallurgy, so that Kyoto's population dropped from some 400,000 before 1650 to 350,000 by 1700.[25]

Edo's growth was even more striking. As noted in chapter 5, the village of 1590 grew to a castle town of some 5,000 dwellings (roughly 30,000 people) by 1600 and continued expanding by leaps and bounds after Ieyasu began converting it into a shogunal headquarters. The regularization of sankin kōtai helped stabilize the samurai population, laying a foundation for growth of the commoner populace, and the city grew precipitously during the next two decades, overrunning villages on all sides of the castle. By 1657 Edo's population probably numbered over half a million, and it reportedly doubled during the next half-century. By 1720 its residents numbered well over a million, roughly half a million being of samurai status. And the densely packed city was absorbing more and more nearby villages, sprawling beyond Yotsuya in the west and into Asakusa on the north.[26]

The growth of Edo and Osaka was fostered in significant part by the regularizing of sankin kōtai. It stabilized Edo's consumer populace and Osaka's crucial role as entrepôt: western daimyo traded goods there to help fund their Edo establishments. Growth was simultaneously expedited by improvements in transportation and communication, which helped transform marketing from regional to countrywide scope.

To elaborate, from early in the century, the bakufu fostered road work, and highway upkeep became a regular task for villagers along the way. Bakufu and han, using local corvée labor, organized the initial building of roads and bridges, and local labor was employed thereafter

25. Scholars offer differing figures for Osaka's population. Innes, *Door Ajar*, 2: 438, 440, gives the estimate of two hundred thousand for 1610 and the figures for Kyoto. William B. Hauser, "Osaka: A Commercial City in Tokugawa Japan," *Urbanism Past and Present* 5 (Winter 1977–1978): 35, presents a chart suggestive of the city's demographic evolution.

26. Sources estimate Edo's population variously. Yazaki, *Social Change*, p. 134, reports 1.4 million. Sketch maps at p. 169 show the spatial growth of Edo in the 1630s, 1650s, 1670s, and 1830s.

5. Highway and Barrier in Sagami. This Tōkaidō highway barrier was in Kanagawa, just south of Namamugi. One can easily envisage the trouble that would arise if two daimyo retinues collided on this narrow road or a fire broke out among these closely packed buildings. Courtesy of the Study and Documentation Centre for Photography, University of Leiden, Collection Bauduin, Neg. No. BR-8.

to maintain them. Villagers swept the roads to remove debris, patched rough areas, graded the surface so that water would drain, kept roadsides grassed to prevent erosion, repaired bridges as necessary, planted and nurtured trees to shade travelers, and established and maintained distance markers, which consisted of trees planted on large mounds of soil.

Situated along the roads were official post stations that handled the needs of travelers.[27] As generations passed, their number grew, and by the later Tokugawa period there were some 250 stations spotted irregularly at intervals of about 5–10 kilometers, most of them post towns with resident populations of from five hundred to three thousand people. At each town a manager's office supervised the station's activities, while inns furnished lodging and shops provided entertainment, footgear, meals, medicines, and other essentials. In addition, each town was

27. These comments on post stations are based on Constantine Nomikos Vaporis, "Overland Communications in Tokugawa Japan" (Ph.D. diss., Princeton University, 1987).

supposed to maintain a specified number of porters and packhorses to move goods and people.

Initially, the stations were supported through a combination of tax-free land grants, government stipends for managers and resident couriers, and a scale of fees charged to travelers. The fee scale provided free service to officials traveling on essential business, imposed modest rates on the rest of officialdom, and established a third "free market" rate that travelers of commoner status negotiated with porters. This rate was about twice that charged officialdom. With the regularizing of sankin kōtai and overall growth in the volume of travel, post stations outgrew their sources of income, and the rulers resorted to poorly paid corvée labor and animal levies to supply the stations with porters and packhorses. For the rest of the century, corvée levies imposed on nearby villages—*sukegō*, or "assisting villages,"—enabled highway stations to keep pace with commercial expansion, thereby helping cities grow.

The rulers also promoted messenger services, some operated by the bakufu and others by daimyo. Within a few decades, these official organs were largely supplanted by entrepreneurial postal services whose runners linked the major cities and towns of the realm. By late in the century, there were some eighty-six express messenger services in Kyoto and nine in Osaka, along with a few in Edo. As the economy grew, messenger trips multiplied and they moved message packets further and faster. Initially, the 500-kilometer run between Edo and Osaka had required six days, but by century's end, by skipping layovers and running nights as well as days, messengers were covering the distance in less than four.[28]

Other changes that helped Osaka and Edo grow were improvements in maritime transport, which reduced the cost of hauling bulk goods for mass consumption. Most notably, during the 1660s and 1670s the bakufu sponsored Kawamura Zuiken's reorganization of coastal shipping to form two major routes. One ran from the Sea of Japan coast around western Honshu and through the Inland Sea to Osaka and Edo; the other, from the Sea of Japan northward through Tsugaru Strait, down the Pacific coast, and around the Bōsō peninsula to Edo. The former route bypassed an expensive, time-consuming, and difficult transshipment arrangement in which goods from the Sea of Japan littoral were landed at Tsuruga or Obama and carried by man or beast overland and

28. Katsuhisa Moriya, "Urban Networks and Information Networks," in Chie Nakane and Shinzaburō Ōishi, eds., *Tokugawa Japan* (Tokyo: University of Tokyo Press, 1990), pp. 106–13.

6. Courier Conveying Message Container. Muscular runners with hardened feet provided the courier service that linked cities and the hinterland during the Tokugawa period. Courtesy of Vereeniging Nederlandsch Historisch Scheepvaart Museum p/a 's Lands Zeemagazijn, Amsterdam, Album 1, p. 6, Neg. No. 216.

via Lake Biwa and the Yodo River system to Kyoto and Osaka. The latter circuit bypassed a route in which goods came down the Pacific coast to below Mito, where they were off-loaded to Tone River boats, hauled upstream to the south branch of the Tone, sent down that branch to Edo Bay, and finally shunted across the bay to the city.

In sum, expansion of rural production, governmental control of part of the output, growth of marketable urban goods and services, and advances in transportation and communication all helped sustain urban growth and vitality, especially that of Edo and Osaka. As the decades passed, moreover, more and more commercial activity came to be handled by merchants operating as entrepreneurs rather than as quarter-masters, and that change involved changes in market organization.

CHANGES IN MERCHANT ORGANIZATION

Major changes in merchant organization were prompted during the seventeenth century by declining government interest in urban growth and by the changing scale of cities and of the provisioning activity that sustained them.

The dominant merchants in Hideyoshi and Ieyasu's day, men like Suminokura Ryōi, provided daimyo with quartermaster and administrative services. They supplied war-making matériel or peacetime commodities as needed and played key roles in rice transactions. They were especially active in mining and minting, in providing timber, rock, and other building materials for castles and towns, and in organizing and financing overseas trading ventures. Paid in salaries, gifts, and honors, their connections also provided opportunity for entrepreneurial profit. Thus, itowappu merchants sold the yarn unwanted by the authorities, and the lumbermen who provided timber for Edo Castle were allowed to sell the pieces left over from government-sponsored construction.

From about the 1630s on, merchants with government ties found their situations deteriorating. They had fewer chances to profit from foreign trade after being forbidden to go abroad, and as castle work petered out, rulers had less and less need of their services. By then, however, large numbers of urban commoners and samurai required provisions for both daily life and reconstruction after the fires that repeatedly ravaged their wooden towns and cities. Accordingly, merchants gradually shifted from official provisioning of government to entrepreneurial purveying to the general public. The shift presented challenges and led to changes in merchant organization and merchant-ruler relations.

The challenge in purveying to the general public was that it required success in an open marketplace. Late-sixteenth-century lords originally promoted open markets (*rakuichi*) to dislodge entrenched merchants and lure more amenable ones to their castle towns. The policy proved so successful that Edo favored unregulated markets well into the seventeenth century, despite growing discontent among the very merchant families that originally benefited from them. In some areas of commerce, mostly those touching samurai households, the bakufu did try to control market conditions by sanctioning trade associations (*na-*

kama) that it could regulate.[29] These included nakama for "pawnbrokers, second-hand dealers, old gold and copper traders, and the imported silk (*itowappu*) merchants." For major commodities, however, non-regulation persisted, and, as noted above, the bakufu even abolished the itowappu in 1655, and restored it later only after much protest.

For established merchants, the marketplace became larger, more complex, and more difficult to manage as the century advanced. With the codification of sankin kōtai, daimyo needed to transport more goods from their han to the great cities to trade for cash and necessities, and the merchants handling that work had to assemble the needed venture capital and devise means of conducting long-distance transactions. The tasks required collaboration by merchant houses (*ton'ya*) that functioned as "wholesale merchants, consignment agents, or receiving agents, while others supervised processing industries or served as shipping agents." Merchants promoted trade organizations as a way to manage these elaborate transactions.

As the growth in urban numbers and tax receipts slowed later in the century, market competition became more intense. Irregularities in production and consumption, particularly those associated with crop failure and urban fire, produced erratic prices and spot scarcities and gluts that could bankrupt merchants. Their vulnerability was heightened, moreover, by the growing shortage of specie, which forced them to conduct more business on the basis of promissory notes and other assurances. The need for funding also gave rise to *nakagai*, jobbers whose capital facilitated transactions but who also took a piece of the profit. These conditions prodded merchants to defend themselves by forming private trade organizations (*kumiai*) and seeking government protection.

The problems of entrepreneurship were harshly revealed by the Meireki fire of 1657. As the city rebuilt, prices gyrated wildly, and the low quality of building material generated discontent and bitter recrimination. Those difficulties, which rippled along supply lines out into the countryside, upset bakufu leaders, persuading them that merchant organization of some sort was needed to assure deliveries and regulate the price, quality, and quantity of goods. From the 1660s on, they permitted groups of ton'ya, mainly in Osaka, to form nakama with authority

29. The two quotations below come from William B. Hauser, *Economic Institutional Change in Tokugawa Japan: Osaka and the Kinai Cotton Trade* (Cambridge: Cambridge University Press, 1974), pp. 13, 14. He lists Osaka ton'ya of 1679 on p. 21.

to regulate wages, prices, and the quality and quantity of goods and services in key areas of business. Nakama also allocated markets and sources of supply and policed participating merchants and artisans.

For the rest of the century, nakama managed major markets in cloth, rice, timber, and other goods. They provided enough stability for business to flourish—*vide* Nagasaki—and by the 1680s merchant houses were handling a wide range of activities. By one listing, for example, Osaka contained some 380 ton'ya, some organized by province or locality, most specialized by product, and many concentrated on a segment of a business. They handled diverse forest products, foodstuffs, textiles, marine products, dried goods, and manufactured items.

Established merchants found even this level of nakama organization less than satisfactory, however, because much of the bakufu's involvement was limited to Osaka, and policy was inconsistent. Leaders in Edo did not necessarily prevent other merchants from trying to enter business and could not be depended on to intervene to protect merchants or enforce their nakama regulations against either external or internal challenges. Until the 1720s, however, the bakufu adhered to its policy of selective organization and local enforcement, and merchants had to make do.

By the early eighteenth century, the era of dramatic economic growth had passed. It left Japan with a countrywide economy, well-developed transportation and communication webs, a large and complex urban society, and an elaborate entrepreneurial system of commerce. It also left Japan with a more closely controlled foreign trade and a domestic economy in which resource constraints and commercial instability were becoming more acute and demanding more active political intervention. How effectively bakuhan leaders would respond to those demands was to be a major theme in later Tokugawa history.

The Blossoming of Political Thought

Creation of an Intelligentsia
  Fostering Samurai Learning
  Scholarship and Careers
Dimensions of Scholarly Thought
  Legitimizing the Regime and Justifying Samurai Privilege
  Naturalizing Confucian Thought and
    Elucidating the Native Legacy
Two Notable Intellectuals
  Nakae Tōju
  Itō Jinsai

As the routines of peace became entrenched, government disciplining of cultural activity was routinized in the form of hortatory edicts and sumptuary legislation that sought to regulate material consumption and daily behavior by linking them to hereditary status and high principle. Within this hierarchically stratified order, the boundaries of acceptable thought were only roughly defined and sporadically enforced. Little was taboo except Fujufuse Buddhism and Christianity, so considerable space for intellectual inquiry existed, and in the absence of warfare, more and more samurai pursued schooling, teaching, and writing. From about the middle of the seventeenth century on, an intelligentsia emerged that produced a flood of learned treatises on government, society, and the nature of being.

CREATION OF AN INTELLIGENTSIA

Both bakufu and han encouraged learning to keep samurai peacably occupied in the pursuit of study and self-discipline. Governments did little more than advocate, however, and most samurai actually received their educations at home or from private scholars. They pursued schooling, moreover, less as a response to government urging than as an avenue of career advancement in a world where military skill offered few rewards.

FOSTERING SAMURAI LEARNING

From early in the century on, lords encouraged vassals to study. The idea that samurai should cultivate both the civil and military arts (*bun* and *bu*) was enshrined in the Laws for the Military Households (*Buke shohatto*) and endlessly reiterated in government admonitions. In the 1615 version of the Laws, the first of thirteen hortatory clauses translates this way: "The study of literature and the practice of the military arts, including archery and horsemanship, must be cultivated diligently."[1] An appended commentary followed each of the thirteen injunctions to explain or justify it, in this case invoking a classic Chinese aphorism: "'On the left hand literature, on the right hand use of arms' was the rule of the ancients. Both must be pursued concurrently."

Such rhetoric notwithstanding, however, exhortation was nearly the extent of government involvement in samurai education. Not until 1630 did Hidetada help Hayashi Razan establish a school at Shinobugaoka in Edo, near the newly built Kan'eiji. Ikeda Mitsumasa opened one in Okayama in 1641, and a few other daimyo set up domain schools in later years, but until the eighteenth century such efforts were exceptional, and most samurai were schooled privately. The scholar-teachers commonly were ronin or sons of ronin: for example, Nakae Tōju, Yamaga Sokō, and Yamazaki Ansai. But a few, such as Fujiwara Seika, were former priests, and a few, such as Matsunaga Sekigo, were sons of scholars. One of the most successful was Itō Jinsai, a Kyoto merchant's son whose descendants sustained his school, the Kogidō, until the late nineteenth century. As a commoner's son, Jinsai also foreshadowed many of the best scholars of later generations.

Most of these scholars taught in Kyoto. With its long tradition of learning and cultural elitism—which successive generations of emperors and nobles worked to sustain—the city continued to dominate intellec-

1. David John Lu, *Sources of Japanese History* (New York: McGraw-Hill, 1974), 1: 201. In Chinese imagery the left hand, and by implication literature, was given precedence, but the 1615 commentary devoted two more sentences to military preparedness, which suggests that it still loomed larger than literature in the eyes of the Laws' framers.

tual life, and the most influential schools operated there. Early in the
1600s, Fujiwara Seika resisted blandishments from Ieyasu to move east,
instead remaining in Kyoto. In 1648 a major new school opened there,
that of Kinoshita Jun'an, whose teacher, Matsunaga Sekigo, had studied under Seika. Another influential Kyoto academy was the Kimon
school, established in 1655 by Ansai, and a third was the Kogidō, founded
a few years later by Jinsai.

Other scholars operated in the provinces: for example, Nakae Tōju,
who taught in a village near Lake Biwa, and Kaibara Ekken, who taught
near Fukuoka. Even Razan's school at Shinobugaoka was something of
a provincial school, despite its limited connection to the bakufu, because the newly risen city of Edo was still a cultural outlier. Razan's
decision to stay there sustained his family's ties to the bakufu and assured him of a stream of samurai students, but it kept the Hayashi
school at the periphery of intellectual life, which may have fostered the
sense of professional vulnerability that he displayed in his attack on
Kumazawa Banzan during the Yui Shōsetsu affair.

The curricula of these independently operated schools varied, but
Confucianism and Chinese learning were their core. Students learned to
read and write the language, practiced calligraphy, studied the classics,
and read Chinese and Japanese history, poetry, or other works, depending on their teacher's preferences. At the larger schools they attended
lectures, where the teacher expounded his views, and they met to discuss subjects with the teacher or with one another. By the time students
completed their studies, whether in a few months or years, they generally were literate, versed in the materials, and adherents to their teacher's opinions.

SCHOLARSHIP AND CAREERS

Scholars operated schools for diverse, entwined reasons: to earn a living, make a name, sustain a family, promote an intellectual agenda. Of
course, not all samurai needed vehicles to advance their careers, thanks
to the mechanism of hereditary succession. But even some of the most
favored seventeenth-century daimyo, to say nothing of the shogun Tsunayoshi, did pursue and promote scholarly activities.

One of the most notable daimyo-scholars was Tokugawa Mitsukuni,
grandson of Ieyasu and lord of Mito. He fostered learning by nurturing
such scholars as the émigré Ming loyalist Chu Shun-shui, but his finest
legacy was *Dai Nihon shi,* a monumental history of Japan that traced

the imperial dynasty from its legendary origin in 660 B.C. to the end of a century-long schism in 1392. So immense was the project that though Mitsukuni started it in 1657, the main portions were not completed until fifteen years after his death, and the remaining sections not until 1906. The published edition of 1928–29 fills seventeen volumes.

Another scholar-daimyo was Hoshina Masayuki, also a grandson of Ieyasu. As lord of Aizu and regent to the child shogun Ietsuna, he arranged official bakufu sponsorship for *Honchō tsugan,* a Ch'eng-Chu-inspired chronology of the imperial family that was prepared by Hayashi Razan and his son, Gahō. He also brought scholars such as Yamazaki Ansai and Yoshikawa Koretaru, the head of the Yoshida Shintō school, into his service. He collaborated with Ansai in the preparation of two gazetteers of Aizu and three texts of the Ch'eng-Chu school for use in Aizu's newly established domain academy. He actively promoted study of both Confucianism and Shintō at Edo, helping consolidate Ch'eng-Chu and Yoshida Shintō in official circles.

Few samurai were grandsons of Ieyasu, however, and few were as comfortably ensconced as daimyo. With the coming of peace even the finest of warriors discovered that military prowess no longer guaranteed a career; the times demanded new strategies. Many became bureaucrats; a few, bandits or buccaneers. Many more became merchants, farmers, or laborers; others, artisans of one or another type. And yet others pursued an academic strategy, becoming physicians, teachers, or scholar-advisors, which were essentially three expressions of a single career path that seems nicely captured by the term *savant.*

Two factors made a career as a savant particularly appealing to ronin. First, it was a status that transcended the formal Confucian categories of samurai-peasant-artisan-merchant (*shi-nō-kō-shō*), probably because physicians were valued for the effectiveness of their therapies and scholar-advisors for the quality of their advice rather than for their pedigrees. If reputed to be able, a ronin savant could expect to be hired and with luck become physician or scholar-advisor to a daimyo, acquiring prestige and a comfortable stipend, and, if all went well, recovering his family's samurai status.

Second, *kanpō,* the holistic Chinese medicine then being practiced, was but a segment of the larger body of Chinese thought. One's mastery of medical knowledge—that is, one's understanding of yin and yang, the five basic elements, their relationship to the five bodily organs and other anatomical structures and physiological processes—and hence one's presumed skill at therapy were tied to mastery of the Way and humankind's place in that Way. So a person acquired extensive knowledge of Chinese thought while learning kanpō. Should his medical practice not flourish, he could shift to a teaching career, and success as a teacher— attracting students and producing disciples—depended on skill in propounding one's own views. The teacher who did that well might gain an official post as scholar-advisor to someone of note and thereby reap the same benefits as a physician. A career as a savant thus offered a ronin two or three ways to make a living, rehabilitate his family, and possibly even achieve personal power and glory.

Successive heads of the family line descended from Hayashi Razan were among the most successful practitioners of the savant strategy. Razan, reputedly the son of a ronin, was a student of Fujiwara Seika. Like his mentor he abandoned Buddhist doctrine to become an advocate of Confucianism. As a young man, he took employment with Ieyasu and served as scribe and consultant to Hidetada, Iemitsu, and Ietsuna until his death in 1657 at the age of seventy-four. His influence grew only slowly, however, as death claimed the generation of warriors who had known the fury of war and the solace of Buddhism. After 1630, when Hidetada finally granted him funds for a school at Shinobugaoka, he began advocating Ch'eng-Chu thought and Shintō teachings. But not until his last years, when he was a venerable sage and one of the few still alive who had known Ieyasu personally, did he enjoy much influence among bakufu leaders.

After Razan's death, his son Gahō operated the family's school and Confucian shrine, aided by additional funds from the bakufu. In 1690– 91, as part of his general promotion of Confucianism, Tsunayoshi awarded Gahō's shrine government sponsorship, setting its annual income at 1,000 koku. He ordered it moved to Yushima, nearer the castle, where he equipped it and its accompanying school with a building complex of some twenty structures. He named the slope (*saka*) where it was located Shōheizaka, the characters for Shōhei being those of Confucius's natal village, Changping. Furthermore, he granted the head of the Hayashi family samurai rank and the hereditary title of *daigaku no kami* (head of the university). By the eighteenth century, the Hayashi thus had formal rank and status and a school situated adjacent to a government-sponsored Confucian shrine near Edo Castle. There it became established as a bastion of Confucian doctrine, predominantly in the Ch'eng-Chu tradition.

Razan and his descendants had achieved what many sought: they had negotiated successful passage through decades that saw the destitution and demoralization of innumerable samurai families. Nor was their intellectual strategy unique. Like them, many samurai scholars staked out distinctive positions to attract followers and build their reputations as socially valued thinkers.

Elements of the savant strategy were visible in the career of Yamazaki Ansai, whose school was arguably Japan's most influential center of Ch'eng-Chu teachings. Born the son of a ronin-turned-physician in Kyoto, Ansai was schooled in Buddhist temples and in 1636, at the age of eighteen, went to Tosa as a Zen monk. Discovering the ideas of Chu Hsi, he embraced the Way, left the priesthood, and returned to Kyoto. He stridently repudiated Buddhism in 1647 and opened a school in the city eight year later. He also studied Shintō, traveled to Edo for further scholarly work in 1658, and divided his time between the two cities from then until 1673, when, after Hoshina Masayuki's death, he settled in Kyoto for a last decade of teaching.

"Single-minded, doctrinaire, and intolerant," Ansai did not limit his criticisms to Buddhist thought. He also became a severe critic of rival Confucianists, asserting that only through undeviating acceptance of Chu Hsi's teachings, or, more precisely, his own understanding of them, could one comprehend the Way and thereby establish it in Japan. He attacked Hayashi Razan and Gahō—and others—for their corruptions of the Truth and lack of religious commitment to it.[2] Of Razan he wrote: "Mr. Hayashi! What sort of a man is he! The whole world knows about his unfiliality. He has served under four shoguns but has never expounded the Way of Yao and Shun before them. . . . What kind of learning does he have! . . . His mind is dark and his knowledge blocked." Benefiting not only from his own strident assertions of correctness but also from Kyoto's cultural éclat, Ansai moved to Edo soon after Razan's death and established himself as a scholar-advisor there, serving Masayuki for several years as a part-time lecturer. By the time he returned to Kyoto, he was esteemed as a scholar of great influence and exceptional insight.

Doubtless Ansai's appeal was strengthened by the sense of certitude

2. These quotations come from Herman Ooms, *Tokugawa Ideology* (Princeton: Princeton University Press, 1985), pp. 207, 210. Razan's "unfiliality" lay in the fact that he taught at Shinobugaoka in tonsure and monk's habit because the bakufu regarded philosophical teaching as a monk's profession. For a close analysis of Ansai's thought, see also Okada Takehiko, "Practical Learning in the Chu Hsi School: Yamazaki Ansai and Kaibara Ekken," in Wm. Theodore de Bary and Irene Bloom, eds., *Principle and Practicality: Essays in Neo-Confucianism and Political Learning* (New York: Columbia University Press, 1979), pp. 233–57.

that he projected. He sustained the confidence of students by restricting their reading to the six Confucian texts that he approved. He also seems to have used intimidation to instill loyalty, one of his students recalling that "each time we entered the door of our teacher's home, we were filled with fear. It was like going into a prison. Upon leaving, we would sigh with relief as if we had escaped from the den of a tiger."[3] Ansai's techniques worked, however, and his message was received. His lectures on both Shintō and Chu Hsi drew large audiences of scholars, priests, and eager students, and some of them passed his teachings on to later generations. The result was the flowering of a rich body of learning known as Suika Shintō and the "Kimon" school of Ch'eng-Chu Confucianism.

Central to the savant strategy was a scholar's assertion that his views were superior to those of others because they were more "correct" or, more commonly, because they were somehow more useful, more appropriate to the time and place, a proposition embodied in the term *jitsugaku*: "real," "useful," or "practical" learning. In Razan's early days, when Buddhists such as the Zen monk Ishin Sūden and the venerable Tendai monk Tenkai were key advisors to Ieyasu, scholars employed the term *jitsugaku* to juxtapose Confucian learning to Buddhism. Razan wrote,

> Now, Confucianism is "jitsu" (real) and Buddhism is Kyo (empty). Indeed the delusion as to what is real and what is empty is prevalent in the world. If one is asked which he would take, the real or the empty, who will choose the empty and discard the real? Thus, those who prefer Buddhism, which is not real, to Confucianism do such a thing only because they have not heard of the Way.[4]

In much the same spirit, in 1638 Asayama Irin'an, a lapsed Zen monk who became Confucian advisor to two major daimyo, wrote *Kiyomizu monogatari,* a popular tract that explained the virtues of Ch'eng-Chu ideas and contrasted their practicality with the uselessness of Buddhism.

By then, however, many had "heard of the Way," and the political role of Buddhist scholars was declining. Not even the vigor of the hatamoto-turned-Zen monk Suzuki Shōsan, who retooled for peacetime service by trading swords for sutras, could reverse the decline. In

3. Richard Rubinger, *Private Academies of Tokugawa Japan* (Princeton: Princeton University Press, 1982), p. 43.
4. Ryoen Minamoto, "The Development of the Jitsugaku Concept in the Tokugawa Period," *Philosophical Studies of Japan* 9 (1975): 65. A revised version of this essay appears as "Jitsugaku and Empirical Rationalism in the First Half of the Tokugawa Period," in de Bary and Bloom, eds., *Principle and Practicality,* pp. 375–456.

his role as elderly proponent of higher insight, Shōsan devoted three years to the practical task of consolidating the Tokugawa order by converting Christian adherents to Buddhism after the Shimabara Rebellion.[5] But the future lay elsewhere: by the 1650s and 1660s such major lords as Masayuki of Aizu, Mitsukuni of Mito, and Mitsumasa of Okayama were actively attempting to suppress Buddhism in their domains.

As the claims of Buddhism lost persuasiveness, intellectuals turned to closer scrutiny of Confucianism and Shintō as means of identifying the "useful" and distinguishing their teachings from those of others. Scrutiny of Confucianism entailed examination of its basic categories, notably principle (*li*) and its manifest form (*ch'i*), their relationship, and their functional implications. As explained by Razan on one occasion, the basic nature of reality was a duality of li and ch'i, in which li took precedence:

> The Principle (*li*) which existed constantly before and after heaven and earth came into being is called the Supreme Ultimate (*t'ai chi*). When this Supreme Ultimate was in motion, it created the *yang,* and when it was quiescent, it created the *yin.* The *yin* and *yang* were originally of the same substance (*ch'i*) but were divided into two complementary forces. They were further divided into the Five Elements which are wood, fire, earth, metal and water. When the Five Elements were further divided, they became all things under heaven. When these Five Elements were brought together to take shapes, people were also born.[6]

Razan, as well as other proponents of Ch'eng-Chu thought, then used this categorizing strategy to describe a properly structured universe, with Heaven above and Earth below, the four classes hierarchically ordered in their places, and the five human relationships basic to all people.

5. Ooms, *Tokugawa Ideology,* p. 125. In addition to an essay by Royall Tyler, "The Tokugawa Peace and Popular Religion: Suzuki Shōsan, Kakugyō Tōbutsu, and Jikigyō Miroku," in Peter Nosco, ed., *Confucianism and Tokugawa Culture* (Princeton: Princeton University Press, 1984), see Tyler's book, *Selected Writings of Suzuki Shōsan,* East Asia Papers, no. 13 (Ithaca, N.Y.: Cornell University China-Japan Program, 1977). Two other, very dissimilar assessments of Suzuki are contained in George Elison, *Deus Destroyed: The Image of Christianity in Early Modern Japan* (Cambridge, Mass.: Harvard University Press, 1973), and Nakamura·Hajime, "Suzuki Shōsan, 1579–1655 and the Spirit of Capitalism in Japanese Buddhism," *MN* 22-1/2 (1967): 1–14. Nakamura, who is presenting Suzuki as a forerunner of modernity, admires him; Elison, whose interest is limited to Suzuki's critique of Christianity, does not.

6. Lu, *Sources,* 1: 235. Several essayists in de Bary and Bloom, eds., *Principle and Practicality,* offer careful analyses of Razan's thought, drawing valuable distinctions between the diverse forms of "Neo-Confucian" thought. Minamoto, "Jitsugaku and Empirical Rationalism," pp. 384–86, discusses Hayashi's uncertainties about the li-ch'i relationship. In romanized Japanese, *li* and *ch'i* appear as *ri* and *ki.*

The pursuit of ontological issues thus carried scholars far beyond the verifiable and opened the way to diversity of interpretation. As the century advanced, that diversity appeared, with disagreements that circled around the concepts li and ch'i expanding into more general study of the various interpretations of Sung and Ming thought, including that of the scholar Wang Yang-ming (Ōyōmei). Beyond that, scholars compared Sung-Ming thought with the classics of Confucius's own day, a field of learning that became known as *kogaku*, or "ancient learning." And they commonly made their cases in terms of the "uselessness" of the view under attack. For example, Yamaga Sokō denounced the impracticality of Ch'eng-Chu thought in this way: "It is needless to compare those who read books of literature and do not know 'jitsugaku' with wise men well versed and practised in world affairs. . . . The scholars of letters do not know the trend of the times. . . . In general, if we do not learn 'jitsugaku,' the knowledge of letters is in effect a form of self-poisoning."[7]

The study of Shintō involved a comparable scrutiny of the Japanese legacy as a whole, most especially the creation myths, dynastic histories, and rich corpus of poetry and prose. Key objectives of this scholarship were to identify distinctively Japanese qualities and to show how they related to continental culture.

In the fields of both continental and indigenous learning, scholars thus built their careers by "pushing back the frontiers of knowledge." They wrote treatises that were read and discussed, refined understanding by criticizing others' interpretations, attracted students to their schools, and gained positions as advisors to daimyo and shogun.

DIMENSIONS OF SCHOLARLY THOUGHT

Seventeenth-century scholarly production had unpretentious beginnings in the search by would-be rulers and their advisors for practical solutions to immediate problems. Throughout the century such concerns remained central to scholarship as samurai intellectuals labored to justify the Tokugawa regime and, more broadly, to legitimize samurai privilege. Other purposes also acquired importance, however, and learned writing became ever more complex as scholars wrestled with inconsistencies and inadequacies in the body of thought they were studying.

7. Minamoto, "Development of the Jitsugaku Concept," p. 69.

The most troubling inconsistencies touched ethnic self-awareness. These thinkers drew heavily on foreign ideas, most notably Confucian doctrines that came to Japan directly from China or via Korea. For those ideas to serve their advocates' purposes, they could not be associated with the proscribed doctrines of Christianity and had to seem "naturalized"—that is, appropriate to Japan. In particular, intellectuals somehow had to rearrange the cultural conceit of Chinese thought that defined China as the source and center of civilization and Japan as part of the barbarian periphery. To that end much energy was devoted to transvaluing Chinese thought and harmonizing or integrating it with the intellectual traditions of Japan, especially those associated with the politico-religous legacy of Shintō.

Even when a general reconciliation was achieved, the application of many aspects of Chinese thought continued to pose problems because China and Japan differed in many particulars, such as adoption and burial customs, and those differences sustained generations of debate about the propriety of specific rituals and practices.[8] Nevertheless, by century's end, Japan's intelligentsia had made great strides in legitimizing the regime, justifying samurai privilege, naturalizing Confucian thought, and elucidating the native legacy.

LEGITIMIZING THE REGIME AND JUSTIFYING SAMURAI PRIVILEGE

From Ieyasu's day on, as noted in chapter 6, Tokugawa leaders actively employed cultural devices to lend credence to their regime, and scholar-advisors contributed to the effort. Later scholars did too.[9] In conjunction with Iemitsu's reconstruction of the Nikkō mausoleum during the 1630s, for example, Tenkai, the shogunate's centenarian Tendai advisor, drafted a founding document for the new shrine. In it, the shrine's god, Sannō Gongen—"the fundamental god of life for Heaven, Earth, and Man," which had manifested itself through Ieyasu—described himself in these words:

8. See I. J. McMullen, "Non-Agnatic Adoption: A Confucian Controversy in Seventeenth- and Eighteenth-Century Japan," *HJAS* 35 (1975): 133–89, on the issue of adoption, especially in the period 1670–1740. Adoption was critical to the maintenance of patrilineages, so the issue of adoption criteria generated heated controversy.

9. The following quotations from Tenkai and *Ieyasu's Testament* come from Ooms, *Tokugawa Ideology,* pp. 177, 66, respectively. Sannō Gongen had long been associated with Tendai Buddhism. See also Kate Wildman Nakai, *Shogunal Politics* (Cambridge, Mass.: Harvard University Press, 1988), pp. 178–80.

I am the mysterious god of Japan. . . . I do not fathom yin and yang, neither do I make the creation. I reside in the nature of the law of the mind; transformed I bring down the way of truth. The Great Vow Buddha is inferior [to me]. My mind protects the country. . . . This whole world is mine and all the people are my children.

Other writings invoked other sanctions, most notably the concept of *tendō,* the Heavenly Way. In *Tōshōgū goikun,* an essay also associated with Iemitsu's Nikkō project, the survival of Tokugawa rule for three generations was used implicitly to demonstrate the propriety of Tokugawa rule: "When as ruler of the realm, one enjoys trust and support, tendō accepts his authority over the realm; if one loses the realm, one's house will completely perish."

In 1652, when for the first time a child held the shogunal title, Hayashi Gahō prepared a brief historical work, *Nihon ōdai ichiran,* that championed the Tokugawa family cause. According to Gahō, Ieyasu had received the Confucian Mandate of Heaven at Sekigahara when "evildoers and bandits were vanquished, and the entire realm submitted to Lord Ieyasu, praising the establishment of peace and extolling his martial virtue. [May] this glorious era that he founded continue for ten thousands upon ten thousands of generations, coeval with heaven and earth!" [10] And, finally, in explaining the relationship of emperor and shogun, Yamaga Sokō conflated Confucian and Shintō rationales for Tokugawa supremacy in this way:

The Imperial Court is the Forbidden Precinct. Happily, the line descended from Amaterasu has possessed hereditary authority for countless generations. Accordingly, even though a military general has grasped the power and directs government and letters within the four seas, this is nevertheless for the reason that he has been commanded to oversee all state affairs on behalf of the Imperial Court, and his serving of the Imperial Court diligently, without the slightest negligence, is in accordance with the Great Propriety obtaining between lord and subject. [11]

This melange of rationales was not without its inconsistencies, and as conditions worsened and complaints proliferated during the later Tokugawa period, critics began to question the adequacy of Tokugawa rule, to challenge its authority, and in the end to deny the regime's very

10. Kate Wildman Nakai, "Tokugawa Confucian Historiography: The Hayashi, Early Mito School, and Arai Hakuseki," in Nosco, ed., *Confucianism and Tokugawa Culture,* p. 79.
11. David Magarey Earl, *Emperor and Nation in Japan* (Seattle: University of Washington Press, 1964), p. 43.

right to exist. As long as peace and prosperity held, however, few raised strong protests and the rhetoric served its purpose.

Besides legitimizing the regime, political thought also served more broadly to sanction samurai privilege. An early formulation by Hayashi Razan anchored that privilege in Ch'eng-Chu doctrine:

> The five relationships governing ruler and subject, father and son, husband and wife, older and younger brother, and friend and friend have been in existence from olden days to the present. There has been no change in these basic relations, and they are thus called the supreme way. . . .
>
> Heaven is above and earth is below. . . . [I]n everything there is an order separating those above and those below . . . , [and] we cannot allow disorder in the relations between ruler and subject, between those above and those below. The separation into four classes of samurai, farmers, artisans and merchants, like the five relationships, is part of the principles of heaven and is the Way which was taught by the Sage (Confucius).[12]

This rationale for samurai supremacy, with its premise of a timeless Way to which society should conform, was propounded not only by the Hayashi in Edo but more effectively by Kinoshita Jun'an and Yamazaki Ansai in Kyoto.

Some scholars questioned the concept of a timeless, unchanging Way and found a more sharply defined basis for samurai privilege in their monopoly of military duties. Most notably, Yamaga Sokō formulated what came to be known as *bushidō,* the Way of the Warrior, and his name has ever since been closely identified with the notion of bushi ethics and the rights and responsibilities of bushi rule.

When Sokō was born in 1622, his father was a ronin temporarily supported by a senior retainer of Aizu han. Five years later a change in Aizu lords cost the father his job. He moved to Edo, where he practiced medicine to support his family. Hoping Sokō would be able to rebuild the family position, he sent the lad to study with Razan for about two years and later to study martial arts with other distinguished instructors. Sokō also studied Shintō, but his teaching and writing concentrated on Confucian thought and martial skills. As a precocious youth he lectured to a number of daimyo, officials, and others but declined several invitations to serve lords in hopes of receiving an appointment from Iemitsu. Iemitsu's death thwarted the hope, and the Yui Shōsetsu incident later that year led authorities to press ronin such as Sokō into employment. Reluctantly, he became a military instructor for Asano

---

12. These passages are quoted, with grammatical simplifications, from Lu, *Sources,* 1: 236.

Naganao, the daimyo of Akō han. He served Asano until 1660, when he resigned and returned to Edo to study, write, and teach independently.

Sokō's writings reveal his concern to provide samurai with useful and appropriate instruction. In particular, he saw the discipline of the military arts as valuable, arguing that in the absence of warfare, the samurai's task was to discipline himself to fill properly the peacetime role of society's leader and culture model. He produced works on military ethics from the mid 1650s on, stating his view this way in a later essay: "The samurai is one who does not cultivate, does not manufacture, and does not engage in trade, but it cannot be that he has no function at all as a samurai. . . . The business of the samurai consists in reflecting on his own station in life, in discharging loyal service to his master . . . and in devoting himself to duty above all." He contrasted this function with that of the lower classes. Although they have family obligations comparable to those of samurai,

> the farmers, artisans, and merchants have no leisure from their occupations, and so they cannot constantly act in accordance with them and fully exemplify the Way . . . ; should there be someone in the three classes of the common people who transgresses against these moral principles, the samurai summarily punishes him and thus upholds proper moral principles in the land. It would not do for the samurai to know the martial and civil virtues without manifesting them. . . . Within his heart he keeps to the ways of peace, but without he keeps his weapons ready for use. The three classes of the common people make him their teacher and respect him. By following his teachings, they are enabled to understand what is fundamental and what is secondary. . . . Herein lies the Way of the samurai, the means by which he earns his clothing, food, and shelter.[13]

Continental political thought thus helped to legitimize the Tokugawa order and its hereditary elite. It could do so because scholars developed arguments that successfully naturalized ideas of foreign provenance, relating them effectively to indigenous traditions and enabling them "to fit the time and place."

NATURALIZING CONFUCIAN THOUGHT AND ELUCIDATING THE NATIVE LEGACY

The process of naturalizing Confucian thought was a complex one that involved philosophical hairsplitting and a tad of sophistry. In essence

13. These two passages come from Ryusaku Tsunoda et al., comps., *Sources of the Japanese Tradition* (New York: Columbia University Press, 1958), pp. 398–400, quoting *Shidō*.

the process changed ideas from an initial form in which Chinese culture was represented as unique and superior to forms in which cultural elements were construed as universalistic phenomena found in Japan and China alike or else as evidence of Japan's superiority.

From early in the seventeenth century on, scholars engaged in this process of ideological manipulation and transvaluation.[14] Razan claimed that the Shintō concept of deity, or *kami,* "is the soul of heaven and earth," those basic categories of Confucian thought. Kumazawa Banzan extended the argument, claiming that the Confucian Way was universal and synonymous with Shintō: "That the Way is the Shinto of heaven and earth is the same as that there are not two suns in the sky. . . . One may say it is the way of the kami (*shintō*) of Japan while at the same time it is the way of the sages (*seidō*) of China." In his Suika Shintō, Yamazaki Ansai articulated one of the richest identifications of Shintō and Confucianism. He wrote:

> In Japan at the time of the opening of the country, [the gods] Izanagi and Izanami followed the divination teachings of the Heavenly Gods, obeyed yin and yang, and thus correctly established the beginnings of ethical teachings. In the universe there is only One Principle, [although] either Gods or Sages come forth depending on whether it concerns the country where the sun rises [Japan] or the country where the sun sets [China]. The [two] Ways [of Shinto and Confucianism] are, however, naturally and mysteriously the same.[15]

In 1675 Yamaga Sokō described in his *Haisho zanpitsu* the logic by which he overcame his initial excess of Sinophilia. Having read avidly about China, he wrote:

> I thought that Japan was inferior to China in every way because it was a small country, and that only in China could a sage be born. This was not just my own view; scholars of all ages thought the same way and were devoted to Chinese studies. Only recently did I realize that this view was mistaken. Truly, it is an incorrigible vice of scholars that they believe their ears but not their eyes, and that they reject what is near and take up what is far away.

Sokō then explained his corrected understanding. Noting that "wisdom, humanity, and valor are the three virtues of a sage," he proceeded

14. The following passages are quoted from Kate Wildman Nakai, "The Naturalization of Confucianism in Tokugawa Japan: The Problem of Sinocentrism," *HJAS* 40-1 (June 1980): 160, 163. See also Harry D. Harootunian, "The Functions of China in Tokugawa Thought," in Akira Iriye, ed., *The Chinese and the Japanese* (Princeton: Princeton University Press, 1980), pp. 9–36.

15. Ooms, *Tokugawa Ideology*, p. 234. See also Okada, "Practical Learning in the Chu Hsi School," pp. 247–48.

to show that in those terms Japan was superior to China. Japan's imperial line had reigned "from the age of the gods down to the present
day" thanks to the absence of "intrigues or outrages by rebels and trai-
tors," which reveals that "the imperial line has possessed the virtues of
humanity and justice." Emperors have all been virtuous and their officials sagacious, as proven by the country's long peace and stability. As
for valor, Sokō asserted that, "no alien had ever conquered even part
of Japan," whereas Japan had twice conquered Korea and had "always
won martial glory throughout the world." By the criteria of "wisdom,
humanity, and valor," he concluded, "we find that Japan is far superior" to China and should, therefore, be called the Middle Kingdom
(*chūka*).[16]

Sokō had upended Sinocentrism to his own satisfaction, using Confucian categories to validate Japanese worth. His was not the last word,
however, and during the eighteenth century the debate continued, with
charges of ethnocentric obscurantism and Sinophilic abasement flying
back and forth as scholars staked out their turf and argued their cases.

As these paragraphs suggest, the naturalization of Confucianism was
accompanied by the elucidation of Japan's own legacy. The process had
several facets, and one can argue that they culminated near century's
end in the literary scholarship of the Buddhist monk Keichū. One such
facet (noted in chapter 6) was the publishing and study of ancient literature and art, which with the imperial court's encouragement continued throughout the century (as discussed more fully in chapter 10).
Cumulatively that work yielded splendid new scrolls of the *Genji monogatari,* numerous representations of Ariwara no Narihira, the perfect
lover and celebrated poet of the *Ise monogatari,* and beautiful poem-
pictures of the poetry—the 31-syllable waka in particular—of the classic poets Fujiwara no Teika and Ki no Tsurayuki.

A second facet of this revitalized interest in the Japanese legacy was
historical study, and here the most notable work of the Tokugawa heyday was Tokugawa Mitsukuni's celebration of the imperial line, *Dai
Nihon shi,* which was written in literary Chinese, infused with Confucian principles, inspired by Chinese historiographical precedents, and
organized in the manner of dynastic histories. Its purpose was "to in-

16. The quotations from Yamaga are taken, with stylistic modifications, from Shuzo
Uenaka, "Last Testament in Exile: Yamaga Sokō's *Haisho Zampitsu,*" *MN* 32-2 (Summer 1977): 147–48. See also Harootunian, "Functions of China," pp. 13–16, for a discussion of these passages. Earl, *Emperor and Nation,* pp. 42–51, discusses Sokō's views
on Japan at some length.

dicate the legitimate emperors of Japan and to exemplify the proper attitude of subjects toward the imperial house," thus consolidating the historiographical tradition that claimed for the Japanese imperial lineage a unique function as "the embodiment, mystic or symbolic, of Japanese society and nationhood."[17]

A third facet of this retrospective interest was the study of Shintō, which Razan, Ansai, and so many other Confucian scholars promoted. The rituals of Shintō religious practice also underwent resuscitation and standardization at the hands of such Yoshida Shintō scholars as Yoshikawa Koretaru. His association with Hoshina Masayuki led, as earlier noted, to the bakufu order of 1665 that all priests who maintain Shintō shrines be certified as competent in Yoshida principles and practices.

These several strands of nativist revival came together in 1690 in a major poetic commentary, the Manyō daishoki, produced by Keichū at the behest of Mitsukuni.[18] Born a cadet son of an Amagasaki han samurai in 1640, Keichū made his career in the priesthood, becoming chief priest of the Myōhōji, a Shingon temple in Osaka. Because of his knowledge of classical waka, Mitsukuni asked him to prepare a commentary on the Man'yōshū. Keichū accepted the task and through careful philology tried to penetrate the many obscurities of the ancient poems and reveal their true meaning. He brought to the job a belief that the kami Susanoo, unruly brother of the sun goddess, Amaterasu, created the waka poetic form and the conviction that readers of the Man'yōshū must "try to forget the spirit of your own age and enter into the spirit of ancient man." He described primordial Japan in this way:

> Japan is the land of the gods. Therefore in both our histories and our government we have given priority to the gods and always placed man second. In high antiquity our rulers governed this land exclusively by means of Shinto. Since it was not only a naive and simple but an unlettered age as well, there was only the oral tradition which they called "Shinto," and there was no philosophizing of the sort one finds in Confucian classics and Buddhist writing.

The ideas were not original with Keichū, but by linking them to careful poetic scholarship, he enhanced their credibility, and they became central themes of national learning (kokugaku) as it developed in later centuries.

17. Herschel Webb, "What Is the Dai Nihon Shi?" JAS 19-2 (Feb. 1960): 135, 139.
18. This topic is skillfully explored in Peter Nosco, "Keichū (1640–1701) Forerunner of National Learning," Asian Thought and Society 5-1 (Dec. 1980): 237–52. The following two quotations are from p. 244.

By the end of the seventeenth century, then, scholars had revitalized the domestic intellectual legacy and used it to make Confucian thought acceptable to Japan, thus establishing precedents for the later adoption and adaptation of other alien ideas. At the same time, they had created a basis for repudiation of Sinocentrism and, beyond that, repudiation of any body of "foreign" ideas.

TWO NOTABLE INTELLECTUALS

The patterns here imposed on seventeenth-century thought—creating an intelligentsia, legitimizing the regime, justifying samurai privilege, naturalizing Confucian thought, and elucidating the native legacy—may seem apparent in retrospect, but scholars at the time did not see themselves as bit players in such scenarios. Rather, they were individuals coping with the exigencies of their lives. As thinkers, they wrestled with the particulars of the text or comment under consideration and strove to "correct" the "misunderstandings" they encountered. Their analyses and criticisms were highly idiosyncratic because the subject matter was amenable to creative manipulation and because each scholar's interpretation was shaped by the circumstances of his life and the texts he was studying.

Select aspects of the lives and thought of major scholars—Hayashi Razan, Kumazawa Banzan, Yamaga Sokō, and Yamazaki Ansai in particular—have appeared in the preceding pages, but such fragmentary treatment conveys no coherent sense of their lives as individuals. Two other scholars—Nakae Tōju and Itō Jinsai—may well have been less influential in their own day, but their reputations endured and their influence on later generations was substantial. Brief scrutiny of their careers will reveal in a somewhat more orderly fashion the tenor of scholarly lives in seventeenth-century Japan.

NAKAE TŌJU

Born in 1608, Nakae Tōju was among the very first of the century's distinguished Confucian scholars. He also was one of the first to criticize Hayashi Razan, doing so nearly two decades before Yamazaki Ansai took up the cudgel. Born to a peasant woman in the province of Ōmi, Tōju was adopted as a child by his grandfather, a samurai in the employ of the Ōzu han on Shikoku.[19] In his schooling at Ōzu, Tōju learned Ch'eng-Chu thought, and in 1632, as a rigorous proponent of Chu Hsi, he attacked Razan for wearing Buddhist garb when teaching Confucianism in his new school at Shinobugaoka:

> Hayashi Dōshun [Razan] has a very good memory and is a man of erudition. Yet in preaching the Way of Confucius, he vainly embellishes his words. Also in imitation of the way of the Buddhists, he has had his head shaved and has abandoned his family duties. He has left the right way and does not follow it. He is what Chu Hsi called a parrot that speaks well.[20]

Whether this attack on Razan created problems for Tōju or simply reflected broader dissatisfactions is unclear, but two years later he resigned his samurai status and returned to his mother's home on the western shore of Lake Biwa. There he busied himself studying and writing about philosophy, medicine, and other topics. From 1634 until his death, he taught there, most of his students being samurai from the region, others coming from the vicinity of Ōzu, and a few from elsewhere.

In time Tōju's fervor for Chu Hsi cooled, perhaps because the stable social hierarchy envisioned by Ch'eng-Chu thought seemed to restrict social mobility and hinder unemployed scholars such as himself.[21] Finding that Chu Hsi's "prescribed modes of conduct were often out of harmony with the times and circumstances," he extended his reading to other classics and the works of more recent scholars. He was most influenced by writings that followed the views of the Ming scholar-official Wang Yang-ming (Ōyōmei), which Tōju came to embrace during the 1640s. Following the Ming scholars, Tōju gave priority to ch'i, rather than li, which put him at fundamental philosophical odds with adherents of Ch'eng-Chu, such as Razan and Ansai.

Furthermore, the Ming interpretations valued intuitive insight and were less formalistic, more mystical and nonrational, and more attentive to individual human nature than those of the Ch'eng-Chu school. In a critique of Chu Hsi's followers, Tōju wrote:

19. An old but still serviceable summary of Tōju's life is Galen M. Fisher, "Nakae Tōju, the Sage of Ōmi," in *TASJ* 36-1 (1908): 25–94. A more recent exploration of his thought is Yamashita Ryūji, "Nakae Tōju's Religious Thought and Its Relation to 'Jitsugaku,'" in de Bary and Bloom, eds., *Principle and Practicality*, pp. 307–30. It is unclear whether Tōju's father was a casualty of the postwar demobilization.

20. Minamoto, "Jitsugaku and Empirical Rationalism," p. 388.

21. The following quotations are taken from Yamashita, "Nakae Tōju's Religious Thought," pp. 309, 314, 317, 320.

Not understanding that the Way exists in their own minds, men recognize as the Way only the laws laid down by the sage kings of old or deeds carried out by the sages and excellent individuals; they define the good in terms of conventions frequently observed in society; they affirm as true principle the modes of reasoning that are current in society. And since men exert themselves to correct their minds and cultivate their bodies according to these codes and conventions and reasonings, the original, active mind which can adapt spontaneously to circumstances is correspondingly diminished.

Far better, he argued, "to follow the course which is appropriate to the time, the place, and one's own lot—this is what is good."

Tōju may have seen his teachings as particularly useful because they called for conduct to fit the day, and thus be practical, but they also constituted a challenge to the Hayashi school. His early attack on Razan, if known in Edo, surely invited retaliation, and some later aspects of his teaching made him even more vulnerable to criticism. As his thinking evolved, he broke with Razan and Ansai in his attitude toward Buddhism. Where they denounced it, he subsumed it and all other teachings within his own, holding that "all men who dwell in the world—the sages and wise men, Sakyamuni and Bodhidharma, Confucians and Buddhists, myself and other men—are the descendants of the August High Lord [Huang Shang-ti]." Furthermore, he said, "the great man regards Heaven, earth, and the myriad things as one body. He regards the world as one family and the country as one person." One of his disciples reported of Tōju that in 1641, after reading a recent work by a late Ming scholar,

> he was moved by the new views found in this work, and on the first day of every month he purified his body and worshipped T'ai-i shen, the great original god who created the myriad things. In ancient times the Son of Heaven worshipped Heaven and there were no ceremonies of worshipping Heaven for the literati or common people. But Tōju regarded this ceremony as the way the literati and common people could worship Heaven.

In his teachings Tōju offered a challenging alternative to Razan and Ansai, one that could be seen as erosive of the established hierarchical order. A suspicious critic could even associate his view with the proscribed Christian teaching about a transcendent God to whom one must pray and owe allegiance. Tōju's untimely death in 1648 while Iemitsu still lived may well have spared him the painful consequences of his erudition. His student Kumazawa Banzan, as noted earlier, fared less well.

ITŌ JINSAI

Nearly alone among seventeenth-century scholars of note, Itō Jinsai was born into a merchant family, made no pretensions to samurai status, and never engaged in political life. In a sense he was the purest of the century's philosophers, approaching his study, not as a way to assist the rulers or advance his family, but as a way to promote insight into existence itself. He is remembered for his seminal role in the formation of ancient learning (*kogaku*) as a coherent line of thought and as founder of the Kogidō, one of Tokugawa Japan's most influential schools.

Jinsai was born in 1627, the eldest son in a Kyoto merchant family that had for some years engaged in lumber marketing. With the general slowing of construction work by the 1620s, the business fell on hard times, and his family abandoned it. The family also included physicians, however, and as future head of his lineage, young Jinsai was encouraged to study medicine. When instead he began studying Confucianism at the school of Matsunaga Sekigo, his kinsmen pressured him to stop. In Jinsai's words, they warned that "Confucianism would not make me any money and that medicine would be more profitable. But their advice fell on deaf ears, and I never did as they advised. Yet they never stopped admonishing me and were unrelenting in their criticism."[22] Alienated from his family, Jinsai left home, deriving solace from Ch'eng-Chu studies, which he supplemented with readings in Buddhist and Taoist texts.

From the early 1660s on, his mood and his family relationships both improved. His family evidently accepted his career choice, and he returned home and began teaching Confucian thought to a small study group that shortly became formalized as the Kogidō. By then his wish to affirm the legitimacy of human feelings by situating them in original human nature had caused him to grow dissatisfied with basic aspects of Chu Hsi's thought and to pursue his studies more eclectically. During several years of intellectual searching, he read works by Wang Yang-ming and other Ming scholars and subsequently the classics themselves.

His scholarly efforts culminated in 1666 in his major written work, *Gomō jigi,* in which he asserted that the basis of the cosmos was not an

---

22. Quoted in Samuel Hideo Yamashita, "The Early Life and Thought of Itō Jinsai," *HJAS* 43-2 (Dec. 1983): 457. See also the old but useful work by Joseph John Spae, *Itō Jinsai,* Monumenta Serica, no. 12 (Peking: Catholic University of Peking, 1948), pp. 82ff. On pp. 209–12, Spae lists Jinsai's publications, identifying their dates of composition where possible.

unchanging principle, li, as followers of Chu Hsi held, but dynamic material force, ch'i, which made the Way a "ceaseless movement of the coming and going of the two forces, yin and yang."[23] Moreover, he used philological techniques to argue that the corrupting influence "of Buddhist and Taoist quietism—the suppression of natural desires and the immobilizing of the will in the process of achieving a single-minded concentration on the original nature" had caused later scholars to misunderstand the meaning of the ancients.[24]

That analysis, which resonated with the broader anti-Buddhist criticisms of the day, asserted the illegitimacy of Sung-Ming opinion and freed Jinsai to seek his own understanding of the original Confucian texts. In 1673, in the short essay Dōjimon, he cleanly juxtaposed his own view of ch'i as basic against Chu Hsi's li, which he relegated to a posterior or secondary role: "In living things, there is the principle of living things. In dead things, there is the principle of dead things. In man, there is the principle of man. In things, there are the principles of things. But a single primal material force is the basis, and principle is posterior to material force."[25] In Dōjimon, Jinsai also continued his attack on Buddhism and Taoism, charging that they ultimately "lead to the abandonment of human relations and the discarding of all decorum and good taste. This is the way of deviation and heterodoxy."

Jinsai directed a more frontal attack against Ch'eng-Chu scholars, denouncing their emphasis on reverence and seriousness as "a deadening, life-denying attitude." They take, he wrote, "a cautious and calculating, inch-by-inch, pinch-penny attitude toward things. They are restrained and reserved, lest they give anyone the chance to find so much as a minuscule fault in their behavior. Therefore they are severely handicapped in their own power to do good, and they cannot appreciate magnanimity in others or a warm open-heartedness."[26] Far better, he asserted, to be like the ancients, who "did not neglect the investigation of the principles of things, . . . [but] considered cultivating the self and governing the people as the main tasks of learning." Such practical tasks require, he asserted, not quiet meditation on principle, but active engagement with daily reality. "When it is ordinary, it is real. When it is

23. The words are those of Minamoto, "Jitsugaku and Empirical Rationalism," p. 436.
24. Wm. Theodore de Bary, "Sagehood as a Secular and Spiritual Ideal in Tokugawa Neo-Confucianism," in de Bary and Bloom, eds., Principle and Practicality, pp. 149–50. The phrasing is de Bary's.
25. Minamoto, "Jitsugaku and Empirical Rationalism," p. 446, quoting Dōjimon.
26. De Bary, "Sagehood as a Secular and Spiritual Ideal," pp. 148, 151.

lofty, it is surely empty. Therefore learning does not scorn the ordinary and the familiar." And success in undertaking practical tasks, which depends on ability, requires one to cultivate not proper appearances but "humaneness," which Jinsai defined as a "mind of compassionate love." Doing so will eliminate "even the smallest hint of cruelness or cold-heartedness." And that outcome constitutes real virtue and will lead one to success because, "when real virtue exists, then real talent follows."[27]

Talent, and hence the potential to succeed, was thus a quality that everyone could nurture. That egalitarian predilection helped Jinsai "naturalize" Confucian thought.[28] Citing Confucius creatively, he argued in 1683 that the sage had wished to leave China for Japan in the belief that it was a less decadent land. Although a barbarian tribe, the Japanese could be civilized because, as Jinsai interpreted Confucius, "no matter where under Heaven or where on earth [they may live], *all men are equally men.* Even a barbarian, if he but possesses ritual and righteousness, is a part of the Middle Kingdom. Even a Chinese, should he lack ritual and righteousness, cannot escape being barbarian." Jinsai combined that proposition with the prevailing notion of Japan's long and unbroken imperial line to assert Japan's superior adherence to Confucian virtue. Whereas Chinese dynasties had come and gone, he wrote, "here in Japan the statuses of sovereign and minister have been strictly upheld down to the present day. We revere our sovereigns as though they were Heaven, and we honor them as though they were divinities. Truly, in this respect China is not our equal." In short, Japan was a worthy realm and the wisdom to be gleaned from Chinese sources was entirely appropriate to it.

Despite personal misfortunes, including his wife's death, a fire that destroyed his home and library, and the deaths of his parents, which required three years' mourning, by the 1680s Jinsai had established a substantial reputation as a helpful teacher and original scholar. His monist perspective based on ch'i provided a foundation for addressing to his own satisfaction that "quintessentially practical question—how best to experience virtue." One did so not by "sitting in disciplined meditation or searching for the principle underlying all things," as Ch'eng-Chu

27. From *Dōjimon,* as quoted in Minamoto, "Jitsugaku and Empirical Rationalism," pp. 434, 439, 446–47.
28. The two following quotations come from Bob Tadashi Wakabayashi, *Anti-Foreignism and Western Learning in Early Modern Japan* (Cambridge, Mass.: Harvard University Press, 1986), pp. 25, 26. Italics in original.

thought prescribed, but by the active, practical "nourishment" of virtue.[29] His writings began to circulate, and the Kogidō flourished, with its enrollment expanding sharply to exceed two hundred names during the 1680s. The majority were townsmen, primarily merchants and doctors, and most of the other students were samurai, with enrollees coming from all over the country.[30]

During the 1660s, despite his forthright criticism of the proponents of Ch'eng-Chu, Jinsai had not, like Banzan and Sokō, attracted nervous government attention, perhaps because he was a merchant-scholar who mostly taught merchants and said little about the martial arts. By 1683, however, his fame was so great that he was finally asked to submit to the authorities material explaining his opinions. He presented a revised version of Dōjimon, but officials evidently found nothing to censure and he continued to flourish, remaining an esteemed mentor until his death in 1705.

Upon Jinsai's death, the Kogidō was taken over by his mature son Tōgai, who had a much richer sense of family mission than his father. In one of Japan's most successful exercises in filial piety Tōgai compiled a formidable library of his father's writings, prepared an intellectual biography of him, and maintained the Kogidō as a bastion of Ancient Learning, thus preserving a remarkably complete legacy of Jinsai's works for future generations and sustaining the family legacy to an extent that Razan would surely have envied.

As these brief comments and biographical sketches suggest, from about 1630 on, Tokugawa intellectuals began producing a body of scholarship that helped consolidate the regime and entrench the ruling bushi class, even as it enriched Japan's philosophical legacy. From the beginning that body of learning embraced conflicting formulations, and as the century progressed and new perspectives were introduced, the range of interpretation broadened, a trend that was to continue during later centuries.

Seventeenth-century thinkers established a philosophical foundation for two basic political propositions: that the established bakuhan system was legitimate and that the hereditary samurai caste—and all lower castes—had worthy peacetime functions that required each to recognize and adhere to its place. By its nature, society was an integral structure,

29. Yamashita, "Early Life and Thought of Itō Jinsai," pp. 474–75, 478–79.
30. Rubinger, Private Academies, pp. 53–56.

with its parts all essential to one another's well-being, but with the several parts unequal in value and hence deserving of unequal treatment. This organic vision of society as a coherent structure consisting of separate and unequal parts underlay legislation and determined how the rulers allocated scarce goods. In our own day, differences in "function," which putatively reflect differences in "merit," are invoked to justify socioeconomic inequality, whereas in seventeenth-century Japan differences in "function" that were determined by birth or adoption served the same purpose of securing the privileges of the superordinate few.

In that ideology of stratification, however, the way social tasks had been assigned meant that economic functions devolved upon the mercantile elite, and therein lay a slowly growing problem for the rulers. Although they viewed politics as primary, economics had by the end of the century emerged as a crucial determinant of social process, and that trend empowered merchants, even though the empowerment was illegitimate. *Chōnin,* members of the merchant class, acquired a sense of self-esteem commensurate with their economic worth, and that esteem began to be reflected not only in the writings of men such as Itō Jinsai but even more so in the other main element of seventeenth-century culture, the *ukiyo,* or "floating world," culture of townsmen.

TEN

Aesthetics and the Rise of *Ukiyo*

Aesthetics of the Elite
  Garden Architecture
  Painting
The Rise of *Ukiyo* Culture
  Printing
  Theater
  Poetry
  Prose
  Art
Genroku Arts and Letters
  Ihara Saikaku and *Ukiyo Zōshi*
  Chikamatsu Monzaemon and Genroku Drama

The decades of pacification, as noted in chapter 6, embodied conflicting tendencies in regard to cultural creativity. On the one hand, peace and prosperity encouraged a burst of cultural activity; on the other, Japan's rulers moved, especially after 1600, to guide elite culture and discipline the masses, doing their best to channel the creative impulses of society. In a general sense, the channeling bore fruit, at least for a while: uplifting arts and letters were promoted, theater was disciplined, prostitution was contained, and feared religious creeds were suppressed. As the century advanced and cities blossomed, however, cultural creativity flourished despite the outpouring of sumptuary rules and the ideological rhetoric of scholar-advisors. By century's end, a vibrant *ukiyo*, or "floating world," culture was setting the tone of urban life.

It is tempting to think of this ukiyo culture as a culture of the urban merchant, or *chōnin*, class and to juxtapose it to the samurai class culture that rulers and ideologues sought to establish. In fact, however, the segregation of elite and commoner—or "feudal" and "bourgeois"—culture remained largely stillborn. A number of factors militated against their segregation, of which three deserve specific note: the seminal cultural role of Kyoto, the complexity of social stratification, and the emergence of a gentlemanly ideal that transcended class lines.

Throughout the seventeenth century, Kyoto remained not only the home of courtly cultural production but also the center of samurai intellectual activity, as noted in the preceding chapter. In addition, it was the city where ukiyo culture flourished most vibrantly until near century's end.[1] In Kyoto, therefore, the philosophy, literature, art, and drama of courtier, samurai, and merchant constantly interplayed. During the later decades of the century, Osaka began draining off Kyoto's industry, and as it did, cultural production also migrated downriver, extending the old city's cosmopolitanism to a major entrepôt, from whence it diffused through the realm. The Osaka taste that arose was reputed to be more mercantile and frugal than Kyoto's, but the two cities were close enough to permit constant interaction, creating a cultural identity reflected in the name "Kamigata," which treats the Kyoto-Osaka region as an entity, distinct from Edo. As people from Kamigata took employment in Edo and other castle towns, they spread the socially diffuse Kyoto·culture across the country.

Higher culture's capacity to transcend social boundaries was also facilitated by the actual structure of society, which was far more involuted than an indigenized Confucian four-caste theory could represent, to say nothing of a European two-class theory. Courtiers, priests, physician-scholar-teachers, and pariahs fitted into none of the stock categories, and each of the four major castes (*shi-nō-kō-shō*) was itself a variegated grouping that lacked any basis for internal coherence. The richest chōnin had more wealth—and hence more capacity to nurture cultural skills and acquire elegant artifacts—than most daimyo. And many people of middling merchant stature, as well as the most substantial landholding villagers, were better off than all but the higher strata of samurai. The lowest levels of samurai were men who retained their petty positions and incomes, but who led lives more similar to those of marginally employed commoners than to the ruling elite's. In addition, for much of the century, Japan contained a population of ronin fami-

---

1. In his essay on "Popular Culture" in *The Cambridge History of Japan,* vol. 4, *Early Modern Japan,* ed. John W. Hall (Cambridge: Cambridge University Press, 1991), pp. 706–69, Donald Shively examines the important cultural role of Kyoto.

lies, many of which struggled to reenter the noble estate but ended up as common folk.

Finally, there emerged a gentlemanly ideal that enabled cultural norms to transcend the ruler-ruled (or feudal-bourgeois) distinction. The scholarly expression of that ideal was the "savant" or physician-scholar-teacher mentioned in chapter 9; an analogous cultural persona, the devotee of *yūgei,* or "polite accomplishments," appeared among the aesthetically oriented. To explain, Tokugawa ideology grouped higher cultural attainments in two categories, *bu* and *bun,* military and civil (or literary) arts, and admonished samurai to cultivate both. They were urged to perfect a particular civil skill, but were expected to show some interest in *bun* more generally. And *bun* embraced reading and writing, Chinese thought, poetry, history and literature, nō dance and drama, tea ceremony, and diverse other customary upper-class arts. As the century advanced, this ideal of the broadly cultured samurai evolved into an ideal, identified by the term *yūgei,* that embraced commoners as well as samurai.

The overlap between *bun* and *yūgei* is evident in this list, prepared sometime before 1685, of skills that an urban gentleman was expected to cultivate: "Cultural activities cover many fields, and so medicine, poetry, the tea ceremony, music, the hand drum, the nō dance, etiquette, the appreciation of craft work, arithmetic and calculation are all included, not to mention literary composition, reading and writing. There are other things as well."[2] Unsurprisingly, since the samurai ideal itself clearly owed much to the classic ideals of Chinese and Japanese civil aristocracy, the flowering of yūgei was most visible in Kyoto. There teachers of calligraphy, tea ceremony, music, dance, and various games joined doctors, scholars, poets, and artists in disseminating their tastes and skills to learners of diverse backgrounds. As epitomized by Suminokura Soan, Tōfukumon'in, and the resident artists of Takagamine, wealthy merchants came into contact with kuge, aesthetes, and the culturally oriented samurai who gravitated to the city. Although the codes of merchant households warned against indulging in them, aesthetic pursuits remained a popular venue for contact across status lines, and yūgei had become entrenched as a widely held urban ideal by century's end.

Under these several influences, cultural alignments cut across the categories of "feudal" and "bourgeois," or samurai-peasant-artisan-

2. Moriya Takeshi, "*Yūgei* and *Chōnin* Society in the Edo Period," *AA* 33 (1977): 38–39.

merchant, the rhetoric of Confucian ideologues notwithstanding. Admittedly, if one looks at the very top of the elite—the households of shogun, daimyo, and senior kuge, and the temples of major prelates—one can identify a culture of tasteful elegance that stood apart from the daily-life culture of the rest of society, if only because its cost denied it to lesser folk or its esoteric quality restricted its appeal to connoisseurs. But even there one can see the insidious role of Kyoto shaping the character and content of higher culture and obfuscating the boundaries of ruler and ruled that shogun, daimyo, and their apologists labored with such dedication to maintain.

AESTHETICS OF THE ELITE

The creativity, splendor, and display of Azuchi-Momoyama culture persisted for decades, evolving by midcentury into a more mannered and less imaginative culture of elegant discipline and correctness. The trend was evident in many areas: for example, the highborn continued practicing the tea ceremony, but it and its utensils became more formal and refined. They continued staging nō dramas, but by Ietsuna's day, both tea ceremony and nō were marks of good breeding, not vehicles of creative expression. The trend toward stylization and domesticity was particularly evident in construction and decoration, most notably in the proliferation of landscape gardens. Only in selected areas, decorative painting most famously, did the seventeenth-century elite continue to produce cultural accomplishments of distinction.

A second trend, the spreading awareness of Japan's courtly legacy, also merits note here. As foreshadowed in the Saga books, seventeenth-century Kyoto experienced a "neoclassical" revival, particularly in painting, as aesthetes celebrated the glorious attainments of ancient aristocratic culture. They restored old court ceremonies, republished books, and produced works of art that celebrated ancient accomplishments. Because courtly and mercantile elites mingled so freely in the city's aesthetic life, the revival introduced classical arts and letters to a wider public, giving that cultural legacy, and the imperial court with which it was inextricably linked, an appreciably broader metropolitan base. Moreover, because of Kyoto's continuing cultural dominance, the influence of this revival reached beyond Kamigata to Edo and the hinterland.

This Kyoto-centered artistic production had several effects. It reinforced the Shintō scholarship that fostered the later rise of *kokugaku* (national learning), with its emphasis on the centrality of the imperial

institution to Japan's political culture. It elevated the aesthetic standards of yūgei, paving the way for the ideal of the *bunjin,* or cultural
adept, that emerged later in the eighteenth century, as subsequent chapters report. And it added another sparkling segment to the cumulative
legacy of Japanese civilization. More pertinent to this chapter, it contributed artistic polish to the popular ukiyo culture that emerged as the
seventeenth century advanced.

GARDEN ARCHITECTURE

The bombastic building projects of Azuchi-Momoyama evolved by the
1630s, as mentioned in chapter 6, into the rococo architecture of the
Nikkō Tōshōgū and daimyo mansions in Edo. Nikkō has survived, but
the Meireki fire consumed most of the mansions, and a combination of
timber scarcity and fiscal dearth resulted in less elegant replacement
construction.

Lacking the resources for monumental construction, daimyo turned
to landscape architecture to display their status and cultural polish.
Walking gardens, which required little timber but much tasteful planning and manual labor, could demonstrate cultural polish because of
Japan's sophisticated tradition of landscape design, which had been
nurtured during the Momoyama period and was being sustained and
enriched by projects such as the Katsura villa. As sankin kōtai became
systematized, lords everywhere enhanced the pleasantness of mansion
life by laying out elaborate decorative gardens in their compounds, both
at Edo and in their castle towns.

One of the first major landscaping projects in Edo was a garden laid
out during the 1630s by Ieyasu's son, Yorifusa, the lord of Mito. Other
gardens followed as landscaping became a regular element of mansion
decor, but in 1657 the Meireki fire destroyed the structures in several
of them, including Yorifusa's. Within twelve years his son and successor, Mitsukuni, had reconstructed the garden with advice from the émigré
scholar Chu Shun-shui. They produced an elaborate 25-hectare (63-
acre) layout that included "a lake with walks, stone lanterns, arched
stone bridges and trees, all arranged skillfully in harmony with their
surroundings. There were also miniature imitations of noted Japanese
and Chinese scenic beauties, including the West Lake of Hangchow and
Mount Lu of Kiangsi."[3] Mitsukuni named his garden Kōrakuen, taking

3. Julia Ching, "The Practical Learning of Chu Shun-shui (1600–1682)," in Wm.
Theodore de Bary and Irene Bloom, eds., *Principle and Practicality: Essays in Neo-*

the name from a noted essay by a Sung dynasty statesman. His "garden of later pleasures" survived into the twentieth century, and a much diminished version can still be seen today.

One of the last fine gardens to be laid out near Edo was the lovely Rikugien, "Garden of the Six Virtues." Rikugien was a quiet retreat built north of the city in 1695 for Yanagisawa Yoshiyasu, the favorite advisor of that most Confucian of shoguns, Tsunayoshi.[4] Even more handsome gardens appeared in the great castle towns: Rakurakuen at Hikone in 1665, Kenrokuen at Kanazawa around 1680, Kōrakuen at Okayama in 1686, and other splendid products of the landscape architect's art at Kumamoto, Nagoya, Takamatsu, and scores of other castles about the countryside.

Surely the construction of these elegant gardens, which so thoroughly mocked the original military function of the castles they adjoined, was a measure of how fully the great lords had come to accept the Tokugawa civil order's claim to permanence. In the spirit of that order, moreover, the gardens helped separate rulers and ruled by providing the former with gracious space in which to live out their lives, safely sheltered from the masses crowded into surrounding city blocks.

PAINTING

As grand construction waned, officially sanctioned art was also scaled down, in the process becoming more polished and less vibrant. One can argue that this art, like domesticated castles, fostered a peaceful civil order, but where walking gardens distanced rulers from the ruled, art bridged the gap between them. In the words of Robert Treat Paine, its purpose, "was to ennoble man, to illustrate models of conduct, to serve in the purpose of good government, and to suggest virtues symbolically."[5] Much of the painting originated in Kyoto, and its influence reached well beyond the ruling elite, obscuring the cultural distinction between ruler and ruled, even as it provided images of order and righteousness.

Confucianism and Practical Learning (New York: Columbia University Press, 1979), p. 202.

4. The present-day Rikugien is approximately half the size of the original. Its name translates as something like "six virtues" or "righteous land," depending on the character used for *riku*.

5. Robert Treat Paine and Alexander Soper, *The Art and Architecture of Japan* (London: Penguin Books, 1974), p. 107. Paine's comment on Tan'yū quoted in the following paragraph is from p. 106.

During the heyday of Hideyoshi and Ieyasu, the dominant pictorial art had been the great murals and screens of the Kanō school, which decorated castles and mansions, and the bright but highly mannered paintings of the Tosa school, as used to illustrate the Saga books. The grand decorative tradition of Momoyama continued for a time, as suggested by the dragons that Kanō Tan'yū painted for the Yōmeimon at Nikkō around 1636. But by then decorative art had become more disciplined, the bold, sweeping brush strokes of Eitoku giving way to more graphic, romantic, and delicate treatments. Even in Tan'yū's work one can see that "the artistic freedom of the Momoyama age is a thing of the past, and elegance and dignity have succeeded gorgeousness and boldness." The elegance of Tan'yū's work is self-evident; the dignity is implicit in his painting of such subjects as *Confucius and Two Disciples,* which celebrates the virtues of reverence and filial piety.

Tan'yū settled in Edo as an official painter for the bakufu, working from there on such projects as Nagoya and Nijō castles. Kyoto remained the center of artistic life, however, and other members of the Kanō school, as well as Tosa artists, flourished there, producing screens and smaller works for aristocratic, military, religious, and mercantile patrons.

Many of these artists were associated with Hon'ami Kōetsu's artist colony at Takagamine, which drew on both the Kanō and Tosa traditions and produced ever more works for wealthy commoners. Besides the Saga books, Kōetsu and his collaborator Tawaraya Sōtatsu (who remained in Kyoto) created innumerable "poem squares" (*shikishi*) and poem scrolls, such as the delicately elegant *Deer Scroll,* on which Sōtatsu's painting served essentially as backdrop for Kōetsu's calligraphy. When Kōetsu died in 1637, and his major collaborators not long afterward, Takagamine's heyday ended. However, the merchant-artist group associated with it remained active for several more decades, benefiting from the patronage of the retired emperor Gomizuno-o and his wife, Tōfukumon-in, whose Edo connections helped support the court's artistic ventures until her death in 1678.[6]

The artists around Kyoto drew heavily on Japan's past for stylistic inspiration and thematic material: for example, stories of famous monks, warriors, and literati, the *Genji monogatari,* incidents in the Genpei

6. Information on Takagamine can be found in Masahiko Kawabara, *The Ceramic Art of Ogata Kenzan* (Tokyo: Kodansha, 1979); Hiroshi Mizuo, *Edo Painting: Sōtatsu and Kōrin* (New York: Weatherhill, 1972); and Bernard Leach, *Kenzan and His Tradition* (London: Faber & Faber, 1966).

7. Kanō Tan'yū, *Confucius at the Apricot Altar and His Two Disciples*. A set of three panels; ink and color on silk; each 104.2 x 74.8 cm. Confucius, seated beneath a flowering apricot tree, his face heavy with wisdom, speaks to reverent disciples from his raised platform. Courtesy of the Museum of Fine Arts, Boston. Fenollosa-Weld Collection. Acc. #11.4399–4401.

wars of the twelfth century, and powerful religious images, both Buddhist and Shintō. Two classics enjoyed especial popularity, the *Ise monogatari* and *Shinkokinshū*.[7] The *Ise* was a tenth-century poetic narrative of Ariwara no Narihira, paragon of virtue and ideal Heian lover. The first Saga book was a new edition of the *Ise,* and it provided motifs for paintings, textiles, and lacquer ware, making imagery of ancient court life a common part of refined culture. The *Shinkokinshū* was an elegant poetic collection by Fujiwara no Teika, who also collated the definitive version of the *Ise*. Artists produced sets of poem scrolls and shikishi as decorative and illustrative contexts for calligraphic presentations of Teika's poems, making the combined poem-painting a dominant artistic form.

Inspired by these and other classics, artists produced works whose stylish elegance has come to define Kyoto taste. Representative is a pair of six-panel screens, *Teika's Poems on Flowers and Birds of the Twelve Months*—one of twenty treatments of that topic—painted in the 1690s by Yamamoto Soken, the son of a Kanō-style artist. Soken painted the twelve panels and placed at the top of each a seasonally appropriate poem by Teika as written by one of twelve court nobles noted for their calligraphy.[8]

This artistic output, which became part of the yūgei repertoire, transformed the courtly aesthetic into the property of a much broader public, thereby spreading and consolidating public awareness of Japan's cultural legacy and suggesting that one could find in it inspiration for the present. The works established a close linkage between that legacy and the imperial court and thus broadened public consciousness of the imperial heritage, even as the bakufu worked to minimize the court's social visibility and political influence.

Of Kōetsu's many successors, the most influential was Ogata Kōrin, born in 1658. Kōrin's sixteenth-century ancestors had been warriors, but his grandfather went into business as a dry-goods merchant, becoming an official purveyor to Hidetada's government in Edo, and from the 1620s on serving as dressmaker to Tōfukumon'in. Thanks to her wardrobe purchases, the Ogata textile business flourished, and Kōrin's father could afford to become an artist and join the colony at Takagamine.

---

7. The material in these two paragraphs is based on the essays in Carolyn Wheelwright, ed., *Word in Flower: The Visualization of Classical Literature in Seventeenth-Century Japan* (New Haven: Yale University Art Gallery, 1989), and on the exhibit that accompanied its publication.

8. Ibid., pp. 28, 40–41, 110.

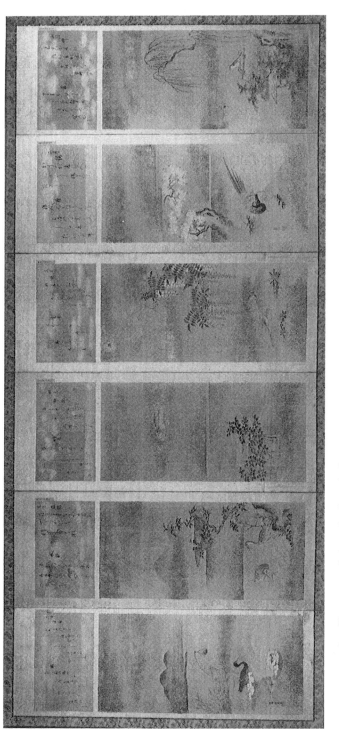

8. Yamamoto Soken, *Birds and Flowers of the Twelve Months*. One of a pair of six-fold screens; in ink and color on paper, with decorated poetry papers inscribed with two poems each. Six-fold screen 5'3" x 12'. In this celebration of classical aesthetics, the six panels starting from the right illustrate poems by Fujiwara no Teika for the first six months of the year; the other six-panel screen completes the series. Courtesy of Yale University Art Gallery, New Haven; The Director's Discretionary Fund, Archer M. Huntington, 1897h, Charles Stetson, B.A. 1900 and Wison R. Foss, Jr. Funds. Acc. #1986.5.1.1.

Kōrin thus grew up exposed to wealth, the aesthetics of luxury textile design, and the artistic traditions of Kōetsu and Sōtatsu.

In the spirit of yūgei, young Kōrin cultivated the many arts of elite culture, including nō, music, and the tea ceremony, and he associated with the finer classes of the city. The Ogata textile business collapsed after Tōfukumon'in's death in 1678, but Kōrin inherited enough wealth to sustain his yūgei style of life for several years. Eventually he had to borrow, however, relying on the generosity of friends and his brother, Kenzan.

Kōrin had studied painting under his father and Yamamoto Soken, and in about 1697 he finally began painting to support himself. His painting income failed to accommodate his luxury-loving taste, however, and in 1704 he went east to Edo in hopes of finding more generous patrons.[9] He was befriended there by a wealthy timber merchant, set himself up in comfortable circumstances again, and in 1707 accepted the daimyo of Himeji (named Sakai) as his patron. Before long, however, he began to chafe at the restrictions of samurai life, and early in 1709 he wrote a friend in Kyoto announcing his intention to return.

> I am sick of Edo. I have no further desire for high life. To be poor gives a man more ease and freedom. I am tired of the restrictions implicit in living as a dependent of the Sakai family. Day and night I am subject to the wishes and habits of my superiors and am not free to go out at nightfall. . . . I see the daily life of feudal lords, but do not envy them. I would not mind being poor if I could be free.[10]

Doubtless Kōrin had discovered the unwelcome constraints that daimyo society imposed on artists, but one suspects that nothing in life had really equipped him to know what being poor would mean. At least, after he frittered away his patrimony some years earlier, he had always been able to borrow when necessary to sustain the life he loved.

Back in Kyoto, Kōrin's painting career reached its apex. His mature works exhibit "a sense of space, of pure design, and a rather soft modeling of forms that was rarely found in Momoyama painting."[11] His most celebrated paintings are elegant landscapes and studies of flowers

9. Yamane Yūzō, "Ogata Kōrin and the Art of the Genroku Era," *AA* 15 (1968): 69–86. Paine and Soper, *Art and Architecture*, p. 117, provide a more colorful explanation of Kōrin's move to Edo.

10. Leach, *Kenzan and His Tradition*, p. 88. Leach gives a translation of a debt agreement Kōrin made in 1694.

11. Doanda Randall, *Kōrin* (New York: Crown, n.d.), p. 5. In fact, Kōrin's work so dominated the decorative painting of his day that scholars refer to the whole decorative tradition as Rinpa art, literally art of the "Kōrin [*rin*] school [*ha*]."

and animals exemplifying the emphasis on stylization and design at the expense of adventuresome originality that emerged during the seventeenth century. Indeed, Kōrin recapitulated most of Sōtatsu's themes, often by the simple expedient of copying the master's work, as in his six-panel screen *Waves at Matsushima,* with its clustering pine boughs, walls of bare rock, and busily rhythmic lines of foam and waves.[12]

When he died in 1716, Kōrin left artistic precedents that influenced generations of painters. His move to Edo helped him propagate his artistic style there, and it also represented a broader trend, in which the center of cultural activity shifted from Kamigata to Edo. That shift, which intensified in the following decades, also became evident in the chōnin-centered ukiyo culture that emerged as the most creative facet of seventeenth-century arts and letters.

THE RISE OF *UKIYO* CULTURE

By Iemitsu's day, government measures to regulate culture had brought most urban leisure pursuits under control. Brothel activity was herded into licensed quarters (*yūkaku*), notably Yoshiwara in Edo (1617), Shinmachi in Osaka (1629), and Shimabara in Kyoto (1641), and an elaborate organization for managing the quarters was rapidly taking shape. In castle towns, the suppression of lascivious entertainment was even more thorough. There the rhythms of peace asserted themselves, and routines of the year, from New Year's celebrations through the Bon festival of midsummer and the numerous other seasonal holidays, became central to the recreational life of commoners.

Restraining recreational excess did not, however, eradicate popular entertainment or its producers. One scholar has described Kyoto's leisure district at midcentury in these terms:

> The Shijō theater area and riverbank was a large amusement center in which kabuki was one of many dozens of diversions. There were smaller playhouses, puppet theaters, and a number of wayside entertainers who recited tales from military epics, the *Taiheiki* and *Heike monogatari.* There were fortune-tellers, dentists, *sumō* wrestlers, jugglers, and tightrope walkers. There were sideshows exhibiting such freaks as the female giant and the armless woman archer. There were exotic animals—tigers, bears, porcupines, eagles and peacocks, performing monkeys and dancing dogs. Teahouses, restaurants, and refreshment stands lined the streets. Paintings of the period show

12. This description of the *Waves at Matsushima* paraphrases Paine and Soper, *Art and Architecture,* pp. 118–19.

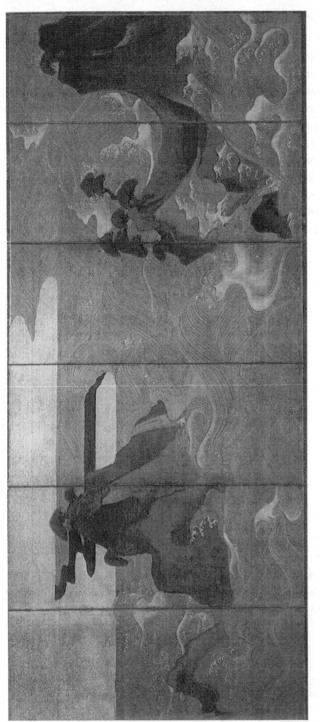

9. Tawaraya Sōtatsu, *Waves at Matsushima*. Color and gold on paper six-fold screen, 152.0 x 355.7 cm. This six-fold screen by Sōtatsu and the one by Kōrin in fig. 10 are the right-hand sets of pairs of screens by the two artists. In Sōtatsu's original version, the waves are less assertive, the color contrasts less sharp, giving a quieter, more fluid sense overall. Kōrin's reprise of the scene offers more dramatic wave and rock formations. Courtesy of Museum of the Freer Gallery of Art, Smithsonian Institution, Washington, D.C. Acc. #06. 31.

10. Ogata Kōrin, *Waves at Matsushima*. Six-panel screen; ink, color, and gold on paper, 154.7 x 369.4 cm. Courtesy of Museum of Fine Arts, Boston; Fenollosa-Weld Collection. Acc. #11.4584.

these establishments crowded together, thronged with people of every description.[13]

While daimyo enjoyed their garden pleasures and the wealthy their poem scrolls and other expressions of yūgei, urban hoi polloi thus pursued a wide range of diversions. Some deserve fuller exploration: theater, literature, and art, and the printing industry that facilitated them.

PRINTING

The printing industry produced the advertisements, theater handbills, librettos, literary works, guidebooks, and artistic prints that linked cultural producer to consumer. As the industry developed during the seventeenth century, printing techniques changed. Most notably, movable type gave way to wood blocks.

In Ieyasu's day, as mentioned earlier, printers utilized movable type, especially in presses of Korean provenance, but wood-block printing later replaced it. Exactly why is uncertain, but blocks had several advantages.[14] Printers could use movable type for text, but it discouraged calligraphic creativity. Movable type also hindered the artistic integration of text and picture that was so valued by literate consumers. Block printing's capacity to combine text and picture enabled printers to reach a readership that ranged from the highly literate to illiterate, and that capacity was crucial for creating a large consumer base. In the Saga books, illustrations were prepared on wooden blocks, while text used movable type, but that procedure required the printer to maintain two complete printing technologies.

From the 1630s on, the use of movable type declined. Printers increasingly employed blocks for the complete production of literary works, whether classics or newly written prose or poetry, and by the 1650s blocks had completely displaced movable type. Prints were black and white, but from the beginning, as in the Saga books, makers embel-

13. Donald H. Shively, "The Social Environment of Tokugawa Kabuki," in James R. Brandon et al., eds., *Studies in Kabuki* (Honolulu: University Press of Hawaii, 1978), p. 11.
14. Donald Keene, *World within Walls* (New York: Grove Press, 1976), pp. 3–4, has attributed "this retrograde step" to the aesthetic inadequacy of movable typeface in representing Japanese script. David Chibbett, *The History of Japanese Printing and Book Illustration* (Tokyo: Kodansha, 1977), p. 78, argues that the cost of maintaining an adequate supply of bronze typeface for multiple publications exceeded the capital resources of publishers. One might add that this likely became a more acute problem after the 1630s as copper coinage came into fashion, which gave the bakufu more reason to control copper production and restrict its use.

lished pictures with splashes of hand-painted color, usually green and orange. This coloring technique continued well into the eighteenth century.

For many purposes, black-and-white prints sufficed. From midcentury on, block printing facilitated the proliferation of travel diaries and gazetteers (*meishoki*) that guided pilgrims and pleasure seekers—often one and the same—to temples, shrines, and other famous places, notably the licensed quarters of the great cities. The six-volume *Kyō warabe*, a guide to Kyoto written in 1658 by the young physician Nakagawa Kiun, was the first of some fifty such guidebooks to appear in the next four decades.[15] Their existence reveals the vitality of the publishing industry and also suggests that the decades of peace and prosperity had made travel safe and given Japan a consumer populace that could afford recreational touring.

The industry continued to grow throughout the century but remained centered in Kyoto. By one calculation, 701 publishers operated there at one time or another before 1700, while 185 appeared in Osaka and 242 in Edo.[16] By Genroku these firms were producing a range and volume of works that dwarfed earlier output. They published summaries, librettos, and commentaries for kabuki and the puppet theater, volumes of poetry, prose, philosophy, and other scholarship, and works of art, design, and advertising. They updated classics, portrayed historical incidents and current events of public interest, offered practical instruction on diverse topics, and transmitted religious teachings and stories of magic and mystery.

THEATER

The two new dramatic forms *ningyō jōruri* (puppet theater) and kabuki were central to the vibrant culture of early Tokugawa cities and became a source of both business and inspiration for printers.[17] By the 1590s, as noted in chapter 6, storytellers were producing skits that combined puppets, stories, and samisen music, and over the next few decades their productions enjoyed widespread popularity. They were not really plays, however, being more like "short works of fiction recited by one or more chanters and mimed by puppets." More interested in scenic description

15. Chibbett, *History of Japanese Printing*, pp. 127–28.
16. Katsuhisa Moriya, "Urban Networks and Information Networks," in Chie Nakane and Shinzaburō Ōishi, eds., *Tokugawa Japan* (Tokyo: University of Tokyo Press, 1990), p. 115.
17. The quoted passages are from Keene, *World within Walls*, pp. 237, 238.

than dialogue, they were literary in intent and enjoyed aristocratic favor. They did not rely on gusto and titillation, so did not run afoul of the censor after 1600, when popular culture was being disciplined and, instead, continued to flourish. By the 1670s, chanters had developed guidelines for technique, principles of performance, and a substantial if undistinguished repertoire of plays.

Kabuki experienced a more hectic passage to maturity. In contrast to early jōruri, early kabuki "consisted of songs and dialogue and relied more on impromptu remarks than on written texts." It was more or less a front for prostitution until edicts issued and reissued for several years after 1629 banned women from the stage. Their ouster left the field open to another recent type of dramatic troupe, *wakashū*, or "youth's" kabuki, which was intimately associated with pederasty. Wakashū kabuki operated for another generation, until authorities closed the theaters in 1652, after Iemitsu's death deprived the troupes of an influential patron.

Facing ruin, theater owners reluctantly agreed to strict control of boys' participation, and the authorities allowed the theaters to reopen. Producers lured audiences back by giving more attention to plot and offering skits and eventually full-length productions in which mature professionals played all roles, making the quality of story and acting central to theatrical success. Plots still turned on affairs in the licensed quarter, but more and more incidents involving famous people appeared, some deriving from the medieval corpus of nō drama and others from war tales (*gunki monogatari*). Nō also influenced kabuki in terms of dancing, posturing, and such aspects of staging as the *michiyuki*, or "poetic journey." In the michiyuki, an actor could build powerful dramatic tension by slowly making his way across stage as he told his story. Kabuki's link to male prostitution persisted, but after a few years and a few more bouts with officialdom, it came to function as legitimate theater, its primary product being the stage presentation itself.

POETRY

The rise of new theatrical forms was accompanied by a flowering of popular literature. Early in the century, the main new literary form was a poetry called *haikai*. Growing out of the frivolous medieval poetic tradition, *haikai no renga*, or comic linked verse, haikai was developed into a respectable genre primarily by the poet Matsunaga Teitoku. He received formal training in one of the secret poetic traditions of Kyoto, but then, in defiance of custom, began giving public lectures on the subject, much to the irritation of his poetic betters. In the 1620s he opened a school for aspiring poets, and over the next two or three decades, he and his disciples developed rules for their poetry of "wild verses." In the process they transformed the "spewing forth of whatever came to one's lips," as one disgruntled poet characterized haikai, into Japan's most popular poetry.[18]

At that stage, haikai was mostly written by the leisured of Kyoto, for many of whom it was a mere diversion from the serious business of composing renga. Its canons were rapidly changing, however, even as its popularity spread to Osaka and Edo, and a noisy battle of poets—openly expressed in print—continued into the 1680s. Haikai finally achieved poetic legitimacy through the works, most especially, of Matsuo Bashō.

Bashō's life and attainments are revealing of both his era and his art. They show the prestige of successful poets, the role of poetry as a mark of cultural polish, the mingling of samurai and merchant cultures, the spread of cultural influences from Kyoto to Edo and throughout the countryside, and the extent to which travel had become safe. In Bashō's poetry, one sees how thoroughly haikai had matured from the new poetic style created by Teitoku to a subtle and deeply moving art.

Bashō was born in 1644, a younger son of a minor samurai in the Tōdō lord's branch headquarters at Ueno, some sixty kilometers by road southeast of Kyoto. As a boy he was befriended by his lord's son, two years his senior, and became his companion and official page. Through him, Bashō was introduced to haikai and to the Kyoto poet and literary figure Kitamura Kigin. When Bashō was twenty-two, however, his lord and friend suddenly died. He revealed his sense of loss some twenty years later during a visit to places they had shared in Ueno:

> How many many things
> they bring to mind—
> the cherry blossoms.[19]

Bereft of companion and career but unsure where to turn, Bashō lingered at his home in Ueno, visiting Kyoto on occasion, until 1672. By then, however, his mentor Kigin had gone to Edo, and finally Bashō broke loose and also went east. In Edo he pieced a life together while

18. Ibid., pp. 29, 36.
19. This translation is a composite of versions offered by Keene, ibid., p. 75, and Harold G. Henderson, *An Introduction to Haiku* (New York: Doubleday, Anchor Books, 1958), p. 17.

building his reputation as a poet, taking students from 1677. He gradually became dissatisfied with the mannered and mechanical quality of haikai as Teitoku had passed it on, and an apocryphal story suggests the sensitivity to nature that he wished to capture in his poems. While walking through a field with Bashō one day, his student Kikaku was inspired by the darting dragonflies to compose this verse:

> Red dragonflies!
> Take off their wings,
> and they are pepper pods!

"No!" said Bashō, "that is not haiku. If you wish to make a haiku on the subject, you must say:

> Red pepper pods!
> Add wings to them,
> and they are dragonflies![20]

By 1680 Bashō was a major poet and sought-after teacher, with many students from samurai households and others from chōnin families. He was already publishing volumes of poetry, both his students' and his own, and for the rest of his life he continued doing so.

By then he was breaking away from the established style of haikai, with its "flashes of wit and take-offs on contemporary mores."[21] But he was still not satisfied with his own work and spent much of the next four years living in relative isolation in a hut in Fukagawa on the outskirts of Edo. There he explored Zen Buddhism, studied Chinese literature and medieval Japanese poetry, and produced poems that frequently were marked by a strong sense of loneliness, including one of his most famous:

> On a withered branch
> a crow has settled—
> autumn nightfall.[22]

The poem illustrates nicely how Bashō used image rather than phrasing to create mood and how he juxtaposed two seemingly dissimilar images to reveal their commonality—the smallness and immediacy of the crow, the immensity and amorphousness of nightfall, and their shared qualities of dark, lonely presence.

In 1684, after learning of his mother's death in Ueno, Bashō took a

---

20. Henderson, *Introduction to Haiku*, pp. 17–18.
21. Keene, *World within Walls*, p. 77.
22. Henderson, *Introduction to Haiku*, p. 18.

trip back west. It was the first of a number of journeys that marked a
new phase of his life and became the basis for several travel accounts.[23]
When he began his decade of travel, he evidently expected it to be fraught
with mortal danger, for he opened his account of that trip, which is
usually titled *Nozarashi kikō,* with this poem:

> Bones exposed in a field—
> at the thought, how the wind
> bites into my flesh.

In fact, however, he discovered that travel was safe, and by the time he
reached Ōgaki, he was able to write,

> When I left Musashi Plain and set out on my journey, it was with a vision of
> my bones lying exposed in a field. Now I wrote:

> > I haven't died after all,
> > and this is where my travels led—
> > the end of autumn.

As his fame spread, Bashō became a traveling celebrity, and former
disciples and admirers throughout the country—daimyo, lesser samurai, priests, merchants, and scholars—competed to entertain and house
him. Indeed, it was on such a journey that he discovered his happiest
dwelling place: the small castle town of Zeze perched on the southwest
shore of Lake Biwa, at the foot of lush green hills. A high official of
Zeze loaned him a summer home in the mountains overlooking Biwa,
and a local priest put him up at a nearby temple later in the year. Zeze
came to hold such a place in Bashō's affections, in contrast to Edo, that
he ordered his ashes interred there.

As Bashō composed successive travel accounts, combining prose and
poetry to describe real and imagined experiences, he slowly perfected
the genre. He produced his finest account, *Oku no hosomichi,* after a
six-month trek in 1689 that took him north from Edo to Sendai and
beyond, west to the Japan Sea coast, and south via Kanazawa to Ōgaki.
He evidently made the journey "to renew his art by visiting the places
that had inspired the poets of the past."[24] En route north from Sendai,
he visited Hiraizumi, a sleepy village near remains of a once-grand capital of regional warrior rulers. Standing on a wooded bluff overlooking

---

23. The following passage and poems from *Nozarashi Kikō* are quoted from Keene,
World within Walls, pp. 81, 85–86. Keene offers a full translation of that travel account
in *Landscapes and Portraits* (Tokyo: Kodansha, 1971), pp. 96–105.

24. Keene, *World within Walls,* pp. 98–99. He discusses the fictional element in *Oku
no hosomichi.*

the broad rice plain of the Kitakami river, amidst overgrown ruins where mighty warriors had once lived, fought, and died, he composed this poem:

> The summer grasses—
> all that remains
> of the warriors' dreams.[25]

After reaching Ōgaki, Bashō, whose health was troubling him ever more frequently, spent two years in the Kamigata region. He made his home at Zeze, and later in Kyoto, happily joining disciples for sessions of renga versification.[26] When he returned to Edo, admirers built him a comfortable new house, but he was generally discontent and stopped seeing disciples for a time. In the spring of 1694, he once more left the city, heading west by palanquin. Again he stayed in Zeze, Kyoto, and Ueno and more than ever was besieged by callers, whom he tried to avoid.

That autumn he left Ueno for Osaka despite exhaustion, hoping to reconcile quarreling disciples. He became ill en route and barely made it to the city, where he was cared for by his followers. But he did not improve and from his bed dictated a beautifully moving poem that proved to be his last:

> On a journey, ill,
> and over fields all withered, dreams
> go wandering still.[27]

PROSE

While Teitoku was establishing haikai and Bashō beginning to perfect it, another literary genre was getting its start. This was *kana zōshi*, prose works of diverse types written in Japanese rather than Chinese and published mainly to entertain and edify samurai. Most grew from medieval literary traditions that included tales of mystery, didactic religious narratives, and improbable stories of hardship and happy endings. One type dated from the age of pacification and appealed particularly to

25. This translation, by R. H. Blyth, is reproduced in Ogata Tsutomu, "Five Methods for Appreciating Bashō's *Haiku*," *AA* 28 (1975): 42-61. Other translations may be found in Keene, *World within Walls*, p. 104, and Henderson, *Introduction to Haiku*, p. 27. Henderson points out the difficulty of translating this particular *haiku*.
26. Etsuko Terasaki, "*Hatsushigure*: A Linked Verse Series by Bashō and His Disciples," *HJAS* 36 (1976): 204–39.
27. Henderson, *Introduction to Haiku*, p. 30.

samurai women who had experienced the turbulence of warfare and the later disruptions of daimyo transfer and punishment. This was the anonymously authored stepdaughter love story, in which a provincial girl, born to hardship or abused by family, survived various hazards, miraculously to discover love, wealth, and well-being while her tormentors received the punishment they so richly deserved.[28]

For some time, most fictional pieces continued to serve Buddhist didactic functions. A delightful example is *Nezumi no sōshi*, an illustrated, ten-page tale of unknown authorship that was written sometime between 1590 and 1640. In the tale, a mouse and a Zen monk engage in a cheerfully insightful discussion of the relative merits of their species. Only cats come off worse than humans, which gives the tale-teller occasion to slip in his Buddhist lesson.[29]

A kana zōshi that reflected one aspect of the age was the ten-page *Chōja kyō,* whose author is unknown, which was published in 1627. Written when rulers still had money to spend, castle towns were growing rapidly, and entrepreneurs with government connections were flourishing, it celebrated the prospects of enrichment, describing how frugality, planning, and sharp-eyed usury could raise one from poverty to wealth and listed for those aspiring to wealth the "principles to cherish at all times."[30]

By the late 1630s, enough books were selling to make kana zōshi profitable to publish, enabling some authors to survive as professional writers. Travel diaries and guidebooks were especially popular around the middle of the century, giving the curious both real and vicarious access to far places and fast people.[31] Other works foreshadowed the later *ukiyo zōshi* (stories of the floating world), notably the rudimentary novel *Ukiyo monogatari,* published in 1661 by the prolific writer Asai Ryōi. Ryōi prepared the reader for his story by contrasting the older Buddhist ukiyo, or "floating world" of transient sadness or suffering, with the newer sense of insouciant dedication to pleasures of the nonce:

> Living only for the moment, turning our full attention to the pleasures of the moon, the snow, the cherry blossoms and the maple leaves; singing songs,

28. Chieko Irie Mulhern, "Cinderella and the Jesuits," *MN* 34-4 (Winter 1979): 409–47, describes these tales briefly. Her essay explores connections between Cinderella stories and women of Christian daimyo households, Hosokawa Gracia most notably, to argue for a Jesuit-related authorship.
29. D. E. Mills, "The Tale of the Mouse," *MN* 34-2 (Summer 1979): 167–68.
30. Keene, *World within Walls,* p. 198.
31. Teruoka Yasutaka, "The Pleasure Quarters and Tokugawa Culture," in C. Andrew Gerstle, *18th Century Japan* (Sydney: Allen & Unwin, 1989), pp. 16–19.

drinking wine, diverting ourselves in just floating, floating; caring not a whit for the pauperism staring us in the face, refusing to be disheartened, like a gourd floating along with the river current: this is what we call the *floating world.*[32]

Ryōi was an eclectic author who wrote on diverse subjects: "comic adventures, ghost stories, guidebooks, and historical romances."[33] Benefiting from the economics of block printing and growth in the reading public, he became "the first popular and the first professional writer in Japanese history." Besides *Ukiyo monogatari,* he wrote extensively on Buddhist subjects and produced a number of kana zōshi in which he gave voice to midcentury discontents, criticizing daimyo greed and waste, denouncing merchant rapacity, lamenting the hardship experienced by poorer samurai, and deploring the exploitation of farmers.

The prominence of licensed quarters in popular writing is evident in the work of Fujimoto Kizan, who "became fascinated with the usages of the world of prostitutes and at an early age decided to consecrate his energies to learning [about] and glorifying them, establishing a Way, in the manner of the Confucianists." Fujimoto's *Shikidō ōkagami,* completed in manuscript in 1678 after twenty years of work, reflects his approach, detailing the sensual joys of the quarter while quoting learnedly from Chinese and Japanese classics. Once placed at the center of popular fiction, the licensed quarter, its courtesans, clients, and cares, remained there throughout the Genroku years and for the rest of the Tokugawa period.

ART

Along with the rise of popular theater and fiction came growth of a popular art, *ukiyo-e,* or floating-world art. The genre included paintings, especially in Kyoto, and prints, mostly in Edo at first but popular in all three cities by century's end.[34]

Distinguishing "schools" of art in seventeenth-century Japan is difficult because the artists who created what later scholars have dubbed ukiyo art were themselves schooled in the Kanō and Tosa styles, and

32. Richard Lane, *Images from the Floating World* (New York: G. P. Putnam's Sons, 1978), p. 11. Italics in original.

33. The quoted phrases relating to Asai Ryōi and Fujimoto Kizan are from Keene, *World within Walls,* pp. 156, 159, 162.

34. Scholars have difficulty agreeing on a definition of *ukiyo-e.* Thus, Lane, whose main interest lies in *ukiyo-e* wood-block prints, defines as *ukiyo-e* works that Chibbett, whose focus is on book printing and illustrating, tends to classify as Tosa-style. In consequence, Lane sees *ukiyo-e* emerging in the early seventeenth century, whereas Chibbett treats it as rising much later in the century.

they only slowly and partially diverged from their mentors. Ukiyo-e emerged through two forms of deviation: focus on new subjects and application of new techniques. Even in Kōetsu's day, some painters trained in the Kanō and Tosa styles were foreshadowing ukiyo-e by representing aspects of daily life and leisure rather than exotica, and common folk, especially courtesans, dancers, and other beauties, rather than aristocrats. From the 1620s on, such subjects became ever more common. In terms of technique, artists began abandoning a number of customary conventions, such as the extensive use of "clouds" in laying out a picture. And compared to Tosa practice, they made human figures central to a picture, rather than incidental.

Ukiyo-e did not, of course, displace all other styles of art. One of the finest artistic accomplishments of the century was the sixty-volume edition of *Genji monogatari* that appeared in 1650 with handsome illustrations in the Tosa style. Moreover, Ogata Kōrin's work, mentioned earlier, reminds us that vital art was still being produced independently of the ukiyo style even at century's end. Nevertheless, the main stream of artistic development was flowing elsewhere. In the disapproving words of one scholarly authority: "We see a gradual drift from genre works depicting the general public to a more limited form showing the world of pleasure. This depiction becomes increasingly decadent with the passage of time."[35]

In particular, the licensed quarters provided a new focus for artists, who produced small paintings, hanging scrolls, long horizontal scrolls, and even large multi-panel folding screens depicting courtesans, their clients, negotiations between the two, and the pleasures of their association. Explicit and boisterously exaggerated pictures of the techniques of lovemaking (*shunga*, or "spring pictures") became from the outset an established segment of the genre. Initially, the works were sold to the Kyoto elite, daimyo, and lesser members of the samurai class, who still controlled most of the discretionary wealth, but as the century advanced, more and more of the ukiyo art was produced for chōnin consumption.

The stylistic ambiguity of early ukiyo paintings is nicely captured by an exquisite work of the 1660s, *Courtèsan and Courtier*. Richard Lane describes the unattributed work this way:

> The man seated on the right is clearly modeled on the great ninth-century court poet, Narihira, hero of the *Tales of Ise*. He not only wears ancient court robes but is even depicted in the traditional Tosa art style. The girl he

---

35. Mizuo, *Edo Painting*, p. 75.

11. Kambun Master, *Courtesan and Courtier*. Medium-sized *kakemono* in colors and gold wash on paper. In this painting from around the mid 1660s, the unknown artist has captured both the elegance of classical Tosa art and, particularly in the courtesan's bold stance and flaring sleeves and robe, the ukiyo sense of human vitality. Courtesy of the Collection of Dr. Richard Lane, Kyoto.

is courting, however, is the heroine of a new, seventeenth-century world: the stylish courtesan. She stands aloof in all the glory of her elaborate kimono, arms withdrawn into her garment in a subtle, vaguely erotic gesture typical of courtesans. Between the courtier and the courtesan chrysanthemums bloom on a rustic but stylish fence. Such elements—like every part of the scene with the exception of the girl—are all traditional Tosa work. Indeed, the first impression is that a modern girl has stepped into a ninth-century scene.[36]

Elegant paintings of this type were much in demand among the wealthy of Kyoto. In Edo, however, a city still recovering from the Meireki fire, wealth was less available and the most promising market for ukiyo-style art was the more plebeian, artistically less sophisticated samurai class. Instead of paintings, this market responded to cheaper, less polished prints that treated the same subjects: licensed quarters, actors and beauties, urban life in general, and lovemaking in particular.

One of the first and most representative of the early ukiyo print prod-

36. Lane, *Images*, p. 30. Lane designates the unknown painter the "Kambun Master."

ucts was *Yoshiwara makura,* an unknown artist's combination sex manual and "courtesan critique" dating from 1660. As manual it illustrated the forty-eight "standard positions," and as critique it offered "guides to the famous courtesans of the day, sometimes providing their portraits and verse eulogies but more often detailing their beauties and faults, where the girls could be located and at what price obtained."[37] Another example of early ukiyo art, also from Edo, is found in the illustrations in Asai Ryōi's *Musashi abumi,* an account of the Meireki fire that he published in 1661. In one illustration, the unknown artist, although trained in the Tosa style, omitted patches of cloud, filling his picture instead with figures of Edo commoners crowding onto rooftops, plummeting into a river, and struggling through the waves to escape the advancing wall of flame.[38]

Prints ultimately proved more central to ukiyo-e than paintings, their popularity spreading from Edo back to the Kamigata cities. In the process, the influence of ukiyo-e penetrated and modified Tosa art, even in Kyoto, and it had emerged as the dominant style of illustration by century's end.

Hishikawa Moronobu is credited with developing ukiyo-e into an artistically sophisticated, independent genre. Raised in the home of a tapestry embroiderer in the small town of Hota near the entrance to Edo Bay, Moronobu early in life acquired the decorative artistic skills that he later honed as a student of the Tosa and Kanō styles of painting. In the 1660s he settled in Edo and began producing pictorial art, and through the 1670s and 1680s, when he was at the height of his powers, he created ukiyo paintings, single-sheet prints, and, more important, the art work for some 130 picture books (*ehon*) and written texts. His book art included "picture-guides to Edo and elsewhere, illustrated anthologies of poetry, pictorial versions of *The Tales of Ise* and later classics, collections of battle-pieces, designs for fans and screens and gardens, striking erotica of all kinds, together with many other books full of the spirited people of the *ukiyo.*"[39] Moronobu's ukiyo-e style, with its strong sense of design and voluptuous sensibility, as seen in the 1682 print *Flirting Lovers,* proved so appealing that he and his disciples came to dominate the genre into the 1690s.[40] His success gave Edo a primacy in

---

37. Lane, *Images,* p. 37.
38. Chibbett, *History of Japanese Printing,* p. 126, reproduces the print in question.
39. Howard Hibbett, *The Floating World in Japanese Fiction* (London: Oxford University Press, 1959), p. 68.
40. Reproduced in Lane, *Images,* p. 47.

12. Hishikawa Moronobu, *Flirting Lovers*. Woodblock print from a *shunga* set, 1680s. In this lush, boldly executed, and closely focused print, an impetuous young samurai eagerly seeks the pleasures of a more mature and self-controlled woman. Courtesy of the Art Institute of Chicago. Clarence Buckingham Collection. Acc. #1973.645.4. Photograph © 1991. All Rights Reserved.

the emergence of ukiyo art that offset Kamigata dominance in the fields of ukiyo zōshi, ningyō jōruri, and kabuki.

The artistic, literary, and theatrical facets of seventeenth-century ukiyo culture were deeply entwined because they all developed in the same great cities and catered to the same expanding clientele. Moreover, they took their themes from the same environment, primarily the cities, and most especially their licensed quarters. Also they relied more and more on the same publishing firms, which displayed their creations through every sort of theater handbill, libretto, literary work, picture book, and artistic print.

Finally, the key role of wood-block printing merits repeating. The techniques of block-making and printing permitted the joining of word and picture in innumerable combinations and the production of print runs large enough to sell at publicly accessible prices while keeping the producer solvent. Whereas Ieyasu and others used tax receipts to pay for publishing, and wealthy aesthetes like Suminokura Soan plowed commercial profits into their ventures, the publishers of ukiyo works were sustained by their buyers. That they could be testifies to both the ingenuity of the wood-block printers and the size of the market for such work.

The spirit of ukiyo was entertaining, titillating, irreverent, at times scolding, occasionally mocking of the rulers, and at a deeper level richly empathic of the lives of city people. Around century's end, it reached an apex of sorts in the literary and dramatic works of Ihara Saikaku and Chikamatsu Monzaemon, the predominant figures in Genroku ukiyo culture.

GENROKU ARTS AND LETTERS

To speak of "Genroku ukiyo culture" is to imply the existence, ca. 1688–1704, of a cluster of interlinked cultural activities embodying the qualities of the "floating world." There was such a cluster, and its rise was abetted by the fascination urban connoisseurs felt for the life of the yūkaku, or licensed quarter. By Genroku those neighborhoods of prostitutes and attendant personnel had matured into highly structured urban systems with hierarchies of authority and status, an elaborately formalized etiquette, and a rich body of tradition. The orderly arrangements of yūkaku life facilitated the handling of clients and linked the quarters to the rest of society in a stable manner.

The women of the quarters and their relationship to outsiders became major themes of drama, prose, and art, the connection between theater and prostitution being especially close. As noted previously, kabuki was from the outset tied to the skin trade, and even after the bakufu separated the two, linkages persisted. Rulers continued to regard both as sources of social pollution and viewed actors and courtesans as unworthy creatures, ideally to be fenced off from "decent" society and restricted to special neighborhoods. Theater-going was similar to yūkaku-going, although women customers normally enjoyed only the former. Actors and courtesans were favorite subjects of artists, who presented brothel and theater in the same manner, in the ultimate popular achievement depicting hero and heroine locked in carnal engagement. The two were regular topics of critical booklets (*hyōbanki*), which offered the public gossipy commentary and assessments of their relative merits. The two participated in "the fluid exchange of fashion, language, and . . . the latest slang. . . . Styles in weaving and dyeing, in color and pattern of dress, in cosmetics, hairstyles, combs and bodkins, constantly passed between them. . . . The music, the popular songs, the styles of recitation were shared. The standard instrument of both

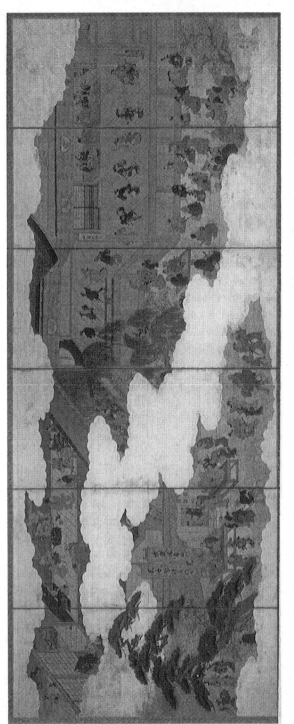

13. Hishikawa Moronobu, *Scenes from the Yoshiwara Pleasure Quarters*. Six-panel screen; ink, color, and gold leaf on paper; late 1670s–early 1680s. In this six-panel screen, Moronobu linked Yoshiwari and kabuki by portraying a kabuki-style stage on which women performers entertain while other entertainers wait to perform at upper left and customers enter at lower left. Courtesy of Museum of Fine Arts, Boston; Gift of Oliver W. Peabody. Acc. #79.468.

quarters was the samisen, [and the] two worlds were also linked by styles of dance." [41]

While the licensed quarters offered a focus for ukiyo culture, the woodblock publishing industry provided the mechanism of its cohesion. The mechanism is exemplified by the career of the artist Torii Kiyonobu. He was born in 1644 to an Osaka kabuki actor who specialized in women's roles but also designed and painted theatrical posters and playbills. In 1687 father and son moved to Edo, bringing Kamigata acting and art to the eastern city. In Edo, Kiyonobu came under the influence of Hishikawa Moronobu's ukiyo-e style, and he combined "the dynamic, disciplined vigor of Moronobu with the bombast and hyperbole of Kabuki" in a manner that dominated the worlds of art and theater for decades. [42] He continued the family craft of producing kabuki advertising posters and actor prints, but he also illustrated prose tales (ukiyo zōshi) and summaries for kabuki plays. In addition, he created a number of picture books (ehon), volumes of prints unified by theme or subject, such as a hundred-print collection of portraits of actors, with accompanying poems, and a nineteen-print book of courtesans.

Kiyonobu's prints were basically black-and-white, in the manner of the day, but he used black to effect areas of color and went beyond the usual technique of hand-coloring (tan-e) to experiment with lacquered printing (urushi-e) and rose-colored tinting (beni-e), forerunners of the later full-color prints. His art celebrated the beauty of the kimono and helped make textile design a flourishing field of aesthetics, while the actors' costumes that he portrayed often set fashion trends. In this one printmaker, then, the fields of advertising, drama, pictorial art, poetry, prose, prostitution, and textile design came together to influence one another's development. Kiyonobu's work also spanned the worlds of Edo and Kamigata and linked past and future ukiyo-e styles.

As this last comment suggests, Genroku ukiyo was far from a static monolith. Each artist, writer, and cultural field had unique characteristics, certainly, but there also were clear distinctions between Kyoto and Osaka on the one hand and Edo on the other. The Kamigata cities remained the dominant force in cultural life, more active and sophisticated than Edo. The Tosa and Kanō styles of art continued to be taught there, and paintings were still favored over prints. The publishing in-

---

41. Shively, "Social Environment of Tokugawa Kabuki," pp. 50–51. Shively also treats actors and prostitutes in "Popular Culture," pp. 742–61.

42. Lane, *Images*, p. 58.

dustry was still centered there, producing literary works in great pro-
fusion, including new and reworked classics of prose and poetry and a
substantial quantity of scholarship.

Edo, viewed as hopelessly boorish by Kamigata's finest, was less polished but more dynamic. It emerged during Genroku as the most vigorous—if not the most elegant—center for wood-block printing, particularly in the celebration of courtesan beauty. Just picture all those samurai
in town for a year of sankin kōtai duty, decorating their barracks and
rental houses and being charmed out of their money by teahouses and
more. With its samurai-centered political culture, Edo also was known
for its dramatic kabuki period pieces (*jidaimono*) whereas Kamigata
audiences favored domestic plays (*sewamono*), which were less bombastic, more realistic, and more openly based on recent incidents of
commoner life.

Genroku culture was characterized by temporal as well as regional
variation, and the changing times were reflected in the works of Ihara
Saikaku, writer of fiction, and Chikamatsu Monzaemon, dramatist. In
brief, the 1680s, Saikaku's heyday, were years of cultural creativity whose
insouciant vitality surely derived from the century's continuing prosperity. However, the 1690s, the very heart of Genroku, were comparatively barren years. As rural unrest grew more intense and monetary
problems disrupted the urban price structure, Saikaku's works became
more somber, and after his death in 1693 the writing of prose tales
stagnated. Theatrical creativity also slackened, the most popular plays
dealing with disorder in daimyo houses (*oiemono*), a preference that
reflected the intensifying fiscal and political difficulties of the day.

Not until about 1700 did major new developments start to occur
again. Chikamatsu returned to writing for the puppet theater, and two
puppet theaters in Osaka competed vigorously for popularity. Ejima
Kiseki began writing ukiyo zōshi, and a number of artists began producing prints, picture books, and illustrated works of great appeal. It
seems appropriate to find in the darkening tone of later Genroku, especially the fascination with love suicide (*shinjū*), the sobering effects
of a tightening economy on a firmly disciplined society.

IHARA SAIKAKU AND *UKIYO ZŌSHI*

The tenor of early Genroku urban life was captured in the oeuvre of
Ihara Saikaku, the Osaka haikai poet who became a prolific writer of
ukiyo zōshi during his last decade. Indeed, to a striking degree, he cre-

ated the genre, and it made no appreciable literary advances after his death.

The twenty-five or so books that Saikaku wrote during his decade of prose composition were essentially collections of tales organized around some theme or topic. Encouraged, perhaps, by the success of other popular authors, Saikaku tried his hand at prose fiction in 1682, when he wrote the entertaining, salacious, and lightheartedly didactic *Kōshoku ichidai otoko,* whose fifty-four chapters recount the lustful conquests of an insatiable hedonist from his initial venture in lovemaking at age seven until his departure for paradise—an island populated solely by women— at age sixty. The book's commercial success inspired Saikaku to ring the changes on physical love, and for the next five years they dominated his output: heterosexual love from the perspectives of both men and women and male homosexual love.[43]

From about 1687 on, however, perhaps because the market for erotic tales was sated, Saikaku shifted to other topics. In works that profoundly enriched the genre and gave it most of its enduring value as a window on the age, he produced collections of tales exemplifying unfilial behavior, the principles of merchant conduct, vendettas among samurai, and the samurai ethic of duty. Other writings treated bizarre tastes and interests, judicial decisions of the bakufu's administrator in Kyoto, incidents involving actors, the hardships of debtors, and the difficulty of getting ahead in life.

The evolution of Saikaku's works betrays changes in his understanding and assessment of life. His early pieces, hedonistic and insouciant in tone, described human foibles and pratfalls and usually attributed their outcome to defects of individual character or behavior, or to simple chance. But even when their characters ended up impoverished or dead, these tales conveyed a basic spirit of optimism or at least devil-may-care acceptance of life as it is. In later works, however, he dwelt more on issues of propriety—on how samurai should act as samurai or merchants as merchants lest they come to no good end, in the process ruining or disgracing their families as well as themselves. His last notable works were tales of hardship infused with a tone of pessimism, and they suggested that the hardship stemmed not from personal failure or random chance so much as from the character of society. In his 1692 work *Seken munesan'yō,* the poor go into debt and, in attempting to escape,

43. The apparent lack of a companion literature of lesbian love doubtless reflects values and structural characteristics of the age, which seem neither to have sanctioned nor offered locations for overt expression of lesbian affection.

try all sorts of devious schemes that make matters worse, or at best buy some time, in the process revealing the frailties of human character.[44]

Saikaku was of comfortable chōnin origin himself, and his comments on the hardship of life did not acquire the bitterness found in works earlier produced by Asai Ryōi, the declassed samurai. Without being maudlin, however, his best works do convey the complexity and moral ambiguity of life and show how people trapped in the social obligations and institutional arrangements of their existence can mismanage affairs and suffer accordingly.

At his death, Saikaku left several unpublished manuscripts, the best being *Saikaku oridome,* a collection of five tales, evidently written in 1689, whose main theme is "the difficulty, and often impossibility, of getting ahead in the world without capital." In his words:

> There are all kinds of ways to make your way in the world if you have to. But the merchant without capital can rack his brains to the utmost, yet end up nevertheless by spending his entire income on interest, working all his days for other people. The man with a good financial backer naturally is free to trade as he pleases. He can always judge when the time is right for buying, and he frequently makes a profit.[45]

The message is unlike that of his own earlier works, and it stands in sharp contrast to the easy optimism of the above-noted *Chōja kyō* written in 1627. Indeed, one of the tales in *Saikaku oridome* explicitly contrasts the tenuous quality of contemporary affluence with the security of business in the Kan'ei period (1624–1644).

Following Saikaku's death, other writers continued to turn out prose tales. Most, however, did little more than vary his themes, frequently plagiarizing words as well as content.[46] The most successful of these later writers was Ejima Kiseki, son of a well-to-do Kyoto shopkeeper. A "satiric realist whose humour is without bitterness," Kiseki spun tales of "misers, flatterers, drunkards, boors, braggarts, gluttons, lechers." His character sketches, most of which appeared in the twenty years after 1699, were produced on good-quality paper and graced with handsome illustrations by the noted printmaker Nishikawa Sukenobu.

44. Ben Befu, *Worldly Mental Calculations* (Berkeley and Los Angeles: University of California Press, 1976), offers a complete, extremely well annotated translation. A partial translation may be found in Ivan Morris, *The Life of an Amorous Woman* (New York: New Directions, 1963).

45. Keene, *World within Walls,* p. 207. For another example of Saikaku's posthumously published later writings, see Virginia Marcus, "A Miscellany of Old Letters: Saikaku's *Yorozu no Fumihōgu,*" *MN* 40-3 (Fall 1985): 257–82.

46. The quoted comments on Kiseki are from Hibbett, *Floating World,* pp. 50, 62–63. That on Sukenobu is from Chibbett, *History of Japanese Printing,* p. 137.

The works brought fame and fortune to Ejima's Kyoto publisher, the Hachimonji-ya. However, Sukenobu "evidently had an obsessional interest in the portrayal of women of all classes of society," and "Kiseki had too much of the unreflective Genroku spirit" to engage in deeper social scrutiny. Instead, his works were limited to the meretricious worlds of kabuki and yūkaku, so their contemporary value as popular entertainment is not matched by historical value as source of insight into the later years of Genroku. In the genre of ukiyo zōshi, Saikaku had said it all.

CHIKAMATSU MONZAEMON AND GENROKU DRAMA

Insofar as cultural production can provide insight into Genroku history, the works of playwrights offer more than ukiyo zōshi. Towering above his rivals was Chikamatsu Monzaemon, who provided for puppet theater and kabuki the disciplinary standards that Bashō did for haikai and Saikaku for ukiyo zōshi.

Until the 1680s the puppet and actor theaters were separate and dissimilar, but as competition for audience intensified, they "borrowed" from one another.[47] They copied dramatic techniques: for example, the two-foot-tall puppets aped noted kabuki actors as a way to personalize their characterizations, while actors emulated the mechanical motion of puppets to heighten the visual impact of their movements. And they began using one another's scripts, most especially those by Chikamatsu, whose popularity at the box office delighted theater operators.

Chikamatsu was born in 1653 to a samurai father who resigned his post in Echizen and moved to Kyoto as a ronin when his son was a youth. Having no family prospects, young Chikamatsu took service as a page in the household of a court noble, studied haikai poetry and classical literature for a few years, and when about thirty, or possibly earlier, began writing jōruri scripts for chanters in the puppet theater. In 1684 he began writing for kabuki actors as well, and soon made a name for himself as a dramatist. During the 1690s, he concentrated on writing kabuki librettos for the celebrated Kyoto actor Sakata Tōjūrō, mainly producing oiemono, which were then in high vogue.

Oiemono were theatrical treatments of disturbances in the houses of

47. A skillful, illustrated examination of the puppet-*kabuki* relationship is James R. Brandon, "The Theft of Chūshingura: or The Great Kabuki Caper," in Brandon, ed., *Chūshingura: Studies in Kabuki and the Puppet Theater* (Honolulu: University Press of Hawaii, 1982), pp. 111–46.

daimyo. The greatest disturbances, as noted in chapter 7, were the oie sōdō that convulsed a number of domains during the seventeenth century, and the popularity of fictionalized stage versions reveals the voyeuristic interest that urban people, both samurai and commoner, had in affairs of the highborn. Back in 1644 the bakufu had forbidden the use of contemporary names on stage, so playwrights used fictional names and placed their stories in ill-defined historical settings as jidaimono. Nevertheless the contemporary events behind them and even the names of principal participants were known to the audience. Oiemono pitted good people against bad: scheming vassals and relatives who usurped positions and frittered away a patrimony against the rightful and righteous, who suffered, endured, and eventually prevailed.

Oiemono, with their samurai subjects, rough "masculine" vitality, and triumphs of righteousness, however implausible, were popular in Edo. In Kamigata, by contrast, domestic plays, or sewamono, with more believable scenes, more natural movements, tighter plots, and closer attention to mental states and individual personalities, gained appeal. By custom, however, theatrical programs consisted of jidaimono, with sewamono added at the end to provide variety, so during the 1690s Chikamatsu tried to make oiemono more attractive to his Kamigata audience by locating some of the action in licensed quarters and enriching the plots with daily-life materials of the sort they enjoyed.

The popularity of sewamono was boosted by another current phenomenon, the lovers' suicide (shinjū). The first kabuki version of a lovers' suicide appeared in 1683, and others followed, a dramatized suicide of 1695 becoming a hit that ran 150 days. When Chikamatsu produced his first suicide play in 1703, he did it as a jōruri piece for the Osaka chanter and theater operator Takemoto Gidayū. The play, Sonezaki shinjū, was based on the recent suicide of a shop assistant and a prostitute in Osaka. Characterized as "the first pure sewamono," it was so successful it saved Gidayū's theater from bankruptcy and helped give the puppet theater popularity enough to flourish for half a century.[48]

Dramas that treated shinjū spoke deeply to theater audiences. The suicides were ultimate expressions of a broader practice wherein "lovers demonstrated to each other the strength of their love." Methods of demonstration included "writing vows of undying love, inflicting burns

48. Donald H. Shively, *The Love Suicide at Amijima* (Cambridge, Mass.: Harvard University Press, 1953), p. 13. On programmatic aspects of Gidayū's popularity, see Yūda Yoshio, "The Formation of Early Modern *Jōruri*," *AA* 28 (1975): 20–41.

or wounds on themselves, cutting off fingers, shaving the head, tattoo-ing, and pulling out the fingernails and toenails."[49] In theatrical repre-sentations, therefore, lovers' suicide may be seen as an ultimate expres-sion of such devotion, a townsman's version of the samurai's seppuku, or suicide of honor.

The real-life phenomenon of shinjū surely cannot be explained in those terms, however. In Genroku Japan, seppuku was an official form of punishment that the rulers occasionally imposed on samurai; it was not a matter of genuine choice or an expression of sincere loyalty. Con-ceivably love suicides, which seem to have proliferated in the late 1600s, and to have become even more common in the early 1700s, were a cultural fad encouraged by romanticization on stage. More likely they reflected human stress as Confucian ethical principles and social regu-lations became more pervasive and restrictive even while economic growth slowed, coinage was debased, and the situations of minor chōnin house-holds grew more vulnerable, especially in Kyoto, which was losing jobs and people to Osaka.

Indeed, Chikamatsu treated financial problems as a factor in most of his love suicides. Whatever caused their growing frequency, the bakufu, evidently fearing that life imitates art, tried to discourage them in 1722, following the theatrical success of another suicide play by Chikamatsu. It forbade their treatment on stage, punished those who attempted sui-cide unsuccessfully, and dishonored the corpses of those who suc-ceeded. Those measures discouraged the practice of shinjū and reduced its presence in plays. But by then it had become established as a major theme in early modern drama.

Chikamatsu did not, however, require shinjū to make a play out of the tensions between social duty (*giri*) and human feeling (*ninjō*). In his 1706 play *Horikawa nami no tsuzumi,* also based on an actual incident, his heroine was the young wife of a samurai. Longing for her husband, who was in Edo with his lord on a year of sankin kōtai duty, she began drinking for solace and one night drunkenly bedded down with her stepson's teacher. Later she was appalled at what she had done, but when her husband returned and found her pregnant, he made her com-mit suicide and then hunted down and killed the teacher.[50] Chikamatsu could have used the story to preach high-toned morality, but he chose,

49. Shively, *Amijima*, pp. 24–25.
50. Donald Keene, *Major Plays of Chikamatsu* (New York: Columbia University Press, 1961), p. 18.

instead, to dwell on the pathos of the situation, in which the law permitted execution of wives for adultery while sustaining institutional arrangements that invited just such an outcome.

By 1705 Chikamatsu's favorite actor, Sakata Tōjūrō, had decided to retire. With *Sonezaki* a smashing success on the puppet stage, Chikamatsu stopped writing for kabuki and moved to Osaka, where he scripted a number of suicide plays for puppets. In them, he employed the michiyuki, or "poetic journey," of nō and kabuki to heighten the sense of tragedy, explore lovers' feelings, and provide them with Buddhist redemption.

Chikamatsu also wrote a number of jidaimono, of which his most successful was *Kokusen'ya kassen,* a visually overwhelming work loosely based on an episode in the Ming resistance to Manchu conquest. He wrote it in 1715, following the death of Gidayū, again to rescue the Takemoto theater from bankruptcy, and the work so delighted audiences that it ran for seventeen months and saved the theater. His career culminated a few years later in a series of fine scripts that included his masterpiece of 1720, *Shinjū ten no Amijima,* in which he probed the complex sensibilities that entangled the young owner of a paper shop, his wife, and a prostitute whom he loved. The puppet version opened in Osaka at year's end, and within months a kabuki version appeared in Edo, its success spurring the bakufu to outlaw suicide plays. By the time Chikamatsu died four years later, he had authored some hundred jōruri and about thirty kabuki plays, and his legacy dominated the Japanese stage into the twentieth century.

The seventeenth century witnessed remarkable cultural developments. At higher social levels, arts and letters rescued the courtly aesthetic heritage from obscurity, giving it new visibility, richness, and esteem, especially in Kyoto. Across the country, the samurai elite defined peaceable and polished cultural norms for castle towns and their samurai populations, in the process blunting more raucous forms of public entertainment in all but the greatest cities.

In those cities, new forms of "floating world" art, literature, and drama gradually arose. Through the earlier years of Genroku, they were notable for their risque tone and meretricious character, but as Genroku advanced, ukiyo culture gained sophistication and came to speak more richly to and for its urban public. Saikaku's works, in their evolution from the erotic to the socially compassionate, and Chikamatsu's, in their deepening insight into the difficulties of human life, contributed centrally to those trends.

In his suicide pieces, Chikamatsu created moving stories of ordinary people trapped by their situations—constrained by obligations (*giri*) and driven by affection (*ninjō*)—who finally asserted their dignity, refusing to abandon their love for one another despite the cost of insistence. In Donald Keene's apt words, "the little men who appear as the heroes of Chikamatsu's sewamono, like the heroes of many modern plays, are trapped by financial and other circumstances which they are powerless to alter, and in the end their daggers are turned against themselves, and not against an enemy."[51]

By the eighteenth century, ukiyo culture had developed the capacity to reflect the triumphs and tragedies of daily life. It was less effective, however, as a tool of political criticism. To some extent that may reflect its concentration on a commoner clientele, people officially excluded from political life. A more substantial reason for the limitation is that while the censors only sporadically intervened, their shadow was ever-present. Recall that during the years when Saikaku was cranking out sybaritic sex tours, the bakufu instructed Itō Jinsai to submit materials for inspection (1683), created a new office to inspect imported Chinese books at Nagasaki (1685), and ordered old Kumazawa Banzan into house arrest for commenting on public affairs (1687). It is unsurprising that Saikaku kept his stories light, laced them with homilies, and steered clear of political commentary.

In the later Genroku era, even when grounds for complaint were greater, political constraints still kept commentary within bounds, especially in Edo. Consider the fate of Edo artist Hanabusa Itchō. In the 1690s he produced a work of political satire in the shape of a picture book (*ehon*) of paintings of high-class women that he titled *Hyakunin jōrō,* signifying "A hundred noble ladies," using a character that permitted the alternative reading "A hundred prostitutes." One of the paintings mocked a rumored recreational activity of Tsunayoshi by depicting a shogunlike figure chanting and poling a boat that carried his favorite mistress while she accompanied him on a drum. For portraying the shogun and ridiculing the privileged, Itchō was exiled in 1698 to Miyakejima, an islet in the Pacific 170 kilometers south of Edo. Had

51. Keene, *World within Walls,* pp. 262–63.

Tsunayoshi not been promoting the ideal of compassion, Itchō doubt-less would have fared worse; as it was he remained in exile until after the shogun's death in 1709.

Writing in Kamigata, Chikamatsu was less exposed to risk than those in Edo, but he avoided punishment mainly by exercising prudence. Five years passed after Hanabusa's exile before he poked cautious fun at the shogun in a play whose title used the same phrase as Hanabusa's scur-rilous ehon. And his most scathing ridicule of Tsunayoshi appeared a decade later, after the man was safely dead and government lay in the hands of the child Ietsugu and his advisors, notably Arai Hakuseki, who was credited with repealing Tsunayoshi's laws of compassion.[52]

Chikamatsu had good reason to be cautious while Tsunayoshi lived, as an Edo playwright discovered when he tried to turn a stunning con-temporary incident to dramatic profit in 1703. Two years earlier Asano Naganori, the young lord of Akō han, having drawn his sword and slashed an abusive bakufu official in Edo Castle, paid for his pique with seppuku and loss of his domain. At the end of 1702, forty-seven of his vassals, now reduced to ronin, wreaked their revenge on the offending official, delivering his head to their lord's grave before surrendering to the authorities. Early in 1703, after debating whether the ronin's action constituted honorable conduct by loyal retainers or criminal violation of the prohibition on unauthorized vendettas, Tsunayoshi settled the affair by compromise. He judged them criminal but ordered them all to commit suicide in the honorable samurai manner. An Edo playwright promptly transformed this horrific incident into a kabuki play, but the authorities censured him and closed the production three days after it opened. The playwright had fared poorly; the ronin fared worse. Chi-kamatsu heeded the lesson.[53]

52. Donald H. Shively, "Chikamatsu's Satire on the Dog Shogun," *HJAS* 18 (1955): 159–80.

53. Jacqueline Mueller, "A Chronicle of Great Peace Played Out on a Chessboard: Chikamatsu Monzaemon's *Goban Taiheiki*," *HJAS* 46-1 (Jun. 1986): 221–67, notes that Chikamatsu did not produce a drama related to the Akō incident until after Tsunayoshi's death. And his work then scrupulously avoided criticism of the authorities.

ELEVEN

Ecological Trends

The Period of Growth

Depletion: Minerals and Forest Growth
The Downstream Ramifications of Land Clearance

Japan changed a great deal during the century and a half prior to 1710, and the effects of that change reached well beyond society to the eco-system within which the human drama was being played out.

Preceding chapters examined social aspects of that change. Popula-tion burgeoned, enlarging established villages, creating new ones, and sustaining the growth of towns, cities, and the travel infrastructure that linked them. The measuring, managing, and milking of rural society led to changes in village organization and operation and in the relationship of rulers to ruled. Foreign relations expanded dramatically and then were chopped back to politically acceptable dimensions and maintained as a set of stable trade arrangements. Domestic political organization grew in scale and regularity, and the political center of gravity shifted from the Kinai, where it had resided for more than a millennium, to the Kantō, where it has been ever since. Politically inspired urbanization permanently rearranged both the population and the flow of goods and services among groups and locations. Formation of cities and domains fostered changes in the role of merchants and the scale of mercantile organization and influence. And the promotion and manipulation of cultural production—art, architecture, scholarship, poetry, prose, drama, and other entertainments—affected the aesthetic and intellectual life of society.

Each of these changes, needless to say, influenced the development of the others, and all depended on the capacity of Japan's ecosystem to provide the requisite goods, whether derived from grains, trees, bamboo, other vegetable growth, birds, land animals, marine life, water, subsurface minerals, rock, soil, or clay. Unsurprisingly, society's rapid growth placed unprecedented demands on existing biomass, accumulated soil and subsoil resources, and on the annual increment of rainfall and biomass production.

These demands were unprecedented not because they were of a new type. In particular, they did not lead to serious pollution, primarily because this was a preindustrial society lacking modern humankind's capacity for chemical manipulation and secondly because it was poor and technologically stable enough for recycling to become pervasive as scarcities intensified. Rather, the century's growth escalated traditional needs—for food, fodder, fuel, clothing, building material, and the myriad implements of daily life. The dramatic rise in population and scale of urban society, along with the entrenchment of privilege, created a demand for resources that depleted accessible supplies of unrenewable resources and selectively outpaced the reproductive capacity of the biosystem.

The most rapidly depleted minerals were gold and silver, and the most rapidly depleted biological item was tall timber, while other forms of forest growth, such as the coppice that yielded fuel wood, were also subjected to intense exploitation. Land reclamation, which directly destroyed large tracts of wilderness, proceeded so rapidly that by century's end very little potentially arable land remained unexploited.

In general, resource limits do not appear to have become a chronic source of social hardship until the eighteenth century. On the other hand, measures to allocate scarce resources appeared as early as the era of pacification and proliferated in later decades. Indeed, one can characterize the Tokugawa ideology of rule as a culture of regulation whose key function was to facilitate allocation by legitimizing a system of rationing. Especially in the countryside, where most people lived, rules eventually applied to the production, distribution, and consumption of nearly every sort of yield. As the century aged and society kept growing, more goods became scarce and more environmental problems demanded attention, eliciting more and more rules and restrictions. That trend, already evident by the end of the seventeenth century, became even more pronounced later and was a central characteristic of the period of stasis.

Resource depletion also led to strategic substitution and innovation as users offset particular resource inadequacies by exploiting alternatives and modifying forms of use until further insufficiencies again drove them to devise anew. During the seventeenth century, those processes were most evident in the use of wood and precious metals; later they appeared most vividly in the utilization of arable land, water, and fertilizer materials, as subsequent chapters will indicate.

The people of early modern Japan did no better than humans elsewhere in recording the biological consequences of resource exploitation, so their impact on species diversity and biomass output is impossible to ascertain with any degree of reliability. Clearly wood cutting and land clearance changed the relative abundance of various species of trees, grains, and other vegetation, and one suspects that they changed the faunal community as well. Wood use and reclamation also had consequences for downstream biota, and after 1700, some of these effects intensified and, together with developments in agronomy, even began to affect marine life.

DEPLETION: MINERALS AND FOREST GROWTH

Technological improvements of the late sixteenth century enabled Hideyoshi, Ieyasu, and Hidetada to exploit Japan's mines with unprecedented thoroughness. As a result, Ieyasu built up a substantial hoard of treasure: by one account, his estate included gold and silver valued at 1,950,000 ryō.[1] Hidetada nurtured the hoard and passed it on largely intact. Iemitsu drew the reserves down, and by the end of Ietsuna's reign in 1680, "the ordinary reserves had been exhausted, and minting began of the special store of ingots Ieyasu had set aside for use only for a military emergency."[2] Some of the dissipated treasure came to reside for varying periods of time in the lesser hoards of merchants and other domestic accumulators of wealth, some went into fabricated objects, and the rest was exported or put into domestic circulation as a medium of exchange.

As noted in chapter 8, Japan was a major exporter of silver, especially in the first half of the seventeenth century, and in later decades copper also left in great quantities. Considerable gold flowed outward, but at times it returned in exchange for silver. By century's end, how-

1. George Sansom, A History of Japan, vol. 3, 1615–1867 (Stanford: Stanford University Press, 1963), p. 5.
2. Kate Wildman Nakai, Shogunal Politics (Cambridge, Mass.: Harvard University Press, 1988), p. 98.

ever, monetization of the domestic economy rather than trade had become the decisive factor creating demand for bullion.

Early in the century, metal was used in transactions primarily as dust or ingots, but more and more was minted into coins, whose convenience led to their use on ever more occasions. As decades passed, difficulties created by shortages of metal were ameliorated by mechanisms of substitution, such as promissory notes and letters of credit. Those solutions were never complete or fully satisfactory, however, and from the 1690s on, scarcity of silver—and the accompanying prospect of a minter's profit—led the regime to debase its existing coinage. By then bullion dearth was also generating pressure to terminate, or at least reduce substantially, silver and copper exports. Even in combination, however, debasement and trade constraint did not solve the problem, and the issues of coinage and trade remained major political concerns well into the next century.

Both war and peace fostered deforestation, and problems arising from scarcity of renewable forest resources, wood in particular, proved even less tractable than those stemming from mineral depletion. In 1560 most of Japan was forested, and most of it was still forested 150 years later, as it is today. However, in 1560 the woodland of Honshu, Kyushu, and Shikoku covered considerable lowland as well as mountainside, whereas by 1710 timber was limited almost entirely to steep slopes, while flatter areas were in tillage or supported scrub growth. Furthermore, in 1560 the islands contained a great deal of old growth timber, which constituted hundreds of years of accumulated biomass. By 1710 most of the old-growth timber that was accessible, given the technology of logging, was gone, replaced by mixed growth with little timber content.

The feverish building and burning that accompanied the wars of pacification consumed woodland at a hectic pace. Most notably, Hideyoshi's timber consumption so exceeded the yield of his own domains and nearby areas that he requisitioned supplies from all over the realm. Even the lord of Akita, far to the north, felled rich old-growth stands to provide the high-grade lumber Hideyoshi needed for his fleets, castles, and other grand projects.[3] The rampant exploitation prompted lords to intervene to protect their woodland and its yield. Some did so because their domains were poorly forested and wood had many military uses, others because forest wealth was a source of income, and others because careless woodland use was having harmful downstream effects. They restricted wood cutting and other forest use, tried to prevent slash-

3. Conrad Totman, *The Origins of Japan's Modern Forests: The Case of Akita* (Honolulu: University of Hawaii Press, 1985), pp. 13–14.

and-burn agriculture, and fostered the planting of protection forests to control erosion and riverine damage.

In Ieyasu's day, timber for castles and their satellite towns continued to be consumed at an unsustainable rate. Around jōkamachi such as Hirosaki and Matsumoto, construction work stripped mountains of forest cover. Ieyasu himself purposely seized most of the good timber areas of central Japan, including the Yoshino and Yamaguni regions in the Kinai and the Kiso and Tenryū river valleys to the east. Still finding accessible timber inadequate to his wants, he launched major river-clearing projects that enabled loggers to extract wood at unprecedented rates. Nevertheless, to build his huge castles at Edo, Sunpu, Nagoya, and Nijō, he still required daimyo to haul timber from Shikoku, Kyushu, and distant regions of Honshu.

After 1615, daimyo slowed their castle construction, but major parts of Osaka Castle were rebuilt following Hideyori's defeat, and expansion of Edo Castle continued, along with mansion building and general urban growth. By the 1630s, much of the accessible high-grade timber south of Hokkaido appears to have been consumed. When Iemitsu ordered the Nikkō Tōshōgū built, neither bakufu nor daimyo was able to provide the high-quality lumber needed for the project. So provisioning was turned over to the merchant Naraya Mochizaemon, who searched widely for the wanted types of wood. His success in obtaining it reportedly made him one of Japan's richest men.[4]

Forest depletion had several ramifications. The harvesting of poorer stands and dependence on longer, more labor-intensive supply lines drove prices up, made construction work more prohibitive, and led to reduction in the quality and size of what was built. Depletion exacerbated price fluctuations, gave rise to conflicts over woodland use, and generated a plethora of regulations that dealt with forest products at the production site, in transit, and at the place of consumption.

The Meireki fire of 1657 highlighted the problem. Like so many fires of the Edo period, it was a creature of the dry, windy, winter weather characteristic of Japan's more populous regions. It erupted north of Edo Castle in a temple in Hongō shortly after New Year's Day and rapidly spread in all directions. Raging on for three days, it overran some 60–80 percent of the city and, before finally dying down, consumed most daimyo mansions (some 500 of them) along with 779 hatamoto residences, 350 temples and shrines, and 400 blocks of densely packed commoner neighborhoods. It destroyed most of the castle's buildings,

---

4. Conrad Totman, "Lumber Provisioning in Early Modern Japan, 1580–1850," *Journal of Forest History* 31-2 (Apr. 1987): 61.

including its great central keep, and killed over a hundred thousand people, perhaps one in five city residents.

This worst urban catastrophe of the Tokugawa period created a huge demand for lumber, and calls for wood went out all over the country. Timber began to come in, but delays and deficiencies in provisioning led to intense complaints and denunciation. The lord of Tosa, whose forests had been among the country's best in Ieyasu's day, reported: "The mountains of our domain are exhausted; we have neither *sugi* nor *hinoki*. We are unable to provide good lumber as requested by the shogun."[5] He may well have been exaggerating for effect—Tosa did end up providing considerable lumber of usable quality—but it is clear from the history of Tosa forest industry that the han had indeed depleted its timber resources.

Because timber did not arrive quickly enough, lumber merchants came under harsh criticism, and bakufu leaders, trying to expedite matters, denounced their cartel arrangements and ordered changes in regulations on marketing procedure and product quality and price. They firmly restricted the scale and elegance of daimyo mansion construction and called on other city residents, as well, to build simply. Moreover, they delayed and in the end abandoned plans to reconstruct the castle's mammoth wood-and-plaster keep, which at 58.4 meters in height—equivalent to a fifteen-story building—was the largest ever built in Japan.[6]

After Meireki, Edo never regained its earlier opulence. It grew bigger, but its days of architectural glory were gone. Throughout the country, a lumber-rationing system took shape. Restrictions on construction proliferated, with timber size and wood quality being tied to status in ways designed to minimize conflict and discontent by anchoring allocation in ideology. And Japan's forests, whose condition had been deteriorating for decades, were shown to be sadly inadequate to the needs of society's wooden cities. All along the Kiso river, whose forests were still fabled in Ieyasu's day, loggers had felled the accessible stands by the 1660s. As far away as Akita, timber scarcity was apparent by the 1670s, with logging costs rising and the quantity and quality of timber declining.

---

5. Conrad Totman, *The Green Archipelago: Forestry in Preindustrial Japan* (Berkeley and Los Angeles: University of California Press, 1989), pp. 74–75.

6. William H. Coaldrake, "Edo Architecture and Tokugawa Law," *MN* 36-3 (Autumn 1981): 249, 252, 257, 269–72. Coaldrake explains these construction restrictions in terms of an imputed governmental interest in tightening status distinctions for ideological reasons. To me they sound like a rationing system designed to conform to the social values of the decision makers, just as such systems are in other societies.

The demand for heating and cooking fuel also depleted woodland, especially near the great cities. Several industrial processes, notably salt, tile, ceramic, and metal production, also consumed fuel wood. In the case of salt-making, seawater provided ample salt, but in some areas, notably along the Inland Sea, fuel for the evaporators that boiled off the water was becoming scarce by century's end. Salt makers were compelled to purchase wood brought by horseback or boat from more distant areas, and during the eighteenth century even that source became inadequate.

Throughout the realm, boundary disputes erupted as woodsmen worked their way into inner valleys until they encountered others approaching from other directions, and during the latter half of the century, bakuhan officials adjudicated numerous boundary disputes between villages and han. In the northeast, for example, Akita and Morioka quarreled over their mutual boundary until a bakufu ruling ordered the two to compromise and to stay out of the disputed area unless they did so. For years the disputants stood fast, unwilling to settle for half a loaf, but finally in 1677, when Akita's other timber resources became inadequate, its leaders agreed to partition the area so that they could commence logging their portion.

Depletion also fostered conflicts over types of forest use. Land that grew timber could not efficiently grow fuel wood, fodder, or green fertilizer. Similarly, areas repeatedly cut over for fertilizer material could never produce tall timber. From the latter part of the century on, disputes over woodland use and regulations determining who could do what on which parcel of land became legion, and conflicts over land use were forcing a reorientation of basic government policy by century's end.

To elaborate that last point, throughout the seventeenth century, bakufu and han alike promoted land clearance, attaching much more value to arable than woodland because its tax yield was so much greater. By the eighteenth century, however, more and more legislation reflected awareness that forest products, especially building timber, fuel, and green fertilizer, must be nurtured even at the expense of further clearance or even by reforesting areas already in tillage. This reorientation was never complete, however, because tax shortfalls persisted and governments were under chronic pressure to increase agricultural yield. As a consequence, policy constantly swung between support for and resistance to reclamation. How best to balance the need for both woodland and arable was a dilemma that early modern Japan never resolved.

THE DOWNSTREAM RAMIFICATIONS
OF LAND CLEARANCE

Land clearance, by permanently reducing woodland acreage, had a direct, usually negative, impact on forest production and woodland biota. It also could prove disruptive for downstream settlements and existing arable. These forms of environmental damage were the trade-offs that seventeenth-century society accepted, wittingly or not, for the gains in food production that sustained its rapid growth.

During the centuries before 1560, severe environmental deterioration was evident in only a few situations. By and large logging, conversion of woodland to arable, reclamation of abandoned farmland, wildfire, and other forms of human intervention do not appear to have caused extensive flooding or dessication, deterioration in soil fertility, or widespread extinctions owing to destruction of wildlife habitat. In a few spots, however, one does find signs of environmental stress caused by overexploitation, most notably in the Kinai basin, which had been extensively deforested during the Nara and early Heian periods, and where soil subsequently deteriorated.

This legacy of overuse made the Kinai region particularly susceptible to trouble, and the heightened exploitation of the seventeenth century produced a rate of soil erosion, stream silting, flooding, and drought that forced government to take remedial action. A bakufu directive of 1666 addressed the Kinai condition in this way:

> Recently, upland vegetation has been torn out by the roots. As a consequence, during rain storms soil and gravel wash into streams and obstruct the flow of water. Henceforth, such uprooting of vegetation is to be prohibited.
>
> Item: Beginning this spring, seedlings are to be planted to halt erosion on denuded sites above streams.
>
> Item: Paddy land and dry fields are not to be formed on the edges and floodplains of rivers; and areas of bamboo, trees, miscanthus, or other reeds are not to press in upon streambeds.
>
> These clauses are to be enforced. This notice is being sent to intendants who, starting this spring, must despatch investigators to ensure that its clauses are not violated.[7]

In following decades, government concern with riparian problems caused by careless woodland management persisted, and river management became a perennial activity in later centuries.

7. Totman, *Green Archipelago,* p. 95.

Before the 1700s, there is, outside of the Kinai, only scattered evidence of difficulties clearly attributable to upstream exploitation. Assessment is difficult, however, as suggested by the Kan'ei famine of the 1630s–40s, whose social aspects were discussed in chapter 7. Logging and land reclamation may have abetted that crisis. To explain, logging proceeded aggressively during the half century prior to 1630, facilitating land reclamation, which meant that substantial areas were newly converted to tillage. On newly opened sites, soil quality commonly was poor, slowing plant growth and making crops unusually vulnerable to fluctuations of weather. Because considerable woodland had recently been logged, moreover, pioneer growth had had little time to replace old vegetation, which reduced the forest's capacity to modulate fluctuations in air temperature and to hold and warm rainwater before releasing it into streams. Consequently, local temperatures fluctuated more severely, streams flowed more irregularly, and the water was colder, all of which hurt crop development. At that juncture, it appears, a general downturn in temperature shortened growing seasons, and in northeastern Japan the yamase effect—irregular flows of cold northern air—exacerbated the cooling. The factors of floral and climatic change thus combined to cause a crop failure that was more widespread and thorough than would have been the case had either variable been absent.

In any event, the trauma of the Kan'ei famine prompted Iemitsu's government to pursue an array of responses, as noted earlier. And after the immediate crisis had passed, the bakufu undertook to survey its lands, to determine its population of people, trees, and bamboo, and to encourage the planting of trees by arguing that they would help villages recover and reduce the need to buy fuelwood.

In a sense, then, the costs of aggressive logging and reclamation may have begun to be extracted from the human population almost as soon as pacification was completed. In the following decades, however, construction petered out and logged areas threw up new growth that restored much of their capacity to soften climatic extremes. Moreover the soil in newly opened lands matured, and no doubt villagers learned which fields were particularly susceptible to drought, flood, heat, and cold, learned how best to crop them, and discovered which to return to woody growth. Perhaps for these reasons, although crop failures and spot famines periodically occurred, the country was not wracked again by a comparably widespread famine until the 1720s, when Japan's population was double that of 1640.

PART FOUR

Struggling to Stand Still, 1710–1790

As foreshadowed in chapter 3, the latter half of Japan's early modern history can be perceived in its entirety as a period of stasis. But within that period, one can identify two successive stages. During the eighteenth century, social energies were mostly directed at "making the system work," primarily by tinkering or trying harder, despite pervasive evidence that society was overloading its environmental base. During the nineteenth century, however, while there still is ample evidence of environmental overload and resulting social distress, one can see many signs of creativity and iconoclasm in economics, village affairs, intellectual and cultural life, and even politics.

Neither the magnitude of the shift nor the preciseness of timing should be overstated. New and dissident views and initiatives appeared in the eighteenth century, and conservative defenders of the established order were visible in the nineteenth. But the former were few, and what the latter defended ofttimes was quite unlike what they claimed to cherish. The timing of the shift cannot be pinpointed: it occurred gradually and at different times in different areas of activity. Indeed, in the realms of basic human-environment relations and higher cultural production, the "stages" so overlap that topical rather than sequential treatment seems to illuminate matters better. Insofar as diffuse and gradual changes can ever be dated, however, 1790 or thereabouts seems to be the moment when the balance tilted.

Because the condition of the environment impinged so strongly on later Tokugawa human affairs, Part IV begins with a two-chapter scrutiny of the human-environment relationship, as a way of establishing the context within which human actors pursued their political, social, intellectual, and cultural attempts to make the system work. Environmental constraints were most harshly manifested in crop failure and famine and in demographic trends, but they also showed up in changing patterns of work and production, social tension, and public discourse. Through ingenuity and hard work, people found ways to maximize the biosystem's immediate utility. And, especially from late in the century on, they slowly expanded their society's ecological foundation, in the process enlarging its "niche" but also laying up debts for future generations to pay.

Within this restrictive context, the central questions of politics and daily life were how to maximize and how to distribute current yield— that is, issues of taxation, marketing, and production: who would get how much; who would have to do without; and how matters would be arranged so as to minimize the social trouble arising from the rationing of scarce goods. The dominating role of these issues was apparent in the Kyōhō reform of the 1720s, the boldest and furthest-ranging attempt at political and socioeconomic revitalization of the entire Tokugawa period. And their intractable nature was evident in the political life of subsequent decades.

In the intellectual realm, the agenda of elite concerns that dominated seventeenth-century thought was displaced by a broader set of concerns as schooling spread in response to needs, difficulties, and opportunities of the day. As rising social tension fostered intellectual fracturing, thinkers labored to transcend the disagreements. As the social basis of intellectual life widened, commentators tried to legitimize the claims of more diverse social groups, devise strategies for solving problems of the day, and identify and clarify ultimate priorities of self and society.

Finally, in the arena of arts and entertainment, much of the century was given over to elaboration of Genroku themes and genres, most notably in drama and printmaking. But as the first chapter of Part V indicates, the latter half of the century also saw new developments in art and literature that broke new ground and eventuated in an early-nineteenth-century burst of creative energy.

TWELVE

Ecological Trends

The Period of Stasis (I)

Crop Failure and Famine
   The Kyōhō Famine
   The Tenmei Famine
   The Tenpō Famine
   Crop Failure: An Examination
Allocating Resources
   Sumptuary Regulation
   Reorganization of Rural Society
Population Control
   Positive Checks
   Preventive Checks

By the end of Genroku, Japan's environmental situation had changed considerably from that of a century earlier. Very little of the remaining woodland could be opened to cultivation. Few additional dry fields could feasibly be converted to paddy culture. Forest production had dropped sharply from its heyday early in the century. And gold and silver mines were largely exhausted. These forms of resource depletion were the price exacted from the land by a century of socioeconomic growth that had more than doubled the human population to some 30 million, dotted the realm with cities and towns and their high-living privileged classes, and created a complexly integrated nationwide polity and economy.

   The process whereby this society adapted to its tightening ecological circumstances can be examined in terms of five facets: (1) unsolicited forms of adaptation, namely, crop failure and famine; (2) purposeful attempts to control the allocation of scarce resources, notably sumptuary regulation and reorganization of village land control; (3) population control; (4) measures to maximize resource exploitation; and (5) strategies to expand the realm. The first three facets constitute this chapter; the last two comprise chapter 13.

Historically, of course, none of these five facets sprang into being in the year 1700; aspects of each were visible in earlier decades. But most became far more consequential from the early eighteenth century on. In practice, moreover, the five were inextricably entangled, each shaping the others. However, their characters and trajectories stand out most clearly when we disaggregate them, insofar as that is possible.

CROP FAILURE AND FAMINE

Crop failure and famine had a long pre-Tokugawa history, and local sieges of hunger were frequent. During the centuries before 1600, crops most commonly failed owing to drought, but early Tokugawa irrigation work ameliorated that problem. Still, the scourge of crop failure persisted. As land was cleared and rice production shifted to the northeast, unseasonably cold, rainy weather abetted by the yamase effect became the main cause. By one count, there were 154 crop failures during the early modern period, and cold weather was implicated in most of them. In particular, the great famines of the Tenmei and Tenpō periods (1780s and 1830s), which were most devastating in the northeast, were primarily products of cold, wet summers. Chilly rain also contributed to the 1732 crop failure that ravaged the southwest.

The seventeenth century experienced famines, notably that of the Kan'ei period, but after 1700 their frequency, severity, and geographical scale increased substantially. The factors behind these trends are not easy to identify. An array of human actions contributed, of course, but quirks of nature were also involved. Sieges of irregular weather, such as typhoons or monsoon rains, early or late freezes, or cold, wet summers, could wreak havoc. Or disasters such as insect infestations could contribute, their impact magnified by nutritional dependence on rice monoculture. A number of major earthquakes inflicted regional destruction, the eruptions of Mount Fuji in 1707 and Asama in 1783 being especially notorious. Combinations of natural factors proved most devastating, however, as brief narratives of the major famines of 1732, the 1780s, and the 1830s will suggest.

THE KYŌHŌ FAMINE

The Kyōhō famine of 1732–33, the first of the three great killer famines, was produced by a combination of cold rain and an infestation of leaf hoppers (*unka: Cicadula sexnotata*) that ruined crops in the south-west.[1] Poor harvests and vigorous rice-tax collection during the 1720s reduced food reserves in the hinterland, paving the way for trouble, and during 1732, forty-six southwestern han lost nearly 75 percent of their crop, some primarily to bad weather, others to insects. Authorities re-corded 12,072 deaths from starvation, and 2,646,020 people report-edly suffered from hunger.

One of the worst hit areas was Matsuyama han in western Shikoku, and its experience, while extreme, reveals what occurred in much of the southwest that year. After a cold, wet spring ruined the winter grain crop, heavy monsoon flooding disrupted transportation and damaged fields. Chilly summer rain then caused part of the rice crop to rot in the fields, and leaf hoppers finished the rest. Indeed, the hoppers were so thick they consumed other crops and wild growth as well, defoliating valleys and hillsides. Villagers consumed their emergency stores of grain, chestnuts, cultivated and wild roots, and even rice hulls and, finally, farm animals. When nothing remained, they fled if able, going to Ma-tsuyama to beg or heading for areas said to be less devastated than their own. Where rice could still be found, its market price had soared from an undervalued 30 monme per 2 hyō in 1731 to 550 in late 1732, reach-ing 750 in the hinterland. Only the well-off could afford that, so the poor starved. In late 1732, the han reported to Edo that 3,489 people (2,213 males and 1,276 females) had died, along with 1,694 cows and 1,403 horses.

This evidently was the first major crop failure in Matsuyama history, and officials responded belatedly, imposing rice rationing on vassals, distributing modest amounts of relief rice, and trying to restrain prices. They moved to import rice but had to get it from afar because nearby han, having lost their own crops, forbade exports. They exempted vil-lages from taxes and other duties and at year's end lifted all restrictions on the crops villagers might grow. In early 1733 they began distributing salt, seaweed, miso, and lumber, as well as seeds and sprouts for start-ing new crops.

Despite its regional character, the Kyōhō famine had an impact across Japan, because the bakufu tried to ease the hardship by shuffling stored rice from place to place and in the end failed to meet demand anywhere. Better harvests improved conditions for a few years after 1733, but over

1. This material on the Kyōhō famine is from Kageura Tsutomu, "Kyōhō kikin to Iyo shohan no sanjō" [The Kyōhō famine and the pitiful situation of several han in Iyo prov-ince], in *Edo jidai no kikin* [Famine in the Edo Period] (Tokyo: Yusankaku, 1982), pp. 85–94.

the next few decades local crop failures and pervasively heavy taxation sustained a high level of rural suffering and unrest. And during the 1780s all of Japan was ravaged by the series of crop failures that produced the Tenmei famine.

THE TENMEI FAMINE

The crop failures of Tenmei were precipitated by volcanic eruption and cold rain. During the summer of 1783, Mount Asama on the Shinano-Kōzuke border northwest of Edo belched smoke and ash irregularly for two or three months and then erupted in a monstrous explosion during the hot summer night of August 4 (1783/7/7–8).[2] The blast, reportedly heard as far away as Osaka and far northern Honshu, threw out a huge quantity of rock and mud, which descended the volcano's north slope at tremendous speed. The roiling rivers of mud engulfed villages, sweeping along household goods and the corpses of people and animals. A portion of the debris-laden mud smashed into the Agatsuma River, temporarily damming it up. When the river breached the barrier, it collapsed and the mucky water thundered eastward down the narrow valley to Shibukawa. There the torrent surged into the Tone and on out across the Kantō plain east to the Pacific and south into Edo Bay. As the tidal rush of the river advanced, it spilled over banks and levees, wrecking fields and villages along its course.

While the wild muck rushed eastward, the volcano continued pumping out lava and ash in a flashing, rumbling din that continued until nearly noon the next day. A sea of red-hot lava spread laterally over three kilometers of the north slope and flowed downhill for eighteen kilometers before cooling enough to stabilize. Meanwhile, devastation rained down from the sky. The initial blast threw rocks as much as a meter in circumference so far into the sky that some fell to earth over three kilometers from the crater. And ash, stone, and gravel kept falling for miles around, smashing buildings, flattening crops, and starting fires.[3] Carried by wind, the ash spread across the Kantō and into the northeast, darkening the sky for days and slowly settling as a blanket of fine, choking dust. In the mountains directly east of Asama, ash piled up to

2. Asama's history of activity is reported in Saitō Yōichi, "Edo jidai no saigai nen-pyō" [A chronology of Edo-period natural disasters], and Minakami Takeshi, "Saigai to nōmin—Tenmei no Asamayake kara" [Natural disasters and the peasantry: The 1780s eruption of Mount Asama], Rekishi kōron 47 (5-10) (Oct. 1979): 10–20, 51–59.

3. Uemae Jun'ichirō, "Asama-yama funka to Furansu kakumei" [Mount Asama's eruption and the French Revolution], Bungei shunjū 67-9 (July 1989): 211, estimates that the force of the blast was sufficient to throw half-inch pebbles some eleven miles into the air.

depths of a meter and a half. At the village of Myōgi, some thirty kilometers to the southeast, the accumulation measured sixty centimeters.
At Takasaki, some forty five kilometers away, it was twenty centimeters, and even at Chōshi, on the sea far to the east, seven or eight centimeters accumulated. In Edo itself, which was south of the fallout path,
about two and a half centimeters of ash were deposited.

The blast, flood, and fires left some two thousand people dead and
eighteen hundred houses destroyed. Between the flooding and ash blanket, crops over much of the Kantō were ruined, and in stricken areas of
Kōzuke and Shinano, villagers went on rampages of smashing in desperate quests for food and other necessities.[4] In the longer run, the eruption reduced the fertility of vast acreages of land and diverted an inor-
dinate amount of labor to removing ash and repairing flood damage.
And as the ash gradually worked its way into waterways, it added to
the silt buildup that villagers would have to keep dredging for decades
to protect their irrigation systems and prevent flooding and further ruin.

Years before these longer-term costs accrued, the effects of the eruption reinforced bad weather to give Japan its worst famine to date.[5]
Already in 1781 there were signs of deteriorating weather, and the next
year Japan west of Nagoya experienced crop failure, rice-price jumps,
and widespread local protests. During the spring of 1783, cold, wet
yamase winds blew out of the northeast at rice-planting time, damaging
the crop at the outset, and as summer advanced the winds persisted.
Then dust from Asama's summer-long venting darkened the sun, with-
ering rice ears, slowing growth, and delaying the harvest. By late in the
eighth lunar month, farmers in the Kantō and Tōhoku regions knew
their harvest would be slender, and in late October (early 83/10) snow
fell, ruining what little remained. Crop losses in the small han of Hachinohe north of Sendai, for example, "ran to an astonishing 96% that
summer, with losses of 84% the following and 38% the previous year."[6]

Villagers did their best, eating sprouts, wild greens, and bark, digging

4. Kären Wigen-Lewis, "Common Losses: Transformations of Commonland and
Peasant Livelihood in Tokugawa Japan, 1603–1868" (M.A. thesis, University of California, Berkeley, 1985), p. 104, says the impact of the eruption was felt much farther away,
disrupting the summer weather so badly that one site in the northeast "recorded rain for
fifty-three out of ninety-two days; only nineteen days brought unambiguously clear skies."
The argument of Uemae Jun'ichirō, cited above, for that matter, is that the eruption had
a global impact on the climate, its ash darkening the sky enough to contribute to crop
failures in Europe that helped precipitate the French Revolution.

5. Save as noted, this material on the Tenmei famine is from Mori Yasuhiko, "Kikin
to ikki" [Famine and protest], and Nanba Nobuo, "Tenmei kikin to bakuhan taisei no
shomujun" [The Tenmei famine and contradictions in the Tokugawa polity], in Edo jidai
no kikin, pp. 52–62, 95–104.

6. Wigen-Lewis, "Common Losses," p. 104.

up roots, and even consuming work animals, although doing so substituted future poverty for present starvation. As conditions worsened late in 1783, local disturbances multiplied, occurring from Tōhoku to the far southwest. Some sixty incidents of violent protest (*ikki* and *uchiko-washi*) convulsed eastern Japan alone between late summer and the spring of 1784. By winter, conditions were desperate for poorer villagers. Robbery became common, along with arson, as people punished the privileged or covered their own criminal tracks. The vulnerable were abandoned, thrown out, and some eventually cannibalized.[7]

Hachinohe reported losing nearly half its population of 65,000, and a study of one area in the han indicates that between that fall and the next summer, 899 fled and 1,984 died out of 7,184. In Sōma han, south of Sendai, the daimyo set up a relief hostel, and on the day it opened (1784/2/1), 468 people sought admission. The numbers grew as word got around, but food was short, many admittees were too weak to recover, and several victims died daily in the hostel. By the spring of 1784, 4,416 were dead and 1,843 missing out of Sōma's population of 48,242. Vacant houses numbered 1,371. By summer the dead numbered 8,500, and three years later the han gave its population as 31,667, a drop of 32 percent since 1783. Elsewhere in the northeast the story was similar, if not often as dramatic.[8]

Population figures for the country as a whole, while unreliable as precise measures, suggest the magnitude of suffering. Counts of commoners had assessed their number at 26,010,600 in 1780, but in 1786 they found only 25,086,466, a drop of over 924,000. A third of the loss was recorded in the sparsely populated Tōhoku region, some representing deaths and some departures for cities and regions to the south and west. In many areas the harvest was better in 1784, but cold, wet weather over the next two years reduced yields, preventing accumulation of reserve supplies, and during 1787 the country was again racked by famine. Though less harsh than that of 1783, it produced additional deaths and took more arable land out of production.

---

7. For brief references to travelers' reports of Tenmei starvation, see Mikiso Hane, *Peasants, Rebels, and Outcastes* (New York: Pantheon Books, 1982), p. 8, and Harold Bolitho, "Travelers' Tales: Three Eighteenth-Century Travel Journals," *HJAS* 50-2 (Dec. 1990): 502–3.

8. For a usefully skeptical scrutiny of the Tenmei famine's impact on Morioka han, see Susan B. Hanley and Kozo Yamamura, *Economic and Demographic Change in Preindustrial Japan, 1600–1868* (Princeton: Princeton University Press, 1977), pp. 146–53.

THE TENPŌ FAMINE

For Japan as a whole, difficulties eased after 1790. During the 1820s, however, several harvest shortfalls set the stage for another major disaster, the Tenpō famine of the 1830s, whose savagery was enhanced by outbreaks of disease. The episode was comparable in character and severity to that of the 1780s, with a series of cold, wet summers again ruining crops, most seriously in the northeast.[9] In 1833 the Tōkai region reported only 70 percent of normal yield while the far northeast had only 35 percent, with areas of the Mogami river valley, Sendai plain, and Echigo harvesting next to nothing. The year 1836 was worse, especially in the southwest, with cold dampness and a hard frost late in the ninth month (late October) again ruining what remained. In Shikoku and those Honshu provinces bordering the Inland Sea, the crop yield was 55 percent of normal; in the far northeast it ranged from 28 percent to nothing. For the country as a whole, it worked out to 24 percent of a regular harvest.

Bizen han, where rice and wheat crops yielded only ten to twenty percent of normal, was particularly hard hit:

> Bad harvests had been the pattern since 1833, but 1836 was the first year in which mass deaths occurred in Okayama [Bizen]. The peasants took to the mountains and dug up roots; they ate anything edible. The bodies of the starving swelled up, acute diarrhoea was common. The han government forbade the selling or transportation of foodstuffs outside the han, and it began to dole out small portions of rice gruel to the starving at night so that those not accustomed to charity could hide their shame in the dark.[10]

The country endured poor harvests for most of the next five years, the suffering being compounded by scattered epidemics and insect infestations. The demographic consequences of these events were substantial, even though specific mortality figures must be treated with skepticism. In Hirosaki han, some 35,600 reportedly died and another 47,000 fled between 1833 and 1839. Nineteen thousand horses were said to have died and 9,484 chō of paddy field to have been abandoned. In Akita during 1837, a number of villages reported death rates that averaged about two per household.

9. This material on the Tenpō famine is mostly from Uesugi Mitsuhiko, "Tenpō no kikin to bakuhan taisei no hōkai" [The Tenpō famine and collapse of the Tokugawa polity], in *Edo jidai no kikin*, pp. 105–15.
10. Susan B. Hanley and Kozo Yamamura, "Population Trends and Economic Growth in Pre-Industrial Japan," in D. V. Glass and R. Revelle, eds., *Population and Social Change* (London: Edward Arnold, 1972), p. 483.

Apart from the dead, there were many who took to the roads in search of sustenance, most commonly heading for cities such as Edo and Osaka. They didn't always make it: in one region of the northeast some three thousand reportedly starved to death and another three thousand died of epidemic disease en route. If they did make it, life was far from easy. They were unwelcome, generally had no place to stay until special hostels were erected, and found food expensive unless they received alms. In Edo, for example, the price of rice rose more than threefold from a pre-1830s level of about 60–70 monme per koku to 122.2 monme in 1833, 199.8 in 1836, and 231.3 in 1837. But for the destitute, that was better than staying put, because prices rose faster and farther in hard-pressed areas of the hinterland—for example, rising nearly fifteenfold in Akita between 1833 and the late fall of 1834. The combination of deaths and departures resulted in an overall loss of population in most areas from the far north to western Honshu and a compensatory rise of 2–3 percent in the population of the far southwest.

CROP FAILURE: AN EXAMINATION

As these brief glimpses of three major famines indicate, vagaries of climate and other natural disasters were not trivial events. However, such acts of nature were not unprecedented and by themselves cannot account for the magnitude of hardship that accompanied them. Other factors caused them to exact their unprecedentedly severe social price.

The process of land reclamation, to begin with, increased the proportion of Japan's rice grown in the Kantō and Tōhoku regions, which were more vulnerable to cold weather. Tōhoku, "a climatic zone to which [rice] was only marginally adapted," was especially subject to devastating variations in air temperature and rainfall owing to the yamase effect, which could blanket the northeast with cold, wet air for weeks at a time.[11] As good land grew scarce, clearance brought marginal land under the hoe. Some was closer to volcanoes or on hillsides more prone to slide when shaken by quakes. Much was at higher elevations, in narrower valleys, or on floodplain or swampy areas, and more susceptible to unseasonal freeze, flood, or drought, and yet its yield might constitute the essential margin of survival for people living in the affected locality.

Reclamation and other forms of land use also fostered erosion that

11. The quoted phrase is from Wigen-Lewis, "Common Losses," p. 104.

led to stream silting. River engineering measures addressed the problem, as is noted in chapter 13, but the long-term trend was toward more extensive silting, more elaborate river works, and more severe flooding and damage when the works failed in the face of unusually heavy rainfall or snowmelt.

Furthermore, intensification of agronomic technique in the eighteenth century gave Japan a finely tuned agricultural system. By exercising care in selecting crops, preparing soil, and applying irrigation water and fertilizer, skilled farmers produced crops sufficient to feed thirty million, even while providing a wide range of other goods—as long as the weather held. But precisely because the cropping was so finely tuned, the margin of error was slender and modest irregularities in weather could produce disproportionate fluctuations in crop yields, which quickly translated into scarcities.

The danger in crop failure was exacerbated by crop specialization, which was occurring within the context of a highly fractionalized political order. Where farmers replaced food production with cash crops such as cotton or tobacco, as many did in the vicinity of Osaka, they became more dependent on food from other localities. When income from their cash crop shrank for any reason, they were hard pressed to pay for food. Conversely, when food crops failed, the producing villagers and their rulers restricted exports to other regions lest reserves fail at home, as did Bizen in 1836, and such restrictions could create food scarcities in cash crop areas.

Apart from these changes at the producer level, actions by the rulers also could exacerbate the destructive effect of crop failure. The shogun Yoshimune, as noted in chapter 14, increased the tax yield of bakufu land and inspired daimyo to improve their fiscal performance, which moved rice supplies more completely from the countryside into the cities, reducing the cushion villagers had against crop failure. Beyond that, when hardship threatened the cities, rulers tried to respond even if that meant increasing pressure on the countryside. Thus, in 1783 when Asama's eruption and the subsequent crop failure threatened Edo's food supply, bakufu leaders ordered their intendants to collect more tax rice, ship it to Edo and Osaka, and hike other taxes to generate resources for the cities.[12]

A particularly disastrous case of governmental action occurred in Hirosaki. In 1781 the daimyo tried to reduce his han debt by promoting

12. Nanba, "Tenmei kikin," p. 99.

taxable new production, including cotton and silk cloth, salt, and pottery. The ventures all failed, so the lord turned to more customary alternatives. He resurveyed his lands, increased the tax levy, compelled wealthy villagers to turn over stored rice, withheld part of his retainers' rice stipends, and began shipping the accumulated grain to Edo and Osaka. Then the harvest failed. Even as villagers and townsmen were rioting and demanding cuts in the rice price and cessation of shipments, he pressed on, at one point deploying troops so that freighters could depart Aomori safely. Some vessels made it to Osaka and Edo; some were lost at sea. But all their cargo was denied to the needy of Hirosaki, and the result was a tragedy twice that of the Tenpō years. By a relatively conservative count, 81,702 people died of starvation. Reportedly 17,211 horses perished, and two-thirds of the han's arable land, some 10,399 chō of paddy field and 6,931 chō of dry fields, temporarily went out of production.[13]

Of course, rulers could also ameliorate hardship, but because daimyo governance was local, "virtuous" rule that bettered conditions in one area might worsen them in another. In 1783 the Tōhoku domain of Shirakawa (110,000 koku) reportedly lost nearly all its rice crop. However, the lord, Matsudaira Sadanobu, grandson of the revered Yoshimune, was able through family connections in Edo to buy substantial quantities of rice, some from Osaka and some from nearby areas, including the Aizu, Taira, Nihonmatsu, and Moriyama domains. He distributed the food to his vassals and villagers and reportedly prevented any from starving to death. Saving his people despite massive crop failure helped give Sadanobu a glowing reputation, propelled his political career, and surely was to his credit.[14] He did so, however, by obtaining rice from areas where need was comparable, and by assuring that it was distributed to his own people, not to outsiders, who found the border closed. Had the polity been more integrated, a more sensitive distribution system might well have kept the people of Shirakawa alive without leaving a reported 8,500 dead in nearby Sōma han.

In sum, a wide range of human actions had combined by the early eighteenth century to make demands on Japan's ecosystem that it could not meet as reliably as in earlier decades. When the rhythms of nature

    13. Mori, "Kikin to ikki," pp. 52–53, and Nanba, "Tenmei kikin," p. 98. Other figures for deaths in Tsugaru during 1783–84 range as high as two hundred thousand (Mori, p. 42).
    14. Herman Ooms, *Charismatic Bureaucrat: A Political Biography of Matsudaira Sadanobu, 1758–1829* (Chicago: University of Chicago Press, 1975), pp. 50–57.

faltered, people—the poor most especially—as well as domesticated animals and other species subject to human exploitation all suffered.

ALLOCATING RESOURCES

More severe crop failure and a correspondingly heightened level of public hardship were two results of the increased pressure on Japan's natural resources. A third was proliferation of mechanisms for allocating those resources.

Some of the more familiar mechanisms require only brief note. Hardship itself performed a distributive function within both society and the wider biosystem. It deprived some people, usually the weak and poor, of goods and services they otherwise could have enjoyed. And farther down the chain of exploitation, it converted animal fodder into human food through the slaughter of draft animals and game and diverted other plant species to human use as emergency food supplies. Similarly, social conflict allocated resources by producing decisions, sometimes violently, on riparian rights, the use of common land, the handling of debt obligations, the payment of taxes, or other matters of contention. And commercial transactions, with their associated price fluctuations, provided another basic mechanism for determining who got what.

More extensive comment seems in order on two developments that were central to the allocation of goods and services: government regulation of consumption and long-term reorganization of local land control.

SUMPTUARY REGULATION

From the outset, Japan's early modern rulers attempted to stabilize society and secure their own income by operating a command economy in which they controlled the distribution of resources. As noted in earlier chapters, during the seventeenth century they gradually delineated elaborate status distinctions and, especially during Tsunayoshi's rule, issued a host of sumptuary regulations that linked consumption to status. In toto, the policy created a pervasive system of rationing that distributed goods and services in accordance with the recipient's social rank.

Leaders of both bakufu and han continued to elaborate this rationing system in later decades, even though much economic activity had shifted by then from command to market arrangements. From the 1730s on,

Yoshimune relied on sumptuary decrees to regulate consumption after his deflationary monetary policy collapsed. And during the 1790s the reformist bakufu leader Matsudaira Sadanobu, of Shirakawa fame, favored them in the belief that such discipline was essential to deter society from consuming more than it produced. Anchoring his argument in Confucian analogues, he wrote: "Just as the Way of Heaven is *yin-yang*, where yin is income and yang outgo, and just as the Way of Man is inhalation and exhalation, so income in economy means storing in storehouses, and outgo means use of the stored goods."[15] To control outgo, he argued, rules should be issued that "are patterned on Heaven" and meet "the need for usage and the trend of the times." Such a policy would curtail consumption and permit accumulation of stored goods, thereby protecting society against scarcities and hardship of the sort that had recently wracked the country during the Tenmei famine.

Daimyo also tried to control consumption by fiat. Many routinely reissued edicts originating in Edo and imposed their own as needed. Timber scarcities produced a wealth of decrees. Aizu domain, for example, began wrestling with timber depletion during the seventeenth century, but its measures failed to suffice. In 1711, in a renewed effort to restore timber stands, the han reissued old restrictions on construction in towns and highway stations and admonished villagers to plan all riparian repair projects that required timber or other materials carefully. It also ordered them henceforth to get approval from village officials before using beams in home construction and placed explicit status-based limits on sizes and quantities.[16]

Bakuhan leaders continually issued restrictive regulations. Many were

15. Ibid., p. 34.
16. Endō Yasutarō, "Aizu han no zōrin seido oyobi sono jigyō ni kan suru ichi kō-satsu" [A study of the afforestation system of Aizu domain and its accomplishments], *Sanrin ihō* 25-2 (1930): 15–16, reports the following village timber-use regulations of 1711:

Household status (in koku)	Size of timbers (in ken)	Total length of timbers (in ken)
1–5	2–2.5	6 (7 for upland villages)
6–10	2.5	8
11–20	2.5 (3 if over 15 koku)	10
Over 20	2.5–3	12

All villagers were allowed an additional 2 ken of timber of the specified size for gates and outbuildings. Village officials (*kimoiri*), regardless of their koku level, were allowed somewhat more timber to maintain their offices. (In what is surely a typographical error, Endō gives a total length of 20 ken for householders of 11–20 koku. I have substituted 10 because that number seems to fit the case and to be the most plausible typographical intent.)

unenforceable, and the very frequency of reiteration casts doubt on their effectiveness. But others achieved their allocative purpose to some extent, even though the marketplace enabled wealth to challenge status as the primary determinant of relative advantage. The regulations could still function because the role of wealth was concealed, and to some extent contained, by status niceties. Much as intellectuals used the savant strategy to secure official positions that gave them access to privilege, so merchants accepted formal appointments by daimyo or bakufu and wealthy villagers took local office to legitimize larger houses, finer garb, and other privileges. In doing so they helped perpetuate the effectiveness of sumptuary regulation as a rationing strategy.

REORGANIZATION OF RURAL SOCIETY

Rearranging land control at the village level was a less obvious mechanism for distributing scarce goods. It performed that function in conjunction with sumptuary regulation, as in the abovementioned instance of home construction in Aizu, where house size was determined by a villager's landholdings, making the allocation of land itself the single most important determinant of a villager's material prospects.

From Hideyoshi's day on, as previous chapters have noted, rulers delineated local organization and relationships through land surveys, censuses, and regulatory decrees, and they linked rural areas to castle towns through official organs and edicts. Forty years later, Iemitsu's government issued a series of regulations that revealed the rulers' vision of a properly ordered rural society—an ideal captured in the term *kyōdōtai,* or "cooperative body"—as an array of unmonetized, self-sufficient villages occupied by hereditary peasant proprietors who lived frugally, worked their lands diligently, shared communal resources harmoniously, accepted responsibility for one another's conduct, and paid their taxes in a timely manner.

As the seventeenth century aged, however, that ideal was threatened by other developments, notably the opening to tillage of most potentially arable land, the conversion to paddy culture of most fields that could be converted, the fullest feasible use of woodland, and the expanding role of money and marketplace in rural life. These developments redefined the possibilities and limits of rural life, setting in motion trends erosive of the kyōdōtai ideal. The timing of those developments varied regionally, occurring first in the Kinai region, long the most populous, most monetized, and most fully exploited part of Japan, and spreading most slowly into the hinterlands of the northeast and far southwest.

In this story of rural change, the key factor is that as villagers ran out of additional land to till, they strove to maximize the output of existing fields.[17] As noted more fully in chapter 13, they increased the mental attentiveness, labor time, and fertilizer applied to each parcel of land. By enabling a household to get by on less arable, this agronomic intensification permitted the formation of smaller farm units. A tiller could exercise more careful husbandry on those units while more intensively exploiting family labor—wife, children, unwed siblings, and elderly parents—because of their sense of engagement and dependence.

Many of these small managerial units arose from the breakup of larger landholdings. Large holdings had been created by local men of power through rude acquisition of land before surveys were conducted late in the sixteenth century and through land clearance during the seventeenth. As decades passed, however, the extended family and quasi-family units that worked these holdings grew too large for effective management and found their sense of familial cohesiveness declining. As long as cities were growing rapidly and unreclaimed land was available, discontented and surplus kin could go elsewhere, thereby easing the stresses on large holdings. But by century's end these "safety valves" were much less available to the much larger populace, and group conflict had to be resolved within the village.

The holders of large farms, finding it more difficult to resolve tensions or use their labor pool efficiently, and being reluctant to support surplus dependents, began renting pieces of land, or even alienating parcels permanently, escaping responsibility for the recipients as a quid pro quo.[18] Generally, the parcels thus "sold" or leased were smaller, relative to the number of people they supported, than the areas landlords retained, and the meagerness of allotment prodded smallholders to intensify tillage. Since the newly created farm units often lacked woodland and wasteland, moreover, their holders became more dependent on communal land, particularly for fertilizer and fuel supplies, even as

17. In this discussion I am relying heavily on the work of Thomas C. Smith, most notably his classic, *The Agrarian Origins of Modern Japan* (Stanford: Stanford University Press, 1959). However, Smith's interest is in economic development and mine is in adaptation to environmental change, so emphasis and explanation in the treatments are dissimilar.
18. Buying and selling of arable land was illegal during the Tokugawa period, but villagers developed arrangements for "indefinite leasing" (*eitai baibai*) of land that accomplished much the same purpose.

those were becoming more scarce. If the smallholder had labor time left over, he was under pressure to hire out or seek by-employment to help feed his family.

This fragmenting of farms was worrisome to the rulers, who knew that smallholders were more likely to fail and default on taxes. The problem was evident in central Japan by the mid seventeenth century: as early as 1656 Bizen han banned the formation of branch households on small plots of land. In 1673 Edo reiterated an older decree that forbade village heads to divide holdings smaller than twenty koku in estimated yield; and common peasants, holdings under ten koku. The pressure to divide grew with land scarcity, but smaller holdings also became more feasible owing to the changes in agronomy. In 1722 Yoshimune brought the regulations more in line with current need and feasibility by eliminating the twenty-koku figure so that only holdings with an estimated yield of less than ten koku (or smaller than one chō in area) were impartible. That decree, too, failed to stop the trend, and micro-farming became pervasive despite its risks for both smallholder and tax collector.

Over time, this change in landholding multiplied the numbers of very small holdings, promoted landlordism and tenantry, and intensified the distance and disparity between well-to-do and poor villagers. As the role of markets and money grew, the economic differentiation that accompanied the rise of micro-farming became ever more decisive in the allocation of goods and services. The wealthy did well; the poor did not. The later Tokugawa period displayed, on the one hand, a widespread population of wealthy landlords who occupied comfortable homes, cultivated diverse arts and letters, and engaged successfully in the life of the marketplace and, on the other hand, a vastly greater population of small holders and landless tenants and laborers who got by as best they could, making their mark in history through the faceless statistics of corvée labor service, rural unrest, famine, and demographics.

POPULATION CONTROL

Crop failure and famine constituted, in effect, an announcement that the ecosystem's capacity to supply food to human society dependably was inadequate to the demand. Whereas sumptuary regulation, differential land control, and the marketplace functioned as key allocative mechanisms for determining who would receive how much of what was available, population control addressed the problem of supply and demand by limiting the overall number of human recipients. It was a major development of the eighteenth century and produced a sharp shift in Japan's demographic trajectory. The questions of how and why the shift occurred are among the most contentious in the historiography of this period.[19]

The basic trajectory of population is reasonably certain. During the seventeenth century, it grew rapidly, from an estimated 12,000,000 to some 30,000,000. From about 1700, however, the growth slackened, particularly in provinces near the great cities, where urban developments most strongly influenced rural life, and in the northeast, where agriculture was most severely affected by vagaries of weather. In those regions, population seems actually to have declined, whereas in the southwest, it continued to grow, but much more slowly, so that for the realm as a whole, population was nearly stable.[20] Growth did not resume for nearly a century, and when it did during the early 1800s, the rate was too low, the trend too irregular, and the documentary evidence too spotty for one to declare a definite change in trajectory until after the Meiji Restoration.[21]

The situation is suggested by the censuses that Yoshimune and later shogun ordered. The first compilation was made in 1721, and a second was decreed in 1726, in an order that set the pattern thereafter:

> As already reported in the sixth year [1721], the farmers, merchants, townspeople, shrine-priests, temple-priests, temple-priestesses and other people shall be fully recorded this year. The whole number in each district shall be given, and recorded from each domain and fief. . . . Of course the report must show

19. In English the main contributors to this demographic study have been Susan Hanley, Akira Hayami, and T. C. Smith. The most notable works are Hanley and Yamamura, *Economic and Demographic Change;* Thomas C. Smith, *Nakahara* (Stanford: Stanford University Press, 1977); and the numerous essays by Hayami, some cited below.

20. Akira Hayami, "Population Changes," in Marius B. Jansen and Gilbert Rozman, eds., *Japan in Transition from Tokugawa to Meiji* (Princeton: Princeton University Press, 1986), pp. 290–94. Smith, *Nakahara,* p. 7, states that "there was no growth of the national population between 1721 and 1846." Griffith Feeney and Hamano Kiyoshi, "Rice Price Fluctuations and Fertility in Late Tokugawa Japan," *JJS* 16-1 (Winter 1990): 1, write that it "neither grew nor declined." In a contrary view, Hanley and Yamamura, *Economic and Demographic Change,* p. 61, state that "between 1721 and 1872, the population of Japan *as a whole* showed a distinct upward trend." However, that statement seems to be based on a comparison of the 1721 census figure for commoners with that of 1872 (33,110,825), which attempts to include the total population.

21. For a different emphasis, see Hayami, "Population Changes," p. 315, who writes that "Japan's national population began increasing from the start of the nineteenth century." His inquiry is concerned with the relationship of population to economic growth, and he recognizes that in fact "mortality crises of 1837–1838 and 1861" wiped out much of the gain. However, he discounts these setbacks as not germane for his purposes, contending that they were "exogenous short-term factors" that had "little connection with national economic conditions" (p. 298).

the month of registration and give the ages. The servants and subordinates, who belong to the samurai, shall not be required to be reported.

Hereafter, even though there are no instructions, in each sixth year . . . the examination and report must be undertaken.[22]

These population registers, which were compiled from the *shūmon aratame chō* (registers of religious faith) that all villages maintained, thus counted most of the commoner class, yielding statistics that indicate the general stability of population.[23] Here are some selected figures:

1721	26,065,425	1792	24,891,441
1732	26,921,816	1804	25,517,729
1744	26,153,450	1828	27,201,400
1756	26,061,830	1834	27,063,907
1780	26,010,600	1846	26,907,625

The figures must be read with caution: they omit several thousand court nobles, some two million members of samurai households, and their "servants and subordinates." Moreover, in ways that varied by locality the census takers left out infants and small children, missing an estimated 20 percent of births. They missed many drifters and probably some of the city poor. In early years they may have seriously undercounted women, at least in the northeast, and as the population became more mobile in later years, they may have both double-counted and omitted more and more people.[24] Whether the earlier or later figures are more unreliable is probably impossible to say, and at best they are rough indicators of the real numbers of commoners despite their seeming exactitude. Equally certain, however, the main story they tell can be credited. The times had changed by the 1720s, and the combination of

22. Eijiro Honjo, *The Social and Economic History of Japan* (1935; New York: Russell & Russell, 1965), p. 147.

23. For a full listing of the census results, with some reports tallied by gender, see ibid., p. 154.

24. An excellent descriptive introduction to *shūmon aratame chō* is L. L. Cornell and Akira Hayami, "The *shūmon aratame chō*: Japan's Population Registers," *Journal of Family History* 11-4 (1986): 311–28. In a number of essays, Hayami notes the problems of omission and double counting in the registers. In his essay, "The Population at the Beginning of the Tokugawa Period," *Keiō Economic Studies* 4 (1966–67): 461, he notes undercounting of women in Kyushu in 1622. Hanley and Yamamura, "Population Trends and Economic Growth," p. 461, speaking of Tōhoku registers, write, "females were definitely under-reported, and by as much as 20 percent. This bias in the figures tended to correct itself over time."

factors that once sustained rapid population growth had been replaced by a combination that promoted overall demographic stability.

Identifying that combination and explaining why it arose and was sustained is where the strongest scholarly disagreement lies. The factors that determined population numbers can be analyzed in terms of "positive" and "preventive" checks on population, meaning, essentially, those factors that killed people sooner than they otherwise would have died and those that prevented births that otherwise might have occurred.[25]

POSITIVE CHECKS

"War, pestilence, and famine" are the positive checks demographers cite most commonly. War, even including the escalating protest activity of commoners, did not contribute significantly to Tokugawa death rates. Japan also was spared many types of pestilence, or epidemic disease: notably bubonic plague, diphtheria, epidemic typhus, malaria, relapsing, scarlet, and typhoid fevers, and, until 1822, Asiatic cholera.[26] On the other hand, the realm did suffer epidemics of dysentery, influenza, measles, and smallpox, and records suggest that they recurred more often after 1700, presumably because the population had become more dense and more mobile and hence more capable of transmitting pathogens from one community to another.

One enumeration of epidemics shows twenty occurring in the fifteenth century, nineteen in the sixteenth, sixteen in the seventeenth, thirty-one in the eighteenth, and thirty-two in the nineteenth. Other listings show a similarly sharp increase in incidence after 1700. Dysentery, influenza, and measles debilitated and could be devastating to individuals and families, but they seem to have had little direct impact on population figures. Smallpox, however, did slow population growth during the

25. The dichotomous categories "positive" and "preventive" are of general analytical utility. However, they are not fully satisfactory for analyzing patterns of death among the newborn because they oversimplify and invite dubious categorization. The problematic category is "infanticide." Surely it should be designated a positive check since the infants were in fact born and subsequently were destroyed, much as combatants in war and victims of serial killers and executioners are born and subsequently die through acts of human will. However, for purposes of demographic analysis, the brevity of the infant's life means that infanticide functioned essentially as a form of stillbirth, and it is, therefore, categorized as a preventive check. A more substantive problem with the term *infanticide* is that its use implies that the newborn died owing to a clearly calculated human decision, whereas *stillbirth* signifies an act of nature beyond human control. Surely Tokugawa reality was more ambiguous, with hard-pressed parents indecisively or accidentally acting or failing to act in ways that led to half-intended or half-wanted infant deaths.

26. These comments on infectious disease are based on Ann Bowman Jannetta, *Epidemics and Mortality in Early Modern Japan* (Princeton: Princeton University Press, 1987). She reports numbers of epidemics on pp. 44, 48–49.

eighteenth century because it was often fatal to children and epidemics recurred locally every few years, infecting children born since the last outbreak. According to one local study, smallpox epidemics killed some 10 percent of all children in the afflicted region.

Even more than epidemics, crop failure and famine became prominent features of later Tokugawa life. Famine killed people outright and, perhaps more harmfully, drove large numbers into desperate flight and temporarily slashed the energy levels of survivors, reducing their capacity to work, produce offspring, and ward off illness. Indeed, many deaths attributed to disease during periods of famine may better be credited to malnutrition. However, because crop failure and famine were highly disruptive and hence highly political events, their demographic effects are difficult to assess. The numbers who actually starved to death may have been lower than claimed, inasmuch as leaders of afflicted villages and han inflated mortality reports to justify requests for tax relief or other forms of assistance.[27]

Nevertheless, during the Kyōhō, Tenmei, and Tenpō famines, food reserves were so inadequate and flight so difficult that starvation appears to have had a significant demographic impact.[28] Countrywide figures for Tenmei and selected numbers for Tenpō were cited above. The Kyōhō famine reportedly killed about 20 percent of the people in Fukuoka han in Kyushu, reducing a population of some 360,000 to 289,000. Many of the dead were fishing villagers, who were unable to fish in choppy winter waters, lacked wasteland where they could forage for roots, tubers, or other wild food, and were "more dependent on the market for rice and other agricultural products and thus more affected by soaring prices."[29] Fukuoka recovered only slowly from that demographic setback.

PREVENTIVE CHECKS

There is ample evidence of the misery caused by famines, but despite their harrowing social impact, even the great ones do not suffice to explain the stable size of the late Tokugawa population. Preventive checks

27. For an examination of highly inconsistent numbers in Morioka han during the Tenpō famine, see Hanley and Yamamura, *Economic and Demographic Change*, pp. 147–53.

28. Hanley and Yamamura, *Economic and Demographic Change*, p. 63. Uesugi, "Tenpō no kikin," p. 109, argues, however, that the Tenpō famine, despite the scope of crop failure, produced less havoc than the earlier ones because it was spread over a longer period and governments were able to respond more effectively to the crisis.

29. Arne Kalland and Jon Pederson, "Famine and Population in Fukuoka Domain during the Tokugawa Period," *JJS* 10-1 (Winter 1984): 47.

that limited the numbers and size of households appear to have been crucial. In essence, couples raised fewer children, with the result that overall fertility declined during the eighteenth century to a level approaching "zero population growth."[30] Several factors were involved: greater difficulty in marrying, women marrying at a more advanced age, reduction in the number of child-bearing years, longer intervals between births, more avoidance of pregnancy, and more abortions, stillbirths, and infanticide.

A discussion of these several factors is essentially a discussion of the peasantry, because peasants, being most of the population, determined demographic trends. It appears, moreover, that most statements about villagers are applicable to samurai and urban commoners as well, except for a couple of differences that warrant mention. The stability of samurai numbers was reinforced by political fiat, because rulers refused to support the branch households of vassals. Owing to the transience and harsh living conditions of the urban poor, moreover, urban commoners were unable to sustain their own numbers, and cities continually drained people from the nearby countryside.[31] Since these conditions probably were about as true of early as of later Tokugawa years, however, they do little to explain the demographic shift, and one has to look elsewhere.

Thomas C. Smith made a crucial observation about fertility when he wrote, "nearly every demographic measure shows either suggestive or statistically significant differences between various groups of holders."[32] That is to say, in most matters that relate to demography, well-

30. Unless otherwise noted, this discussion of preventive measures is based on Smith, *Nakahara,* and Hanley and Yamamura, *Economic and Demographic Change.* Where sources disagree—and they do—I have chosen what seemed the most defensible interpretation.

31. On samurai, see Kozo Yamamura, "Samurai Income and Demographic Change: The Genealogies of Tokugawa Bannermen," in Susan B. Hanley and Arthur P. Wolf, eds., *Family and Population in East Asian History* (Stanford: Stanford University Press, 1985), pp. 62–80. On city transiency, see Robert J. Smith, "Small Families, Small Households, and Residential Instability: Town and City in Pre-Modern Japan," in Peter Laslett, ed., *Household and Family in Past Time* (Cambridge: Cambridge University Press, 1972), pp. 439–41. On urban demography, see Sasaki Yōichirō, "Urban Migration and Fertility in Tokugawa Japan: The City of Takayama, 1773–1871," in Hanley and Wolf, eds., *Family and Population,* pp. 133–53. Hayami Akira mentions the obstacles to a self-sustaining urban population in "Labor Migration in a Pre-Industrial Society: A Study Tracing the Life Histories of the Inhabitants of a Village," *Keiō Economic Studies* 10-2 (1973): 6. Hayami has published a revised version of that essay, with added comparative material from other villages, in Hanley and Wolf, eds., *Family and Population,* pp. 110–32.

32. Smith, *Nakahara,* p. 31. Here I am generalizing a claim that Smith makes only for the village of Nakahara. The generalization is supported by Hayami, "Labor Migration," and by his "Class Differences in Marriage and Fertility among Tokugawa Villagers in Mino Province," *Keiō Economic Studies* 17-1 (1980): 1–16.

to-do peasants and poor peasants behaved somewhat differently. Specifically, the offspring of tenants and smallholders married later, largely because adult sons and daughters were away from home working to help support their families (*dekasegi*) or because daughters were kept at home to help their parent(s).[33] So poorer women started having babies later. They also stopped having additional infants sooner, in part because their marriages ended sooner in death or divorce.[34] The poor raised fewer children; indeed they had so few that many found themselves unable to preserve their family lines. Well-to-do peasants, by contrast, had more children, establishing cadet sons in branch houses that, in effect, replaced the poorer village households that died out. Hayami Akira summarizes his findings for one village this way: "Three-quarters of the daughters of tenants in the lowest class migrated and as a result, in tenant families, succession was frequently difficult, the age at marriage late, and the number of births small, leading to a negative rate of replacement."[35] It thus appears that the rise of micro-farming created conditions that caused a large portion of the populace to reduce its fertility so much as to alter the basic demographic trajectory of the entire society.

How do we explain why poorer households—which were the bulk of peasant households and hence the most important segment in determining overall population trends—had so few offspring that they endangered their own familial existence? One surely cannot call it a matter of free choice. There is no evidence that they were indifferent to the survival of their lineages; on the contrary, the frequency with which smallholders and tenant farmers adopted sons to assure themselves of heirs reveals their wish to sustain their family status (*kakaku*).[36] Moreover, when their economic conditions were good, smallholders raised more children than when times were bad.[37]

33. It actually is difficult to establish age at marriage because, as Hanley and Yamamura note in *Economic and Demographic Change*, p. 246, brides generally "married, became pregnant, and then recorded the marriage in that order." Consequently, infertile marriages might never be recorded, and some marriages were recorded well after they actually occurred. Moreover, an older bride's age might be understated to enhance her nuptial appeal.

34. Smith, *Nakahara*, p. 51, gives these life-expectancy figures for his village:

Size of Holding	Females	Males
Large (12 koku and up)	52.5	49.2
Small (under 12 koku)	48.2	42.8

35. Hayami Akira, "The Myth of Primogeniture and Impartible Inheritance in Tokugawa Japan," *Journal of Family History* 8-1 (1983): 10–11.

36. Hanley and Yamamura, *Economic and Demographic Change*, pp. 262–65, stress the importance to villagers of maintaining their family status.

37. Feeney and Hamano found birthrates fluctuating with harvests, as reflected in rice-price movement, and Hanley and Yamamura seemed to believe that villagers con-

If smallholders wished to sustain their kakaku, why did they fail so often? Susan Hanley has identified their dilemma incisively: "A large number of children on a small farm was almost as disastrous as no children at all."[38] Often they failed to steer safely between Scylla and Charybdis, and it seems plausible that low fecundity—difficulty in producing healthy children—was a contributory factor, although the proposition lacks statistical support.[39] Carl Mosk summarizes nutritional effects this way: "Because calorie, protein, and vitamin intake was drastically limited, the hours of toil long, and the demands for strenuous physical exertion great, the levels of fecundity tended to be low. Spontaneous abortions were frequent and ovulatory cycles were often missed. Moreover, the viability of live offspring was often dubious since many babies appeared sickly, deformed, or weak once delivered."[40] Wealthier peasants may have been able to raise more children in part because their wives were "more fertile than small holders' owing to better nutrition and shelter and less crowded quarters."[41]

Other characteristics of smallholders' lives also fostered smaller households. When a peasant with extra offspring could divide his holding no further, he was compelled to discourage his younger sons from marrying. Instead, they, as well as daughters, best served the kakaku by remaining single, staying home, contributing labor to the household, and leaving when the designated heir was ready to take over. The strategy maximized the proportion of a household's members who were able-bodied adults even as it delayed marriage and reduced the number of married couples in a family, slowing its rate of reproduction.

---

trolled reproduction more firmly in bad times than good. Recently, however, Susan B. Hanley has argued in "Tokugawa Society: Material Culture, Standard of Living, and Life-styles," in *The Cambridge History of Japan*, vol. 4, *Early Modern Japan*, ed. John W. Hall (Cambridge: Cambridge University Press, 1991), p. 699, that birth control was practiced "equally in good times and bad." So listeners may wish to stay tuned.

38. Susan B. Hanley, "Family and Fertility in Four Tokugawa Villages," in Hanley and Wolf, eds., *Family and Population,* p. 197. This view—that the small-farm pattern of Tokugawa villages played a decisive role in shaping reproductive behavior—is supported by the essay of Dana Morris and Thomas C. Smith, "Fertility and Mortality in an Outcaste Village in Japan, 1750–1869," in the same volume, pp. 229–46. They show that outcaste villagers, who were career laborers, reared many more offspring, who could bring wage income into their households.

39. Hanley and Yamamura, *Economic and Demographic Change,* pp. 244–45. Although poorer villagers tended to die younger than their more well-to-do neighbors, scholars point out that the relatively long life span of Tokugawa villagers suggests that they were not severely undernourished. How seriously different levels and forms of malnutrition affect fecundity and life span is not, however, spelled out in the literature.

40. Carl Mosk, "Fecundity, Infanticide, and Food Consumption in Japan," *Explorations in Economic History* 15-3 (July 1978): 275.

41. Thomas C. Smith, *Native Sources of Japanese Industrialization, 1750–1920* (Berkeley and Los Angeles: University of California Press, 1988), p. 123.

Furthermore, in the wake of poor harvests, which proliferated in the eighteenth century, smallholders often could not get by, especially if they lacked sibling help. Some coped by mortgaging land to wealthy neighbors, others by taking by-employment, preferably in the village but if necessary by leaving to work elsewhere (*dekasegi*), often on a seasonal basis.

Dekasegi was rarely a smallholder's policy of choice. Bakuhan leaders, with their ideal of the village kyōdōtai, discouraged by-employment and travel in pursuit of work lest they undercut land-tax yields. And the villagers themselves preferred to stay home. They knew that the surest way to preserve their kakaku was by maintaining enough productive land to support an ample supply of heirs.[42] Dekasegi threatened that goal. A young woman's departure to find work could deprive a man of workmate and spouse. A man's departure placed more burdens on wives and other household members, and because it occurred most commonly during years of hardship when there were few alternatives near at hand, the practice could only have delayed or complicated pregnancies and increased the readiness of women to accept abortion or infanticide.

Moreover, by depriving households of adult labor, dekasegi so disrupted the cropping regimen that in the later Tokugawa period poor villagers ceased cultivating more and more of their most marginal fields despite government objections and even though doing so further weakened the farm's longer-term prospects for survival. In short, although villagers pursued dekasegi to sustain their households, its several effects enhanced the likelihood of a household's disappearance.[43] Nevertheless, the practice of dekasegi, legal and illegal, and mostly by poorer villages, grew ever more common, helping to delay marriage, lengthen birth spacing, and reduce the numbers of children per household.

In several ways then, the circumstances of smallholder life reduced rural fertility, but in the process they endangered kakaku by increasing the likelihood a household would lack an heir or lose its land. They did not, therefore, provide satisfactory solutions to the smallholder's dilemma.

Thomas C. Smith and others have shown, moreover, that sponta-

42. Smith, *Nakahara*, pp. 127–30, points up the crucial role of landholding in family perpetuation.

43. W. Mark Fruin, "Farm Family Migration: The Case of Echizen in the Nineteenth Century," *Keiō Economic Studies* 10-2 (1973): 37–46, concludes from his analysis of who went out to work and who didn't that "overpopulation and poverty were primary motivations for migration in late Tokugawa Japan" (p. 46). *Dekasegi,* or going out to work, was a major form of migration.

neous abortion, stillbirth, and random reduction in fertility through delayed or denied procreation could not produce the regularities in birth
spacing and gender sequence that one finds among village families. Also,
the regularity with which rises in rice prices were followed by declines
in birth rates suggests that purposeful decisions were being made.[44] Some
of the regularity was achieved, no doubt, by adopting children into and
out of families and perhaps by buying or selling them.[45] But induced
abortions and especially infanticide appear to have been key factors.
Whether inducing abortion placed a Tokugawa peasant's wife more at
risk than did full-term birthing is problematic. However, the techniques
of abortion were at best of uncertain effect, unpleasant, or sufficiently
dangerous so that their use could hardly have been desired, at least by
the woman, for whom birthing a few months hence must as a rule have
seemed less frightening than aborting *now*. Infanticide carried much
less risk to the mother, but it, too, could hardly have been welcome.[46]

So why did poor peasants practice abortion and infanticide when
even without it they faced a high risk of family extinction? Not because
the rulers encouraged it; quite the contrary. During the eighteenth century the rulers—motivated by ideals of compassion or stern righteousness, perhaps, but also by a keen desire to sustain tax income—became
alarmed at reports of proliferating abortions and infanticides. As decades passed, they issued more and more edicts denouncing the practices and imposing penalties on those convicted of employing them. The
effort failed to stop infanticide, but it did encourage concealment. The
usual way to conceal was simply not to report a birth. Another way,
where death records were kept, was to record a stillbirth.[47]

Among samurai as well, infanticide was concealed, even though accepted as customary. The disapproving Confucian scholar Nakai Chikuzan put it this way in 1788, late in the Tenmei famine:

> There are an exceedingly large number of poor people in the out-of-the-way
> districts who refuse to bring up their children. Indeed, this custom has be-
> come so widespread that people regard it as if it were a matter of course. . . .
> I have often heard that this evil practice has spread even to the *samurai* class.
> If a baby is born in a *samurai* family, for instance, the friends of the family
> make inquiries among themselves as to whether the baby is going to be brought

44. Feeney and Hamano, "Rice Price Fluctuations and Fertility," pp. 1–30, examine
this topic with care and conclude that infanticide is the most fitting explanation for the
type of linkage they find between prices and birthrates.

45. Honjo, *Social and Economic History*, p. 179, refers to traffic in children.

46. On the techniques of abortion and infanticide, see Hanley and Yamamura, *Economic and Demographic Change*, pp. 233–34, 315–16.

47. Ibid., pp. 377–78.

up. They do not visit the family to congratulate the parents until they are sure that the newly born infant is to be brought up. If they learn that it is not going to be of the living, they pretend to know nothing of the matter, and leave it severely alone. Most families do not take the trouble to bring up any except the first-born. If any family chooses to bring up two or three children, it is held up to ridicule by others. This is simply outrageous.[48]

A samurai, whose social position and level of income were reasonably predictable, even if marginal, may have found infanticide helpful in maintaining his lineage. And a well-to-do peasant, whose lands could sustain the main household and even a branch or two, may have found that infanticide judiciously practiced helped preserve a sturdy family line. For them the advantages may indeed have outweighed the unpleasantness and the risk of legal trouble.

Among poorer peasants, however, given the other factors hindering procreative abundance, fertility control commonly led to family extinction. Yet they appear to have employed infanticide more aggressively than their betters, which suggests that they saw it as the least unsatisfactory method of producing neither too many nor too few children, a task made imperative by the spread of economically marginal and unreliable micro-farming. Infanticide became a preferred way of managing the smallholder's difficult situation because it limited the mouths to feed while maximizing parental capacity to rear the preferred combination and number of sons and daughters, thereby giving the lineage its best chance of survival. The strategy constituted, in short, an attempt to preserve one's kakaku in a social, technological, and environmental context that made its preservation highly problematic for a large portion of the populace. As an unintended consequence, the strategy played a major role in stabilizing overall population size. Without it, one suspects, suffering and famine among the later Tokugawa populace would have been vastly more common.

48. Honjo, *Social and Economic History*, p. 180. Honjo is quoting Nakai's *Sōbō Kigen*, which he presented to Matsudaira Sadanobu in 1788.

THIRTEEN

Ecological Trends
The Period of Stasis (II)

Maximizing the Existing Resource Base
  Recycling and Using Waste
  Intensifying Labor Inputs
  Improving Labor Efficiency
  Intensifying Agricultural Production
  Enhancing Forest Output
  Maintaining Rivers and Rice Production
Expanding the Realm
  Ground Coal
  Fisheries
  Ezo

The methods of resource allocation and population control examined in chapter 12 constituted attempts by later Tokugawa society to function within the limits of existing natural resources. People also tried to maximize yield from the existing resource base and to enlarge that base. Their efforts yielded a gradual increase in society's output, further inroads into the ecosystem, and, by some measures, an increase in productivity.

MAXIMIZING THE EXISTING RESOURCE BASE

Rulers and ruled alike tried to maximize the yield of resources already under exploitation. Their methods included "recycling" and greater use of "waste" products, fuller human self-exploitation, more efficient labor utilization, and more thorough use of arable, forest, and riparian resources.

260

RECYCLING AND USING WASTE

Some forms of recycling, most notably the reuse of construction timber, were of hoary vintage in Japan, but other forms became widespread during the eighteenth century. Logging waste, industrial byproducts, and night soil deserve particular attention.

In Hideyoshi and Ieyasu's heyday, loggers were selective in terms of tree species and size, taking only the most valued timber and leaving tops, branches, and poor trunks to decay in the woods. Well before Genroku, however, inferior pieces and wood from less desirable species were being utilized, and smaller, less elegant timbers became acceptable to builders. Logging waste acquired sufficient value for governments and villages to develop rules for the disposition of limbs, brush, and wind-felled trees previously ignored as worthless. Similarly, whereas loggers in the era of pacification were content to throw pieces of wood into rivers, free-float them to a landing, snare them, and heap them up until needed, at the risk of losing substantial amounts to flood and fungus, later generations of lumbermen improved rafting and storage procedures to assure that pieces would not wash out to sea or be lost to decay.

Seventeenth-century land clearance increased demand for fertilizer even as it destroyed green fertilizer sources. The rise of commercial cropping, notably cotton and tobacco, which consume soil nutrients voraciously, reinforced the trend. As fertilizer demand grew, its market worth rose and substitution became feasible, especially near cities and castle towns. Meanwhile, the manufacture of soybean products, sake, and vegetable oils was generating organic wastes such as seed hulls and pulp that had potential value as fertilizer, and in the later Tokugawa period, the sale and use of such industrial byproducts became well established.

One of the most valued organic wastes was night soil, that is, human bodily waste, which had long been employed as fertilizer material in the immediate environs of cities. By the eighteenth century, it was acquiring unprecedented market value. Indeed, in villages around Osaka, where much cotton was grown, its price was so high by midcentury that "poorer farmers had difficulty in obtaining sufficient fertilizer, and incidents of theft began to appear in the records, despite the fact that going to prison if discovered was a real risk."[1] And around Edo, where night soil had

1. Susan Hanley, "Urban Sanitation in Preindustrial Japan," *Journal of Interdisciplinary History* 18-1 (Summer 1987): 11.

been free for the taking in the early seventeenth century, it became a marketable commodity, its price rising until "the cost of fertilizing fields and paddies became, in the peasants' view, unreasonable."[2] By 1790 disputes over price led to complicated, government-mediated negotiations between sellers, dealers, and village users and to the creation of mechanisms for stabilizing and, users hoped, lowering the price. The effort was only modestly effective, however, because continuing demand kept encouraging dealers to bid up the price.

These measures of recycling and waste utilization did not overcome the scarcities that created them, but they did constitute elements in the larger process whereby the populace of Japan attempted to sustain itself by maximizing the human value of its resource base.

INTENSIFYING LABOR INPUTS

In several ways the late Tokugawa populace intensified its self-exploitation, meaning, in the main, fuller exploitation of those below by those above. Rural change in particular facilitated fuller use of human labor in ways that need only be itemized here since they are treated in other contexts elsewhere:

1.   The emergence of an agricultural order based on small households encouraged maximal exploitation of household members of all ages.

2.   The intensification of agriculture led to more attentive, disciplined work routines.

3.   The expansion and systematization of corvée labor for road and river work created an onerous burden for the rural populace.

4.   The rise of by-employments fostered night work and off-season employment.

5.   The emergence of a landless laboring class created a population that was more mobile, more available for employment away from home, and less able to control its work routines than could the adequately landed.

Moralists high and low reinforced the trend toward greater industry by celebrating the virtues of hard work and dutiful performance and warn-

2. Anne Walthall, "Village Networks: Sōdai and the Sale of Edo Nightsoil," MN 43-3 (Autumn 1988): 293–302. The quotation is from p. 296. Peasants asserted that night soil costing 20 ryō in 1740 cost 60–70 ryō by 1789 (p. 295, n. 52).

ing against the evil consequences of indolence and irresponsibility. Writers of all sorts admonished people to be frugal and work hard, thereby nurturing their patrimony and demonstrating their virtue. Two examples from the writings of village moralists may suffice to illustrate the values that came to pervade late Tokugawa Japan:[3]

> If a man is foolish and brings his family [*ie*] to ruin, he commits a crime against his parents that will last for generations. But if the lessons of hard work and good farming are not forgotten, a man's conduct will conform to Heaven's way, and he will achieve the greatest filial piety.
>
> (Ōbata Saizō)

> From the age of 8 boys should gather grass for the animals, pick up horse dung from the road, make rope, and help with other light work. When they work well, they should be praised and given a coin. When coins accumulate to a sufficient sum, the children should be allowed to buy something they want. Also, when they are given clothes they should be told it is a reward for work. Thus their childish hearts will develop the spirit of industry and perseverance. If they are given suitable work in this way when young and taught farming skills as they get older, by age 14 or 15 they will be industrious and meticulous farmers.
>
> (Musumi Takehachi)

IMPROVING LABOR EFFICIENCY

Besides developing ways to make people work longer and harder, later Tokugawa society experienced an array of changes that contributed cumulatively to more efficient utilization of that work force.

Several of these developments have been noted in other contexts. The environmental stress that forced people to abandon interior mountain valleys, especially in the northeast, relocated many of the survivors closer to continuing work sites, enabling them (or others) to make better economic use of their time. The shrinkage of Osaka and many lesser castle towns that accompanied government fiscal difficulty relocated workers to production centers in the countryside, where they were farther from fire-prone city blocks and closer to food supplies, raw materials, and less crowded transportation routes and storage facilities. The processes of crop specialization and regional economic differentiation that aggravated the threat of famine also yielded improved efficiencies of production by fitting types of output to particular locations in terms of comparative economic advantage. And monetization of the economy, even

---

3. Quoted in Thomas C. Smith, *Nakahara* (Stanford: Stanford University Press, 1977), pp. 108–9.

as it helped pauperize the unlucky, created credit institutions that helped others launch new ventures and survive short-term economic downturns.

In addition to structural changes such as these, discrete technical developments also improved the efficiency of labor use. Mid-Tokugawa farmers devised specialized sickles and hoes, such as the four-pronged Bitchū hoe that enabled tillers to penetrate and open fallow soil more deeply and easily than hitherto. Other inventions, notably a multi-toothed threshing frame (*senba koki*), hand-powered winnowing fan, and gravity-flow inclined screen, speeded the threshing and winnowing of grain.[4] Attempts to employ waterwheels for milling the grain were less successful because farmers objected to merchants disrupting streams with their dams and wheels. In the eighteenth century, however, waterwheels did come into use in some areas for industrial processing: cleaning grains and other seeds for sake and oil production and crushing clay for pottery and ore for metal.[5]

INTENSIFYING AGRICULTURAL PRODUCTION

Most of the changes in labor use, as the above comments suggest, enhanced farm production. In broader terms too, agriculture was the arena in which output maximization was pursued most vigorously. As land reclamation became more costly and the quality of new arable declined, villagers concentrated on increasing the output of existing fields. The techniques they employed were discussed in the farm manuals (*nōsho* or *jikatasho*) of the day, whose proliferation aided in their diffusion. Combining information from Chinese, Korean, and earlier Japanese works with knowledge derived from authorial experience and practicing farmers, the manuals gave detailed advice on myriad facets of village life and work.

Miyazaki Antei's *Nōgyō zensho* (1697) described and explained many horticultural points in detail and formulated an enveloping rationale for prudent, thoughtful, and industrious stewardship of the land. Although not the first such work, it was the most encyclopedic to date and became the standard reference for many later manuals.[6] In articulating his

4. Tsuneo Satō, "Tokugawa Villages and Agriculture," in Chie Nakane and Shinzaburō Ōishi, eds., *Tokugawa Japan* (Tokyo: University of Tokyo Press, 1990), pp. 68–69.

5. Ryoshin Minami, "Water Wheels in the Preindustrial Economy of Japan," *Hitotsubashi Journal of Economics* 22-2 (Feb. 1982): 3–4, 7–9.

6. The following passages are taken from J. R. McEwan, *The Political Writings of Ogyū Sorai* (Cambridge: Cambridge University Press, 1962), pp. 24–25.

rationale, Antei cut directly to the heart of the problem: "In no class of society are rich men so few and poor men so many as among the peasantry. Unless they lay up stores of money and grain, they run the very great risk of dying of starvation in bad years. Peasants should always bear this in mind, being humble in their persons and practising economy." He went on to expound Chinese precedents for right conduct, defined the elements of proper behavior, lamented the decadence and profligacy of the times, and took an explicit swipe at the greedy, who suffer from "the chronic disease of avarice and who desire nothing better than to gather to themselves as much gold, silver, money and grain as they can, storing it up and leaving it unused." When poor peasants fail to conserve and then experience harvest failure, he warned, "they are forced to sell their property, mortgage their land and pay great sums in interest to rich merchants, and at once they are reduced to extreme poverty." Antei recognized, in short, that for self-sustaining smallholders, the acceptable margin of agronomic error was slender indeed, and his advice was intended to help them avoid overstepping it.

Following the appearance of Antei's opus, manuals multiplied. Bakufu and han provided official guidance, and diverse authors, including officials, scholars, and village leaders, prepared essays on matters of interest to farmers.[7] Some were aimed at villagers and in a spirit of encouragement offered moral guidance and practical advice on how to farm and live. Others were directed at officials, to assist them in overseeing rural affairs.

One of the most important government-oriented works was *Jikata hanreiroku*, which fills two volumes in its modern edition. It was written during the 1790s, as the Kantō recovered from the Asama eruption and Tenmei famine, by Ōishi Hisayoshi, a district intendant of Takasaki han.[8] Ōishi began his loosely organized but highly articulated essay by discussing the supervision of rural affairs in general, adumbrating its historical development and geographical particularity. He went into de-

7. On the general character of *jikatasho*, see Jennifer Robertson, "Japanese Farm Manuals: A Literature of Discovery," *Peasant Studies* 11-3 (Spring 1984): 169–94, and Marti, "Intellectual and Moral Foundations of Empirical Agronomy in Eighteenth Century Japan." For a closer examination of one work in the genre, see Thomas C. Smith, "Ōkura Nagatsune and the Technologists," in Albert Craig and Donald H. Shively, eds., *Personality in Japanese History* (Berkeley and Los Angeles: University of California Press, 1970), pp. 127–54. A thoughtful study of the way ideologues could use farm manuals as a vehicle for disseminating their views is Jennifer Robertson, "Sexy Rice: Plant Gender, Farm Manuals, and Grass-Roots Nativism," *MN* 39-3 (Autumn 1984): 233–60.

8. Ōishi Hisayoshi, *Jikata hanreiroku* [An exegesis on practical affairs], ed. Ōishi Shinzaburō, 2 vols. (Tokyo: Kondō Shuppansha, 1969).

tail on measuring, assessing, and taxing the many types of land and rural production. He explained village customs, specifics of the rural economy, and the many official regulations that applied to rural folk. He discussed problems in weights, measures, and units of currency. He spelled out the customary practices of local officials, the types of help that supervisory officials might expect of villagers, and details of sundry gift giving and other customs. He explained the funding and staffing of village offices and the handling of such tasks as fire control, public surveillance, disaster relief, communal construction and repair, riparian engineering, forest management, and numerous corvée obligations.

Doubtless works such as Ōishi's, while intended to help government exploit the hinterland, also helped increase agricultural yield by enabling supervisory officials to furnish advice that could boost taxable production. However, manuals aimed at farmers, such as Antei's *Nōgyō zensho,* surely did more to increase output per acre and per person. Their authors gave various rationales for their interest in farm production, but most saw the vitality and stability of farm families as essential to those larger ends, and they repeatedly asserted that villagers should apply the recommended techniques because doing so would help perpetuate their families. They shared, that is to say, the goals of the micro-farmers who engaged in dekasegi, infanticide, and other desperate measures to preserve their kakaku.

One of the most influential producer-oriented writers was Ōkura Nagatsune, a villager from Kyushu whose father produced wax from lacquer trees.[9] Born in 1768, Nagatsune became a mendicant scholar, working at diverse trades as his studies took him about Kyushu and eventually eastward to Kyoto and Edo. Wherever he went, T. C. Smith writes, "he asked questions of skilled farmers about local soils, seed, fertilizers, irrigation, and tools, taking down what they had to say and making detailed sketches of plants, tools, and operations." His first book, published in 1802, explained how to cultivate lacquer trees profitably, and he subsequently issued twenty-seven other treatises, "one on ethics, two dictionaries, two on nutrition, two on government policy, one on education, and all the rest on the technology of farming and farm by-employments."

Persuaded that villagers could make their lands more productive by careful use of the best tools and techniques, as demonstrated by successful farmers, Nagatsune wrote in great detail about the particulars

9. Smith, "Ōkura Nagatsune and the Technologists," pp. 129–30, 139–40, 143.

of all types of agronomy. One passage on cotton growing may illustrate his approach:

> In choosing cotton seed, pick a bush of medium height with luxuriant shrubbery and no dead branches, and take cotton bolls in full bloom with heavy fibers from a branch three or four branches from the bottom. [Do this] when half the bolls on the tree have opened. The choice of the seed is extremely important. . . . Good seeds have a slightly black look, bad ones a reddish hue. Also knead the seed with the fingers. Round seeds generally are poor; pointed seeds generally are good. For storage, remove the seed from the surrounding cotton and dry it in the sun. Then take it out from time to time to expose it to the sun in order to keep it absolutely free of moisture.

And here is Nagatsune on footwear:

> *Tsuranuki* [leather footgear worn in winter by Kinai peasants] have other advantages over straw sandals. One can go into the fields earlier in the morning and work better because they keep the feet warm and supple, and they eliminate the need for hot water to wash the feet daily. These are not great advantages in a single day, but day after day over a lifetime they become significant.

Driven by tax obligations and the wish to sustain their lineage despite scarcity of land and the caprices of weather and marketplace, farmers gradually adopted the techniques advocated by writers of jikatasho. They employed better tools, more appropriate crops and cropping techniques, and improved processing and storage methods. Most important, they used more fertilizer and as its cost rose, paid closer attention to fertilizing procedure. Cumulatively, the measures increased rural output, sustaining a population of some 32 million even as villagers shifted more and more arable to producing the raw material—for example, cotton, tobacco, rapeseed, dyes, and sedge—for diverse consumer goods and lamp oil to illuminate the workplaces of their makers.

Ironically, these measures, promoted as ways to help villagers save their families, fostered the very system of micro-farming that made the task so difficult. The system was highly labor-intensive, with humans replacing draft animals in the attentive manipulation of tiny plots of land, and in the context of a stable overall population, it absorbed most available labor. It required, moreover, that the labor be skilled and that it be deployed in accordance with the finely tuned rhythms of each crop, which meant that a crop could easily be endangered if the tiller found his work routine disrupted by illness, corvée duty, or the need to work away from home. And loss of a crop could force a debt-burdened smallholder to mortgage his land to a well-to-do neighbor, reducing him to a tenant or even a landless laborer.

The tendency of smallholders to fail inspired yet more jikatasho to lament the loss of household continuity. It did not, however, reverse the trend toward greater productivity per acre of arable and lifetime of work, partly because the rise of a system of tenantry facilitated continual recruitment of hard-pressed but able-bodied people to till arable land as landlords rented parcels to needy villagers. The process eroded large kinship units and communal cohesiveness, giving rise to a more rigorous, production-oriented village order that rewarded the diligent and fortunate while driving the vulnerable and less diligent or less competent out of business, thereby making their land available to others. Gains in output were achieved, that is, at a cost to community that expressed itself in social tension, alienation, and disorder, as noted in subsequent chapters. However, the gains also meant that arable land was being manipulated in ways that maximized its value to the human populace as a whole.

ENHANCING FOREST OUTPUT

Woodland, like arable, received more attention in the later Tokugawa period, and users gradually induced it to yield up more products for human consumption. In essence, they achieved the gain by replacing "useless" biota with species yielding consumable goods. Near villages, in particular, more and more fruit trees and tea bushes were planted on hillsides that had once supported mixed natural forest. Villagers replaced natural growth with mulberry bushes whose leaves fed silk-worms, chestnut trees that yielded food and fuel, and monoculture growth of bamboo or other tropical grasses that had myriad uses.

Most significant, perhaps, late in the eighteenth century the long-term decline in timber production began to reverse as tree-planting slowly spread, supplementing older policies that had tried to sustain timber stands by restricting wood consumption and forest abuse. The story having been told elsewhere recently, it requires only summation here.[10] Suffice it to say that writers of jikatasho discussed ways to enhance forest production and grow trees; bakufu and han encouraged it; and entrepreneurs, villagers, and domains undertook it. By the early nine-

10. The development of afforestation techniques and the rise of plantation forestry are topics central to Conrad Totman, *The Green Archipelago: Forestry in Preindustrial Japan* (Berkeley and Los Angeles: University of California Press, 1989).

teenth century, several forms of long-term woodland management had developed that permitted plantation forestry, and woodland holders were planting seedlings and cuttings and nurturing them over the several decades necessary to yield useful lumber. In much of Japan, reforestation remained dependent on natural seeding and survival, but clearly the basic trend was toward increased production through plantation forestry wherever that was economically feasible.

MAINTAINING RIVERS AND RICE PRODUCTION

It took most of the eighteenth century to convert the idea of plantation forestry into widespread practice, but after that gestation, the policy paid off in gradually expanded forest production. The story of river management, which was pursued primarily to maximize agricultural production, had a more ambiguous outcome.[11]

By Genroku, reclamation work had brought into paddy culture most of the land that could be irrigated from natural and manmade ponds and small, easily managed streams. In the main Honshu watersheds of the Kinai, Nobi, and Kantō regions, large rivers became the main object of river management efforts thereafter, in part because they were the major source of additional irrigation water but in ever greater part, it appears, because they became more and more destructive and their containment more crucial to the preservation of nearby villages and their taxable production.

Acts of nature contributed to river turbulence: typhoons, monsoon downpours, abrupt snowmelt, but most seriously volcanic eruptions, whose ash silted streams and fouled both river and irrigation systems. However, human exploitation of the ecosystem was the main cause of heightened riverine destructiveness. Most important, woodland use and reclamation work produced erosion and silting that led to flooding and drought. These developments complicated irrigation activity and created shortages that led to disputes over water use, or *mizu mondai* as they are known, making them a common form of conflict within and between villages. River maintenance during the later Tokugawa period was primarily an attempt to deal with those problems.

11. For an introduction to river work in the Kinai, Nobi, and Kantō regions, see Conrad Totman, "Preindustrial River Conservancy: Causes and Consequences," *MN* 47-1 (Spring 1992): 59–76. William Kelly, *Water Control in Tokugawa Japan: Irrigation Organization in a Tokugawa River Basin, 1600–1870,* East Asian Papers, no. 31 (Ithaca, N.Y.: Cornell University, 1982), is a detailed study of irrigation arrangements along the Aka River, a major tributary of the Mogami.

River maintenance entailed mobilizing huge gangs of laborers to patch riverbanks, straighten meanders, clear debris, dredge riverbeds, and pile silt up to form levees, which were reinforced with stone, timber, bamboo, brush, and reeds. Once begun, the work never ended, because every advance in control created conditions that required constant attention and further advances. Huge amounts of poorly paid but unavoidable work were thus one of the major, lasting legacies of river control.

From early in the eighteenth century, the bakufu developed and continually modified its river-control policies. It created and enlarged supervisory and engineering offices to oversee the work, issued, revised, and re-revised funding rules that committed its own resources as well as those of daimyo and villagers, and defined and redefined manpower and supply obligations and arrangements. In this welter of actions, two trends stand out. The cost of river work kept rising and became an intolerable burden, which bakufu, han, and villages continually tried to foist on one another. And the scale of projects kept expanding, compelling the bakufu to extend its supervisory authority further and further into the domains.

The burden of river management was so great partly because of mishandled work. But problems of mismanagement aside, at base the bakufu was relentless in its demands on lords and villages because streamflow was relentless in its assault on the riverworks that hemmed it in. The problem persisted until the twentieth century, when industrial technology expanded radically the scale and durability of the structures used in the task.

EXPANDING THE REALM

Writers commonly characterize early modern Japan as a "closed country" (sakoku) because Tokugawa leaders carefully regulated Japan's dealings with other societies, ending that policy only from necessity in the 1850s. When one views this history from a broader ecological perspective, however, it becomes apparent that in some ways Japanese society subverted its leaders' restrictive policies by extending its activities into new and uncharted territories, especially from the eighteenth century on. And political leaders themselves began taking tentative steps to extend their dominion by late in that century.

The extension encompassed both time and space. As in preindustrial societies elsewhere, most of early modern Japan's biomass exploitation was current—consumption of the living. The most notable retrospective use occurred during the seventeenth century when old growth forest was felled, which extended the exploitative reach back in time to encompass about a century's worth of forest biomass. When the Japanese began burning ground coal near the end of the seventeenth century, they were projecting their reach backward millions of years. In terms of space, during the eighteenth century, they extended their activity outward into the surrounding seas by developing and expanding maritime fisheries. And by century's end they were very tentatively entering the uncharted northern region known as Ezo through trade, exploration, and political contact.

GROUND COAL

Late in the seventeenth century, after a hundred years of intensive woodcutting, villagers near coal seams in Kyushu began burning ground coal as a substitute fuel (they had used charcoal for millennia). Then expanding industrial production during the eighteenth century created fuel needs that exceeded nearby woodland capacity in much of Japan. In particular salt and sugar makers and potters from the Nobi Plain westward encountered fuel shortages that drove up prices enough to lure more and more of them into replacing fuel wood with ground coal.

The substitution was not entirely welcome, however, despite its economic advantage to producers. Burning coal produced noxious fumes and sticky, destructive fallout. Both mining and burning caused water pollution that led to conflict, litigation, instances of compensation, and efforts at regulation. From about the 1780s on, wastewater runoff near coal mines in Kyushu began polluting downstream rice fields, generating protests, forcing villagers to pursue more riparian work, and prompting the authorities to close mines and encourage reversion to wood burning. In some areas villagers opposed the use of coal in salt-making because its smoke and ash damaged crops and disrupted those trying to work nearby.[12] During the 1830s, for example, villagers some thirty-five kilometers east of Hiroshima protested the use of coal by nearby salt makers on the grounds that "the soot and smoke stick to the fruit and leaves of rice, wheat, soy beans, red beans, cow peas, buckwheat, tea, and everything else, smearing them with oily smoke, and

12. Andō Seiichi, "Kinsei no sekitan kōgai" [Early modern coal pollution], *Osaka sangyō daigaku sangyō kenkyūjo hōkoku* 12 (Nov. 1989): 139–55, examines this problem and provides useful bibliographical information.

causing them to wither or ripen poorly, much like a general crop failure."[13]

Not even the users were necessarily pleased with coal. Salt makers traditionally heated their boilers with pine boughs, which produced a "soft" heat that precipitated the brine into fine, white crystals. Coal evidently generated a more intense fire that yielded larger, irregular, cloudy crystals, reducing its appeal as table salt for city dwellers. The lower-grade salt was adequate for pickling processes and commercial manufacture of soy products (miso and shōyū), however, and despite its defects could be sold for household use in poorer regions of the country. In consequence, as pine boughs became scarce and expensive, salt makers began switching to coal, faute de mieux. They used it in Kyushu and far western Honshu from the 1770s on, in the salt fields of Akō and eastern Shikoku by the 1820s, and in Okayama by the 1840s, despite protests of neighbors and those upland villagers who depended on the high price their fuel wood had commanded.[14]

The scarcity and consequent dearness of firewood caused coal use to continue expanding despite its undesirable qualities and the objections aroused by its mining and burning. Its use constituted one form of expanded Japanese exploitation of the ecosystem and marked Japan's entry into the "modern" age of global human dependence on ancient biomass.

FISHERIES

The people of Japan have exploited rivers, lakes, and coastal waters since prehistoric times, but the scale of activity expanded greatly in the Tokugawa period.[15] Expansion was encouraged initially by the restoration of peace and subsequent restricting of foreign travel, which compelled seafarers to settle down and find new uses for their skills and

13. Watanabe Noribumi, "Mae kindai no seien gijutsu" [The techniques of early modern salt manufacture] in Engyō-gyogyō [The salt and maritime industries], vol. 2 of Kōza Nihon gijutsu no shakaishi [A symposium on the social history of Japanese technology] (Tokyo: Nihon hyōronsha, 1985), p. 114.

14. Chiba Tokuji, Hageyama no kenkyū [A study of bald mountains] (Tokyo: Nōrin Kyōkai, 1956), pp. 152–55. Watanabe, "Mae kindai no seien gijutsu," pp. 112–16.

15. This section on fisheries is based on Ninohei, "Kindai gyogyō gijutsu no seisei," and Nihon gakushiin, comp., Meijizen Nihon gyogyō gijutsushi [A history of fisheries technology in pre-Meiji Japan] (Tokyo: Nihon gakujutsu shinkōkai, 1959). The latter is an exhaustive treatment of fisheries technology but does not place the material in a social context. A careful examination of fishing organization in Kyushu is Arne Kalland, "Sea Tenure in Tokugawa Japan: The Case of Fukuoka Domain," Senri Ethnological Studies 17 (1984): 11–36.

equipment. As the seventeenth century advanced, moreover, coastal shipping spurred creation of small ports and semi-agricultural coastal settlements. Changes in landholding and lack of reclaimable land forced more and more villagers to find new means of enhancing their income, and jikatasho, some of which discussed techniques of marine production, gave further impetus to fishing during the eighteenth century. Fishing villages proliferated in the bays and inlets that dotted the archipelago's convoluted coastline, with householders using lines and small nets, some from shore and some from little boats operated by one or two people, extracting ever more yield from the sea.

During the later Tokugawa period, this small-scale fishing grew into a diversified, highly specialized occupation. The varieties of fish at market multiplied, coming to include bonito, cod, flounder, flying fish, gray mullet, herring, mackerel, salmon, saurel, sea bream, tuna, turbot, yellowtail, and others, including species lacking English names.[16] Fishermen caught crab, eel, shark, shrimp, and squid, and such mammals as dolphins, seals, sea otters, sea lions, and whales. Seaweed of diverse types also became an important marine product. From Amakusa to Aomori, fishermen developed tools and techniques to fit the particular habits and habitats of the species they pursued. The techniques of line fishing—the types and deployments of baits, floats, hooks, lines, poles, and sinkers—all were adapted to special requirements of the locality. Similarly, the techniques of net fishing were refined, with fishermen developing innumerable varieties of drag nets, hand-held nets, set nets, and throw nets. Cormorant fishing, ice fishing, and trap fishing all became established.

Part of the expanded catch went for human consumption. At least as important, however, was the provision of fertilizer material for crop use. As green fertilizer became scarce and demand for soil nutrients grew, night soil and industrial by-products came into fuller use, as noted above, but fishmeal also became a major part of the nutrient supply, a part less tied to castle town and city. Its provision fostered large-scale fishing by allowing fishermen to be undiscriminating in their work: nearly any fish of any size would produce usable fertilizer material. The opportunity to harvest in bulk led to development of large nets operated

16. Translations of fish names are a bit confusing, since species vary from place to place. Nihon gakushiin, comp., *Meijizen Nihon gyogyō gijutsushi*, pp. 135ff., 187ff., and 227ff., mentions these fish: *aji, ankō, ayu, bora, hamachi, hatahata, hirame, ikanago, inada, iwashi, karei, kashiki, katsuo, maguro, muroaji, nishin, saba, sake, sanma, sawara, shirauo, tai, tara,* and *tobiuo.*

by entrepreneurs employing two or even four vessels and anywhere from fifty to a hundred fishermen per net. Some used large capstans on board ship and on the shore to reel in huge nets filled with teeming schools of fish. These economies of scale facilitated the extension of early modern exploitation into the surrounding seas.

In the rich fisheries off western Kyushu and the eastern shore of the Kantō, where the warm Japan current meets the two south-flowing arms of the cold Okhotsk current, large-scale commercial fishing developed by the nineteenth century. South of Japan, commercial whaling flourished. And along the shores of Hokkaido, maritime exploitation arose, particularly kelp mining promoted by merchant shippers who wanted cargo for return voyages to the Kinai. In toto, fisheries development constituted a major expansion in the resource base of the Japanese, supplementing the terrestrial base to which their rulers had restricted them. Indeed, the caloric boost that these marine nutrients gave the Japanese directly and via fishmeal fertilizer may have been the key factor limiting demographic shrinkage after the 1720s, despite the nutrient loss represented by persistent soil erosion and the shift of arable land to nonfood production.

EZO

The rise of Japanese interest in Ezo late in the eighteenth century seemed to foreshadow terrestrial expansion. After a few years in which proponents viewed Ezo as a promising new frontier, however, interest waned, and in the end Ezo proved less consequential than fisheries or even ground coal as a venue for enlarging the early modern resource base.

To eighteenth-century Japanese, Ezo was an ill-defined region that lay to the north, beyond the pale.[17] Ezo began where Japanese civilization and political control ended in southern Hokkaido (as the island is now known). Occupied by "primitive" native peoples, most notably the Ainu (or Ezo), it included the rest of Hokkaido and whatever other islands and areas might be supposed to exist further north.

Early in the seventeenth century, the bakufu assigned the frontier area of southern Hokkaido to the daimyo Matsumae. His jurisdiction reached northward as far as imagination might run, but the heart of his domain was Oshima peninsula, the arm of land that projects south-

17. Bob Tadashi Wakabayashi, *Anti-Foreignism and Western Learning in Early Modern Japan* (Cambridge, Mass.: Harvard University Press, 1986), p. 73, discusses the meaning of the name Ezo.

westward from the island proper. By the late eighteenth century, Oshima reportedly held a Japanese-speaking populace of nearly thirty thousand, roughly equaling the Ainu population of Ezo.[18] Because Matsumae's domain lay too far north for rice culture, his chief source of income was trade in marine products. By the 1750s, shippers from Osaka and elsewhere conducted regular trade with him, and his trading posts dotted the Hokkaido coastline eastward as far as the southern Kuril islands.

For nearly two centuries, Matsumae lords pursued their exploitation of Ezo with little attention from the rest of Japan. From the 1770s, however, affairs in the north began to capture wider notice, and some bakufu and han officials, advisors, and collaborating merchants began to nurture the vision of a promising new frontier. From then until about 1815, Japan experienced an "Ezo boom," whose history has two notable characteristics. First, it reflected regional concerns that were given sharp focus by the Tenmei famine. Specifically, those advocating Ezo's development were mostly from the northeast, and they were moved by the hope that frontier development could overcome their region's backwardness and economic hardship. Those resisting development represented, in part at least, southwestern interests, especially Osaka and Nagasaki merchants who feared competition for their comfortable arrangements with the Dutch or disruption of existing trade arrangements in Ezo.

The second characteristic of the "Ezo boom" was that the nature of interest in the region changed as time passed. It began during Tanuma Okitsugu's tenure as bakufu leader in the form of economic and fiscal interests reinforced by a secondary strategic wish to keep the realm secure in the face of encroaching Russian traders and adventurers. But it evolved very quickly into a predominantly strategic concern, which was sustained for a while by hopes of economic benefit. During the early 1800s, however, as discussed at some length in chapter 20, Russo-Japanese relations became tense, and official interest in Ezo was transformed into a wish for political disengagement, largely out of fear that defense of the region constituted a bottomless fiscal quagmire.

The vision of Ezo as frontier was expressed most eloquently by Honda Toshiaki of Echigo. As early as 1792, he memorialized the bakufu leader Matsudaira Sadanobu urging him to settle Ezo as a way to establish a clear frontier between Japan and Russia, resettle criminals, and exploit

18. George Alexander Lensen, *The Russian Push toward Japan: Russo-Japanese Relations, 1697–1875* (Princeton: Princeton University Press, 1959), p. 179, speaks of the Japanese numbering "less than 27,000 in 1765."

the region's mines, cropland, and timber. In 1798 he followed with two major essays that provided information on Europe and a prolix argument for developing areas to the north as the start of a great Japanese empire that could counterbalance Russia and England. Badly overestimating the salubriousness of Sakhalin (Karafuto) and Kamchatka, he described how northward extension of settlement would overcome flaws in current policy.

> Once great cities spring up in Karafuto and Kamchatka, the momentum will carry on to the islands to the south, and the growing prosperity of each of these places will raise the prestige of Edo to great heights. This, in turn, will naturally result in the acquisition of the American islands, which manifestly belong by right to Japan.

"If these plans are put into effect," he concluded, "there will unquestionably come to be two supremely prosperous and powerful countries in the world: Japan in the East and England in the West." [19]

Pursuing that vision was easier said than done. Bakufu investigators visited Ezo sporadically from the 1770s, but no intervention followed. In 1798, however, Edo learned of Russian settlers reaching Uruppu, the third Kuril island east of Hokkaido, where they began introducing Russian culture, including Christianity, to the Ainu. Reports said the settlers were also moving onto Etorofu, the large second island, and other reports indicated that a foreign ship was surveying in the Ezo region.

This flurry of information prompted bakufu leaders to despatch more investigating teams. On Etorofu, the team member Kondō Jūzō, a minor bakufu official, claimed the island for Japan by tearing down crosses and posters erected by Russians and replacing them with a pillar bearing the words "Dai Nihon Etorofu." [20] The team also initiated a policy of countering the Russians by cultivating the goodwill of the Ainu and introducing them to Japanese culture. The real wish of the Ainu, no doubt, was to be left alone, but as the two sides jockeyed for position, that wish seemed unlikely to prevail.

Even as this team was extending Japanese jurisdiction to Etorofu, Edo was moving to substantiate the claim. In 1799 the bakufu transferred eastern Ezo from Matsumae to bakufu control and despatched

19. These quotations from Honda are from Donald Keene, *The Japanese Discovery of Europe, 1720–1830* (Stanford: Stanford University Press, 1969), pp. 222–23, 226. The "American islands" seem to refer to the Aleutians and to some large but imaginary islands northeast of Japan. For a good discussion of eighteenth-century misconceptions of northwestern Pacific geography and their gradual rectification, see Lensen, *Russian Push,* pp. 22–60.
20. Lensen, *Russian Push,* p. 186. Jūzō is also known as Morishige.

troops to guard the region against Russian intruders. Edo also ordered Morioka and Sendai han to deploy 500 men apiece to defend Hakodate. Seeing the Kurils as the gateway to Hokkaido, Edo put Kondō in charge there, with a staff that grew to "about 350 officials, engineers, doctors, and provincial levies."[21] Moreover, the bakufu authorized Takadaya Kahei, the operator of an Osaka-to-Hokkaido shipping line, to open a new route to Etorofu, presumably to improve lines of communication and counter the trading activity of Russians on Uruppu.

For some years the bakufu continued its forward policy in Ezo, surveying and exploring, and in 1802 giving fuller organization to its new administrative headquarters (bugyōsho) at Hakodate. But almost from the moment it took over eastern Ezo, problems multiplied. The policy of wooing Ainu made some progress but also encountered setbacks. Kondō imposed an administrative system on Kunashiri and Etorofu, built roads, introduced new fishing techniques, promoted other developmental activities, and fostered adoption of Japanese dress and deportment. Some of his measures may have been welcome, but others generated resentment, particularly decrees requiring Ainu to cut their hair in the Japanese manner, abandon their bear festival, and cease tattooing and ear-piercing. The measures even prompted several tens of Ainu to flee to Uruppu, where Russian residents offered shelter against the pressure to "Japanize."

The Russians on Uruppu thus constituted continuing rivals for Ainu goodwill, and from 1801 bakufu officials in Ezo tried driving them from the island by halting their trade with Etorofu, which provided daily necessities. The pressure bore fruit, and over the next few years Russian settlers left and the abandoned Ainu moved to Etorofu. The forward policy seemed to be achieving its goal of consolidating Japanese control of the Ezo frontier. But the gains were probably less apparent to officials in Edo, where other considerations weighed more heavily.

Most immediately the forward policy—deploying guard forces, despatching explorers, and staffing new administrative organs—cost money. Daimyo too were being burdened with new guard and patrol duties. Costs could only continue to rise, moreover, because the development of coastal defenses would require cannon and seagoing vessels. And cannon not only were expensive but required copper, which was so scarce that in 1790 the bakufu slashed the volume of Dutch trade by 50 percent to reduce the drain of silver and copper, a move that gave mer-

21. John J. Stephan, The Kuril Islands (London: Oxford University Press, 1974), p. 69.

chants at Nagasaki one more reason to oppose northern development. Moreover, every official mission or troop deployment meant added corvée work for villagers along the highways, and such work was one of the public burdens most likely to elicit resistance. Sadanobu, realizing the gravity of the highway problem, had forbidden increases in levies of porters and packhorses a full decade earlier, but the Ezo activity led to increases anyway, and in 1804 villagers in Hitachi and Hachinohe mounted strong protests against their duty.

Finally, as noted in chapter 20, from 1803 foreign approaches from the south began shifting bakufu attention away from Ezo and hardening its opposition to all foreign contacts. One factor hardening the rulers' posture was their enduring fear that foreigners might induce the Japanese masses to turn against them. That fear, central to the suppression of Christianity, was reinforced by reports of Japanese castaways, who spoke favorably of their treatment by Russians, and by some reports of Ainu attitudes toward Russia. Honda Toshiaki, for example, reported hearing that "the natives trust the Russians as they would their own parents," and "the barbarians of islands east, south, and west of Kamchatka all seem to be attracted like ants to the sweetness of the Russian system."[22]

That assessment of Russo-Ainu relations was rather off the mark, but it contrasted sharply with Edo's belief that Matsumae han pursued a harshly exploitative policy that was willy-nilly alienating the Ainu from Japan and making them potential allies of any Russian invaders. Distrust of Matsumae had been growing for years as investigations revealed illegal trading, abuse of the Ainu, and persistent attempts to conceal affairs. In 1805 the bakufu again sent examiners to Hokkaido to investigate the condition of Matsumae's remaining holdings. Their report, received by Edo in early 1807, persuaded leaders to reduce the danger of subversion from the north by reclaiming the holdings and ordering Matsumae into house arrest for mishandling affairs.

During the next few years, further alarms from the north elicited more attempts to strengthen defenses, but for the bakufu the image of Ezo as a promising economic frontier seems to have evaporated, in part because of its fiscal impact and in part, no doubt, because the limited agricultural prospects of the region had become clearer. By 1815 what had initially looked like a field of opportunity had degenerated into a huge quagmire, from which Edo was only too glad to escape. Modest

22. Keene, *Japanese Discovery,* pp. 83, 182.

trade between Hokkaido and nearby islands continued after that year, but after Matsumae regained his domain a few years later, the trade remained a minor and largely secret activity of Matsumae han and its handful of collaborating merchants.

Nevertheless, the vision of Ezo as a frontier whose opening could enrich the northeast survived, reappearing from the 1830s in attempts by the dynamic leaders of Mito han to gain control of the region. Their efforts foundered, however, on bakufu opposition. When Edo's interest in the northern border revived in the 1850s, it did so as one small facet of a radically exacerbated set of foreign problems, and in no way was Ezo then perceived as a solution to a problem of domestic resource insufficiency.

During the later Tokugawa period then, the Japanese began extending resource exploitation far into the past through coal mining, but intensive use of coal did not occur until after the Tokugawa collapse. Expansion of fisheries was much more substantial, and extension of the realm through maritime exploitation was well under way by the nineteenth century. Terrestrial expansion to the north was pursued tentatively around 1800, but the venture sputtered out, reviving only after a more powerful central regime seized control in 1868.

Early modern Japan's capacity to sustain its highly differentiated population of 32 million must be credited to a combination of intensified self-exploitation, enhanced maritime exploitation, and more aggressive terrestrial exploitation within the confines of the existing realm. As the mechanisms of demographic stabilization and resource allocation reveal, the costs and benefits of stasis were distributed inequitably, and as decades passed, society found it ever more difficult to resolve the tensions and disputes generated by problems of allocation, as subsequent chapters will show.

FOURTEEN

Yoshimune and the Kyōhō Reform

The Genroku period (1688–1704), with its burst of fiction, theater, and art, is popularly viewed as the glorious heyday of Tokugawa urban culture, and that surely is an important part of the story. But the full story was more ambiguous, as earlier chapters have suggested, with opulence and accomplishments balanced by difficulty and discontent. Genroku was at once an end to one era—an era of dynamic growth— and the start of another—an era of general social stasis. The main attributes of the new era were clearly delineated for the first time during the Kyōhō period (1716–1735), when the wide-ranging reform efforts of the eighth shogun, Yoshimune, and the problems that led to them, dominated the scene.

Tokugawa Yoshimune was born in Wakayama in 1684, third son of the daimyo of Kii. Thirteen years later the lad was designated daimyo of Sabae han, but in 1705, after his elder brothers died, he was reassigned to Kii. Following the death of seven-year-old Ietsugu in 1716, bakufu leaders named Yoshimune his successor, giving Edo a leader already experienced in administering a major domain. The new shogun lacked ties to any group in the bakufu, but he gradually placed his own appointees in key offices and by the early 1720s was securely in control.

Certain characteristics of his rule stand out. Whereas Tsunayoshi had, for better or worse, adhered to policies anchored in a sturdy ideology, Yoshimune bobbed and weaved in response to circumstances; his adaptability is suggestive of Ogyū Sorai's political thought. His reform began cautiously, prompted by difficulties inherited from the preceding administrations of Tsunayoshi and his successors, Ienobu and Ietsugu. From the early 1720s on, however, the range of reform expanded sharply in apparent response to the combined impact of recoinage policies already in effect and a rash of crop failures and social unrest. That expanded range, which made the years from 1721 to 1728 the heyday of the Kyōhō reform, drew the bakufu more deeply into the management of society than at any time in its past.

Managing the large, complex, highly monetized, and environmentally constricted society of eighteenth century Japan proved unwieldy, however. After reaching an apex of success in 1728, Yoshimune devoted five years to battling harsh agricultural difficulties—the Kyōhō famine—and wild rice-price fluctuations that severely disrupted samurai life. The hardship forced him to rethink basic policies and in 1736 to implement a radical shift in monetary strategy. The shift ushered in a fifteen-year period of governmental stability that was achieved despite or, more correctly, at the price of, continuing rural hardship.

FORESHADOWINGS: ARAI HAKUSEKI
AND THE CURRENCY

Following Tsunayoshi's death in 1709, the regime of his nephew and successor, Ienobu, addressed problems that had appeared during Genroku. Mostly, however, Ienobu's accomplishments were limited to a shake-up in officialdom and repudiation of Tsunayoshi's policies, notably his laws of compassion for animals. His sudden death late in 1712 brought the child Ietsugu into office, during whose brief tenure reform policy, currency reform in particular, began to accelerate.

Arai Hakuseki, scholar-advisor to Ienobu, was highly critical of the coinage policies of Tsunayoshi's fiscal chief, Ogiwara Shigehide, seeing them as evidence of moral decay and corrupt rule.[1] Blaming Ogiwara's several currency debasements for contemporary fiscal disorder, economic turmoil, and social hardship, Hakuseki drew up detailed plans for monetary reform. In one facet, for example, he advised that since silver mines yield little bullion (for reasons that he explained), Edo should recall all old silver-bearing coins and control other silver usage to obtain enough metal for recoinage. To recover old coins, the bakufu should offer paper money in exchange and promise to redeem it later for new copper coins. To sustain the worth of the copper, it would be redeemable at face value for the finer silver coins that were to appear. Similar procedures were to be used for gold. In the process of reform, he stressed, care must be taken to maintain exchange ratios, heed supply and demand lest inflation erupt, and act concurrently in Edo and the Kamigata cities lest regional imbalances arise.

Despite the careful detail of Hakuseki's proposals, during Ienobu's years he could do little more than reactivate a comptroller post (*kanjō ginmiyaku*) earlier used to watch for fiscal abuses, gradually reduce Ogiwara's ties to the shogun and senior officials, and induce Ienobu to create a committee to plan the new minting. Not until a month before Ienobu's death was Ogiwara finally dismissed, and not until the fallen minister died a year later did the bakufu actually begin to implement a new coinage policy. The child shogun ordered a new currency issued, and during the next year gold, silver, and copper coins were minted and policies for their circulation established. In 1715 Edo announced plans to take all Genroku gold coins out of circulation.

Minting required bullion, but the recovery of old coins proved difficult and attempts to increase mine output bore no fruit. The bakufu also tried to obtain metal by controlling domestic use and restricting export. Hakuseki justified export restrictions by arguing that "the Five Metals are like the bones which are not produced a second time. . . . there are few places which produce these and the yield is not constant. Spending the useful wealth of Japan in exchange for useless foreign

---

1. The fullest study of Hakuseki in English is Kate Wildman Nakai, *Shogunal Politics* (Cambridge, Mass.: Harvard University Press, 1988).

goods is not a far-sighted policy." In 1712 he informed Ienobu that, "in exchange for useless foreign goods," Japan had lost "one quarter of the gold and three-quarters of the silver [it had mined]." Two years later, having apprised himself of more trade figures and the domestic complications of bullion scarcity, he asserted that "in another century we shall have lost half our gold, and all the silver will have gone before that period is out. As for copper, not only is what we have now not enough for foreign trade, but insufficient for internal needs as well."[2]

Driven by the conviction that foreign trade was exacerbating fiscal and economic disorder and propelling Japan toward ruin, the bakufu tightened trade limits and procedures at Nagasaki. It reiterated old proscriptions against secret foreign trade and prescribed punishments for violators. It ordered daimyo in western Japan to be on the alert for foreign vessels and seize any they discovered, and in ensuing years numerous reports reached Edo of measures taken by daimyo to locate ships and interdict illicit trade.

By the time of Yoshimune's succession in 1716, the bakufu had thus adopted a new currency policy and in conjunction with it had tightened control of domestic metal usage and foreign trade. The economic effects of the recoinage showed up during his years as shogun and seem, in retrospect, to have severely complicated his attempts to govern. By then Hakuseki had lost his influence on affairs, eclipsed by a man whose ideas proved more congruent with, and possibly even influenced, Yoshimune's policies, the Confucian scholar, Ogyū Sorai.

OGYŪ SORAI AND THE PRINCIPLES OF REFORM

Sorai was born in Edo in 1666, son of a doctor serving Tokugawa Tsunayoshi, daimyo of Tatebayashi and brother of the shogun Ietsuna. The lad reportedly began studying in the Hayashi school at Shinobugaoka, but his father became entangled in a dispute that led in 1679 to the family's exile to a village in Kazusa province, across the bay from Edo. Finding himself in the classic dilemma of the gifted ronin, young Sorai continued his study of Chinese and the Confucian classics. Eleven years later, Tsunayoshi, now shogun, allowed the family to return, and Sorai tried to establish a medical practice in Edo. The attempt failed, so he began teaching Confucianism and the Chinese language, displaying his erudition in 1692 by publishing *Yakubun sentei*, a guide to written

2. Joyce Ackroyd, *Told Round a Brushwood Fire: The Autobiography of Arai Hakuseki* (Princeton: Princeton University Press, 1979), pp. 178–79, 247.

Chinese. His reputation as a skilled linguist grew, and four years later he realized the ronin's dream of finding service among the powerful when he was hired by Yanagisawa Yoshiyasu, senior bakufu official, confidante of the shogun, and builder of Rikugien.

For thirteen years Sorai moved among the mighty, and his stipend rose to a thoroughly comfortable 500 koku.[3] However, in 1709 when Tsunayoshi died and Yoshiyasu was drummed from office, he prudently took his leave. By then he enjoyed a reputation as a well-connected expert on Chinese philology and Confucian learning, and he established a Confucian school at Nihonbashi in the city. He designed a curriculum to produce students thoroughly schooled in classical Chinese thought and soon acquired followers, including such noted scholars as Dazai Shundai.

In 1714 Sorai began publishing philosophical essays, initially as attacks on Itō Jinsai. His later, less vituperative essays consisted of broader analyses of politics and political thought, and four merit specific note. Two were essays of 1717, *Bendō* and *Benmei*, which together articulated his understanding of Confucianism. And two were the later *Taiheisaku,* probably written around 1721–1723, but possibly earlier, and *Seidan,* probably written in 1725 but usually dated by its presentation to Yoshimune in 1727. These two spelled out policy proposals for the shogun's consideration.

SORAI'S THOUGHT

As a lad, Sorai first learned the Ch'eng-Chu interpretations prevalent in Edo at the time, and he initially criticized Jinsai for deviating from that understanding. By 1717, however, he had adopted the basic ancient learning (*kogaku*) proposition that Jinsai had helped pioneer, namely, that Confucian thought of the Sung dynasty and later was a corruption of a fundamentally correct classical legacy. He continued to attack the deceased merchant-scholar, however, in essence charging that he had not understood the Ancient Way correctly and had instead advanced his own intellectual agenda, in the manner of Sung Confucianists.

Sorai's mature understanding undergirded his policy proposals of the 1720s. His basic concern was political: how to establish and preserve peace and contentment. That is difficult, he argued, because human na-

3. An examination of Sorai during his service for Yanagisawa is Olof Lidin, "Ogyū Sorai's Journey to Kai Province in 1706," *Journal of Intercultural Studies* 2 (1975): 29–41.

ture is diverse and people generally are ill informed, so the task devolves upon government. To govern successfully, a ruler must address the problems of the day in a manner that accommodates the diversity of human nature and the specifics of the situation. Policy-making must therefore be creative, but it also must have proper ultimate goals, and those were established by the Early Kings of China. As Sorai asserted time and again, "The Way of the Early Kings was the way by which all under Heaven were brought peace and contentment."[4]

To govern wisely, therefore, one must understand the Way of the Early Kings, who, "by virtue of their high intelligence and perspicacity, received the Mandate of Heaven and ruled the world."[5] But the only guide to the Early Kings' rule is the writings, notably the Six Classics, of the ancient Sages, who recorded the Way of the Kings accurately and without embroidery. His authority for that assertion was Confucius himself: "Confucius said, 'I have transmitted what was taught to me without adding anything of my own.' ... Even Confucius, who was endowed with a sage's intelligence, was satisfied merely to cherish the Way of the Early Kings."[6]

Since then, however, there have been no Sages. Men no longer know the Way because, as time passes, "the world changes, carrying with it language; language changes, carrying with it the Way."[7] One can recover the ancient Way only by mastering the ancient language and adhering to ancient rites and rituals, which are recorded and hence can be known as elements of sound governance. Indeed, "there is no such thing as the Way apart from rites, music, law-enforcement, and political administration."[8] Chinese and Japanese scholars, even down to Jinsai, have failed to master the ancient language and apply their mastery to scrutiny of the classics and hence have failed to understand the Way. Instead they have presumed to improve on the Sages and Early Kings, and as a result their teachings distort the Way and confound attempts to govern properly.

4. Olof G. Lidin, *Ogyū Sorai's Distinguishing the Way* (Tokyo: Sophia University Press, 1970), pp. 12, 24, 36, 38, 48, 58, 74, 110.

5. Ibid., p. 24.

6. Samuel Hideo Yamashita, "Nature and Artifice in the Writings of Ogyū Sorai (1666–1728)," in Peter Nosco, ed., *Confucianism and Tokugawa Culture* (Princeton: Princeton University Press, 1984), p. 141.

7. Minamoto Ryōen, "Jitsugaku and Empirical Rationalism in the First Half of the Tokugawa Period," in Wm. Theodore de Bary and Irene Bloom, eds., *Principle and Practicality: Essays in Neo-Confucianism and Practical Learning* (New York: Columbia University Press, 1979), p. 442. The full text is translated in Richard H. Minear, "Ogyū Sorai's *Instructions for Students:* A Translation and Commentary," *TASJ* 36 (1976): 16.

8. Lidin, *Ogyū Sorai's Distinguishing the Way*, p. 16.

Happily, however, as he informed a friend, his own philological understanding and accomplishments had ended that long benighted era:
"Ah! It is more than 1,000 years since Confucius died; and today for
the first time the Way has become clear. How could this be of my own
strength? Heaven has willed this. Even should I die, this assures that I
'will not decay.' "⁹ Sorai thus saw himself as uniquely qualified to give
sagely advice on governing, and he did so in *Taiheisaku* and *Seidan,*
which together surely rank among the preindustrial world's most detailed schemes for authoritarian social management.

Like other Japanese Confucians, Sorai faced the dilemma of how to
accept the Chinese categories of civilized and barbarian without seeming to heap calumny on Japan's own legacy. One of his most influential
solutions was to argue that whereas China had deteriorated since the
time of the Sages, Tokugawa Japan with its decentralized (*hōken,* or
"feudal") polity embodied a true expression of the Ancient Way. As he
put it in 1716 in describing the hōken model that the Tokugawa order
supposedly represented:

> The period of the Three Dynasties [in ancient China] was that of a *hōken*
> state. The Han and later dynasties, down to the T'ang, Sung, and Ming, were
> all *gunken* [centralized bureaucratic] states. . . . In a *hōken* state the country
> is divided up among feudal lords, and only a small part of it is ruled directly
> by the Emperor. The retainers of the feudal lords receive hereditary emolu-
> ments and hold land in fief which descends from generation to generation.
> Although exceptional men may be given advancement, in general a man's
> position is determined by his status at birth. Thus the descendants of gentle-
> men, senior retainers, and feudal lords retain these positions in perpetuity.
> Thus a *hōken* age is one in which men's minds are fixed and settled. Law is
> little developed and rule is based on personal obligation between superior
> and inferior, while the greatest consideration is given to the preservation of
> a sense of honour. The feudal lords and their senior retainers rule over their
> lands as their own property.¹⁰

In a centralized (*gunken*) state, by contrast, the system of peripatetic
officials invites irresponsibility and greed within officialdom and self-
ishly ambitious conduct by people in general because they are permitted
to rise in life. So the Way and its virtues are lost, as is evident in contemporary China, with its barbarian rulers and bankrupt philosophy.

By thus identifying the Tokugawa order with the ancient Way, Sorai

    9. Minear, "Ogyū Sorai's *Instructions for Students,*" p. 75.
    10. J. R. McEwan, *The Political Writings of Ogyū Sorai* (Cambridge: Cambridge,
University Press, 1962), p. 21. Italics added; parenthetic Japanese originals of several
nouns deleted.

abetted Japan's claim to being guardian of the Way. His analysis affirmed the legitimacy of Tokugawa rule, advocated energetic and creative policy-making to sustain that rule, and defined its proper objective as preservation of society's hōken character.

SORAI'S POLICY POSITIONS

In *Taiheisaku* and *Seidan*, Sorai assigned economics a central role in affairs.[11] Once a dynasty's founder has imposed order and erected proper institutions, he wrote in *Seidan*, peace and contentment prevail. However, the permanance of that outcome cannot be assumed:

> After conditions of peace have continued for a long time, impoverishment gradually overtakes the upper and lower classes alike, the political structure is disrupted and the result is civil war. It is clear in every case in history that the transition from a state of peaceful rule to one of civil war has come about because of the impoverishment of society, and for this reason the basis of all government consists in ensuring before all else that the country shall have ample wealth. . . . When one is so poor that one is in want of food and clothing, one loses all regard for propriety. Unless there is respect for propriety among the lower orders, it is obvious that there must be unrest, and eventually civil war.

In *Taiheisaku*, Sorai had previously argued that men of the founder's day "are of simple habits but of great capacity," whereas later generations become petty and inept, which leads via profligacy to poverty. To avoid that outcome, the Sages established "Rites and Music and other regulative institutions," which "remain in force without undergoing any change" and hence are able to counter the natural tendency toward extravagance. In the Tokugawa case, regrettably, Ieyasu died before establishing all the necessary institutions, and while the requisite changes might have been implemented before Tsunayoshi's rule, "thirty or forty years have passed since that time, impoverishment is much more marked, there are many stupid men in high office, and I fear that it may be too late to do this."

That being the case, the situation was desperate. But corrective measures could still be taken. He proposed in *Seidan* that although the sankin kōtai system of hostages originally was valuable for preventing the re-eruption of civil war, today, "the daimyo are completely powerless and their poverty is very real, [so] it is inevitable that some relief from

11. The next several quotations are from McEwan, *Political Writings,* pp. 31–32, 34–35, 37–38, 45–46.

their compulsory attendance in Edo should be granted." Daimyo poverty was exacerbated, he noted, by the levies that Edo imposed on them and by their attempts to adhere to "the style proper to their station," which dictated their food, dress, servant staff, and ceremonial practices.

Lesser samurai had also been impoverished by living in "proper style." Their existence as a captive consumer populace had created a class of exploitative merchants who encouraged extravagance and "the fashion of trivial bustle." These nefarious merchants could "demand any price they please" for whatever they purveyed because they were "in communication with one another" throughout Japan, knew how to corner markets and hoard goods, and had "now devised means by which they can obtain a livelihood without even carrying on trade but merely by acting as middlemen."

Sorai wished to restore the physical vigor and fiscal well-being of samurai by ending their habits of urban indolence, extravagance, and dependence on merchants.[12] So he recommended their transfer from cities back to the land. That would restore samurai concern for the peasantry and peasant respect for their superiors, with the result that "good order would be preserved in the district." Moreover, it would give samurai direct control of the rice crop, and thus "the merchants, who will be forced to buy the rice in exchange for money, will be utterly confounded, and it will be possible to bring down prices to any level desired." While samurai consumed cheap rice in the countryside, "the price of rice [in the city] could be made very high and all the chōnin of Edo would be obliged to eat coarse grains. In this way there would arise a distinction between the food of the rulers and the ruled which is also in accordance with the ancient Way."

By these measures, he argued, proper hōken social relationships would be restored. To assure that affairs did not deteriorate again, thorough censuses should identify who lived where and careful measures of highway control should keep track of travelers. To help people conduct themselves in accord with their stations, sumptuary legislation should grant privilege "according to the degrees of office, precedence, honorary ranks and emoluments at every level from the daimyō to the lowest ranks of the military class and should comprise everything from dress to apartments, furnishings, food and retinue."[13] Equally stringent reg-

---

12. The three quotations in this paragraph are from McEwan, *Political Writings*, pp. 60, 62–63.

13. This quotation and the next several, all from *Seidan*, derive *seriatim* from McEwan, *Political Writings*, pp. 71, 97, 77, 80, 81, 78, 79, 82–83.

ulations for commoners would identify the many articles of food, dress, and equipment they were forbidden to utilize.

Citing the classics, he spelled out how bakufu administration should be reformed to enhance its effectiveness. Although he advised relaxing sankin kōtai to ease daimyo poverty, he did not wish lords strengthened vis-à-vis the bakufu and recommended that major domains be divided so that the largest would not exceed 300,000 koku in production. Moreover, he wrote, "mountains which produce timber or which have mines bearing gold, silver, copper, iron, lead or other metals, and places where there are fisheries or salt-pans should not be given in fief." To undermine the power of merchants, he urged the bakufu to requisition all goods, whether food, cloth, or other necessities, directly from producers, thereby cutting out the entrepreneurial middleman and restoring samurai dominance.

Reforming administration and coping with the myriad problems of the day required one more thing: competent officials. "It is a general and lasting principle of the natural order that old things should pass away and new things be brought into existence," and thus as generations pass, the progeny of daimyo and high officials become less and less competent. They "become more and more stupid [because] all human ability is produced by suffering difficulties and hardships," which they never encounter. Quite the contrary, "they are reared in the midst of the praise and adulation of their household retainers, so that they become conceited in a wisdom which they do not possess," Sorai observed. As a result of this pampered upbringing, he believed, "persons of ability will disappear from among the upper class and in the course of time an age of disorder will come, in which men of ability will appear among the lower classes and overthrow the dynasty."

To avoid that grim prospect, the able must be promoted and the inept demoted. Doing so would place the realm in conformity with the "natural order," assuring that "the will of those above is diffused throughout the lower classes" and "the sufferings of the lower classes and the general state of society are made known to the rulers." This reintegration of society would create harmony among the classes and result in "the enjoyment of good government by the state and in a universal increase in wealth similar to the natural growth which takes place in spring and summer."

Sorai spelled out more fully why the elite were incompetent, but knowing that his readers were themselves of high status, he eventually backpedaled to a less exposed position:

Acceptance of the principle of promoting men of worth and talent does not imply driving out all those who have held high positions in the past and reversing the position of rulers and ruled. If only two or three, or even only one or two, men of worth and talent are promoted from the lower classes, the hitherto unbroken precedent of hereditary succession will be destroyed and everyone will adopt a new attitude, each working with great diligence in imitation of the men who have been promoted, and thus by one stroke the entire country will be transformed to a better state.

It seems plausible that one of the "one or two" he had in mind for everyone else to imitate might be the sagely man who had been toughened by his years of youthful exile in Kazusa.

Sorai also wrote at length on coinage, the topic that had dominated government fiscal policy for three decades.[14] Rejecting the bullionist view that currency devaluation was at the heart of Genroku inflation, he claimed that Hakuseki's program of recoinage was wrongheaded and ineffective. The real cause of inflation was government failure to control human extravagance, which allowed people, especially those in cities, to live luxurious lives, in the process bidding up prices. To control inflation, the rulers must enforce sumptuary regulations and reduce consumption. Other factors also spurred price rises—excessive land rents, increased costs of transportation, exploitative mortgage and loan agreements, and short-term wage labor—but those, he argued, were amenable to firm government management. In any case the basic solution was to get samurai back to the land and the rustic simplicity of their forebears. Sorai thus transformed the debate on prices from a question of monetary policy to one of social policy, fitting it into his larger vision of a society shaped by forceful, enlightened government initiative.

By these several policies, Sorai proposed to revitalize the polity, restore samurai well-being, and reconsolidate the social hierarchy. Some of his ideas, particularly his condemnation of profligacy and calls for sumptuary regulation, reflected well-established positions. Others, such as the return of samurai to the land, expressed a view that never gained favor among samurai in general. Yet others, such as his castigating of merchants in particular and urban life-styles in general, provided ammunition for the growing number of observers who found in those targets fitting scapegoats for the escalating economic stresses of the day. Lastly, some proposals, such as reduction of sankin kōtai duty and flexibility in promoting lesser samurai to higher posts, provided ideological

14. These comments summarize material in McEwan, *Political Writings*, pp. 95–109, and Neil Skene Smith, "An Introduction to Some Japanese Economic Writings of the 18th Century," *TASJ*, 2d ser., 11 (1934): 68–79.

backing for specific policy decisions that Yoshimune was in the process of making.

There is enough similarity between both the general thrust and specific aspects of Sorai's proposals and Yoshimune's reform policies of the 1720s to tempt one to attribute the policies to Sorai. From what little we know of the dates of actions and essays, however, and of the infrequent contacts Sorai had with Yoshimune's officials, it seems wiser to view the two as concurrent expressions of ideas then under discussion and of choices in the process of being made. In some matters, essay preceded act; in others, action preceded essay. But both essay and action were responses to problems of the day, and the problems in turn were shaped by the larger context of society and environment.

THE CONTEXT OF REFORM

Many of the problems that precipitated the Kyōhō reform were becoming visible by Genroku, and they became more pronounced thereafter, providing the situational context within which Yoshimune undertook his reform. That context can be examined in terms of problems in the city and hinterland that most concerned Tokugawa leaders, namely, Edo and the Kantō, and in terms of the monetary instability that disrupted Yoshimune's early years as shogun.

PROBLEMS IN EDO

Two of Edo's problems particularly troubled bakufu leaders, because they burdened the treasury and complicated the task of governing. The first was the tendency of city-bound samurai to overload with debt. The bakufu's immediate concern was shogunal vassals, the hatamoto and gokenin. They had tended to live beyond their means throughout the seventeenth century, borrowing from merchants and then disputing their obligations. By midcentury, lawsuits over their debts cluttered judicial dockets, and the bakufu began ordering them settled out of court by mutual consent, which improved a debtor's chance of obtaining partial forgiveness.

From the mid 1690s on, the problem was temporarily "solved" by Ogiwara Shigehide's currency debasements, which increased the volume of money in Edo, reducing its value relative to rice. Shogunal vassals were paid much of their income in rice, so when they sold it at market, they received larger sums of money, which made it easier to carry debt and buy other goods and services, whose prices rose more slowly than rice. The flood of debased currency, which was fed into the marketplace by licensed wholesalers, enabled usurers to make loan funds readily available, and shogunal retainers appear to have seized the opportunity to borrow and spend more freely than ever. In the process they sustained their comfortable lives and Genroku's tone of luxury—but they also slipped further into debt.

By the end of Tsunayoshi's rule, many were deeply in the red, their situation suggested by the domestic records of one high-ranking hatamoto, who in the year 1711 had income valued at about 483 ryō in gold.[15] His expenses that year totaled 890 ryō, distributed in the following manner:

Food	75 ryō	Gifts	23 ryō
Fuel	35	House maintenance	15
Personal expenses	40	Exceptional expenses	86
Wages of servants	159	Debt service	426
Other domestic expenses	31		

The hatamoto's income was sufficient to maintain his house and staff and even meet the exceptional expenses of 86 ryō associated with the birth of a child. But accumulated debt was swamping him; he could carry the burden only if rice prices remained high. If they fell, the area of expense he could most advantageously trim was the cost of servants, but some of them were rear vassals, part of the bakufu's military force.

Hatamoto indebtedness thus posed a direct threat to bakufu military capacity. It was also a fiscal liability if the regime felt compelled to bail out insolvent retainers and a political liability should it not do so. In short, by 1710 core personnel of the regime presented its leaders with problems having the potential to threaten its survival.

The second problem was Edo's size. The city had become a huge burden on the bakufu for several reasons, notably its acute vulnerability to fire. All of Japan's cities and castle towns were ravaged by fire, and

15. Kozo Yamamura, "The Increasing Poverty of the Samurai in Tokugawa Japan, 1600–1868," *Journal of Economic History* 31 (June 1971): 397. The expenses as given here omit fractions of *ryō*. I have also combined several of Yamamura's more specific figures. Thus what I label debt service, Yamamura lists as payment for past debts (254 *ryō*); payment for current debts to merchants (21); payments for various debts of peasants (54); and interest payments (97).

the constant demand for construction materials steadily consumed timber stands, but conflagrations in Edo had the furthest-reaching impact, because of the city's immense size and the concentration of political power there.

An important factor in the fire problem was the city's roofing. After the Meireki fire, the bakufu outlawed tile roofs, even for daimyo. As a result thatch roofs, which were highly flammable and had become rare in earlier decades, again became common, making fire a greater risk than ever. Bakufu leaders tried to reduce the risk by encouraging use of mud daubing, but fires remained a major menace.

This seemingly irrational response to conflagration probably reflects the deteriorated condition of Japan's forests. Timber scarcity, as noted in chapter 11, torpedoed plans to rebuild Edo Castle's central keep and created an array of problems in the city. It also seems the probable cause of the decision to proscribe tile roofs. At that time, thick, semi-tubular *hongawara,* whose pieces were held in place by a bed of clay spread over roofboards, were the only available tiles.[16] To assure watertightness, the alternating convex and concave courses of tile overlapped from ridge to eave, making the roof extremely heavy and necessitating large framing timbers and a solid board underroof. Before 1657 such roofs, being limited to buildings of the wealthy, were a mark of elegance, and their prohibition struck a blow at an expensive, timber-intensive style of roof that reflected the daimyo penchant for debilitating competitive display. But the prohibition also created an extremely fire-prone city, which over the years may in fact have consumed more timber than one covered with hongawara.

City fires drained the treasury, disrupted lives, and devoured timber. Edo's seventeenth-century growth also created such a voracious appetite for heating and cooking fuel that it depleted bakufu fuel lands on Izu Peninsula, led to harsh disputes over extraction rights, and produced a complex and costly organization for getting fuel to the city. By Yoshimune's day, disputes over the quality, quantity, and price of fuel and building timber were chronic, and the fires that repeatedly ravaged Edo kept the issues in the public eye. The situation, in short, gave bakufu leaders compelling reason to want a smaller, less densely populated, less fireprone tinderbox of a city, and measures to address that want showed up in the Kyōhō reform.

16. William H. Coaldrake, "Edo Architecture and Tokugawa Law," *MN* 36-3 (Autumn 1981): 253–61. Coaldrake emphasizes considerations of status rather than cost in explaining why tiling was discouraged during the seventeenth century.

PROBLEMS IN THE KANTŌ

In the country at large, the agricultural economy was more productive than ever by the 1690s, thanks to a century of reclamation and riparian work. But land for further expansion was nearly gone, and the rural populace seemed to be experiencing increasing economic difficulty. Popular hardship and unrest began building from the mid 1690s, usually as disputes over tax policy and land surveys. A few incidents impinged on Edo during the quarter century prior to 1720,[17] but most occurred in the west, especially along the Sea of Japan, an area almost entirely under daimyo jurisdiction. In 1721 the trouble finally reached the bakufu's own lands when a protest erupted in the district of Minamiyama, on the northern edge of the Kantō. That disorder struck close enough to home to really capture Edo's attention.

Minamiyama was a cluster of narrow, north-facing, agriculturally marginal river valleys in the mountains southwest of Aizu. A buffer area periodically assigned to Aizu or reclaimed by Edo, Minamiyama had a history of peasant protests against tax- and rice-collection policies. In 1713 Edo resumed control of the area, and during the next few years the intendant raised the tax rate, undertook a new land survey, and shipped to Edo rice supplies stored locally as reserves against crop failure. Late in 1720, after their local complaints had been ignored, villagers assembled and marched in force to the intendant's headquarters, where they demanded "reduction of the tax rate, lower taxes on beans and secondary crops, commutation of the entire land tax, halting of rice exports [to Edo], and abolition of the office of chief headman." [18]

The intendant rejected the petition, so the villagers organized a small delegation, which bypassed his office and went directly to Edo. Officials there buried the appeal in bureaucratic stalling, causing the frustrated delegates to return home. The protest leaders then began organizing a tax strike, and when news of that reached Edo during 1721, officialdom paid attention. Authorities ordered hundreds of troops to the area to suppress the strike, arrest the leaders, and interrogate everyone involved. Before the process ran its course, "more than ten thousand peasants had been interrogated and three hundred and fifty jailed or

17. W. Donald Burton, "Peasant Struggle in Japan, 1590–1760," *Journal of Peasant Studies* 5-2 (1978): 154–55.

18. Stephen Vlastos, *Peasant Protests and Uprisings in Tokugawa Japan* (Berkeley and Los Angeles: University of California Press, 1986), p. 51. The phrasing is Vlastos's. Chief headmen were government appointees who served primarily as local expediters of government policy.

placed under house arrest." Over forty were fined or had lands confiscated, nine died in prison, and six leaders were executed and their heads posted for local edification.[19]

Certainly one can imagine bakufu leaders in their great castle at the center of Edo perceiving these rural rumbles as something very far away. However, Tsunayoshi, Ienobu, and Yoshimune all served as mature daimyo before becoming shogun, and most senior officials were themselves daimyo or fief-holding hatamoto. Few could afford to disregard evidence of growing rural disorder. Though they might ignore the toll on villagers, none could forget that domanial disorder was a major cause of daimyo dismissals. Moreover, no one was indifferent to the fiscal implications of unrest, as suggested by Edo's brisk response to the threatened tax strike in Minamiyama.

PROBLEMS IN THE MONETARY SYSTEM

Yoshimune sustained Hakuseki's monetary reform program during his first years as shogun. Initially, Edo experienced some difficulty getting its new coins into circulation and the old ones out, but by 1718 the recoinage policy was working. Urban rice prices had dropped sharply, undermining the market value of the rice tax that enabled the bakufu and its retainers to carry indebtedness. Basic commodity prices in Edo also showed a downward trend after 1716, as this index of Edo consumer prices indicates:[20]

1710:	100	1730:	59.7
1711:	95.2	1733:	75.8
1713:	139.7	1740:	99.0
1716:	209.5	1745:	89.4
1726:	64.4	1750:	89.6

Their decline lagged behind that of rice, however, so for a few years samurai were selling rice at lower prices while buying necessities at comparatively higher ones.

The deflation that hurt samurai also injured urban commoners, many of whom were servants of samurai or depended on them as customers.

19. Ibid., p. 54.
20. Yamamura, "Increasing Poverty," pp. 381, 387–89, 405. Yamamura's price index (p. 405) is a composite of prices for bean paste, salt, soy sauce, sake, and lamp oil. He continues the series to 1857.

As samurai saw the value of their income falling, they borrowed if possible, and when that did not suffice, cut expenditures, most notably by trimming servants' wages or simply dismissing them. And servants tried to pass their losses on to the townsmen who serviced their needs.

The people of Edo, who had previously been major beneficiaries of currency devaluation, now bore the brunt of currency "improvement." So it is unsurprising that the problems dominating central politics during the early Kyōhō years were those affecting the city and, in particular, the rulers and their vassal forces. Of most immediate concern were samurai purchasing power and urban order and safety, which directly affected the regime's closest supporters and its claims to competence and virtue. But beyond those matters, the Kyōhō reform also addressed larger issues of social control and ideological order.

HEYDAY OF THE KYŌHŌ REFORM, 1721–1728

In broadest terms, Yoshimune intended to reconsolidate the Tokugawa order by revitalizing the samurai class, strengthening government control of affairs, and reducing public discontent. His reform began slowly during his first years as shogun, but from about 1721 on, with supporters well entrenched and rural unrest becoming more worrisome, he started implementing a wide range of policies, some quite unorthodox. The most striking reforms date from the difficult period 1721–23, but the shogun continued his programs in following years, and by 1728 the situation—at least that of the rulers—seemed sharply improved.

Most of Yoshimune's reforms during the 1720s dealt with Edo's fiscal dilemma, but they also addressed an array of other issues: the finances of shogunal vassals, city security, daimyo performance, merchant conduct, schooling, bakufu administrative practices, and peasant conditions. Finally, certain policies aimed to expand the output of society as a whole, but those longer-term initiatives became more pronounced in the 1730s, after the harrowing years of the Kyōhō famine, so they are treated later.

AIDING RETAINERS AND SECURING EDO

The deflation that came with recoinage undermined the ability of hatamoto and gokenin to finance their debts, prompting Yoshimune to force them to retrench by making further borrowing difficult. He did so by expanding an older policy that had made it easier for them to abrogate outstanding obligations. Some weeks after Ienobu's death in 1712, the bakufu reiterated its seventeenth-century policy prohibiting creditors from seeking monetary reimbursement in bakufu courts, and in 1719 after the great slide in rice prices, Yoshimune expanded that policy by decreeing that any loans offered in future also could not be recovered through bakufu courts. This broadened policy, which was kept in place for a decade, discouraged merchants from making new loans to shogunal retainers, at least until they devised ways of securing their funds despite the edict.

As intended, the policy made borrowing more difficult for hatamoto, but because it was implemented when recoinage was undermining their purchasing power, its effect percolated through the city economy, forcing the bakufu to take relief measures that undermined its own fiscal situation. And that problem led it to tighten tax collection in places such as Minamiyama. In essence the rulers were dealing with their problems by passing them downward through the city and outward to rural areas.

The problem of Edo's flammability held Yoshimune's attention from his first years as shogun. Just a few months before he became shogun, two winter fires damaged Edo severely, creating widespread hardship and forcing the bakufu to provide costly assistance to the homeless. At first he attacked the problem by the customary tactics of reforming and expanding city fire-fighting units and creating open areas as firebreaks. But those measures did not suffice, and after fire wracked the city again in 1720, he adopted a new and more radical strategy of trying to fireproof the city, most notably by promoting general use of roofing tile.

The tiling problem, as noted above, lay with the hongawara tile, but late in the seventeenth century, a new, flat roof tile, the *sangawara* (the sort that can still be seen on houses today), was invented. Being a thinner and lighter tile, it required less clay and less fuel for firing and thus was cheaper and more resource-efficient to produce. It also required less overlapping and needed no clay bed, and hence could be installed more easily and faster, with less underroofing and lighter framing.[21] In short, it sharply altered the economics of construction and enabled Yoshimune to promote tiling as a key strategy for reducing the city's incendiary potential.

After the fire of 1720, the bakufu called on rebuilders to use whitewashed walls, caked-mud warehouses, and tile roofs. Fires in 1721,

21. Coaldrake, "Edo Architecture and Tokugawa Law," p. 261, notes that the bakufu initially insisted on use of clay beds with the new tile (lest the tile fall, I presume).

14. Vista of Tile Roofs in Osaka. By the mid nineteenth century, tile roofs, mainly the flat *sangawara* type, were normative in Japan's cities. Fireproof storehouses and fire outlook towers, as in this photograph of Osaka, contributed to urban fire safety. Courtesy of the Study and Documentation Centre for Photography, University of Leiden, Collection Bauduin, Neg. No. BR-32.

1723, and 1725 led to further edicts urging tile construction and offering assistance to those who switched to tile. With those actions, Edo began a gradual conversion to the use of tile and other fire-proofing techniques that reduced the frequency and scale of fires, contributing over time to social savings and preservation of forest resources.

AIDING AND EXPLOITING DAIMYO

Some of Yoshimune's policies were designed to help daimyo govern better; others, to steer daimyo resources to bakufu service. One of his concerns, with lords as with lesser retainers, was their fiscal condition, and in the customary manner he exhorted them to trim expenses. He also urged them to enhance their tax bases by promoting agriculture, improving tax collection, and reducing the role of merchants in their domains.

The admonitions had little effect, however, in part because the fiscal difficulties of daimyo were to a significant degree self-inflicted: since Hidetada's day, most had insisted on bringing more retainers and servants to Edo than the bakufu required, and in Edo, they engaged in competitive gift giving and display despite repeated shogunal attempts to curtail the custom. As Edo blossomed into a vibrant cultural center, more and more lords and vassals wished to spend time there, and repeated bakufu orders failed to halt the tendency. The daimyo behavior troubled bakufu leaders because it was costly to lords, imposed a huge burden on villagers along the highways, and contributed to the overcrowding and overpricing of Edo itself.

In 1721 Yoshimune tried once again to trim *sankin kōtai* retinues by issuing new guidelines, but the measure had little effect. The following summer he attacked daimyo gift giving by slashing "monetary gifts [to the shogun] to one-tenth and other gifts to about one-third of the amounts presented up to this time."[22] That action was reinforced by a more radical measure, an order that sankin kōtai duty be reduced by half. He issued the order despite contrary advice from his elderly scholar-advisor, Muro Kyūsō, who said it would undermine Edo's control of the daimyo. The new policy would reduce daimyo expenses and, at least as important to the bakufu, it would ease Edo housing density and thus the problem of major urban fires. And it would cut demand for—and hence the cost of—food and other necessities in the city.

In explaining his decision to the lords, Yoshimune revealed another policy objective. The reduction in sankin kōtai duty was a quid pro quo for daimyo assistance in dealing with bakufu fiscal difficulty. He explained that over the years the costs of Edo's retainer force had risen and now, finally, the regime could no longer meet its payroll: "Accordingly, though this is something unheard of in the past, all those with fiefs yielding 10,000 koku and above will be commanded to present rice [to the bakufu]. We take this shameful step since otherwise we have no alternative but to deprive several hundreds of our retainers of their allowances." Yoshimune defined the rice levy as an annual 1 percent tax on fief production, the first regularized bakufu tax on daimyo. To help lords bear the new burden, he said they would henceforth be required to spend only six months out of two years in Edo. Presumably the savings they could realize from the shortened stay, together with reduced

22. This quotation, and the next, come from Toshio G. Tsukahira, *Feudal Control in Tokugawa Japan* (Cambridge, Mass.: Harvard University Press, 1956), pp. 69, 117.

gift giving, would cover the new tax. The principal losers would be Edo townsmen who had fewer lords to service, but Yoshimune wanted fewer townsmen anyway.

Yoshimune's interest in controlling lords and his readiness to exploit them was even more evident in his policy of river management. From 1703, when Edo first turned to daimyo for help in river work, it invoked the policy of daimyo-assisted public works (*otetsudai bushin*), which it had previously used for castle-building projects, with lords being assigned certain tasks and left largely unsupervised to complete them. Edo adhered to that policy for nearly twenty years, despite chronic complaints of negligence and mismanagement and consequent modifications of procedure.

In 1720 Yoshimune changed the policy. That year he wished to repair rivers on predominantly bakufu lands in the Nikkō vicinity, but he was unprepared to pay the cost. So he devised a new policy called *kuniyaku bushin*, or "construction service for the domain." Its regulations placed the primary burden for repair work on local people, compelled daimyo to participate to the extent that their land was involved, and limited the bakufu to supplemental funding as necessary. To assure Edo's control of such projects, in 1724 he created a new construction agency, the *fushin yaku*, initially assigning it twelve people and four years later expanding its staff to eighty-six. Through these moves he tried to shift the burden of river work away from Edo while tightening shogunal control of projects, regardless of whether they were initiated by bakufu intendants, han administrators, or villagers.

During the 1720s, Yoshimune applied the policy to repairs still needed because of Mount Fuji's eruption of 1707 and to projects in other areas where bakufu and daimyo lands were mixed together. For several years the new policy gave him, despite Edo's budgetary problems, enough supervisory reach and fiscal resources to cope with the growing need for river control. And the lords, having just had their sankin kōtai obligations reduced, were ill placed to complain about the more regularized levies and tighter discipline.

CONTROLLING MERCHANTS AND GUIDING SCHOOLING

Yoshimune took several steps to weaken merchants and bring them under tighter control. He forbade their use of bakufu courts to recover bad debts, as noted above. He restricted their right to acquire land and issued new regulations on usury and pawnbroking. Periodically he prohibited price increases and ordered prices reduced after city fires or other disruptions. And he repeatedly attempted to regulate rice prices by establishing bakufu control over the Osaka rice market, efforts that created a mutually frustrating, long-drawn-out legal struggle between the bakufu and Osaka merchants over how the rice market was to operate and who would be in charge of it.

Yoshimune also codified wholesale merchant organization, accepting the principle of licensed oligopoly that established merchants had long desired. For decades uncertainties of the marketplace had led them to seek government protection of their commercial positions, and in 1721 he tried to turn that merchant wish to government advantage by granting groups of artisans and merchants specific commercial "fiefdoms" that amounted to functional analogues of daimyo domains. He proscribed the creation of any new enterprises or the sale of any new goods of an inessential nature in Edo and soon after ordered the formation of *kabu nakama,* or chartered trade associations.

In these charter arrangements Yoshimune recognized the production or marketing rights of designated groups of artisans or merchants and forbade, or at least discouraged, outsiders from competing in the chartered activity. In return, nakama members were to handle their business responsibly, policing themselves and bringing stability to pricing, supply, and quality of goods and services. By 1724 the charters covered a wide range of businesses, from diverse luxuries to some twenty-three commodities of daily use, including "ginned cotton, cotton cloth, bleached cotton, silk pongee, textiles, paper, tea, tobacco, bean paste, soy, rice, salt, sake, and lamp oil."[23]

Yoshimune's readiness to grant commoners specific "fiefdoms" in return for service was also evident in the realm of schooling. He licensed schools to provide commoners with appropriate instruction, much as the Hayashi school at Shōheizaka provided it for samurai.

During the seventeenth century, both bakufu and han established a few schools (*gōgaku:* literally, "village" or "local" schools) to provide moral and practical instruction to village and town leaders. Some daimyo also took steps to foster Confucianism and discourage Buddhism,

---

23. William B. Hauser, *Economic Institutional Change in Tokugawa Japan: Osaka and the Kinai Cotton Trade* (Cambridge: Cambridge University Press, 1974), p. 35. See also Nakai Nobuhiko and James L. McClain, "Commercial Change and Urban Growth in Early Modern Japan," in *The Cambridge History of Japan,* vol. 4, *Early Modern Japan,* ed. John W. Hall (Cambridge: Cambridge University Press, 1991), pp. 570–79.

as noted in chapter 9. The policy of guiding moral education was manifested at a higher level by Tsunayoshi when he designated the Hayashi
family shrine and school a stipended, officially recognized center for the
ritual honoring of Confucius. In 1717 Yoshimune gave bakufu interest
in Shōheizaka a more explicitly educational emphasis by initiating regular lectures there and having them delivered primarily, but not entirely, by proponents of Ch'eng-Chu thought.

In much the same spirit, in 1723 he provided land and construction
funds so that Sugeno Kenzan, a ronin follower of a disciple of Yamazaki Ansai, could establish a school for samurai and commoners in Edo.
In his school, the Kaihodō, Kenzan taught writing for daily use and
gave instruction on basic Confucian texts. Three years later, after months
of negotiation, the shogun granted land and a tax-exempt charter to
Nakai Shūan, an Osaka merchant-scholar, who founded an autonomous merchant academy, the Kaitokudō, in Osaka. Known locally as
the Nakai family school, the Kaitokudō provided an appropriately
practical Confucian education to successive generations of Osaka merchants.

Two years after approving Nakai's request, Yoshimune appears to
have received a petition from Kada no Azumamaro, an elderly scholar
who had long provided antiquarian services to the bakufu and who ran
a school of ancient Japanese studies (*wagaku*) in Fushimi.[24] Azumamaro asked for a grant of land and the implicit recognition that his was
the authorized school of Japanese studies. He contended that correct
study of ancient texts would preserve Japanese wisdom by overcoming
ignorance and misunderstanding. It would reduce the present imbalance in favor of foreign learning and so conduce to the well-being of
society and the Tokugawa order, whose praises he sang with the enthusiasm appropriate to a petitioner. It seems, however, that his appeal was
rejected, perhaps because of its imprudent criticism of Chinese studies
or perhaps because he seemed more intent on promoting a doctrinal
viewpoint than on fostering the orderly education of a definable social
constituency.

Educational guidance could mean broadening the range of approved
learning, as in the case of books on Europe. Before 1720 Edo had rig-

24. Azumamaro's petition, which some scholars consider a later forgery, is translated
in Ryusaku Tsunoda et al., comps., *Sources of the Japanese Tradition* (New York: Columbia University Press, 1958), pp. 511–14. Peter Nosco, *Remembering Paradise* (Cambridge, Mass.: Harvard University Press, 1990), pp. 90–95, discusses the petition and its
historiography.

orously proscribed any books containing even a hint of Christianity, but official fear of subversion was considerably ameliorated by then, while concern with finances, production, and social order had intensified. So Yoshimune altered policy to improve access to books containing information on astronomy and calendar-making, along with other useful learning. The decree of 1720 specified that "books directly related to the Christian creed shall be prohibited as before. But those directly describing mere episodes concerning Christians may be sold to or purchased by common people, not to mention translations by the Bakufu for official purposes."[25] After that decree, the import of Chinese and European-language books on European subjects started to accelerate, and within a few decades their impact began to appear in art, astronomy, and medicine.

IMPROVING ADMINISTRATION AND EASING RURAL HARDSHIP

Like Iemitsu, Yoshimune was a "hands-on" ruler who saw effective administration as the heart of good governance. In customary fashion, he tinkered with organization, tightened controls, cashiered incompetent men, and replaced them with others. He reorganized and elaborated Edo city administration. He had officials develop new regulations for censuses, land surveys, and riparian work, and for settling disputes over boundaries and use rights on arable and untilled land. He reorganized his system of intendants (*daikan* and *gundai*), tightening Edo's control over them and pressing them to oversee their territories more carefully. For example, intendants customarily deducted their operating costs from tax receipts, forwarding the balance to Edo. The procedure invited abuse, so he ordered them, starting in 1725, to send all tax proceeds to Edo in return for an office allowance set by senior finance officials.

Yoshimune also addressed a more basic administrative problem. By the eighteenth century, a close link existed between hereditary family status and access to bakufu office, and he found it restricting his flexibility in appointing officials. The problem was compounded by burdensome costs that office holders customarily faced. In 1723 he tried to solve both issues by establishing *tashidaka,* or supplemental stipends, for men whom he named to posts higher than those appropriate to their

25. Itō Tasaburō, "The Book Banning Policy of the Tokugawa Shogunate," *AA* 22 (1972): 42. Itō lists all the books that are known to have been banned.

hereditary status. The supplements sanctioned such appointments and, more to the point, given the financial squeeze then affecting hatamoto and gokenin, helped induce men to accept the burdens of office.

One of Yoshimune's best-known measures, which may have been aimed at defusing public discontent more than improving government, was the installation of complaint boxes in which people could deposit petitions on matters of concern. He had one periodically placed near the bakufu's judicial offices (*hyōjōshō*) in Edo beginning in 1721 and another near the city administrative office of Osaka from 1727. The boxes seem to have had little value, however, and they were modified and their use discontinued a few years later.

A basic goal of Yoshimune's administrative tinkering was to improve bakuhan fiscal effectiveness. However, given the straitened environmental context and the spread of micro-farming, success in that endeavor could only intensify stress among taxpayers, and matters were worsened during the 1720s by crop failures that plagued the countryside, precipitating sporadic local turmoil.

Aspiring to so pluck the goose, in the words of Jean Baptiste Colbert, Louis XIV's minister of finance, "as to obtain the largest amount of feathers with the least amount of hissing," Yoshimune tried to minimize local administrative abuses lest they exacerbate disorder and confound tax collection. To that end he warned daimyo against harsh rule, reprimanded some lords and intendants, revised lax administrative procedures and tax regulations, reworked penal and judicial rules, and forbade "excessive" use of punitive banishment (which deprived localities of able-bodied workers and filled cities with vagrants). And in 1724 he ordered temporary reductions in tax levels as a way to provide short-term rural relief.

Yoshimune also tried to halt the trend to micro-farming and the rise of landlordism. As noted in chapter 12, he forbade villagers to divide holdings unless they exceeded one chō in area or had an estimated yield greater than ten koku. He sought to ease the burden of peasant debt to moneylenders by sharply limiting legal interest rates. And during 1722, when the Kantō and northeast were most severely wracked by hardship and turmoil, he fought land alienation by flatly prohibiting mortgages on paddy fields. Since the measures attacked the symptoms rather than the causes of difficulty, however, land continued slipping into merchant hands.

Unable to prevent the failure of micro-farmers, Yoshimune tried to guide the process of land alienation, decreeing in 1726 that rights to land could be transferred to others engaged in cultivation but not to people of merchant (chōnin) status. The implication seemed to be that even though the maintenance of high tax rates might ruin producers, merchants at least were not to profit from the situation.

By 1727–28 the fiscal condition of bakufu, han, and lesser retainers was much improved. Yoshimune's initiatives seemed to be succeeding on a broad front, in their totality revitalizing the Tokugawa order and validating Edo's claim that it ruled by right as a virtuous and effective regime. Although Yoshimune did not display Tsunayoshi's enthusiasm for scholastic Confucianism, he did consider it his duty to promote a stable, properly ordered hōken society and thereby to demonstrate shogunal virtue. In the spring of 1728, he finally felt he had done so, and in a gesture intended to suggest that the years of crisis were past and all was well, he made an expensive pilgrimage to Nikkō to pay his respects to the spirits of the great founders, Ieyasu and Iemitsu.

The grand trek to Nikkō proved, however, to be the high point of the Kyōhō reform. Even before it occurred, signs of trouble were reappearing, and during the next few years Yoshimune found himself struggling, in effect, with the destructive consequences of some of his greatest successes.

REFORM DISRUPTED, 1729–1735

One of Yoshimune's earliest objectives had been to replace a debased currency with a high-quality coinage, and the effort was successful. The new coins appeared and drove urban rice prices sharply downward by 1718, holding them below earlier levels even during the crop failures of 1720–21, and from 1722 sending them back down again for the rest of the decade.

Another goal had been to enhance bakufu tax receipts, and by the mid 1720s he was succeeding, as figure 15 indicates.[26] As the rural crisis passed and rice harvests improved, he issued new rules tightening tax collection and regularizing reductions for villages hurt by natural calamities. In 1727 he restricted reductions to villages experiencing crop loss of 20 percent or more, and a year later he raised the threshold for relief to 25 percent. By then, however, the policy of tightening tax ob-

26. Conrad Totman, *Politics in the Tokugawa Bakufu, 1600–1843* (Berkeley and Los Angeles: University of California Press, 1988), p. 79.

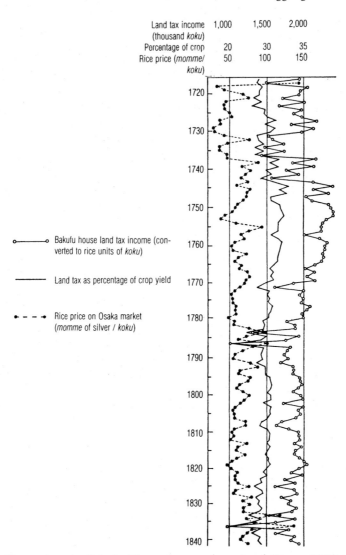

Land tax income (thousand *koku*)	1,000	1,500	2,000
Percentage of crop	20	30	35
Rice price (*momme/ koku*)	50	100	150

○———○ Bakufu house land tax income (converted to rice units of *koku*)

——— Land tax as percentage of crop yield

●- - -● Rice price on Osaka market (*momme* of silver / *koku*)

15. Fluctuations in Bakufu House Income from Land Taxes, 1710–1840. Adapted from Furushima Toshio, "Shōhin ryūtsū no hatten to ryōshu keizai," *Iwanami kōza Nihon rekishi* 12 (1963): 78–79.

ligations only exacerbated the new problem, which was too much rice flowing into a city whose population had been cut by the reduction in sankin kōtai duties even as daimyo shipped rice there instead. An ample harvest in 1729 caused the urban rice price to drop yet again, creating havoc among daimyo and retainers. Hatamoto, for example, found that in 1729 the purchasing power of their rice-tax income was only about half what it had been three years earlier.

The success of recoinage and improved tax collection was thus having the unintended result of sabotaging two of Yoshimune's dearest—and most elusive—goals: stable prices, especially for rice, and stable living costs for samurai. Instead, he was generating sharply erratic price movements and general dismay among people of consequence. That outcome precipitated several years of emergency maneuvers, reversal of the twenty-year policy of currency reform, and finally abandonment of sustained attempts at price control.

To elaborate, at the end of 1729, as lords and vassals in Edo grew desperate, Yoshimune tried to ease their situation by ordering frugality among retainers and lower interest rates on monetary loans. To facilitate borrowing, he repealed the standing prohibition against merchants bringing money suits to bakufu courts. A fortnight later he ordered the prices of other commodities reduced in parallel with that of rice. And a month later he ordered that rice be sold through a bidding procedure, which supposedly would pit buyers against one another, helping to shore up the price daimyo and shogunal vassals received when marketing their tax rice.

That flurry of midwinter measures launched a two-year campaign to cope with the collapse of rice prices, winning Yoshimune the sobriquet "the rice shogun." Most visibly, he instructed daimyo in the spring of 1730 to cease bringing rice to the city and instead to resume their former sankin kōtai schedules—measures to cut food imports while increasing mouths to feed. A few months later he took two more steps to drive up rice prices. To shrink the supply of marketable rice, he ordered daimyo to store it against future crop failures. And to increase the money supply, he authorized lords to issue paper money (*han satsu*), as they had before its issuance was prohibited in 1707.[27]

In a spate of actions that continued through the summer of 1732, the bakufu reiterated orders to han to buy and store rice and sent out inspectors to assure that the order was obeyed, particularly in the Kinai district, with its large bakufu-controlled cities. Edo also tinkered some more with its regulation of rice merchants and marketing, essentially abandoning efforts to manage the Osaka rice market and allowing merchants there to engage in speculative buying, probably in hopes that this would reflate prices.[28]

While working to enhance daimyo income, Yoshimune also tried to

27. Sakudō Yōtarō, "Domain Paper Currencies and Money Merchants in the Tokugawa Period," *AA* 39 (Oct. 1980): 65–66.
28. Sakudō Yōtarō, "Growth of Securities Market in Feudal Japan," *Osaka Economic Papers* 8-2 (Mar. 1960): 31, 37–38.

reduce their expenditures, the restoration of sankin kōtai notwithstanding. Early in 1731 he ordered a three-year program of general frugality and two years later a three-year cancellation of daimyo gift obligations to the shogun. To underline his resolve, he singled out for denunciation two of the most powerful and prestigious daimyo in the land, the Tokugawa lords of Owari and Kii, reprimanding them for extravagance and unseemly conduct.

By then, however, a new scourge had appeared that soon confounded his efforts to achieve an orderly rise in urban rice prices. As reported in chapter 12, bad weather and an infestation of leaf hoppers in 1732 ravaged crops in western Japan, creating unprecedented misery and slashing the tax income of bakufu and daimyo alike. In response to the famine, Yoshimune authorized westward shipment of rice stored in Osaka, but the quantities released proved thoroughly insufficient to prevent starvation, even though they threatened to leave Osaka short.

Lest too much rice flow out of Edo, the shogun limited exports from the city, but the restriction proved inadequate. Despite his earlier attempts to fatten rice reserves, urban supplies grew scarce, and during the winter of 1732–33, city rice prices shot up. Samurai with tax rice to sell may have gained, and merchants who happened to have reserves on hand certainly did. But for townsmen in general any trickle-down effect proved too little too late. As urban hardship intensified, Edo, Nagasaki, and the intendancy at Takayama were all hit by a new form of violence, *uchi kowashi*, or incidents of urban smashing in which commoners vented their wrath on merchants benefiting from the sudden price surge. Yoshimune was able to prevent similar trouble in the Kinai cities only by distributing relief rice in Kyoto and shipping additional supplies to Osaka from the northeast.

In the outcome, the food crisis of 1732–33 passed almost as abruptly as it appeared. Weather improved, the leaf hoppers did not return, and when new harvests came in, urban rice prices promptly dropped back to earlier levels. The bakufu made some attempts to control prices in 1735 and 1736, but Yoshimune seems by then to have adopted a radical new tack in his quest for price stability: he abandoned his twenty-year policy of currency reform.

Finally persuaded, it appears, that Ogyū Sorai was correct in seeing sumptuary regulation rather than recoinage as the key to orderly prices, he repudiated Hakuseki's policy of currency reform and returned to Ogiwara's strategy of debasement. In 1736 he authorized the debasing of Ietsugu's gold and silver coins. To get the new issue into circulation, however, he, unlike Ogiwara, sacrificed the immediate gain of debasement by allowing holders of the old, more valuable coins to turn them in at a premium. The tactic worked. The new coins flowed into the market, and rice prices rose, enabling governments and samurai to sell their tax rice at profit and thus to recover their fiscal strength. Indeed, for nearly a quarter of a century, "the Shogunate's budget stayed in the black by the greatest margin of the Tokugawa period and the reserves of gold and silver in its treasury reached 3 million *ryō*."[29] Not until a decade after Yoshimune's death did the fiscal stimulus lose its value to the rulers.

THE LATER YEARS OF REFORM

The year 1736 was a fitting moment for conditions to change. The preceding spring Emperor Nakamikado had stepped down, after twenty-five years on the throne, in favor of Sakuramachi. And in the spring of 1736 a new year-period was announced, with Kyōhō giving way to Genbun. Yoshimune remained shogun for another decade, until the autumn of 1745, when he turned the title over to his disabled eldest son, Ieshige, whom he oversaw as retired shogun until his own death six years later at the age of sixty-seven.

During these last fifteen years of Yoshimune's life, rural hardship and disorder persisted and prices and tax yields continued to fluctuate. But the topic of rice ceased to dominate affairs, with the bakufu issuing directives on its price and provisioning only at moments of immediate difficulty. As figure 15 suggests, vigorous rice-tax collection sustained bakufu income and city food reserves throughout the period. And Edo's acceptance of speculative buying by licensed rice wholesalers may have helped even out swings in the market price: at least prices tracked more steadily after 1739 than they had at any earlier time in Yoshimune's rule.

In these new circumstances the shogun's interests seemed to grow more eclectic. Going well beyond the role of a "rice shogun," he oversaw a remarkably comprehensive managerial state.[30] That managerial

29. Takehiko Ohkura and Hiroshi Shimbo, "The Tokugawa Monetary Policy in the Eighteenth and Nineteenth Centuries," *Explorations in Economic History* 15 (1978): 105–6.
30. For a longer-term interpretation of Tokugawa political history that presents it as a gradual growth of central state power, see James W. White, "State Growth and Popular Protest in Tokugawa Japan," *JJS* 14-1 (Winter 1988): 1–25. For other aspects of Yoshimune's legal reform, see Tsuji Tatsuya, "Politics in the Eighteenth Century," in Hall, ed., *Early Modern Japan*, pp. 446–48, 454–55.

impulse included a heightened attention to policies for enhancing society's overall production. And the attentiveness was sustained, no doubt, by the continuing escalation of river problems, which made a shambles of Edo's kuniyaku bushin policy and saddled daimyo with backbreaking obligations.

THE MANAGERIAL SHOGUNATE

In a sense, Yoshimune's post-1736 policies as a whole, not just his coinage program, reflected the Sorai view that a properly stratified social order and shogunal control of that order depended on exhortation, sumptuary regulation, and other forms of governmental supervision.

The most enduring element in Yoshimune's attempt at comprehensive social management was the legal compilation known to historians as *Ofuregaki kanpō shūsei*. In 1742 (the second year of the Kanpō period) he ordered officials in key offices—secretaries, inspectors, and ministers of finance—to compile by subject matter and in chronological order the documents of their offices from 1615 to the present. In response they produced a collection of 3,550 decrees organized in eighty categories and bound in fifty fascicles (*kan*). A massive body of precedent for administrative law, the compilation served as model for three similar projects of the 1750s, 1780s, and 1830s, forming in toto a comprehensive record of bakufu legislation.

Yoshimune intended the *Ofuregaki kanpō shūsei* to guide policymakers in overseeing society, a task that relied heavily on exhortation. From the start he had repeatedly admonished daimyo and lesser samurai to be frugal and conduct themselves responsibly. In his later years he issued frequent calls for frugality, aiming them at diverse groups: officialdom, lords, the rich, and the general public. He also issued explicit decrees regulating clothing, women's decorations, behavior of nuns, daimyo recreation, highway usage, and manners and morals in general. He insisted on periodic population censuses and issued decrees relating to mortgage and sale of land, sale of women, abandonment of children, secret adoption, and unauthorized wearing of swords or use of family names.

He broadened the scope of kabu nakama arrangements and issued decrees regulating such diverse commerce as coastal shipping, forest products, cinnabar, birds, ginseng, and vegetable waxes and oils. He defined the seasonal limits on sales of fish, fowl, and vegetables. And because of continuing irregularities and commercial abuses, he had weights and measures investigated throughout the realm. To control fires in Edo, he continued advocating roof tile, in 1740 ordering thirty-two lords to tile all the roofs of their mansions. In the face of continuing rural unrest, he reiterated or strengthened regulations for village mutual-responsibility groups (*gonin gumi*). He forbade absconding, forming of mobs, or presenting of appeals; specified punishments for violation of those decrees, and established rewards for people who cooperated in restoring order.

During these later years, Yoshimune continued trying to manage the flow of precious metals by discouraging unauthorized domestic trading, the export of bullion, and hoarding (other than his own). He reduced the volume of silver the Dutch might export and, starting in 1738, levied a surcharge on the special silver coins that Tsushima han was allowed to use in its Korean trade, a move that soon shrank the Pusan silver trade and ended it by 1754.

In 1747 Yoshimune took direct control of another silver mine in the northeast, but by then gold and silver mines had long since ceased yielding bullion adequate for domestic currency needs.[31] Indeed, silver had become so scarce that it was actually being used for very little coinage, the monetary silver in circulation having fallen nearly 60 percent between 1714 and 1736.[32] Instead, the metal formed a sort of bullion reserve, and Yoshimune moved to replace it in the marketplace with copper currency. He tightened Edo's control of copper mining and use and substantially increased the supply of copper coins (*zeni*) by activating new mints in Edo (at Koume) and Osaka. To slow copper exports, he reduced Chinese trade at Nagasaki from twenty-nine to twenty-five vessels per year in 1736, and six years later slashed the number to ten. And he limited copper per vessel to 150 *kin* (approximately 180 pounds). In 1741, in apparent testing of an alternative export money, the bakufu minted some iron coins in Nagasaki.

ENCOURAGING PRODUCTION

Yoshimune clearly wanted little left to chance in his managerial actions, most of which were designed, in essence, to avoid or resolve disputes

31. Kozo Yamamura and Tetsuo Kamiki, "Silver Mines and Sung Coins—A Monetary History of Medieval and [Early] Modern Japan in International Perspective," in J. F. Richards, ed., *Precious Metals in the Later Medieval and Early Modern Worlds* (Durham, N.C.: Carolina Academic Press, 1983), p. 345, gives some figures on quantities of silver the bakufu received from mines in Sado, Ikuno, and Iwami.

32. E. S. Crawcour and Kozo Yamamura, "The Tokugawa Monetary System: 1787–1868," *Economic Development and Cultural Change* 18-4 (July 1970): 491–93.

over how the pie of nature's bounty and society's production was to be distributed. But another aspect of his policy, which began in the 1720s and intensified after the Kyōhō famine, was an array of initiatives designed to increase the size of the pie by fostering output. Unsurprisingly, given the food situation he faced, his main interest lay in expanding and diversifying agricultural production.

Basic to expansion was acquisition of useful knowledge. After easing restrictions on the import of foreign books in 1720, he gathered texts with botanical and zoological information. He assembled data on foreign flora and horticultural practices from Chinese gazetteers and had experts compile information on the useful biota of Japan. In 1722 he established a horticultural testing area of about five acres at Koishi-kawa, north of Edo Castle, and had agronomists test plants there. To aid the work, Nagasaki officials asked Chinese traders to supply information on "the cultivation of ginseng, extraction of ambergris, and cultivation of sugar cane and techniques for the refinement of sugar . . . and to bring seeds for seventeen varieties of flora pharmacopoeia."[33] As that list of products suggests, Yoshimune tried in particular to substitute domestic goods for imports. Like others before him, he promoted the manufacture of high-grade silk, and from the 1720s on, the silk output was sufficient to start driving down the price of imports. Prices continued falling during the 1730s, and by the 1750s the Korean silk trade had been abandoned, killed in the end by the increased cost of the silver that paid for it.[34] From the late 1720s on, Yoshimune also promoted cultivation of rape and Chinese sesame, whose seeds produced oils and wax for diverse uses. And from the 1730s on, domestic production of ginseng commenced, in a few decades reducing imports from Korea.

Yoshimune actively promoted sugarcane production. Imports from Taiwan were substantial from the seventeenth century on, but only Satsuma, with its warm climate and Ryūkyūan connection, had domesticated the technology of cane cultivation and refining. To protect its profitable monopoly, Satsuma kept the technology secret until 1726, when Yoshimune began seeking information on cane culture. The next year he had a Satsuma vassal grow some at the shogun's seaside villa

    33. Quoted with permission from Ohba and Toby, "'Seek Knowledge throughout the World,'" pp. 54–55. The Koishikawa horticultural area is today's Tokyo University arboretum.
    34. Tashiro Kazui, "Tsushima han's Korean Trade, 1684–1710," *AA* 30 (1976): 98, 101.

(Hamagoten) and at selected test sites elsewhere. And in 1734 after the famine was past, he extended cane growing to Koishikawa and Fukiage, a capacious garden area within the castle. In later years he distributed seedlings, promoted compilation and publication of handbooks on sugar production, and sent experts about the country giving instruction. Cane culture spread, and by the nineteenth century, Japan had largely ceased to require sugar imports.

The sweet potato (*kansho* or *Satsuma-imo*) may have been the most significant of the new crops in terms of public value. A tropical tuber, it was cultivated in the Ryūkyūs by about 1600, was introduced to Kyushu as an exotic during the seventeenth century, and later was promoted as a valuable food source by Miyazaki Antei. Its virtues were several. It could be grown on small, unused patches of ground, fared well despite climatic irregularities, was safe from many insects and vermin, and yielded a large amount of nutritious food per plant.

Sweet potato cultivation spread slowly, being adopted on the island of Tsushima and in western Honshu during the 1720s. In 1733 Yoshimune learned that the tuber had staved off famine in parts of Kyushu during the preceding year, and that news led him to order its cultivation in Koishikawa and Fukiage. The man most commonly associated with the effort is Aoki Kon'yō, the son of an Edo fish merchant, who studied at Itō Jinsai's Kogidō in Kyoto, opened a school in Edo, and caught the attention of a shogunal official.[35] It is unclear whether Aoki helped grow Yoshimune's first crop of tubers, but he was involved by 1735, and within a year or two his potato crop enabled the shogun to provide relief for the needy and distribute thousands of tubers to officials for propagation purposes, particularly in the famine-prone Izu islands south of the Kantō. Aoki continued to promote the potato's use, and it evidently proved its worth as an emergency food supply, because in following decades its cultivation spread throughout much of Japan.

In the long run, Yoshimune's horticultural work reduced some forms of import dependence and provided crop diversity. Whether it eased hardship among the general populace is less clear, because the level of rural unrest and other symptoms of difficulty did not abate. It may well be, however, that without those horticultural efforts the public situation would have been worse and the eighteenth-century demographic slide more pronounced. In any case, a concurrent trend that was adding to public hardship, creating problems for the rulers, and spurring Yo-

---

35. Patricia Sippel, "Aoki Kon'yō (1698–1769) and the Beginnings of *Rangaku*," *Japanese Studies in the History of Science* 11 (1972): 127–62, examines Aoki's role briefly.

shimune's managerial impulse was the deteriorating condition of rivers.

During the 1720s, Yoshimune's kuniyaku bushin policy enabled him to pursue and pay for major river repair projects. As a way to cut bakufu expenses, however, the policy soon backfired, becoming instead a way for villages assigned to minor daimyo to secure bakufu funding for their own escalating riverine needs. Then price gyrations, heavy rains, and the Kyōhō famine added huge fiscal burdens, and by 1732 the bakufu's kuniyaku bushin expenses had become unsustainable. With his treasury stretched to the breaking point, Yoshimune suspended the policy, shifting more of the costs onto local and daimyo shoulders.

The river problem would not go away, however. Instead it worsened, its magnitude heightened by typhoons in 1742. Yoshimune's orders to daimyo that year constituted a resort to the pre-1720 policy of otetsudai bushin, but on an unprecedented scale. And that action foreshadowed the future, as river repair and maintenance grew into an endless task that drained treasuries, generated political tensions, and consumed incalculable amounts of village labor.

When he died after thirty-five years of energetic rule, Yoshimune left a record remarkable for dedication and range of initiatives. He displayed more creative imagination than any other shogun, except possibly Ieyasu, came far closer than Tsunayoshi to being a model ruler, and showed a pragmatic readiness to assess and adjust policy that seems exceptional. His long adherence to currency revaluation bears the stamp of ideological rigidity, but even that changed in time. His reliance on exhortation strikes us as naive, but it may well have been more effective, given the structure and values of eighteenth-century society, than we care to acknowledge. That later generations looked back on his regime as a model of good government was a fair measure of his performance.

One is struck, therefore, by the modesty of his accomplishments. If one posits that the bakufu was tottering when he took over and that restoring its position was his task, then surely he deserves high marks for reasserting Edo's leadership, shoring up the samurai ruling elite as a whole, and improving its mechanisms of control over the rest of society. Even there, however, one can argue that he shored up the samurai by hammering down their standard of living and subjecting daimyo to more intensive exploitation. He revived Edo's standing in the end only by abandoning the currency revaluation, rice-price control, and kuniyaku bushin policies that were central to his rule before 1732. And while he may have shared Ogyū Sorai's wish to enfeeble the merchant class and pursued policies to achieve as much, he in fact settled for giving established merchants a more secure position in the marketplace, closer links to the samurai establishment, and greater control of the economy. Ironically, although those outcomes hardly enfeebled the chōnin, they probably strengthened the Tokugawa order by broadening the community of interests that it protected.

If one posits that the shogun's task was to secure the well-being of the populace as a whole, Yoshimune's record is even more dubious. His years of rule appear to have seen more hardship and unrest, both rural and urban, than the reign of any earlier Tokugawa shogun. He had the unhappy distinction of being shogun during the creation of uchi kowashi, and between 1716 and 1751, the trends of both hardship and unrest seem to have been upward, not downward. In part, of course, this was because Yoshimune's overriding concern was with the rulers, and main elements of his social policy—his census taking, tax reforms, sumptuary regulation, and landholding decrees—were designed to assure that government would be able to tax any increase in production as effectively as possible. His success as tax collector, that is to say, contributed to his failure as meliorator of public hardship.

More basically, however, Yoshimune-the-benevolent was thwarted by changes in Japan's ecological condition. The reserves of exploitable resources that had once permitted ruler and ruled alike to improve their condition had been consumed by a century of population growth, land clearance, and economic development, and he was powerless to undo those changes. His efforts to foster new crops addressed the problem, but they were long-term ventures whose payoff came later, and even then, they were modest gains. Insofar as improvement in the commonweal could be achieved, it depended in the main on those incremental efforts at extension and intensification of production and orderly management of consumption, most notably by population control, that chapters 12 and 13 examined. And those developments were in their early stages during Yoshimune's rule, with the consequence that his years encompassed some of the most harrowing in the painful process of social change that moved early modern Japan from an era of growth to one of stasis.

FIFTEEN

The Politics of Stasis, 1751–1790

Problems of the Social Order
  Varieties of Protest and Response
  Crop Failure and Famine
  Common Land
  Corvée Duty
Problems of the Fisc
  Producing Money
  Licensing, Monopolizing, and Milking Business
  Confronting Price Gyrations
Political Issues
  Takenouchi Shikibu
  Yamagata Daini
  The Rise and Fall of Tanuma Okitsugu

For four decades after Yoshimune's death, domestic problems consumed the energy of political leaders. As the years passed, political attention focused on a series of incidents involving combinations of court officials, bakufu leaders, han administrators, intellectuals, and common villagers. However, long-term developments that fostered public hardship and unrest, along with the worsening state of government finances, set most of the rulers' agenda. Those issues, needless to say, antedated 1751 and persisted long after 1790, so their examination here will range rather freely over the period of stasis.

One topic was notable for its near absence during these decades and indeed until the 1840s: overt conflict between the bakufu and individual daimyo. A few minor lords ran afoul of Edo, but great lords managed almost entirely to avoid harsh confrontations for nearly a century. Tensions of a more generalized sort, mostly over public works and fiscal policy, were present, but they did not produce the kind of dispute that so frequently had led in earlier years to daimyo attainder or other harsh punishment. The lines of tension and conflict that dominated political affairs lay between those above and those below, not between those in the ruling elite, who had a shared interest in perpetuating the status quo.

PROBLEMS OF THE SOCIAL ORDER

Several trends discussed in chapters 12 and 13, together with tax policies of the Kyōhō period, raised the level of public hardship, particularly in rural areas, making unrest a more serious political issue. The long-term increase in rural disorder is suggested by this tabulation of incidents.[1]

Period	Total	Annual rate
1601–1650	209	4.2
1651–1700	211	4.2
1701–1750	422	8.4
1751–1800	670	13.4
1801–1850	814	16.3
1851–1867	373	22

At best such a counting is a rough approximation, and doubtless the figures reflect more complete reporting for later decades, but the trend is still unmistakable. Urban protests as well, most visibly *uchikowashi,* or "house smashings," also increased in frequency and scale.

Besides occurring more often, incidents of rural unrest changed in character and size. During the seventeenth century, absconding was common, but as unreclaimed land grew scarce, it became difficult and unusual. In the early years, moreover, when villagers and officialdom collided, village leaders presented the petitions that were the other main form of protest. Later, however, members of the village elite often stood

1. Stephen Vlastos, *Peasant Protests and Uprisings in Tokugawa Japan* (Berkeley and Los Angeles: University of California Press, 1986), pp. 46, 75.

318

o

at odds with their poorer neighbors, caught in a rich-poor, landlord-tenant polarity that undermined village solidarity, made them opponents or reluctant participants in protest, and fostered more frequent and violent intravillage disturbances. Finally, the scale of protest grew, with thousands and eventually tens of thousands of poorer villagers drawing together in regional protests, commonly directed against their richer neighbors and the rulers with whom they were associated.

VARIETIES OF PROTEST AND RESPONSE

Unrest had a wide variety of causes, manifested itself in diverse ways, and elicited a broad array of government responses. By the later eighteenth century, however, certain issues had become predominant. Crop failure and the threat of starvation provoked many outbursts. The changes in village society discussed in chapter 12 also fostered unrest, especially local disputes over the use of such essential communal resources as water and common land (*iriaichi*). Disputes over taxes were probably the most common and most important form of conflict between rulers and ruled. Of the numerous tax issues that elicited protest, the escalating demand for corvée labor, primarily for highway and river duty, may have become the politically most worrisome form of tax protest by the 1750s.

In general, rulers seemed to fear public unrest less because it might turn the world topsy-turvy than because it hurt the fisc. Unrest commonly threatened treasuries directly through petitions and demonstrations that explicitly denounced tax increases, demanded tax reductions, protested the form of a tax, or objected to forced loans (*goyōkin*) or other special levies. Moreover, unrest resulted in lost labor time, property damage, and the costs of negotiation and suppression, all of which hurt treasuries.

Villagers could be tactful in their demands, or blunt. A formal petition for redress commonly spelled out the hardship that justified it; assured the addressees of the petitioner's dutiful humility; reminded them that without productive peasants, they too would be in trouble; and specified the concessions sought. As negotiations advanced, however, the comments could grow more shrill. During the crop failure of 1721, protesting peasants reportedly denounced officials in words to this effect:

> You relentless thieves! Monstrous exploiters! From now on we shall do as we please. If your punishments are severe, we won't pay taxes. . . . We shall

choose under whom we shall serve according to the severity of his punishments.[2]

Protesters recognized that conflicts of interest pitted them against their superiors. In 1783, during the crisis in Matsushiro han that followed Mount Asama's eruption, one peasant made his case this way, when discussing his village's petition with han officials: "Right now everyone in the Yamanaka district down to the smallest peasant is suffering excessive hardships. . . . Even if [our demands] are bad for the lord, that is unavoidable. . . . The taxes on people in this domain are unjust."[3] When petitions failed, action often followed. During the Tenmei famine, Fukuyama han imposed an array of heightened and special taxes on its peasants. Aggrieved villagers identified the levies as the handiwork of an official named Endō and mounted a protest near the end of 1786. According to one lively summary of the incident, "the entire populace rose up like a disturbed nest of bees. Signal fires lit up the night sky while battle cries shook the mountains and rivers. It so happened that over forty thousand people gathered and they all said, 'Let's get Endō to satisfy ourselves!' Ultimately, they lived outdoors for over sixty days. Discipline was broken and the government and public terrorized."[4] Initially, the han rejected their demands, deploying some twelve hundred samurai and jailing about seventy villagers in the course of suppression. In the end, however, it repudiated a number of the tax measures, cashiered Endō, and placed him under house arrest.

Besides taxes, villagers denounced monopoly and licensing policies that seemed to create unfavorable prices or destroy marketing rights. They objected to paper money, which they blamed for inflation or viewed as an ill-concealed way for government to purchase goods and services on the never-never. And more and more they protested corvée work. In short, every kind of government exaction sooner or later became a target of protest.

Villagers strengthened their claim to redress by developing a heroic literature of legendary peasant rebels such as Sakura Sōgorō, reputedly a village headman (in Sakura han) who was crucified in the 1650s for daring to petition authorities for famine relief. Having died on behalf of their communities, righteous men (*gimin*) like Sōgorō were idolized

2. Yoshio Yasumaru, "Rebellion and Peasant Consciousness in the Edo Period," *Senri Ethnological Studies* 13 (1984): 416.

3. Anne Walthall, *Social Protest and Popular Culture in Eighteenth-Century Japan* (Tucson: University of Arizona Press, 1986), p. 30.

4. Herbert P. Bix, *Peasant Protest in Japan, 1590–1884* (New Haven: Yale University Press, 1986), p. 122.

as "gods" (*kami*), becoming inspirational models—as well as caution-
ary examples—for later generations of protesters, who invoked their
names, beseeched their spiritual support, and offered thanks when it
was manifested, usually through the decision of authorities to offer
concessions or aid.[5]

Less directly threatening to the rulers than anti-tax actions were
uchikowashi, in which gangs of villagers or townspeople smashed the
shops of moneylenders or others whom they judged guilty of unacceptably callous or exploitative behavior. But even uchikowashi became
worrisome as time passed and mobs began attacking the residences of
government officials and even the headquarters (*jin'ya*) of minor domains and district administrators. Indeed, in 1787 massive rioting and
smashing in Edo were instrumental in routing the remnants of Tanuma
Okitsugu's leadership group and allowing Matsudaira Sadanobu to gain
power.

The rulers reacted to unrest in many ways. Often they tried to forestall it by pursuing concessive and ameliorative policies. When years of
good weather yielded a succession of bountiful harvests, the bakufu
would repeatedly urge daimyo and rice merchants to store surplus grain
as a way to build reserves against future crop failures and stem price
declines that hurt shogunal retainers and triggered peasant protest. After
poor harvests, Edo often decreed reductions in sake production as a
way to moderate price hikes, save rice for food, and reduce the availability of alcohol. And rulers forestalled trouble by distributing warehouse rice to the needy or setting up relief hostels for the homeless and
hungry.

When prevention failed, governments responded with ad hoc measures. Sometimes, as in Fukuyama, they reversed the policy that had
precipitated disorder, whether it be a new tax, corvée demand, monopoly arrangement, or issue of paper money. Sometimes they provided
assistance, particularly in cases of city fire or natural disaster that had
generated demands for help. And sometimes they simply suppressed the
protest, usually after attempts to settle peacefully had failed. Most com-

5. An early version of the Sōgorō legend is translated in Michiko Y. Aoki and Margaret B. Dardess, *As the Japanese See It* (Honolulu: University Press of Hawaii, 1981),
pp. 275–82. Anne Walthall discusses this genre of popular literature in ch. 8 of *Social
Protest and Popular Culture* and in her essay, "Japanese *Gimin*: Peasant Martyrs in Popular Memory," in *American Historical Review* 91-5 (Dec. 1986): 1076–1102. Peasant
rhetoric and narratives are also treated in essays by Walthall and Irwin Scheiner and
translated by Herbert P. Bix, J. Rahder, and Heinrich M. Reinfried in works identified in
Conrad Totman, "Tokugawa Peasants: Win, Lose, or Draw?" *MN* 41-4 (Winter 1986):
471–76.

monly, they combined carrot and stick, suppressing and then decreeing concessions and punishments, or promising aid or adjustments to quiet the situation and then punishing offenders—or at least scapegoats.

Doubtless these efforts at social management helped ease the difficulties of the day, and thus reduced the level of public disorder, but often they were overwhelmed by more severe crop failures, more heated disputes over common resources, and heightened resentment at escalating corvée labor duties. And they were continually compromised by the ceaseless government quest for funds.

CROP FAILURE AND FAMINE

The importance of the specter of starvation in social protest is suggested by the persistent correlation between major occasions of crop failure and major spasms of rural unrest.[6] Like statistics on the incidence of rural unrest, figure 16 shows turmoil in the countryside rising to a new level early in the eighteenth century and a yet higher level during the nineteenth. It also reveals extreme peaks of disorder during the Tenmei and Tenpō famines.

Nor was the link between hunger and upheaval merely a statistical correlation. In both word and deed, villagers revealed time and again how the fear of starvation prodded them to act. Those put at risk refused to acquiesce in their fate and instead petitioned for relief. If that failed, they moved on to the many forms of resistance and protest that characterized later Tokugawa life, as when they rioted to stop rice shipments from Aomori during the famine of 1783.

The following excerpts from a petition of 1787 submitted by villagers in the province of Sagami to their intendant exemplify the presentations villagers made when seeking relief from severe hardship:

> In 1786 the paddies and dry fields of all the villages suffered crop failures, and we had nothing at all to eat. In the 12th month we . . . [petitioned for loans of food, but] you told us that you would not be able to do anything, and since you explained in exhaustive detail how you wanted to have the village officials manage things so that somehow we would survive, we returned to our villages and explained all this even to the small peasants. . . . [However,] since there was an extraordinary crop failure in 1786 coming right after the great crop failure of 1783, not a single person was able to store any grain. During the crop failure of 1783, people who were able sub-

6. The graph is from Hugh Borton, "Peasant Uprisings in Japan of the Tokugawa Period," *TASJ*, 2d ser., 16 (May 1938): 207. Recent scholarship has uncovered many more incidents, but it has not changed the overall pattern.

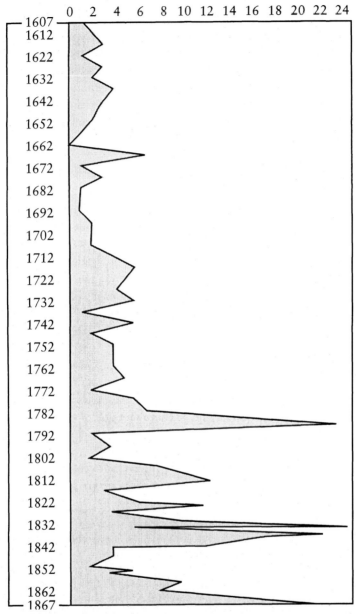

16. Incidence of Peasant Uprisings, 1607–1867. Source: Hugh Borton, "Peasant Uprisings in Japan of the Tokugawa Period," *TASJ*, 2d ser., 16 (May 1938): 207.

mitted food and money for supplies to be loaned to those truly unable to
survive, grain was purchased in other provinces, and we dug up vines, ferns,
and tubers in the mountains. For that reason, when we dig for food now, we
find nothing, and since we cannot repay the loans made in 1783, we cannot
make any more. . . . Since many people are starving, the village officals have
all worked together in buying grain, and we are happy to have been able to
survive. Nevertheless, we have exhausted the products of fields and mountains, we can contract no more loans, and truly we suffer extreme hardships.
We are fearfully aware that it would be the fault of the village officials were
someone to die of starvation. . . . Once again in fear and trembling all of our
representatives offer up an appeal for you please in your compassion to loan
us food.[7]

The rhetoric of these appeals was calculated and purposeful in evoking the ethical values of the day. When villagers petitioned under circumstances such as those of the Tenmei famine, however, they could
not afford to lose, so their argument had to present a sufficiently plausible account that official readers would not reject it as disingenuous.

If petitioning did not suffice, the needy often defied authority, despite
the risks involved. After Mount Asama's eruption, villagers in devastated areas petitioned for relief, denounced merchants for hoarding, decided to attack when no help came, warned other villagers to collaborate or see their homes burned to the ground, and on the agreed-upon
night commenced their action. They smashed warehouses, pawnshops,
and grain stores, and demanded food, drink, and money, continuing
until suppressed by local forces or hostile villagers or until their energies
petered out. On other occasions, protesters aimed more directly at the
rulers, and while they often won concessions, their leaders were commonly punished. In dubious compensation for the price they paid, leaders' names might be added to folklore's list of gimin, whose legendary
deeds inspired subsequent generations of protesters.

COMMON LAND

Disputes over water (mizu mondai) and village common land proliferated as decades passed. By their nature these usually were parochial
disputes that could be addressed locally, and higher authority was rarely
involved. However, problems of large-river control and of pollution
from coal and copper mining and metal smelting did reach bakufu leaders, especially during the nineteenth century.

During the eighteenth century, the most frequent source of quarrels

7. Walthall, *Social Protest and Popular Culture,* pp. 49–50.

among villagers themselves seems to have been use rights on common land, or *iriaichi*. To explain, early Tokugawa land surveys identified which households were entitled to till which fields in return for designated taxes, but uncultivated land, unless claimed by local strong men, was generally recorded as being held in common by village members, who used it in accordance with locally sanctioned customary rights. The importance of those rights cannot be overstated. "Nothing was more critical in the maintenance of the remarkable productivity of [the Tokugawa agricultural] system than the nutrient subsidy continuously culled from the agricultural hinterlands," Kären Wigen observes.[8] Villagers living near town gradually replaced scarce green fertilizer with purchased nutrients, most commonly fish meal and organic wastes, but many farmers deeper in the hinterland could not afford them and simply had to compete for such green fertilizer growth as was still available.

For villagers the provision of this nutrient subsidy was iriaichi's key function, but it was only one of several. Common land supplied fodder for work animals, fuel for cooking and heating, and bamboo, thatch, and other construction material for buildings and equipment. It provided wild foods, most crucially in times of famine, and served an array of other functions, "as indispensable sources of earth and rocks for terrace construction; as cemeteries and horse-burial grounds; as watersheds for irrigation; and as a potential new-field frontier."

Land clearance reduced the area of common land even as population growth, intensive agriculture, and the spread of by-employment increased pressure on what remained. These colliding trends, along with changes in landholding arrangements, heightened tensions among villagers and eroded old understandings of fair commmunal usage. One man's just claims became a neighbor's thievery, and disagreements could lead to years of litigation, animosities, and even violence. Persistent quarrels over iriaichi encouraged its partition among households, and given the disparities of wealth and power within villages, that often meant distribution among the favored few.

The partition of iriaichi deprived poorer villagers of their source of fertilizer, fodder, and fuel, compelling them to travel farther and work

8. This discussion of *iriaichi* is based on Kären Wigen-Lewis, "Common Losses: Transformations of Commonland and Peasant Livelihood in Tokugawa Japan, 1603–1868" (M.A. thesis, University of California, Berkeley, 1985). The quotations come from pp. 28, 33.

longer and harder to scavenge the necessary goods. But many had to do so, even at the risk of denuding hillsides, fostering erosion and stream silting, and sabotaging the land's future value. Or else they could—and often did—enter reserved forests or the woodland of others, even though they might be caught and prosecuted by village leaders or higher authorities. Or they set fire to woodland to convert it to the scrub growth that produced what they needed.

Finally, the loss of sufficient healthy iriaichi reduced the wild food supplies—nuts, tubers, shoots, bark, and grass—so precious to the poor in times of crop failure, enhancing the likelihood that failure would lead to starvation. In short, loss of common land exacerbated the difficulties of poorer villagers in a number of ways, making them more vulnerable to hardship and more disposed to engage in coercive protest.

CORVÉE DUTY

Disputes over common land pitted villagers against each other. Most of the larger-scale conflicts that pitted them against government stemmed from grievances against the tax collector, who kept devising new ways to pick their pockets. Doubtless the collector was a preferred object of protest in part because he, unlike bad weather, scarce land, or inadequate food, might respond to pressure. Corvée labor duty, whether for river work, highway service, or other tasks, was only one form of taxation, but it became a major grievance in the eighteenth century. Anticorvée protests emerged as a prominent type of disturbance, and dealing with them became a common item on government agendas after 1751.

The problem of increased river work is noted elsewhere; here let us examine the highway situation. Road construction and maintenance dated from Ieyasu's time, but the burdens of porter-packhorse duty and upkeep-repair work grew along with the economy. In 1694 Edo regularized the duty by extending it into daimyo domains and designating villages near highway stations as *sukegō*, or "assisting villages." Sukegō were expected to provide porters and horses when requested by the post station to which they were assigned, doing so at the rate of two porters and two horses for every 100 koku of village output. Highway use kept growing, however, and the rates of sukegō duty rose dramatically. Villages serving the Honjō station on the Nakasendō, for example, were expected to provide 15 horses and 18 porters in 1694, but by 1773 the

17. Sakawa River Crossing, Tōkaidō in Sagami. The highway system required immense amounts of poorly paid corvée labor. One of the worst tasks was transporting travelers across rivers, most of which lacked bridges primarily because frequent, destructive floods made them nearly impossible to maintain. Courtesy of Vereeniging Nederlandsch Historisch Scheepvaart Museum p/a 's Lands Zeemagazijn, Amsterdam, Neg. No. 7944.

numbers were 91 horses and 140 porters, or about one able-bodied person per household.[9]

Even in moderation, sukegō duty was resented. It was heaviest during the cropping season, when travelers were most numerous. As farm units became smaller and agronomic techniques more refined, the diversion of prime labor from crucial tasks—commonly for about three days at a stretch—became more hurtful. In addition, the work was onerous, requiring villagers to walk miles to the station, then to trek along the highway or back and forth through the river hauling people and goods— or to sit in idleness if no travelers happened by—and then to hike home again, all for a wage that was a fraction of a regular laborer's pay. Also the work forced villagers to deal with the highborn, who might simply be arrogant and exploitative but who, even if decent, were likely to be

9. Constantine N. Vaporis, "Post Station and Assisting Villages: Corvée Labor and Peasant Contention," MN 41-4 (Winter 1986): 389.

tired, uncomfortable, peeved at the delays and irritations of travel, resentful of the need to bribe for adequate service, and as a result uncommonly disposed to be churlish and even violent in their treatment of porters.[10] At best, sukegō duty was unpleasant. It might be downright dangerous, and only dire hardship made it acceptable work.

By the early eighteenth century growth in sukegō duty was prompting villagers to resist assignments and lobby for reduced obligations. By the nineteenth, reports Constantine Vaporis, "assisting villages were declaring themselves impoverished and applying for reductions and exemptions in such great numbers that the system seemed in danger of collapse."[11] The gap between labor supply and demand forced Edo repeatedly to increase the number of villages providing service, turning to villages farther from the stations, making the work that much more hateful, and adding to rural resentment of the system.

The discontent generated by sukegō service was most commonly expressed through failure of workers to appear on time or in the required number. But it could develop into incidents of violence, doing so on at least twenty-one occasions after the middle 1700s. Of these incidents one of the most significant was that of 1764, the Meiwa *tenma sōdō*, or "post-horse rebellion" of the Meiwa period.

On that occasion extra sukegō duty that Edo assigned for a planned shogunal pilgrimage to Nikkō set off a surge of resistance, initially among peasants from villages around Obata han. The protest soon included villagers from bakufu and daimyo lands in four provinces and numbered some two hundred thousand at its peak. Marching along the Nakasendō toward Edo, the villagers accumulated supporters as they went and at Kumagaya swept aside a force of musketeers and other troops deployed, at Edo's behest, by the daimyo of Oshi (100,000 koku). From Kumagaya the protesters trudged on, halting their advance only after a respected bakufu official came from Edo, met them, and agreed to rescind the new impositions.

They then turned their ire on others, destroying "the homes and storehouses of village officials, rich peasants, sake merchants, and moneylenders," which suggests how villagers when lifted out of quotidian routine by one complaint could go on to address other grievances with

---

10. A semi-fictional autobiography that evokes nicely highway conditions in the vicinity of the Kiso River during the 1860s is Shimazaki Tōson, *Before the Dawn* (Honolulu: University of Hawaii Press, 1987).

11. Vaporis, "Post Station," pp. 408–9.

equal vigor.[12] It was a pattern that could only make rulers uneasy, as suggested by Matsudaira Sadanobu in this comment of 1815:

> When it comes to peasant revolts, there is no need to be concerned just because a lot of people are involved. And that they are bitter about headmen and lower officials and start riots to demonstrate about that doesn't amount to much either. But when they're close to starvation because of famine and decide to rise up rather than starve to death, and attack the homes of the wealthy and the rice dealers, or start setting fire to everything, it's time to look out. They are strongest when the fief holder's government is bad, for then they make him out to be the enemy. Moreover these risings are worst when there are additional complaints because of long-standing despotic government with heavy demands for taxation, transport, corvée, and forced loans.[13]

PROBLEMS OF THE FISC

Bakuhan officials fretted about finances and labored diligently at fundraising to pay their regular costs of personnel, programs, and plant, to cover interest charges on debts to moneylenders, to pay for more and more river work, and to respond to such periodic disasters as crop failures and city fires. They habitually reduced their largest single cost—the stipends of their vassals—by routinely withholding ("borrowing") a portion of those stipends, but by the late eighteenth century, little more could be saved there. Around 1770 one observer noted that samurai "sold vegetables, made pottery for sale—and all for gain. All suffered from poverty."[14] A few years later, another commented:

> For years now, the samurai have suffered from poverty and their minds have been occupied by making a living. "Buy this, sell that" and "pawn this to pay for that" has become all of their lives. Even for those dedicated to their duties, it was inevitable to debase themselves and to engage in unsavory conduct [i.e., trading]. Even the wives of those who were earning as much as 200 *koku* busied themselves in trading and in shops.

By 1750 further economizing at the expense of vassals was impractical, so daimyo, like the bakufu, scurried after funds.

12. Ibid., p. 412.
13. Marius B. Jansen, "Japan in the Early Nineteenth Century," in *The Cambridge History of Japan,* vol. 5, *The Nineteenth Century,* ed. Jansen (Cambridge: Cambridge University Press, 1989), p. 80.
14. These two quotations on samurai poverty are from Kozo Yamamura, "The Increasing Poverty of the Samurai in Tokugawa Japan, 1600–1868," *Journal of Economic History* 31 (June 1971): 401–2, n. 66.

And scurry they all did. An axiom of fiscal policy everywhere is that the dedicated tax collector goes where the money is, and the truism was especially apt following Yoshimune's death. By then development of a diversified and monetized commercial marketplace had created many new sources of taxable wealth even as income from the grain tax (*nengu*) began to shrink in the face of hardship and rural unrest. Unable to sustain the grain tax and finding that other levies on primary production (*komononari*) yielded little additional income, revenue officials devised stratagem after stratagem to tap into the new wealth despite a rhetoric of fiscal orthodoxy that said only agricultural production should be taxed.

Essentially their strategies were elaborations of two established government practices: the issuance of coinage and paper money and the licensing, taxing, and even monopolizing of commercial enterprises. Pursuit of these policies contributed to price gyrations, however, even as increased reliance on monetary income made governments more vulnerable to them, and that development heightened government interest in stabilizing prices.

PRODUCING MONEY

Until 1760 the vigorous land tax collection and other fiscal measures of the Kyōhō reform sustained the bakufu, but in that decade Edo's income fell sharply. To offset the losses, finance officials tapped into reserves of silver that had accumulated in Osaka.[15] Since the seventeenth century, silver had been the preferred medium of exchange there, but convenient silver coins had not developed. Instead, silver was transacted by weight and fineness, a procedure so cumbersome that merchants substituted paper certificates (*tegata*) backed by silver. The silver to back the paper resided in their warehouses.

Finance officers decided to use the horde, and during the 1760s they transferred silver worth some 1.6 million gold ryō from Osaka to Edo. In 1765 they used the bullion to mint bulky, oblong coins of low-quality silver alloy, pegging their exchange rate at 12 per ryō. They expected the issue to circulate in the Kantō, where the ryō was the basic monetary unit and where economic development had created a scarcity of

15. This summary of the 1760s–1770s minting effort is based on Taya Hirokichi, "The Modernization of the Japanese Currency System," *AA* 39 (Oct. 1980): 81–85.

useful coins. Users found the new coins cumbersome, however, and were distrustful of their worth, so they failed to circulate.

The regime's fiscal condition continued to deteriorate, so officials made another attempt to use their horde in 1772. After a major fire in Edo created strong demand for currency, they minted a new silver coin, the Nanryō *nishugin,* also denominated in gold ryō. The exchange rate of eight *nishu* per ryō was embossed on the coin's face, and it contained a finer-quality silver than the 1765 issue, making it smaller and easier to use. Being convenient to handle and exchangeable at a clearly speci-fied rate, the nishu overcame initial merchant resistance and soon gained commercial acceptance. The coin's actual silver content was well under what current gold-silver market ratios called for, so the bakufu turned a handsome profit on the minting, and because it appeared at a time of heavy commercial demand when usable currency was scarce, its fiscal value was not lost to an inflationary surge. Its success implies that "face value" was replacing "bullion content" as the determinant of a coin's market value.[16]

Besides its silver issue, the bakufu periodically minted penny cash (*zeni*) that were officially valued at 4,000 per gold ryō. In theory, zeni were copper coins, but as copper supplies shrank during the eighteenth century, the government minted brass and even some iron coins. As more zeni came into circulation, however, especially in heavy mintings of the 1760s and 1770s, they tended to depreciate, and by the late To-kugawa period they were circulating at some 6,700 per ryō.[17]

The bakufu printed no paper money before the 1860s, but the paper certificates issued by licensed merchants performed much the same commercial function. And insofar as the bakufu obtained fees and other monies (*unjō, myōga, goyōkin*) from such merchants, the certificates aided the fisc. Daimyo, on the other hand, did issue paper money as well as coinage.

Some lords had minted coins in the early seventeenth century, but as bullion became scarce and Edo tightened control of its use, the last han coinage disappeared in the 1660s, not reappearing until after Yoshi-

---

16. Tsuji Tatsuya, "Politics in the Eighteenth Century," in *The Cambridge History of Japan,* vol. 4, *Early Modern Japan,* ed. John W. Hall (Cambridge: Cambridge Univer-sity Press, 1991), p. 464, notes that the 1772 coin did not end the dual gold-silver cur-rency system.

17. Sakudō Yōtarō, "Monetary System in Feudal Japan," *Osaka Economic Papers* 5-1 (Aug. 1956): 54. E. S. Crawcour and Kozo Yamamura, "The Tokugawa Monetary System: 1787–1868," *Economic Development and Cultural Change* 18-4 (July 1970): 492, 507.

mune reversed his policy of monetary purification in 1736. From the following year on, a few han minted coins from time to time, but the scarcity of copper, cost of minting, bakufu opposition to use of such coins outside the domain of origin, and public resistance to their use within the domain combined to prevent minting from becoming an important fiscal instrument for daimyo.

Domain paper money (*han satsu*) proved more successful.[18] It appeared from the 1660s after Edo outlawed han coins, and forty-six lords are known to have issued paper by 1707. In that year, however, as the bakufu tried to get its own debased currency to circulate, it proscribed domain paper, and the prohibition survived until 1730, when Yoshimune reauthorized domain notes as a means of reflating rice prices. To preserve order in the use of han satsu, he required daimyo to obtain Edo's permission for both new issues and reissues. He also set limits on their life spans—twenty-five years in han of 200,000 koku and over; fifteen years in lesser domains—and ordered their use restricted to the territory of the issuing domain. The regulations remained in force until the Restoration, but it appears that han leaders were less than punctilious about observing them.

After being reauthorized in 1730, han satsu became common, with 240 domains issuing some 1,700 kinds of paper during the Tokugawa period as a whole. When properly managed, the notes facilitated economic activity by supplementing scarce bakufu currency. And some lords used them as instruments of public relief by loaning them to the needy. Mainly, however, daimyo issued them for fiscal reasons, using them to purchase government necessities and goods destined for sale through han monopolies. Recipients of domain notes initially used them to defray land taxes or other obligations to the han, but as years passed, they used them in more and more private transactions, mostly within the han, but also when dealing with merchants in the great cities.

Despite the care given their handling, domain notes remained a source of contention. Issuers commonly placed them in circulation by fiat, which hardly enhanced their appeal. Also notes often depreciated before holders could redeem them, even when a han and its collaborating merchants limited them to what the economy could absorb, promised to redeem them at set rates, issued new notes for old at face value, or set

18. Sakudō Yōtarō, "Domain Paper Currencies and Money Merchants in the Tokugawa Period," *AA* 39 (Oct. 1980): 61–77, is a valuable survey of *han satsu*. See also his much earlier "Currency in Japanese Feudal Society," *Osaka Economic Papers* 4-1 (June 1955): 17–30.

aside currency, bullion, rice, or other resources as backing. Although depreciation made han satsu even more fiscally advantageous to the domain, it reinforced the general distrust of domain paper and on occasion became an ingredient in public protest and disorder.

Paper money, in short, became an important element in han finance after 1750. But it did so at the price of making daimyo more dependent on the collaboration of merchants, including such major Osaka and Kyoto firms as Mitsui, Sumitomo, and Kōnoike, who often handled the transactions and provided reserves to back the issues. And the paper constituted another source of popular discontent with daimyo rule.

LICENSING, MONOPOLIZING, AND MILKING BUSINESS

Besides producing money, leaders of both bakufu and han licensed and monopolized business for fiscal reasons. They also fostered taxable production. The rationale of bakufu policy was more complex than that of daimyo, however, and the trajectory of its efforts less consistent.

In daimyo domains, license fees and monopoly arrangements long antedated 1750, but they proliferated thereafter. Han tried to control a wide array of markets, including cotton, indigo, paper, salt, silk, sugar, vegetable oil, wax, wood products, and even rice, in hopes of generating income and preventing the outflow of currency. Satsuma's sugar monopoly was one of the most successful. By the nineteenth century it was reportedly turning an annual profit of some 120,000 ryō despite the spread of sugar production within Japan.[19] Less spectacularly, Chōshū established an early and profitable monopoly on wax production and by 1770 had added "oil, linen, raw cotton, cotton cloth, indigo, and other products" to its list of items whose sale by licensed merchants generated income for the han.[20]

Han commonly tried to protect domestic markets by excluding outside peddlers from the domain, even while promoting external sales of their own products, as with Satsuma's sugar marketing in Osaka. Han leaders fostered the import of useful new technology and new crops and offered producers technical and monetary assistance in hopes of gener-

19. W. G. Beasley, *The Meiji Restoration* (Stanford: Stanford University Press, 1972), p. 54.
20. Albert M. Craig, *Chōshū in the Meiji Restoration* (Cambridge, Mass.: Harvard University Press, 1961), p. 66. Other examples of han exploitation of commerce can be found in Hall, ed., *Early Modern Japan*, pp. 223–24, 588–89.

ating production that would then become taxable, as in the disastrous case of Hirosaki in the early 1780s. Despite frequent setbacks, these measures to exploit commercial wealth proved effective enough cumulatively so that han leaders intensified them during the nineteenth century.

The bakufu, of course, had long since set precedents for monopolizing and licensing. From the outset it handled foreign trade in that manner, and domestically it tried to monopolize the production and use of precious metals. By the mid eighteenth century, it controlled commerce in such other high-value goods as alum, cinnabar, and ginseng. And it regulated shipping and highway traffic through licensing and inspection arrangements that helped cover the travel costs of its own personnel.

Edo's reasons for expanding license and monopoly activity during the eighteenth century were more complex than those of daimyo. Yoshimune managed commerce for several reasons: to counter price fluctuations and economic disorder; to control the quantity, quality, price, and distribution of goods and services; to contain the spread of tabooed activity; to cozen licensees into cooperative behavior. Ultimately, he hoped, doing these things would maintain the established social hierarchy and value system and the privileges of the ruling elite.

Licensing also generated income. As Edo's land-tax income declined after 1750, fiscal need became a dominant consideration in licensing, and the bakufu began assessing fees (*myōgakin*) on chartered trade associations, treating licensed commerce more and more like a "cash cow." It was able to do so because established merchants faced intensifying commercial competition and were willing to pay for government support against it. Some fees were substantial, others more token in nature, and they were never fully regularized, but over the years they constituted an additional source of revenue.

Besides fees, the bakufu obtained more and more forced "loans," or *goyōkin,* from licensed merchants. Thus, in 1761–62 it collected goyōkin valued at some 700,000 ryō from Osaka rice brokers despite vociferous protests by the Osaka merchant community.[21] In the following decades, it periodically levied similar demands, as in 1788, when it demanded 338,000 ryō from a newly licensed group of Edo merchants. During the nineteenth century, Edo continued extracting goyōkin from the merchant community.

21. Beasley, *Meiji Restoration,* p. 53. It seems likely that these funds were part of those used in the issue of silver-alloy currency in 1765 and 1772.

CONFRONTING PRICE GYRATIONS

Abrupt price fluctuations, fostered by irregularities in supply and demand and inconstancy in the value of monetary instruments, accompanied monetization of the economy. Some monetary inconstancy was owing to regional differences, notably the primacy of silver in Osaka and gold in Edo, but most was because of manipulation of the currency by Tsunayoshi and later rulers.

In view of the economy's countrywide linkages, daimyo had little capacity to control prices, so price management was largely a bakufu task. Throughout the period of stasis, Edo employed an array of tactics to combat price instability, all of them foreshadowed during Yoshimune's rule. To examine the tactics briefly, Edo continually tried to manage prices by edict and exhortation. During inflationary episodes it denounced hoarding, ordered merchants to lower prices of specified goods, and issued calls for austerity. Following city fires, it forbade merchants to raise the price of building materials. After Edo began ordering daimyo to dredge rivers and build levees, it routinely followed such orders with edicts forbidding anyone to boost the price of goods and services required by such projects.

The bakufu also strove to influence prices through monetary policy and management of the rice supply. During periods of rice-price inflation, it tried to drive prices down by shrinking the volume of monetary instruments. One strategy was to limit the issuance of rice certificates to those backed by grain in storage, while forbidding issues backed by goods in transit or goods anticipated from the next harvest. Edo also tried to manage the price of rice by regulating supply, authorizing more sake production in years of good harvest; less in bad years. Similarly, in good years it ordered daimyo and merchants to store rice and in bad years cancelled storage orders, released its own supplies, and ordered daimyo and merchants to do the same. Edo also repeatedly investigated pricing and punished people for hoarding, cornering markets, or violating price regulations.

Despite all the effort, price gyrations persisted. Doubtless the constant attempts to contain them had some effect, but the complexity of the money system, mutual incompatibility among Edo's monetary goals, and political barriers that obstructed movement of goods undercut policy effectiveness. And the absence of an adequate margin of safety because the populace was fully utilizing the ecosystem's yield meant that short-run fluctuations in commodity output expressed themselves in monetary instability so severe as to transcend the system's managerial capacity.

POLITICAL ISSUES

Vexing and intractable long-term problems of society and the fisc preoccupied bakuhan leaders for much of the time during the years 1751–90, but shorter-term matters also commanded attention. Incidents involving the scholars Takenouchi Shikibu and Yamagata Daini and the politician Tanuma Okitsugu seem to merit particular attention because they reveal the contents of political life and illuminate the interplay of ideology and politics during those decades.

In 1745, while still in good health, Yoshimune decided to retire, as had Ieyasu and Hidetada, and oversee his eldest son Ieshige's handling of office. Ieshige is reputed to have been "sickly, feebleminded, and afflicted with a stammer so severe as to render him incoherent."[22] Yoshimune chose him despite his infirmities in the belief that adhering to primogeniture at the highest level would minimize the risk of succession disputes throughout the political order. Besides, Ieshige already had an 8-year-old son whom Yoshimune viewed as a promising successor to his enfeebled father. If the 61-year-old ex-shogun lived even another decade, he would be able to train his grandson, ease his son out of office, and turn the reins of government over to a young but competent successor. In addition, Yoshimune had already taken the precaution of assigning Ieshige's two younger brothers ranks as highly stipended pseudo-daimyo that held them in reserve as potential regents or replacements for Ieshige or his son.

As it worked out, Yoshimune died in 1751, and officialdom, notably Ieshige's personal attendant Ōoka Tadamitsu, handled matters during his remaining decade as shogun. Ieshige's tenure was dominated by the longer-term issues of public unrest, river work, and fiscal maneuver, but an unusual problem of momentary concern to the political elite did appear, the matter of Takenouchi Shikibu.

TAKENOUCHI SHIKIBU

Takenouchi was born a physician's son in Niigata in 1712. He went to Kyoto and studied the Shintō-Confucian teachings of Yamazaki Ansai,

22. Harold Bolitho, *Treasures among Men* (New Haven: Yale University Press, 1974), p. 191.

later opening his own school for courtiers and commoners.[23] He could
not have been unaware of the hardship and unrest of the day and taught,
in essence, that even though the times were perilous, the court was powerless to act because its officials were poorly schooled and incompetent.
If, however, they trained themselves adequately, they could assert the
imperial court's proper role as sovereign authority and confront the
perils facing Japan.

Senior court officials, who likely found his ideas more insulting than
insidious, became alarmed when younger courtiers welcomed them. After
an investigation, the court in 1756 forbade them to study with him, but
some were defiant, and disputes continued, with the discontented invoking their teacher's ideas in attacks on court leaders. After a brief
inquiry early in 1757, bakufu officials concluded that Takenouchi was
guilty of no crime, so he continued lecturing. Even young Emperor Mo-
mozono became a keen follower, however, to the discomfort of his mother
and other court elders. They may have been upset because Takenouchi's
views were encouraging younger nobles to challenge them, but they
argued that his teachings were dangerous because they would cause
trouble between court and bakufu.

In 1758 court officials drafted a long set of charges against him and
asked bakufu officials in the city to intervene again. Reluctantly they
did, arresting and interrogating him. When asked why he considered
the times so perilous, he explained in Confucian terms that,

> When the country is in possession of the Way, rites, music, and punishments
> proceed from the sovereign. When the country lacks the Way, they proceed
> from the feudal lords. When they proceed from the feudal lords, it is rare
> that these do not lose their power in ten generations.[24]

Ieshige was the ninth Tokugawa shogun, and Takenouchi's meaning
surely was not lost on the investigators, but they appear to have seen
his reasoning as that of a concerned, if naive, subject, not that of a
subversive.

During a year of sporadic inquiry and interrogation, the investigators
found no evidence that he had given courtiers illegal military training,
and they ended up charging him only with "disregarding established

23. Details of the Takenouchi affair can be found in a rambling account by Yoshi S.
Kuno, *Japanese Expansion on the Asiatic Continent* (Berkeley and Los Angeles: University of California Press, 1940), 2: 143–66. Kuno's treatment reflects the moderate imperial loyalist orientation of its Japanese scholarly sources.
24. Quoted in Herschel Webb, *The Japanese Imperial Institution in the Tokugawa
Period* (New York: Columbia University Press, 1968), pp. 249–50.

usage" in his teachings, concluding that they were "on the whole, wrong, misleading, and injurious."[25] To appease court leaders, they imposed a minimal sentence, ordering Takenouchi and his son exiled from the city. Meanwhile, senior court officials ordered punishment for a few more obdurate young courtiers, and those actions quieted the situation. When Takenouchi left as required, going east and settling in Izu, the issue seemed closed.

A few months later, Ōoka Tadamitsu died, and Ieshige was eased into retirement in favor of his son, Ieharu. The new young shogun began his rule vigorously, benefiting momentarily from improved harvests and a decline in popular unrest. His administration tried to promote mining, encouraged the export of marine products as substitutes for metal, promoted rice storage, took other measures to stabilize prices, formally received Korean and Ryūkyūan delegations, exercised active but proper shogunal leadership of daimyo, and energetically pursued river repair. In 1766, however, another instance of political criticism captured bakufu attention, and this one it took far more seriously than that of Takenouchi.

YAMAGATA DAINI

The immediate object of bakufu concern in 1766 was Yamagata Daini, a man who imprudently bit the hand that fed him. He did so at a time when the bakufu was experiencing renewed concern with intellectual deviance, and, worse yet, he did so in a way that entangled him with both the post-horse rebellion of 1764 and the unfortunate Takenouchi Shikibu. Under these circumstances, Daini's imprudence proved fatal.

Born near the bakufu's intermontane outpost of Kōfu in 1725, Daini was adopted as heir to a police captain (*yoriki*) in the bakufu garrison. He seemed destined for a safely obscure life, having received local schooling, taken nearby jobs, and married the daughter of a wealthy villager. However, in about 1752 after a step-brother reportedly killed another samurai in a quarrel, he left bakufu service, returned to his natal household, and then moved to Edo as a ronin. Like so many before him, he tried the career path of savant, making his way as a doctor. Somehow he acquired a post as physician to Ieshige's favorite, Ōoka

---

25. The judgement is quoted in Kuno, *Japanese Expansion,* p. 163.

Tadamitsu, but apparently left before long to open a school, in which he lectured on military and civil affairs.

One suspects that Daini was dismayed by the disparity he observed between the worlds of Tadamitsu and poor commoners, because in 1759 he drafted a biting polemic, *Ryūshi shinron,* in which he castigated the rulers for corruption and abuse. The regime, he argued, ought to use its power to succor the people, but it actually was using it to perpetuate itself at the expense of the people, all the while concealing its performance behind a rhetoric of virtue. Tetsuo Najita has summarized Daini's view this way:

> It was common knowledge, he observed, that there were serious problems afflicting the land: the growth of population; rising cost of goods and crushing taxes of 50 and 60 percent of rice production; high interest rates on loans; and the inability to channel the "profits of commerce" for the national good. The Bakufu's failure to cope with these problems was not due to ignorance or lack of information about them. As a "system," however, it could not act because it depended on the support of the samurai. Thus, it was compelled to satisfy the narrow interests of that class. ... [and it chose, therefore,] to rule in arbitrary fashion, giving power to "small men" and keeping the prince "exiled in the fields" and the people poverty stricken and oppressed.[26]

Daini then pursued the implication of his analysis by spelling out his understanding of what the situation required: "Why should law punish only the people? Any person, even a prince, should be punished for committing a crime. Should this [justice] not prevail, an army should be raised. ... To kill a prince can be humane. Let us identify ourselves with the feelings of the people."[27] Had they discovered the essay, bakufu officials could hardly have welcomed it. Not only did its critique score a number of direct hits; it also advocated assassination of a "prince," meaning, no doubt, the pathetic Ieshige, and later, young Ieharu. Officialdom may not have heard of it, however—Daini evidently did not publish it until 1763—or perhaps they chose to ignore it as the ranting of a maniac.[28]

Whatever the reason, for several more years Daini continued teaching undisturbed. In the meantime, however, other events were setting

26. Tetsuo Najita, "Restorationism in the Political Thought of Yamagata Daini (1725–1767)," *JAS* 31-1 (Nov. 1971): 23. For a lengthy paraphrase of *Ryūshi shinron,* see Kuno, *Japanese Expansion,* pp. 168–75. Ryūshi was a name Daini was using at the time he wrote the essay.

27. Najita, "Restorationism in the Political Thought," p. 24.

28. John W. Hall, *Tanuma Okitsugu (1719–1788)* (Cambridge, Mass.: Harvard University Press, 1955), p. 129, gives the publication date of 1763.

the stage for his entrapment. New information that physicians had recently acquired from European medical texts had precipitated an unseemly academic quarrel over questions of anatomy and the cause of illness, and the disputants soon sought political support. In 1762, Kumamoto han moved to prevent medical confusion in its castle town by requiring that local doctors certify the program of medical instruction in its recently established domain school. The bakufu took a stand three years later, granting land to the shogunal physician Taki Motonori (Angen) so that he could establish a school to train Chinese-style doctors. Taki opened the Seijukan as an officially sanctioned medical school, and the bakufu advised those interested in medicine to study there.[29] Later that year, in a move that suggested fear of Christian influence more than a wish to unify medical thought, the bakufu struck another blow for intellectual correctness by confiscating a newly published translation of a Dutch work on botany because it reproduced the Dutch alphabet "in cursive, Latin and gothic scripts."[30]

In this context, with scholarly disagreement roiling the scene and raising the hoary specter of Christianity, a major disturbance occurred that further alarmed bakufu leaders and reduced their tolerance for rhetorical excess. This was the earlier-noted post-horse rebellion of 1764, the anti-corvée uprising that erupted in the vicinity of Obata han and grew until it threatened Edo. The highway duty orders that triggered it had been given in conjunction with a plan for Ieharu to make a shogunal pilgrimage to Nikkō, much as his grandfather had done in 1728. The march on Edo alarmed bakufu leaders because it overwhelmed Oshi han's considerable military force and momentarily threatened the Tokugawa citadel. Moreover, it humiliated them by thwarting their plans for a shogunal pilgrimage that had been scheduled to commence some five months hence. They responded in 1765 by jailing hundreds of protest leaders and launching extensive interrogations.

The links between the uprising and Yamagata Daini are indirect. For some time his students had included Yoshida Genba, a senior official of Obata han, and some forty of his followers, a faction of Obata vassals. Stirred by Daini's teachings, they urged his appointment as advisor to their lord. The proposal elicited strong protests from Yoshida's rivals, who said Daini's extremism would endanger their lord's good name.

29. James R. Bartholomew, *The Formation of Science in Japan* (New Haven: Yale University Press, 1989), pp. 27, 29, 36, 44.
30. Grant K. Goodman, *Japan: The Dutch Experience* (London: Athlone Press, 1986), p. 85.

To forestall the appointment, some Obata vassals informed bakufu officials late in 1766 that Daini and others were plotting a rebellion. The bakufu arrested the accused and launched a thorough investigation. They learned that, in conjunction with his lectures on military tactics Daini had discussed with one of his students, a disciple of Takenouchi, means of attacking the castles at Edo and Kōfu.

In the outcome the investigators concluded that the accusations of rebellious intent were unfounded. But, they said, Daini had encouraged a craving for war, had been unacceptably alarmist about affairs and critical of the shogun, and had been guilty of recklessly discussing ways to overrun shogunal castles. Accordingly, he and Takenouchi's disciple, whose misdeeds were much the same, were sentenced to death. And Takenouchi himself, although found innocent of complicity, was exiled to Hachijōjima (he died en route) for having illegally made visits to Kyoto despite the earlier ban. Daini's other students, including Yoshida, were exonerated, but those who brought the charges were exiled for having made false accusations. The lord of Obata was ordered into retirement and house arrest, and his heir was reassigned to a lesser domain far to the north.

Daini may have died for his ideas, as some scholars have suggested, or for seeming to engage in a regicidal plot. However, the pattern of punishments suggests that he was executed in 1767, whereas Takenouchi had only been exiled a decade earlier, because his case became entangled with the nerve-rattling post-horse rebellion at a time when bakufu officials were unusually fretful about the dangers of deviant thought. Daini, after all, was influencing leaders of Obata, and they had, at the very least, been derelict in dealing with the post-horse upheaval. Or perhaps they had been complicit. Neither possibility was acceptable. And in any case the lord of Obata had failed to control his vassals, allowing them to drift toward an *oie sōdō,* or household disorder, of the sort that periodically disrupted political life. Indeed, to fretful leaders, the affair could well have had the odor of a cabal involving dissident courtiers, radical ideologues, leaders of a *tozama han,* and peasants. To forestall further trouble, the ideologues were removed from the scene on grounds of malfeasance, Kyoto's isolation was reaffirmed, and while the involvement of Obata men in the case was minimized, they and their lord were punished for maladministration by being transferred to an unappealing domain far from Edo.

Whether any of this punishing would have occurred had the Takenouchi incident and medical disputes not sensitized officials to the disruptiveness of deviant ideas or the post-horse rebellion not grown so unnerving is impossible to say. But the problem of public disorder may have been the decisive factor; at least bakufu concern with peasant unrest was strongly evinced during the next few years whereas comparable concern with intellectual discipline did not reappear until the 1790s.

The later 1760s were years in which crop failure, public hardship, and social unrest escalated dramatically, and Edo leaders responded firmly. They ordered administrators to tighten control of shogunal lands, cracked down with unusual severity on incidents of peasant unrest, and ordered the arrest of "vagrants" throughout the Kantō. They sent orders to daimyo to suppress peasant unrest rigorously, authorizing them to collaborate and even use firearms in such efforts. And they warned them to discipline their vassals carefully. The disposition of the Obata case constituted an object lesson for any daimyo inclined to be blasé about the warning.

There is, finally, one last possibility in the Daini affair. As the comments above suggest, he may have died not for saying the wrong things but for saying them to the wrong people at the wrong time. It is possible that the issue of timing related not to public flare-ups, bakufu fears, or Obata factions but to the ambitions of a politician rising to preeminence in Edo, Tanuma Okitsugu.

THE RISE AND FALL OF TANUMA OKITSUGU

Tanuma was the most powerful non-shogunal leader in the history of the Tokugawa regime. He epitomized a common type of bakufu leader, a man who acquired the confidence of the shogun and used it to parlay his way to fame and fortune. Yanagisawa Yoshiyasu had operated in that manner during Tsunayoshi's rule, and Ōoka Tadamitsu with Ieshige.

Tanuma's ancestors were minor retainers of the lord of Kii, and his father, a daimyo's page, had accompanied his lord Yoshimune when he assumed the title of shogun in 1716.[31] Tanuma, born three years later, became a page to Ieshige and after he became shogun in 1745 gradually advanced through the ranks of attendent personnel, garnering grants of land sufficient to convert his initial 600 koku into a minimal daimyo domain of 10,000 koku by the time of Ieshige's death in 1761. He successfully adapted to Ieharu's regime, continued serving as a close atten-

31. This material on Tanuma Okitsugu is derived from Hall, *Tanuma Okitsugu.* The quotations come from pp. 37, 55, 66.

dant, received more land, and in 1765 was among the officials who went to Nikkō as substitutes for the aborted shogunal pilgrimage.

Tanuma had thus been a participant in the active rule of Ieharu's early years. During 1767, even as the investigation of Daini was being concluded, he was promoted above all other shogunal advisors to the position of grand chamberlain (*sobayōnin*). He also received enough additional land to make a han of 20,000 koku and was allowed to build a castle on his coastal fief at Sagara in Tōtōmi. Surely this man, whose fortunes were linked to Ieharu's success and who was sitting in on judicial deliberations, had a hand in the Daini verdict. One suspects he was a keen defender of shogunal interests and that his rewards in land and honors reflected Ieharu's approval of the way the affair was being handled. Daini's loss, that is to suggest, may have been Tanuma's gain.

During the two years following Daini's execution, popular unrest became more widespread and intense, as noted above. The bakufu responded by pressing daimyo to keep their vassals under control and restore order among commoners. And all the while, Tanuma continued to advance. In 1769, as John W. Hall has written, he surmounted

> the most difficult hurdle of his career when he was appointed to Rank Equivalent to Senior Councillor [*rōjū kaku*]. On this occasion he received a further increase of 5000 koku and a promotion in court title to Court Chamberlain. It was further ordained that he should continue his close attendance upon the person of the Shogun in addition to maintaining the schedule of duty followed by the Senior Councilors. On the days on which he sat on the Supreme Court of Justice all orders were to bear his name. In his movements to and from the Shogun's court he was permitted to display two spears.

Tanuma had acquired a uniquely advantageous position at Edo, and surely it enabled him to exercise a major, if not completely dominant, influence on policy.

Three years later he was designated a regular *rōjū*, and as the years passed, he kept accumulating lands, honors, and power. He packed the bakufu with men who owed him favors, received marks of shogunal appreciation, and handled diverse special assignments, as when he played a key role in the shogunal progress to Nikkō, which finally occurred in 1776. Most important, perhaps, he headed the commission to select an heir for Ieharu in 1781, following the death of the shogun's son. The day after the commission chose a near cousin of Ieharu's as heir, a nephew of Tanuma's was named special attendant to the boy. Meanwhile his own son had been steadily acquiring titles and promotions and late in 1783 was designated a junior councillor (*wakadoshiyori*), which positioned him to follow his father to the heights of power. Few ambitious samurai ever did as well.

The 1770s were Tanuma's heyday, however, and by 1783 his luck was faltering. He already was the most durable and influential non-shogunal leader in Tokugawa history, but his regime had a fair-weather quality that undermined it during the 1780s.

From 1771 on, the turbulence of the late 1760s gave way, despite the occasional drought, to generally improved harvests and quiescent villages. Doubtless the harshness of suppression during the late 1760s contributed to the relative calm, as did the failure of tax collectors to restore land taxes to earlier levels. Instead, as noted above, they sought alternative income. Tanuma in particular tried to monopolize and license, especially in the areas of mining, metallurgy, and vegetable oil. The oil was lucrative because cooking oil had a large, captive market and the use of lamp oil grew as by-employments proliferated. He expanded minting, but after his success with the Nanryō nishugin in 1772, he did it so vigorously that overproduction of coins began to undercut their value. And proliferating coinage types led to commercial confusion and widespread resentment.

In the area of foreign trade, he enjoyed considerable success. Earlier leaders had made long-term efforts to stem bullion outflows by indigenizing imports such as ginseng and fine silk and developing export substitutes such as marine products. The efforts finally bore fruit in commercial agreements of the 1760s and 1770s that required Dutch and Chinese traders to bring specified quantities of gold and silver to Japan to pay for export goods. Those imports offset copper exports, which continued, and provided the bakufu with bullion for its new coins.

During the 1770s, Tanuma thus pursued fiscally advantageous policies with considerable success. He did little, however, to prepare the realm for hard times. He made little apparent effort to build up rice reserves, perhaps because there was little surplus. When rice prices rose, he did not order cutbacks in sake production to save food stocks. Instead, he chose short-term gain by taxing brewery output. He nearly ceased deploying daimyo for river work, which surely made it easier for them to rebuild their Edo mansions after the conflagration of 1772 but also allowed silt to accumulate in river beds.

The reduced level of river work may have been a quid pro quo for another aspect of Tanuma's regime, the bribery that facilitated the luxury his officialdom reputedly enjoyed. Ritual gift giving was deeply imbedded in the bakuhan system, but its customary limits were gener-

ally recognized. Tanuma evidently saw no logic to limits and encouraged maximal gift giving, primarily to enrich himself, although he purported to see it as proof of a donor's sincerity. He is quoted as explaining
the meaning of gifts in terms a Saikaku chōnin could appreciate:

> Gold and silver are treasures more precious than life itself. If a person bring
> this treasure with an expression of his desire to serve in some public capacity,
> I can be assured that he is serious in his desire. A man's strength of desire
> will be apparent in the size of his gift.

Tanuma discovered that many men were serious in their desire, but in
the process he gained a reputation for corruption that came to haunt
him in the 1780s, when bad weather, volcanic eruption, flooding, crop
failure, and widespread famine and upheaval sharply altered the context of political life.

 When Tanuma did belatedly attempt to cope with food scarcity, his
policy backfired. In 1782 he approved one of the most ambitious river
projects of the Tokugawa period, a scheme to reclaim a large area of
Kantō swampland by draining Inbanuma, a long, convoluted, and shal-
low lake east of Edo that functioned essentially as overflow area for the
Tone and other major rivers of the northern Kantō. The draining of
Inbanuma and another overflow area, Teganuma, had been studied in
the past, but this time work actually began. Even as huge crews dug a
canal to divert water southward to Edo Bay, however, rain and eruption forced postponement. When the project was resumed in 1786, heavy
rains "brought to the Kantō area the worst flood in its remembered
history," inundating the region, backing up flood waters into Inbanuma, and creating raging torrents that destroyed the work in progress.

 By then Tanuma was in serious trouble. Having lived lavishly, he and
his supporters had not converted money-raising ventures into treasury
reserves. When rain and eruption forced him to undertake major repairs
in the Kantō, he had nothing to fall back on except dunning daimyo,
milking merchants, manipulating the currency, and calling for austerity
and price restraints, none of which endeared him to many people. He
alienated key relatives of the shogun, the shinpan daimyo, by disregarding their advice. His attempts to control prices by restricting the issue
of rice certificates angered those lords who relied on the certificates as
cash advances on the upcoming rice crop. And other lords were embittered when he ordered them to mobilize and direct corvée crews in
dredging and diking operations.

 In the spring of 1784, personal disaster struck. A castle guard attacked and mortally wounded his son, the junior councillor, to avenge a number of personal and family insults. The assailant committed suicide as ordered by the bakufu, but within weeks Tanuma's son also died. When reports of the incident circulated, the assailant rather than the victim received general sympathy, soon being idolized as a savior or *yonaoshi daimyōjin* (great august deity of the rectification of the world).[32]

During the next two years, as Tanuma's regime struggled to cope with widespread hardship and unrest, he frenetically sought money to finance its operations. He extracted contributions from Osaka shipping merchants, minted more coins, and licensed more usurers, boatmen, and other businessmen. He established a monopoly on the sale of sulphur, explored the feasibility of a wax monopoly, and drafted an ambitious plan to impose forced loans on temples, shrines, merchants, artisans, and villagers throughout the country, nominally to create a pool of loan funds for indigent daimyo, who would then pay interest to the bakufu on the monies they borrowed. He even sent investigators to Ezo to explore trading possibilities there. And for the longer term, he restarted the Inbanuma work, as noted above, commenced ditching at Teganuma, and authorized other reclamation projects.

The schemes encountered diverse obstacles and amounted to little or nothing. And even as they were being pursued, Tanuma's rivals were getting themselves organized. Late in the summer of 1786, 51-year-old Ieharu fell ill and rumors of poisoning filled the castle. Seizing the moment, those rivals, most notably the great shinpan lords, moved in and tried to take charge. They halted Tanuma's loan and reclamation schemes, cashiered some of his officials, and accepted the resignation that he prudently tendered on grounds of ill health.

Ten days later the shogun's death was announced, and within weeks Tanuma's closest financial officers were cashiered and he was stripped of key perquisites of high office. Beyond that, however, his critics were unable to move. Much of his political machine remained in place, and early in 1787 his allies close to the new shogun not only managed to stall moves to put his arch-rival, Matsudaira Sadanobu, in high office but even began suggesting that Tanuma should be restored to a commanding position.

For some months the political stalemate dragged on, but the food shortage caused by the crop failure of 1786 finally precipitated an upheaval so great that it discredited the old guard, opening the way for a

32. Herman Ooms, *Charismatic Bureaucrat: A Political Biography of Matsudaira Sadanobu, 1758–1829* (Chicago: University of Chicago Press, 1975), p. 73.

new regime. The crop failure had caused over a hundred disturbances throughout the country, according to Herman Ooms, and "by the end of 1786, elderly men and women from the surrounding countryside swarmed into Edo, beggars who sang and danced in an eerie, trancelike fashion."[33] The influx of homeless and hungry only added to the pressure on city food prices, and during 1787 they reached unprecedented heights. Throughout the country, protests continued to erupt, some nineteen convulsing cities and towns during the fifth month alone. The greatest of them occurred in Edo:

> The riot that broke out on 1787/5/20 was the worst Edo had ever known. In a few days, 980 rice shops and hundreds of licensed merchant stores, pawnshops and *sake* shops were destroyed. It was also the first riot that was clearly of the *yonaoshi* type [with overt calls for "world renovation"] ... ; the destruction was carried out by people who, in their desperation hoped in a semireligous way for a new, more egalitarian world order. Low-class Shugendō exorcists and magico-religious reciters seem to have been the spiritual leaders of the movement, which obviously had political overtones. ... From the bakufu's viewpoint the situation looked frightening. After two days of turmoil a militia totaling three thousand men was sent into the city to restore order.

The heavy deployment of military force, unlike that of Oshi han during the post-horse rebellion of 1764, sufficed to restore local order. But such turmoil so near the shogun discredited Tanuma's backers. Within days they were drummed from positions close to the shogun, and the word went out that Sadanobu, who was at his castle in Shirakawa, should come south to Edo to assume office. Popular upheaval had achieved what machinations of the political elite had failed to do.

In succeeding weeks the new leaders wreaked their revenge. Tanuma was stripped of his daimyo title. His mansion in Edo and his lands at Sagara were confiscated. His castle was torn down, and his heir—like the heir to Obata han two decades earlier—was assigned a small domain far to the north. When Tanuma died in the summer of 1788, the story goes, "townspeople heard of it and gathered to throw stones at his remains as they were taken through the streets on the way to their final resting place."[34]

33. The politics of Tanuma's fall are laid out in ibid., pp. 71–76. The quoted passages appear on pp. 75–76. Italics added.
34. Hall, *Tanuma Okitsugu*, p. 141.

With Tanuma's fall, Edo came into the hands of Matsudaira Sadanobu, who saw his task as restoring the vigor and virtue that presumably marked the bakufu during the rule of his grandfather, Yoshimune. Sadanobu's rhetoric suggested that policy was being changed drastically, but he faced the same basic constraints as his predecessor in terms of social order and the fisc, and policy changes at that level were neither radical nor consequential. More important in the longer run were the uses he made of ideology and his reoriention of foreign policy, two issues that acquired increasing importance from his day. In those areas his initiatives established trends that became central to the history of the next half century, as noted in chapter 20.

Thought and Society

The Eighteenth Century

During the seventeenth century, samurai dominated philosophical output, while commoners directed their cultural creativity to the literary and visual arts. That division of interests was far from perfect, however, with gifted chōnin, samurai, and especially ronin in their pursuit of the savant career path engaging in both philosophical and aesthetic production.

After Genroku, the distinction between philosophy and popular culture became even more obfuscated as social strata grew more entangled. Philosophical discourse became the property of more people and broadened in scope and diversity. Later Tokugawa intellectual and cultural production was so voluminous, however, that it must be segmented in some manner, and the way chosen in the next four chapters is, again, to examine philosophy and social thought as one category and the visual arts, popular literature, and drama as another.

Seventeenth-century thought was so fully dominated by a samurai agenda that it is amenable to examination in terms of that agenda, but the subsequent spread of philosophical production altered priorities. Following a brief look at how the samurai agenda played out, the issues that invite attention are the spread of education, which undergirded the diffusion of thought, and the main functions of the thought that was disseminated, functions that reached well beyond the concerns of the samurai elite.

EPILOGUE TO THE SAMURAI AGENDA

The dimensions of seventeenth-century scholarly thought that seemed to warrant attention in chapter 9 were these: its role in educating samurai and providing them with career opportunities, in legitimizing the Tokugawa regime and justifying samurai privilege, and in "naturalizing" Chinese thought and elucidating Japan's own legacy. We also noted that the idea of *jitsugaku,* or "practicality," was commonly invoked by scholars as a criterion for judging a proposition's worth. One can follow thought of later decades in these terms, as the following comments may suggest.

Schooling samurai and giving them careers. The educating of samurai continued during the eighteenth century, primarily through the proliferation of private schools (*shijuku*), where they studied along with growing numbers of commoners. From late in the century on, the shijuku were supplemented by more and more han academies devoted to the instruction of samurai. However, because samurai schooling became so entangled with that of commoners, it seems best to examine it as part of the broader spread of education.

The importance of scholarship as vehicle for samurai careers—the "savant strategy"—declined as time and economic growth reduced the ronin population during the later 1600s. Ogyū Sorai and Yamagata Daini epitomize extremes of savant success and failure among eighteenth-century ronin. By then samurai knew that their hereditary stipends were practically assured—even if meager and subject to partial confiscation by lordly edict or price fluctuation—so few had compelling need for alternative careers, though many sought supplemental income. As a career vehicle, scholarship, in medicine especially, became more valuable for commoners than samurai because it enabled them to "rise" from townsman or villager to an ambiguous intercaste status in which accomplishments as doctor or teacher could open doors of opportunity. Itō Jinsai was forerunner to a large number of later Tokugawa commoner savants.

Nevertheless some gifted samurai still turned to scholarship as a way to enliven their days, address social issues, supplement their salaries, or, in a few cases, leave lordly service altogether. And as noted later in examining literary culture, during the eighteenth century some samurai began adopting the life style of the *bunjin,* or aesthete, a sort of Taoist sagely alternative to dutiful Confucian service as a loyal samurai.

Legitimizing the regime and justifying samurai privilege. By the eighteenth century, a sturdy rationale for the regime was in place, but scholars continued to present arguments new and used to justify shogunal rule, including an abortive attempt by Arai Hakuseki to award the shogun "the comprehensive kingly authority that once had been possessed by the *tennō.*"[1] More and more, however, and especially during the nineteenth century, writers seemed to affirm shogunal authority as a ritual way of disclaiming seditious intent when actually criticizing government or its leaders for particular failings.

The right of samurai to their hereditary status was such a thoroughly internalized dogma by the 1700s that few writers bothered making a case for it. One of the last and most influential statements of *bushidō,* "the Way of the Warrior," was *Hagakure,* a discursive essay on samurai ethics and purpose completed in 1716 by Yamamoto Tsunetomo, a vassal of Saga han.[2] The routinized character of samurai status was reflected in the ritualization of military skill, with fighting styles evolving into highly fragmented and doctrinaire academic disciplines. *Honchō bugei shōden,* written by an obscure samurai named Hinatsu Shigetaka in 1714, is suggestive of the stylized military arts of the day.[3] It consists of brief sketches of some 150 warriors renowned for their mastery of one or another of nine martial arts that had been secretly transmitted (*hiden*) by successive masters. It is both a hagiology and an attempt to clarify, preserve, or resurrect the styles, primarily in archery and swordsmanship, that Hinatsu favored. In the following decades a number of similarly didactic works of samurai retrospection appeared.

One of the most pugnacious defenses of samurai supremacy was made by Ogyū Sorai, as discussed in chapter 14. Even his writings marked a shift in the debate, however, in that his concern was less with justifying samurai rule than explaining how to maintain it in the face of mounting socioeconomic woes, and that issue engaged many later thinkers. Otherwise, insofar as the issue of samurai privilege was addressed, it often was by scholars of commoner status who were arguing against it, frequently by attacking Sorai.

    1. Kate Wildman Nakai, *Shogunal Politics* (Cambridge, Mass.: Harvard University Press, 1988), p. xii. Italics added.
    2. A fragment of *Hagakure* is translated in David John Lu, *Sources of Japanese History* (New York: McGraw-Hill, 1974), 1: 251–52.
    3. John M. Rogers, "Arts of War in Times of Peace: Archery in *Honchō Bugei Shōden,*" *MN* 45-3 (Autumn 1990): 253–84. Rogers continues the translation in subsequent issues.

Naturalizing Chinese thought and elucidating Japan's legacy. Some scholars continued to work at naturalizing Chinese thought. As decades passed, however, they were met by a growing number of scholars of national learning (*kokugaku*) who insisted, as noted below, that "Chinese" thought was alien and unworthy and should be repudiated so that a purely Japanese world view and value system could prevail. By the nineteenth century, the process of naturalization was being applied not to Chinese but to European thought, or "Dutch learning" (*rangaku*) as it was called because most of it entered Japan via the Dutch trading station at Dejima.

Advocating "practicality." Finally, writers continued to advocate *jitsugaku*, or "practicality." Indeed, as the environmental context tightened and public distress and government difficulty intensified, it became a prominent theme in intellectual discourse. For many observers, Buddhism remained the epitomy of the worthless, but as scholarly viewpoints proliferated, new candidates for impracticality appeared. Nearly all commentators considered practical ideas and actions to be those that could ease hardship and improve social well-being and tranquillity. For samurai, practicality remained centrally the political utility of an idea or program, whereas for commoners it was usually a question of economic or horticultural effectiveness.

The idea of practicality provided ammunition for inter-Confucian disputes, and it was invoked by—and against—proponents of national learning. From Yoshimune's time on, a minor aspect of the quest for practical learning was inquiry into European learning, but by the nineteenth century, as interest in rangaku grew apace, the claim to practicality became a key tenet in its naturalization.

As this review of topics suggests, later Tokugawa thought can be approached via the categories used in chapter 9. However, they tend to distort, focusing on some minor, residual matters and nearly ignoring some key topics, notably the spread of schools for commoners, the rise of commoner thought about polity and society, and the emergence during the nineteenth century of popular religious movements.

THE SPREAD OF EDUCATION: *SHIJUKU*

For most of the eighteenth century, shijuku, private or proprietary schools, dominated formal education. From late in the century, as chapter 19 relates, three other types of school also began to proliferate: han academies for samurai, together with their branch schools (*gōgaku*); schools affiliated with religious movements, which mainly taught commoners; and small local schools (terakoya) that sprang up in both town and hinterland to provide instruction for neighborhood youngsters. They all became important during the nineteenth century, but proprietary schools remained influential, expanding in number and diversity as the century advanced.

For most of the eighteenth century, the preeminence of proprietary schools was unchallenged. They had existed throughout the seventeenth, when such scholars as Fujiwara Seika, Nakae Tōju, Kinoshita Jun'an, Yamazaki Ansai, and Itō Jinsai offered instruction, mostly in Confucian studies. Later, in the words of Richard Rubinger, shijuku proliferated into "a bewildering array of institutional arrangements running from small and intimate tutorial types to huge centers with elaborate administrative machinery, from writing schools scarcely distinguishable from terakoya to advanced research institutes."[4]

Operated by individual scholars, often in their own homes, most private schools continued to offer a Confucian education. The most famous were found in the three great cities, but a few esteemed academies were situated in out-of-the-way places, where they offered instruction to local townsmen and members of richer rural families, as well as to a sprinkling of samurai. One such was Baienjuku, dating from about 1766 and located in the village of Tominaga north of Kizuki, a small castle town on the east coast of Kyushu. It was operated by the idiosyncratic Confucian rationalist, Miura Baien. A generation later, Hirose Tansō established another distinguished school, the Kangien, in Hita, a bakufu intendancy west of Kizuki.[5]

For samurai, shijuku in the major cities were most accessible. And probably the single most important one was Ogyū Sorai's school in Edo, where samurai were reminded of their high calling as the leaders of a properly ordered society. Many of Sorai's pupils set up their own schools or became key figures in han schools as they were established, and by the 1740s they were an influential part of a fragmented and argumentative Confucian scholarly community.

Shijuku were also central to the education of commoners. The Kogidō of Itō Jinsai and his successors in Kyoto was perhaps the best-

---

4. Richard Rubinger, *Private Academies of Tokugawa Japan* (Princeton: Princeton University Press, 1982), p. 8.

5. Rubinger, *Private Academies*, pp. 60–98, examines the Kangien at length. He mentions Baienjuku on pp. 57–58. On Miura Baien, see the intellectual biography by Gino K. Piovesana, "Miura Baien, 1723–1789," *MN* 20-3/4 (1965): 389–421.

known. Others included the Gansuidō, established in Osaka in 1717 as a Confucian school addressing the needs of local people, and the Senjikan, also in Osaka, where during the latter half of the century Asada Gōryū gave instruction on scientific topics, largely to commoners. Many other urban shijuku arose to teach townsmen, and most served a local clientele, although widely known schools such as these two enrolled students from all over the country.

Some proprietary schools—such as the previously mentioned Shōheikō of Hayashi Razan, Kaihodō of Sugeno Kenzan, and Seijukan of Taki Motonori in Edo and the Kaitokudō of Nakai Shūan in Osaka—were officially authorized academic "fiefdoms," which presumably performed a service for the rulers akin to that of vassals or licensed merchants. Where they essentially served commoners, however, they might experience tension between their need to retain official goodwill and their wish to meet the needs of their students as chōnin in a samurai-dominated society.

The tension was evident in the Kaitokudō. When Nakai Shūan secured its bakufu charter in 1726, he tended to stress the "officialness" of the school, insisting that its directors be allowed to wear two swords when visiting a government office and permitting samurai to sit at the front of the classroom, provided they arrived before lecturing started. He insisted that only those formally approved by the school authorities be admitted and that students pay for their schooling. In the 1730s, when Tominaga Nakamoto, one of the Kaitokudō's brightest students and son of one of its sponsors, began propounding a defiant iconoclasm that seemed to risk government displeasure, he was expelled and stripped of all connection to the school and its merchant backers.[6]

As the century advanced, however, and relations between Edo leaders and Osaka merchants grew more strained, mostly for fiscal reasons, the Kaitokudō tended to favor its merchant connections. It relaxed admission procedures but still insisted on fees for learning, which increasingly placed poorer samurai at disadvantage. And under the leadership of Shūan's son, Chikuzan, it eliminated samurai seating privileges by 1760. These changes gave fuller expression to the school's instructional ideal that "interchange among students will take place without regard to high or low status and entirely as colleagues of like mind."[7]

6. A new study of Tominaga that contains translations of his work is Michael Pye, *Emerging from Meditation* (London: Duckworth, 1990).
7. Tetsuo Najita, *Visions of Virtue in Tokugawa Japan* (Chicago: University of Chicago Press, 1987), p. 80.

The shift in emphasis did not, however, change the content of Kai-tokudō instruction. It continued to give the children of Osaka merchants elementary schooling in reading, writing, use of the abacus, and the basic Confucian ethics of loyalty, trust, and filial piety, while mature students received advanced training in the reading and interpretation of Confucian texts. Nor did the school ever forget its status as an officially authorized institution. The Confucianism it espoused always fell within parameters acceptable to Edo leaders, and Chikuzan labored energetically to strengthen his ties to Edo even as he enhanced the role of commoners in class.

Most people attended no formal schools during the eighteenth century. They were socialized and acquired basic vocational training at home in the course of growing up. Many commoner boys learned vocations as apprentices in commercial houses or in adoptive homes to which they would eventually succeed, and numerous young women acquired skills while serving as maids and ladies-in-waiting in the houses of the more highly born.[8]

Most of those who did receive formal schooling were urban folk. But whereas urban schooling had been largely for samurai in the seventeenth century, by the mid eighteenth century it had become normative among more well-to-do urban commoners. And in the great cities this meant large numbers of people. According to one observer of the day: "Tuition has become extremely inexpensive, and school-registration procedures simplified. It amounts to a bargain sale on education, and as a result, even people of low status have enrolled in terakoya, to the point that nowadays 'brushless people' [*muhitsu*—those who can't write] are a rarity. This is a very good thing."[9] Doubtless the writer was overstating affairs a bit, but other records also reveal the spread of schooling. During the years 1760–1785, according to one study, there were "nine *shijuku* in Edo . . . with one hundred students or more, one with over one thousand; four in Kyoto with over two hundred, one with three thousand; one in Osaka with over one thousand students."[10] Un-

8. On apprenticeship training, see Irie Hiroshi, "Apprenticeship Training in Tokugawa Japan," *AA* 54 (1988): 1–23. For a nineteenth-century example of women's education, see Edwin McClellan, *Woman in the Crested Kimono* (New Haven: Yale University Press, 1985), pp. 23–29.

9. Katsuhisa Moriya, "Urban Networks and Information Networks," in Chie Nakane and Shinzaburō Ōishi, eds., *Tokugawa Japan* (Tokyo: University of Tokyo Press, 1990), p. 120.

10. Rubinger, *Private Academies*, p. 56, n. 37. Italics added. These figures presumably represent total enrollments, not average attendance for those years. Rubinger observes that their accuracy is difficult to ascertain.

surprisingly, this diffusion of schooling was accompanied by a broadening of intellectual vistas as learning came to serve the needs of a more diverse clientele.

THE FUNCTIONS OF SCHOLARLY THOUGHT

Late Tokugawa thought may be classified, as has been done, in terms of "national packets," Chinese, Japanese, and Dutch (European).[11] Doing so has certain merits: it identifies the geographical source of major strands of thought and highlights major categories of mutual vilification, as scholars accused one another of being intolerably Sinophilic, uncritically accepting of indigenous myths, or dangerously infected with *ranpeki* or "Dutch mania."

On the other hand, treating the thought in terms of such "packets" tends to exaggerate their distinctiveness and obscure their interplay. It seems more useful, therefore, to approach thought in terms of its major functions: namely, ameliorating social tension and reenforcing the existing order by transcending disputes among fractious Confucians, establishing the worth of commoner lives and careers in a samurai-dominated order, advocating "practical" solutions to problems of the day, and defining the indigenous legacy and establishing its contemporary pertinence.

TRANSCENDING INTELLECTUAL DISPUTES

Following medieval precedents, scholars such as Hayashi Razan had expounded both Shintō and Confucian doctrines from the early seventeenth century, noting compatibilities and proposing identities. Later, even as sectarian distinctions became sharper, Yamazaki Ansai formulated Suika Shintō, his "highly personal synthesis of Shintō and Neo-Confucianism," which he taught along with his own version of Ch'eng-Chu thought.[12]

During the eighteenth century, even as thought became more diverse, efforts to transcend that diversity grew more intense. Miyake Sekian, the Kaitokudō's first major lecturer, was so eclectic that he was teased by his successor, Goi Ranju, who said of him: "He sounds like a mys-

11. R. P. Dore, *Education in Tokugawa Japan* (Berkeley and Los Angeles: University of California Press, 1965), p. 160, coined the term.
12. Herman Ooms, *Tokugawa Ideology* (Princeton: Princeton University Press, 1985), p. 263.

terious night bird. His head is Neo-Confucian; the backside resembles
Riku Shō Zan; the arms and legs are like Ōyōmei; and his language
reminds one of a physician." Goi, an Osaka merchant-scholar, espoused a more firmly defined Ch'eng-Chu (Neo-Confucian) view. But
he also used classics of Japanese literature, which he viewed from a
Buddhist perspective, and spoke favorably of Dutch rejection of superstition, their "substantial command of astronomy," and the precision
of their calculations.[13]

Shingaku, a religious movement begun by Ishida Baigan, was even
more inclusivist in impulse than Kaitokudō scholars. Baigan drew ideas
from Buddhism, Shintō, and Ch'eng-Chu, finding "no difference at all
between spiritual attainment realized through Buddhism and the Way
of Confucianism."[14] And Shingaku sustained the principle of respecting
those doctrines, as in this axiom of a later Shingaku teacher: "Revere
Shintoism, Buddhism, and Confucianism and cherish sincerity in all."[15]

By the early 1700s, however, the harshest disputes were not between
proponents of those three bodies of thought but between warring factions of Confucianists, most notably disciples of Sorai and followers of
Ansai or Jinsai. As the eminent scholar Okada Takehiko has pointedly
observed, because of the popularity of Sorai's teachings, other Confucian scholars "likewise set up their own schools and vied for originality.
They promoted their independent theories, rejected the restrictions imposed by their teachers, and became self-appointed authorities on Confucianism. As a result the traditional decorum of Confucian studies was
lost."[16]

As intra-Confucian disputes flourished, other scholars strove to reconcile them. One of the first was Inoue Kinga, the son of a daimyo's
physician. Facing the bitterly conflicting interpretations of Jinsai and
Sorai, he worked out a synthesis that in essence accepted the Sorai proposition that time changes and politics must change with it, but denied
his corollary that Ch'eng-Chu scholars were therefore in error and that
only the ancient kings had known the true Way of governance. In Tetsuo Najita's words, "Inoue had provided a theory of flexible selection

13. The two quotations from Goi are in Najita, *Visions of Virtue*, pp. 123, 142. Riku
Shō Zan is the Chinese scholar Lu Hsiang-shan (1139–92), who taught ideas akin to
those of Wang Yang-ming (Ōyōmei).
14. Najita, *Visions of Virtue*, p. 137.
15. Robert N. Bellah, *Tokugawa Religion: The Values of Pre-Industrial Japan* (Glencoe, Ill.: Free Press, 1957), p. 173.
16. Takehiko Okada, "Neo-Confucian Thinkers in Nineteenth-Century Japan," in
Peter Nosco, ed., *Confucianism and Tokugawa Culture* (Princeton: Princeton University
Press, 1984), p. 217.

of historical ideologies, thus allowing the ideas of Ogyū Sorai and of Neo-Confucianism to coalesce within a single framework in which, [depending on] the circumstances, one or the other could be given emphasis."[17]

These syncretist Confucian teachings, known as *setchūgaku*, or "eclecticism," were welcomed by bakuhan authorities, who were far more interested in academic quiescence than doctrinal originality or purity. They promoted setchūgaku to reconcile quarreling scholars, and in following decades a number of Confucianists expounded it, Hosoi Heishū being one of the best-known.[18] Although differing in particulars, these scholars agreed on the virtue of "rejecting factional extremes and searching for the right way by 'adopting the strong and supplementing the weak' in all schools of thought."[19] They broke little new theoretical ground but continued to promote setchūgaku for the rest of the Tokugawa period. Their approach surely encouraged the intellectual scrambling and adaptation—the interplay—that became common as scholars wrestled with the escalating disjunctions between social ideal and reality.

SANCTIONING COMMONER LIVES

The pragmatic founders of the Tokugawa order did not presume that commoners were unworthy. Politically subordinate for practical reasons of state they certainly were, and subjected to onerous exploitation. But as samurai scholars elaborated Confucian ideology, they overlaid these utilitarian considerations with a legitimizing ideology of socioethical discrimination that was expressed most aggressively by Ogyū Sorai and his followers. Predictably, perhaps, the articulation of an ideology purporting to show the moral inferiority of commoners generated counterclaims of plebian worth, which were actively championed during the eighteenth century. Several scholars challenged the Sorai view that only samurai had a use for higher learning and that only they, as models for the "stupid commoners," deserved esteem. They promoted instead two

17. Tetsuo Najita, "Method and Analysis in the Conceptual Portrayal of Tokugawa Intellectual History," in Najita and Irwin Scheiner, eds., *Japanese Thought in the Tokugawa Period* (Chicago: University of Chicago Press, 1978), p. 15.
18. An example of Hosoi's thought is "A Sermon by Hosoi Heishū," in Michiko Y. Aoki and Margaret B. Dardess, *As the Japanese See It* (Honolulu: University Press of Hawaii, 1981), pp. 59-72, reprinted from *MN* 31-4 (Winter 1976): 400-13.
19. Masao Maruyama, *Studies in the Intellectual History of Tokugawa Japan* (Princeton: Princeton University Press, 1974), p. 141.

other propositions: that the seeds of virtue lie in all humans and that all honest walks of life are meritorious.

During the seventeenth century, as noted in chapter 9, the belief in universal human potential was expressed by Nakae Tōju and Itō Jinsai, and followers of the two continued to promote their views in later centuries. The defense of callings other than rulership began to be made not many years later, two early voices being those of Nishikawa Joken and Ishida Baigan. Thereafter assertions of occupational worth became common.

Nishikawa Joken was born into the house of a licensed Nagasaki textile merchant in 1648. He studied Confucianism in Kyoto and European astronomy, calendration, and mathematics in Nagasaki. He ably advised merchant houses and later taught astronomy and geography. In 1719 Yoshimune summoned the aged Joken to Edo for consultation because of his reputation for broad practical knowledge, but he returned to Nagasaki shortly before dying in 1724. In the course of his full and productive life, Joken wrote a number of treatises that pointed out the important role merchants had come to play in society. As he put it in 1719,

> For a long time the merchants have been regarded as inferior to the peasants, but ever since the money economy grew to country-wide proportions, everyone has been borrowing money from them. . . . Nowadays the peasants, and even the samurai, engage in commercial activities. Moreover, most [professionals]—Confucian scholars, doctors, poets, tea-ceremony masters—are *chōnin*.[20]

Lest social success merely invite hedonistic greed, however, he proposed a concept of wealth that helped legitimize merchant careers by defining them as a type of public service. He defined wealth, whether money or goods, as public property:[21] "Wealth does not remain stationary in a single place for any length of time. As soon as it stops, it already has reversed itself and begun to scatter about. This is in accordance with natural principle." Wealth thus could not be a "private" possession, because it was in constant motion, as evidenced in the marketplace and in the rise and fall of wealthy households, and the function of merchants was to expedite its flow—a perspective that surely helped Yoshimune accept *kabu nakama* as commercial fiefdoms.

20. Jennifer Robertson, "Rooting the Pine: Shingaku Methods of Organization," *MN* 34-3 (Autumn 1979): 312.

21. The next several quotations are from Najita, *Visions of Virtue*, pp. 49–51, 87, 92–93, 155.

In return for a just profit, Joken argued, merchants use their skill at carefully calculating supply and value to assure that wealth circulates in a rational and orderly manner, avoiding scarcities and wild price fluctuations and thus benefiting all of society. What deters merchants from indulging in exploitative greed, he argued, is that the natural spirit of human beings partakes of the virtue inherent in nature.

Joken also held that stratification is normal, that societies differ one from another—citing China and Holland in support of his thesis—and that it was natural for Japan to be structured as it was. Merchants had no reason, therefore, to feel any less worthy for not being samurai. After all, he reasoned, the stratification of Japanese society is a product of custom, not of innate human differences: "When all is said and done, there is no ultimate principle that establishes superior and inferior among human beings. These distinctions result from upbringing." So parents in all social strata have every reason to rear their children carefully and to expect them as a result to live worthwhile lives.

In this same spirit, at the inaugural lecture of the Kaitokudō, which followed its official licensing in 1726, the principal lecturer, Miyake Sekian, cited the *Analects of Confucius* and *Book of Mencius* in declaring "an intrinsic goodness innate to all human beings" regardless of their status. Drawing on both Ch'eng-Chu and Ōyōmei teachings, he argued that reason and empathy should both be nurtured and urged his audience to select knowledge widely within the limits of reasoned righteousness. He reminded them that "the diligent flourish, the ineffectual languish," and held that if merchants practice righteousness, they will realize an appropriate profit.

Nakai Chikuzan, who became the intellectual leader of the Kaitokudō around 1760, affirmed that view: "Human beings are endowed by heaven at birth with a virtuous essence, consisting of compassion, righteousness, propriety and wisdom." Concerning the merchant's profession, Chikuzan wrote, "Like the stipend of the samurai and the produce of farmers, the profit of merchants is to be seen as a virtue."

The same themes of human worth and merchant usefulness were developed by Ishida Baigan, the founder of Shingaku. Born into a farming household northwest of Kyoto in 1685, Baigan went to the city as a young man to work in a merchant house, eventually rising to the position of chief clerk (*bantō*). Over the years his quest for religious insight took him into Confucianism, Shintō, Buddhism, and Taoism, until finally in 1729 he began preaching to any who would listen, directing himself essentially to Kyoto townsmen. Reflecting his own religious ex-

perience, he promoted meditation as a means of attaining enlighten-
ment: "The good person makes his heart united with heaven and earth
and all things. . . . If he makes heaven and earth and all things himself,
there is nothing which he cannot attain."[22] Baigan also advocated as-
ceticism and "devotion to one's obligations and occupation,"[23] ideals
the authorities encouraged as they struggled to maintain social order.

Like Kaitokudō scholars, Baigan was critical of Sorai, arguing that
his doctrines were "mere intellectual reflection" that failed to grasp the
true character of human nature and its oneness with heaven and earth.
He quoted Mencius approvingly: "He who exhausts his mind, knows
his nature. Knowing his nature he knows heaven."[24] And since people
of all stations can attempt that, samurai had no monopoly on access to
truth. Indeed, all shared the Way; all had their proper roles. Whereas
Sorai wished to eliminate merchants, Baigan argued, "If the merchants
all became farmers and artisans, there would be no one to circulate
wealth and all the people would suffer. . . . The trade of the merchants
assists the empire. . . . The profit of the merchant too is a stipend permitted by the empire." And more broadly: "Although the *samurai*,
farmers, artisans and merchants differ in occupation, since they all appreciate the same principle if we speak of the Way of the *samurai*, it
goes for the farmers, artisans and merchants, and if we speak of the
Way of the farmers, artisans and merchants, it goes for the *samurai*."[25]

Baigan's successors, who developed his teachings into the widely
propounded doctrines of Shingaku, continued to promote these ideas.
Tejima Toan, a disciple of Kyoto merchant extraction, regarded occupational reciprocity as essential to society's proper functioning: "The
contentment of the sellers and the contentment of the buyers should be
the motives of business. [To sell] at such a profit as to result in a loss to
the buyer, or [to buy] at depressed prices, resulting in a loss to the seller,
is no different from gambling."[26] So the merchant, like the samurai,
has criteria of right and wrong to guide him, and his adherence to them
enables him, just as much as any samurai, to contribute to society's
well-being.

During the eighteenth century, as these examples suggest, exponents
of universal human worth were mainly addressing chōnin and talking

22. Bellah, *Tokugawa Religion*, pp. 150–51.
23. Ibid., p. 152. The words are Bellah's.
24. Robert N. Bellah, "Baigan and Sorai: Continuities and Discontinuities in Eighteenth-
Century Japanese Thought," in Najita and Scheiner, eds., *Japanese Thought*, p. 145.
25. Bellah, *Tokugawa Religion*, pp. 157–58.
26. Robertson, "Rooting the Pine," p. 313.

about their worth. By the nineteenth, few still evinced a need to justify either chōnin or their calling. For them, the debate had moved on to the question of what role merchants should play in managing society as a whole. Spokesmen and women for the peasantry, however, were slower to make their case, few becoming vocal before the nineteenth century.

The social gap between eighteenth-century peasants and their betters is suggested by the tone and reasoning of Andō Shōeki, an obscure physician-scholar. Shōeki is said to have been born around 1710, perhaps to a samurai family of Okudono han in Mikawa.[27] But he was adopted by a family in Hachinohe in the far northeast, studied medicine, and by the 1740s was a practicing physician there. At some point he traveled to Nagasaki and learned a bit about Europe, and in the early 1750s he published essays that revealed his wide-ranging interests and idiosyncratic philosophy. He had a few disciples, mostly from the northeast, but despite his extensive writing, he was little known in his own day.

Shōeki matured during the years when Yoshimune was revitalizing tax collection and the rural populace was mastering the grim arts of birth control and otherwise learning to cope with scarcity of reclaimable land. For villagers they were harrowing years, and Shōeki developed a powerfully disillusioned view of the existing order. His iconoclasm was even more radical than that of his near-contemporaries Tominaga Nakamoto and Yamagata Daini, and the scorched-earth tenor of his polemics may explain why he had so few disciples and was unknown and nearly unpublished.

Shōeki does not seem to have disputed individual scholars of the day, but he savagely denounced scholars as a group, priests, physicians, samurai, merchants, prevailing creeds, and the ruling order itself.[28] The only people who really deserve respect, he asserted, are those who till the soil: "Peasants who engage in direct cultivation and weaving, clothe and feed themselves happily, are free from avarice and disorder and are the real children of Nature. They are neither noble nor humble, superior nor inferior, wise nor foolish, but are free from all arbitrariness, conforming to the laws of the universe." Shōeki's vision of the good society was essentially the communal village (kyōdōtai) that Iemitsu had sought to establish during the 1640s and that Yoshimune aspired to revive in

27. Seiichi Iwao, *Biographical Dictionary of Japanese History* (Tokyo: Kodansha, 1978), p. 165.
28. The following quotations come *seriatim* from E. Herbert Norman, "Andō Shōeki and the Anatomy of Japanese Feudalism," *TASJ*, 3d ser., 2 (Dec. 1949): 243, 221–22, 155.

the 1720s. But where the village was for these shogun the foundation that supported higher castes in the Tokugawa order, to Shōeki it was to be the whole society. He described his utopian ideal this way:

> In the world of Nature, human beings work in accordance with the operation of Heaven and Earth; there is not the least divergence between man and Nature. Spring comes both in Heaven and Earth giving life to blooming flowers and all other livings things; in consonance with it, men begin to sow the seeds of the five cereals and various vegetables. Summer . . . Autumn . . . Winter [proceed similarly, and this] cycle of seasons and human labour has neither beginning nor end.

In this world of ceaseless work and infrangible harmony with Nature, there are no luxury, no money, no social stratification, no immorality, no misery, and "no ruler who exploits the ruled."

Had Japan not been corrupted by the alien creeds of Confucianism and Buddhism, it would be such a land, because "Japan is situated in the east of the Universe. It is the native land of the Sun Goddess and the centre of all countries. Therefore men cultivate diligently and have honest and innocent minds. They are loved by the gods and the five cereals grow abundantly. . . . It is a righteous country where god and man are one." But the alien creeds were introduced and the primal virtue was lost. Shōeki had to look elsewhere for the good society, and his premier example was Ezo, where the fruits of nature were abundant and the native people lived simply and productively without laws, social inequality, money, or greed. Almost as appealing was Holland where, despite the confusion and danger of Christianity, diligent burghers lived simple, productive lives.

To get from Japan's current disastrous condition back to the Way of Nature, he argued, the vassal forces of daimyo should be radically reduced and returned to the soil. Merchants and officials should be returned to the soil and land given to the unemployed. The use of money should be abolished; entertainers, beggers, and other useless types put to work; and a unitary polity established. Shōeki, in short, didn't even try to sanction peasant life within the existing order. The only way to realize the dignity of peasants, in his view, was to carry out radical social change.

ADVOCATING PRACTICAL POLICIES

As previously noted, the stresses facing eighteenth-century Japan prodded scholars to value "practicality," an emphasis evident in the views of Nishikawa Joken and those associated with the Kaitokudō. Among samurai scholars, followers of Ogyū Sorai displayed an especially strong interest in practical solutions to problems of governance, and rangaku began to emerge during the eighteenth century as an important source of practical knowledge.

Dazai Shundai, a sometime-ronin from Iida han, was one of Sorai's most influential disciples. In 1729, a year after Sorai's death, and amidst the shambles of Yoshimune's monetary reform, he drafted an essay that explained what was wrong and what should be done about it. Writing in a contemporary style that made his essays accessible to a broad readership, he addressed the problems of society as a whole. Like his mentor, however, he was most concerned with samurai. Defying established verity, including that of Sorai, he claimed that bakufu fiscal policy was fundamentally wrongheaded, because it was based on agriculture rather than trade. The bakufu ought to foster commercial activity, he argued, as should the daimyo. In Tetsuo Najita's paraphrase:

> A *han*'s most efficient avenue to increased cash wealth is not in agriculture *per se,* but in the process of buying and selling goods. The greater the volume of exchange, the greater the income. A *han,* therefore, should maximize production of goods best suited to its environment. Anything and everything that is useful to human beings and has cash value in the process of exchange should be vigorously produced. Above all, useful and valuable goods should be manufactured because they increase the total wealth of the political community, and [do] not merely *supplement* the subsistence needs of a household.[29]

Later generations of Sorai's followers also argued their case in terms of utility, as did scholars of national learning and other persuasions. It was Dutch learning, however, that seemed to profit most from the interest in practicality, being aided in that regard by aspects of national learning and Sorai's thought that helped create an intellectual "niche" for it.

Eighteenth-century proponents of kokugaku, as noted below, cited the indisputable verity of Japan's ancient myths to celebrate the mysterious wonders of life that are beyond human ken and must be exempted from critical scrutiny. By leaving study of those wonders to thinkers of other persuasions, they helped give scholars of rangaku a special hold on the niche of physical science. Sorai's contribution, which was similar, derived from his cosmology. He anchored his understanding in the

---

29. Tetsuo Najita, "Political Economism in the Thought of Dazai Shundai (1680–1747)," *JAS* 31-4 (Aug. 1972): 834. Italics in original.

words of the Sages, advancing the corollary that "the teaching of the
sages represents perfection. How can one outdo and surpass them? What
the sages left unsaid generally does not need to be said. If it needed to
be said the Early Kings and Confucius would already have said it. How
could there be anything left for later men to discover and reveal? It is
simply unthinkable."[30] From this premise, Sorai concluded that the world
of natural phenomena could not and should not be studied, because
doing so constituted disrespect for the Sages and undermined one's understanding of them and of the Way:

> There are things even a sage does not know. . . . The mysterious workings
> of Heaven and earth, which are not limited to wind and snow and thunder
> and rain, cannot be reached by man's knowledge. From the blossoming and
> fruition of the grasses and trees, and the flowing of water and the towering
> up of mountains, even to the flight of birds, the running of animals, and the
> movements of man: we do not know how they work.[31]

The upshot was that while Sorai's teaching encouraged practicality and
flexibility in thinking about political matters, it restricted the field of
acceptable inquiry, leaving broad areas for later thinkers, and rangaku
was a major beneficiary of that self-limitation.

One of the first areas in which rangaku proved useful was Sorai's
"mysterious workings of Heaven and earth," or more prosaically, astronomy. Chinese astronomical lore prevailed during the seventeenth
century, when Chinese-language books on European subjects were
banned, but early in the eighteenth century a Confucian scholar at Nagasaki persuaded the authorities to admit a Chinese book on European
astronomy. Nishikawa Joken and others then used the work in their
discussion of the universe and man. To Joken it revealed that Europeans
were "ingenious in manipulating figures and instruments" and had
"thoroughly mastered the art of navigation," but were inferior in such
larger matters as metaphysics and cosmology.[32] A few years later,
Yoshimune attempted to develop a new calendar using this Sino-Jesuit
astronomy, but his effort was thwarted by hereditary astronomers at
the imperial court who saw the effort as a usurpation of their preroga-

30. Wm. Theodore de Bary, "Sagehood as a Secular and Spiritual Ideal in Tokugawa
Neo-Confucianism," in de Bary and Irene Bloom eds., *Principle and Practicality: Essays
in Neo-Confucianism and Practical Learning* (New York: Columbia University Press,
1979), p. 166. For an alternative translation, see Olof G. Lidin, *Ogyū Sorai's Distinguishing the Way* (Tokyo: Sophia University, 1970), p. 98.
31. Richard H. Minear, "Ogyū Sorai's *Instructions for Students:* A Translation and
Commentary," *TASJ* 36 (1976): 45.
32. Shigeru Nakayama, *A History of Japanese Astronomy* (Cambridge, Mass.: Harvard University Press, 1969), p. 109.

tives. They denounced it as an attempt to popularize European ideas and managed, after his death in 1751, to have the project completed in Kyoto according to their own lunisolar principles.

In the following decades, official bakufu interpreters at Nagasaki and physicians working independently in Edo gradually supplemented Chinese-language sources on European science with Japanese translations of Dutch works. During the 1770s, the interpreter Motoki Ryōei completed a translation that introduced at least the name of Copernicus's heliocentric theory to officialdom, and he prepared a fuller exposition of the theory in 1792–93.[33] A few scholars had access to his works, and one, the Edo artist-literatus Shiba Kōkan, used them in writing three books that popularized Copernican theory.

In Osaka, meanwhile, the scholar-physician Asada Gōryū was actively studying astronomy and teaching Dutch learning at his school, the above-noted Senjikan. Formerly physician to the daimyo of Kizuki han and friend of Miura Baien, Asada had taught himself astronomy and in 1769 resigned from his lord's service and went to Osaka. There he supported himself as a doctor while teaching and continuing his studies. He made measurements with such instruments as telescopes, a pendulum clock, quadrant, transit, and eclipse meter, establishing his reputation as an expert in the field. By the 1790s, the recently constructed court calendar was so out of step with the seasons that bakufu leaders sought to correct it. Aware of the merits of European calendarial techniques, they wanted the new calendar prepared on that basis, but their own astronomers could not handle the task, so they invited Asada. He declined in favor of Takahashi Yoshitoki and another of his students, and they accepted the challenge and used European measurements to complete the project in 1798.

After 1800, to complete this story quickly, more up-to-date works on European astronomy reached Japan, and by the 1830s they had been translated and published. They were used for another calendar revision in 1841 and provided material for scholars trying to reconcile the new learning with established calendarial principles. Their effort was flawed, but at the time domestic and foreign difficulties were making life dangerous for scholars of Dutch learning, and astronomers evidently found it safer to let old dogmas lie, which meant that irreconcilable ideas remained in place until after the Tokugawa regime's collapse some thirty years later.

33. Ibid., pp. 175–76, discusses the problem of how much information on Copernicus Motoki actually introduced.

As noted elsewhere, European art and medicine also attracted eighteenth-century scholarly attention because of their "practicality," and their study experienced vicissitudes similar to those of astronomy. When diplomatic problems escalated during the nineteenth century, European military techniques also began receiving closer attention because of their perceived utility.

INTERPRETING THE NATIVE LEGACY

The most energetic and influential interpreters of the native legacy were the scholars of national learning. Negatively their purpose can be viewed as a sustained attempt to "denaturalize" Confucianism, or at least to discredit the notion of Chinese cultural superiority. Positively it can be viewed as the articulation of links between the mythological past, the recorded history of the aristocratic few, and the daily lives of common folk. In the process they created an ideological foundation for the national self-consciousness of a later day. And more immediately they encouraged belief that one's local affairs were deeply imbedded in and contributed to the fate of the broader realms of Japan and its gods (*kami*).

Eighteenth-century scholars built on the accomplishments of their predecessors. During the 1600s, as noted in chapter 9, Japan's cultural legacy was resurrected in three main ways. Scholars revitalized Shintō thought and ritual and produced new histories of Japan, and poet-painters, inspired by classical traditions of poetry and art, produced a grand array of new works that celebrated Japan's aristocratic inheritance. Near century's end, this study of the native heritage (*wagaku*) was given a sharper focus by the Shingon monk Keichū, whose commentary on the *Man'yōshū* centered subsequent wagaku on ancient poetics and the legacy of Shintō.[34]

Kada no Azumamaro, the son of a priest at the Inari shrine in Fushimi, reaffirmed the focus on poetics and Shintō. He taught poetry at the imperial court for two years, then spent over a decade in Edo, lecturing on Shintō, teaching and writing about the *Man'yōshū,* and providing scholarly service to the bakufu. Around 1713 he returned to teach in Fushimi, but he still provided antiquarian services to Edo and on occasion went there to lecture. He also continued studying the *Man'yōshū, Kojiki,* and other ancient texts. During his lifetime he produced, in

34. A concise examination of early modern scholarship on the *Man'yōshū* is Peter Nosco, "*Man'yōshū* Studies in Tokugawa Japan," *TASJ,* 4th ser., 1 (1986): 109–46.

addition to poetry, numerous commentaries on ancient histories, poetic collections, and other works. He also instructed a number of students in Shintō, among them Kamo no Mabuchi, the son of a Shintō priest in Hamamatsu, whom he retained as a teacher at Fushimi.

Azumamaro's essential contribution to nativist thought was to separate it from Confucianism and, in Peter Nosco's words, to present it "in terms of an adversarial relationship with such non-native doctrines as Buddhism and Confucianism and thereby set the tone for the next century of nativist thought." [35] He left to later scholars the thorny tasks of sorting out what was native and what alien in the wagaku heritage and erecting a hierarchy of excellence in the literary components of that heritage.

By the late 1720s, Azumamaro's place in Edo was taken by his adopted heir, Arimaro, who acquired a stipended post as specialist in Japanese learning (*Wagaku goyō*) to Tokugawa Munetake, a well-schooled younger son of Yoshimune.[36] In 1742 Munetake instructed Arimaro to prepare a piece on Japanese poetics, and the scholar drafted the essay *Kokka hachiron,* in which he wrote: "Since versification is not one of the original Six Accomplishments, it was never intended to be of benefit to the governing of the state, nor is it of any help in the realm of daily affairs." That view meshed nicely with the opinion of Ogyū Sorai, whose arguments were in high vogue at the time. However, Munetake, properly trained in Ch'eng-Chu Confucianism, was displeased. In written rebuttal he asserted that verse was indeed among the Six Accomplishments and that skill in poetics was important for governing society. Arimaro was in trouble.

Six years earlier, Azumamaro's disciple Mabuchi had left Fushimi and moved to Edo, following his teacher's death. Lacking fruitful ties to officialdom, he was making a living as a teacher of classical poetry and the *Tale of Genji* when Munetake asked him to draft a rebuttal to Arimaro. He did so, in the course of it cautiously opining that "poems might appear useless, but they calm the heart and bring a man to peace, and who could possibly not realize that they can be of broad use as an aid to government." Especially valuable, he went on, were poems of long ago, because "the poems of ancient man were spontaneous (*ono-*

---

35. Peter Nosco, *Remembering Paradise* (Cambridge, Mass.: Harvard University Press, 1990), pp. 72–73.

36. These quotations from the *Kokka hachiron* controversy come from Peter Nosco, "Nature, Invention, and National Learning: The *Kokka hachiron* Controversy, 1742–46," *HJAS* 41-4 (June 1981): 85–87.

zukara) expressions of human sensitivity where a person sang about his feelings whenever they arose. It was by this very same process that the age was automatically (*onozukara*) governed." In the present world, he added: "When those above enjoy poetry, those below will follow suit; if those above use the ancient spirit and ancient words, those below will likewise return to antiquity." In short, to secure social order today, one should foster the study of ancient poetry, because through it any Japanese can recover that ancient spirit of rectitude that makes good governance occur naturally. Munetake approved, and in 1746 Mabuchi replaced Arimaro as his *Wagaku goyō*, holding the post until 1760 and remaining in Edo until his death nine years later.

After the *Kokka hachiron* controversy, Mabuchi went on to become a major figure in the study of wagaku, or kokugaku, as it was increasingly called. He was basically a literary scholar, and the bulk of his rich output was commentary on the classics, most notably the *Man'yōshū*, but also the *Genji, Ise monogatari,* and other works. In addition, he crafted essays on prose and poetic styles and on what he considered the unique beauty of the language. His belief that poetics and politics were inseparable led him to write on the *Kojiki* and other early historical and political treatises, which, he contended, revealed the purity of primeval Japan. He also wrote critical essays that compared China invidiously with Japan and explained how one should understand ancient Japan and why doing so was important.

Mabuchi's views, like those of all vital intellectuals, changed as he aged, but certain ideas became central to his mature thought. As he saw it, after one overcomes the misunderstanding caused by Chinese studies, he can master the language of ancient Japanese poetry. The surest method is to study the *Man'yōshū* because the antiquity of its poems makes them the best entrée to the original Japanese heart and mind. Mastering the language unlocks the textual record of ancient Japan, of which the *Kojiki* is most important, because it was written in Japanese, whereas the *Nihon shoki*, which earlier scholars had favored, was written in Chinese. In the *Man'yōshū* and *Kojiki,* one discovers the original Japanese "manliness" and true heart (*magokoro*) that enabled government to flourish "automatically" in the heyday of imperial rule before about A.D. 700. In that grand age, he contended, "the Emperor displayed majesty and manliness in accordance with the Way of the Heavenly *Kami*, and the ministers governed in his service, professing valor and directness over all."[37] Subsequently, however, the infiltration of Chinese in-

37. Muraoka Tsunetsugu, *Studies in Shinto Thought* (Tokyo: Ministry of Education, 1964), p. 117. Italics added.

fluences set Japan on a path of decline, which Mabuchi found evident in the "effeminate" poetry of the *Kokinshū*.

Mabuchi reasoned that retrieving those original virtues and with them a proper reverence for the emperor—which constitutes the Japanese Way of gods and emperors (*kamusumeraki no michi*)—will aid in the governing of present-day society by promoting social tranquillity. That outcome is assured because the ancient Japanese "worshiped the imperial deities, had no foulness in their hearts, venerated their emperors, and committed no transgressions."[38] And present-day Japanese, if they master the poetics of the *Man'yōshū* and thereby regain access to the Japanese Way, can recover the pure spirit that lies within themselves despite the encrustation of Chinese learning.

Mabuchi thus went well beyond Azumamaro in identifying the uniquely native and virtuous in Japan's heritage. By celebrating the *Man'yōshū* and *Kojiki* at the expense of the *Kokinshū* and *Nihon shoki*, moreover, he had begun ranking the classics in terms of their merit as vehicles for retrieving those virtues. And whereas Arimaro had said poetry was there simply to be enjoyed, for Mabuchi it had a much more "practical" role.

Mabuchi applied his views to current affairs with circumspection. Despite his proximity to shogunal authority, he evidently had nothing to say on behalf of Takenouchi Shikibu or Yamagata Daini in their time of troubles. And even as he decried problems of the day, he was as careful as Azumamaro to honor the Tokugawa regime, crediting Ieyasu with having understood and restored the essence of Japan's original Way. While he saw adulation of China and of Confucianism as central to society's problems, he balanced his attacks on Confucianists with criticism of such Shintō scholars as followers of Ansai's Suika Shintō, who failed, in his view, to penetrate to the spiritual heart of antiquity. Both, he held, needed to purge erroneous thought so they could apprehend the purity of the original Japanese Way.

Moreover, he was careful to direct his criticisms of Confucianism most squarely at the interpretations of Sorai and Dazai Shundai, which Munetake also disapproved. In 1765 he denounced Confucian teachings, or at least Sorai's view of them, as "no more than a human invention which reduces the heart of Heaven and Earth to something trivial." By contrast ancient Japan "was governed in accordance with the natural laws of Heaven and earth."[39] And he attacked Shundai by belit-

---

38. Nosco, *Remembering Paradise*, p. 130.
39. Quoted in Ryusaku Tsunoda et al., comps., *Sources of the Japanese Tradition* (New York: Columbia University Press, 1958), pp. 515–16.

tling as impractical his central concept of "political economism," or
keizai:

> Now, those who have studied a little are apt to discuss *keizai*. . . . However,
> since there has been not a single occasion when Confucianism, on which the
> theories of those people are founded, was actually practised in politics, how
> could it be useful when imported into this country? It is because man does
> not understand the reality of heaven, earth, and nature that he thinks man
> by nature must adhere to some teaching.[40]

Instead of such misplaced attention he called for the sound study of
antiquity. Indeed, "if there should emerge a man on high who loves
antiquity and who hopes to put the world right, the world will be entirely put right within less than ten or twenty years. It is too soon to
think it cannot be put right easily. Through the thought and feeling of
one man on high, the world can certainly be changed."[41] When Sorai
called for the raising of "one or two" good men to office during the
1720s, his call came complete with detailed policy suggestions. Mabuchi, calling for one good man on high during the years of Tanuma's rise
to power, settled for abstractions. His silence on issues of the day may
in fact have reflected a lack of interest in current politics: after all, the
malfeasance and misery of the moment were inconsequent compared
with the basic issues of political culture that he was exploring. Or he
may simply have had a good instinct for survival in a risky political
climate. He may have recognized that his sponsor, Munetake, son,
brother, and uncle of three successive shogun, could ill afford to shelter
an imprudent scholar, lest he be suspected of harboring untoward designs on the shogunal title.[42]

As the years passed, Mabuchi's fame as a scholar grew, spread by his
writings, his some three hundred students, and his occasional travels.
During the 1750s he came to the attention of a young physician living
in the small highway town of Matsusaka, a few miles from the Ise Shrine.
The young man was Motoori Norinaga, destined to become the most
distinguished scholar in the kokugaku tradition.

40. Ōkubo Tadashi, "The Thoughts of Mabuchi and Norinaga," *AA* 33 (1973): 79,
quoting *Kokuikō.*
41. Muraoka, *Studies in Shinto Thought,* p. 127. The quotation is from *Kokuikō,*
written sometime between 1765 and 1769. See Sajja A. Prasad, *The Japanologists: A
History,* pt. 3 of *The Patriotism Thesis and Argument in Tokugawa Japan* (Guntur, India:
Samudraiah Prakashan, 1984), p. 490.
42. Indeed, Tsuji Tatsuya reports in "Politics in the Eighteenth Century," in *The
Cambridge History of Japan,* vol. 4, *Early Modern Japan,* ed. John W. Hall (Cambridge:
Cambridge University Press, 1991), p. 457, that Munetake was placed in house arrest for
three years during the later 1740s because of his father's displeasure.

Norinaga was born to a local cotton-goods merchant in 1730. Raised a Pure Land Buddhist, he was schooled in the Confucian texts appropriate to boys of merchant households. He enjoyed waka poetry and other literature, practiced the tea ceremony, nō, and archery, and was introduced to diverse Shintō deities and worship practices, particularly those of the nearby Ise shrine. The untimely deaths of his father and stepbrother left him in charge of the family business, allegedly revealing to his mother that he was an inept tradesman, and in 1752 she sent him off to Kyoto to acquire a useful education.

For six years he enjoyed the student's life at his mother's expense, studying Chinese medicine, Confucianism, and Japanese literature, including works of Keichū and other nativist scholars. By 1757 he had concluded that Confucianism was of little value to him because it dealt with "ruling a country, pacifying the whole world under heaven, and keeping people content." When one has "no country to rule and no people to gratify, of what use is the Way of the Sages?"[43] Instead, as he admitted, what he loved above all else was waka.

That year Norinaga finished his studies in Kyoto and returned to his mother's home to take up the medical career that would sustain his family. While developing his practice, he continued studying literature, starting to lecture within two years to the local literary circle on such classics as the Man'yōshū and Genji. He also wrote literary commentary, heard more about Mabuchi's attainments, and met him one evening in 1763 when the Edo scholar passed through Matsusaka on his way home from Ise. After that, Norinaga carried on an awkward correspondence with the elder scholar even though he received repeated criticisms for deviating from Mabuchi's views.

Whereas Mabuchi the priest's son had gone to Edo and spent his life hobnobbing with the great, Norinaga the merchant's son stayed home, caring for his mother, practicing medicine, teaching, and writing. Being on the highway to Ise, however, he did meet scholars and others on pilgrimage, and his reputation as scholar and teacher grew until it exceeded that of Mabuchi and the other nativists, even bringing him during his last years into contact with a few daimyo and court nobles. One measure of his spreading influence was the number of his disciples, which grew in three stages as this breakdown of disciples by place of origin suggests:[44]

43. Shigeru Matsumoto, *Motoori Norinaga, 1730–1801* (Cambridge, Mass.: Harvard University Press, 1970), p. 36.
44. Calculated from ibid., table 2 (p. 125).

Period	From Ise	From elsewhere	Total no. per annum
1757–1782	74	4	3.12
1783–1788	51	33	16.80
1789–1801	92	257	29.08

Prior to the Tenmei famine, these numbers suggest, Norinaga was little known outside Ise; indeed, until 1780 all his students came from that province. However, in 1782 he enlarged his house, a move that reflected his decision to shift his attention from medicine to teaching, and from that time on, his enrollments began to grow substantially. Thereafter his fame spread, peaking when Matsudaira Sadanobu was in power, especially in the early 1790s, when, as noted in chapter 20, coincidental problems involving foreigners and court-bakufu relations suddenly erupted, catching the attention of the politically conscious throughout the country.

During his career, Norinaga echoed many views of Mabuchi and others, but he also made his own major contributions. As a scholar, he was most celebrated for his *Kojikiden,* an exhaustive study of the *Kojiki* that he worked on from 1764 until his death in 1801.[45] That project completed Mabuchi's task of establishing the *Kojiki,* rather than *Nihon shoki,* as the text that best reveals Japan's original nature. Whereas Mabuchi had found that nature to be "manly," however, and well evidenced in *Man'yōshū* poetry, Norinaga found it to have been "feminine," its character captured in the elegant poetry of the *Shinkokinshū.* "Manliness," he asserted, was an unfortunate accretion from China. He concluded, moreover, that the *Genji* embodied most perfectly *mono no aware,* that highly developed and uniquely Japanese sensibility in which "man's heart itself is so spontaneously and irresistibly moved that it is beyond his control."[46]

In the tradition of Azumamaro and Mabuchi, Norinaga juxtaposed this virtuous original "Japanese heart" (*mikunigokoro*) to the corrosive influence of "China heart" (*karagokoro*), which had estranged the peo-

45. Sey Nishimura, "The Way of the Gods: Motoori Norinaga's *Naobi no Mitama,*" *MN* 46-1 (Spring 1991): 21–41, describes *Kojikiden* and offers a translation of the introductory section known as *Naobi no mitama.*
46. Matsumoto, *Motoori Norinaga,* p. 44.

ple of Japan from their gods and emperor.[47] Thus, he considered one of life's most elemental qualities to be its wondrous inexplicability, which Confucian rationalists denied:

> If one claims that it is stupid to believe everything one reads, . . . then there is no way to learn about the past. It is those straight-laced stinking Confucians who insist that anything wondrous must be false and cannot exist, and this way of thinking is extremely narrow-minded. . . . There are things in the world that are beyond the [comprehension of ordinary men].

Going beyond Mabuchi, who targeted Confucianism in his attack on Chinese thought, Norinaga added Taoism as a part of the debilitating alien incubus, even charging that it had penetrated Mabuchi himself.

Whereas Mabuchi explained the unique virtue of the ancient Japanese heart as a quality "naturally" inherent in "the way of gods and emperors," Norinaga located a primal mover, announcing that the Way of the gods (*kami no michi*) was "created by the miraculous power of the god Takami Musubi, and all things and affairs in the world without exception are created by his miraculous power." Not only was there a godly prime mover but the gods favored Japan, making it superior to all other countries. As he put it in 1771: "This grand imperial country is the home of the august and awesome divine ancestress, the great goddess Amaterasu, and this is the primary reason why our country is superior to all others. There is not a country in the world that does not enjoy the blessings of this goddess."

Having situated the prime mover in Japan, Norinaga pressed the logic of that construct to completion. Whereas Mabuchi saw the recovery of Japan's original masculine purity through mastery of poetics as the path to contemporary order and well-being, Norinaga saw the quietly working will of the kami as determinative of all acts, events, and other phenomena, good and bad, "without exception." Like determinists everywhere, however, he left leeway for modest human intervention, and that leeway permitted his very tentative engagement in current affairs. If properly apprised of the kami activity through study of the Way of the gods, he argued, the people could conduct themselves in accordance with that ancient Way and thereby help achieve the general good.

His belief that learning can contribute to social well-being prompted Norinaga to aim his teaching at the general public rather than a handful of scholarly disciples and to prepare some texts, such as a simplified

47. The next three quotations come from Nosco, *Remembering Paradise*, pp. 171, 188, 199.

version of the *Kojiki*, for use in public instruction. Norinaga evidently saw himself shaping affairs through such teaching, essentially as a reverent servant of the kami, rather than through instruction of the political elite.

In terms of political engagement at a higher level, he was even more circumspect than Mabuchi. The only suggestion that he might have had political ambitions as a young man was his decision to abandon his merchant family name of Ozu in favor of the name Motoori, which was associated with his pre-1600 samurai ancestors. Rather, he rejected Confucianism as irrelevant to his apolitical situation and spent his life in Matsusaka. He appears never to have gone to Edo after his years in Kyoto, and until his late years he had no contact with figures such as daimyo or court nobles. Even then, his contributions were strikingly cautious. In 1787 Tokugawa Harusada, the elderly daimyo of Kii, who was grappling with difficulties caused by the Tenmei famine, asked him to provide advice on affairs. At the time, Edo was awash with maneuvers to oust the Tanuma faction, and Motoori may have felt that the moment counseled prudence. In any case, he submitted a secret essay that did little more than reiterate verities and advance a few safe and unoriginal suggestions.[48]

Five years later he declined an invitation from the daimyo of Kaga to serve as in-house scholar because at the age of sixty-two he had no wish to leave home. And two years after that he agreed to lecture to the new lord of Kii only after being assured that he could retain his Matsusaka residence. He did travel to Wakayama a few times to lecture on literature and Shintō ritual, and in 1795 he delivered a lecture on the *Genji* to a daimyo who visited him at home.

He was no more aggressive about cultivating contacts in Kyoto, perhaps because he, an upstart merchant scholar with ideas of his own, was resented by the hereditary aristocratic scholars of Japan's literary and mythic legacy.[49] Despite occasional visits to the city, he appears to have met no high court personages before 1793, and not until 1801, just before his death, did he make a major lecture tour there and meet

---

48. John S. Brownlee provides a translation of Norinaga's 1789 revised version of this essay in "The Jeweled Comb-Box: Motoori Norinaga's *Tamakushige*," *MN* 43-1 (Spring 1988): 45–61. Harusada of Kii (1727–89) should not be confused with his younger contemporary, Tokugawa Harusada of Hitotsubashi (1751–1827), father of the shogun Ienari and an active participant in the politics of Tanuma's fall.

49. Thomas J. Harper, "*The Tale of Genji* in the Eighteenth Century: Keichū, Mabuchi and Norinaga," in C. Andrew Gerstle, *18th Century Japan* (Sydney: Allen & Unwin, 1989), pp. 115–17.

several nobles. Certainly his ideology justified the restraint. He taught that all things transpired through the will of the gods and applied the proposition to his own teachings. Writing a disciple in 1797, he expressed pleasure at the news that his message was gaining adherents even in Izumo, adding,[50] "[the Ancient Way] will naturally spread when the time comes; this is a matter for the will of *kami* and is beyond the reach of man's power." On the other hand, he was not averse to giving the kami a friendly nudge. "However," he went on, in the same letter, "Kyoto is a most difficult place in which to propagate this study, although I hear that some followers begin to appear. I hope you will make further efforts to spread it." The main problem in Kyoto may well have been tension between his views and those of court scholars, but he may also have been reluctant to approach the nobility during the early 1790s, lest he become tangled in the dispute over imperial titles then pitting most of the court against Sadanobu in Edo.

Whatever the reason, in his own lifetime he was largely disengaged from the political scene, being content to counsel obedience and moderation. As he phrased it in verse,

> We dare not disobey
> the edicts we receive
> from time to time,
> for they are the bidding
> of the *Kami*.
>
> When I hear described
> the turbulence
> of eras past,
> how reverent I am
> for this era of peace.[51]

As these poems suggest, his political engagement was one of philosophical idealism. The idealism is also suggested by the way he signed the essay *Naobi no mitama* on completing it in 1771, identifying himself as "Taira no Asomi Norinaga, the Emperor's subject, Iitaka county, Ise province."[52]

The legacy of this gifted country scholar was a body of interpretation that explicitly identified the gods as the source of Japan's unique virtue and the unbroken line of emperors as the living embodiment of that

50. The two quotations are from Matsumoto, *Motoori Norinaga,* p. 134. Italics added.
51. The two poems come from Muraoka, *Studies in Shinto Thought,* pp. 159–60. Italics added.
52. Nishimura, "Way of the Gods," p. 41. He translates the title as "A Treatise on the Way of the Gods brought forth by the spirit of the Gods of Naobi" (p. 22).

godly inheritance. The task of those emperors and their designated officials was to cherish the people by ruling in the way of the gods, and the people's task was to obey their superiors reverently. Even more than his predecessors, Norinaga identified his vision of a once-perfect and still-perfectable realm as uniquely Japanese and juxtaposed it to degenerate influences that seeped in from abroad, especially from China.[53] As he saw it in the late 1780s, for his own day this understanding called not for change but for better implementation of the established order, because that order was a modern manifestation of godly will. In his secret memo to Harusada he wrote:

> The present age is one in which, at the discretion of Amaterasu ōmikami and under the trust of the imperial household, the successive [Tokugawa] shogun, starting with [Ieyasu], have conducted the affairs of state, and further, the administration of each province and district is left in charge of its respective daimyo. . . . Hence, the decrees issued by [Ieyasu] and the laws enacted by the successive shogun are the decrees and laws of Amaterasu ōmikami, and therefore, a daimyo should attach special importance to them and observe them well.

Nor should anyone pursue radical change. Since all things occur at the behest of the kami, as he had written a year earlier in another essay he sent to Harusada, "you should not attempt suddenly to cancel or rectify anything which has been established and is difficult to change, even if it is somewhat harmful to your province. If you try forcibly to rectify it all at once, you may possibly be acting contrary to the will of kami, and therefore fail in that attempt." A strict determinist might argue that when one acts radically, one is simply being the vehicle of radical kami will, but Norinaga did not choose to unleash the will of the gods in that direction.

He had, nevertheless, bequeathed an explosive legacy to future generations. He had identified, as the heart of what must be nurtured, a uniquely Japanese virtue that was anchored in the gods and their imperial representatives on earth but that was vulnerable to alien malignancy. And he specified explicitly that the Tokugawa were but trustees of that godly virtue. Should the time come when the alien malignancy manifested itself, not in the form of wrongheaded scholastics, but in the form of foreigners making political demands and backing them with military force, then the problems that in his day were academic issues

53. The following two quotations are from Matsumoto, *Motoori Norinaga*, pp. 138–41. Italics added.

to be resolved in the fullness of time by the eternally acting will of the kami would become immediate issues of political consequence, in which the burden of performance would rest on the bakufu. And on that day the criteria of evaluation would be clear and inescapable: had the evil foreign influences been contained and had the land of the gods, its imperial legatees, and its people been protected?

SEVENTEEN

The Later Years of Early Tokugawa Arts and Letters

The Decay of Elite Culture
  The Stagnation of Bushi Culture
  The Decline of Kyoto's Cultural Primacy
Ukiyo Culture after Genroku
  Haikai
  Ukiyo Zōshi
  Kabuki and *Ningyō Jōruri*
  Ukiyo-e Prints

"Genroku ukiyo culture" seemed a useful concept in chapter 10 because it directed attention to a limited number of interconnected activities pursued by people in a few places for about one generation. Essentially it embraced ukiyo zōshi, *ningyō jōruri* (puppet theater), kabuki, ukiyo-e—and perhaps haikai—in Kyoto, Osaka, and Edo from about 1680 to 1720, and it was the culmination of decades of cultural development whose urbane ideal was a broad mastery of *yūgei,* the "polite accomplishments."

Later Tokugawa cultural trends do not yield a comparably tidy story of development and culmination. Rather, the eighteenth and nineteenth centuries were marked by two categories of noteworthy trends. One covers later stages in the life of earlier cultural forms: the stagnation of samurai and courtly arts and the playing out or enrichment of ukiyo culture. The other consists of new developments in prose, poetry, and art. These latter arose from the later eighteenth century, yielding in the early nineteenth an era of renewed cultural vitality that embraced more people and more varied content than had earlier arts and letters. This chapter examines the former topic; chapter 18, the latter.

As denizens of an age of hyperspecialization, we must bear in mind when examining this cultural output that what we identify as disciplinary trends in drama, prose, poetry, or the visual arts emerged from the activities of individuals who commonly aspired to be cultural cosmopolites rather than specialists in one or another skill. Chapter 10 suggested that the Genroku ideal of yūgei constituted an urban analogue to the samurai ideal of *bun*, or literary accomplishment. The yūgei ideal in turn seems to have encouraged the appearance of *bunjin*, multi-talented gentlemen—or women—of leisure, especially in the fields of literature and art. These bunjin engaged eclectically in many forms of cultural production, both the established practices examined here and the new developments of the next chapter.

Another trend is visible in the movement from *bun* and yūgei to the late eighteenth-century bunjin ideal. In principle a samurai mastered literary and martial arts (*bun* and *bu*) to enhance his effectiveness as society's leader and model. The merchant who pursued yūgei did so despite warnings that it was dangerously seductive and must be restrained lest it ruin his household and business. But the bunjin, an ideal realized in theory far more often than practice, was one who had dissociated himself from the authorities—a samurai who ceased to serve his lord or a commoner who devoted his time to artistic cultivation—because doing so was the way to realize the best possible life or, if he were philosophically inclined, to attain the Way. By the nineteenth century, in other words, the informing spirit of cultural production had ceased to serve the established order and was, instead, justifying social disengagement.

THE DECAY OF ELITE CULTURE

The decay of elite culture affected both samurai (bushi) in their castle towns and court nobles (kuge) in Kyoto.

THE STAGNATION OF BUSHI CULTURE

Seventeenth-century measures to segregate bushi and chōnin were continually offset by factors that obscured the distinction between "feudal" and "bourgeois" culture, as suggested in chapter 10. Nevertheless, rulers tried to maintain the distinction, the earnestness of their endeavor growing in proportion to its futility. By the eighteenth century they had succeeded in the ironic sense that they had throttled creativity in approved areas of bushi culture, forcing the aesthetically creative to opt for the cultural modes of the commoner or the disengaged life of the bunjin.

Token expressions of samurai cultural privilege survived, of course. Seasonal items, such as the first crop of spring tea from Uji, or fresh fruit, fish, or other products, were whisked off to Edo as offerings to the shogun, or taken to Kyoto, castle towns, or local headquarters (*jin'ya*) for ritual presentation to emperor, daimyo, or lesser authorities. Certain ceramics were reserved for daimyo, and sumptuary regulations preserved residual privileges of clothing, hair style, architecture, and travel facilities. And much as court nobles preserved secret poetic and other courtly traditions, samurai experts nurtured the secret traditions (*hiden*) of their particular styles of swordsmanship, archery, hand-to-hand combat, and so on.

However, bushi could no longer deny others most of the goods and services they enjoyed. They still received Confucian educations at shijuku, but so did growing numbers of non-samurai. They continued to master various arts and skills—the tea ceremony, flower arranging, poem writing, meditation, recreational games—but so did more and more commoners. Insofar as they could afford to, they still acquired elegant lacquer ware, ceramics, incense, and textiles, but the producers also sold them to wealthy merchants and, eventually, well-to-do farmers. Cultural attributes that once had signified elite status thus became more common property.

The role of Kanō artists exemplifies the situation. Theirs was the school of approved art, with the highest-ranking Kanō artists officially serving the bakufu, while those of lower formal rank took commensurate employment with daimyo. All were expected to abide by the canons of their school. Kanō Yasunobu, a seventeenth-century head of the main lineage, established the school's priorities, asserting that proper training was more important than natural talent to the creation of consistently good paintings. "To uphold the principles of our art and to pass them accurately on to posterity are the most important tenets of the school, and compared to them the individualism of artists is secondary," he decreed.[1] Strictures on employment and style notwithstanding, lesser Kanō artists supplemented their living by teaching commoners. And while they taught a particular technique rather than artistic crea-

1. Sasaki Jōhei, "The Era of the Kanō School," *Modern Asian Studies* 18-4 (1984): 655. The character of late Tokugawa Kanō painting for the bakufu is nicely conveyed in Penelope E. Mason, "Seisen'in and His Sketches: A Kanō Master and Edo Castle," *MN* 43-2 (June 1988): 187–96.

tivity, their activity spread artistic skills, interest, and taste well beyond the elite.

The rulers abandoned a few cultural practices by choice. Nō, for example, functioned as elite drama during the seventeenth century, thanks to official patronage, but it weakened after 1711, when Arai Hakuseki persuaded the shogun to eliminate it from official functions. Recreational hunting, once an expression of samurai vigor, nearly ceased, despite sporadic attempts by rulers to revitalize samurai skills, and woods and wasteland once reserved for the chase were gradually given over to other uses. But most samurai pretensions fell victim to financial stress. Daimyo and their retainers no longer could afford to build fine gardens or grand mansions or acquire more treasures or hire more actors, artists, or writers; in fact, they could scarcely maintain those they had. Lesser samurai could afford fewer and fewer prized items, and as wealth accumulated elsewhere in society, the goods and services it could buy flowed there as well.

In the end, bushi consumption, which had powered economic growth and sparked cultural life during the early seventeenth century, became a passive force, sustaining some traditional arts and letters but providing the impetus for very little of what was new, creative, and historically significant.

THE DECLINE OF KYOTO'S CULTURAL PRIMACY

The wish of seventeenth-century rulers to keep kuge peacably shut away from politics had the unexpected result, as noted in chapter 10, of mingling courtly accomplishments, chōnin wealth, and resident samurai resources to give the city a century of cultural efflorescence. With the flowering of a more plebeian ukiyo culture, however, Kyoto began sharing its primacy with Osaka, and during the eighteenth century, Edo displaced the two great Kamigata cities as primary source of cultural creativity. With those developments, Kyoto lost dynamism and aesthetic leadership, which may have made nobles all the more protective of their secret traditions and may have contributed to the discontent they evinced during the Takenouchi Shikibu incident and in later decades.

Edo's eclipse of Kyoto was foreshadowed in the careers of the Ogata brothers, Kōrin and Kenzan, whose painting and pottery culminated Kyoto's century of grand decorative (Rinpa) art. Kōrin, as noted in chapter 10, flourished in Kyoto until about 1704 when he moved to Edo, where he accepted daimyo patronage and introduced his artistic style before returning to Kyoto for his final years. His brother, the distinguished potter, also moved to Edo, staying there and actively producing pottery for the rest of his life.

Edo's displacement of Kyoto was implicit in eighteenth-century kokugaku, which was much more closely associated with the former city despite its doctrinal focus on the imperial legacy. Edo's rise is suggested, as well, by the long-term trend in number of publishers in the three cities.

Century	Kyoto	Osaka	Edo
Seventeenth	701	185	242
Eighteenth	536	564	493
Nineteenth	494	504	917

Whereas Kyoto publishing peaked before 1700, that of Edo grew steadily. By the nineteenth century, according to Moriya Katsuhisa, "Edo had come to wield overwhelming power in publishing, surpassing Kyoto and Osaka in both the quality and quantity of its output. This trend is captured in the early modern epigram, 'culture's march eastward.'"[2] One by-product of that shift in publishing was that the Edo dialect gradually displaced that of Kyoto as the norm for representing dialogue, promoting its eventual triumph as the lingua franca of modern Japan.[3]

Finally, Edo's rise to preeminence was apparent in ukiyo culture, as noted below. Kyoto did, of course, remain culturally vital, especially in the world of poetry.[4] However, Kamigata sophisticates no longer had grounds for viewing Edo as a cultural hinterland, their will to believe otherwise notwithstanding.

UKIYO CULTURE AFTER GENROKU

The history of later ukiyo was not all of a piece. Ukiyo zōshi and ningyō jōruri lost vitality, to be replaced by new developments, but haikai,

2. Katsuhisa Moriya, "Urban Networks and Information Networks," in Chie Nakane and Shinzaburō Oishi, eds., Tokugawa Japan (Tokyo: University of Tokyo Press, 1990), p. 115. The publishers' figures appear on the same page.
3. H. B. D. Clarke, "The Development of Edo Language," in C. Andrew Gerstle, ed., 18th Century Japan (Sydney: Allen & Unwin, 1989), pp. 63–72. Cecilia Segawa Seigle, "The Impact of Yoshiwara Courtesans on An'ei-Tenmei Edo," Japan Foundation Newsletter 14-2 (July 1986): 12–16, conveys the flavor of this emergent Edo cultural influence.
4. Leon Zolbrod, "The Busy Year: Buson's Life and Work, 1777," TASJ 4th ser., 3 (1988): 53–81, captures the tenor of this Kyoto poetic life.

kabuki, and ukiyo-e broadened their social appeal and enriched their content.

HAIKAI

Before his death in 1694, Matsuo Bashō single-handedly transformed haikai into a sophisticated poetic form known to versifiers throughout the land, giving it a following that extended far beyond the urban realm of contemporary ukiyo culture. After his passing, afficionadoes wrote haikai by the bushel, but the form tended to revert to its older character as a popular but trivial exercise in wordplay. In Edo, particularly, haikai became a mark of glib cleverness, long on arcane allusions but short on poetic quality. Elsewhere it tended toward a banality only occasionally relieved by gifted poets.

One such was Kaga no Chiyojo, a resident of Kaga province, artisan's daughter, graceful painter, and the most famous haikai poetess. She crafted some exquisite poems:[5]

> The well-rope has been
> captured by morning-glories—
> I'll borrow water.

> The butterfly—
> what are the dreams that make him
> flutter his wings?

Both poems allude to earlier literary works, one Japanese and one Chinese, but both can stand on their own, achieving independent richness of imagery and evoking real feelings with a wonderful economy of words.

Little is known about Chiyojo, even though her poems are among the best of the countrified haikai that valued simple and direct expressiveness.[6] Much more is known about Yosa (Taniguchi) Buson, a haikai poet who reflected several trends of his day.

Buson, born in 1716, was the son not of a samurai, physician, or rich merchant but of a well-to-do farmer in a village on the southeast edge of Osaka. In the manner of successful farm families of the day, his father gave him a good education, schooling him in both Chinese literature and the Japanese classics. At twenty, Buson went to Edo, where he

5. Donald Keene, *World within Walls* (New York: Grove Press, 1976), p. 340.
6. Fumiko Y. Yamamoto, "Haiku Poet-Painters Chiyo and Kikusha: Two Haiku Poets," in Patricia Fister, *Japanese Women Artists, 1600–1900* (Lawrence: Spencer Museum of Art, University of Kansas, 1988), pp. 55–56, provides information on Chiyo.

studied acting, haikai, Chinese poetry, and painting. In 1742 he left the city for a decade of travel and poetic study, paying his way with freelance painting. He settled in Kyoto in 1751, marrying, raising a daughter, and spending most of his remaining years there. He strove to master a variety of skills and imbued his haikai with sharp images and real, if not deep, feelings. Like others in the emerging bunjin tradition, he found himself precariously balanced between the worlds of amateur aesthete and professional artist, and he supported his family through the sale of paintings, ultimately gaining greater fame as painter than poet.[7]

During Buson's active years, the world of haikai experienced a "back to Bashō" reaction against the shallowness of recent decades. The revival culminated in two celebrations of Bashō's craft. The first, in 1783, was essentially limited to Kyoto, but the second, a decade later on the hundredth anniversary of his death, was a countrywide celebration. That change in scope from citybound to countrywide reflected the end of the Tenmei famine and the diffusion of haikai poetry so widely that "amateur poets from all over the country . . . were affected by the craze for *haikai* and the worship of Bashō."[8]

During the early decades of the nineteenth century, haikai became more of an organized social activity. Groups of amateur poets gathered regularly to compose them, and a national register of 600 haikai poets was compiled in 1813 and supplemented with 120 more names in 1821. By then many of the poets lacked formal poetic training, and Edo had emerged as their predominant location, with others living in the northeast more commonly than the southwest.

Of the early nineteenth-century poets, one stands out for his richness of sensibility, Kobayashi Issa, writer of poetry and prose and the son of a middling farmer from a village in northern Shinano province. Schooled in Edo, he spent most of his life there, returning to Shinano in 1813. His haikai were of many styles, humorous, lyrical, or deeply moving as his mood dictated:[9]

> When he looks at me
> what a sour face he makes,
> that frog over there!

7. Zolbrod, "Busy Year," outlines Buson's life. His financial arrangements are explored in Mark Morris, "Group Portrait with Artist: Yosa Buson and His Patrons," in Gerstle, ed., *18th Century Japan*, pp. 87–104.
8. Keene, *World within Walls*, p. 360.
9. Ibid., p. 366. For a valuable introduction and translation of Issa's journal of his father's illness and death, see Robert N. Huey, "Journal of My Father's Last Days: Issa's *Chichi no Shūen Nikki*," MN 39-1 (Spring 1984): 25–54.

But when his young daughter Sato died, he wrote:

> The world of dew
> is a world of dew, and yet,
> and yet . . .

UKIYO ZŌSHI

Haikai thus experienced a revival during the eighteenth century, growing into a popular nationwide recreational activity by the nineteenth.
Ukiyo zōshi left a strikingly less fruitful record after Genroku; indeed
those "stories of the floating world" proved the least viable of its cultural legacies. Ihara Saikaku's death in 1693 left the field to others, and
a number of weak imitators and plagiarists, mostly in the Kamigata
cities, turned his legacy to profit during the next two decades. As noted
in chapter 10, Ejima Kiseki was the most original and effective of his
successors: "though . . . an uncertain moralist, he knew what his readers liked." [10] His stories of the licensed quarters and his character sketches,
most popularly sketches of courtesans, were published by the Hachimonji-
ya in Osaka, but he shrewdly aimed them at townsmen in all three
major cities, assuring their sale in all three markets.

From the 1720s on, Kiseki ceased writing, and only one later author
of ukiyo zōshi, Tada Nanrei, who also wrote for the Hachimonji-ya,
enjoyed notable popular acclaim. Even his pieces, mostly character
sketches dating from the 1740s, seem derivative and detached, and after
his death the genre was unable to sustain a publishing house. Only a
handful of ukiyo zōshi appeared in following decades, and they came
from writers such as Ueda Akinari, who, like Nanrei, treated ukiyo
zōshi as frivolous digressions from their other literary efforts. Invented
during Osaka's heyday, ukiyo zōshi remained embedded in the city, and
the genre was left behind when Edo displaced the Kamigata cities as
Japan's literary center.

KABUKI AND NINGYŌ JŌRURI

The puppet theater (ningyō jōruri) outlasted ukiyo zōshi but fared poorly
compared to kabuki. After Chikamatsu's death in 1724, the two theaters energetically competed for audience appeal, and for a few decades

10. Howard Hibbett, The Floating World in Japanese Fiction (London: Oxford University Press, 1959), p. 61.

puppets retained their favored standing. Later in the century, however, their dominance gave way to a long era of kabuki vitality. The live theater consolidated its gains near century's end, when it successfully shifted its center from Osaka to Edo, gaining popularity among samurai there and leaving the puppet theater to decline along with its home city.

Puppeteers and playwrights in Osaka worked energetically to sustain audience interest after Chikamatsu's death. New plays, while often heavily reliant on his works, came to be characterized by gimmicks, surprises, and exaggerated mixtures of fantasy and "realism," enhanced by ever more complex stage arrangements. Costumes and sets became more lavish and colorful. Puppets became more complicated during the 1730s, acquiring movable mouths, hands that could grasp and later fingers that could flex, eyes that opened and shut and eventually rolled, and even eyebrows that moved. After 1734 three men per puppet were required to operate these elegant devices.

In the 1740s a series of lively new puppet plays appeared, primarily the creations of Takeda Izumo II and his associates at the Takemoto theater in Osaka.[11] Using the recent technical developments to grand effect, their plays made the theater a spectacle for the eyes, whereas Chikamatsu's had appealed primarily to the ear. Besides plays about distraught lovers and daily lives they produced bombastic stories of samurai heroes, culminating in 1748 in *Kanadehon chūshingura,* the most sensational of the many theatrical adaptations of the incident of 1702 (mentioned in chapter 10) when forty-seven ronin wreaked their revenge on a bakufu official for ruining their lord and domain.[12]

In later years the puppet theater never regained its glory of the 1740s, occasional successes notwithstanding, and live theater surpassed it in popularity. Kabuki converted the most successful puppet plays, including *Chūshingura,* to its own use and outdid it in gadgetry and glitter. It left its rival behind in 1796, when Namiki Gohei, the dominant play-

11. Stanleigh H. Jones, Jr., *Sugawara and the Secrets of Calligraphy* (New York: Columbia University Press, 1985), pp. 1–26, provides a valuable introduction to the operation of the Osaka puppet theater during its heyday in the 1740s, and its influence on kabuki and theater in Edo.

12. Donald Keene, tr., *Chūshingura* (New York: Columbia University Press, 1971), consists of a brief introduction, which discusses various dramatic treatments of the incident, and a complete translation of the puppet play. More recent works of note on plays about the Akō incident are James R. Brandon, ed., *Chūshingura: Studies in Kabuki and the Puppet Theatre* (Honolulu: University of Hawaii Press, 1982), which contains a kabuki version of *Chūshingura,* and Jacqueline Mueller, "A Chronicle of Great Peace Played Out on a Chessboard: Chikamatsu Monzaemon's *Goban Taiheiki,*" *HJAS* 46-1 (June 1986): 221–67.

wright of the day, moved from Osaka to Edo, where he successfully tapped into the largest urban audience in the world.

Because kabuki used real people rather than puppets, it easily won the competition to be more "realistic." It also developed more impressive stage devices. In 1727 an Osaka producer constructed a trap lift to elevate scenery to stage level, and during the 1730s trap lifts were added to bring actors to the stage. In 1758 Namiki Shōzō, Gohei's teacher, had a revolving stage installed in his theater in Osaka, and in 1761 a rival Osaka theater added a marvelous contraption, the *gando gaeshi*, which enabled the stage operator to pivot one large piece of scenery onto its side so as to reveal a different one. The devices were employed in Edo, and in 1827 a theater there added a second, counter-revolving, inner stage.

While these successive additions were multiplying the ways in which people and props could reach and move about the stage, the stage itself was becoming larger and more elaborate. It was broadened and deepened, with sections developed to serve as indoor and outdoor settings. And runways passing through the audience (*hanamichi*) were added, one in the 1720s, a second in 1772, and a third that linked the two in 1780. By then, according to Earle Earnst, the layout of a kabuki stage was that shown in figure 18.[13]

The changes in stage arrangement were clearly intended to enhance kabuki as visual spectacle. Playwrights pursued the same goal, devising scripts that included violent and macabre scenes, grotesque characters, and bizarre situations. They loaded their plots with surprises, inventive maneuvers, and ever-quicker changes of garb, scenery, and disguise. They added subplots and even introduced real fireworks and live animals as they successfully pursued popularity among the Edo masses, both men and women.

Meanwhile, the theater itself expanded to handle the larger audiences. One floor of side boxes became two, the rear section of the pit was changed to boxes, and that row raised and converted into two. An unused stage corner was converted to cheap standing-room audience use and later double-tiered. Official size limits were surreptitiously exceeded, and roofs were extended over the pit to make more fully all-weather theaters.

Edo became the heartland of kabuki, but the genre continued to thrive

13. The diagram is adapted from Earle Ernst, *The Kabuki Theatre* (New York: Grove Press, 1956), p. 35.

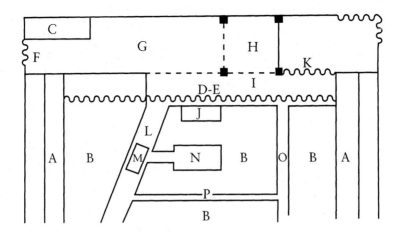

A. Audience boxes
B. Audience seating in pit
C. Audience standing room
D-E. Draw curtains for stage
F. Curtained entrance for actors
G. Bridge to stage
H. Stage proper
I. Forestage

J. Pre-forestage
K. "Hurry door" for actors
L. *Hanamichi*
M. Trap lift
N. Name-calling platform
O. Temporary *hanamichi*
P. Center passageway

18.   Kabuki Stage, ca. 1780.

in the Kamigata cities as well. In all three, kabuki fan clubs (*hiiki ren-chū*) developed by the nineteenth century. They consisted mainly of dilettantish sons of wealthy townsmen who regularly attended the theater, occupied the better seats, lavished gifts on their favorite actors, and handled such chores as theater decoration and seasonal rituals. They also commented freely on plays in progress, applauding their heroes and harassing other actors as they deemed appropriate.[14]

Elsewhere troupes of actors toured the hinterland, producing dramas at theaters scattered about the country and encouraging local folk to put on their own productions. This diffusion of kabuki broadened the genre's social base and worked it into the fabric of a countrywide popular culture.[15]

Nineteenth-century playwrights produced a huge number of kabuki dramas. In more than a hundred full-length, 7–8-hour plays Tsuruya

14. S. Matsudaira, "Hiiki Renchū (Theatre Fan Clubs) in Osaka in the Early Nineteenth Century," *Modern Asian Studies* 18-4 (1984): 699–709.
15. Anne Walthall, "Peripheries: Rural Culture in Tokugawa Japan," *MN* 39-4 (Winter 1984): 379–82, discusses rural theater very perceptively.

Nanboku IV dazzled his Edo audiences with preposterous stories and breath-taking visual effects. And Kawatake Mokuami, the last great figure of the age, produced during his career 130 domestic plays, 90 historical ones, and 140 dance plays. Some were of considerable literary merit, but the popular triumph of kabuki was based on its capacity to appeal to an urban audience that clearly welcomed exciting, escapist spectacle.

Kabuki producers knew as well as Hollywood moguls that sex sells. A critic in 1816 wrote about the decay of public morals:

> Up to seventy or eighty years ago the amorous play of men and women was suggested by an exchange of glances; if the man ever took the woman's hand, she would cover her face with her sleeve in embarrassment. That was all there was to it, but even so, old people of the time are said to have been shocked by what they deemed to be an unsightly exhibition. Women in the audience were also very modest, and would blush even at the famous scene in Chūshingura in which Yuranosuke takes Okaru in his arms as he helps her down the ladder. Nowadays sexual intercourse is plainly shown on the stage, and women in the audience watch on, unblushing, taking it in their stride. It is most immoral.[16]

One suspects that the moralist's memory was a bit faulty, but his comments surely reveal qualities that contributed to kabuki's success as popular entertainment.

In 1841, during the Tenpō reform effort of the bakufu leader Mizuno Tadakuni, a city fire destroyed Edo's three kabuki theaters. Doubtless the salaciousness on stage contributed to Mizuno's decision to order them rebuilt in Saruwaka-chō (modern-day Asakusa), an inconvenient area near the Yoshiwara licensed quarter on the edge of town. He also attempted to resegregate the residential arrangements of actors, to reduce their personal contact with "honorable" people, and to force them to live frugally and produce plays that would "encourage virtue and chastise vice." Within a few years, however, that attempt at moral rectification passed and kabuki regained its central cultural role in the city, continuing it beyond the fall of the Tokugawa regime.

UKIYO-E PRINTS

Ukiyo art originally encompassed both paintings and prints.[17] During Genroku, however, prints came to predominate because they were ame-

16. Keene, *World within Walls*, p. 458.
17. This discussion of *ukiyo* prints is based essentially on Richard Lane, *Images from the Floating World* (New York: G. P. Putnam's Sons, 1978).

nable to a sort of mass production that made them cheaply and widely accessible. Thereafter, prints dominated the genre, although ukiyo painting survived. Like kabuki, printmaking flourished, growing aesthetically richer as decades passed. Indeed, by the nineteenth century it had evolved more than kabuki, broadening its range of interests so effectively and adopting elements from other genres so skillfully that it sustained an appreciably higher aesthetic level than did the late Tokugawa stage.

Several factors contributed to the continuing vitality of ukiyo art. Unlike puppet theater, the print industry was not threatened by Edo's rise, because prints already were a Kantō specialty when seventeenth-century Kamigata aesthetes still preferred paintings. In fact, during the eighteenth century, ukiyo prints were often referred to as *Edo-e,* or Edo pictures. Moreover, printmakers found ways to exploit their craft's mass-production potential without sacrificing the quality demanded by connoisseurs. In addition, they learned how to produce fully colored prints (*nishiki-e*), devised other techniques of representation, and broadened the range of subjects portrayed, thereby sustaining artistic creativity and widening their consumer appeal.

To elaborate, essentially two elements were involved in the mass production of woodblock prints. One was creation of a production team of artist, engraver, and printer that was linked to a funding source, whether publisher or patron. The other was multiplication of prints knocked off from each set of blocks. In the early days, printers produced anywhere from forty to eighty sheets per block before discarding it as worn out. As demand grew, however, the number increased, and by the nineteenth century a single set of color blocks might yield thousands of prints. The blocks retained sharp edges only during production of the first prints, however, so the quality of later ones was clearly inferior, which led makers to identify prints as first, second, and later editions, and to price them accordingly. By producing large issues, printers could keep the price of later editions down, and for many customers the distinctions in quality were immaterial, while the lower cost was crucial.

Printmakers also promoted a mass consumer base by diversifying the sizes, shapes, and functions of prints. Seventeenth-century prints lacked the variety of ukiyo paintings, which were produced as single sheets and in book format, were mounted on screens and horizontal and vertical scrolls, and provided miniatures for use on fans or other small surfaces. But from Genroku on, prints appeared in ever more varied sizes for use in books or scrolls and as single sheets or triptyches. By 1800 printmakers had added yet more sizes of regular prints, developed prints as New Year's cards and calendar sheets, and devised extremely long, thin prints (pillar prints or *hashira-e*) for display on the exposed studs of interior walls.

To retain their wealthy clientele while catering to the masses, printmakers produced private editions for greeting cards, musical programs, private announcements, and vanity verse collections. For such occasions and for regular color prints aimed at the affluent, they used especially costly cherry-wood blocks and superior paper and made more ample use of color from more precious dyes. In the upshot, they succeeded in retaining their choosy rich clientele while selling, as well, to hoi polloi.

The mastery of color technique was the single most striking stylistic development of the eighteenth century. As earlier noted, Genroku prints were produced in black and white and then colored by hand. The decorative splashes of orange and green added to the earliest prints (*tan-e*) gave way during the early eighteenth century to prints colored much more extensively with two or three shades of lacquer (*urushi-e*). The frugality edicts of the Kyōhō reform, the urban stress caused by recoinage, and the hardship of famine and economic disorder during the early 1730s discouraged the print industry for a while, but by 1740, as tax collection improved and urban wealth increased, it revived.

During the 1740s, the print industry enjoyed a revitalization in conjunction with the last flowering of ukiyo zōshi and puppets. Artists produced more elaborate prints, such as the hand-colored representation of the kabuki theater done in 1740 by Okumura Masanobu, which portrays an Edo theater before a second runway and revolving stage were added. Three years later, Torii Kiyotada produced a double-sized *urushi-e* print that replicated Masanobu's treatment of the same theater.[18] More important for the future of prints than largeness of scale, however, were other innovations that began to appear at this time, especially printing in color.

To make colored prints, the engraver carved additional blocks, one for each desired color. The crucial technical requirements were that he carve the additional blocks in exactly the correct places and that the printer align each one with the basic black-and-white print so that it receive the added color precisely where intended. Okumura Masanobu

---

18. Lane, *Images*, p. 77, reproduces Kiyotada's *urushi-e* print.

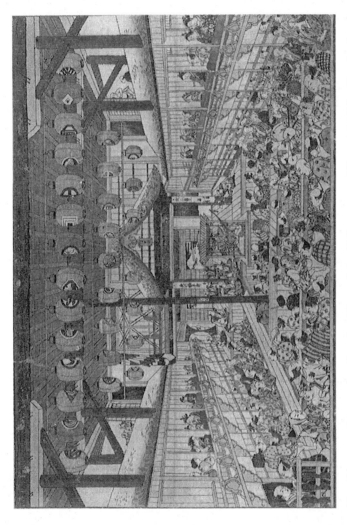

19.   Okumura Masanobu, *Interior View of the Nakamura-za Theater in Edo.* Hand-colored woodblock print, 1740, 46.3 x 67.9 cm. In this large, highly detailed print, Masanobu employed *uki-e* perspective to represent a midcentury kabuki theater with its well-developed stage and audience areas, full roof overhead, and residual nō-stage roof. Courtesy of the Art Institute of Chicago. Clarence Buckingham Collection. Acc. #1925.2285. Photograph © 1991. All Rights Reserved.

of Edo perfected the technique in the late 1730s, initially adding two colors, generally rose and green, to his basic prints. By the 1750s, with sales covering greater production costs, some prints sported three or four colors, but the basic rose-and-green print (*benizuri-e*) dominated ukiyo art for another decade.

It was the Edo printmaker Suzuki Harunobu who established the full-color print, the *nishiki-e* or "brocade print," as the norm. By skillfully appealing to his moneyed clientele, he was able from about 1765 to develop color printing into an elaborate and profitable industry that combined the skills and resources of artist, engraver, printer, publisher, and patron. Once established, brocade prints became dominant, prevailing for the rest of the Tokugawa period despite sporadic attempts by government to contain their luxuriance.

Successive generations of printmakers enriched the genre with other techniques. Besides developing color printing, Masanobu experimented with a technique called *ishizuri,* or "stone rubbing," in which a print's background was blackened and its lines appeared white. Some later print makers used the method, but it never gained wide popularity. Artists tried other background techniques. Suzuki Harunobu, for example, sometimes employed a single solid color and at other times treated the paper to achieve a wood-grain-like effect. Artists often used cloud-like formations to create blank space, but from the late eighteenth century they more often filled their backgrounds with detail as part of a quest for "realistic" portrayal. They also devised ways to depict atmospherics such as rain, wind, mist, or falling snow, the landscape prints of Andō (Utagawa) Hiroshige showing such techniques with particular clarity.

Another area of new technique was adoption, via the Dutch at Dejima, of European artistic elements. Most notable was European-style perspective, as employed by Masanobu and Kiyotada in their representations of the kabuki theater. Utagawa Toyoharu developed the perspective print (*uki-e*) much more thoroughly, during the 1770s and 1780s creating lavish "wide-angle" representations of city scenes, historical vistas, and landscapes that foreshadowed the gorgeous creations of the nineteenth-century artists Hiroshige and Katsushika Hokusai.

As print techniques grew more varied, so too did their range of topics, although urban life and especially the worlds of the licensed quarter and the theater predominated throughout the eighteenth century. Erotic prints remained popular, with artists devising ever-more-preposterous situations in their ceaseless quest for the new and different. The genre

had such intrinsic limitations, however, that the most creative and original print work treated other subjects.

Feminine beauty itself remained the central interest of printmakers.
Most commonly courtesans were the subjects, but later a variety of
women appeared, highly idealized by some artists, treated more realistically by others. Stylistic preferences ebbed and flowed. Early in the
century, Kaigetsudō Ando and his successors painted and printed voluptuous courtesan beauties with boldly colored, gloriously flowing robes
that reflected the kimono style of the day. By the 1760s those images
had been displaced by Harunobu's willowy evocations of eternal girl-
hood and during the 1780s by Torii Kiyonaga's more realistic treatment
of townswomen. Like Kaigetsudō, Kitagawa Utamaro evoked an idealized femininity near century's end, but his women were clothed in less
showy garb, were much more demure and self-possessed, and conveyed
a more subdued, if no less powerful, sensuality.

Kabuki actors were another mainstay of ukiyo prints, and like the
women they were subjected to varying treatment. Especially from the
later eighteenth century on, when kabuki dominated the world of drama,
actors were depicted in their most popular roles, especially as samurai.
The most striking actor prints, those that captured individuality most
powerfully, were by an elusive artist, Tōshūsai Sharaku. Reputedly a
nō actor employed by the daimyo of Tokushima, Sharaku evidently
produced prints for only a few months in 1794–95.

By then printmakers had produced prints on an array of subjects—
children, poets, priests, diverse townsmen, animals, demons, street scenes,
party scenes, people on outings, and a host of historical events—often
using them as vehicles for portraying beauties of the day. A few pictured
travel scenes or rural folk, and from the 1770s on, with full-color printing established and "realism" in vogue, landscapes began to assume
more and more importance. Utagawa Toyoharu, as noted above, used
European-style perspective effectively to portray cityscapes of remarkable liveliness, and Torii Kiyonaga skillfully combined foreground figures and background scenery in handsomely designed, richly textured
prints.

Landscape as subject triumphed in the nineteenth-century works of
Hokusai and Hiroshige. Hokusai, born in Edo in 1760, was an eclectically trained artist who studied the several traditions of Japanese art, as
well as the Chinese and European ones to which he had access. He tried
diverse techniques and a wide variety of subjects during his early years
and from 1798 began producing collections of vistas, such as his *Tōto*

meisho ichiran. After three more decades of active printmaking, he produced another major landscape series, *Fugaku sanjū rokkei.* In that series the natural landscape itself became the focus of attention in several prints, while in others he combined Mount Fuji in the background with some foreground example of human endeavor, such as logging, fishing, boating, or packhorsing.

Hiroshige, born the son of an Edo fireman in 1797, was less well trained than Hokusai and never developed his array of skills. He produced undistinguished prints on the customary themes of women and actors until around 1830 when he, like Hokusai, turned to landscapes. For nearly three decades after that, however, he created series after series on highways, cities, and "famous places," including his *Tōkaidō gojūsan tsugi.* Combining an imaginative sense of design and love of color, he produced works that integrated human figures and landscape with unprecedented warmth and intimacy. His works, like those of Hokusai, appealed to people throughout Japan, helping transform the metropolitan tradition of ukiyo prints into a facet of national culture, much as the spread of kabuki performances and haikai poetry had transformed those urban cultural inventions into elements of the entire country's cultural legacy.

One suspects that Hiroshige's landscape prints won such affection because he invested so much love in them. In 1858, after a life of immense productivity, he composed this farewell verse.

> Leaving my brush behind in Edo,
> I set forth on a new journey:
> let me sightsee all the famous views
> in Paradise.[19]

19. Ibid., p. 184.

PART FIVE

The Erosion of Stability, 1790–1850

This study of early modern Japan began with the formation of the To-kugawa order and ends with its destruction. Like political structures elsewhere, the Tokugawa order emerged from blood-soaked battle-fields. It disappeared the same way. Accordingly, Part II began with an examination of politics and moved on to look at the economic, intellec-tual, and cultural aspects of early Tokugawa history. In Part V the se-quence is reversed, beginning with cultural and intellectual history and ending with a narrative of nineteenth-century politics that focuses on the interplay of domestic and foreign affairs.

Diplomatic matters command attention because during the decades after 1790 unprecedented foreign problems confronted Japan's rulers. The problems were produced by industrializing Euro-American soci-eties that slowly established their commercial, political, and intellectual presence in East Asia. In the process they presented political demands that none of the polities there, the Tokugawa included, was capable of handling. It is obvious in hindsight and it became apparent—slowly and painfully—to participants of the day that the new foreign demands were forcing Japan's early modern order to change radically, and the history of Japan after 1790 can be viewed as the story of that change.

One need not, of course, view the history of Japan from 1790 to 1850 only in synchronic terms of global history. Approaching it in diachronic terms of Japan's own history, one can see it as a segment of the period of stasis that dates from about 1710. As noted in chapter 13, changes in the pattern of natural resource exploitation began appearing in the eighteenth century, and from about 1790 they translated into a modest, erratic, and regionally imbalanced renewal of population growth that suggested the early modern stasis was starting to come unglued.

Within this context of a modestly expanding energy base, a number of cultural changes also appeared. In terms of aesthetics, nineteenth-century kabuki, haikai, and ukiyo-e were supplemented by new styles of art, popular fiction, and poetry and by emergence of the bunjin aesthetic among the urban elite. In education, from the 1780s on, a striking expansion in han academies, *terakoya* (small local schools), and religious schools occurred. It was facilitated by rulers who responded to the worsening problems of the day by trying to improve their retainers' competence while strengthening ideological control over them. Schooling was also bolstered by politicized people who pursued learning in hopes of finding ways to deal with those problems. And it was promoted by landlords who took pride in cultural accomplishments and could afford to promote them among the more well-to-do segments of rural society.

In higher thought, the decades were notable for their politically engaged scholarship—notably Mitogaku, kokugaku, and rangaku—which was more radical or shrill than that of earlier decades. Confucian scholars also evinced renewed vitality, stimulated, as were other intellectuals, by the foreign problem. There were new religious movements of a more popular nature. Some, notably Shingaku and Hōtoku, were basically conservative, system-affirming developments while others, including local cults and millennialist movements, probably should be seen as expressions of alienation from the existing order, although not all were accompanied by politically significant social protest.

In politics, the rulers, spurred by the vigor of intellectual movements that seemed to threaten entrenched interests and values, tried to control opinion more rigorously by guiding thought and restricting its range. That strategy, sharply enunciated by Matsudaira Sadanobu around 1790, was pursued erratically thereafter by bakuhan leaders who tried to manage schooling and suppress unacceptable ideas. Diplomatic crises strengthened the leaders' interest in thought control, as did changes in the scale and tenor of public unrest.

Another thread of late Tokugawa politics was the emergence of "Edo-centrism," a tension between Edo and the hinterland that reflected the city's growth into a monstrous political-economic-cultural center that was both the engine driving Japan and a great octopus consuming society's resources. A related trend that was evident by 1790 was the regionalism that stemmed from the basic tension between northeast and southwest Japan. Rooted in dissimilarities of historical and economic experience, the tension was exacerbated by foreign encroachments.

The political stresses imbedded in thought control, Edo-centrism, and regionalism were fueled by the chronic fiscal problems that ate away at both bakufu and han, most severely during periods of environmental crisis such as the 1830s. The stresses were heightened by the approach of foreigners, which intensified ideological fears and forced governments to expend resources on defense work. That work increased the demand for corvée labor, already straining to handle river work, by requiring porters and packhorses to move more people and goods and carry out fortification projects. More fundamentally, foreign contacts highlighted the intrinsic weakness of the bakuhan system as a structure for coping with external threats. At first, because of Russian encroachment via Ezo, these several effects bore most heavily on the northeast, but from the 1840s Euro-American encroachment from the south forced southwesterners to confront the danger.

The intensified political stresses of the nineteenth century led bakuhan leaders to make greater demands on their vassal forces even as they tried to save money by slashing samurai stipends. Those trends, together with the pressure for ideological obedience that restricted schooling choices and periodically led to punishment of the intellectually incautious, heightened tensions between rulers and vassals and between rulers and politically conscious thinkers. The situation prompted some officials to opt out of service and pursue the lives of bunjin, while other observers pursued reformist lines of thought. During the Tenpō famine, rage led a few people to attempt coups d'état, and from the 1850s on, samurai disillusionment with the established order—or at least with its operatives—grew rampant as foreigners ran roughshod over Japan.

EIGHTEEN

Later Tokugawa Arts and Letters

New Influences in Painting
  Nanga and the *Bunjin* Ideal
  European Art and Realism
New Genres in Literature
  Serious Prose
  Popular Prose
New Trends in Poetry
  Waka
  Kanshi

Late Tokugawa cultural history displayed two notable characteristics. One was the emergence of Edo as the cultural center of the realm; the other was creation of a body of arts and letters that was shared countrywide by urban and rural folk. The enriched traditions of haikai, kabuki, and ukiyo-e that chapter 17 explored were important aspects of that shared, Edo-centered culture. Other aspects were developments in prose, poetry, and art that owed less to the earlier Tokugawa heritage.

The ideal of cultural cosmopolitanism imbedded in the concepts of *bun* and *yūgei* and in the lives of literati such as Yosa Buson was reflected at a cruder public level in the diversity of this broadly shared culture. A passage quoted in chapter 10 described the Shijō entertainment district in Kyoto around 1660, with its eating places, diverse theaters, and myriad wayside entertainers and sideshows. By the nineteenth century, mass entertainment was even more variegated, and the pricing and content suggest that it was pitched to an even more plebeian audience of old, young, men, women, tourists, migrant laborers, and others. A description of the scene near a theater at the Ryōgoku bridge in Edo in the mid 1800s mentions[1]

> the "Three Sisters" female kabuki, peep shows of *Chūshin-gura, Naniwa-bushi* chanting . . . beggar's opera . . . raconteurs, archery booths, barber-shops, massage healers, and around them peddlers of toys, loquat leaf broth, chilled water, . . . confectionery, chilled and solidified agar-agar jelly, *sushi,* tempura, dumplings, stuffed Inari fritters, fried eel livers, insects, lanterns, as well as wandering masseurs and Shinnai balladeers, peddlers of all sorts, blowgun booths, . . . fortune-sellers with lanterns dangling from their collars, vendors of "streetwalker" noodles, drunks, quarrels, pests, public urination.

In the hinterland as well, cultural-recreational activities acquired more variety locally—but more homogeneity overall—as home-grown recreation was supplemented by itinerant troupes and individuals who traveled the highways in pursuit of their trades and/or aesthetic ideals, in the process bringing urban arts and letters to the hinterland. Moreover, the well-to-do villagers who emerged with rural socioeconomic change pursued learning, enjoyed more cultural amenities, and displayed the noblesse oblige expected of them by encouraging religious festivals and other forms of local entertainment. The rulers, who wished villagers to produce much and consume little, might not approve, as in 1827 when a bakufu decree "forbade villagers to provide lodging for traveling players, jugglers, monkey trainers, bell ringers, takers of oaths, reciters of plays, and all other entertainers."[2] But the rulers were too few, too far away, and too full of more pressing concerns to enforce such bans.

The new genres of arts and letters did not arise randomly. Rather, they appeared in almost inverse proportion to the later success of ukiyo traditions. The continuing vitality of kabuki and its skill in appealing to the public obviated the emergence of a new theater. Similarly the popularity of ukiyo prints left little room for rival popular art. Among sophisticates, on the other hand, ukiyo-e did face competition from important new genres of painting despite the attempts of printmakers to cater to refined—or at least monied—tastes. Haikai satisfied the general public's need for poetic expression but proved inadequate for more ambitious intellectual agendas, and other forms of poetry rose to meet that need. Most strikingly, in the field of prose, as ukiyo zōshi sank into

1. Andrew L. Markus, "The Carnival of Edo: *Misemono* Spectacles from Contemporary Accounts," *HJAS* 45-2 (Dec. 1985): 509.
2. Anne Walthall, "Peripheries: Rural Culture in Tokugawa Japan," *MN* 39-4 (Winter 1984): 389.

torpor, a wide array of new forms arose to take its place. So this discussion of new departures examines painting, prose, and poetry.

NEW INFLUENCES IN PAINTING

Not all late Tokugawa art was new or popular. A few artists linked to the kuge in Kyoto preserved the Tosa artistic tradition. A larger number perpetuated the Kanō style, many by providing instruction in Kanō technique even to ukiyo printmakers. Ukiyo prints remained the predominant pictorial art of commoners, at least in the cities, but other popular forms survived, notably Ōtsu-e, which flourished from the 1660s. Ōtsu-e were crude paintings that depicted folk tales and other popular themes, most of them produced by anonymous local artisans for travelers passing through Ōtsu on the Tōkaidō. Finally, some traditional themes such as ghosts and demons enjoyed a vigorous revival during the later Tokugawa period, being represented in both paintings and prints.[3]

Two major artistic traditions of foreign origin were introduced during the eighteenth century. The more influential of the two was *nanga,* or "southern painting." Nanga was associated with bunjin, the literati or leisured artist-scholars of Chinese tradition, and so was known also as *bunjinga (wen jen hua* in Chinese), or literati art. The other was European art, introduced via the Dutch at Nagasaki. Whereas nanga was adopted as an artistic whole, however, European art was exploited selectively by artists working in other styles who wished to achieve more realistic visual representation.

NANGA AND THE *BUNJIN* IDEAL

Literati painting was introduced by Chinese immigrants to Nagasaki.[4] Some were traders who imported works of art. Some were political

3. The art of ghosts and demons is examined in the delightfully illustrated collection of essays, Stephen Addiss, ed., *Japanese Ghosts & Demons: Art of the Supernatural* (New York: George Braziller, 1985). Ōtsu-e is discussed briefly in Cornelis Ouwehand, *Namazu-e and Their Themes* (Leiden: E. J. Brill, 1964), pp. 43–50.
4. The artistic impact of Chinese visitors on Japan was the focus of the exhibition that is presented in Stephen Addiss, ed., *The Japanese Quest for a New Vision: The Impact of Visiting Chinese Painters, 1600–1900* (Lawrence: Spencer Museum of Art, University of Kansas, 1986). See also Addiss, "Ōbaku: The Art of Chinese Huang-po Monks in Japan," *Oriental Art* 24-4 (Winter 1978): 420–32; James Cahill, "Phases and Modes in the Transmission of Ming-Ch'ing Painting Style to Edo Period Japan," and Yu Yiaohu (Joan Stanley-Baker), "The Ōbaku Connection: One Source of Potential Chinese Influence on Early Tokugawa Painting," both in Yue-him Tam, ed., *Sino-Japanese Cultural Interchange: Aspects of Archaeology and Art History* (Hong Kong: Chinese University of Hong Kong, 1985), pp. 65–97, 99–154.

refugees and others were prelates associated with the newly introduced Ōbaku sect of Zen Buddhism, which developed in Japan from the 1660s as a by-product of the Manchu conquest. Ōbaku leaders established their headquarters temple, Manpukuji, at Uji on a parcel of land given them by retired emperor Gomizuno-ō. Connections to bakufu leaders, especially Tsunayoshi, aided the sect's rapid expansion in the Kantō. Ōbaku continued to employ prelates from China, and they offered instruction in nanga as well as other continental arts and letters.

The Chinese at Nagasaki, notably Shen Nan-p'in, who arrived in 1731 and supported himself teaching art, introduced not only nanga but also the broader bunjin ideal that underlay it. In China bunjin were those who abandoned the Confucian role of society's servant-teacher-ruler in favor of the Taoist role of recluse devoted to pursuit of the Way. The posture enjoyed contemporary political éclat as an expression of anti-Manchu sentiment. Bunjin cultivated artistic sensibilities as part of their spiritual quest, and painting was central to the effort. Believing their art to be more creative and individualistic than the stylistically acceptable work of professionals who painted on commission for governments, temples, and wealthy patrons, bunjin set theirs apart by calling it "southern art" and that of professionals "northern art."

Chinese nanga artists stressed the kinship of painting and calligraphy. They were more concerned with the act of painting itself than with the representational fidelity of the result, believing that the quality of brushwork determined how well a painter conveyed his grasp of the "essence of nature."[5] Most often they depicted images inspired by poetic references that expressed the ideal of social disengagement. They used distinctive brush techniques to picture eye-catching scenes, such as mountains towering over diminutive human figures or sheltering primitive huts. In China the genre was venerable, and differences in style were clearly defined by the 1700s. Because Japanese artists initially had limited access to continental nanga, however, they tended to be inventive, ignoring stylistic restraints, injecting humor, and treating subjects that lay outside the canon of Chinese nanga, such as academic bird-and-flower paintings. In consequence they acquired the reputation of eccentrics.

5. Calvin L. French, *The Poet-Painters: Buson and His Followers* (Ann Arbor: University of Michigan Museum of Art, 1974), p. 1. Melinda Takeuchi, "'True' Views: Taiga's *Shinkeizu* and the Evolution of Literati Painting Theory in Japan," *JAS* 48-1 (Feb. 1989): 3–26, examines the rationale by which Japanese nanga painters asserted that their style was superior to both Kanō and Tosa styles and contemporary realistic painting.

In this rather undisciplined way, nanga and the bunjin ideal reached Japan, where they appealed to artists of diverse sorts. Not every painter of nanga succeeded in cultivating the broader polymathic ideal, and some aesthetes pursued the ideal without producing nanga. Surely the yūgei tradition, which also valued broad cultivation, facilitated acceptance of the bunjin ideal. Indeed, the potter Ogata Kenzan, whose life epitomized yūgei, reportedly composed this poem on his deathbed in 1743:

> All my life through
> these eighty-one years
> I have done what I wished
> in my own way—
> the whole world
> in a mouthful.[6]

The statement was untrue by half—of necessity Kenzan supported himself in Edo marketing humdrum ceramic ware—but the sentiment was one a bunjin would have approved.

The bunjin ideal was pursued by some of the most successful nanga artists. A number of them, moreover, were samurai who resigned official posts, sometimes in protest of current policy or conditions, to pursue a life of amateur artistic creativity in the spirit of the Taoist recluse. An early instance was Yanagisawa Kien, a senior retainer of Kōriyama han in Yamato and a student of Ōbaku. He cultivated some sixteen arts, "including calligraphy, poetry, painting, the incense ceremony, sword connoisseurship, and the tea ceremony."[7] He saw himself as a painter in the nanga manner but was in fact an eclectic who freely employed diverse artistic styles.

To retire in favor of the aesthetic life presupposed wealth. For those less privileged or affluent than Kien, the bunjin ideal was harder to realize. Ike (or Ikeno) Taiga, often credited with establishing nanga in Japan, and his artistic wife Gyokuran illustrate the situation.[8] For nearly a decade after they married in 1752, the young Kyoto couple accepted all sorts of painting tasks to eke out a living—decorating outdoor lanterns, tobacco pouches, even fans for dancing girls. Gradually, however, Taiga acquired paying students, and by 1760 both his and Gyo-

6. Masahiko Kawabara, *The Ceramic Art of Ogata Kenzan* (Tokyo: Kodansha, 1979), p. 62.
7. Melinda Takeuchi, "Ike Taiga: A Biographical Study" *HJAS* 43-1 (1983): 150.
8. On Taiga's life, see Takeuchi, "Ike Taiga." Information on Gyokuran is in Patricia Fister, *Japanese Women Artists, 1600–1900* (Lawrence: Spencer Museum of Art, University of Kansas, 1988), pp. 74–75.

kuran's nanga were selling. By the 1770s he was a celebrated artist, having his work exhibited and receiving substantial commissions from diverse sources, which enabled the couple to live a comfortable life despite Taiga's notorious carelessness in domestic finance. In the end they epitomized the mixture of painting for profit and painting for pleasure that characterized Japanese bunjin.

Generally, bunjin were men, but as Gyokuran's experience suggests, some women were able to pursue the bunjin aesthetic ideal. Perhaps the most successful was Kikusha, born in 1753 the daughter of a Chōshū samurai. Well educated as a child, and widowed by the age of twenty-four, but childless, she became a nun and left for the east, trekking through Tōhoku in the tradition of haikai poets. In Kaga she visited the home of the deceased poetess Chiyojo, and at numerous other stops met local masters to study haikai, waka, Chinese poetry (kanshi), calligraphy, and the tea ceremony. In Edo she studied painting and learned to play the seven-string ch'in, a Chinese zither. By 1803 her artistic talents were so well known that the daimyo of Chōshū exchanged verse with her, and in subsequent years she continued traveling about Japan, maintaining a lively engagement with poets and bunjin from Edo to Kyushu.[9]

Yosa Buson, whom we earlier noted as the stellar haikai poet of his day, actually gained greater fame as an artist. His paintings of figures, flowers, birds, and landscapes transcended the bounds of nanga custom, drawing inspiration from both Chinese and Japanese sources, which he reworked to achieve the originality that bunjin valued. What he considered his special contribution, and called haiga, were works that combined painting and poetry. Such combining was a well-established tradition, but Buson aspired to fuse the two, "at a level beyond illustration," by eliminating the arcane and locating the fusion in "the concrete world of familiar objects."[10]

One of Buson's disciples, Matsumura Goshun (Gekkei), went on to combine nanga style with the realistic painting technique of Maruyama Ōkyo, whom we consider below in discussing realism. The result was a new style called Shijō painting, which linked Chinese and European influences and enjoyed considerable popularity into the twentieth century. Nanga itself, however, was so well established by the nineteenth century that the genre lost much of its creativity as artists learned and

    9. Fumiko Y. Yamamoto, "Haiku Poet Painters Chiyo and Kikusha: Two Haiku Poets," in Fister, Japanese Women Artists, pp. 61–67.
    10. French, Poet-Painters, p. 25. The words are those of the author.

heeded the limits of Chinese precedent and the styles of their mentors.

One of the last boldly individualistic nanga painters, and one who epitomized the bunjin ideal, was Uragami Gyokudō. In his own day Gyokudō was a celebrated musician of the seven-string ch'in, but he was also a poet, calligrapher, and painter. His final decade was dominated by his interest in nanga, in which he used powerful brushwork to capture the dynamism of nature.

An official of Okayama han and student of Ōyōmei Confucianism, Gyokudō pursued his artistic interests, music and poetry in particular, while serving his lord. In 1794, however, the fifty-year-old Gyokudō resigned his post after Matsudaira Sadanobu's Kansei reform opened followers of Ōyōmei to ideological criticism, and thereafter he pursued the life of an artistic vagabond. Freed of official duties, he traveled the country, visiting fellow literati, some of them like himself samurai who had left office. He kept up his versifying and ch'in playing but did more and more painting, the proper amount of sake so quickening his hand that, as a friend wrote, "a heavenly refinement would appear in his brushstrokes." With too much drink, however, "one could not perceive the differences between houses, rocks and trees."[11]

Gyokudō suggested his mood at the time of retirement from official life in this little poem, which evinces the stereotypical bunjin self-image:

> Fifty years have passed
>   like a whistle in the wind.
> With clothes patched with lotus leaves,
>   white hair blowing in the breeze,
> I dwell deep in the mist and smoke
>   where no human voice is heard.
> Among the short-tailed deer,
>   I strum my *ch'in*.

He also conveyed the bunjin amateur ideal in an autobiographical comment of about the same time:

> I love to read but have no knowledge of exegesis or etymology. I just read to please my eyes and detest being a "scholar." I love to play the *ch'in* but do not understand its rules; I play just to amuse myself and detest being a "*ch'in* expert." I write not for posterity but merely to transmit my ideas; I detest being a "literatus." I practice calligraphy but do not know the eight rules; I just suit myself and detest being a "calligrapher." I paint without

11. Stephen Addiss, *Tall Mountains and Flowing Waters: The Arts of Uragami Gyokudō* (Honolulu: University of Hawaii Press, 1987), p. 104. The friend was Tano-mura Chikuden, the son of an Oka han physician. Chikuden left his lord's service to become a bunjin. The next three quotations from Gyokudō come from pp. 14, 17, 18.

knowledge of the ancient six laws; it is all done at random and I detest being a "painter."

Another poem written in 1795 captures the mixed sensibility of aging, loneliness, and freedom from duty that he was experiencing as a dedicated bunjin:

> The years have gone by and taken away my rosy cheeks;
> spring comes to greet my white hair.
> A widower alone, unkempt and uncouth,
> I strain my health searching for blossoming trees.
> New worries are expelled by *ch'in* music;
> old faults I wash away in sake.
> Breaking a plum branch, I thrust it into a vase,
> do a drunken dance, and become a child again.

EUROPEAN ART AND REALISM

Interest in artistic realism was stimulated by the enthusiasm for practicality (*jitsugaku*) that we have already seen in the eighteenth-century approach to agronomy, economics, and politics. In art that interest entailed a desire to represent subjects, whether figures, flowers, birds, or landscapes, in a realistic manner, and artists found helpful techniques in both the Chinese and European art styles that reached Japan via Nagasaki.

European art was first introduced to Japan in the Momoyama period, when Japanese painters of *nanban,* or "southern barbarian," art employed European and Japanese techniques to portray European religious, geographic, and social motifs.[12] By 1640 all that was stifled, however, and not until Yoshimune relaxed the ban on information about Europe was a revival of artistic interest possible. When it came, the revival was spurred, no doubt, by fascination with the exotic, but it was sustained by the art's utility in realistic portrayal. From the 1730s a few illustrated Dutch books provided guidance for painters wanting to portray subjects realistically and scholars seeking to depict useful plants and animals. And from the 1740s, as noted in chapter 17, woodblock-print artists began employing a European-inspired perspective in prints known as *uki-e.*

The pivotal figure in eighteenth-century realism was Maruyama Ōkyo,

12. A splendidly illustrated examination of nanban art is Yoshitomo Okamoto, *The Namban Art of Japan* (Tokyo: Weatherhill, 1972).

born a farmer's son in a village just north of Ōtsu in 1733. He initially studied with a Kanō artist in Kyoto but, becoming dissatisfied with Kanō restrictiveness, explored other techniques, including Kōrin's brushwork and the newly popular European perspective. He also studied the style of Shen Nan-p'in and other Chinese artists at Nagasaki, who offered instruction on realistic representation in bird-and-flower paintings. He tried his hand at a wide array of subjects—"figures, landscapes, birds, fish, even puppies"—and during the 1760s emerged as a highly original artist who "painted with enormous care for truthful detail and for actuality of composition."[13] By the 1780s his reputation brought commissions from the imperial family, the bakufu, wealthy merchants, and other patrons. And he operated a school that produced a number of gifted artists, including the above-noted Matsumura Goshun, who consolidated the realist tradition.

Aspects of European-style art were gaining acceptance in Edo and the Kamigata region by midcentury, but serious attention to the genre as a whole came more slowly. Hiraga Gennai, a remarkably eclectic scholar, seems to have initiated serious study of European painting. Born in 1726 the son of a minor samurai in Takamatsu han, Gennai resigned his post after a few years and left home to visit and study in Nagasaki, Edo, and the Kamigata cities. He studied European painting, medicine, botany, zoology, mineralogy, and other sciences, as well as agronomy, practical economics, Chinese thought and literature, and Japanese studies. He advised daimyo on practical affairs, taught European painting, wrote *jōruri* (puppet drama) texts and pulp fiction (*sharebon*), and made pottery.

Gennai's interest in European art developed, it appears, when he visited Nagasaki, possibly as early as 1753 and again in 1770. Although not notably artistic himself, he traveled to Akita in 1773, and there he met the young Akita vassal Odano Naotake, a gifted artist who had studied the Kanō style as well as Chinese realism, and who also produced ukiyo prints. Gennai taught him the basics of European-style perspective and showed him how to depict relief by means of shading, which reportedly "awakened Naotake to the exactness of Western art."[14]

Gennai also taught elements of European art to Naotake's lord, Satake Shozan (Yoshiatsu), and with Shozan's encouragement an art style be-

13. Robert Treat Paine and Alexander Soper, *The Art and Architecture of Japan* (London: Penguin Books, 1974), p. 122.

14. Calvin L. French, *Shiba Kōkan* (Tokyo: Weatherhill, 1974), p. 79.

came established in Akita that combined European techniques and the Chinese realist tradition. Painting should be realistic and practical, wrote Shozan:

> A picture is of value when it accurately represents the thing portrayed. . . . An illustration of a monarch cultivating fields is intended to encourage agriculture; that of a great general in the heat of battle glorifies military strategy. If such pictures are not realistically illustrated, how can they possibly serve their intended purposes?

And in a criticism directly aimed at bunjin artists, he went on: "There is a theory that claims the spirit of a painting is more important than realistic representation; this concept, however, loses sight of the real aim of painting [which is to portray accurately]."[15]

Naotake, meanwhile, moved to Edo to study further with Gennai. There he agreed to illustrate Sugita Genpaku's *Kaitai shinsho,* a translation of a European anatomical text.[16] Naotake died a few years later, but not before encountering Shiba Kōkan, an ambitious and calculating man who went on to become the most distinguished pioneer of the European style in art of the late Tokugawa period.

Kōkan was born around 1740 in an artisan household in Edo.[17] He studied Chinese classics and poetry and Kanō-style painting, but after a year of Kanō he switched to the more realistic bird-and-flower and nanga styles taught by disciples of Shen. By the 1760s he was supporting himself as an artist in the Chinese style, but in 1770 when the celebrated ukiyo print artist Suzuki Harunobu died, he began making and marketing prints. Initially, they were forgeries of Harunobu's work, but after a lucrative year he modified his style and stopped using Harunobu's name. For five years he flourished as a print artist, sometimes using an uki-e perspective, but in 1775 he turned from prints to ukiyo-style painting, which he produced for another five years.

In 1780 Kōkan changed direction again, and the 1780s proved to be a remarkably lively decade for him. His work as an ukiyo artist had spread his reputation through the city, assuring a market for his works.

15. French, *Shiba Kōkan,* pp. 83–84. For the nanga counterargument, see Takeuchi, "'True' Views," pp. 13–14.

16. The story of this translation project is told in Gempaku Sugita, *Dawn of Western Science in Japan* (Tokyo: Hokuseido, 1969). The work that Genpaku and his colleagues translated was *Ontleedkundige Tafelen,* a 1734 Dutch translation by Gerardus Dicten of the 1731 German work, *Tafel Anatomia* (Latin: *Tabulae Anatomicae*) by the German physician Johann Adam Kulmus.

17. This summary of Kōkan's life is based on French, *Shiba Kōkan.* French discusses the problem of dating Kōkan's birth in Appendix V, p. 176.

The more discriminating knew him primarily for his Chinese-style paintings, and he even demonstrated his skills to daimyo and their intimates. Sometime after 1781, he was married, possibly to a woman of samurai status. The marriage was evidently unhappy. Kōkan begot a daughter and then begot himself to bachelorhood again. More important for his artistic career, in 1780 he gained access to a Dutch book on European painting that "described and illustrated in detail methods of sketching, composition, coloring, shading, perspective, landscape painting, portraiture, architectural drawing, ceiling painting, still life, flower painting, and book illustration."[18] The book prompted him to try his hand at the new techniques. Copperplate engraving first caught his fancy and oil painting from about 1784. He gradually gained skill, basing some of his creations on European examples and drawing others from Japanese landscapes, especially during a trip to Nagasaki in 1788.[19]

Thereafter European-style art became Kōkan's forte. He painted a wide variety of subjects—figures, still lifes, landscapes—using both European and indigenous models, but he was most proud of his European-style landscapes, such as *The Shore at Shinagawa*. His technique retained substantial domestic influence, but he came to consider himself "the chief prophet of Western art in Japan," a conviction that led him to attack bunjin art on grounds similar to those used earlier by Satake Shozan.

In 1811 he expanded his critique into a broadside, writing of the Tosa, Kanō and Chinese schools that "none of them knows how to draw Fuji." Kanō Tan'yū was unable to because "he relied exclusively on 'the spirit of the brush' and 'the force of the brush,'" and Chinese-style painters failed because they "paint nameless mountains and call them landscapes." These painters, he said, "draw mountains and water in whatever way strikes them as interesting, giving free play to their brush. This is exactly the same thing as drawing a dream." He also attacked rival European-style artists from the Tōhoku region, notably the copper plate artist Aōdō Denzen, whom Matsudaira Sadanobu patronized. Kōkan complained that he had been painting in the Dutch method for twenty-five years, enjoying great popularity, but people from

18. French, *Shiba Kōkan,* p. 80. The book was Gerard de Lairesse's *Groot Schilderboek* (Amsterdam, 1707). The next several quotations are from pp. 84–85, 114, 107–8, 51.

19. In "Diary of Kōkan's Trip to the West," Donald Keene, *Travelers of a Hundred Ages* (New York: Henry Holt, 1989), discusses Kōkan's trip to Nagasaki and the personality it reveals.

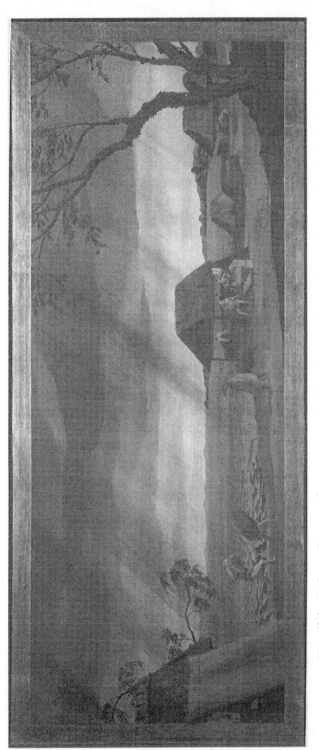

20. Shiba Kōkan, *Shore at Shinagawa*. Panel; ink and color on silk, 59 x 154.5 cm. Kōkan employed European-style perspective and shading in this representation of a rainy-day, highway scene near Shinagawa, just south of Edo. Courtesy of the Museum of Fine Arts, Boston. Fenollosa-Weld Collection. Acc. #11.4686.

the northeast, being "stubborn and opinionated, never changing their minds," had never asked for any of his work: "people from Ōshū have not learned to appreciate my art. How very stupid they are!"

Despite his criticism of bunjin artists, Kōkan shared their impulse to omnicompetence, not only in art but in learning more broadly, going on to become a general advocate of Dutch learning (*rangaku*). And his works on geography, astronomy, and other aspects of European learning had an impact, being used by such later scholars as Satō Nobuhiro. He never developed a group of disciples, however, perhaps because of the disdain he showed other artists, and insofar as interest in European art continued to develop, it did so more as a reflection of the times than as a result of Kōkan's efforts. It should be added, however, that a few years after his death in 1818 the bakufu began mounting sporadic attacks on Dutch scholars, and those assaults could only have intimidated artists inspired by his example.

NEW GENRES IN LITERATURE

The failure of ukiyo zōshi was essentially a failure of popular literature, and most of the prose genres that developed in its place reflected popular literary taste. The intelligentsia also sought vehicles for more serious literary expression, however, and *yomihon,* a new form of serious prose, served that purpose.

SERIOUS PROSE

Ukiyo zōshi never purported to be serious. That Saikaku captured the irony and pathos of life was testimony to his talent, not to the genre's purpose or potential. After him, ukiyo zōshi offered no inspiration to serious writers. Instead, they turned to Japan's older literary traditions and to Chinese fiction for models of serious prose, preparing translations and adaptations that bookstores began selling from about 1750 under the label *shōsetsu,* the modern-day word for fiction.[20] In both China and Japan, stories of heroism and mystery were common, and the shōsetsu, or *yomihon,* "books for reading," as they came to be called, reflected these precedents, telling tales of ghosts, witches, demons, fairy princesses, and heroic warriors. In the custom of moral uplift that rulers expected of literature, moreover, the stories—with varying degrees of dedication—taught virtue and promoted righteousness.

20. Donald Keene, *World within Walls* (New York: Grove Press, 1976), p. 376.

Some writers of the new fiction were of samurai ancestry, others of commoner background. In the spirit of bunjin, the best of them tried their hand at several literary forms, as evidenced in the careers of two pioneers, Takebe Ayatari and Ueda Akinari.

Takebe Ayatari (Ryōtai) was a fallen samurai, the son of a senior official of Hirosaki han. He wrote haikai, became a painter in the nanga style, studied national learning (kokugaku) with Kamo no Mabuchi in Edo, unsuccessfully promoted an archaic style of Japanese poem, and in 1768, during his fiftieth year, tried his hand at prose, inspired by a recent tragedy involving star-crossed lovers. His effort yielded a short, three-part, fictionalized narrative, *Nishiyama monogatari*, written in "pseudo-Heian style" and larded with the "manliness" of Mabuchi's kokugaku and the bushidō ideals of Tokugawa samurai.[21]

Ueda Akinari was of plebeian Osaka origins, born in 1734 to a prostitute but adopted and raised in a retail merchant's house. He wrote haikai and waka, as well as poetic commentary, and, as noted in chapter 17, even produced a pair of ukiyo zōshi in the style of Ejima Kiseki. Except for a time around 1780 when he practiced medicine, however, he saw himself primarily as a scholar of kokugaku and Chinese literature. He vigorously questioned Motoori Norinaga's philology and attacked his claim that the *Kojiki* was literal truth. On the other flank he denounced proponents of Confucian thought, such as the Osaka merchant-scholar Nakai Riken, for doctrinal rigidity and failure to appreciate the inexplicable wonder of life.

In the course of his life, Akinari also wrote two collections of tales that expressed his kokugaku-inspired delight in the mysterious and problematic, *Ugetsu monogatari*, written between 1768 and 1776, and *Harusame monogatari*, dated 1808.[22] The two collections are dissimilar in character. The former is a well-crafted book of ghost stories, some original and others drawn from China and reset in Japan. The latter, written when Akinari was old, nearly blind, destitute, and lonely, is an

21. Ibid., pp. 378–79. Blake Morgan Young, "A Tale of the Western Hills: Takebe Ayatari's *Nishiyama Monogatari*," MN 37-1 (Spring 1982): 77–121, describes the incident and Takebe's involvement in it and offers a translation of Takebe's work. He also discusses Ueda Akinari's treatment of the affair.

22. Translations of these works are available. *Ugetsu monogatari* has been translated by Leon Zolbrod under that title (London: George Allen & Unwin, 1974) and by Kengi Hamada as *Tales of Moonlight and Rain* (New York: Columbia University Press, 1972). *Harusame monogatari* has appeared as *Tales of the Spring Rain*, tr. Barry Jackman (Tokyo: University of Tokyo Press, 1975). Dennis Washburn, "Ghostwriters and Literary Haunts: Subordinating Ethics to Art in *Ugetsu monogatari*," MN 45-1 (Spring 1990): 39–74, explores the role of Akinari's *kokugaku* thought in his tales.

uneven set of semi-fictionalized essays and stories that aspire to greater philosophical insight but generally read less well as literature. Perhaps because he was dissatisfied with *Harusame monogatari,* he never had it published, and his earlier *Ugetsu monogatari* proved the more important in establishing his literary reputation and influencing nineteenth-century fiction writers.

The later author Takizawa Bakin is the most celebrated writer of yomihon. Indeed, because of his "sense of literary purpose and the broad canvases he filled with people and incidents," he has been called "the greatest writer of romances in the history of the Japanese novel."[23]

Bakin, like Ayatari, was a fallen samurai, having been born in the Edo household of a shogunal vassal whom his father served as a personal attendant. Of minor samurai status at best, Bakin's life fell apart while he was a boy. His drunken father died when he was eight, prompting his lord to slash the family stipend, and when he was eleven, his mother left him to look after her other children. Bakin was taken in by his lord but detested the attendant duties required of him and ran away at the age of thirteen. He wandered for five years, survived the Tenmei famine, and returned to Edo in 1785 to discover his mother dying. She pleaded with her children to devote their lives to restoring the family fortune, but misfortune prevailed, and three years after her death, Bakin formally renounced his samurai status.

On his own again, Bakin tried his hand at medicine. Enjoying no success there, he "studied to become a Confucian scholar, a comic poet, a calligrapher, a fortuneteller, and a comedian, but none of these professions suited him."[24] In 1790, however, his luck changed. He became acquainted with the popular Edo author Santō Kyōden, and when Kyōden ran afoul of Matsudaira Sadanobu in 1791 and spent fifty days in manacles, Bakin was able to produce some prose pieces on his behalf. In return, Kyōden taught him the writing trade and helped him publish.[25] Over the next several years, Bakin became an active teacher and writer of fiction, and by 1806 he was able to support himself through writing alone.

Even before meeting Kyōden, Bakin had drafted an amateurish novel,

23. Keene, *World within Walls,* p. 424. In the accolade, Keene is quoting the Japanese scholars Teruoka Yasutaka and Gunji Masakatsu.

24. Leon M. Zolbrod, *Takizawa Bakin* (New York: Twayne, 1967), p. 23. For further detail on Bakin, see Zolbrod, "Takizawa Bakin 1767–1848," *MN* 21-1/2 (1966): 1–46.

25. A concise and informative introduction to Kyōden and his work is Jane Devitt, "Santō Kyōden and the *Yomihon,*" *HJAS* 39-2 (Dec. 1979): 253–74.

whose scenes, he said, served to "censure evil and encourage good." No doubt Kyōden's punishment, and that of other popular but risque authors in following years, reinforced his determination to avoid official displeasure, and his writing always retained its didactic quality. Because his early works, like those of Kyōden, were aimed at the general public, he had to produce what would sell, which meant he tried his hand at the popular new prose genres of the day. Their quality failed to satisfy him, however, and he persistently inserted passages and incidents that pretended to greater sophistication and moral purpose than the genre normally displayed.

Trips to the Kyoto region in 1800–1802 opened new literary vistas to him, and he turned to writing more substantial historical fiction, the yomihon, which became the basis of his enduring fame. In the process, he acquired a favorite theme, the restoration of a family's glory, a theme that reflected his mother's dying plea and his own persistent dream of restoring the Takizawa family's dignity. The virtues that his stories celebrated, such as filial piety, feminine chastity, and dedication to righteousness, came to serve his characters in their great overarching task of restoring their family fortunes.

This elevation in the style and content of Bakin's writing produced a shift in his readership. More and more his works appealed "to samurai, former samurai, civic-minded burghers, and rural gentry interested in art, scholarship, society, and politics."[26] The shift led to a change in his life's routines. He became alienated from other writers, whom he came to see as vulgar, and from about 1818 he drifted into the life of a recluse. He pursued scholarly writing, literary criticism, and biography, and continued working on his major historical novels, notably *Nansō satomi hakkenden,* which he wrote and published in spurts between 1814 and 1841. Set in the Kantō and drawing inspiration from a pastiche of Chinese and Japanese historical and literary works, its 106 volumes (10 modern volumes) tell an elaborate story of medieval warriors, heroism, sacrifice, miraculous happenings, the capriciousness of fate, the power of morality, and the ultimate triumph of virtue in the restoration of the Satomi family to its former glory.

Bakin struggled as persistently to restore his own family's fortunes as he did to produce epic fiction, but the efforts came to nought. Sickness, surliness, sadness, and senility consumed his household, and in the

26. Zolbrod, *Takizawa Bakin,* p. 61. On the quality of Bakin's later years, see Keene, *Travelers of a Hundred Ages,* pp. 370–75.

end it was Bakin's works, not his family, that became etched indelibly in the historical record.

POPULAR PROSE

As Bakin's case suggests, the distinction between serious and popular prose was less clear-cut than the terms suggest. One can, however, identify a number of prose genres, known collectively as *gesaku* (or *kusa zōshi*, "grass pamphlets"), that date from the late eighteenth century and harbored no elitist pretensions. Originally, gesaku was a Chinese term meaning silly or light works and referred to a playful style of poetry. Hiraga Gennai first used the term in Japan around 1770 to distinguish some popular puppet plays he had written from what he regarded as his serious literary efforts. Subsequently, it came to encompass all the new and popular prose genres, including, for some critics, yomihon such as those of Bakin.[27] Here gesaku refers to two general types of works: those that were basically picture books with appended writing (*kibyōshi* and *gōkan*) and those that were mainly text (*sharebon, kokkeibon,* and *ninjōbon*). Kibyōshi and sharebon arose during the eighteenth century, the other three during the early nineteenth.

The central defining quality of gesaku was the use of colloquial language in dialogue. Whereas writers of ukiyo zōshi and Genroku drama retained older formalities and developed new stagy elements, gesaku authors insisted on realistic speech. That usage reflected the influence of oral storytellers (*rakugo* and other types) who flourished in the cities, were acquaintances of gesaku authors, and sometimes wrote such works themselves. And since the characters in gesaku commonly were Edo folk, its rise meant that the language of that city acquired literary preeminence.

Gesaku writers fancied themselves, in the bunjin spirit, as writing and painting for their own and their fellows' entertainment. By the 1800s, however, many had in fact become professionals, making their living as authors whose most popular works sold from ten to twenty thousand copies.[28] Their readership was even more numerous than that thanks to the emergence of lending libraries that put books within reach of towns-

27. J. Scott Miller, "The Hybrid Narrative of Kyōden's *Sharebon*," *MN* 43-2 (Summer 1988): 133–52, alludes to the problem of literary categorization.

28. Robert W. Leutner, *Shikitei Sanba and the Comic Tradition in Edo Fiction* (Cambridge, Mass.: Harvard University Press, 1985), pp. 2–3, 6–7. Leutner gives library figures on p. 114, n. 6.

men who could never have afforded to buy them outright. By 1808, 655 such libraries—commonly a vendor making his neighborhood rounds with a backpack of books for loan—were reportedly operating in Edo and about 300 in Osaka. By the 1830s, Edo numbered some 800 of them, and they made available to a wide clientele both printed books and illicit handwritten manuscripts dealing with scandals and other affairs.[29]

To examine the several types of gesaku briefly, *kibyōshi,* or "yellow-cover" books, amounted to "glorified comic books."[30] They evolved from juvenile to adult satire, many dealing with the licensed quarters but others parodying Chinese and Japanese classics and lampooning historical myths and heroes. They ridiculed examples of pomp and greed, even targeting political figures who seemed particularly deserving. The booklets, of only a few pages apiece, consisted of illustrations whose margins and background areas were written over with text and dialogue. Since the author commonly provided the illustrations as well as the prose, kibyōshi constituted works of popular art as much as they did literature.

Gōkan, or "bound-together volumes," arose during the 1790s as successors to kibyōshi. Sadanobu's crackdown on political satire made the production of kibyōshi risky, especially for samurai, so authors shifted from comic depiction of the licensed quarters or other forms of satire to serious treatment of "more worthy" subjects. These included historical tales, fairy tales, and currently popular stage plays, but most notably stories of vendettas, which enjoyed tremendous popularity in Edo in the early 1800s. To tell longer stories, the writers extended their picture-narratives over several kibyōshi-size pamphlets of five double pages or so, bound them together, and sold them as units called *gōkan.* Most remained short works, but the single-volume format could be multiplied to make longer works on more elaborate topics.

An outstanding example of an expanded gōkan is Ryūtei Tanehiko's *Nise Murasaki inaka Genji,* an illustrated version of the *Tale of Genji,* set in medieval times, simplified to make it manageable, and enriched with plot devices from kabuki and the puppet theater. The work appeared in installments between 1829 and 1842 and proved extremely

29. P. F. Kornicki, "The Enmeiin Affair of 1803: The Spread of Information in the Tokugawa Period," *HJAS* 42-2 (Dec. 1982): 503–33, examines the role of lending libraries in disseminating handwritten manuscripts.

30. Keene, *World within Walls,* p. 399.

popular among women readers. Tanehiko rough-drafted its illustrations, and the print artist, Utagawa Kunisada, produced them.[31]

Tanehiko was a Tokugawa retainer, Edo resident, and bunjin. He wrote several yomihon, evidently hoping to make a career of them, but settled for gōkan in the belief he could never compete with Bakin. His literary ambition found expression even in his gōkan, however, which he invested with shards of moral purpose and a tone of aloof gentility. Tanehiko also wrote haikai and explicitly comic poetry, and he painted, performed in amateur kabuki productions, published lavishly illustrated booklets outlining kabuki plays of the day, and authored some valuable bibliographical works.

Sharebon, or "witty books," which first appeared in the Kamigata cities during the cultural boom of the 1740s, were prose works modeled on erotic pamphlets from China. They portrayed the licensed quarter and its clients, pointedly satirizing those who bungled the local etiquette. And they used dialogue and other verbal and visual devices, rather than kibyōshi-style pictures, to evoke the world of their characters. They later became popular in Edo, with Santō Kyōden publishing them to great effect until he collided with Sadanobu in 1791. By the 1800s, sharebon had evolved into less witty, more melodramatic, and more widely popular stories of the romantic entanglements and social quandaries of the quarter, focusing on "the personal, non-professional relationships among courtesans, patrons, entertainers, and brothel keepers."[32]

The term *kokkeibon*, or "humorous book," came into use in the 1820s to identify sharebon-like works of a comic nature. Like sharebon they relied heavily on dialogue. They were also influenced by the techniques of storytellers and by parodies of itinerant preachers' sermons, which gave them their insistence on colloquial language and their readiness to point up the disparities between reality and social convention.

A celebrated master of kokkeibon was Jippensha Ikku, a minor shogunal vassal who left bakufu service to become a comic poet, artist, and prolific writer of kibyōshi and later kokkeibon. His most successful work was the travel burlesque *Tōkaidōchū hizakurige,* which proved so pop-

---

31. For an insightful, illustrated discussion of the art work and appeal of *Nise Murasaki,* see Eiko Kondo, "Inaka Genji Series," in Matthi Forrer, ed., *Essays on Japanese Art Presented to Jack Hillier* (London: Robert G. Sawers, 1982), pp. 78–93.

32. Leutner, *Shikitei Sanba,* p. 61. Miller, "The Hybrid Narrative," offers an insightful discussion of *sharebon* literary devices.

ular when its first part appeared in 1802 that Ikku followed up with
one addendum after another until he had issued some forty-three installments by 1822.[33] It was a sprawling story about the pratfalls and
tomfoolery of two cheerfully coarse scoundrels, Kita and Yaji, as they
traveled along the Tōkaidō to Osaka and subsequently along other
highways, endlessly getting into scrapes, ogling women, and demonstrating the insouciance and boorishness for which Edo residents were
notorious.

Shikitei Sanba, another successful kokkeibon author, also was a multi-
talented bunjin, writing stories using the kibyōshi, gōkan, and sharebon
formats as well as kokkeibon. Born the son of a woodblock carver in
Edo in 1776, he learned the publishing trade before turning to writing
in 1794. Over the next few years he borrowed heavily from other authors and published rapidly, until his sharp wit got him into trouble in
1799. That year he wrote a historical tale cast in kibyōshi format that
poked savage fun at some Edo firefighters who had engaged in a brawl
the year before. Fellow firemen took umbrage at the tale and trashed
the houses of Sanba and his publisher. The bakufu was displeased and
settled the incident by jailing the firefighters, fining the publisher, and
manacling Sanba for fifty days for having caused the brawl by writing
about current events.[34] The incident chastened Sanba, much as Santō
Kyōden's punishment had intimidated him, and he "never again wrote
anything that dealt satirically with current events or recognizable contemporary individuals or groups."

That affair, together with a spate of domestic problems, slowed Sanba's writing for a few years, diverting him to study, literary compilations, comic versifying, and sundry other activities, until he gradually
returned to prose writing of less controversial sorts. He loathed the
vendetta story for its excess of seriousness, but by 1805 it was all the
rage, and he finally capitulated to his publisher's insistent pressure, declaring: "If the vendetta is in fashion, then I shall imitate everyone else,
submit to the publisher's urgings that I write a vendetta story, and at
long last take up my brush again, even though a plot that is all seriousness is an affront to the spirit of playfulness implicit in the word gesaku." Active again, he cranked out a number of vendetta stories, as

33. *Tōkaidōchū hizakurige* has been translated by Thomas Satchell as *Hizakurige, or
Shanks' Mare* (Rutland, Vt.: Tuttle, 1962; reprint of a 1929 Kobe edition). Satchell's brief
introduction sketches Ikku's life and notes some of his story's internal inconsistencies.
34. The following four quotations come from Leutner, *Shikitei Sanba*, pp. 31, 44,
64, 69.

well as other pieces, mostly employing the gōkan format. Over the next decade and a half, he helped develop it into a major literary form, eventually delighting in his own authorial success.

During those years he also continued expanding his circle of friends and associates to include calligraphers, print artists, publishers, theater people, and storytellers. Their importance to his career is revealed in his comment on the origin of *Ukiyoburo,* which he wrote in installments between 1809 and 1813:

> One evening in Utagawa Toyokuni's lodgings, we listened to Sanshōtei Karaku telling *rakugo* stories. . . . Beside me that evening, laughing as hard as I was, sat a publisher. Greedy as ever, he suddenly asked me if I would put something together based on these stories of the public bath, leaving out the parts about the licensed quarter and emphasizing the humor in commonplace people and events. I agreed to try.

Ukiyoburo, which skillfully used dialogue to evoke the life and people of a public bath, turned out to be a fairly uncontroversial piece, and most of Sanba's works were intended to be entertaining in an unsavage way. But they still offered social commentary. In a few works, writes Robert W. Leutner, Sanba's "basic point is serious: self-deception and pretense, hypocrisy and expedience are the rule in human affairs." Sanba mocked the response of Edo folk to epidemics, pooh-poohed attempts by some authors to celebrate or uplift the culture of the hinterland, and ridiculed the samurai heroes of *Chūshingura* and the antiquarian scholars who celebrated them. And others of his works portrayed drunks, liars, hypocrites, gossips, or the flaws and foibles of other ordinary folk.

Ninjōbon, or "books about human feelings," another literary category of the 1820s, derived from the later, more romantic sharebon. But unlike their antecedents, ninjōbon were aimed at women of samurai and merchant households. Their authors developed the personalities of female characters, usually prostitutes, making the heartaches, jealousies, and devotion of the women the emotional center of the stories and presenting their men as weak but caring, rather than debonaire and heartlessly cavalier. Ninjōbon were written in colloquial Japanese and were erotic but in a highly circumspect way that did not offend their readers.

The most successful author of ninjōbon was Tamenaga Shunsui. Born of Edo merchant ancestry in 1790, Shunsui operated a lending library, later worked as a professional storyteller, and finally emerged as an author in the 1820s. In 1832–33, after a prolific decade, he published *Shunshoku umegoyomi,* a twelve-volume story that followed the tense and tangled relationship of the geisha Yonehachi, the unfortunate Tan-jirō, whom she loves, and Ochō, a neighborhood girl whom Tanjirō has known since childhood. The story was wildly popular, which led Shun-sui to double its planned length and later write a sequel. Despite its digressions and rambling quality, it has enough narrative coherence and emotional persuasiveness to prompt Donald Keene to characterize it as "perhaps the best work of fiction composed in Japanese between the novels of Ueda Akinari [ca. 1800] and Futabatei Shimei [ca. 1900]."[35]

In the summer of 1842, Shunsui's good fortune ended when he fell victim to the broad-ranging repression of Mizuno Tadakuni's Tenpō reform. Accused of undermining public morals, he was manacled for fifty days. His publisher and illustrator were fined, and the blocks for several of his books were destroyed. Sixteen months later he died, aged fifty-three.

NEW TRENDS IN POETRY

Haikai was by far the most popular of late Tokugawa poetic forms, but among the intelligentsia, and proponents of kokugaku in particular, waka continued to enjoy esteem. During the eighteenth century it began escaping the restrictions of form and content that poetic traditionalists had maintained until then, acquiring new vitality as a result. Concur-rently kanshi, or Chinese poetry, also gained new popularity as a longer and more flexible type of poem that permitted expression of richer im-ages.

WAKA

During the seventeenth century, the ancient 31-syllable waka was pre-served primarily by orthodox court poets (dōjō). They purposely ad-hered to Kokinshū and Man'yōshū precedents on the ground that the poems in those collections were perfected expressions of human feelings and a complete catalogue of subjects appropriate to poetry. Even non-dōjō poets rarely strayed beyond the structure, sensibility, and subject matter of those models.

By century's end, however, the traditionalist versifying of dōjō poets was coming under attack. Scholars of wagaku, notably Keichū and Kada no Azumamaro, as noted in chapter 16, undertook scholarly analyses

35. Keene, World within Walls, p. 419.

of the *Man'yōshū* that stressed the importance of the spirit informing ancient poetry, not the formalities of poetic style and subject. And in a symptom of the rising Edo challenge to Kyoto's cultural pretensions, the Edo poet Toda Mosui mounted a savage and sustained attack on the myriad restrictions and secret practices required by dōjō poetics.

During the eighteenth century, the eclipse of Kyoto and rise of wagaku/kokugaku combined to break the dōjō grip, and waka became an effective vehicle for addressing contemporary concerns. As the century passed, poets discussed the character of the spirit informing waka, declared it either "masculine" or "feminine," and argued the relative merits of *Man'yōshū*, *Kokinshū*, and *Shinkokinshū* poems. By late in the century, Motoori Norinaga was using waka to express the many facets of his kokugaku persuasion.[36]

Poetic debate continued during the nineteenth century, with the rearguard efforts of dōjō poets challenged by others arguing for freer use of waka to portray actual experience and express present feelings. Ryōkan, a Sōtō Zen priest in Echigo, drew inspiration from the *Man'yōshū* for poems that evoked local scenes, children playing, and the vicissitudes of life:[37]

> You mustn't suppose
> I never mingle in the world
> of humankind—
> it's simply that I prefer
> to enjoy myself alone.

Ōkuma Kotomichi, from a scholarly merchant family in Fukuoka, was less restrained in expressing sentiment. Poking fun at himself, he spoke for so many of us:

> It doesn't matter what—
> I never get anything straight;
> the only sure thing
> is that I have become old,
> without an idea of my own.

And of his own poverty:

> In this house where I have lived
> in poverty all these years

36. Muraoka Tsunetsugu, *Studies in Shinto Thought* (Tokyo: Ministry of Education, 1964), contains many of Norinaga's poems. The translators are Delmer M. Brown and James T. Araki.
37. The following poems by Ryōkan, Ōkuma, and Tachibana are from Keene, *World within Walls*, pp. 497, 501–2, 504–6.

> there is nothing to do;
> I sweep the garden again,
> the garden I have already swept.

Finally, Tachibana Akemi, son of a paper merchant from Fukui, found in waka a vehicle for expressing a wide range of experiences. After visiting a bakufu silver mine, he wrote:

> Stark naked
> the men cluster together;
> swinging great hammers,
> they smash into fragments
> the lumps of unwrought metal.

A keen student of kokugaku, after visiting Ise and Kyoto in 1861, he wrote:

> It is a pleasure
> in these days of delight
> in all things foreign:
> I come across a man who
> does not forget the divine land.

And on a less public subject:

> My sweetheart and I,
> sleepy faces side by side,
> look out at the pond
> covered with snow and watch
> the mandarin ducks floating.

KANSHI

Chinese-style poetry, or *kanshi*, had a long history in Japan, and in the Tokugawa period it was esteemed as a facet of Chinese culture. During the seventeenth and eighteenth centuries, much of it was derivative, as bound to Chinese precedents as waka was to Japanese. But from the late eighteenth century on, as the rise of new thought and new literary styles broke down older formalisms, poets turned kanshi into an effective means of expressing real feelings and concerns. They made it, according to Nakamura Shin'ichirō, "the predominant literary expression of the intellectuals of this period."[38]

Kanshi was favored by bunjin whose disengagement from Confucian

---

38. Nakamura Shin'ichirō, "New Concepts of Life of the Post-Kansei Intellectuals: Scholars of Chinese Classics," *Modern Asian Studies* 18-4 (1984): 624.

social roles, as in the case of Uragami Gyokudō cited above, made them more willing to ignore the formalities of the genre's established poetics. One peripatetic nineteenth-century poet even wrote a 290-line kanshi describing a smallpox epidemic.[39]

Disengagement from Confucian social roles had a notable corollary effect: it encouraged the transcending of proper "female" conduct, and during the nineteenth century more women established reputations as poetesses.[40] The most renowned was Ema Saikō, born in 1787 in the home of a physician in Ōgaki. Saikō became a bunjin skilled in kanshi, calligraphy, and nanga, and an active presence in the literati circles of Kyoto. Celebrated as a painter, she is also known for her poems. Here she recalls a night's stroll with her lover, probably the poet-historian Rai San'yō:

> A little drink enjoyed in the east of town;
> windy rain of the late autumn
> hitting the blinds and banners.
> City lights still unlit
> and lanterns dark,
> we shared an umbrella all the way—
> such tenderness![41]

Years later, regretting that her father had forbidden her to wed San'yō, she wrote this bitterly sad remembrance:

> Lonely room, fiddling with a brush as the years go by;
> one mistake in a lifetime, not the kind to be mended.
> This chaste purity to rejoice in—what do I resemble?
> A hidden orchid, a rare bamboo—sketch me in some such cold form.[42]

Like waka, kanshi could give voice to the broader public concerns of the day. The samurai Sakuma Shōzan, having studied rangaku, wrote of Czar Peter the Great this way:

> He pushed back the eastern borders three thousand miles,
> learned the Dutch science and taught it to his people.
> Idly we sit talking of our long-dead heroes—
> in a hundred years have we bred such a man?[43]

39. Burton Watson, *Japanese Literature in Chinese* (New York: Columbia University Press, 1976), 2: 12.

40. Fister, *Japanese Women Artists*, pp. 97–100, discusses this expanded role for women. The biographical information on Saikō is from pp. 100–103. For a glimpse of another late Tokugawa woman, see "The Diary of Iseki Takako," in Keene, *Travelers of a Hundred Ages*, pp. 376–82.

41. Slightly modified from Nakamura, "New Concepts of Life," p. 630.

42. Watson, *Japanese Literature in Chinese*, p. 58.

43. Ibid., p. 66.

21. Ema Saikō, *Landscape*. 1856. Hanging scroll, ink on silk,
118.5 x 43.2 cm. Saikō demonstrated her mastery of classic
nanga brushwork, subject matter, and spirit in this representation of an ideal Chinese landscape. In it, human affairs find
their properly peaceful and modest place in the realm of nature, thus expressing the harmony of the Way. The poem has
been translated as follows:

How many places have I once traveled,
where pure streams rushed between white rocks?
As I grow old, I can no longer freely roam,
so I pick up the brush to depict those hills and mountains.

Courtesy of the Spencer Museum of Art, University of Kansas;
Jennifer de Gasperi Memorial Fund. Acc. #86.55.

There were other, more fervent ways to say much the same thing. Shōzan's poetry teacher, Yanagawa Seigan, born in a village in Mino province in 1789, studied poetry in Edo and later married the poetess Kōran,
with whom he wandered about Japan for a decade before returning to
Edo. In later years the diplomatic crises of the day dismayed him,
prompting him in 1846 to move to Kyoto. His rage at bakufu weakness
was captured in this poem:

> You, whose ancestors in the mighty days
> roared at the skies and swept across the earth,
> stand now helpless to drive off wrangling foreigners—
> how empty your title, "Queller of Barbarians"![44]

In the end, barbarians overwhelmed the queller, and the Tokugawa regime died on the battlefield at the end of 1867. Aizu han chanced to
become tightly linked to the regime in its last years, and Aizu became
the victors' primary scapegoat. Some of the most vicious fighting of the
civil war occurred around Aizu Castle, and Ogasawara Gokyō (Katsu-
naga), a poet and scholar of the han, said this of the battle and its
outcome:

> At dawn I gathered up the bones in the fields,
> nights took shelter in a village in the fields,
> village empty even of dogs and chickens,
> sorrow in my heart I cannot describe:
> my lord disgraced, yet I could not die for him;
> my homeland destroyed, I could not save it.
> Amid the grasses I seek to go on living,
> shamefaced before those ghosts who've gone below.[45]

44. Keene, *World within Walls*, p. 556.
45. Watson, *Japanese Literature in Chinese*, p. 73.

Thought and Society, 1790–1850

Patterns of thought change slowly, and neither 1790 nor any other single year witnessed a decisive break in Japanese intellectual history. Indeed, one can trace developments of the next several decades in terms of themes already explored in chapters 11 and 16. Continuity is especially evident in the further spread of schooling, the persistent interest in "practicality," and the "naturalizing" of alien thought, and less so in the sanctioning of commoner lives.

On the other hand, around the turn of the century, Japan's intellectual landscape also experienced considerable change, and just as the "samurai agenda" of the 1600s was inadequate for examining thought of the 1700s, so developments of the nineteenth century invite scrutiny in categories other than the four "functions" used in chapter 16. One thread that seemed to run through nearly all articulate thought of the 1800s was deepening disbelief in the adequacy of the established order, at least as currently managed. That disbelief—so sharply sounded in the poet Yanagawa Seigan's howl of rage at bakufu ineffectuality toward foreigners—manifested itself in two dissimilar but entangled trends.

The less visible trend was "disengagement from authority," especially by poor commoners. It entailed a growing disregard for existing authorities and proprieties and more reliance on transcendent powers. It showed up in transient phenomena such as pilgrimages and spontaneous celebrations and in the rise of more durable religious movements.

More visible than this trend to disengagement was a countertrend toward more active scholarly involvement in political life. More and more scholars wrote critically on current affairs, even though escalating tensions made such comments riskier than ever. Some commentators based their arguments on Confucian thought, some on Dutch learning, and some on the imperial legacy as expressed in kokugaku and *Mitogaku* teachings. But unlike political thinkers of the 1600s, most were trying to rectify current problems, not ratify current practice.

THE FURTHER SPREAD OF EDUCATION

During the eighteenth century, formal education, mostly provided by urban, proprietary schools (*shijuku*), offered samurai and more wealthy urban commoners instruction in reading, writing, Confucianism, and diverse other skills and subjects. From late in the century, schools proliferated in both town and hinterland, reaching a far larger number and range of people. Part of that increase was in shijuku, but more was in official domain schools, locally organized schools (*terakoya*), and schools operated by religious movements, most notably Shingaku.

PROPRIETARY AND DOMAIN SCHOOLS

Shijuku continued to proliferate, providing instruction in a widening range of subjects. One area of notable growth was *rangaku*, or Dutch studies, in which a key pioneering role was played by Ōtsuki Gentaku. His Shirandō in Edo offered instruction, primarily in Dutch medicine, to some ninety-four students during its thirty-seven years of operation before his death in 1827.[1]

The Tekijuku of Ogata Kōan, which operated in Osaka for twenty-five years after 1838, proved to be the most important school of Dutch studies. It flourished during the few years after bakuhan leaders cautiously accepted European learning and before English displaced Dutch as the preferred European language. A total of 630 students from all over Japan studied at Tekijuku, enrolling for three years apiece on average. In an atmosphere of striking informality and competitiveness, they worked at the Dutch language and such subjects as medicine, gunnery, botany, and chemistry. Initially, most were commoners, but from the mid 1840s, after the last spasm of rangaku persecution subsided, the school enrolled ever-larger numbers of samurai. By the later 1850s, some 40 percent of its students were of samurai status.[2]

A few shijuku, such as the Ibukiya of Hirata Atsutane in Edo, focused on Japanese studies (kokugaku), but most remained dedicated to Confucianism, even as they spread into the hinterland. Thus Hirose Tansō's Kangien at Hita in Kyushu enrolled a total of some four thousand students during the half-century he operated it after 1805. A handful of those students were samurai, and about a third were Buddhist priests, but the majority were "doctors, merchants, farmers, village heads, poets, artisans, Shintō priests, and assorted other commoner groups."[3] Most came from Kyushu, but the school's fame drew others from all over the country. At any one time it listed some 150 enrollees, adding about fifty each year and teaching them for enough months or years to satisfy their curiosity, exhaust their energy, or complete the school's highly structured curriculum, which usually required two to three years but might take six. Hirose's students, who were of widely varying age but mostly sixteen to twenty-one, were tested and grouped by ability. They studied Chinese language and classics in a combination of lectures, seminars, and drill sessions designed to produce well-disciplined

1. Richard Rubinger, *Private Academies of Tokugawa Japan* (Princeton: Princeton University Press, 1982) examines the Shirandō (pp. 107–11) and Tekijuku (pp. 127–51).
2. For a participant's lively recollection of Tekijuku in the mid 1850s, see Fukuzawa Yukichi, *The Autobiography of Fukuzawa Yukichi* (New York: Columbia University Press, 1966), esp. chs. 3–5.
3. Rubinger, *Private Academies*, pp. 93, 95. The Kangien is also treated in Rosemary Trott, "Hirose Tansō and His *shijuku*, Kangien," *Papers on Far Eastern History* (Canberra) 23 (Mar. 1981): 1–37; and in Yoshimi Inoue, "The Kangien: A Private School for Chinese Classics and Its Disposition toward Western Learning," *Philosophical Studies of Japan* 11 (1975): 121–37. Inoue, who stresses the Kangien's importance in the promotion of *rangaku*, notes that Tansō's successors continued Kangien operations until 1871, and Trott reports that the school survived until 1897.

students with a deep "reverence for Heaven" and solid basic preparation for "practical" careers.

The growth of shijuku was so great that by 1872, 1,482 are known to have been established. They have been classified as follows: [4]

Specialty	Number	Specialty	Number
Chinese studies	612	Writing	30
Calligraphy	415	Japanese studies	9
Calculation	175	Other subjects	26
Western studies	47	Unknown	149
Military studies	19		

Unquestionably, increased shijuku activity contributed to the rising literacy and political consciousness that was so apparent during the nineteenth century. But other forms of schooling also grew rapidly, and for samurai, growth in domain schools was a key factor.

Only a few daimyo established schools for their vassals during the seventeenth century, but later on new foundings multiplied, especially after 1770: [5]

Period	No. of schools	Schools/year
1620–1690 (70 yrs.)	8	0.11
1690–1770 (80 yrs.)	38	0.48
1770–1860 (90 yrs.)	144	1.60

Some domains established more than one school, and from the 1780s on, many of the larger ones established branch schools (gōgaku) to provide basic instruction to children of retainers living in branch fiefs, in secondary towns, or on scattered parcels of domain land. As of 1850

4. Rubinger, *Private Academies*, p. 13. Of the 1,482 *shijuku* identified by Rubinger's sources, only about 300 were established before 1830 and 1,100 before 1867.

5. Derived from R. P. Dore, *Education in Tokugawa Japan* (Berkeley and Los Angeles: University of California Press, 1965), p. 71, table l. Rubinger, *Private Academies*, p. 5, using a different periodization, gives somewhat different figures, as does Herman Ooms, *Charismatic Bureaucrat: A Political Biography of Matsudaira Sadanobu, 1758–1829* (Chicago: University of Chicago Press, 1975), p. 138. Scholars continue to discover evidence of other han schools that existed at one time or another, and Rubinger (p. 49, n. 19) cites a study of 1976 that reports nine han schools established before 1688, and eleven during the period 1688–1703.

432   The Erosion of Stability

about ninety-five han, mostly smaller ones, still had no han school, but most samurai were in domains that did, which helped assure them a formal education in either a domain school or private academy.

As R. P. Dore shows in his classic study of han schools, they were thoroughly Confucian, aiming to produce a cultured and moral ruling elite. Some of those founded in the seventeenth century appear initially to have admitted commoners as well as vassals, but that practice soon ended as ideology deepened the ruler-ruled cleavage. As the eighteenth century aged and domanial conditions worsened, observers began faulting han schools for not admitting and advancing students on the basis of ability rather than hereditary family status. Despite the complaints, however, commoners continued to be excluded from most of them. Moreover, normal school practice favored sons of higher-ranking vassals, although many teachers devised infomal means of rewarding achievement without regard to a pupil's parentage.

By the late 1700s, observers were also faulting curricula. Some said they should be more "practical." In 1787 a senior official of Aizu han urged that vassals study "fiscal matters, village administration, ceremonies and protocol, military affairs, criminal detection and law, and public works and utilities."[6] And some schools did gradually introduce such instruction to supplement the philosophy, moral training, and Chinese language drill that was central to existing programs.

Japanese studies as propounded by scholars of kokugaku and Mitogaku were another curricular addition, especially from the 1830s on. Although viewed by some as hostile to Chinese learning, the subject was usually introduced as useful supplementary instruction. One han school advised students in their study of kokugaku not to scorn Buddhism and Confucianism: "Range widely over the chronicles, the histories, prose and poetry, and above all approach these studies with the firm resolve to make them of practical value as an aid in 'ruling the country and giving the people peace.'"[7]

Also from the 1830s on, practical aspects of Dutch learning, medicine in particular and then military topics, began cautiously to be introduced into han schools. During the 1840s, the trend accelerated, but not until after 1853 did it really win broad support. And even then han schools remained largely wedded to the system-affirming Confucian education they had originally been designed to propagate.

6. Dore, *Education*, p. 205. The phrasing is Dore's.
7. Ibid., p. 158.

TERAKOYA AND *SHINGAKU* SCHOOLS

Most people attended neither proprietary nor domain schools.[8] For them, formal education meant instruction at terakoya, meaning locally organized schools, and most terakoya appeared in the nineteenth century, when their numbers grew dramatically. By one count, only 558 terakoya were established before 1803, but 3,050 during 1803–43, and 6,691 during 1844–67. Of the 6,000 or more operating in 1850, however, some 1,200 are said to have been in Edo, while many rural areas had none.

The teachers of terakoya pupils were of varied backgrounds. In the early 1600s some 45 percent had reportedly been Shintō and Buddhist priests and another 27 percent commoners, but the role of commoners grew while that of priests shrank, and one study gives this composition for late Tokugawa terakoya teachers:

Commoners	38%
Samurai	23%
Buddhist priests	20%
Doctors	9%
Shintō priests	7%
Other	3%

Teachers commonly offered instruction at their homes, either in one room or in two or three combined if enrollment warranted. Some operated terakoya as a career, but most provided instruction as an esteemed public service.

Whereas gōgaku schooling was aimed at local leaders and contained a substantial moralizing content, terakoya serviced a more plebeian clientele, providing basic literacy and preparation for daily life. Their copybooks were often of ancient or medieval derivation, and while the mixed Buddhist and Confucian ethics were intelligible, much of the content could have made little sense to the pupils, who mostly used them in learning to pronounce and write characters. For substantive instruction, teachers employed a wide range of texts. Some covered diverse

8. The two tables are from Herbert Passin, *Society and Education in Japan* (New York: Teachers College Press, 1965), pp. 15, 27, with supplemental figures from pp. 28, 30. Despite their exactness, the figures are based on scattered and incomplete information and should be viewed as rough indicators.

topics of presumed interest. A few were written explicitly for female
pupils. Others were more job-oriented, such as texts on commercial
matters for use in urban schools or materials on farming and country
life for rural schools.[9]

Terakoya were mostly secular institutions, but other schools arose in
conjunction with religious movements. The most noteworthy were schools
associated with Shingaku, whose ideals, as expressed by the founder,
Ishida Baigan, were noted in chapter 16. Starting with a single lecture
hall in Kyoto in 1765, Shingaku schools proliferated thereafter.[10]

Date	Number of schools	In number of provinces
1786	22	14
1789	34	?
1795	56	?
1803	80	25
1834	134	34
by 1867	over 180	?

Organized under the Meirinsha, a central college in Kyoto, Shingaku
schools (kōsha) ideally consisted of buildings with a standard set of
eight adjoining rooms whose sliding doors could be pushed back during
lectures to create sufficient seating space for attendees.[11] All kōsha had
a religious purpose, which was reflected in their operation. Thus, the
main lecture hall contained a decorative alcove "in which hung a scroll
on the favorite Shingaku theme of loyalty and filial piety." Furthermore, "above and to the right of this was a small shrine to Amaterasu,
and above and to the left the likeness of the master of the kōsha."[12]
The master usually lived at school with his disciples. He was assisted by
a few administrative aides, some preferably merchants who could cover
any school expenses not met by voluntary contributions.

Subordinate teachers shared the task of delivering lectures. The lectures, whether aimed at regular students or visitors, generally were drawn
from classical texts and everyday experience. They contained much

9. Dore, *Education,* pp. 275–90, discusses copybooks and texts.
10. Robert N. Bellah, *Tokugawa Religion: The Values of Pre-Industrial Japan* (Boston: Beacon Press, 1970), pp. 166–72.
11. Jennifer Robertson, "Rooting the Pine: Shingaku Methods of Organization," *MN*
34-3 (Autumn 1979): 311–32, describes Shingaku school organization. The quotation is
from p. 317.
12. Bellah, *Tokugawa Religion,* p. 167.

practical advice on daily affairs and used parables freely to convey the desired ethics. For regular students the lectures were supplemented by meditation, question and answer sessions, and reading and discussion in small groups.

Shingaku spread, with the blessing of daimyo, through the work of itinerant lecturers whose encouraging message and skillful use of folksy parables and didactic illustrated texts, pamphlets, and handbills were widely appreciated. Like kōsha masters these lecturers were disciples who had received certificates testifying to their mastery of the teachings. This control of the Shingaku staff by leaders at the Meirinsha helped sustain the movement's consistency of doctrine and practice despite its rapid growth.

By 1868 these several forms of education were bringing formal schooling to a large number of people—some 40 percent of boys and 10 percent of girls by one estimate.[13] Herbert Passin offers figures that suggest the trajectory of late Tokugawa enrollment growth, although they may err on the side of caution because of paucity of statistics:[14]

Type of school	To 1829	1830–1853	1854–1867
Terakoya	219,604	593,790	921,720
Domain schools	51,502	61,982	63,750
Gōgaku	9,752	14,695	29,990
Shijuku	44,574	96,798	121,708
Shogunal schools	—	—	6,000
TOTAL	325,432	767,265	1,143,168

Those enrollments, Passin notes, were biased in favor of larger cities and castle towns, where most youngsters attended terakoya or other schools. Far fewer—perhaps a quarter of the children—attended in the hinterland. About a fifth of the attendees were female, most of them in the cities, while few attended in lesser towns and villages. Everywhere,

13. Dore, *Education,* p. 254. He discusses the problems in attendance figures in Appendix 1, pp. 317–22.
14. Passin, *Society and Education,* p. 44. The one figure on shogunal schools is a rough estimate; there are no estimates for prior periods. In Appendix 3, pp. 310–13, Passin discusses the problems of Tokugawa educational statistics and why he considers these figures a substantial underestimate.

needless to say, the more affluent were better educated, but for society as a whole, an estimated 40 to 50 percent of the male populace was literate by the final decades of the Tokugawa period.[15] And mostly they acquired their literacy at school.

NATURALIZING THE ALIEN AND SANCTIONING THE LOWLY

Early Tokugawa scholars labored to "naturalize" Confucian thought, but from the late 1700s the process was applied to rangaku, or Dutch learning. As noted in chapter 16, "practicality" was persistently cited as a reason for studying and utilizing rangaku, and that argument encouraged adoption of fragments of European thought even by people who sought to prevent the adoption of other aspects. From late in the century on, a more inclusive argument also emerged, which held that in its fundamentals European learning was not alien to Japan.

While some scholars sought to legitimize the study of rangaku, others labored to sanction the lives of rural commoners within the existing order, much as earlier scholars had done for chōnin. Ninomiya Sontoku stands out most strongly as a nineteenth-century proponent of peasant worth. As noted later, however, his position was almost quixotic and seems quite out of step with the main thrust of nineteenth-century peasant attitudes.

NATURALIZING DUTCH LEARNING

By the late eighteenth century, "useful" aspects of European art, astronomy, and medicine had been introduced to Japan. Given the earlier taboo on European thought, however, domestication could proceed smoothly only if scholars reconciled this new body of knowledge with existing thought. The process developed along several lines, and ideas and information of European provenance—including a charted geography of the globe, the concept of a heliocentric universe, the notion of a creator deity as core religious concept, new interpretations of physiology, a verifiable anatomy, artistic perspective and shading, and principles of balance-of-power and overseas empire—all gradually entered the arena of acceptable discourse. They did so, moreover, even as samurai suspicion of European intentions, and hence samurai fear of Eu-

15. Passin, *Society and Education*, p. 47. Passin offers more figures on *bakumatsu*-Meiji literacy on pp. 57–58.

ropean thought, grew in tandem with diplomatic imbroglios involving foreign ships.

During the nineteenth century, the practicality of rangaku remained one of its most attractive qualities. In 1813 the Confucian pragmatist Kaiho Seiryō attacked the prevailing dogma that pursuit of profit was a selfish and unworthy act. To validate his contention that even governments engage in transactions, he reached out to Europe: "The warrior laughs when told that the King of Holland engages in commerce. But he himself buys and sells commodities; it is a law of the universe that one must sell in order to buy, and hardly a thing to be laughed at." [16] Proponents of Ezo development, such as Honda Toshiaki and Satō Nobuhiro, also drew on Dutch learning to buttress their arguments. For these scholars, information about Europe supported arguments that addressed essentially economic concerns.

Proponents of kokugaku and Mitogaku also gave credence to elements of Dutch learning by employing them to affirm Japan's virtue or superiority. Thus the kokugaku scholar Hirata Atsutane wrote of Japanese learning:

> It is just like the great sea into which flow and mix the waters of many rivers.
> . . . Thus we see that a man who wishes to attain the pure and correct Way of Japan must know all these kinds of learning. Foreign though they are, they can help Japan if Japanese study them and select their good points. It is thus quite proper to speak of Chinese learning, and even of Indian and Dutch learning, as Japanese learning. [17]

Hirata cited specifics to support his case. He welcomed the ideas of a heliocentric solar system and solar calendar as confirming the importance of the Sun Goddess. He attacked Sinophilia by invidiously contrasting things Chinese with European analogues. He explained that European medicine was so superior and Japanese medicine so backward because Europeans lived in filthy, unhealthy regions where medicines were essential, whereas Japan, before being polluted by foreign diseases, had not needed medicine because of its divine creation and salubrious climate. Even Christian theology was grist for his mill, the

16. The quoted passage is from Ryusaku Tsunoda et al., comps., *Sources of the Japanese Tradition* (New York: Columbia University Press, 1958), p. 502, from *Keikodan*, Kaiho's final essay, written in 1813. For a discussion of Kaiho's thought, see Tetsuo Najita, "Method and Analysis in the Conceptual Portrayal of Tokugawa Intellectual History," in Najita and Irwin Scheiner, eds., *Japanese Thought in the Tokugawa Period, 1600–1868* (Chicago: University of Chicago Press, 1978), pp. 23–36.

17. Donald Keene, *The Japanese Discovery of Europe, 1720–1830* (Stanford: Stanford University Press, 1969), pp. 158–59.

story of Adam and Eve helping confirm that of the gods Izanagi and Izanami and the Christian creator god apparently inspiring his celebration of a transcendent creator deity at the expense of other figures in the Shintō pantheon.[18]

In a similar vein, in 1834 the Mitogaku scholar Fujita Tōko advised his readers that "to adopt the strong points of countries overseas extensively and thereby strengthen the Divine Land, information from Holland should not be cut off completely."[19] Shortly afterward, he argued that one proof of Japan's superiority was its capacity to adopt and make use of "the strong points of other countries." Or, as he put it in an essay drafted in the early days of 1846, "to take the strengths of other countries and to try to compensate for the weaknesses of one's own country were consistent with the principle of heaven and earth, and that . . . was precisely what the sages had striven to do."[20] Rangaku could thus be used to advance diverse agendas, even agendas fundamentally hostile to European thought. However, to domesticate it as fully as earlier generations had domesticated Confucian thought required a more basic level of legitimization.

Gradually that deeper acceptance was achieved, a process mediated by Confucian thought itself. Until the nineteenth century, most European texts reached Japan in Chinese translation and most rangaku scholars were trained Confucians. Unsurprisingly, they saw European knowledge through Tokugawa Confucian eyes, and it was mainly through selective citing of Confucian ideas that they created the image of rangaku as fundamentally conformable to established Tokugawa thought.

Deep interest in Dutch learning initially appeared among government interpreters in Nagasaki and physicians in Edo, and by the 1770s scholars were beginning to promote and use it seriously. One of the first was Sugita Genpaku, a daimyo's physician, who berated "hidebound Confucians and run-of-the-mill doctors of Chinese medicine [who] don't know how large the world is" and attempted to make the new learning acceptable in terms of Confucian categories. "The Way is not something established by the sages of China. It is the [universal] Way of Heaven and Earth. Wherever sun and moon shine, wherever dew and

18. Ibid., pp. 159–61, 166, 169. For a careful examination of Christian sources in an early essay by Hirata, see Richard Devine, "Hirata Atsutane and Christian Sources," *MN* 36-1 (Spring 1981): 37–54.
19. Richard T. Chang, *From Prejudice to Tolerance* (Tokyo: Sophia University Press, 1970), p. 55.
20. Ibid., p. 55, as paraphrased by Chang.

frost form, there are nations, there are people, and there is the Way," he asserted in an essay written in 1775.

Sugita's colleague, Maeno Ryōtaku, the son of a daimyo's physician, also turned to Dutch studies as an adult, becoming a vigorous exponent of European excellence, which he expressed in these Confucian terms in 1777: "Through *Naturkunde* [natural science] they revere Heaven, honor the deities, conduct government, seek out the truth, become conversant with affairs and proficient in techniques, correct [defective] goods, and make effective use of tools. Thus, their emperors disseminate virtuous teachings, their princes maintain the state, their people are secure in their livelihoods, and their arts and crafts attain perfection. *Their sphere of moral suasion must truly be vast!*"[21]

Yamagata Bantō, a successful Osaka financier, saw himself as a disciple of Confucian scholars at the Kaitokudō, but he also studied European science and found in astronomy the most advanced discipline of all. In a seminal essay crafted around 1800, he explained the revelations of astronomy in terms of Confucian categories:[22] "The universe exists prior to all else. The earth follows, and after that come human beings and moral norms. Compassion, righteousness, propriety, filiality and loyalty are all parts of the way men order society and do not exist prior to the universe." Therefore the most basic thing one must understand is the universe. And astronomy as practiced by Europeans offers the means to do that: "Westerners have accumulated discovery upon discovery. And as the Japanese and Chinese too have begun to adopt their approaches, the errors of the ancients can now be shown through actual experimentation. Moreover, as knowledge not yet known is gradually uncovered in the future, the errors of today will be made clear." Treating astronomy as the basic source of sound knowledge against which all other received wisdom could be tested and evaluated, Bantō pro-

21. The quoted fragments from Sugita and Maeno are from Bob Tadashi Wakabayashi, *Anti-Foreignism and Western Learning in Early Modern Japan* (Cambridge, Mass.: Harvard University Press, 1986), pp. 44–45, 47.

22. The two following quotations come from Tetsuo Najita, *Visions of Virtue in Tokugawa Japan* (Chicago: University of Chicago Press, 1987), pp. 255–56. The linkages of astronomy and *jitsugaku* are evident in Takano Chōei's 1835 survey of European thought, "*Seiyō gakushi no setsu;* The Theories of Western Philosophers," *MN* 27-1 (Spring 1972): 85–92, tr. Gino K. Piovesana. A valuable discussion of Bantō is in Albert Craig, "Science and Confucianism in Tokugawa Japan," in Marius B. Jansen, ed., *Changing Japanese Attitudes toward Modernization* (Princeton: Princeton University Press, 1965), pp. 133–60. On the general issue of science in early modern Japan, see ch. 1 of James R. Bartholomew, *The Formation of Science in Japan* (New Haven: Yale University Press, 1989), which will guide one to other references.

ceeded to attack Shintō mythology and other "foolish" superstitions. He sketched an understanding of Japanese history that distinguished it clearly from China's, that presented the Tokugawa regime as legitimate, and that led into a discussion of its shortcomings and measures to remedy them.

The later scholar Sakuma Shōzan, son of a minor vassal of Matsushiro han, was well trained in the classics and became an exponent of Sun Tzu's military doctrines and Ch'eng-Chu thought. The domestic and foreign crises of the late 1830s shook his faith, however, forcing him to examine the sources of Europe's strength, particularly its military power. Rather than abandon his Ch'eng-Chu convictions in favor of European thought, he sought to reconcile the two. In the autumn of 1847 he wrote:

> If we follow the system of Ch'eng Yi and Chu Hsi [i.e., the doctrine of the extension of knowledge through the investigation of things], we may see that even Western learning is nothing more than part of our learning. . . . [Indeed], when one accepts [Ch'eng and Chu], widely adopts even the theories of Westerners, and elucidates the principle, one reaches the point where one can discern even the errors of [Ch'eng-Chu thought].[23]

Sakuma eventually propounded a principle of "Eastern ethics and Western techniques," presenting European thought as an enrichment of Sung, a filling of its lacunae:[24] "If we follow the meaning of Ch'eng-Chu, even Western skills will become part of learning and knowledge, and will not appear to be outside our framework." And "there are not two real principles of the universe that reside in different places. The learning skills developed in the West are conducive to the learning of the sages."

By midcentury, scholars had formulated original understandings of the basic relationship of established thought to that intruding from Europe, in the process providing new ground for viewing its adoption as acceptable.

SANCTIONING RURAL COMMONERS

One notable nineteenth-century commentator championed peasant dignity within the context of the established order. He was Ninomiya Son-

23. Chang, *From Prejudice to Tolerance*, pp. 150–51.
24. These two fragments are from H. D. Harootunian, *Toward Restoration: The Growth of Political Consciousness in Tokugawa Japan* (Berkeley and Los Angeles: University of California Press, 1970), p. 147.

toku, a man celebrated for his teachings, although his accomplishments as a rural leader seem more impressive than his ideas.

Sontoku was born into a reasonably comfortable peasant household in Sagami province in 1787, but when he was about five his family was ruined after the nearby Sakawa river flooded, ravaging the family's lands. Despite later floods and other hardships, he managed to gain an education and by laborious repair of ravaged cropland did well enough as a farmer to restore his family. By the time he was twenty-six, his success caught the attention of a senior vassal of Odawara han, who put him to work revitalizing some villages ravaged by the Tenmei famine. He succeeded, so the Odawara lord hired him in the 1820s to repair a set of devastated villages. The capacity of those villages to survive the Tenpō famine so enhanced Sontoku's reputation as sage and rural rehabilitator that his advice was widely sought, and in 1847 he reluctantly accepted a bakufu request to revive some villages near Nikkō that had been ravaged by famine and flood.

In the course of his career as restorer of villages, Sontoku propounded his ideas on human and village affairs, labeling them Hōtoku, "returning one's blessings." In essence he taught that the mere fact of existence, as well as whatever good fortune one may experience in life, imposes moral burdens on everyone, but by repaying them with care and persistence, one will prosper. Much as Kaitokudō scholars promoted the dignity of chōnin, he thus asserted the virtue of all who work, which to him mainly meant peasants.

His message was eclectic in the spirit of *setchūgaku*.[25] "There is," he declared, "only one true way under the sun. Shintoism, Confucianism and Buddhism are nothing but the names of the entrances [to it]." Moreover, "without either being taught or studying, one naturally knows what is the true way. . . . Everybody grasps its meaning by himself and does not forget it." He reinforced this argument for a universal, untutored, natural wisdom with the assertion that "though there are so many men well versed in Shintoism, Confucianism or Buddhism, few of them are of any good to society." Rather than indulging in useless study, he said, one should pursue his vocation with sincerity and diligence.

"Every one of us is respectable," he held, but only by attentiveness and hard work can we realize "the way of man" and enjoy satisfying lives. As "a million koku of rice is but accumulation of small grains of

25. The following fragments of quotation are from Ishiguro Tadaatsu, *Ninomiya Sontoku* (Tokyo: Kenkyusha, 1955), pp. 80, 77, 86–87, 98, 150–51, 156, 203–4. See also Bellah, *Tokugawa Religion*, pp. 126–31.

the cereal," just so, "if people pay attention to small things . . . they are sure to accomplish great things, but one who neglects small things can never achieve anything great." Accordingly, Sontoku recommended "industry, thrift and concession. Industry means efforts put forth for the production of goods needed for clothing, feeding and sheltering mankind, while thrift is endeavour not to waste such goods and concession [or giving] is the act of transference by one to others of such goods owned by him. By living thus, people can return the blessings [hōtoku] they have received through four 'natural laws'—the blessing of earthly life given by Heaven, the blessing of individual life given by parents, the blessing of a happy maturity given to one another by husband and wife, and the blessing of well-being given by agriculture."

Sontoku was asserting for villagers a claim to dignity comparable to the one other scholars had made for chōnin. And like them he held that the best way to live was by industrious participation in the established order. It was a view that landlords and rulers had reason to applaud. But it did not jibe with current trends among the poorer peasantry, and one suspects that despite Sontoku's estimable career, his views would have been lost to posterity had they not been seized upon and promoted by leaders of later generations who found them useful for their own political purposes.

DISENGAGING FROM ESTABLISHED AUTHORITY

Villagers were disinclined to take the troubles of life lying down, and in the nineteenth century their readiness to protest violently intensified, as noted in chapter 15. Other forms of unauthorized conduct also became more visible, revealing the public's greater readiness to disregard established authority and dogma and rely instead on their own willpower and the aid of higher forces. Disengagement could, of course, turn into disorder, but it usually entailed nonviolent styles of defiance. It took several forms: pilgrimage, spontaneous celebration, other expressions of millennialism, and participation in unauthorized local cults.

These forms of nonviolent defiance, as well as the rebellions and smashings (ikki, sōdō, uchikowashi), can be viewed as expressions of a widely held commoner outlook on life.[26] One way villagers coped with

26. Winston Davis, "Pilgrimage and World Renewal: A Study of Religion and Social Values in Tokugawa Japan, Part II," History of Religions 23-3 (1984): 216–17. Also Anne Walthall, "Peripheries: Rural Culture in Tokugawa Japan," MN 39-4 (Winter 1984): 373.

the worry and tedium of daily existence was by envisioning life as a cyclical process of energy slowly dissipating, to be revitalized (*hare*) through some disrupting activity. As one stirs the soil to start crops, which then grow vigorously, gradually mature, and go by, and as soils are energized with fertilizer but slowly lose their vitality, or human sexual energies wax and gradually wane, so community life is spurred, flourishes for a time, and then slips into dullness and lethargy.

In ordinary times, periodic religious festivals (*matsuri*) offered such revitalization. The authorities, wanting peasants to live frugally and yield their "surplus" to the tax collector, fretted about such matsuri, habitually urging villagers to avoid "excessive" celebration. Instead, festivals grew more frequent and elaborate as the Tokugawa period advanced. In unusually good times, villagers achieved exceptional renewal through pilgrimages and spontaneous celebrations that could easily take on a millenarian quality. Conversely, in times of exceptional communal hardship they sought group renewal as well as redress through riot and rebellion. If the hardship were personal rather than collective, it could produce individual religious experiences, and during the nineteenth century, a number of those led to the emergence of new religious groups.

THE PILGRIMAGE

A form of disregard for authority evident throughout the early modern period was the pilgrimage, or *okage mairi*, a sporadic communal undertaking that involved large numbers of peoples. The largest occurred in 1705, 1771, and 1830, but there were another dozen or so involving people from all areas of the country and many more of local extent. Pilgrims usually visited the Ise Shrine, particularly the Outer Shrine dedicated to Toyouke, a deity of fertility, going there to obtain blessings and give thanks.

Ise pilgrimages occurred during the seventeenth century, but they were modest in scale and religious in character. From the early eighteenth century on, more and more villages set up communal savings funds (*kō*) to defray costs for their participants, and pilgrimages grew into massive events that could number millions of people. They also became more secular, serving not only as a way to give thanks or gain godly help or forgiveness for self, kin, or community, but also as an escape from work and occasion for sightseeing or recreation. Some people participated because the temptation to join was compelling or because no one else was left at home.[27] Okage mairi served their function of renewal not only by providing the pilgrims with a major break in quotidian life but by giving their neighbors something to anticipate and by providing the amulets, blessings, and stories that pilgrims brought back to their village.

Pilgrimages were marked by riotous behavior, including licentious dance (okage odori; Ise odori), that was quite at odds with the norms of daily life. This ditty from the Ise odori captures the sense of joy, wonder, and promise associated with the idea of pilgrimage:

> Even in Kantō and Tōhoku far away,
> young and old, men and women together . . .
> How wonder-ful the pilgrimage!
> Dancing, dancing
> the Ise dance;
> if people have fun
> the country will prosper forever . . .
> How wonder-ful![28]

Pilgrimages were joined by more and more people who, in defiance of edicts and employers, simply went (nuke mairi). When crowds overloaded the highways, creating severe hardship for travelers and disruptions to communities en route, the authorities were unable to reduce the numbers. The best that rulers and rich could do was to humor the pilgrims, provide them with resources, and hurry them along lest they pay their way, as sometimes happened, by extortion or intimidation.

Pilgrims had goals other than Ise, and those too became more popular as people disrupted the tedium and restraint of pervasively regulated lives. Whereas rulers discouraged the traveling, to little effect, people along the way tended to welcome the travelers—so long as their numbers were not excessive—offering free food, lodging, sandals, or medicine. At times, no doubt, they did so to avert trouble, but more often it was in hopes of sharing in the religious benefits of the pilgrimage. Custom held that gods, Buddhas, and holy men occasionally traveled incognito, and, after all, "the pilgrim might be Kōbō Daishi in disguise. And kindness to a disguised holy man or divinity, as innumerable legends attest, brings good fortune. Niggardliness, stinginesss or the churlish

27. Winston Davis, "Pilgrimage and World Renewal: A Study of Religion and Social Values in Tokugawa Japan, Part I," History of Religions 23-2 (1984): 105.
28. Davis, "Pilgrimage and World Renewal . . . Part II," p. 217.

rebuff, on the contrary, invite a curse which may leave the village permanently impoverished."[29]

SPONTANEOUS CELEBRATIONS AND OTHER EXPRESSIONS OF MILLENNIALISM

Local eruptions of raucous celebration or *eejanaika* ("Ain't it great!") also appeared in the later Tokugawa period. In eejanaika, which generally were preceded by reports of magical amulets falling from the sky, common folk took to ecstatic dancing, in disregard of the authorities, often seizing the occasion to barge into the homes of rich neighbors for a "dance-in" (*odorikomi*) that settled old scores.[30] As one participant recalled the well-documented eejanaika of late 1867: "We went to the houses of chaps we used to hate or to the homes of people who pretended they were big shots and danced right in shouting 'ain't it great, ain't it great!' We'd destroy the floor mats and doors, taking any good-looking furniture, and dance around." Another man recollected: "While we were dancing around from shrine to shrine, completely naked and without a penny, when we came to the house where amulets had fallen, we'd dance at the doorway and shout 'ain't it great, ain't it great!' And then we'd force our way in—with muddy feet, straw sandals or whatever—and dance around the house. Then the people in the house would panic and give us something to eat and drink."

In addition to pilgrimages and eejanaika, commoners increasingly looked to saviors of one sort or another to redress grievances and renew the realm. One savior was Miroku (Maitreya, the "Buddha of the Future"), who would descend and put all things right. Although traditionally a millennialist ideal of incomprehensibly distant promise, Miroku was sometimes invoked in the late Tokugawa period as a power that was rectifying the world through the actions of the people themselves. In popular parlance, "The world has reached the end of the kalpa, the end of an age. Miroku's ship has arrived."[31]

Miroku became the central deity in the Fujikō, a cult that based its worship on pilgrimages to Mount Fuji, which drew most of its followers from the Edo vicinity. Dating from the early Tokugawa era, the

29. Carmen Blacker, "The Religious Traveller in the Edo Period," in *Modern Asian Studies* 18-4 (1984): 606.

30. The two quotations are from Davis, "Pilgrimage and World Renewal . . . Part I," p. 116, n. 60.

31. Carmen Blacker, "Millennarian Aspects of the New Religions in Japan," in Donald H. Shively, ed., *Tradition and Modernization in Japanese Culture* (Princeton: Princeton University Press, 1971), p. 592.

Fujikō enjoyed a sharp revival in the mid eighteenth century, developing a fuller organization and establishing faith in Miroku as its core tenet. In 1789, as the crisis of the Tenmei famine waned, the cult leader's wife petitioned the bakufu: "It has not yet reached the ears of those in authority that Miroku is initiating his age, and renewing all things, for as long as this world shall last, and for as long as heaven and earth shall endure. We therefore beg that the Age of Miroku be proclaimed. . . . [so that] there will be no more calamitous rains or droughts."[32] The bakufu declined the request, but later, and especially in the disastrous 1830s, the cult flourished among townsmen and villagers, who established local shrine groups that functioned as communally managed, mutual-assistance units. Some of the cult's leaders became more vocal, espousing imperial loyalist (sonnō) sentiments, and in 1849 the bakufu suppressed the movement. It revived only after the regime fell in 1868.

A less coherent millennialist impulse became incorporated in the folk explanation of earthquakes, which said they were caused by movements of the namazu, a great catfish that lay beneath the earth's surface. Originally an evil force to be pacified, in the nineteenth century the namazu became an ambiguous figure: brute, mischief maker, victim of popular rage, savior, or avenging force that purified society. An earthquake that devastated Edo in 1855 provoked a large output of anonymous namazu prints that showed the catfish ruining lives and turning the world topsy-turvy.

In some prints, the populace, ravaged by the quake, berate and batter the namazu. In others, the fish is a force for good, performing heroic feats and supporting the poor against the rich. In one print, bearing the caption, "Herewith we [the people] attained our cherished desire," the namazu admits his cruelty in causing the quake and in penance slits open his belly, allowing gold coins to pour out for the assembled people. In other prints, the catfish forces the rich to vomit up and excrete coins for the poor. In the landlord-tenant dialogue on one print, the tenant asks to borrow money for sandals, and when the landlord protests, the tenant retorts, "It's an earthquake and that's why I came to extort it from you!" In another, a construction worker observes, "With your help, Mr. Namazu, we make such a lot of money at present, that we don't know how to thank you for it."[33]

32. Royall Tyler, "The Tokugawa Peace and Popular Religion: Suzuki Shōsan, Kakugyō Tōbutsu, and Jikigyō Miroku," in Peter Nosco, ed., Confucianism and Tokugawa Culture (Princeton: Princeton University Press, 1984), p. 117.
33. Cornelis Ouwehand, Namazu-e and Their Themes (Leiden: E. J. Brill, 1964), pp. 14–15, 31, 32–33. The latter print is shown as plate 11.

A more broadly and more frequently invoked talisman of rectification and renewal was the *daimyōjin* ("divine rectifier" or "savior"). Daimyōjin usually sprang from the memory of historically credible figures—but sometimes from suprahuman forces such as the namazu itself—who, believers asserted, had sacrificed themselves in the struggle against injustice. Those struggles were elevated to great moral attempts to renew the world (*yonaoshi*) much as a matsuri or pilgrimage renewed a village and its folk. The label *yonaoshi daimyōjin,* with its sense of "world savior," was applied to such diverse people as the bakufu official who killed the son of Tanuma Okitsugu in 1784, the leaders of some nineteenth-century peasant rebellions, and Ōshio Heihachirō and Ikuta Yorozu, who led putsch attempts in the 1830s. By midcentury these saviors were being invoked by peasant protestors who identified themselves as "the gods of *yo-naoshi* who have come to give punishment."[34]

NEW RELIGIONS

During the nineteenth century, commoners defied authority in another, less public way. They began responding to individuals propounding new and unsanctioned religious beliefs, accepting their teachings not as transient deviants but as more or less permanent congregants, in the manner of Fujikō adherents. The founders were ordinary people whose faith sprang from emotionally devastating personal experiences, and the movements reflected their origin. They commonly involved faith healing, a willfully optimistic outlook on life, strong faith in the founder's religious power and concern for the well-being of his or her followers, and sometimes mystical involvement in cult rituals.

Three noteworthy new faiths (*kyō*)—Kurozumi, Konkō, and Tenri—emerged before 1868; others appeared later. Kurozumi arose near Okayama around 1815 from the preaching and healing activity of Kurozumi Munetada, the priest of a local Shintō shrine, who lost his parents to dysentery in 1812, nearly died from tuberculosis in 1813, and vowed, "When I die and have become a god (*kami*), I shall devote myself to . . . healing the diseases of mankind."[35] He lingered on and some months later prayed to the sun, "inhaled the sun's rays deeply [and felt

34. Irwin Scheiner, "The Mindful Peasant: Sketches for a Study of Rebellion," *JAS* 32-4 (Aug. 1973): 588.
35. Charles William Hepner, *The Kurozumi Sect of Shintō* (Tokyo: Meiji Japan Society, 1935), p. 61.

the sun] come down out of the sky, enter his mouth, and pervade his entire body, as if he had swallowed it."[36]

Munetada believed he had become a kami while still alive (*ikigami*). After regaining his strength, he preached "The Way of Amaterasu Ōmikami," the sun goddess. It was an idiosyncratic doctrine that subsumed the virtues of gods and Buddhas in the creator-god Amaterasu and defined the "heart of man" as a "separated part" of Amaterasu.[37] He practiced intense devotions, made a half-dozen pilgrimages to Ise, and employed divination, purification rites, prayers, and medicinal pills and powders to help people avoid dangers and cure illness. Amaterasu's powers of assistance were accessible to all who had faith, he taught, and ranged "from simple cures to the prolongation of life, abundance, having children, easy delivery, increased success in trades and business, bumper crops, and larger fishing catches."[38] Thanks to the apparent efficacy of faith in Amaterasu, Munetada gradually developed a following. By the 1830s, his disciples included Okayama samurai as well as commoners, women as well as men, and during the 1840s he gave fuller organization to the sect.

When Munetada died in 1850, he left some eight hundred adherents. Most had joined during his last five years, primarily because of his reputation as a venerable healer who could direct Amaterasu's curative powers to aid the faithful, purify well water, and restore "spoiled rice, soy-sauce, plants, [and] herbs"—matters of importance to the poor.[39] His disciples carried on the proselytizing after his death, and in 1856 the Head of Shintō affairs (*Jingi kanryō*) in Kyoto designated him a daimyōjin. Despite flaccid bakufu attempts to suppress the sect, it won followers at court and received formal imperial recognition in 1862.

The Konkō sect also arose near Okayama, emerging from the preaching of Kawate Bunjirō, who was born to a poor farmer in 1814. Like Munetada, Bunjirō endured severe hardships, losing children and other relatives to smallpox and suffering disastrous farming losses in the 1840s. He blamed these calamities on his failure to pacify the demonic kami Konjin. Five years later he grew desperately ill and experienced a kami

36. Helen Hardacre, *Kurozumikyō and the New Religions of Japan* (Princeton: Princeton University Press, 1986), p. 52. The words are Hardacre's.

37. Hepner, *Kurozumi Sect*, pp. 108ff., offers an explanation of Munetada's teaching in terms of the main analytical categories and concerns of Christianity—for example, creation, monotheism, faith, salvation, sin, evil.

38. H. D. Harootunian, "Late Tokugawa Culture and Thought," in *The Cambridge History of Japan*, vol. 5, *The Nineteenth Century*, ed. Marius B. Jansen (Cambridge: Cambridge University Press, 1989), p. 223. The phrasing is Harootunian's.

39. Hepner, *Kurozumi Sect*, p. 177.

possession that led him, after recovery, to devote himself to Konjin. As Konjin's medium he helped fellow villagers deal with the troublesome deity, and another possession in 1858 convinced him he had become a living kami. He started calling himself Bunji daimyōjin and gave spiritual aid to more and more people despite protests by other religious leaders. He quit farming and in 1867 was officially recognized as a Shintō priest. After that his teachings spread, and his adherents became an organized sect during the 1880s, following his death.[40]

The Tenri sect arose just south of Nara during the 1850s, founded by Nakayama Miki. She was born in 1798 to a farmer and his devout Jōdō Buddhist wife. Unhappily married from the age of thirteen to a prosperous nearby farmer, Miki suffered a series of family crises in the late 1830s and experienced godly possession while helping exorcise a malevolent spirit from her son. In 1838 the possessing kami declaimed: "I am the True and Original God. I have a predestination to this Residence. Now I have descended from Heaven to save all men. I want to take Miki as the Shrine of God."[41] Persuaded of her religious mission, and in line with her compassionate nature, Miki began giving away the family's possessions, despite intense protests by kin and neighbors. Her actions helped ruin the family farm in a few years.

After her husband died in 1853, she gave away most of the family's remaining goods, keeping eight acres of land and a hut to live in. There she began performing incantations and faith cures, mainly to assure nearby peasant women of painless childbirths. Her following grew thanks to her healing powers, and in 1861 she began holding religious services. Her success provoked resistance from local Buddhist monks and others, but in 1867 the court's head of Shintō affairs recognized her as Tenri daimyōjin. She died in 1887, but her teachings evolved into an organized movement despite sporadic persecution by the Meiji government.

None of these three new faiths constituted a purposeful political enterprise. All encountered resentment and sporadic harassment from suspicious regimes or religious groups that saw them as competitors, but none was so feared as to be crushed. Nevertheless they reduced the emotional engagement of followers in the established social hierarchy and its traditional religious arrangements by giving them new foci of

40. Delwin B. Schneider, *Konkōkyō* (Tokyo: ISR Press, 1962), examines Konkō doctrine.

41. Clark B. Offner and Henry Van Straelen, *Modern Japanese Religions* (Leiden: E. J. Brill, 1963), p. 45. Also quoted in Blacker, "Millennarian Aspects of the New Religions," p. 575.

commitment and gratitude. And by their very existence they held out to others the promise of an alternative to traditions that evidently were failing to meet basic human needs.

ENGAGING IN MACROPOLITICS

The celebration of godly intervention in human affairs and the aggressive good humor of eejanaika, to say nothing of peasant uprisings, were forms of political activism, whether they involved explicit demands or merely defiant insouciance. However, they were the activism of people so far removed from positions of high authority that they were rarely able to reach Japan's rulers through literate argument. Scholars could do so, however, and from about 1790 more and more began memorializing the rulers about current affairs. Their actions reveal that they presumed the right and competence to advise and that they viewed the troubles of the day as too grave to ignore despite the risks involved in taking a stand. As years passed, more fully articulated political statements emerged, developing most forcefully from the functionally apolitical legacy of Motoori Norinaga and the pro-Tokugawa legacy of Mito scholarship, but also from the "practical" worlds of business, agronomy, political economy, and Dutch learning.

The role of Confucian thought itself was more ambiguous. On the one hand, it provided scholars with some of their firmest rationales for advising rulers, and into the early nineteenth century, one can see them doing so. On the other hand, Confucian ideas were so deeply linked to the established order that scholars had difficulty finding in them a solid basis for a radical critique of the system as a whole. Confucian scholarship enjoyed a striking revival during the century, but it also seemed to withdraw from the political arena to a position of doctrinally enforced ineffectuality. That it should play such a marginal or defensive role in political discourse, even though the scholars engaged in its revival were responding to the stresses of the day, surely was a measure of how radically the times were changing.

THE LIMITS OF CONFUCIAN ENGAGEMENT

Confucian scholars in official posts influenced affairs during the nineteenth century. Their role was strengthened by Matsudaira Sadanobu, who revived the Hayashi school at Shōheizaka during the 1790s and defined Ch'eng-Chu thought as "orthodox" Confucianism. Under the energetic hand of Hayashi Jussai, who guided the school from 1792 to 1837, Ch'eng-Chu influence was strengthened throughout officialdom. Government scholars performed a watchdog function, guiding samurai education and discouraging unapproved study. In a notable instance, as reported in chapter 21, around 1840 Jussai's second son, serving as a bakufu inspector, was the key figure in a harsh crackdown on scholars of Dutch learning.

Except for those officially supporting the established order, however, scholars who consciously adhered to Confucian positions made very few contributions to political thought. The few dedicated Confucian scholars who did engage in political action, such as Ōshio Heihachirō and Ōhashi Totsuan, were criticized by their fellows for failing to act in accord with proper principles.[42] According to these critics, one could successfully address the crises of the age only by working at "the meritorious act of broad self-cultivation," as Kusumoto Tanzan put it.[43] Through energetic study of human nature and principle, one could come to grasp the Way, and then one would know what the times required. Those who chose instead to take precipitate action would only make matters worse.

Namiki Rissui, a student of Totsuan, complained that nowadays scholars yearn to become great heroes rather than great sages. As a result, "men's minds are demoralized, behavior has degenerated, and many blindly follow heretical doctrines." Reflecting on the situation, he went on:

> There has never been a country wherein faithfulness, sincerity, courtesy and deference flourished that had disorder. There has never been an instance of great men of wisdom to appear and govern the country when doctrines of heroics are popular. . . . I dare say that scholarly circles of the early-modern era have completely changed. The origins [of this change] came from Rai San'yō, and the followers of Fujita Tōko and Sakuma Shōzan encouraged it. They were so-called heroic great men. Therefore their popular abuses have overwhelmed the country. Their ill effects have been most severe.

Instead of heroic action, Namiki and others argued, the times called for renewed dedication to teaching, because only that could counter the

42. Carmen Blacker, "Ōhashi Totsuan: A Study in Anti-Western Thought," *TASJ*, 3d ser., 7 (Nov. 1959): 147–68, discusses Ōhashi's essay, *Hekija shōgen,* published about 1854.
43. Takehiko Okada, "Neo-Confucian Thinkers in Nineteenth-Century Japan," in Nosco, ed., *Confucianism and Tokugawa Culture,* p. 232. Namiki and Ikeda are quoted from pp. 240–41, 243–44. A careful study of one rigorous late-Tokugawa Confucian philosopher is Robert L. Backus, "Tsukada Taihō on the Way and Virtue," pts. 1 and 2, *HJAS* 50-1 (June 1990): 5–69, and 50-2 (Dec. 1990): 505–60.

malign influence of erroneous doctrine, European thought in particular. As the Ōyōmei scholar Ikeda Sōan warned: "Unless our scholars and great men exert themselves in the study of [Confucian] teachings, how are they to realize that the disorder of schools we have had thus far in our own country is not comparable to that in the West. This is why I am so deeply concerned." All of which doubtless was true, but it left the field of action to others. Those others, almost to a man, were well versed in Confucian thought, and the right to advise that they presumed to enjoy had been most vigorously propounded by the likes of Ogyū Sorai. Nevertheless, they wrestled with the issues of the day in terms other than those demanded by committed Confucians such as Tanzan and Sōan.

"PRACTICAL" ADVICE ON POLITICAL ECONOMY

The scholars who proffered advice did so because they saw society as facing real problems for which they wanted effective solutions. One source of pragmatic thought was the Confucian legacy of Sorai and Dazai Shundai. Kaiho Seiryō, cited above, reflected their influence when he advocated government engagement in the economy. During the nineteenth century, however, other sources of thought proved more effective in sanctioning reformist proposals. One was the corpus of Dutch learning; another, the real world experience of merchant scholars and agronomic reformers.

As foreign contacts revived from the 1790s, information and opinion about Europe became ever more common in political debate. Honda Toshiaki used knowledge derived from rangaku to buttress his arguments. Reputed to be from a samurai family in Echigo, Honda went to Edo, studied, and from 1767 taught mathematics, astronomy, geography, and surveying. A few years later he left to travel the realm, observed the devastation wrought by the Tenmei famine, and concluded that overseas trade and colonization were essential to the country's recovery. He actively sought information on affairs abroad, studying Dutch, interviewing widely, and traveling in the Ezo region. Although he held no official position, he submitted a series of unsolicited, confidential essays to the Edo authorities during the 1790s, in which he discussed public affairs and proposed several bold policy initiatives, including, as noted in chapter 13, creation of a great northern empire.[44]

A wide range of scholars used information derived from rangaku in

44. See Keene, *Japanese Discovery*, esp. ch. 5 and the appended translations of Honda's writings.

their essays and memorials on affairs. Some, such as Sakuma Shōzan and Aizawa Seishisai, occupied official positions that customarily allowed them to express views. Others, such as Hirata Atsutane and Satō Nobuhiro, lacked such posts, at least initially, but they expressed their views anyway in both independent essays and memorials prepared for official consideration.

Men of commerce also became more outspoken. Since the days of Ieyasu, they had played key roles in bakuhan finances, but they later found their talents resented, leading many to reciprocate with feelings of contempt for the fiscal ineptness of lords and officials. From the late 1700s on, Confucian-schooled merchants began asserting that commercial expertise qualified them to advise government. In 1789, when Sadanobu solicited the views of Nakai Chikuzan, head of the Kaitokudō, Chikuzan responded with a long essay, *Sōbō kigen,* which ranged widely over domestic and foreign affairs, argued against development of Ezo, suggested a number of reforms, and boldly promoted a larger national educational role for the Kaitokudō and himself.

In the same spirit, around 1800, the Osaka merchant-scholar Kusama Naokata wrote a treatise on the history and character of money, in which he discussed monetary policy and problems at length. Good merchant that he was, he criticized the authorities for erratic monetary policies, remission of samurai debts, and sporadic levies (*goyōkin*) on the Osaka merchant community. Those acts, he asserted, were dishonorable, hurt the economy, and revealed official incompetence and irresponsibility. Merchants, by contrast, handled affairs competently and responsibly, giving the economy such effectiveness as it still had. So, he argued, if the rulers really want to salvage the situation, they should turn to the experts: "No doubt it would be embarrassing for the samurai to seek the advice of lowly commoners, but [they know less than merchants] about price, money, and trade and should, therefore, consult them."[45]

Like merchant scholars, students of practical agronomy date from the early Tokugawa period, but their influence became pronounced much later, as in the cases of Ōishi Hisayoshi and Ōkura Nagatsune, cited in chapter 13. The most remarkable figure in this tradition was Satō Nobuhiro (Shin'en), who was born in 1769 into a rural physician's family with a long tradition of scholarship in horticulture and rural economics.[46]

---

45. Najita, *Visions of Virtue,* p. 247.
46. Satō Nobuhiro has generated diverse, strong opinions among Japanese scholars, but despite (or because of?) the abundance of his scholarly output, he has received almost

Like so many of the later Tokugawa reformist thinkers, Satō derived from the northeast, being reared in an inland village south of Akita. When he was twelve, his father took him on a trip to the Ezo frontier. From there they headed south, observing the effects of the Tenmei famine as they traveled. They reached Shimotsuke in 1784, where they visited the Ashio copper mine, but there Satō's father died of a sudden illness, leaving the boy to reach Edo by himself. He found lodging in the city with the Dutch scholar Udagawa Genzui and under the tutelage of Genzui and others studied Dutch texts, Confucianism, astronomy, geography, surveying, and calendography. He spent some years traveling about southwest Japan and later settled in the village of Mamesaku some 90 kilometers north of Edo, not far from where his father died. There he pursued his agricultural studies until 1806, when he returned to Edo.

During the next two years, while the city was in the grip of its first "Russian scare," he put his Dutch learning to use. He published one essay that was the first Japanese-language history of Europe and another on foreign affairs that called for vigorous overseas trade.[47] In 1808 he took a job as advisor to the lord of Tokushima han, writing and teaching on defense work, gunnery, and related military matters. After a year in Awa, he returned to Edo, where he published his first essay on horticulture. He studied for a while with the bakufu's official Shintō scholar and seems to have found in those teachings deeper reason for caring about the well-being of the imperial land and its god-given flora and fauna. In 1810 he returned to Mamesaku to continue his agricultural studies.

At some point, Satō began reading the works of his fellow provincial Hirata Atsutane, whose idiosyncratic kokugaku teachings were popular in Edo. Inspired by Hirata, he went again to the city in 1814 to found a center for the discussion of Shintō. The venture soon aborted, however, because his interpretations—or perhaps his abrasive personality and uncouth demeanor—provoked a hostile reaction from the bakufu's Shintō scholars. When Satō refused to modify his position, he was banished from Edo.

Back in Mamesaku, he continued studying and writing, mostly on

no attention in English. This summary derives mainly from Kanō Kyōji, *Edo jidai no ringyō shisō* [Forestry thought in the Edo period] (Tokyo: Gannandō, 1963), pp. 43–53, a somewhat dated source that provides a brief biography and convenient review of the secondary literature before looking more carefully at Satō's writings on forestry.

47. Grant Goodman, *Japan: The Dutch Experience* (London: Athlone Press, 1986), pp. 219–21, describes Satō's foreign policy views briefly.

horticulture and agricultural economics. His main goal was to stimulate production as a way to cope with famine, rural hardship, government debt, and social demoralization, but inspired by Hirata's sense of unique Japanese virtue, his vision expanded to messianic proportions. During the 1820s, he wrote a number of major essays, including *Suitō hiroku*. It described a rigorously centralized state that would enable Japan's leaders to solve domestic problems and establish a global empire capable of assuring Japan's prosperity and bringing imperial blessings to people everywhere.

The centralized state he proposed in *Suitō hiroku* was modeled on the T'ang imperial government. Six ministries would handle all affairs, and all people would be assigned to one of eight functional classifications—"plant-cultivation, forestry, mining, manufacturing, trading, unskilled occupations, shipping, and fishing"—and the law would "strictly prohibit anyone from trying his hand at another occupation." As he envisioned it,

> the six Ministries will care for the groups of people assigned to them, inducing them to study their occupations and making them devote their attention constantly and exclusively to the performance of their occupations without faltering or becoming negligent, and to the fullest extent of their energies. In this way, as the months and the years pass, each industry will acquire proficiency and perfect itself, providing steadily increased benefits for the greater wealth and prosperity of the state.[48]

Those ideas, and his contemporary calls for creation of an empire, might have found few listeners in the 1820s, but a half-century later they seemed considerably less bizarre.

Satō's fame continued to spread, mainly owing to his less expansive advice on domestic economics, which he imbedded in appealing kokugaku images of Japan's divine origins and special virtues. People kept seeking his views, and in 1832 he violated his ban and went to Edo. He was caught, sent into house arrest in a village northeast of the city, and ordered to stay out of town. In his new home he continued writing, even as the Tenpō famine racked the land, and many scholars and notables corresponded with him and even trekked to his house for advice. His contacts included the rangaku scholars Watanabe Kazan and Ozeki San'ei, and his connection with them nearly tangled him in the anti-rangaku crackdown of 1839. His admirers saved him from prosecution, however, and in 1846 he was allowed to return to the city, where he

48. Tsunoda et al., comps., *Sources*, pp. 572–73.

pursued his writing until his death four years later at the age of eighty-one.

In the course of his life, Satō was consulted by bakufu officials and by daimyo, heirs, and senior officials of such domains as Kagoshima, Uwajima, Tsuyama, Kurume, and Tawara, as well as Tokushima. Some of his 25-odd essays, including *Suitō hiroku,* were written as independent treatises, but many of the more technical ones were drafted specifically at the behest of bakufu leaders or particular daimyo or han officials.

Modern scholars have criticized Satō for plagiarizing and garbling the views of other authors, and his essays do draw eclectically and not always carefully from the writings of Hirata, agronomists, rangaku scholars, and others. Neither his authoritarian approach to social management nor his expansionist ideas win many plaudits today, but his corpus still stands as a monument to attentive husbandry, dedicated ethnicity, radical institutional theorizing, and a broad-ranging curiosity, all directed to the problems of the day. Said to be of unbending will and forceful mind, imprudent in expressing himself, and utterly indifferent to his own appearance, Satō never formed a school of followers. But his writings reflected both the concerns of the age and the readiness of scholars to address them. And bits and pieces of his ideas influenced many an official both then and later.

POLITICIZING THE IMPERIAL LEGACY

As things worked out, the scholars whose ideas loomed largest in the realm of macropolitics were proponents of the imperial legacy, the nativist scholars of Mitogaku and kokugaku. They succeeded in transforming bookish traditions into compelling political messages, doing so by anchoring them in ethnic awareness in a way that gave them relevance to issues of the day. Their message as a whole was powerful because it defined an ideal that nearly all Japanese could cherish, an enemy all could wish to overcome, and a scapegoat to blame for obstacles encountered in pursuing those goals.

In institutional terms the message was not expressly pro-court or anti-bakufu. Rather, it was an inclusivistic cultural message that worked at a higher level of concern, defining the well-being of Japanese society as a godly responsibility and holding those in positions of power accountable. As long as they performed acceptably, they retained legitimacy; should they fail to succor the sacred realm and its people, they earned denunciation and, implicitly, displacement.

The scholarly tradition of Mito, noted in chapter 9, was thoroughly academic, centered on production of *Dai Nihon shi,* the great Chinese-inspired history of Japan's imperial institution. The kokugaku of Motoori Norinaga and his predecessors, as noted in chapter 16, was highly literary, philological, and religious in character. Moreover, it aimed its arrows of criticism at Chinese studies, which rallied few and angered many.

From the 1790s, however, when Europeans reappeared in the seas around Japan, nativists began transforming their scholarly legacies by declaring that the times were critical. The barbarian was at the gate; domestic affairs were a mess because the stewards of the Tokugawa order were mishandling their responsibilities, and disaster could be averted only if the realm were thoroughly revitalized. Mito scholars, being in service to their lord, defined their ideas in domanial terms, making them substantive in content and explicit in issues and objectives. Hirata Atsutane, on the other hand, addressed issues at a more abstract level, dealing more purely with issues of Truth and Falsehood in the nativist legacy as they related to the daily lives of individuals and their sense of ethnic identity and location. Being an independent scholar, his efforts yielded results indirectly, mainly via the work of disciples—over five hundred during his lifetime and hundreds more in later years—who introduced his ideas to the imperial court, daimyo domains, and commoners in towns and villages across the realm.

These dissimilarities between Mitogaku and kokugaku meant that the former enjoyed a political impact sooner than the latter. But because it was tied to Mito han and the established political structure, it also had a more limited potential, and from the 1850s on, developments rapidly rendered it obsolete. Even as Mitogaku was losing effectiveness, kokugaku, with its focus on basic issues of ethnic community and individual persona and its lack of structural fetters save for an idealized imperial institution, rapidly gained popularity as a message that inspired some political activists and was skillfully exploited by others in struggles for political supremacy in Japan.

Naiyū gaikan, or "internal troubles and external catastrophes," was a hoary Confucian formulation that acquired striking pertinence to politically conscious residents of northeastern Japan late in the eighteenth century. The Tenmei famine and then reports of Russian activities to the north alarmed observers like Fujita Yūkoku, a seminal figure in nineteenth-century Mitogaku, spurring them to scholarly activism. The son of a Mito townsman, Yūkoku was schooled locally by the distinguished scholar Tachihara Suiken and through him acquired a position in the han bureau (Shōkōkan) where *Dai Nihon shi* was being compiled.

In 1791 young Yūkoku addressed issues of the day in *Seimeiron,* an academic essay that reflected his schooling in Mito Confucian thought.[49] In the essay, which he presented to Matsudaira Sadanobu upon the latter's request, he argued that society's problems could be overcome only if proper human relationships were clearly understood and integrity restored to current practice. Japan's unbroken imperial line, which was descended from the gods, embodied a unique virtue that the shogun as regent to the emperor was obligated to make manifest. He was to do so with the loyal and dedicated assistance of his hierarchically arrayed daimyo and officials, down even to dutiful villagers, whom those above were to cherish.

Although Yūkoku cast that essay in terms appropriate to the realm as a whole, his main concern was Mito, as shown by his major opus, *Kannō wakumon* (1799), which focused on village conditions and problems of agriculture. In his view the problems of the countryside included growing disparities of wealth, inequities in taxation, oppressive corvée burdens, public unrest, and the habit of luxury, which overly wealthy peasants encouraged. To solve them, he called for compassionate, attentive, and responsible government and measures to discourage luxurious habits and improve equity in living standards, taxation, and other obligations. To achieve those goals among han retainers, he advised that they be "returned to the land."[50]

Yūkoku's diagnosis and prescriptions, while unoriginal, identified key problems that had become more pronounced during the eighteenth century. The problems transcended Mito, as he recognized, and required treatment at a countrywide level. And he knew that his lord had a special obligation in those larger affairs because Mito was one of the *sanke,* the three major cadet branches of the shogunal line, which were expected to be especially attentive to the main Tokugawa line at Edo. Thus in 1797, with Sadanobu out of office and the bakufu reform impulse waning, he memorialized his lord, Harumori:

49. J. Victor Koschmann, *The Mito Ideology* (Berkeley and Los Angeles: University of California Press, 1987), pp. 43–48, discusses *Seimeiron.*
50. Harootunian, *Toward Restoration,* pp. 78–80.

The Three Houses [*sanke*] stand like a tripod, a great buttress upholding all within the seas. Moreover, Your Grace is superbly endowed of high virtues; the hopes of men turn to you, the whole land has great expectations of you. If some day the Bakufu requires your counsel, should Your Grace then rest irresolute and fruitlessly silent?[51]

Yūkoku's hopes notwithstanding, Harumori's voice no longer carried weight in Edo and little reform occurred in either Edo or Mito. Thanks to improved environmental circumstances, however, "internal troubles" seemed to abate.

"External catastrophes" did not diminish, and Yūkoku's student, Aizawa Seishisai, found them particularly alarming. As an old man recalling his youth, he wrote:

In 1792 when I was at the tender age of eleven, the Russian barbarians arrived in northern Ezo. When Master Yūkoku told me about their fearsome, cunning nature, my blood began to boil and I resolved then and there to drive them away. I built an earthen statue of [the Russian emissary] Laxman and derived great pleasure by lashing it with my riding whip. From then on I vowed to devote myself to learning.[52]

Aizawa may well have been reading later rage back into his youth, but during the 1790s he was sufficiently concerned with the Russian issue to study it strenuously.

In 1801 he completed a manuscript, *Chishima ibun,* designed to inform his countrymen about Russia and the lands north of Japan. He outlined an alleged legacy of ancient Japanese conquests that had long ago brought the Kurils and continental northeast Asia under imperial rule. That age of glory had subsequently been lost, however, and Russia was currently overrunning realms that properly were subject to imperial suzerainty. "According to Honda Toshiaki, Kamchatka was formerly part of Ezo, and as such, should be under Matsumae control. But we have been ignorant of this for more than a hundred years since that territory was stolen from us," he wrote. Using earlier reports by foreigners and by explorers such as Mogami Tokunai, along with other sources of information and misinformation, he described the areas coming under Russian control, the Russians' cunning strategies, and their alarming success in fashioning a great and flourishing empire. Now,

51. Yukihiko Motoyama, "The Political Thought of the Late Mito School," *Philosophical Studies of Japan* 11 (1975): 104.
52. The quotations of Aizawa are from Wakabayashi, *Anti-Foreignism and Western Learning,* pp. 70, 78, 80.

"the only islands left to us are Kunashiri, Etorofu, and Karafuto [Sakhalin]. All the rest were snatched away before we knew what was happening." The Ezo question loomed large in the minds of many Tōhoku observers during the next several years, but Aizawa found himself occupied serving his lord at a number of posts in Edo and Mito, and his most notable sortie into foreign and imperial affairs came two decades later.

In 1825, as chapter 20 reports, the bakufu hardened its policy against foreign ships, and Aizawa seized the moment to prepare *Shinron*, a long and richly articulated statement that he presented to his lord Narinaga in hopes it would spur him and the bakufu to initiate the energetic reform he believed essential if society was to cope with its problems. He stated his premise and his dominant concern at the outset:[53]

> Our Divine Realm is where the sun emerges. It is the source of the primordial vital force sustaining all life and order. Our Emperors, descendants of the Sun Goddess, Amaterasu, have acceded to the Imperial Throne in each and every generation, a unique fact that will never change. Our Divine Realm rightly constitutes the head and shoulders of the world and controls all nations. . . . But recently the loathsome Western barbarians, unmindful of their base position as the lower extremities of the world, have been scurrying impudently across the Four Seas, trampling other nations underfoot.

In the body of the essay Aizawa explained the special character of the Japanese nation (*kokutai*), its godly origins, the vicissitudes of the imperial family, and how "Great Heroes" have appeared at critical moments to save it. Now, he noted, a hero such as Tokugawa Ieyasu was needed to take charge of the realm, prod the daimyo to rearm, and revive the fighting capacity of samurai so that they could stop the barbarian encroachment. He discussed the domestic and foreign influences that had corrupted Japan over the centuries, leading to its present parlous condition—"shaman cultism, Buddhism, the ideas of perverse Confucians, petty scholasticism, Christianity," and, of late, Dutch Studies. The main domestic problems that required remedy were those Yūkoku had earlier identified—urban samurai lacking martial qualities and an economy marked by luxury and inequities—and only by addressing them could a foundation be laid for repelling the barbarians.

He drafted short chapters explaining current world conditions and the history of the barbarian advance on Japan and then dwelt at length

53. The quotations from *Shinron* come from ibid., pp. 149, 165, 275–77. For an examination of Aizawa's conceptual categories, see Koschmann, *Mito Ideology*, pp. 56–80.

on the means of coping: internal reforms to envigorate Japan, measures of coastal defense and military strengthening, and for long-term security, reviving the basic virtues of the imperial land through restoration of proper customs, proper understanding, and proper relationships. In closing, he returned to his observation that Edo's decision to repel foreign ships had set the stage for vigorous action: "If we resolutely achieve the tasks bequeathed by Amaterasu at home, and establish impenetrable safeguards against subversion from without, the foreign beasts will never be able to beguile our people no matter how hard they try." It is essential first to straighten the country within, because "only then will we rescue all nations in the world from suffering, only then will we eliminate every vestige of the Western barbarians' occult religions from the face of the earth, and only then will we spare the children of our Middle Kingdom from barbarian cunning." To this end, he had explained what must be done:

> Elucidating "what is essential to a nation" (*kokutai*), being informed on world affairs, understanding fully the barbarians' nature, strengthening national defense, and establishing a long-range policy—these represent the best form of loyalty and filial devotion, the best method of recompensing Imperial Ancestors and Heavenly Deities, and the best way for bakufu and daimyo to rescue their peoples and dispense benevolent rule for eternity.

But in the final analysis, he noted, "the *Book of Changes* says, 'The Way does not implement itself; that requires the Man of Talent and Virtue.' To solve difficult problems as these arise and to devise methods of dealing with changed situations—these tasks await the appearance of the Great Hero."

Narinaga, it turned out, was not the Great Hero. He even declined to show *Shinron* to Edo leaders lest it offend them. But in 1829 he died and his brother Nariaki succeeded. Nariaki was a reformer, aspired to be the Hero, and found the ideas of Aizawa, Fujita Yūkoku, and Yūkoku's son, Tōko, thoroughly appropriate. Under his guidance, as noted in chapter 21, the reformist ideas of Mitogaku were given vigorous expression in political action. By the late 1840s they were even having an impact, however begrudged, on bakufu policy.

The politicization of kokugaku proceeded differently. The seminal figure in that process was Hirata Atsutane, who was born in 1776, the fourth son of a minor vassal of Akita han.

As a boy Hirata studied Confucianism with a disciple of Yamazaki Ansai's and medicine with an uncle. His childhood, which encompassed the Tenmei famine years, was said to be unhappy, and he left his family and moved to Edo at age nineteen. There he studied the martial arts, works of noted Japanese Confucians, and materials on Buddhism, Hinduism, Taoism, and rangaku. He also gained access to some Chinese-language works on Christianity and in 1801 discovered the writings of Motoori Norinaga, which aroused a strong interest in kokugaku. From this eclectic menu, he fashioned his own view of Truth, teaching it at the Ibukiya, his school in Edo.

Hirata styled himself a disciple of Norinaga's, and his first written work, in 1803, was an attack on Dazai Shundai quite in the manner of earlier kokugaku scholars. Thereafter, however, he grew more adventuresome, and Norinaga's other followers disputed his claim of discipleship and attacked his scholarship as erroneous. Most of them retained Norinaga's interest in poetry and philology and his belief that their mastery was essential for understanding the ancient Japanese spirit. Hirata, in contrast, placed Shintō and religion at the center of his teachings, rejecting poetry as an obstacle to understanding.[54] His may have been the deviant view, but in the end it triumphed, dominating kokugaku thought into the twentieth century. It did so, one suspects, because it addressed issues of public concern whereas his rivals spoke mainly to scholars.

One of the first issues he dealt with reflected his reading in kokugaku and Christianity. An essay he drafted in 1806 reworked traditional creation stories to give unprecedented clarity to the concepts of a transcendent creator deity and an afterlife clearly linked to temporal existence. The mystery of life's relationship to death held his interest, prompting him in later years to question hermits about their powers, study reports of goblins (tengu), and interview a person "who claimed to be the reincarnation of a dead man."[55] His later writings reiterated the notions of a transcendent creator deity and an afterlife closely linked to this world, so that those who die are not simply consigned to "the dreaded and dark world" of yomi.[56]

Even while combining ideas of diverse provenance to buttress his interpretations, however, Hirata also asserted the superiority of native thought. We earlier noted how he defined Japanese learning as the sum of all understandings, so that foreign teachings "can help Japan if Jap-

54. H. D. Harootunian, *Things Seen and Unseen* (Chicago: University of Chicago Press, 1988), p. 133.
55. Devine, "Hirata Atsutane and Christian Sources," p. 39.
56. H. D. Harootunian, "The Consciousness of Archaic Form in the New Realism of Kokugaku," in Najita and Scheiner, eds., *Japanese Thought*, p. 96.

anese study them and select their good points."[57] He also warned that careless acceptance of foreign learning may damage the mind, which will prevent one's grasping the unique virtue of the Japanese spirit. Not only Japanese thought, but even the people "differ completely from and are superior to the peoples of China, India, Russia, Holland, Siam, Cambodia, and all other countries of the world." This is so because "we, down to the most humble man and woman, are the descendants of the gods." And, as people throughout the world know, the gods, not only of Japan but of all the world, "were without exception born in Japan. Japan is thus the homeland of the gods."[58]

Hirata's religious views, it appears, contributed to the popular appeal of his teachings. And his lively insistence on Japanese superiority anchored them in ethnic pride, giving them an appeal that was especially salient in decades when the diplomatic evidence conveyed a less reassuring verdict.

Among the elite, Hirata scored triumphs of a visible sort that helped spread his teachings. Shintō studies at the imperial court had encompassed two traditions for generations, and Hirata attacked them both. He denounced the Suika Shintō tradition that traced back to Yamazaki Ansai for being riddled with Chinese thought and the older Yoshida Shintō tradition for containing Buddhist influences. By 1823 the two schools had modified their teachings enough to accommodate his interpretation of the founding myths, and that new formulation became official orthodoxy later in the century.

This obscure man of the north had thus established himself as both a popular teacher and the arbiter of religious Truth at the highest political level. In 1838 he was even invited to serve as advisor to the lord of Akita, the prodigal son vindicated. In the course of his life he produced a body of writings that celebrated Japan to an unprecedented extent, excoriated Chinese learning in particular, warned of the dangers in rangaku, while crediting it with virtues that surpassed Chinese thought, and in the end etched his name indelibly in Japan's history.

In the process, Hirata created enemies among disciples of Norinaga, Shintō scholars, and others whose views he denounced, and his prominence finally brought him to grief. In 1839, as mentioned earlier, the bakufu was convulsed by a spasm of anti-rangaku persecution spurred on by Hayashi Jussai's son, a disciple of Ch'eng-Chu Confucianism. Hirata's disciple, Satō Nobuhiro, was a suspect in the case, and one can

57. Keene, *Japanese Discovery*, pp. 158–59. The source is *Kodō taii,* dated 1811.
58. Also from *Kodō taii,* as quoted in Tsunoda et al., comps., *Sources,* p. 544.

imagine that Hirata's own qualified expressions of admiration for Dutch learning raised a few eyebrows, but he emerged unscathed. In 1841, however, he fared less well. After he published *Tenchō mukyūreki*, a work that elaborated his own view on the imperial legacy, bakufu leaders, who were launching their Tenpō reform, with its claim to pervasive managerial authority, denounced him and ordered him out of Edo, much as they had banned Nobuhiro a quarter of a century earlier. He returned to Akita, where he died two years later. His ideas did not die, however, and from the 1860s on, they inspired many men to risk their lives in pursuit of their convictions.

Between 1790 and 1850, the tenor of Japanese political thought changed profoundly. The noisy quarrels of Confucian dogmatists and risque chatter of popular writers that displeased Sadanobu in 1790 sounded like parlor patter compared to the angry denunciations and visionary rhetoric that echoed around the realm by midcentury. From plebeian celebrants of disorder to academic theoreticians and political reformers, the range of ideas and magnitude of schemes had grown exponentially.

That transformation in thought was linked to changes elsewhere in society. At lower social levels the long-term changes in rural social organization—and the heightened inequities and hardships they produced—laid a foundation for disbelief and disengagement. Among the more fortunate, the spread of schooling broadened intellectual horizons and created a clientele for attractive ideas. And among the more politically conscious the combination of exacerbated domestic difficulties and unprecedented foreign complications discredited old verities, reactivated old fears, and forced people to think anew. The following chapters examine the political developments that spurred and were spurred by the new thought and that eventuated in the dismantling of the early modern order.

The Best of Times, 1790–1825

Early-nineteenth-century Japan presents a curious face to the historian. Following the horrific years of the Tenmei famine, the realm enjoyed four decades of comparatively quiet prosperity, which gave way in the 1830s to years of hardship akin to Tenmei. Japanese scholars know the period of prosperity as *kaseiki*. At one level the term is simply a neologism denoting the Bun*ka*–Bun*sei* year periods (1804–29), but by a slight change in the character for *sei,* it also means a period of "change" or "transformation." The term suggests a period in which matters were in flux, going from an older condition to a newer one. As to what changes were occurring and why, scholars find ample room to disagree, but the changes in arts and letters discussed in chapters 18 and 19 were among the more visible ones. The domestic contextual issues and growing foreign contacts discussed below were other areas of substantial change.

The image of the decades after 1790 as comfortable ones must, of course, be qualified. The Kantō still suffered aftereffects of Mount Asama's eruption, and rural discord continued to become more pronounced. The rulers kept wrestling with fiscal problems, and poorer samurai bore the brunt of their efforts. The articulate loser's view of the times is preserved in a rambling essay of 1816, *Seji kenmonroku*, whose author, allegedly an Edo ronin, used the nom de plume Buyō Inshi. In contrast to the virtuous old days of responsible rulers, stoic, frugal vassals, and a well-ordered status system, he saw decadent, wasteful lords, soft city samurai, commoners disrespectful of their betters, monks and priests utterly corrupt, wealth residing in all the wrong places, money-grubbing the rule, and rich and poor bitterly at loggerheads.

Clearly the domestic *kasei* were not to Buyō's liking. Foreign affairs were no more reassuring, because these decades witnessed an unprecedented series of diplomatic incidents that alarmed the political elite and led the bakufu to modify its foreign policy, eventuating in 1825 in the adoption of a more rigid posture that seemed for a while to bring the foreign threat under control. Later, however, that "success" in kaseiki diplomacy contributed to the agony of Tenpō.

THE CONTEXT OF PROSPERITY

If one is to view the later Tokugawa period as an era of stasis, then the evidence of early-nineteenth-century socioeconomic growth requires explanation. One can point to several factors that abetted it, and in toto they constitute evidence of a momentarily improved ecological balance between available resources and human demand. This altered balance grew out of prior circumstances and was sustained during the decades to 1825 by acts of god and man.

As noted in chapter 13, the people of eighteenth-century Japan expanded salt-water fishing, devised systems of plantation silviculture, and began using ground coal. In the early nineteenth century, these areas of activity grew rapidly, expanding society's energy base, while the side effects of resource depletion and pollution became pronounced only in later generations. Concurrently, means of agronomic intensification spread widely, and thanks to generally favorable weather the negative potential of the new horticultural regimen did not manifest itself harshly in the country at large until the 1830s.

Expansion of the resource base coincided with demographic changes that also proved a boon after 1790. As noted in chapter 12, the population spurt of the seventeenth century ended during the eighteenth as several kinds of social change reduced the numbers of children per household. By century's end the patterns of mobility, marriage, and birth control that kept families small were well entrenched. Moreover, the Tenmei famine hammered total population downward, in the process effecting demographic rearrangements that benefited survivors. The famine may well have left a population containing fewer unproductive—elderly, sickly, or very young—members. More certainly it drove people out of marginal locations, notably the northeast, leaving more of the survivors situated in the areas that benefited most from concurrent changes in agronomy, forestry, fisheries, and coal use. When weather patterns improved, then, the abandoned areas became a frontier for rehabilitation work of the sort that Ninomiya Sontoku handled so well.

These basic changes in the relationship of resources to human demand worked to society's advantage after 1790 for a number of reasons. The archipelago's long period of generally favorable weather optimized the benefits of agronomic change and river and reclamation work. Reproductive practice meant that improved economic conditions translated into only modest demographic growth, the officially recorded 24,891,441 commoners of 1792 growing to 27,201,400 in 1828. So it seems plausible that economic gains per capita were enjoyed by at least a part of the populace. Finally, during the Tenmei famine, the rulers lost some of their ability to tax rural production, and the Kansei reform of 1787–93 did less to restore tax collection than to drive down elite consumption. As a result, the increased output of the post-Tenmei decades flowed more broadly to the general public. This occurred, it appears, even though the long-lived shogun Ienari (r. 1787–1837) and his coterie of followers gained notoriety for their luxury, in part no doubt because their standard of living contrasted so sharply with the grim condition of lesser samurai, who created much of the historical record.

Out of this combination of factors emerged the flourishing cultural life noted in preceding chapters. For the rulers themselves, however, the years 1790–1825 were less reassuring: in essence domestic affairs muddled from better to worse and foreign affairs from worse to better.

DOMESTIC ISSUES

There is a tedious familiarity to the bulk of government activity during these years. As in the eighteenth century, fiscal problems towered over other domestic concerns, eliciting persistent attempts to cut expenses and generate income. To cut expenses, bakuhan leaders called for austerity, trimmed vassal salaries, tried to contain the costs of river work, and did their best to minimize the expense of coping with foreign visitors. Their income policies included minting, printing, borrowing, manipulating prices, and monopolizing and licensing commerce, all practiced with mixed success.

For example, the bakufu minting of *nishugin* in 1772 proved very profitable, as noted in chapter 15, and when finances again grew chaotic after 1818, Edo leaders issued another gold-convertible nishugin and also *isshugin*, coins worth half a *nishu*. They both circulated well. With the flood of red ink approaching an all-time high, the bakufu began debasing a number of its other coins as well, both gold and silver. By one calculation that activity generated nearly 6 million ryō of income by 1830.[1]

Much of Matsudaira Sadanobu's Kansei reform addressed fiscal problems, and most of the reform's other facets are familiar because his main concerns were essentially those of his revered grandfather, Yoshimune. He attempted to improve the bakufu's administrative effectiveness, enhance the condition of shogunal retainers, maintain the city of Edo, control merchants, and ease rural hardship.[2] Certain aspects of his policy merit explicit attention, however, because their impact was distinctive and substantial—namely, his concern with moral and intellectual propriety, his dealings with the imperial court, and his concern with Edo.

Edo's condition continued to hold bakufu attention after Sadanobu left office because it was closely tied to broader issues involving the Kantō region and the overall organization of the economy. During the kasei period, his successors wrestled continually with those matters.

1. Takehiko Ohkura and Hiroshi Shimbo, "The Tokugawa Monetary Policy in the Eighteenth and Nineteenth Centuries," *Explorations in Economic History* 18 (1978): 110, n. 18.

2. The most comprehensive treatment of the Kansei reform in English is Herman Ooms, *Charismatic Bureaucrat: A Political Biography of Matsudaira Sadanobu, 1758–1829* (Chicago: University of Chicago Press, 1975). On monetary and fiscal aspects of Sadanobu's policy, see also Isao Soranaka, "The Kansei Reforms—Success or Failure?" *MN* 33-2 (Summer 1978): 151–61.

SADANOBU AND INTELLECTUAL DISCIPLINE

From the earliest days of their regime, Tokugawa rulers had been concerned about ideas and values, seeking to taboo views subversive of the regime. During the seventeenth century, certain Buddhist sects and Christianity had been main foci of attention; during the eighteenth century, however, emphasis moved to a more diffuse interest in quieting discordant voices of all sorts, whether they be Confucians, physicians, or others. Sadanobu favored sharper intellectual priorities, promoting them among shogunal vassals in particular but in society at large as well. His policies for guiding thought and values entailed both carrot and stick: the carrot of acceptable schooling and the stick of punishment for commentators who strayed beyond the pale.

His best-known decree on scholarship was the ban on heterodoxy (*igaku no kin*) of 1790. Arguing, erroneously, that Ch'eng-Chu teachings were the "orthodox" learning favored by successive shogun since Ieyasu's day, Sadanobu designated them the only instruction acceptable at the Shōheikō, the Hayashi school at Shōheizaka. He had revealed his belief in the efficacy of Ch'eng-Chu thought six years earlier in a light fictional piece, *Daimyō katagi*, in which he satirized a foolish young lord who pursued the military arts excessively, then indulged in vacuous Confucian rhetoric, only to become an addict to kabuki theater. Not until he had a dream in which a Chinese sage lectured him sternly on Ch'eng-Chu proprieties did the young man come to understand the path to true understanding of the Way.[3]

Almost as soon as Sadanobu became active at Edo in 1787, he moved to make the Shōheikō a citadel of appropriate instruction. Yoshimune had promoted Confucian studies there, and Sadanobu wished to enhance the school's role, but doing so would require great effort because enrollments had been declining from the 1730s. After Yoshimune's death the shrine and school had been neglected and become dilapidated, and the last of its fine buildings were consumed by fire in the 1770s and 1780s. In 1787 the bakufu began reconstructing the school, and the following year Sadanobu started naming distinguished scholars to direct it. In the ban of 1790 he informed the school's directors that

> in recent times a variety of novel doctrines have been preached abroad, and
> in some cases the prevalence of heterodoxy has ruined public morals; if this
> is really due to a decline of orthodoxy, it is altogether inexcusable. . . . Now

3. A translation of *Daimyō katagi* is included in Haruko Iwasaki, "Portrait of a Daimyo: Comical Fiction by Matsudaira Sadanobu," *MN* 38-1 (Spring 1983): 1–48.

you are commanded to . . . sternly forbid heterodoxy to the students; and, further, you shall not confine it to your own school but shall make every effort to reach agreements with other schools to pursue the orthodox learning and to advance men of ability.[4]

Sadanobu revealed his wish for intellectual order—and his impatience with scholarly babble—in this way:

> Who shall support scholarship if this superfluity of scholars—one could count them by the dozen and ship them by the cartload—continue to argue and abuse one another with their various theories, like the bubbling of boiling water or the twisting of strands of thread. . . . [Better that] the study of Sung Confucianism should be continued. Its orthodoxy has stood the test of time; it has commanded the respect of the majority of good men and a good many men have respected it; one can well say that one is least liable to err if one puts one's trust in the Sung teachings.[5]

The ban pressured samurai to focus on Ch'eng-Chu teachings, and more and more of them turned to the Hayashi school to get an education that they knew higher authorities would approve. The school also benefited from expanded bakufu funding, completion of physical reconstruction, delineation of a full curriculum, recruitment of additional scholars, and expansion of staff and regulations. As a result the Shō-heizaka gakumonjo, as the school was known after 1797, enjoyed strong enrollments until the latter part of the nineteenth century:[6]

Period	Enrollments	Yearly average
1774–1786	100	8.0
1787–1792	130	21.7
1793–1838	796	17.7
1839–1867	517	18.4

4. Robert L. Backus, "The Kansei Prohibition of Heterodoxy and Its Effects on Education," *HJAS* 39-1 (June 1979): 57. For other translations of the decree, see Ryusaku Tsunoda et al., comps., *Sources of the Japanese Tradition* (New York: Columbia University Press, 1958), pp. 502–3, and Ooms, *Charismatic Bureaucrat*, p. 132. On the motivation of Sadanobu and his Confucian advisors in issuing the *igaku no kin,* see Backus, "The Motivation of Confucian Orthodoxy in Tokugawa Japan," *HJAS* 39-2 (Dec. 1979): 295–338.

5. R. P. Dore, *Education in Tokugawa Japan* (Berkeley and Los Angeles: University of California Press, 1965), p. 27. Ooms, *Charismatic Bureaucrat*, p. 132, also quotes selectively from this comment, which Sadanobu wrote in 1812.

6. Backus, "Kansei Prohibition," p. 88. I have rounded off the figures for yearly averages. Backus discusses problems in the sources of the numbers, which probably cause them to understate enrollments after 1838.

In Robert Backus's apt phrase, with the changes enacted by Sadanobu, the center at Shōheizaka was "transformed from a temple with a school attached into a school with a temple attached."[7]

Sadanobu intended to use reformed education in staffing government offices. Accordingly he had his scholars design an examination system based on Ch'eng-Chu readings to test candidates for appointment and promotion. The first exams were given in 1792, and after problems in the examination process were resolved by trial and error, bakuhan leaders employed more and more testing in their schools. However, the relationship of tests to office-holding remained modest, overridden by the customary criteria of status and connections.

The establishment of a major school at Shōheizaka was Sadanobu's principal educational achievement, but he also moved to strengthen Ch'eng-Chu by providing the scholar Hattori Rissai with land and funding to operate a school in Edo. A follower of Yamazaki Ansai and a former student at the Kaitokudō in Osaka, Rissai established his school and dutifully provided the expected instruction until his death in 1800.[8]

Politician more than ideologue, Sadanobu was mainly concerned with the competence of bakufu officialdom and beyond that with social order and industry. Hence his attention focused on schools in Edo, especially that at Shōheizaka, which he expected to function as a training center for bakufu vassals. Knowing that some han leaders favored other schools of thought, he encouraged but did not impose his views on them. Nevertheless, in the country at large his educational changes shifted the intellectual trajectory, causing han to favor Ch'eng-Chu in more and more schools and prompting scholars to convert from the doctrines of Sorai or other Confucians. This revitalization of Ch'eng-Chu learning was evident, as noted in chapter 19, in the lively debates of Confucian scholars. And their unease with political engagement may have stemmed as much from reluctance to attack institutions that supported them as from the content of their thought.

Sadanobu also addressed disputes over Chinese and Dutch medicine that had first flared in the 1760s. Although he agreed that Dutch medicine had value, in 1791 he designated the Seijukan, the Taki family's medical school, an official institution, with the task of providing instruction in Chinese medical techniques. In the following decades the

---

7. Robert L. Backus, "The Relationship of Confucianism to the Tokugawa Bakufu as Revealed in the Kansei Educational Reform," *HJAS* 34 (1974): 135. The handsomely reconstructed buildings of the Shōheikō were destroyed in the earthquake of 1923.

8. Backus, "Kansei Prohibition," p. 73.

school's staff pursued the study of Chinese medicine with considerable energy, and the bakufu reaffirmed its Chinese specialization in 1849.[9]

Sadanobu's interest in spiritual guidance ran well beyond the proper education of samurai and physicians, and in that broader arena stick prevailed over carrot. At the level of public morality he was troubled by the reckless lack of restraint that he perceived in popular culture. Kabuki and its related arts, for example, had become so popular among daimyo and lesser samurai that it prompted one disgusted bakufu official to write this in 1802:

> The samisen became extremely popular during the 1740s–60s. Eldest sons of good samurai families and even other sons all took lessons; from morn till night samisen sounds were always to be heard. Eventually they began to perform other Kabuki music and full dramas etc., and followed this depravity to the extent of performing amateur Kabuki plays in residences. High hatamoto officials mimicking riverbed beggars (actors), aping female impersonators and stage heroes![10]

He added, however, that with Sadanobu's denunciation of such frivolities, excesses were checked.

Sadanobu also saw popular fiction as harmful to public morality, especially when authors took ill-concealed potshots at government. In 1790, after a number of popular works (*kibyōshi*) mocked the authorities, he announced that "newly published books are to be regarded as strictly undesirable if they are depraved or a medley of unorthodox ideas."[11] In that spirit he revived long-standing but laxly enforced orders regulating the content of handwritten manuscripts and publications. To assure that publishers and authors took him seriously, in 1791 as noted earlier, his censors made an example of Santō Kyōden, one of the most popular fiction writers of the day, convicting him of violating the law and handcuffing him for fifty days. Later bakufu leaders followed that precedent when they punished Shikitei Sanba in 1799 and Tamenaga Shunsui in 1842.

In a narrower political sphere, Sadanobu disapproved of the punditry that accompanied renewal of foreign contacts. As unauthorized

9. Edwin McClellan, *Woman in the Crested Kimono* (New Haven: Yale University Press, 1985), pp. 161–62, 165–73.

10. C. Andrew Gerstle, "Flowers of Edo: Kabuki and Its Patrons," in Gerstle, ed., *18th Century Japan* (Sydney: Allen & Unwin, 1989), p. 40.

11. Peter F. Kornicki, "*Nishiki no Ura*: An Instance of Censorship and the Structure of a *Sharebon*," *MN* 32-2 (Summer 1977): 156. In this essay Kornicki conveys nicely the logic and immediate effect of Sadanobu's book censorship. Regarding hand-written manuscripts, see Kornicki, "The Enmeiin Affair of 1803: The Spread of Information in the Tokugawa Period," *HJAS* 42-2 (Dec. 1982): 503–33.

ships began reaching Japan, rulers again became concerned lest the "stupid people" be seduced by Christian propaganda smuggled in from abroad. They also believed, however, that leaders must learn more about the Europeans, especially about their military techniques, but about other aspects of their culture as well, and that such knowledge was most accessible through rangaku. Dutch learning, in short, was necessary but dangerous. Some years after retiring from office, Sadanobu spelled out the logic of its control:

> The barbarian nations are skilled in the sciences, and considerable profit may be derived from their works of astronomy and geography, as well as from their military weapons and their methods of internal and external medicine. However, their books may serve to encourage idle curiosity or may express harmful ideas. It might thus seem advisable to ban them, but prohibiting these books would not prevent people from reading them. There is, moreover, profit to be derived from them. Such books and other foreign things should therefore not be allowed to pass in large quantities into the hands of irresponsible people; nevertheless it is desirable to have them deposited in a government library.[12]

How to introduce the desired information to those with "a need to know" without allowing it to fall into the hands of others was a problem the rulers addressed frequently but never fully resolved.

The problem appeared in 1792 during the first of a series of "Russian scares," when, as noted more fully below, Sadanobu jailed the scholar Hayashi Shihei for publishing *Kaikoku heidan,* an unauthorized analysis of foreign relations that he considered alarmist and unacceptably critical of bakufu policy. In 1811 after further diplomatic incidents had alarmed Edo leaders, they moved to tighten control of information from abroad by establishing an office of translation and documentation (*bansho wage goyō*) in Edo, assigning it duties previously handled by scholar-translators in Nagasaki.

SADANOBU AND THE COURT

Even more vexing to Sadanobu than writers and scholars were senior figures in the authority structure, especially the emperor Kōkaku. Sadanobu inherited from Tanuma Okitsugu an absurd little issue that festered all through his six years as bakufu leader and contributed to his

---

12. Donald Keene, *The Japanese Discovery of Europe, 1720–1830* (Stanford: Stanford University Press, 1969), pp. 75–76, quoting Sadanobu's autobiography, *Uge no hito koto.*

resignation in 1793. That issue, the Title Incident (*songo jiken*), grew out of Kōkaku's persistent attempt to have his father, prince Sukehito, designated "retired emperor" (*dajō tennō*) even though he had never served as emperor.[13] The incident was noteworthy both for its residue of ill will and as an indicator that the question of imperial authority, which Takenouchi Shikibu had articulated in the 1750s, was becoming more insistent and that bakufu efforts to suppress it seemed only to exacerbate Edo-Kyoto relations.

During the 1780s, court and bakufu officials in Kyoto sporadically discussed the possibility of conferring the title on the prince, and in 1787, after Kōkaku came of age and Tanuma left office, the court began to press for action. From the outset, Sadanobu appears to have been opposed, perhaps because the plan did not conform to precedents dating from Ieyasu's day or perhaps because he feared it would encourage the shogun Ienari to elevate his own, profligate father to an analogous position as "retired shogun" (*ōgosho*).

Thoroughly versed in the proprieties of Confucian rule, Sadanobu attached great importance to decorous conduct and proper relationships. To avoid an open dispute with the court, he adopted a policy of procrastination and covert resistance pursued through political allies in Kyoto. For two years a proper but desultory correspondence failed to break the stalemate. Near the end of 1791, however, court leaders, their patience exhausted, assembled forty-one officials and advisors and put the question to a vote. In an unprecedented expression of assertiveness, thirty-six of the forty-one voted to defy the bakufu by proclaiming Sukehito's appointment as dajō tennō unilaterally and without further delay. Three nobles favored such an action in due course; only Sadanobu's two allies opposed the motion. The court had at last found the courage to take a stand, at least on internal matters, as Takenouchi had advocated nearly forty years earlier.

When news of the decision reached Edo, Sadanobu realized that the court was mounting an overt challenge to the bakufu: what he had been treating as a matter of propriety had been transformed into a question of authority. To forestall implementation of the vote, he and his colleagues prepared a series of escalating responses intended to intimidate

13. Ooms, *Charismatic Bureaucrat*, pp. 105–19, treats the Title Incident. In 1779 the eight-year-old Kōkaku had succeeded his uncle, Gomomozono, who lacked an heir. For a broader examination of the social function of imperial titles, see Bob Tadashi Wakabayashi, "In Name Only: Imperial Sovereignty in Early Modern Japan," *JJS* 17-1 (Winter 1991): 25–57.

the court and stop it in mid-action. An increasingly tense correspondence ensued, and when the elderly prince fell ill in the summer of 1792, the court decided it could delay no longer. It informed Edo that the titling ceremony would take place three months hence in conjunction with the autumn harvest festival.

The notice proved more than Sadanobu could accept. He directed his delegate in Kyoto to make the court cancel its plan. The court refused. Sadanobu ordered it to send officials to Edo to explain the situation and, implicitly, to receive the orders for punishment that would be presented upon their arrival. With that threat the court agreed to postpone the ceremony but refused to abandon the plan altogether. At that point, even though he might be accused of irreverence toward the court, Sadanobu sent an explicit order to Kyoto that directly forbade the emperor to bestow the title under any circumstances.

That blunt order finally broke the court's resistance and it cancelled the plan. Early in 1793, Sadanobu summoned two court officials to Edo, interrogated them, and then forced the court to dismiss and punish them along with scores of other courtiers who had participated in the scheme. Sadanobu had triumphed. Propriety, if that was what concerned him, had been preserved. Ienari never attempted to elevate his father to ōgosho, and Sukehito's death a year later ended any threat of the issue being revived.

But Edo's victory had a price. Not since the early 1600s had the court shown either such readiness to defy Tokugawa wishes or such ability to achieve near-unanimity on a thorny issue. And the incident was not forgotten: one suspects that the bitter feelings it left helped Motoori Norinaga during his visit to Kyoto in 1801 to cultivate ties with the nobility and promote his ideas about the unique virtue and pristine legacy of the imperial line. In later decades, as nativist teachings gained adherents, the Title Incident stood as evidence of Tokugawa highhandedness and disrespect for the court. Not until 1884, when the Meiji emperor awarded Sukehito the title posthumously, was the matter set right.

More immediately, Sadanobu's insistence in this matter added to his stock of enemies at Edo, and four months after determining punishments for the courtiers, he resigned from his leadership role. Had he accepted Kōkaku's wish at the outset, before the issue escalated into a conflict of authority, it might have passed unnoticed, depriving imperial activists of a cause and sparing Sadanobu severe political embarrassment. Whether such an outcome would have made appreciable difference to either the fate of his rule or the later rise of imperial loyalism is surely impossible to say. But the Title Incident clearly foreshadowed lines of political tension that became prominent during the 1850s and shaped the regime's disintegration during the 1860s.

Finally, the Title Incident added one more facet to Sadanobu's policy of intellectual discipline. He had previously tried to establish correct Confucian thought and orderly medical schooling, to discipline popular culture and limit commentary on diplomatic matters, and following the Title Incident he implemented a measure to control Japanese studies. On the day he resigned bakufu office, seemingly to "take responsibility" for the dispute with the court, the bakufu agreed to fund the Wagaku kōdansho, a school for the study of Japanese history, housing it among hatamoto residences near the castle.

By establishing an approved school under Hanawa Hokinoichi, a noted student of national learning, Sadanobu equipped the bakufu to claim definitive knowledge about ancient Japanese history. That would enable it to assert competence in both matters of court etiquette, such as the Title Incident, and questions of historical interpretation, which unregulated scholars such as Norinaga claimed to propound with authority. Two years later the school was put under the aegis of the schoolmen at Shōheizaka. In the following decades, its scholars collected documents for use in compiling major historical texts that would establish an authoritative Japanese history from earliest times and clarify the role of samurai rule in that history. They also helped Edo control kokugaku, as in the earlier-noted banning of Satō Nobuhiro in 1814 and Hirata Atsutane in 1841.

SADANOBU, EDO, AND THE NORTHEAST

Since its founding the bakufu had given special attention to Edo, its castle town (jōkamachi), placing its well-being before that of all other parts of the realm. And that policy remained unchanged until the 1860s. The position of Edo in Japanese society changed, however, so that by the nineteenth century bakufu attentiveness to the city had very different implications for the country at large than it had had back in the 1600s.

During the seventeenth century, Edo was Japan's political center, but Kyoto was its cultural capital, and Osaka grew into its economic hub. And throughout the rest of the country a large number of vigorous castle towns functioned as regional and local centers that enjoyed a high level of economic and political autonomy. In political, economic, and even cultural terms, the Japan of that day was a highly polycentric society.

During the eighteenth century, all that changed. With "culture's march eastward," Kyoto lost its cultural dominance. And Osaka lost its economic primacy as commercial production migrated into rural areas. Kyoto managed to retain most of its population after 1700, but Osaka slid into a steep and punishing decline, its 1780s population of about 500,000 dropping to some 310,000 by 1860, a process that left it with ruined neighborhoods and grinding poverty. Furthermore, many (but not all) castle towns found their autonomous power eroding as han governments became more dependent on loans from wealthy villagers and urban merchants and costly assistance from Edo. Castle town life also was subjected to greater cultural influence from the cities, which increasingly meant Edo. And, like Osaka, many found their economic strength eroding as production moved into the hinterland and the rise of countrywide commerce caused trade to bypass them.

Edo, by contrast, grew from a predominantly samurai city of perhaps half a million in the mid seventeenth century to a sprawling metropolis of uncounted and uncountable numbers, estimated at a million to a million and a half, the majority of them commoners. In addition to its core populace of samurai, it included by 1800 a large array of interstitial religious figures, scholars, and physicians, and a well-entrenched burgher populace of merchants, shopkeepers, and myriad craftsmen, the brassy Edokko. The base of the social pyramid was a large transient population of menial laborers, male and female entertainers, and assorted poor. These transients, whose presence helped give the Edokko their status pride, were unable to sustain their numbers because of high rates of illness, early death, and movement in search of employment, and because they included many who were unmarried, had married late, or were living apart. They were continually replaced, however, by new waves of immigrants, some coming in search of work, others fleeing famine and local catastrophe in east and northeast Japan.

By 1800 countrywide economic and demographic changes were transforming Japan into an essentially unicentric society. That change in Edo-hinterland relations did not, however, translate directly into bipolar bakufu-versus-han political tension because the change cut through the very heart of domain governance. Major han maintained permanent staff in Edo, so generation after generation of han officials knew the city as their home. Their interests became linked to Edo's, and the more culturally elegant Edo became, the more alienated these people felt from their colleagues back in the hinterland. To many Edo samurai, their castle-town peers were rustics, country bumpkins—"mountain apes" was the term Edo-based samurai of Hirosaki han applied to their fellows up north in the domain.[14] Reasonably enough, those back at the castle commonly viewed their Edo fellows as decadent wastrels undeserving of the name samurai. Edo's rise thus deepened fissures within han, undermining daimyo capacity to oppose bakufu policy, contributing to intradomain tension, and subtly transforming the city from Tokugawa castle town into bastion of the realm's culturally privileged.

This change in Edo's character notwithstanding, bakuhan leaders continued to see their political roles in terms of the original polycentric Tokugawa structure, and bakufu officials continued to treat Edo as their jōkamachi. Sadanobu, in his policy toward the city, mostly followed in the footsteps of his grandfather and other predecessors. He worked to tighten bakufu urban control, weaken the greatest merchants, improve maintenance of streets, waterfronts, and other public facilities, stabilize and even lower commodity prices, return immigrants to their native places, assist the destitute, and build up rice reserves and relief funds against future need.[15]

He went beyond precedent by taking steps to reduce Edo's dependence on Osaka and to forge links between Edo and rural production areas that bypassed Osaka and other castle town intermediaries. For the leader of the bakufu to promote the interests of the shogunal city of Edo at the expense of the shogunal city of Osaka seems especially peculiar, and the explanation for it may lie in a broader tension that pitted northeast Japan against the southwest.[16]

The northeast had long been a frontier zone, whereas the southwest, the Kamigata area in particular, was the ancient seat of civilization. Some degree of tension between the two ran through much of Japan's history, and during the eighteenth century, those vague traditions of difference and hostility were sharpened by intensifying disparities of regional experience in terms of crop failure, famine, and living conditions. While the economy of the southwest continued to experience modest growth, the region from the northern Kantō outward struggled

14. McClellan, *Woman in the Crested Kimono*, pp. 67–68.
15. Ooms, *Charismatic Bureaucrat*, pp. 87–100.
16. The regional distinction made here correlates roughly with the Region I–Region II construct of Susan B. Hanley and Kozo Yamamura, *Economic and Demographic Change in Preindustrial Japan, 1600–1868* (Princeton: Princeton University Press, 1977), pp. 19–24, although their regions are more theoretical than geographical entities.

with hardship and depopulation. The regional tension found one focus late in the eighteenth century, when the possibility of developing Ezo arose, as reported in chapter 13. In debates about the matter, most of the supportive commentators hailed from the northeast, with pundits arguing that development of Ezo would enhance the economy of the whole region. Opposition to the idea seemed to come primarily from interests in Nagasaki and Osaka, who feared competition for foreign trade and diversion of resources from their region.

The northeast also experienced a burgeoning intellectual life that surely fostered regional self-consciousness. Seen in the growing number of Tō-hoku haikai poets, it also showed up in scholarship, with intellectuals from there becoming mainstays of both kokugaku and Mitogaku as well as rangaku. In the spirit of Andō Shōeki of Hachinohe, observers from the northeast provided some of the most radical, late-Tokugawa critiques of the established order and produced some of the most innovative visions of social reconstruction. In the end, intellectuals from the northeast failed to convert their ideas into effective political juggernauts because the region was poorer and less populous than the southwest. Instead, the lead in countrywide reform was seized by southwesterners during the 1860s, and they implemented the vision of change that produced Meiji Japan. But earlier in the century the northeast provided much of Japan's intellectual dynamism, as seen in the writings of Mito scholars, Hirata Atsutane, Honda Toshiaki, Ōtsuki Gentaku, Sakuma Shōzan, and Satō Nobuhiro.

How fully Sadanobu himself saw affairs from a Tōhoku perspective is unclear. Like so many high-status samurai, he was actually born and grew up in Edo, becoming daimyo of Shirakawa han as an adult. He gained fame through his handling of the Tenmei famine in the han, however, and it seems plausible that he would have acquired the northeasterners' resentment of the smug and affluent southwest, especially its great merchants. It is true that when he addressed the issue of Ezo development, he halted it—despite contrary advice from his advisor, friend, and colleague Honda Tadakazu, lord of neighboring Izumi han—nominally for fiscal reasons, but more probably because the project was linked to Tanuma. However, he balanced that action by ordering reductions in the volume of Dutch and Chinese trade at Nagasaki, in toto denying potential gain to the northeast while imposing a net loss on the southwest.

Concern over the imbalance between northeast and southwest seems implicit in Sadanobu's new departures in Edo policy, specifically his

moves to end what he saw as Osaka's overly advantageous role in the
Edo economy. His coinage policies were designed to benefit Edo at the
expense of Osaka merchants. He imposed limits on the amount of sake
they could ship to Edo. To lower the cost of lamp oil in Edo, he ordered
oil produced in the Kinai to bypass Osaka middlemen when destined
for Edo. To displace Kinai cotton goods in Edo, he established direct
links between Kantō producers and Edo merchandisers, and he took
similar steps to replace southwestern paper with paper produced in the
Mito vicinity.[17] Cumulatively, these measures furthered the trend toward
a unicentric society dominated by Edo, and they strengthened the Kantō
and its northern hinterland at the expense of the southwest.

KASEIKI (1804–1829) AND THE KANTŌ

As suggested above, several developments of the eighteenth century enabled Japanese society to obtain maximum benefit from the improved
weather of the early nineteenth century. This "thick glue" at the base
of society contributed to the political stability of the day, but it was
abetted by a layer of "thin glue" at the top, a layer applied by the shogun, Ienari.

Ienari's fifty-year tenure made him by far the most durable of all
shogun, but he remains a shadowy figure to historians. Unlike Yoshimune he appears to have left the details of governance to subordinates,
contenting himself with the pursuit of high-level political alliances. This
he did by taking to wife a lady from the court nobility who had been
adopted by the lord of Satsuma and then by acquiring forty secondary
consorts of good ancestry, of whom sixteen begot him fifty-five children. He subsequently placed his offspring in daimyo houses as adopted
heirs and wives, working mostly with han leaders in Edo rather than
those in castle towns. He consolidated the marriage alliances with gifts
and favors, such as the handsome Akamon, or Red Gate, which he
presented to Maeda of Kaga in 1827 when the lord wed his twenty-
fourth child. The gate was erected at Maeda's mansion in Edo, which
subsequently became the main campus of the University of Tokyo. It
stands there today.

Ienari's energetic pursuit of alliances with courtiers, daimyo, and other
people of consequence neutralized much political criticism. In all likelihood it helped the bakufu continue making onerous demands on dai-

17. Ooms, *Charismatic Bureaucrat*, p. 90.

myo for river work, coastal defense, and other costly tasks. And it likely helped quiet the unrest that Sadanobu had provoked in Kyoto, muffled worries about foreign affairs, and blunted complaints when the bakufu extended its control over the lands of fief holders in the Kantō.

Several factors sustained bakufu interest in tightening control of the Kantō. Edo's great size made its provisioning difficult, and Sadanobu had increased its dependence on Kantō production. But the Kantō was hardly an ideal "breadbasket," because its administration was badly fragmented, with large numbers of petty shogunal vassals and daimyo, as well as the bakufu itself, holding parcels of land in fief. That fragmentation, which commonly spread the tax yield of villages among several fief holders, produced peasant complaints about inequitable taxes, corvée duty, and other burdens. And the complaints sometimes turned into protests that hurt Edo.

Commercialization of the economy further complicated the tasks of governing and taxing.[18] It increased the amount of travel and hence the need to maintain roads, fords, and highway stations, which meant more funding and coordinating of corvée labor. Greater circulation of money brought an increase in gambling, highway robbery, and prostitution, which created more need for effective regional police work. And finally, as noted in chapter 13, the expanding task of large-stream management prodded Edo leaders more and more to encroach on fief authority in the Kantō. Consequently, as Kantō production became more important to Edo, Sadanobu's successors attempted through various initiatives to protect their city's interests by remedying these diverse problems.

Sadanobu had tried to improve Edo's control of bakufu lands in the Kantō by juggling local administrators and putting finance officials in Edo more directly in charge of the lands. His successors tried harder. In 1803 they expanded the finance office's authority to coordinate both preventive and emergency river work throughout the Kantō no matter what domains the rivers traversed. And two years later they revamped their district control system by appointing eight intendants, giving them assistants, and making them responsible for designated parts of the Kantō, regardless of whether the villages therein were assigned to daimyo, minor shogunal retainers, or the bakufu itself.

In subsequent years, other measures were enacted to manage prices of Kantō products, and police attempted to control the lawbreakers.

18. David L. Howell, "Hard Times in the Kantō: Economic Change and Village Life in Late Tokugawa Japan," *Modern Asian Studies* 23-2 (May 1989): 349–71, examines the ambiguities of the early nineteenth-century Kantō economic situation.

During the 1820s, however, as fiscal conditions worsened and the rural situation began to deteriorate, disorder became more troublesome. In 1827 the bakufu enacted a more complete package of administrative changes and admonitions intended to create a more unified and disciplined rural structure to control beggers, gamblers, the disgruntled, and the disobedient in the Kantō.[19] The effort was disrupted a few years later by the Tenpō famine, however, and the problem of Kantō management persisted until the bakufu's collapse.

THE THREAT FROM THE NORTH, 1792–1813

A powerful new dynamic was introduced to Japanese history in the 1790s.[20] By then, as noted in chapter 16, a new perception of Japan's proper relationship to the outside world was rapidly acquiring adherents within the country. This perception, expressed as the kokugaku vision of Japan's unique virtue, and which Motoori Norinaga defined in essentially religious terms, endowed Japan with intrinsic superiority, a superiority of sacred importance because it was anchored in the will of the gods. As this image of Japan matured, the older, simpler notion that Christianity was subversive of the polity and must be controlled for reasons of state and elite convenience—a notion that seems to have lost force within officialdom during the eighteenth century[21]—was displaced by the view that foreign influence was intolerably hurtful because it was a threat not merely to the polity but to elemental virtue itself.

From the 1790s on, this newly flourishing ethnic self-image began to collide with resurgent European global aggressiveness in a way that caused issues of diplomacy and ideology to become desperately entangled,

19. Marius B. Jansen, "Japan in the Early Nineteenth Century," in *The Cambridge History of Japan*, vol. 5, *The Nineteenth Century*, ed. Jansen (Cambridge: Cambridge University Press, 1989), pp. 84–85.

20. This section is based on materials in George Alexander Lensen, *The Russian Push toward Japan* (Princeton: Princeton University Press, 1959), pp. 22–256; Keene, *Japanese Discovery*, pp. 31–59; John J. Stephan, *The Kuril Islands* (London: Oxford University Press, 1974), pp. 57–85; John Whitney Hall, *Tanuma Okitsugu, 1719–1788* (Cambridge, Mass.: Harvard University Press, 1955), pp. 100–105; Ooms, *Charismatic Bureaucrat*, pp. 119–21; Bob Tadashi Wakabayashi, *Anti-Foreignism and Western Learning in Early Modern Japan* (Cambridge, Mass.: Harvard University Press, 1986), pp. 65–68.

21. Thus the discovery of hidden Christians in Nagasaki during the 1790s seems to have produced a cover-up rather than reprisals by the local magistrate. See J. L. Breen, "Heretics in Nagasaki: 1790–1796," in Ian Nish, ed., *Contemporary European Writing on Japan* (Kent: Paul Norbury, 1988), pp. 10–16.

creating unprecedented political stresses that culminated in destruction of the Tokugawa regime, radical changes in Japan's political structure, and a profound shift in the historical trajectory of its society.

Russian explorers, adventurers, empire builders, and traders had been moving about eastern Siberia and adjacent seas since the seventeenth century, and they reached Japan in the eighteenth. They first came to Edo's attention in the summer of 1739, when Yoshimune learned of foreign ships approaching the east coast near Sendai and southeast of Edo. At the latter spot, the foreigners landed, obtained provisions, engaged in a bit of ad hoc trade, and departed. At the time, the Chinese traders in Nagasaki were protesting a reduction in their authorized trade, and not wanting any more trouble, Yoshimune instructed daimyo to deploy enough troops to seize the visitors if they tried to return but to let them depart if they chose.[22]

For decades after that, the Russians were preoccupied elsewhere, and their contact with Japan was sporadic and indirect, mostly carried on through residents of the Kuril Islands. When a Russian expedition did reach Hokkaido in 1778–79, Matsumae officials handled its request for trade locally. They turned it down, instructed the Russians to go to Nagasaki if they desired further contact, and concealed the entire episode from Edo.

By then, however, news of Russian activity was filtering into Japan from other sources, prompting Kudō Heisuke, a physician of Sendai han, to make further inquiries and draft a small essay titled *Akaezo fūsetsu kō* on the subject of the Russians, who were identified as "Red Ainu." Hoping to promote development of the northeast, Kudō downplayed the Russian "threat," arguing instead that the "Red Ainu" really wanted peaceable trade and that it would benefit Japan to develop Ezo and pursue trade with the Russians and other people of the region. Given Ezo's sparse population and rich natural resources, Kudō saw opportunity for colonization and development. Insofar as the Russians might become a threat, he argued, populating the region and making it "Japanese" would strengthen it against their advance.

In 1783 Kudō's essay appears to have caught the eye of Tanuma

---

22. Yoshi S. Kuno, *Japan's Expansion on the Asiatic Continent* (Berkeley and Los Angeles: University of California Press, 1940), 2: 219–26. Kuno gives a translation of the bakufu order on p. 214. Lensen, *Russian Push*, pp. 50–56. Lensen notes that Russian and Japanese versions of the encounter are quite dissimilar, the Russian ones making it sound much more friendly, the Japanese correctly minimal.

Okitsugu. Despite his interest in the matter, however, domestic difficulties kept "Red Ainu" off the bakufu's political agenda for nearly a decade.

THE LAXMAN AFFAIR

In Russia, meanwhile, a new policy toward Japan was being set in motion. In 1791 Catherine the Great chartered an expedition to establish commercial relations, and the mission, led by naval Lieutenant Adam Laxman, reached northeast Hokkaido late in 1792. Laxman was to present his request for trade in Edo, using the return of some Japanese castaways as pretext for the visit, but with cold weather approaching, he decided to winter over at Nemuro. When informed of the situation by Matsumae officials, Sadanobu accepted the wintering arrangement, seeing it as a way to gain time for defense preparation.

Edo leaders were already on edge owing to the recent publication of Hayashi Shihei's essay, *Kaikoku heidan,* mentioned above. The second son of a minor bakufu retainer, Shihei had taken service as a scholar-attendant of the daimyo of Sendai. Around 1770 he became interested in defense matters and proceeded to explore Ezo. Subsequent study convinced him that Japan was intolerably vulnerable to foreign attack, so in 1791 he published his essay, which waved the bloody shirt of a Russian menace advancing from the north.

Shihei argued that coastal cannon and naval forces, including the large seagoing vessels currently prohibited by law, were essential for an island state such as Japan. He charged that the accepted military principles of Chinese origin were inappropriate, that compared to Europe, Japan was militarily backward, and that only by serious attention to samurai training and defense preparation could the realm be protected. Evoking the specter of the thirteenth-century Mongol invasions, he warned of the dire risk from continental aggressors. Russia in particular was a menace, he said, because it was so large and powerful, had expanded as far eastward as it could, had turned southward, and was descending by way of the Kurils toward Japan.

Sadanobu may well have agreed with much of Shihei's analysis, but the author had criticized bakufu law on naval vessels, had presented his views on government affairs publicly and without authorization, and had done so in a way that Edo leaders considered alarmist. In a move that resembled Tsunayoshi's confinement of Kumazawa Banzan after he warned of a Manchu invasion a century earlier, Sadanobu jailed

Shihei and shortly afterward remanded him to house arrest in Sendai, where he died a year later. Sadanobu also ordered copies of his essay destroyed. Within two months of that order, however, news of Laxman's visit forced officials again to discuss the defense of Ezo.

Laxman's arrival seemed to confirm Hayashi's thesis. As diplomats headed north to interrogate the Russians, Sadanobu took charge of coastal defenses. He made inspection tours of the Kantō coastline and, lest daimyo not know what to do, reissued bakufu instructions on the handling of foreign ships. Meanwhile, his officials, together with those of Matsumae, met the Russians for conversations, which continued through the winter. While they talked, Sadanobu ordered coastal han to prepare defenses and conduct training exercises, and he continued inspecting the Kantō shoreline to ensure that if Laxman did indeed proceed to Edo, he could be handled.

In the summer of 1793, negotiators in Hokkaido informed the Russians that they could not return the castaways in Edo, warning that if they tried, they would "be taken prisoner and not accepting any excuses, will be dealt with according to our laws."[23] Lest their refusal to approve Laxman's main purpose lead to confrontation, however, they offered a compromise by giving him a permit to enter Nagasaki harbor, the only place where he would be allowed to pursue any trade negotiations. The permit specified that

> Permission for entrance into Nagasaki harbor is granted to one vessel of the great Russian empire; as explained already, foreign vessels are forbidden to come to places other than Nagasaki, and we repeat that the Christian faith is not tolerated in our country, so that upon arrival there [must] be no sign of it, either in act of worship or oblation; should any agreement be reached, nothing must be done contrary to our laws as laid down in the prescript handed to you by us; it is for this purpose that we give the paper to Adam Laxman.

The permit seemed to offer the prospect of trading arrangements like those of the Dutch. Understanding that a later embassy would be allowed to trade in Nagasaki and possibly even negotiate diplomatic ties, Laxman turned over the castaways in Matsumae and departed without approaching Edo.

As matters worked out, events in revolutionary France so commanded St. Petersburg's attention that a decade passed before the Russians followed up on the Laxman permit. For Edo, however, the incident had a much more immediate effect. It clarified foreign policy and

23. This and the next quotation are from Lensen, *Russian Push*, pp. 113–14.

pushed it in the direction of greater rigidity. Generalizing selectively from particular incidents, Sadanobu claimed, not entirely correctly, that customary policy required all foreign ships to go to Nagasaki. Furthermore, ships from unrecognized countries were to be driven off (*uchi harai*) or impounded and destroyed and their crews imprisoned if they approached Japan at other points.[24] To enforce the posture, he urged consolidation of bakufu control in the north, the casting of more cannon, and improved coastal defense at the entrance to Edo Bay. And to make sure that he himself did not become neglectful of the danger, he inscribed this poem on a drawing of a foreign vessel,

> Not to forget
> even for one moment of sleep
> that these vessels can come here,
> is of utmost importance to the world.[25]

St. Petersburg's failure to follow up on Laxman's visit did not end Edo's northern problem. In 1795 a Russian entrepreneur sent a group of settlers to Uruppu, and for the better part of a decade thereafter the bakufu tried to repel the Russians from the Kurils and strengthen Japan's presence in Ezo, as noted in chapter 13, by deploying military forces, explorers, and administrators to the region.

The furor over Ezo did not go unnoticed by scholars. One of the first to champion an aggressive northern policy was Honda Toshiaki. In 1792 he memorialized Sadanobu, urging him to develop Ezo and warning that the Russians had "displayed such diligence in their colonization efforts that eighteen or nineteen Kuril islands and the great land of Kamchatka have already been occupied. Forts are said to have been built at various places, and a central administration established . . . that rules the natives with benevolence."[26] Other scholars shared his concern, in part because they read his works, as in the case of Aizawa Seishisai of Mito, mentioned in chapter 19.

Despite this emerging concern with the northern frontier, domestic issues obstructed bakufu responses to the Russian advance. From 1803, moreover, developments to the south redirected Edo's attention, reminding officials that foreign dangers did not come solely from the north. That year an American ship reached Nagasaki in pursuit of trade, and almost as soon as its request was denied, two British ships entered the

24. Wakabayashi, *Anti-Foreignism and Western Learning*, pp. 66–67.
25. Quoted in Lensen, *Russian Push*, p. 183. He indicates that *yo* ("the world") is to be understood as meaning Japan.
26. Keene, *Japanese Discovery*, p. 182.

harbor briefly. The following year a Russian vessel bearing an official delegate, Nikolai Rezanov, appeared there, demonstrating that developments north and south were not unconnected and precipitating a new decade of complicated Russo-Japanese relations.

REZANOV AND HIS FRIENDS

The commercial vessel *Nadezdha,* flying an Imperial Russian naval flag, brought Rezanov to Nagasaki via Cape Horn in the autumn of 1804 after St. Petersburg finally decided to use Laxman's permit.[27] In the optimistic view of the Russian press, Rezanov's expedition would "go to Japan in order to open and establish commercial relations for Russia with these islands, where the industry and ignorance of the people are equally surprising, where some skills have reached a degree of perfection unknown to us, but where reason is still in the cradle." The press anticipated agreeable trading because the Japanese, for all their rudeness, "are not such spiteful and cunning swindlers in trade, as our neighbors the Chinese."

This somewhat tentative spirit of goodwill did not long survive Rezanov's contact with bakufu officialdom. He waited six months, confined to his ship and a small residence on shore while officials and information shuttled between Nagasaki and Edo. When the formal answer did arrive in the spring of 1805, it was a lengthy denial of his request. Edo asserted that only Chinese, Koreans, Ryūkyūans, and the Dutch were allowed into Japan; relations with others were impermissible. "This is a hereditary law for the protection of our country's frontiers. How can our government change a hereditary law merely on account of your country?" Trade, the statement went on, would entail exchanging valuable Japanese goods for worthless foreign items and would only create quarrels and moral decay, so "do not come again in vain. You must sail home quickly."

What led Edo to reject Rezanov's request is unclear. Two months after his arrival, the bakufu sent Hayashi Jussai, the highly esteemed head of the Shōheizaka gakumonjo, together with other officials, to Kyoto to tell the court how it was handling foreign affairs. Upon hearing their report, the court may simply have acquiesced in a policy position already taken, but an official in Nagasaki is said to have reported

27. The following several quotations come from Lensen, *Russian Push,* pp. 128, 155, 161–63, 165, 167. On the emperor's role in the Rezanov affair, Lensen cites two Russian sources, which may be presenting garbled information (p. 162).

otherwise, informing the Russians that the emperor had protested and therefore the bakufu had rebutted Rezanov.

That report may simply have been an official's device for deflecting Rezanov's anger, but if true, it helps explain the slowness of Edo's reply. And it has a ring of credibility when viewed in terms of the political maneuvers of the 1840s–1860s, when diplomatic issues became the main arena for court-bakufu infighting. More to the point, perhaps, the feisty emperor Kōkaku, aggrieved party of the Title Incident, was still on the throne in 1805. One suspects that he saw in the Rezanov issue a chance to place Edo in an embarrassing and possibly dangerous position and that he welcomed the opportunity finally to harass those who had denied his father the title of "retired emperor."

Doubtless many at Edo favored that response, anyway, but whatever determined bakufu policy, a few months after denying Rezanov's request, Edo again attempted to reduce the risk of collision by softening its stance. Back in 1793 Sadanobu had asserted that policy required the repelling or seizing of any unauthorized vessel approaching the shore anywhere except Nagasaki, but in the early days of 1806, Edo notified coastal daimyo of its reply to Rezanov and advised that if Russian vessels approached the shore in obvious need of aid, they could be provisioned with food, fuel, and water. Crew members were not to dally or sightsee, however, and if they refused to depart or proved troublesome, they should be driven off by gunfire (*uchi harai*). But at least they could be provisioned, which Sadanobu had not stipulated.

The gesture proved useless because Rezanov wanted more than provisions. A fortnight after being turned down, he left Nagasaki and sailed north through the Sea of Japan to Russian posts on the Siberian coast, having decided to try again, using force this time. He recruited two young Russian naval officers, Khvostov and Davydov, to his scheme, and they made plans, in George Lensen's words, "to destroy the Japanese settlement on Matsumae, dislodge the Japanese from Sakhalin, and spread terror along their shores, and, having deprived them of their fishery and food, to force them to enter into trade relations with Russia." He also proposed to annex Sakhalin for the czar, believing that "a fortified Russian colony on Sakhalin Island could keep the settlement on Matsumae in constant fear and thereby force the Japanese to seek commercial relations with the Russians." As he put it in a letter to Khvostov and Davydov: "Let us proceed with united endeavours, to the execution of this great enterprise, and let us shew the world that, in our happy age, a handful of bold Russians can equal those prodigious actions, to which millions of other nations attain only in a succession of Ages." Honda Toshiaki, that most optimistic of empire builders, could not have said it with greater enthusiasm.

In the autumn of 1806, Khvostov sailed to Sakhalin and launched his operation. Attacking the main Japanese settlement near the island's south end, he burned buildings, boats, and other possessions, stole rice and other goods, seized hostages, and returned to Kamchatka for the winter. After sea ice softened the next spring, he and Davydov resumed work, laying waste an Ainu village and attacking the Japanese head-quarters on Etorofu. Though greatly outnumbered, the Russians routed the three hundred ineptly led defenders. They then managed to burn the settlement to the ground in the course of drunken celebration while the disgraced Japanese commander committed suicide up in the hills. Following that triumph, the Russians sailed on, looting and burning Japanese freighters near Hokkaido, torching a few abandoned buildings on Sakhalin, and then heading home.

By way of explanation and warning, during his initial sortie in 1806 Khvostov posted near the smoking ruins of the Sakhalin settlement a copper plate with a notice that read:

> 1. It is unjust of the Japanese to hinder trade of the Russians on Sakhalin Island.
> 2. If the Japanese should change their decision and wish to trade, they can send notification thereof to Sakhalin Island or to Etorofu Island.
> 3. If the Japanese persist for long in denying the just demand, the Russians will lay waste the northern part of Japan.

Whether the strategy would establish trade remained to be seen, but it did achieve its immediate objectives. Properly terrified by what had occurred and what seemed in store, Japanese residents abandoned Sakhalin and those on Hokkaido reduced their activity in the Kurils. Word of the raids did not reach Edo until mid 1807, however, because survivors of the first attack on Sakhalin were left with no boats to carry the news south.

When the news did get to Edo, it precipitated hectic defense moves. The bakufu recruited more Morioka troops and ordered Hirosaki han to deploy more men to the Soya Strait to defend against invasion from Sakhalin. It placed higher-ranking officials in charge of Ezo defenses and sent them to their stations. It despatched 15,000 koku of rice as emergency foodstuffs for garrisons in Ezo and sent out more investigating teams to determine the scope of the problem. One team included

Mamiya Rinzō, a native of Hitachi, who during the next two years explored much of Sakhalin and part of the lower Amur river region.[28] The bakufu also cashiered officials involved in the debacle on Etorofu and in early 1808 ordered Sendai and Aizu han to join Hirosaki and Morioka in defending Ezo. Sendai reportedly put over 1,000 men on Kunashiri and Etorofu. The cost of securing Ezo was escalating.

When rumors of irresistible Russian invaders swept Edo, the bakufu moved to suppress them and restore public calm, and it took further steps to defend Japan proper. As these measures were being implemented, officials and commentators heatedly discussed and memorialized about the menace. Ranging from the furious, who were ready to fly north and slay the barbarous intruders, to the philosophical, who said trade was preferable to war, the debate wore on for months. But Edo leaders wanted to avoid both trade and war, and devising a formula for that purpose proved difficult.

Eventually the bakufu drafted a statement saying that trade was not possible, especially in view of the recent attacks. If Russia made amends and returned all prisoners, then trade might be arranged, but only if there were no further abuses.[29] Even before that message could be delivered, however, new developments complicated matters again, threatening to push the two governments yet closer to a major confrontation.[30]

GOLOVNIN IN HOKKAIDO

The newest complication began in the summer of 1811 when the *Diana*, a sloop-of-war on a surveying mission under Lieutenant Commander Vasilii Golovnin, sought provisions on Kunashiri. It was fired on by defense forces implementing the "shell and repel" law enunciated by Sadanobu two decades earlier, who still smarted from the humiliation Khvostov and Davydov had inflicted on them. Instead of sailing away, Golovnin moved his ship a short way down the coast and sent crewmen ashore in search of provisions, which they stole from a hurriedly abandoned village. With his immediate needs met, Golovnin continued trying

28. A translation of Mamiya's report on Sakhalin is in John A. Harrison, "Kita Yezo Zusetsu, or A Description of the Island of Northern Yezo by Mamiya Rinsō," *Proceedings of the American Philosophical Society* 99-2 (1955): 93–117.
29. This is a summary of a paraphrase in Lensen, *Russian Push*, p. 195.
30. These paragraphs on the Golovnin episode are based on the richly textured narrative in Lensen, *Russian Push*, pp. 196–256, which depends heavily on Russian sources.

to reach authorities and eventually established contact with a minor bakufu official at a nearby fort.

The parties met to talk, but mutual distrust prevailed, and for his trouble Golovnin was seized along with some crewmen, victims, they soon concluded, of a purposeful trap. The *Diana*'s crew engaged in an ineffectual cannon duel, but lacking sufficient firepower to rescue the captives, they headed back to Kamchatka for reinforcements. The captors transferred their prizes to Hokkaido, marching them overland to Matsumae. There they were jailed and interrogated, quickly entangling themselves in a web of circumstantial evidence and duplicitous testimony.

Meanwhile, officials had notified Edo and asked guidance, and early in 1812 they received instructions: hold Golovnin captive for the time being and "shell and repel without mercy" (*muyōsha uchiharai*) any Russian ships that approach the shore.[31] Gone was the possibility of peaceful provisioning. Accordingly, the captives were moved to better housing, placed in indefinite detention, and employed for the next year and a half as teachers of Russian language and informants about Russian society.

At the time, St. Petersburg was locked in war with Napoleon and unable to indulge in reprisals. Even attempts to effect the captives' release were slowed by Europe's convulsions. In the fall of 1812, however, Petr Ricord, Golovnin's second-in-command, took the *Diana* back to Kunashiri to see what he could do. A local Japanese commander, still hungry for revenge, tried to lure him into battle, but Ricord hesitated and chanced upon a Japanese freighter carrying the wealthy merchant Takadaya Kahei, who in 1799 had established a shipping line between Hakodate and Etorofu. Ricord seized the freighter and after establishing that Takadaya might be a prize he could trade for Golovnin took him back to Kamchatka for the winter.

Takadaya, it turned out, hoped to promote trade with Russia, so he wished the dispute settled amicably and, from the moment of his capture, lobbied for a diplomatic solution. Meanwhile, Golovnin was gradually persuading his captors that Khvostov and Davydov had acted without St. Petersburg's approval, and when Takadaya and Ricord returned to Kunashiri in the summer of 1813, local officials informed them that talk was possible. However, formal disavowal of the raiders by senior Russian officials was essential to any settlement. Ricord man-

31. Inobe Shigeo, *Ishin zenshi no kenkyū* [A study of pre-Restoration history] (Tokyo: Chūbunkan shoten, 1935), p. 253.

aged to obtain that disavowal from authorities in Siberia, and after lengthy negotiations, he and Takadaya won Golovnin's release in exchange for the disavowal. That autumn, in a grand celebration and amidst much relief all around, Golovnin was exchanged for Takadaya, ending the period of strained relations between Japan and Russia.

The two governments had seemed headed for war, but good luck and the prudence of enough people at the right moments overcame the forces of hubris, anger, and ambition to yield a peaceful outcome. Even Golovnin's captivity had not been without value. Many of the Japanese who had contact with the captives learned from them and established a deeper understanding of the world beyond their shores. Russians, meanwhile, learned a great deal about Japan. Whereas Russian writers two decades earlier had spoken of the Japanese as surprisingly ignorant and lacking in reason, Golovnin expressed the opinion in 1818 that "the Japanese are the most educated people in the entire world. There does not exist a person in Japan, who could not read or write, and did not know the laws of his fatherland."[32] If not entirely accurate, this was nonetheless a view that promised better for the future than had the earlier one.

In their final communication, Japanese negotiators reaffirmed that policy was settled: Christianity was still taboo; relations with additional powers were prohibited, and ships approaching Japan except at Nagasaki would be repelled with gunfire.[33] Golovnin believed, however, that there might still be room to negotiate, initially to define the Russo-Japanese boundary in the Kurils and then to explore trade prospects. Over the next five years, a few Russian ships approached the Etorofu vicinity to pursue the matter. For various reasons, however, the initiatives never reached Japanese officials, and after 1818 Russian interest in Japan and the Kurils evaporated.

On the bakufu side as well, interest in Ezo collapsed with striking abruptness. Overwhelmed by the costs and political difficulties of the diplomatic and defense effort, Edo rapidly chopped back both its own and han assignments, leaving the further boundaries of Ezo neither defined nor defended. Had the Russians returned, Tokugawa leaders would have found themselves utterly unprepared to defend what they purported to control.

This vulnerability in the north was compounded, as already suggested, by growing troubles in the south. English speakers were already

32. Lensen, *Russian Push*, p. 250.
33. Inobe, *Ishin zenshi*, p. 256.

replacing Russians as the primary source of concern, so problems of diplomacy continued to loom large in the lives of Japan's political leaders.

THE THREAT FROM THE SOUTH, 1808–1825

The incidents in Ezo were so worrisome to bakufu leaders in part because they occurred in conjunction with others in the south. Ōtsuki Gentaku, at the time one of Japan's most knowledgeable foreign affairs experts, interpreted them as evidence of a foreign plot involving Russians and Britons and even the Dutch and Americans. But the British and Russians were the key villains in his view.

Englishmen traded in Japan for a decade during the early seventeenth century, but finding the profits thin, they abandoned Hirado in 1623. Sporadic merchant proposals to renew the trade were not pursued until the 1670s. When the *Return* reached Nagasaki in 1673, bakufu officials—their fears aroused by a Dutch report that the English king had a Portuguese queen—rejected the request for trade.[34]

As English political and commercial activity spread across India and southeast Asia, desultory inquiries were made through third parties, but traders showed no keen interest in Japan until the 1790s. By 1793 news had reached London of improved trade prospects, and that year the government proposed to renew relations. It instructed Viscount Macartney, recently appointed to negotiate a treaty with China, to visit Japan as well, because "the difficulties of trading there which have so long deterred other nations from attempting it are now said almost to have ceased." The Macartney mission failed in China, however, and never made it to Japan, and other proposals were derailed by the outbreak of war with France.

The Napoleonic wars thus shielded Japan from both Russian and English trading schemes, but in other ways Europe's struggles disrupted life even in Edo Castle. In the name of war on the high seas, English warships entered Japanese coastal waters and demanded provisions. Moreover, the English deployed surveying vessels to locate convenient anchorages, hidden shoals and other dangerous waters, and coves in which enemy craft might hide. Indeed, William Broughton's surveying

34. H. Paske-Smith, *Western Barbarians in Japan and Formosa in Tokugawa Days, 1603–1868* (New York: Paragon, 1968), pp. 70–81, quotes *in extenso* the report of the 1673 expedition. The instructions to Macartney are quoted from p. 128.

around Hokkaido and in the Kurils in 1796–97 contributed to Edo's alarm about the northern frontier.

More seriously, the Napoleonic wars affected Edo by disrupting Dutch trade at Nagasaki. The Dutch, having been forced into alliance with Napoleon, found their annual merchantman threatened by high seas raiders, so they tried to sustain their Dejima trade by using foreign ships that flew Dutch flags when in Japanese waters. Between 1797 and 1817, only eight of the twenty-two merchantmen flying Dutch colors into Nagasaki were Dutch. Nine were American; three, English; one, Danish; and one, from Bremen.[35] To conceal the policy from Edo, the Dutch suppressed news of European developments. However, an incident of 1808, coming a few months after the Khvostov-Davydov affair, thoroughly alarmed Edo, undercut the Dutch strategy, and jeopardized their position at Dejima. That incident was the visit of H.M.S. *Phaeton*.

THE *PHAETON* AT NAGASAKI

The *Phaeton*, one of Britain's most powerful ships of the line, entered Nagasaki harbor in the late summer seeking two Dutch merchantmen. The visitor bristled with cannon at the ready, but it reportedly flew Dutch colors, and Matsudaira Yasuhira, the city magistrate (*bugyō*), despatched a reception boat bearing two Dutchmen to learn the ship's purpose.[36] Before information could be exchanged, British sailors seized the Dutchmen and hustled them aboard for questioning. Yasuhira knew his orders were to shell and repel, or capture and confine, any intruder who behaved lawlessly, so he ordered defenses prepared and instructed his men to rescue the captives. When the British under cover of night deployed boats to sound the shoreline, as though preparing to land, he ordered nearby han to drive the intruder off.

It quickly became apparent, however, that none of the samurai in town, neither those of the magistracy nor those of Saga (Hizen) han, who were there to defend the port, was prepared to bell the cat. Men knew their pikes, swords, bows, archaic firearms, and puny war junks were of little value against the *Phaeton*'s fifty cannon and heavily armed crew. While samurai were avoiding risks and awaiting reinforcements, the city grew panicky. As word of the Dutchmen's capture got about, according to one melodramatic diarist:

35. Wakabayashi, *Anti-Foreignism and Western Learning*, p. 91.
36. Paske-Smith, *Western Barbarians*, p. 130, reports that the *Phaeton* flew Dutch colors, but his report is brief and not entirely reliable.

a great outcry arose in the harbour. In all the Chinese junks the sailors burnt fires and made signals to their countrymen on shore by beating great gongs. Several boats put off to their assistance. On board the Japanese vessels in harbour it was thought that a fire had broken out among the Chinese junks, or that they had been set on fire by the foreigners. On shore, a report was current that the Russians had landed, and many of the towns-people prepared to fly to the hills. Men and women rushed wildly about the streets, and the sound of voices by sea and land was like the noise of great waves breaking on the beach. Rumours of all kinds were afloat,—that a boat full of women had been captured at Inasa—that a fishing-boat had been taken at Kitasezaki—that Hizen soldiers had been made prisoners at Fukahori— that all the provisions had been seized—that the water-gate at Mumegasaki had been broken through, etc.[37]

Rumors—erroneous—that the foreigners were landing fueled the panic. Meanwhile, Yasuhira called for reinforcements, discussed responses with the Dutch, and tried to supervise defense preparations while implementing a general plan to barricade the ship's escape route and then attack and burn it to the waterline with fire ships. Through the night "the noise of the ammunition carts and the shouting of the coolies, as they dragged the guns to the batteries, reverberated among the hills like thunder."

By the next morning the British interrogators were persuaded that their Dutch captives had no information on the merchantmen they were pursuing, so they notified the shore that they would release the Dutchmen in exchange for water, food, and fuel. Yasuhira provided the goods and with the nationality of the vessel established sent a back-dated notice to Edo assuring his superiors that "a foreign ship has entered the harbour, and has seized some Redhairs. The Redhairs will be brought back, and inquiry made into the reason for this unwarranted visit, after which the ship will be burnt, if necessary." In fact that bold posture was already compromised by inadequate resources and insufficient resolve, and the discouraged magistrate gradually realized that his incendiary strategy would not work and that he was powerless in the face of the enemy ship.

The British, judging Yasuhira's provisions inadequate, retained their captives and late in the afternoon made "a further demand for beef, vegetables, and water, accompanied by a threat that if these articles were not supplied, all the Japanese and Chinese vessels in the harbour would be set fire to and destroyed." The note incensed Yasuhira, but at

37. The quotations are from W. G. Aston, "H.M.S. 'Phaeton' at Nagasaki in 1808," *TASJ* 1-7 (1879): 326–31.

Dutch urging he agreed to provide what he could—beef was not available. After receiving those supplies, the British released their hostages, and the second night passed uneventfully while city officials awaited reinforcements. The following morning, after the released Dutchmen apprised him of the *Phaeton*'s purpose, Yasuhira tried to salvage the situation by sending a notice to the ship instructing it to depart. Having no further reason to stay, and with a good wind in its sails, the *Phaeton* shortly did so, even as troops poured into the city and samurai accelerated their preparations to capture and burn the intruder.

The crisis ended as abruptly as it began. But by then the damage was done and belated heroics could not conceal it. Utterly humiliated, Yasuhira escaped punishment for failing to defend the city by committing suicide the night after the ship's departure. When Edo leaders learned details of the debacle, they realized that the *Phaeton* had defied their laws with impunity and that defense forces had performed miserably. They ordered more cannon emplacements readied and other defense work begun. They punished some of the magistrate's military subordinates as well as the lord of Saga for negligence. And to be better prepared another time, they ordered some Dutch interpreters to start learning English, French, and Russian. The foreigners might not be permitted to trade, but they needed to be known.

As of early 1809, then, leaders in Edo were awaiting the return of Khvostov and Davydov, or other trouble in the north, and whatever further collisions might occur as British commanders pursued their war on the high seas. To prepare the realm, they continued working on defenses. They kept explorers in the field, had signal-fire sites set up along the coasts of southern Hokkaido and northern Honshu, ordered Shirakawa and Aizu han in early 1810 to prepare cannon emplacements along the shore south of Edo, and supervised construction of more batteries at Uraga. To improve the handling of foreign vessels and expand officialdom's long-term knowledge of foreigners, as noted above, they moved their official translators from Nagasaki to the bakufu astronomical observatory at Edo. Their task was to receive and translate information on foreign ships, diplomatic matters, and world conditions in general. Even those modest measures strained the treasury, however, and by 1811 Edo leaders were soliciting proposals on how to economize.

During the *Phaeton* affair, leaders in Edo learned of conditions in Europe and realized that the Dutch had been deceiving them. One source of their information was Ōtsuki Gentaku, a native of Tōhoku and scholar of Dutch learning who was serving in Edo as surgeon to the daimyo of Sendai. Ōtsuki had met a castaway returned by Rezanov in 1804 and heard from him about the war that pitted Englishmen and Russians against Frenchmen. He also knew that in 1803 a ship's captain from New England had tried to establish trade relations at Nagasaki. Unaware of the recent colonial revolt in North America, he considered this person English.[38] From these bits of information he inferred that the Dutch at Nagasaki were under English control, that "New" English were really Englishmen, that their ships were spying for England, and that the English and Russians might well be collaborating to displace the Dutch in Japan. These views he expressed in book 1 of his *Hoei mondō*, which he published to edify the authorities in 1807; in book 2, published a year later, he asserted that the *Phaeton* affair confirmed his suspicions—it was, he said, an English spy ship operating on behalf of Russia.[39]

How much influence Ōtsuki or other scholars such as Honda Toshiaki, Aizawa Seishisai, or Takahashi Kageyasu had on senior officials is unclear, but Ōtsuki and Takahashi (son of Yoshitoki, the calendar-maker of chapter 16) were among the first appointees to the new translation bureau. In any case, because of the deception over ship registries, Edo notified the Dutch in 1809 that their trading vessels were banned from Nagasaki for eight years. Even that order proved ineffective, however, because the British seized all Dutch outposts in southeast Asia two years later and in 1813–1814 despatched merchant ships to Nagasaki in abortive attempts surreptitiously to displace the Dutchmen at Dejima.[40] Before that scheme—which seemed to validate more of Ōtsuki's suspicions—developed far enough to trouble Edo, however, the Napoleonic wars ended, the Dutch reestablished themselves, and trade resumed.

38. This shadowy captain, William Robert Stewart, is discussed briefly in Peter J. Fetchko, "Salem Trading Voyages to Japan during the Early Nineteenth Century," in *Beyond Cape Horn and the Cape of Good Hope: North Americans in the Indian Ocean and the Pacific, 1785–1885*, ed. Archibald R. Lewis and W. Stuart Morgan, III (Salem, Mass.: Peabody Museum of Salem, 1986), pp. 50–54.

39. Wakabayashi, *Anti-Foreignism and Western Learning*, pp. 92–93. For a summation of Ōtsuki's Dutch scholarship, see Grant Goodman, *Japan: The Dutch Experience* (London: Athlone Press, 1986), pp. 119–33.

40. W. G. Beasley, *Great Britain and the Opening of Japan, 1834–1858* (London: Luzac, 1951), pp. 5–7. This scheme was the brainchild of Stamford Raffles, an official of the British East India Company and lieutenant-governor of Java during the British occupation of the Dutch colony there.

OTHER BRITISH CALLERS

By 1815 the Golovnin affair was resolved, northern defense forces were
reduced, war in Europe had ended, and tensions at Nagasaki had eased.
Foreign relations seemed to be returning to normal. In fact, however,
the tempo of British activity around the archipelago intensified following a favorable analysis of trade prospects by the abortive Nagasaki
mission of 1814. In that analysis Stamford Raffles of the British East
India Company reported to his countrymen occupying Batavia that the
mission found the Japanese[41]

> a nervous, vigorous people, whose bodily and mental powers assimilate much
> nearer to those of Europe than what is attributed to Asiatics in general. Their
> features are masculine and perfectly European, with the exception of the
> small lengthened Tartar eye which almost universally prevails, and is the
> only feature of resemblance between them and the Chinese. The complexion
> is perfectly fair and indeed blooming, the women of the higher classes being
> equally fair with Europeans and having the bloom of health more generally
> prevalent among them than is usually found in Europe. For a people who
> have had very few, if any, external aids, the Japanese cannot but rank high
> in the scale of civilisation. The Chinese have been stationary at least as long
> as we have known them, but the slightest impulse seems sufficient to give a
> determination to the Japanese character which would progressively improve
> until it attained the same height of civilisation with the European.

Motoori Norinaga might have awarded Raffles two cheers for percep-
tiveness.

The Dutch having Nagasaki, British merchantmen pursued trade at
other ports. The Ryūkyūs were on the line of north-south shipping, and
after Broughton's initial surveys more and more ships began stopping
in the islands for provisions and shelter. In 1816 two British warships
dropped anchor at Naha, Okinawa's capital, and they resurveyed the
coasts during an amicable ten-day visit. Their reports of Ryūkyūan generosity encouraged other Britons to follow.[42]

Aware that Edo was the seat of authority, Britons tried to approach
Japan's leaders more directly, with ships reaching Uraga in 1816, 1817,

41. Paske-Smith, *Western Barbarians*, p. 131. The author, British consul in Osaka,
writing in about 1929, adds that these opinions of Raffles and a Dr. Ainslie "show that
fifty years before the re-opening of Japan there were at least two discerning minds able to
appreciate the difference between the Japanese and other Asiatics."
42. George H. Kerr, *Okinawa: The History of an Island People* (Rutland, Vt.: Charles
E. Tuttle, 1958), pp. 231–34, 252–58.

and 1818. The third of those visits, by the brig *Brothers* under Captain Peter Gordon, most alarmed Edo. Gordon sought a trade agreement, and the bakufu responded by deploying a huge force along the shore in hopes of persuading him to abandon his request. He did, but before sailing, someone on his ship evidently gave local people copies of a Chinese-language Christian Bible, and the books soon fell into official hands. Political custom said that foreign attack would begin as subversion of the populace, to turn them against their rulers, so the distribution of Bibles raised the specter of the earlier Jesuits and the Shimabara rebellion. In recent decades, moreover, ideologues had been warning that Russia was building its empire that way, seducing the Ainu and entering Japan from the north. If more evidence were needed, given the recent British attempts to trade covertly at Nagasaki, the distribution of Bibles written for "native" use surely proved that they, too, intended to conquer the imperial land by subterfuge and subversion.

Accordingly, in 1819 Edo strengthened control of Uraga by appointing a second magistrate for the port. And lest foreigners establish themselves surreptitiously in the Izu islands, as the Russians supposedly had done in the Kurils, Edo set up a new office to supervise trade there.

By then, however, the fiscal condition of many han, as well as the bakufu, was again deteriorating, and defense costs were becoming onerous. To ease the burden, the Uraga magistracy took over Aizu's coastal defense duty in Sagami province in 1820, and the following year Edo cancelled the remaining duty of Morioka and Hirosaki han in Ezo. Encouraged by the recent quiescence on the northern border, moreover, the bakufu terminated its program of defense and development in Ezo and restored the area to the lord of Matsumae, who reportedly paid well for the decision. Two years later Edo released Kuwana han from its coastal duty in the Kantō.

These measures of relaxation were acceptable to Edo because the policy of firmly resisting foreign demands appeared to work. The "New" English had been turned aside in 1803 and Rezanov a year later. Resolute handling of Golovnin had ended Russian demands. The Dutch had been brought up short and the British kept at bay. In 1822 when another British vessel anchored off Uraga and requested food and water, the bakufu responded by applying the more conciliatory of its recent policy positions, despatching officials from Edo to oversee peaceable provisioning of the ship. They told the visitors they could not trade, and a few days later the ship departed.

WHALERS

In 1824 another facet of the foreign problem emerged, the demand of whalers for provisions and safe haven when in distress. The problem grew out of overexploitation of the Atlantic Ocean's cetacean population to meet the growing demand for lamp oil by burgeoning urban populations in Europe and America. In one writer's words,[43]

> When the Yankee whalers of New Bedford, Massachusetts, began, about the year 1750, to find their game leaving them, they sailed into new waters in quest of blubber and bone. They moved their ships down into South American waters. Then they rounded Cape Horn and pushed up into the northern Pacific Ocean. . . . Some of the "black ships" began to loom up in fleets along the coast of Japan.

As whalers learned of exceptional harpooning in the north Pacific, they flocked to the kill, their numbers increasing rapidly from about 1820.

European as well as American crews worked the north Pacific, and when they needed supplies or sought shelter, the nearest inhabited shores commonly were Japanese. The east coast of the Kantō was particularly attractive to whalers because the mixing of warm and cold ocean currents offshore created especially rich marine communities. And the long sweeps of beach were highly approachable.

During 1823 villagers sighted numerous whalers off the Kantō. The following summer a dozen crewmen from a British ship landed in search of provisions at Ōtsuhama, a fishing village on the northern edge of Mito han. Their arrival caused a local flurry, and coast guard forces seized and held them in the village until higher authorities came. Mito officials, along with added guard forces from four other han, reached Ōtsuhama in a few days, and bakufu officials arrived several days later, after the Mito lord asked them to handle the matter. The delegates from Edo, with Takahashi Kageyasu as interpreter, were able to establish the character and purpose of the foreigners. Satisfied that they posed no danger, they notified them of the prohibition on landing, instructed them to depart, and released them.

The whalers departed, and a few days later Mito leaders sent officials

---

43. The writer is W. E. Griffis, as quoted in Ernest W. Clement, "Mito Samurai and British Sailors in 1824," *TASJ* 1-33 (1905): 87.

out to read to coastal residents a long proclamation that nicely captured the rulers' perceptions and fears. It said in part:[44]

> Lately foreign ships are often seen passing from the northwest to the southeast in spring and summer. Pretending to be hunting whales, they anchor off the coast, or come near to the land, in order to spy out our country. They invite our fishermen on board and give them tempting things in an insinuating manner. ... Whether the country be England or Russia or any other country, it believes in the wicked religion of the cross. Outwardly the people are mild and peaceful, but really they are untruthful and full of wickedness. Our people who approach their ships and are tempted to believe in their religion, are greatly to be pitied. Japan is the divine country of Amaterasu Ōmikami; and there is no necessity for introducing any other religion, because it already has a good religion of the gods. Our people are naturally honest thereby. Why then go to a bloody and disagreeable religion and incur the severe punishment of the gods?
>
> Many years ago the teaching of "Kirisutan" was introduced and propagated by the "Namban"; it was first brought by "black ships" of the West, pretending to carry on trade with our people. But their real aim was to conquer our country by means of tempting the people into the wicked religion. So many as 280,000 people were slain as a punishment for their own folly. Since the time when this wicked religion was prohibited by Tōshōgū [Ieyasu], and the Third Shōgun [Iemitsu], that severe prohibition has been strictly observed. Consequently the carrying on of foreign trade was limited to Nagasaki only; and the people of no other countries except Holland were permitted to land in our country. Is not this a law for which one should be grateful? ... Suspicious books or pictures or any other things which remind one of the wicked religion should not be received, even if offered. If there be any who ignorantly receive such things, they should not keep them, but bring them to a neighboring office. When any one discovers suspicious acts of foreign ships, he should at once present himself before an official to give information thereof. One who disobeys this order shall be punished. These things should be kept deep in mind.
>
> The above order should be promulgated among villagers and fishermen by officials in the coast-districts, that one and all may observe it very carefully.

The Ōtsuhama incident thus passed uneventfully, having done little more than cause a local stir, add to defense costs, and elicit a statement of foreign policy attitudes. A few days later, however, a more serious incident occurred on Tamashima, an islet in the northern Ryūkyūs, when men from a British whaler landed to obtain food and water. Dissatisfied with what was offered, they tried under cover of gunfire to steal some

44. As quoted, with changes in the spelling of shogunal names, in Clement, "Mito Samurai and British Sailors," pp. 125–27.

livestock. That led Satsuma men on the island to attack them, killing one of the crew before they made their escape.[45]

That incident seems finally to have prodded Edo to clarify its policy toward foreign vessels. To halt the proliferation of random landings, early in 1825 the bakufu issued new instructions to the daimyo. After summing up the difficulties with foreigners since 1804 and reiterating the dangers of Christianity, the notice stated:

> Henceforth, whenever a foreign ship is sighted approaching any point on our coast, all persons on hand should fire on and drive it off. If the vessel heads for the open sea, you need not pursue it; allow it to escape. If the foreigners force their way ashore, you may capture and incarcerate them, and if their mother ship approaches, you may destroy it as circumstances dictate.[46]

The notice acknowledged that this policy might lead accidentally to firing on Dutch vessels, but it advised nevertheless, "when in doubt, drive the ship away without hesitation [*ninennaku uchiharai*]." Later in the year, in hopes of avoiding such an accident, Edo ordered Dutch vessels to fly a Japanese flag of commerce when approaching the country.

Parts of the 1825 notice were similar to instructions dating back to 1739, but the order to shell and repel "without hesitation" constituted application to all foreign vessels of the hard-line policy first directed at Russian vessels during the Golovnin incident. It eliminated the option of provisioning ships and sending them on their way, the policy articulated after Rezanov's visit and generally applied thereafter. Three decades of persistent foreign intrusions had served only to harden Edo's stance.

Why bakufu leaders chose to escalate their obduracy at that time is unclear. Perhaps they wished to prove themselves as resolutely opposed to Christianity as was Mito: surely many Edo officials shared the convictions expressed in Mito's proclamation. Or perhaps Edo was seizing an opportunity to choke off illicit Satsuma commercial contact with foreigners.[47] In any case, an appealing rationale for *ninennaku uchi-*

45. Robert K. Sakai, "Shimazu Nariakira and the Emergence of National Leadership in Satsuma," in Albert M. Craig and Donald H. Shively, eds., *Personality in Japanese History* (Berkeley and Los Angeles: University of California Press, 1970), p. 211. Inobe, *Ishin zenshi*, p. 320. Tamashima is one of the small islands in the Tokara chain, just southwest of Tanegashima.

46. Wakabayashi, *Anti-Foreignism and Western Learning*, p. 60.

47. Robert Sakai discusses the bakufu-Satsuma trade rivalry in "The Satsuma-Ryukyus Trade and the Tokugawa Seclusion Policy," *JAS* 23-3 (May 1964): 397–402.

harai had been articulated by Takahashi Kageyasu following the whaling incident at Ōtsuhama. He argued that the foreign visitors would leave peacefully if fired on because they were poorly armed whalers, not government representatives, and their objectives were commercial. Repelling them that way would be much less costly than deploying forces every time foreigners landed, and it would help prevent the spread of Christianity among commoners.[48] Repelling by force would thus be a safe, effective, and efficient means of avoiding later, more dangerous developments.

Whatever Edo's motive, its decision sharply reduced flexibility toward foreign vessels at a time when their visits were multiplying. That conjunction of developments seemed destined to cause trouble. For over a decade, however, the troubles were domestic rather than diplomatic. Few foreigners chose to test the new policy; moreover, on several occasions daimyo procrastinated in the face of foreign visits long enough to avoid implementing the order.

As of 1825, then, it appeared that civil firmness would suffice. What Tokugawa leaders did not know and perhaps could not know was that long-range changes affecting the major states of Europe and the United States were destroying the conditions essential to their policy. Its apparent success was utterly a function of the modesty of foreign interest in Japan, and industrialization was equipping the foreigners with military capacity, economic reason, and ideological excuse to demand changes in Japan's relationship to the world.

48. Wakabayashi, *Anti-Foreignism and Western Learning*, pp. 102–5. Also Inobe, *Ishin zenshi*, pp. 321–24.

The Worst of Times, 1825–1850

Popular authors shackled for fifty-day periods. A city magistrate dead by his own hand at Nagasaki. A military commander dead by suicide on a cold, desolate island far from home. These hardly seem tokens of the best of times. And while no tumbrels were rolling, the best of times were not thoroughly good, any more than the worst proved thoroughly bad.

There were, nonetheless, striking changes in degree of unpleasantness between the decades before 1825 and those after. The tenor of domestic affairs changed dramatically in the 1830s, with the Tenpō famine ravaging the populace at large, as noted in chapter 12. It drove total population downward again and produced eruptions of protest and a rash of government attempts to cope. The hardship and attempts to respond lasted into the early 1840s, when improvements in the general situation enabled leaders to undertake a return to "normalcy."

The second change related to foreign affairs, but it did not entail a simple escalation in foreign demands. On the contrary, for more than a decade after 1825, foreign approaches were fewer and less threatening than in preceding years. After 1836, and especially from about 1844 on, the tempo of foreign contacts accelerated, but the level of demand changed very little, still consisting of unassertive queries about trade and requests to repatriate castaways and obtain provisions. The striking change after 1825 was in the way foreign affairs played on the domestic scene. Earlier diplomatic crises had mostly vexed only a handful of officials, and while scholarly observers expressed opinion, none ran afoul of the rulers for doing so. Hayashi Shihei was punished not for his opinions per se but for his manner of expressing them.

From the late 1820s, by contrast, diplomatic issues acquired a political intensity not seen since the seventeenth century as foreign and domestic problems became deeply entangled. The disruptive potential of foreign demands in terms of basic social ideals, bakufu-daimyo relations, and military technology and organization began to be grasped by more and more scholars and officials. And witchhunts for subversives began to destroy men, ruin careers, undermine attempts to respond thoughtfully to the crises of the day, and feed the flames of what may best be labeled ethnic paranoia and political scapegoating.

Still, the impact of foreign contacts on society at large should not be overstated. Neither before nor after 1825 did diplomatic issues elicit any general public response. Around 1806–1808, it is true, Russian pillaging in Ezo terrified ordinary people there; the *Phaeton*'s visit threw Nagasaki into turmoil; and rumors of advancing Russians panicked Edo. But apart from that spate of frightened responses to dangers real and imagined, the general public seems rarely to have been alarmed by the foreigners' peregrinations. Many chose to be prudent and avoid contact when seamen came ashore; some surely were fascinated by their strange encounters with alien visitors.

Among more educated commoners, however, as the spread of kokugaku and Mitogaku fostered interest in Japanese history and culture, a growing number of non-officials became alarmed at the trends and forces that seemed to endanger the imperial country and its people.

Because of the relative sparsity of foreign visitors between 1826 and 1850, this rising ethnic self-awareness only sporadically addressed diplomatic issues. But it meant that when the foreigners did present a renewed threat at midcentury, they elicited a more hostile, more widespread, and intellectually more elegant response than in the days of Laxman and Rezanov. The pattern was foreshadowed in the spy crisis of 1828.

Finally, that spy crisis also foreshadowed the future by hinting at how the interplay of foreign affairs and intellectualized ethnic self-awareness would contribute to a striking aberration in central politics, an aberration that appeared during the 1830s and persisted through the 1850s. In theory, the bakufu stood above all the daimyo, making demands on them and distributing benevolences among them as seemed appropriate to Edo leaders, and, in fact, from Ieyasu's day until the 1830s, no daimyo outside the official structure of bakufu office had ever exercised an intimidating influence for a sustained period.[1] During that decade, however, Tokugawa Nariaki, lord of Mito and leader of an ideologically inspired renovationist movement, thrust himself onto the national scene in unprecedented fashion.

Nariaki presented his advice and policy positions with such vigor and insistence that for the first time in Tokugawa history someone outside the authorized structure of control became the single most influential voice in politics. Bakufu leaders continually tried to appease, oppose, or ignore Nariaki and his vocal supporters while pursuing their own disorderly and difficult agendas, and in 1844 his persistence finally goaded Edo into stripping him of his daimyo position. His influence soon revived, however, becoming even greater during the 1850s. Indeed, the political movement that he had shaped outlasted his death in 1861, finally being devoured in the bloodshed and brutality of civil war three years later.

THE SPY CRISIS OF 1828

By 1825 the decades of foreign intrusion had exacted a price. Policy toward foreign vessels had gradually hardened, culminating in the *ni-*

---

1. Hoshina Masayuki of Aizu was influential during the 1650s and 1660s, but for much of that time he served as regent to the child shogun. Mitsukuni of Mito was influential later in the century, but he did not intimidate Tsunayoshi or noticeably shape policy.

nennaku uchiharai order, and the tone of policy debate was growing shrill as charges of treasonous gullibility began to be hurled about. The tenor of affairs seemed reminiscent of the 1650s and 1660s, when Christians and Fujufuse Buddhists were under assault and Kumazawa Banzan and Yamaga Sokō were both subjected to official punishment. The new surge in ideological politics yielded its first batch of victims in the Siebold spy scare.

MITOGAKU AND FOREIGN AFFAIRS

The fearful distrust of foreigners that underlay the shrillness of debate—and the way that distrust could reinforce itself—was evident in Aizawa Seishisai's attempt to interview the whalers detained at Ōtsuhama in 1824. He went to Ōtsuhama at the behest of his lord, Tokugawa Narinaga, who considered him the domain expert on foreigners. Aizawa presumed that the captives were Russian but was able to establish, through gestures and fragments of speech and writing, that they were English. He asked their purpose in coming to Japan and through gestures was told whaling, which he disbelieved, writing in his report of the interview that, "I did not like it that he should conceal the real purpose of their coming there; and gazed earnestly into his face." Already convinced of their aggressive designs, he was able to misconstrue fragments of information to confirm the suspicion, regarding one gesture as proof that the man being questioned "must have meant to include even Japan under the domain of England . . . a most unpleasant thing to hear." And later he reaffirmed his suspicion that the English had a "plan of landing for the purpose of encroaching on our country."[2] It was a view of the whalers, as noted in chapter 20, that was not shared by Takahashi Kageyasu and other bakufu officials on the scene.

A year later, after the bakufu instructed daimyo to shell and repel foreign vessels, Aizawa composed his *Shinron,* whose overall character was adumbrated in chapter 19.[3] On current events, he observed:

> The bakufu has just ordered that barbarian ships be destroyed on sight. It has publicly declared that it, along with the whole realm, regards foreigners

2. These fragments are from Ernest W. Clement, "Mito Samurai and British Sailors in 1824," *TASJ* 1-33 (1905): 93, 95, 97.

3. The following quotations come from Bob Tadashi Wakabayashi, *Anti-Foreignism and Western Learning in Early Modern Japan* (Cambridge, Mass.: Harvard University Press, 1986), pp. 164, 150, 164, 169.

as the enemy. Everyone in the realm took heart after learning of this decree and [they] now eagerly await the chance to execute it. Such is the indomitable strength of the people's spirit!

He took sharp issue with the reasoning by which Takahashi justified the ninennaku uchiharai policy, attacking unnamed figures who argue,

"They are only barbarians in merchant ships and fishing boats. They pose no serious problem; there is no grave danger." Such skeptics rely on the barbarians' staying away, on their not attacking; they rely on something not within our power to control. Should I question them about our military preparedness or immunity to attack, they would be dumbfounded. Ah, how can we prevent the world from falling prey to the barbarians?

His answer was straightforward: "If we induce spiritual unity throughout the Divine Realm, how can armed expulsion be beyond our power? A chance like this will not come again in a thousand years—we must exploit it!" Later, in discussing the intellectual forces that had harmed Japan over the ages, he resumed his attack on scholars who, like Takahashi, studied rangaku uncritically:

The harm comes when some dupe with a smattering of second-hand knowledge of foreign affairs mistakenly lauds the far-fetched notions spun out by Western barbarians or publishes books to that effect in an attempt to transform our Middle Kingdom to barbarian ways. There are, moreover, many curiosities and concoctions from abroad that dazzle the eye and entice our people to glorify foreign ways. Should the wily barbarians someday be tempted to take advantage of this situation and entice our stupid commoners to adopt beliefs and customs that reek of barbarism, how could we stop them?

The foreign threat was so perilous, Aizawa argued, because of domestic demoralization, disorder, and decay. Reform was imperative if the foreign menace was to be overcome, particularly because without it, the "stupid commoners" would remain alienated from the rulers and susceptible to the subversive influence of Christianity, the preferred instrument of infiltration. Three years later he published a tract, *Kikōben,* in which he expanded on the malevolent nature of the alien creed. Aizawa may have been extreme in his views—and a mite presumptuous in denouncing others for "a smattering of second-hand knowledge"— but his writings reveal how thoroughly foreign policy was becoming entangled in ideology and through it with domestic politics.

Aizawa's attack on Takahashi, an Osaka native, may have been an expression of the northeast-southwest tension; more surely the harshness of discourse on foreign affairs was exacerbated by a general deepening of domestic woes. After three decades of favorable overall conditions, Japan again was experiencing crop failures and proliferating peasant protests. The bakufu again was devaluing coins, to the detriment of monetary order, and tensions between Edo and certain daimyo were rising as conflicts over commercial policy became more pronounced. Ienari still nurtured his ties to major lords, but in some han that put him in the camp of Edo-based "city" samurai who were opposed by reform-oriented colleagues centered on the castle towns. And his regime's reputation for corruption provided grounds for the dissatisfied to express criticism.

Most notably, Tokugawa Nariaki, the brother of Narinaga, favored the reformist views of men such as Aizawa, and he rapidly emerged in the late 1820s as an articulate and energetic critic of Ienari. That posture was reinforced, no doubt, by factional divisions within Mito, which led one group of officials to urge that a son of Ienari be named successor to the childless Narinaga, while the rival faction supported Nariaki.[4] At Narinaga's death the issue was still unsettled, but the latter group found a document allegedly indicating that the deceased had wished Nariaki to succeed, and that settled the issue in his favor. He became daimyo in 1829 and promptly began circulating copies of Aizawa's *Shinron,* which his predecessor had suppressed lest its tone and content anger Edo.

Under these circumstances of heightened ethnic self-awareness and deepening domestic tension and difficulty, a man's views on foreign policy began to function as a litmus test of his integrity and loyalty. Knowledge of Dutch learning became increasingly dangerous, especially if it led one to a favorable view of foreigners, and some of the most accomplished Dutch scholars of the day fell prey to vilification and denunciation. The first well-known victim of this new era of ideological politics was Takahashi Kageyasu, principal figure in the Siebold Incident.[5]

THE SIEBOLD INCIDENT

Philipp Franz von Siebold, a German physician, came to Dejima in 1823 to serve as doctor for the Dutch.[6] A year later he opened a school where

4. Richard T. Chang, *From Prejudice to Tolerance* (Tokyo: Sophia University, 1970), pp. 23–24.

5. Kondō Jūzō (Morishige), another of the bakufu's Dutch scholars and a leader of Edo's exploration and development of Ezo, enjoyed career promotions until 1826, when he was dismissed and placed under house arrest. The cause of his downfall is unclear.

6. This summary of the Siebold affair is based primarily on Grant Goodman, *Japan: The Dutch Experience* (London: Athlone Press, 1986), pp. 184–88, and Donald Keene,

he taught European science to visiting Japanese scholars in return for information about Japan. He visited Edo in 1826 and met Takahashi, who had studied at Nagasaki some years earlier, and the two traded books about Europe for geographic materials that included one or more maps of Japan recently prepared by the bakufu cartographer Inō Tadataka.

By bakufu regulations, as Takahashi knew, such "classified material" was strictly forbidden to foreigners, but in 1828 leaders in Edo discovered that Siebold had acquired some and that Takahashi, their own official, had provided it. The discovery was cruelly fortuitous: Siebold, readying to sail for home, had stowed his possessions, but bad weather beached the ship in Nagasaki Bay. When his goods were unloaded to permit repair of the vessel, they were routinely inspected as incoming freight, and the contraband was discovered. The authorities promptly arrested him and held him in Nagasaki for a year, much as they had earlier held and interrogated Golovnin at Matsumae. They arrested Takahashi and nearly forty other scholars and translators in Edo and Nagasaki, sealed off and searched Dejima for incriminating material, and closed the translation center (*bansho wage goyō*) at Edo while investigating what they evidently regarded as a major spy case.

In the course of interrogating Siebold, officials learned that he was German, not Dutch, which prompted them to wonder if he were a spy for Russia. The thought was not original: twenty years earlier Ōtsuki Gentaku had warned bakufu leaders that Englishmen, Russians, and other foreigners were in collusion, and the idea still made sense. As the spy case unfolded during 1829, Fujita Tōko, son of Yūkoku, colleague of Aizawa, and advisor to Nariaki, updated the idea, warning his lord that the Dutch were working with the Russians and English and should be denied trading rights at Nagasaki. He argued that the foreign spy should be punished along with his domestic collaborator, Takahashi. Besides disciplining the foreigners and punishing the criminals, he argued, the bakufu must invigorate the realm and prepare for foreign invasion, because even if the foreigners "get solidly together and attack Japan, there will be nothing Japan needs fear so long as the souls of ten thousand people here have been animated."[7] Coming late in the investigation, Tōko's opinion had little influence on the outcome, but it does suggest how observers could perceive the affair.

The Japanese Discovery of Europe, 1720–1830 (Stanford: Stanford University Press, 1969), pp. 147–54.
7. Chang, *From Prejudice to Tolerance*, p. 50.

The public's perception is also revealed by the diary of Iseki Takako, the wife of a hatamoto and a student of kokugaku. She wrote of Takahashi: "It was revealed that he had turned over to the foreigner not any ordinary maps of our great country but copies he himself had made of the official charts. He died while under investigation for this crime, but since he was no commonplace criminal, they say his body was pickled in salt so that the investigation could continue."[8]

The climate of the time was so unnerving that as the investigation proceeded, other Dutch scholars distanced themselves from Takahashi. Two translators at the center in Edo wrote officials to plead that they were "translating Chomel's Encyclopaedia. We have no connection with the men captured in the Siebold-incident—Kageyasu TAKAHASHI and the interpreters. We are innocent. Besides, we are confident that our translation is of great value to our country. Please let us resume this translation work at once."[9] More important to the outcome, Mamiya Rinzō, a native of Hitachi province whose findings as an explorer of Ezo had helped Inō and Takahashi in their map work, allegedly shared his superiors' conviction that geographic information was of crucial strategic importance, and he was said at the time to have denounced Takahashi for his indiscretion.

After jailing Takahashi, the authorities confiscated his books and papers. A few months later he died in prison, but the judges, determined to make him an example, posthumously convicted him of spying, beheaded his corpse, and exiled his two sons. In Nagasaki, Hatasaki Kanae and three other translators were jailed, and in Edo many others were punished. Siebold was expelled from the country and forbidden to return. Mamiya went on to serve the bakufu as a domestic spy and investigator and Mito as a supporter of Nariaki's administration.

THE TERRIBLE THIRTIES

Following the Siebold incident the years passed quietly in terms of foreign affairs. The Dutch, their position at Dejima jeopardized by the spy scare, abided by the customary restraints on trade and labored to regain credibility at Edo by providing periodic reports on world affairs. Chinese residents in Nagasaki did forcefully protest added commercial restrictions in 1835, but local officals quickly restored order. Elsewhere dip-

8. Donald Keene, *Travelers of a Hundred Ages* (New York: Henry Holt, 1989), p. 381.
9. Goodman, *Japan: The Dutch Experience*, p. 187.

lomatic problems were minimal. Attempts by British settlers in the Bonins to have London claim the islands as a colony made no progress, and whatever Edo knew of the activity, it merely reiterated restrictions on trading in the islands. Of the few ships that approached the coast, only two appear to have been driven off by gunfire: an unidentified vessel that approached eastern Hokkaido in 1831 and an American merchantman, the *Morrison,* that tried to trade and proselytize at Uraga and later at Kagoshima in the summer of 1837. The calm continued until 1839, when ideology-ridden factional conflict re-erupted in another siege of witchhunting.

Instead of wrestling with foreign demands, Japan's leaders found their time and energy consumed by the hardship, unrest, and disruption of the Tenpō famine and its culminating political events, the insurrectionary attempts in 1837 of Ōshio Heihachirō at Osaka and Ikuta Yorozu at a district office of Kuwana han in Echigo. In a number of domains, the troubles of the day prompted leaders to initiate reform programs, but in Edo reform did not became possible until Ienari finally acknowledged his mortality in 1841.

THE BAKUFU AND THE TENPŌ FAMINE

The Tenpō famine, as noted in chapter 12, was mainly a catastrophe of the northeast. But it affected all Japan. Many people fled to the cities, especially Edo, in search of aid, multiplying the urban destitute. And even in the southwest mortality was distressingly high. As Hayami Akira has noted: "The immensity of this Tempō mortality crisis is beyond doubt. . . . Between 1834 and 1840, only eight of Tokugawa Japan's sixty-eight provinces registered a population increase, while twenty-seven showed a decrease of 5 percent or more."[10] Not until the late 1840s did the population regain its pre-crisis level.

Two of the most striking characteristics of the bakufu response to this famine were its inadequacy and the extent to which it focused on Edo in disregard of more severely wounded regions even as reports and instances of riot, smashing, protest marches, famine, and flight inundated the city. A chronology of major bakufu actions follows:

10. Marius B. Jansen and Gilbert Rozman, eds., *Japan in Transition from Tokugawa to Meiji* (Princeton: Princeton University Press, 1986), p. 295.

Year/month	Measure
1833/8	provides assistance to the poor in Edo
/8	forbids cornering the market in rice
/10	orders a one-third cut in sake production
/10	gives more relief rice to Edo poor
/11	forbids hoarding and orders dispensing of rice
/12	orders a policy of frugality for five years
1834/1	orders rice brought to Edo from all Kantō provinces
/1	again forbids hoarding of grain
/5	forbids secret storing of rice in Osaka and orders rice shops to lower their prices
/6	provides relief rice to the poor of Edo
/6	orders han to send rice to Osaka
/6	controls usury by grain retailers in Osaka
/9	forbids unfair rice marketing by Osaka grain dealers
/10	forbids shipment of rice from Osaka to other places
1835/3	assists poor in Edo
/7	authorizes gokenin to obtain an advance against winter's rice allotment
1836/1	erects relief hostels and assists the poor in Edo
/10	erects more relief shelters to house the starving
/11	restricts shipment of grain from Osaka
1837/3	assists the poor in Edo
/4	disseminates information on simple remedies and measures to counter epidemics then spreading through the provinces
/5	again assists the poor in Edo
1838/4	orders a new period of frugality
/9	forbids shipping grain out of Osaka[11]

11. These entries are culled from *Nihonshi nenpyō* [A chronology of Japanese history] (Tokyo: Kawade shobō shinsha, 1973), pp. 322–24.

It appears that the bakufu expended most of its energy and resources during the first two years of crisis. And except for pious utterances, its attention was riveted on Edo, with secondary concern limited to Osaka, even to the point of pursuing policies that deprived other areas of food. To some degree, this response reflects the scale on which desperate villagers fled to cities during the crisis. But surely it also reveals the limits of bakufu capability—little more than keeping the peace in its capital city—and confirms the Edo-centric focus evident in preceding decades. Individual han pursued their own relief measures, of course, but nowhere was the response adequate to the need, as shown by the extent and ubiquity of suffering.

ŌSHIO HEIHACHIRŌ AND IKUTA YOROZU

Like earlier famines, that of the 1830s generated widespread protest by the poor and desperate. Unlike them, it also produced two noteworthy attempts at political rebellion by samurai, the first since the ronin plots of 1651. Whereas those of 1651 had the earmarks of men promoting their own interests, moreover, those of 1837 were basically expressions of outrage at social injustice and elite irresponsibility. The first plot was that of Ōshio Heihachirō in Osaka, which triggered the second, that of Ikuta Yorozu in Echigo. The two suggest how current conditions, personal situations, and individual outlooks could combine to produce risk-laden ventures.

Ōshio Heihachirō, born in 1793 to a minor shogunal vassal in Osaka, was reared by a grandmother after his parents' death. He later moved among adoptive homes of bakufu police officers (*yoriki*) in the city, eventually succeeding to his adoptive father's post as one of Osaka's sixty yoriki and in 1818 marrying the daughter of a rich farmer. In his career as a city police official, he revealed his moral rigor and growing religiosity. He refused the bribery customary to his post and tried instead to wipe it out, despite the resentment his effort generated among fellow officers. Around 1827, prior to the Siebold spy scare, he found and arrested a number of Christians in the city, and in 1830 he prosecuted several Buddhist monks for breaking their vows. His righteous service drew little praise, however. Embittered by the corrupt indifference of fellow officials, he resigned in favor of teaching and study, ending a fourteen-year career as dedicated bakufu official.

Ōshio made a pilgrimage to the Ōmi home of his intellectual hero, Nakae Tōju, and nearly drowned in a boating accident while returning on a storm-tossed Lake Biwa. The terror of that incident convinced him he must transcend his self, and for the next few years he studied and taught Nakae's Ōyōmei thought at Senshindōjuku, his school in Osaka. In 1833 he compiled and published his lectures and in another indication of growing religiosity burned one copy as a tribute to the kami at Ise and placed another in a cave on Mount Fuji, sacred place of the flourishing Fujikō cult.

His students were drawn from all classes, and many became dedicated followers of their intense, intolerant teacher. They were especially moved by his insistence that all people can know the goodness of their true nature intuitively—that is, can "transform their personalities into sages"—because "the fundamental spirit of the ordinary man is no different from that of the sage . . . , [that of] the wretched man identical with the aristocrat." [12] Knowing their nature, men can and should act to rectify injustice, thereby attaining unity with the absolute. "What is this thing called death?" he asked rhetorically. "We cannot possibly begrudge the death of the body; but the death of the spirit—that indeed is to be dreaded." [13] Ōshio also was an elitist, however, who believed that he, as the sage hero, had the moral duty "to save the people from the hell of the past and . . . establish paradise before their very eyes." If he failed to act when the need for action was apparent, he could not claim really to know the nature of truth. [14]

For decades Osaka had been growing poorer as it lost business and population, and when the Tenpō famine overtook the city in 1837, Ōshio petitioned that reserve rice be given out. The city magistrate (*machi bugyō*) rejected the request, so Ōshio sold his library and prepared to act. He gave some of the proceeds to the poor and used some to buy a small cannon, a few shoulder arms, and several hundred swords. He then drafted a summons to revolt, addressed it to villagers and village officials in nearby provinces, and had it distributed. The summons denounced officialdom for corruption and extravagance, for abusive taxation, for shipping rice from Osaka to Edo even when it was scarce and dear, and for failing to punish merchants guilty of exploitative accumulation of wealth and land. These conditions being intolerable, he called for a rebellion:

12. Tetsuo Najita, "Ōshio Heihachirō (1793–1837)," in Albert M. Craig and Donald H. Shively, eds., *Personality in Japanese History* (Berkeley and Los Angeles: University of California Press, 1970), pp. 155–79. The two quoted fragments are from pp. 166, 165.
13. Ivan Morris, *The Nobility of Failure* (New York: Meridian, 1975), p. 196.
14. Najita, "Ōshio Heihachirō," p. 170.

First we shall execute those officials who torment and harass those who are lowly. Next we shall execute those rich merchants in the city of Osaka who are accustomed to the life of luxury. Then we shall uncover gold and silver coins and other valuables they hoard as well as bags of rice kept hidden in their storage houses. They will be distributed to those who do not own fields or . . . have a hard time supporting fathers, mothers, wives and other members of the family.[15]

He evidently intended with his twenty companions, several of them samurai, to attack the magistrate's office and fire the homes of rice merchants. The smoke would signal nearby villagers to join the fray.

Betrayal scrambled Ōshio's plans, but he hurriedly launched the rebellion anyway. His rebel band, carrying banners emblazoned "Save the People" and "The Great Shrine of the Goddess Amaterasu," torched houses of officials and merchants as they went. The fires raged, but despite the monetary enticement, few villagers responded, and the townsfolk who joined turned to looting instead of challenging authority. Guard forces suppressed them within a few hours, but when the fires died out a day later, a quarter of the city lay in ruins. Ōshio and his followers fled, some committing suicide. Ōshio returned to the city six days later, was discovered after a month of hiding, and killed himself just before being captured.

Word of Ōshio's revolt raced across the country, and one of those most moved by it was Ikuta Yorozu. Born in 1801, the son of a middle-ranking vassal of Tatebayashi han, as a youth Ikuta received a Confucian training at the han school. His family favored Ōyōmei teachings, but he reportedly was impressed by an old essay of Asami Keisai's, *Seiken igen*, in which Asami extended his principle of loyalty beyond child-parent and vassal-lord to the ideal of utter loyalty to Japan. After reading works of Kamo no Mabuchi and Motoori Norinaga, Ikuta went to Edo in 1824 and entered Hirata Atsutane's Ibukiya. He did well as a student of kokugaku and over the next three years produced essays that denounced Confucianism and its proponents, charging that their blindness to the truth of kokugaku prevented people and kami from achieving their proper and mutually beneficial relationship.

In 1827 Ikuta returned to Tatebayashi and wed the daughter of a han vassal. At the time the han was in dire straits, having borrowed heavily from its samurai and peasantry. The contrast between the relatively easy life of Edo and the grim state of the domain prompted Ikuta

15. David John Lu, *Sources of Japanese History* (New York: McGraw-Hill, 1974), 2: 8.

to draft a long and eloquent reform proposal, which he submitted to Tatebayashi leaders the following spring. The proposal's particulars were hoary and familiar: cut domain costs by trimming officialdom and effecting economies of operation, reduce luxury spending and promote frugal life-styles, and most important, return samurai to the land. More bluntly than most pundits, he urged his lord to cut the stipends of senior officials. In the tradition of horticultural writings, he stressed the centrality of agriculture and called for practical knowledge to nurture crops. And he warned, as had numerous others, that the lack of benevolent and attentive administration above invited upheaval below and that those in power should, therefore, not lose touch with the general condition of the people.[16]

He was advised not to present the proposal to his lord, perhaps because it questioned the perquisites of his superiors or because his earlier anti-Confucian tracts had offended people. He insisted, but the essay was poorly received and he was ordered into house arrest. Unable to bear confinement, a few months later he fled with his wife and child into the hinterland, where they endured three difficult years of hand-to-mouth living before Tatebayashi officials allowed him to return. By then his parental family had made other succession arrangements, so he lost his samurai status. A ronin, he headed for Edo, but eventually retraced his steps and settled in the small town of Ōta a few miles northwest of Tatebayashi. There he started a small school to teach neighborhood children.

Misfortune notwithstanding, his reputation as a teacher, or perhaps as a kokugaku scholar, seems to have spread, for in 1836 a Shintō scholar invited him to move to Echigo to teach in the coastal town of Kashiwazaki, which contained a regional administrative office (*jin'ya*) of Kuwana han. There he opened the Ōen, a school for Japanese studies. At the time, Echigo was suffering harshly from bad weather, crop failure, escalating food prices, and usury, and many were dying of starvation. The Kuwana regional intendant, whose primary task was to collect tax income for shipment to Kuwana, had close ties with wealthy local merchants. He lived comfortably despite the hardship round about and seemed unresponsive to the crisis.

Ikuta was appalled by the evidence of official indifference and wrote three or four petitions for remedial action, but nothing was done. Learning of Ōshio's insurrection, he gathered his students, other followers, and

16. H. D. Harootunian, *Things Seen and Unseen* (Chicago: University of Chicago Press, 1988), pp. 285–89, stresses the originality and radicalness of Ikuta's proposals.

the poor, and three months after Ōshio's effort, he led them in an attack on the Kashiwazaki jin'ya. Local police responded promptly and dispersed the attackers. Ikuta fled and committed seppuku before the police caught up with him. His son died in jail.

In the end, then, these two putsch attempts of 1837 fell far short of their intended goals. That of Ōshio served at the time primarily to ravage much of Osaka and secondarily to alarm many samurai. To later generations, it exemplified the activist potential of Ōyōmei political thought and transmuted a frustrated ex-official into a *daimyōjin,* a quasi-mythical hero. That of Ikuta seems to have caused almost not a ripple, perhaps because its immediate impact was so dwarfed by the disaster in Osaka. Because the revolts accompanied the hardship and disorder of the Tenpō famine, however, they surely contributed to the reform efforts that proliferated during the next several years.

DOMAIN REFORMS: SATSUMA, CHŌSHŪ

The rhythms of domain politics were always idiosyncratic, shaped heavily by changes in han government personnel, especially changes of daimyo. To some degree, however, all han responded to political pulses emanating from Edo, and all were influenced by the ebb and flow of climate, economy, and public condition. During Tenpō, one sees a few domains initiating policy changes early, notably Satsuma in 1831 and Chōshū in 1838. But most han reform awaited the death of Ienari in 1841 and the subsequent initiation of bakufu reform by Mizuno Tadakuni, head of the senior council (*rōjū*).

Everywhere the dominating issue was the same: the treasury. As in the eighteenth century, the goals of fiscal policy were to increase revenues and cut expenses without seriously compromising vested political interests. And everywhere solutions were essentially the same: on the income side, produce money, manipulate prices, license and monopolize existing trade, and promote new commerce for its fiscal value. On the expense side, trim waste, debt burdens, and program costs. Specifics varied among han, of course, and some enjoyed substantially more success than others.

Reformers addressed other issues as well. One common concern was the insolvency of retainers; others, the problems of samurai morale and the politico-military value of vassal forces. Beyond the samurai caste were problems of public hardship and disorder owing to the Tenpō famine. And some domains were concerned with foreign affairs and the broader enveloping issue of the imperial land as a whole.

One of the first Tenpō reforms occurred in Satsuma, where officials promoted one of the period's least imaginative, most forceful, and fiscally most successful reform programs. In the outcome, they rehabilitated their treasury and produced a large cash reserve for future use. In 1831, leaders summarily eliminated the bulk of a han debt that exceeded 300,000 kan of silver by repudiating all obligations to merchants in the domain and slashing payments to merchants in Osaka and Edo by unilaterally rescheduling debts to a 250-year lifetime. On the credit side, they tightened control of wax and rice production and processing, making sales yield greater profits in Osaka. And most valuably, they maximized income from sugar production. In the words of Albert M. Craig, they established in their sugar-producing islands,

> a despotic plantation type system. No crops could be raised on those islands other than sugar; their paddy lands were all destroyed. All other commodities—literally all other commodities, 457 items ranging from rice, cloth, wood, to pots and pans—had to be obtained within the moneyless economy established on these islands by barter for fixed amounts of sugar. Rice for example cost, in terms of sugar, six times what it was worth at the Osaka market. . . . Private sales of sugar were punishable by death. . . . Altogether it resembled nothing so much as a penal colony producing delights which its inmates were forbidden to consume.[17]

One can only wonder if these arrangements reflected the influence of Satō Nobuhiro, whom Satsuma officials had consulted during the 1820s.

Chōshū also was spurred to address its fiscal problems by accumulated debt. Its reform, initiated in 1838 when a new daimyo took office, was led by Murata Seifū, an official committed to revitalizing the moral calibre of the domain. Murata cast his reform in broad ethical terms of restoring old virtues and reversing moral decline, issuing an array of sumptuary regulations to discourage luxury and establishing more schools in which han samurai could improve their martial skills and study the civil arts. As in Satsuma, however, the core of his effort was fiscal.

For decades Chōshū leaders had done their best to milk commercial production with licenses and monopolies. During the 1830s, however, peasant uprisings targeted han tax and monopoly policies, prodding officials to seek alternative ways of handling their 90,000 kan debt. By 1838 they evidently had trimmed that to 60,000 by the simple expedi-

17. Albert M. Craig, *Chōshū in the Meiji Restoration* (Cambridge, Mass.: Harvard University Press, 1961), p. 71.

ent of ceasing to honor the remainder. From that starting point, Murata moved to cut costs by budgeting more closely, urging frugality, and renegotiating the remaining debt to reduce annual payments. To enhance income, he "borrowed" from han retainers by withholding portions of their stipends. He appeased villagers by abolishing various monopoly and guild arrangements, but to offset the income loss, the han sold licenses to any who wished to pursue commercial activities. And it expanded a profitable monopoly on rice transshipment, storage, and marketing at the port of Shimonoseki. That arrangement, which generated income from goods originating in other domains, reflected Murata's mercantilist view that "the first principle of finance is to sell all the goods produced in Chōshū to other *han* in exchange for gold and silver and not to let any gold or silver produced in Chōshū out of the *han*." [18] Less draconian than the Satsuma measures, those in Chōshū also had a less dramatic impact on the fisc. But they did enable the han to meet expenses without dipping into a separate domain investment fund, the *buikukyoku*, a major reserve account maintained for emergency use.

By the late 1830s, then, some of Japan's most powerful domains had undertaken reforms designed to revitalize their capacity to govern. At Edo, Ienari still lived and bakufu reform was stalled, which discouraged reform in many domains. But in Mito the accession of an energetic new daimyo in 1829 had already set in motion one of the most ambitious and fundamental attempts at renovation that Japan had experienced since Yoshimune's reform of the 1720s.

RENOVATION AT MITO

As in other han, fiscal inadequacy lay at the heart of Mito reform: had the han treasury been full, there almost surely would have been no Tenpō reform there. However, it was far from full, and Mito leaders viewed that condition not merely as a problem of income and outgo but as a symptom of more basic defects of the domain and, broadly, of the realm.

To Nariaki, the reform's leader, the well-being of the imperial realm was indivisible. Reform in Mito, rehabilitation of the country, and adequate management of Japan's external relations were interdependent enterprises. Or rather, they were all facets of the single enterprise of restoring a properly ordered and smoothly functioning universe. [19] How

18. Craig, *Chōshū*, p. 74. Italics added.
19. Matthew V. Lamberti, "Tokugawa Nariaki and the Japanese Imperial Institution, 1853–1858," *HJAS* 32 (1972): 97–123, skillfully summarizes the political roles of Mito and Nariaki.

one attacked the task was a matter of tactics. Accordingly, throughout the 1830s he made periodic requests of bakufu leaders and submitted opinions and advice to them. However, in the face of their non-cooperation he devoted most of his attention to han reform, laboring to repair the treasury as evidence that the larger tasks of renovation could also be handled.

Fiscal repair proved very difficult, in considerable part because Mito suffered from two liabilities that Satsuma and Chōshū were spared. Whereas they were situated in the more fruitful southwest and had access to considerable commercial revenue, Mito was located northeast of Edo in a less productive region and off the main arteries of trade. Secondly, while Satsuma and Chōshū as *tozama han* had no responsibility for the realm as a whole, Mito, as one of the three main Tokugawa branch families (*sanke*), did. That obligation—which gave institutional legitimation to Nariaki's political activism—diverted both resources and government energies.

Mito's role as a *sanke han* was especially burdensome because of its importance to the domain's self-esteem. Mito was the least of the sanke, derived from the youngest of the three founders, lower in formal rank than the other two, and by far the smallest in domanial assets. Its holdings were so much smaller than those of Owari and Kii that whereas they chose to understate the actual yield of their domains, Mito leaders felt compelled to overstate theirs to justify ritual privileges that symbolized their status and their success, so to say, in keeping up with big brother. And they adhered to this large-domain claim even as their producer population was decimated by crop failure and famine, falling from 318,475 in 1726 to 229,239 in 1798.[20] Successive Mito leaders squeezed their peasants to sustain their pretensions, but doing so only worsened matters by making absconding and abandonment of fields a chronic problem in the domain.

During the nineteenth century, Mito's broader obligations as a sanke lord were reinforced by proponents of Mitogaku, whose concerns, as noted in chapter 19, embraced a wide array of issues. These included the thorny question of the proper relationship of emperor and shogun, the legitimacy of the Tokugawa order, the proper roles of lord, vassal, and commoner, the basic principles of good governance, the best means of handling foreigners, and Japan's rightful place in the world.

When Nariaki became daimyo, he believed that the times required

---

20. J. Victor Koschmann, *The Mito Ideology* (Berkeley and Los Angeles: University of California Press, 1987), p. 86.

action and that it was proper for him to take the lead in promoting it. As he wrote in late 1830 to the trusted rōjū Ōkubo Tadazane, lord of Odawara and employer of Ninomiya Sontoku:

> Since the Three Houses and [major fudai daimyo] have the duty of advising the shogun of impropriety among the *rōjū* . . . ignorant though I am, because the Three Houses have been charged with this obligation I intend to speak up, with all due respect, in cases adversely affecting shogunal authority; and I am determined in the bottom of my heart to do so though it cost me my life.[21]

Nariaki was supported in this view by his reformist advisors, although they tended to advise caution in matters less directly important to Mito.

Thanks to the appearance of whaling vessels, the foreign problem that had vexed Aizawa Seishisai from afar at the beginning of the nineteenth century became a matter of direct concern to Mito officials in the 1820s, as noted above. That development gave the larger problems of the realm an immediacy that further conflated Nariaki's roles as domanial lord and advisor to the shogun. Consequently, when he and his advisors began planning reforms around 1830, they saw themselves as engaged in enterprises that were far more basic and far more important than merely balancing the budget.

Fiscal issues clearly were important, but because of Mito's poverty, even they were treated as more elemental economic problems. The fiscal aspects of reform were neither remarkable nor particularly successful: in 1830 during the first effort, they included advocating frugality, "borrowing" from samurai, and trying to establish han monopolies in such areas as paper and tobacco production. From the start, however, the reformers also pursued a more basic expansion of Mito's economic foundation, attempting with little success to introduce or enhance such industries as tea, silk, glass, lacquer, and pottery. Beginning in 1832, they outlawed infanticide and paid villagers to rear more children as ways to repopulate villages, reopen arable land, and expand taxable rural production.

The following years of inclement weather, crop failure, and distress stymied much of Mito's reform effort, and Nariaki did little at the level of the general public beyond implementing emergency measures. He did pursue the expansion of local schooling, however, opening the first of four planned regional schools in 1835. He opened the second two years

21. Yukihiko Motoyama, "The Political Thought of the Late Mito School," *Philosophical Studies of Japan* 11 (1975): 105.

later, the third in 1839, and the fourth in 1850. Fujita Tōko originally envisioned the schools as enhancing public virtue, by which he meant the peoples' diligence and obedience to han authority, so as to yield the desired "unity between ruler and subject."[22] But Nariaki, holding that education was wasted on peasants, seems to have hoped the schools would improve rural health, evidently as a way to help repopulate the countryside. So the schools were directed toward the training of local doctors.

Nariaki's concern with public health was also evident in his approach to Dutch learning.[23] He shared his advisors' view on the dangers of alien religion, but like many at the time he regarded technical aspects of rangaku, medicine in particular, as useful and believed that in proper hands they would aid Mito's renovation. That belief led him in 1832 to hire Aochi Rinsō, an Edo physician who had studied Chinese and Dutch medicine and translated for the bakufu several European works on medicine and physics. Until his untimely death early the next year, Aochi lectured to Mito men on Dutch learning and instructed three Mito doctors in European medicine.

Nariaki also valued Dutch military knowledge and had Aochi translate works on gunnery and large ships. After Aochi's death he hired Hatasaki Kanae, a former employee at Dejima who had been convicted and jailed in the Siebold affair and later escaped from prison. In Mito's employ, Hatasaki translated military works until 1837, when Nariaki sent him to Nagasaki to acquire Dutch books on shipbuilding. There he was captured by bakufu officials and returned to prison, where he died five years later. Despite that setback, Nariaki continued trying to acquire Dutch works on naval architecture and other military matters.

In 1836 Nariaki initiated another aspect of reform, the return of samurai to the land. Despite bitter protests from "city" samurai, he moved many Edo families back to Mito and deployed a few men to coastal villages for purposes of shoreline defense. Mito leaders justified the policy on grounds advanced long before by Ogyū Sorai and others: to reduce the burden on the treasury and hence on the peasantry, to weaken the role of merchants, and to revitalize samurai élan. A new argument—that such redeployment would strengthen the han against foreign invaders—was important enough to shape the initial fief assignments.

22. Koschmann, *Mito Ideology*, p. 123.
23. Chang, *From Prejudice to Tolerance*, pp. 61–62. Goodman, *Japan: The Dutch Experience,* pp. 152–53.

The next year, as relief measures eased public unrest, han leaders drafted a revitalized reform plan, and they began its implementation after Ōshio's rebellion passed without repercussions in Mito. A key element in that plan was a resurvey of the domain to improve the effectiveness and equity of tax collection.[24] A major, multi-year task, the survey did overcome inequities, bringing the system more in line with what reformist theory called for. However, its fiscal effects were almost nil, and it pleased the payers no more than any other tax program: "The rich peasants are bitter, the poor peasants are not particularly happy," Tōko reported.

While the land survey was in progress, Nariaki initiated a new phase of educational expansion. In 1841 he opened Mito's new domain academy, the Kōdōkan, so that his retainers could learn how to "serve the Ancient Way of Japan and supplement it with the Confucianism of China." And that autumn he staged a military review of Mito retainers on the outskirts of the castle town, thus giving expression to his goal of revitalizing both the military and civil arts.

During the years of reform, Nariaki also addressed the larger agendas of the imperial realm and foreign affairs. Two issues particularly deserve attention, his requests to take charge of Ezo and to build large ships.

As noted earlier, observers from the northeast had been interested in Ezo from the late eighteenth century. During Nariaki's tenure, the Ezo matter arose in the context of Mito's financial dilemma. In 1829, vassals suggested that he ask the bakufu for more land on grounds of fiscal need, but Nariaki demurred, proposing instead that Mito request Ezo to improve its defenses. Tōko objected that developing Ezo would further impoverish the han, but Nariaki insisted, saying Mito should take it over because Matsumae was failing in its defense responsibility. Beginning in 1834, he repeatedly asked the bakufu for Ezo and repeatedly was turned down. His advisors urged him to request an alternative area, but he vetoed the idea, evidently seeing the defense issue rather than Mito's fiscal need as the key consideration.[25] Instead, when it became clear that Mito would not get Ezo, he advised the bakufu to take direct charge of its defenses.

Tōko opposed the Ezo scheme as uneconomic, but he urged Nariaki to seek repeal of the bakufu prohibition on construction of ocean-going

---

24. The next two quotations are from Koschmann, *Mito Ideology*, pp. 99, 117.
25. Chang, *From Prejudice to Tolerance*, pp. 41–42. Chang argues that the fisc, not defense, was Nariaki's primary concern in the Ezo matter, but Chang's narrative suggests that the fisc was his vassals' primary concern, while his own was defense.

vessels so that daimyo could build warships for coastal defense. Initially, Nariaki resisted, saying Edo would refuse because having such ships would tempt people to go abroad, which was illegal, and increase the risk of conflict with foreigners. But he did seek information on European-style ships, as noted above, and from 1834 when he first petitioned for control of Ezo, he also urged Edo to lift its ban on large-ship construction.

Nariaki also pursued other defense work, promoting training and reorganizing his military system to improve its effectiveness. He also fostered rearmament by casting firearms and cannon, even when that meant collecting and melting down the bells of Buddhist temples to get the needed metal. Bakufu leaders regularly refused his advice on Ezo and shipbuilding, and they gradually became distrustful of his rearmament activity. They also turned aside his other advice on national policy, most notably his suggestion that they abolish the Dutch trade at Nagasaki. Doing so, he argued, would halt the outflow of gold, silver, and copper and close another loophole by which Christianity was smuggled into the country. Nariaki was undeterred by the rebuffs and continued lobbying on larger affairs in subsequent years.

DEEPENING ENTANGLEMENTS

Central politics became dreadfully messy during the late 1830s. Just as the stresses of the Tenmei famine had produced harsh infighting between the Tanuma faction and its challengers, so the Tenpō famine filled the bakufu with tension as impatient reformists tried to initiate new policies while Ienari and his allies clung to power. As officials jockeyed for position in 1839, a new siege of witchhunting erupted, producing more victims comparable to those of the Siebold incident. By the time that siege played out in 1842, Ienari was dead and political energies had refocused on domestic issues. Mizuno Tadakuni's reformists were in power, issuing a rash of edicts on domestic policy that generated enough resentment and resistance to produce yet more political turmoil, and by late 1843 the reformists themselves were the objects of denunciation.

FACTIONAL FEUDING AND FOREIGN AFFAIRS

Factions, or cliques, the clusters of officials and collaborators who made government work, were as old as the bakufu itself.[26] Well-led, well-

---

26. Conrad Totman, *Politics in the Tokugawa Bakufu, 1600–1843* (Berkeley and Los Angeles: University of California Press, 1988), pp. 179–203.

structured factions could operate the bakufu reasonably well, but the replacing of one faction with another could produce months or even years of infighting and policy deadlock analogous to the oie sōdō of daimyo domains. The late 1830s were one such period. In 1837, following the putsch attempts of Ōshio and Ikuta and with famine still gripping the land, Ienari finally retired and his mature son Ieyoshi succeeded as shogun. Ieyoshi constituted a new authority figure around whom reform-minded men could cluster, but he was unassertive and his father kept control of policy. The reformers, notably the rōjū Mizuno Tadakuni, could do little more while he lived than mark time and build their alliances.

The tension among officials was exacerbated by the rising tide of ideological rhetoric that warned of the dangers presented by policy failure. Ōshio's rebellion gave advocates of Ch'eng-Chu Confucianism, as taught in the Shōheizaka gakumonjo, reason to fear Ōyōmei thought as expounded by "reckless" activists. Hirata Atsutane's emperor-oriented kokugaku views, which had inspired Ikuta Yorozu, generated so much distrust among orthodox Shintō scholars and others in Edo that he was ordered out of the city in 1841. And from Mito came unwelcome admonitions about Ezo and armaments, warnings to stand firm against all foreigners who approached Japan, and advice to close Dejima to keep the metal in and mischief out.

This last theme, the belief that uncontrolled dissemination of rangaku was intolerable because it would allow the introduction of Christianity or other harmful ideas, was one on which proponents of diverse viewpoints agreed. Most regarded the managed adoption of practical European learning as desirable, but its entry had to be regulated at the gate. And bakufu officials were the gatekeepers on whom ideologues depended to keep the realm safe. Fortunately for them, one of the gatekeepers was the inspector (*metsuke*) Torii Tadaaki, who had special responsibility for coastal affairs. Born the second son of Hayashi Jussai, the long-time head of the Shōheizaka gakumonjo, Torii was dedicated to upholding Confucian proprieties and keeping Japan safe from corrupting foreign influences.

Torii was at the center of the faction-driven ideological politics that erupted in the summer of 1839 with the arrest of Watanabe Kazan. Kazan was a senior official of Tawara han with special responsibility for coastal defense, and he was also a bunjin of sorts, especially as an afficionado of European art and learning. He participated in a group of some twenty-five Edo samurai and scholars who were interested in rangaku and met periodically to discuss current events and exchange information on Europe. Unluckily for Kazan, Torii heard him lecture to the group and was displeased with his enthusiasm for Dutch learning, seeing in the rangaku circle an uncontrolled subversive influence.

Torii was particularly alarmed that Kazan's group enabled bakufu officials, including Egawa Tarōzaemon, one of Edo's most influential intendants (*daikan*) and a proponent of coastal defense strengthening, to learn about Europe via unauthorized channels. To rectify this dangerous situation, he obtained an arrest warrant that accused Kazan of being one who "likes Dutch studies" and

> gathers about him other men with a curiosity about such things and gives talks on Western books. Together with Hatazaki Kanae, Takano Chōei, and other scholars of the West, Kazan studies foreign countries and criticizes the government. He knows about the foreign ships visiting the offshore islands of Ōshū Kinkazan, and he once publicly expressed his wish to hire local fishermen to ferry him to meet the ships.[27]

Other charges named Kazan, wrongly, as the author of certain books critical of Japan and identified Egawa and other bakufu officials who allegedly were being subverted by his teachings.

After Kazan's arrest, investigators found some essays he had written, including a pathetically garbled discussion of the so-called *Morrison* affair in which he wrote critically of bakufu reliance on obsolete Chinese military theory and ended up deploring Edo's current leadership as corrupt, decadent, and comparable to the Ming dynasty shortly before its collapse. The investigation gave Torii evidence enough to charge Kazan and his fellows with planning an illegal trip abroad, and he recommended that Kazan and the scholarly Takano Chōei, an Edo physician, be executed. If their crimes merited death, he presumably reasoned, Egawa and others would be more cautious in future about toying with rangaku.

Pressured by friends of the accused, Mizuno Tadakuni intervened just before year's end and commuted Kazan's sentence to house arrest in Tawara. Kazan went as ordered, but near the end of 1841 he committed suicide. Chōei's sentence was commuted to life imprisonment, but he escaped during a prison fire in 1844, hid for a time in Shikoku, and later sneaked back into Edo, but was discovered there in 1850, whereupon he too committed suicide. A third member of the group,

27. Bonnie Abiko, "Persecuted Patriot: Watanabe Kazan and the Tokugawa Bakufu," *MN* 44-2 (Summer 1989): 209–10. Kinkazan is the seaward islet at the tip of the Oshika peninsula, east of Sendai.

Ozeki San'ei, committed suicide at the time of Kazan's arrest, fearful
that officials would learn he was translating a life of Christ. And Hatasaki, as noted above, had already been captured while in Nagasaki on
behalf of Nariaki and in 1838 was confined at a castle town in Aki
province. The group of scholars dissolved, and officials became more
prudent about their scholarly associations.

After disposing of the Kazan case, Torii examined the procedures for
handling Dutch matters at Nagasaki. He was displeased at the evidence
of laxity and drafted a ten-point proposal for tightening access to information about Europe to ensure that only authorized officials and physicians receive it.[28] In the summer of 1840, Edo leaders accepted some
of his suggestions, appreciably reducing legal access to rangaku.

From about that time, news began reaching Nagasaki of British attacks on China, and by year's end Edo knew that China had lost the
Opium War. During the autumn, awareness of those developments
prompted a minor Nagasaki official, Takashima Shūhan, to propose
to his local superior, and thence to Edo, that the bakufu adopt the
European-style gunnery techniques and tactics of maneuver that he was
teaching his own men.[29] When Torii saw the proposal, which seemed
to confirm the reports of laxity in regulating rangaku at Nagasaki, he
attacked it on the ground that the practices would have no military
value for Japan. The China news shocked others, however, and after
Ienari's death in early 1841, leaders called Shūhan to Edo for a demonstration. He brought his company of 125 uniformed men together
with their weapons and in the summer put them through their drill
paces to the sound of commands given in Dutch. Despite the bizarreness
of puppetlike figures pivoting in unison one way and then another in
response to strange utterances, senior officials authorized Shūhan to
return to Nagasaki and continue the training. They did not, however,
recommend its wider adoption.

Torii disapproved any accommodation, but he was unable to van-
quish Shūhan or even Egawa, with whom he was also at loggerheads
over coastal defense policy. He continued, however, to retain the goodwill of Tadakuni, who was clearly in control and who was relying on
him in his pursuit of domestic reform. Indeed, near the end of 1841
Tadakuni promoted Torii to Edo city magistrate (*machi bugyō*), making him one of the most powerful figures in the bureaucracy.

28. Abiko, "Persecuted Patriot," p. 216, lists Torii's ten stipulations.
29. A laudatory treatment of Takashima is G. B. Sansom, *The Western World and
Japan* (New York: Knopf, 1951), pp. 248–53.

Then in mid 1842 a new development enabled Torii to reopen the question of Shūhan's activity. A Dutch report said the British were still angry that the *Morrison* had been fired on in 1837. With China subdued, a British fleet was about to visit to "inquire into the 'misconduct' of Japan, even at risk of war."[30] That report sent consternation through the bakufu, raising doubts about the prudence of its ninennaku uchi-harai law. After intense debate, Edo moved to reduce its exposure:

> In 1825 it was ordered that foreign vessels should be driven away without hesitation. However, as befits the current comprehensive reforms, in which we are recreating the policies of the Kyōhō and Kansei eras, . . . in the event that foreigners, through storm-damage or shipwreck, come seeking food, fuel, or water, the shogun does not consider it a fitting response to other nations that they should be driven away indiscriminately.[31]

Henceforth fuel, food, and water were to be provided peaceably to any vessel that requested them, the vessel to be informed that it should then promptly depart. Only if it lingered were cannon to be employed.

That policy change enabled Torii to argue that Shūhan's alien-style training was no longer necessary because the risk of war had been sharply reduced. At the time he was engaged in harsh factional struggle, and in the fall of 1842, evidently in hopes of tarnishing his rivals' reputations, he accused Shūhan of maintaining unauthorized contacts with foreigners. In all likelihood the charge was true. As city magistrate, moreover, Torii had great influence in the judicial process, and in the ensuing trial Shūhan was convicted and imprisoned. Three years later the bakufu reduced his term to lenient house arrest, but it did not fully rehabilitate him until 1853.

Shūhan's conviction halted the new forms of gunnery practice for a few years and deepened the chill on rangaku studies. But it also marked the end of the late Tenpō spasm of witchhunting. In following years the study of rangaku revived, the Tekijuku flourished in Osaka, and more and more han schools added Dutch studies to their curricula. Only a faint echo of anti-Dutch sentiment sounded in 1849, when the bakufu reaffirmed the 1791 decree that forbade instruction in Dutch medicine at its medical school, the Seijukan, and ordered that all manuscripts on medicine be approved by school authorities before publication.

30. Chang, *From Prejudice to Tolerance*, p. 138.
31. Harold Bolitho, "The Tempō Crisis," in *The Cambridge History of Japan*, vol. 5, *The Nineteenth Century*, ed. Marius B. Jansen (Cambridge: Cambridge University Press, 1989), p. 146.

MIZUNO TADAKUNI AND BAKUFU REFORM

The conviction of Takashima Shūhan was one of Torii's last successes because he and his superior, Tadakuni, were encountering more difficulty as the bakufu's Tenpō reform generated opposition. Tadakuni had launched the reform in the summer of 1841, four months after Ienari died, by informing officialdom that the bakufu was to be renovated in line with policies of the Kyōhō and Kansei eras. His goal, it appears, was to restore the ideal order in which rural folk lived frugally and produced vigorously, samurai lived lives of simple dedication, and merchants accepted properly inferior roles.

There was no intrinsic disagreement between Tadakuni's ideal and the vision espoused by Mito reformers. However, Nariaki's unsolicited advice so offended him that one of his first moves after announcing reform was to commend the Mito lord for his splendid administrative record and instruct him to stay at his castle for five years. With Nariaki out of town, Tadakuni addressed the accumulated problems of the regime. He instructed shogunal vassals to rededicate themselves to the military and literary arts and soon afterward reminded daimyo to abide by their sankin kōtai travel schedules. Over the next two years he issued a plethora of edicts to break up merchant oligopolies, improve morals, reduce luxury, expand rice reserves, and lower prices. He pressured recent Edo immigrants to return to their villages and tried to put the urban unemployed to work. To restore status distinctions, he forbade diverse employments to women, by-employments to villagers, and martial arts to merchants. And to help the treasury, he manipulated the currency and obtained contributions from chōnin.

Inevitably, some of Tadakuni's policies brought him into conflict with powerful people. Four such policies deserve note. First, to eliminate trade practices that interfered with the flow of goods and pushed up commodity prices in Edo, he outlawed commercial monopolies in daimyo domains. The order of late 1842 read:

> Of late, daimyo [from Kyoto westward] have been, by various methods, buying up the products not only of their own domains, but of other domains also; . . . sending them to their warehouses, and then selling them when the market price is high. . . . This is most irregular, particularly bearing in mind our frequent instructions to reduce prices.[32]

Chōshū's policy at Shimonoseki was a case in point; there were many others.

32. Bolitho, "Tempō Crisis," p. 151.

Second, Tadakuni arranged a costly shogunal pilgrimage to Nikkō, presumably in the spirit of Kyōhō when Yoshimune's visit announced the success of reform. Third, to expand Kantō food production, he put Torii in charge of the oft-discussed plan to redirect Tone river waters and drain the Inbanuma swamp. Fourth, to eliminate the long-standing administrative confusion in Kantō landholding and improve bakufu control of its several towns and their productive environs, he announced that all fief lands within ten *ri* of Edo and areas adjacent to the other towns were to be returned to the bakufu in exchange for land elsewhere.

All these moves caused Tadakuni grief. By forbidding han monopolies, he angered powerful lords who stood to lose income. The Nikkō trip and Inbanuma project imposed heavy burdens on many people. The land transfer scheme upset a plethora of daimyo and lesser samurai who held small fiefs and parcels of good land within easy distance of Edo or other towns. By the time Tadakuni ordered the surrender of land near Edo in the early autumn of 1843, his Inbanuma project was already embroiled in factional fighting and charges of corruption. The ten-ri order created a new batch of opponents and did Tadakuni in. Less than a month after the order was issued, it was rescinded. Six days later, Tadakuni was dismissed, and bakufu reform ground to a halt, although two years of convoluted political maneuver would ensue before he was finally and permanently driven from power.[33]

During the two years of Edo's reform, a number of han followed its lead. Some fiscal improvements and other changes were made, but the abrupt collapse of the bakufu effort undercut reformist élan, and for the country as a whole the Tenpō reforms seemed to have little lasting impact. Differential success caused some shifts in relative strength, at least in the short run, but one can only speculate whether matters would have developed very differently had no reform efforts been undertaken at all.

RESTORING NORMALCY, 1843–1852

Compared to the 1830s, the decade after 1842 was a tranquil time in Japan. As in the 1790s, the return of favorable weather helped survivors of famine to reopen fields, rebuild communities, and get on with life. Some aspects of Tenpō reform policy may have improved the situation,

33. Conrad Totman, "Political Succession in the Tokugawa Bakufu: Abe Masahiro's Rise to Power, 1843–1845," *HJAS* 26 (1965–1966): 101–24, recounts the intricacies of political maneuvering.

and the canceling of other aspects doubtless cheered many. Finally, Edo's post-Tadakuni leadership labored to quiet political tensions, extending the improved tenor of affairs upward to the ruling class.

This favorable domestic situation was compromised, however, by the growing frequency of foreign visits and requests, which prodded bakuhan leaders to direct ever more resources and attention to defense preparation. Escalating foreign contacts also thrust diplomatic issues more deeply into bakufu-daimyo politics, most notably the relationship between Edo and Nariaki. For the first time since the reign of emperor Kōkaku, moreover, Edo felt it must apprise the court of how it was handling foreign affairs.

FOREIGN CONTACTS AND BAKUFU RESPONSES

Of the numerous occasions when foreign ships were sighted offshore or approached Japanese ports during the 1840s, two were of particular consequence. In 1844 the Dutch warship *Palembang* brought a message from King William II. Two years later French and American warships arrived, seeking to establish formal relations. The visits spurred measures of coastal defense and led to more intense debates about foreign policy.

The letter from William warned that the British were coming in search of trade: if Japan failed to accommodate them, it would suffer the fate of China. To avoid such a dire outcome, he wrote, Japan should accept Dutch assistance in return for expanded relations. At the time Edo was hobbled by the continuing struggle between Tadakuni and his rivals, and the last thing those men wanted was to make more hard decisions. Besides, any who wished to disbelieve the bad news could point to past instances of self-serving Dutch misinformation, and this letter had the earmarks of another such ploy.

So Edo procrastinated. The Dutch embassy was politely assured that an answer would be forthcoming, and the *Palembang* was told to depart, which it did. For another half year the rivals at Edo maneuvered, until early 1845, when the power struggle was finally resolved in favor of young Abe Masahiro, who became head of the council of rōjū.[34] Four months later the rōjū formally and tactfully notified the Dutch that ancestral law forbade the establishment of treaty relations, and

---

34. For a disparaging assessment of Abe's political performance, see Harold Bolitho, "Abe Masahiro and the New Japan," in Jeffrey P. Mass and William B. Hauser, *The Bakufu in Japanese History* (Stanford: Stanford University Press, 1985), pp. 173–88.

"such is the strictness of the ancestral law, that no other course is open to us."[35] Together with the repeal of uchiharai in 1842, the reply to William meant that Edo had universalized the policies applied to Rezanov in 1805–6.

By then the Opium War treaties had expanded commercial, diplomatic, and military activity in the waters off Japan, and an unprecedented number of European and American vessels reached Japan and the Ryūkyūs in 1846. They were seeking trade and other forms of contact, and news of the two most important requests reached Edo almost simultaneously that summer. One was a request for trade in the Ryūkyūs, which French Admiral Jean-Baptiste Cecille submitted from there. The other was a request by American Commander James Biddle, whose two ships, "one, a formidable 74-gun ship of the line," anchored off Uraga, to arrange American access to Japanese ports.[36]

Abe responded to the two requests in dissimilar ways. That of Biddle he rejected with little ado because it constituted a direct challenge to the diplomatic position he had just affirmed to William. The French request was more problematic because it referred to the Ryūkyūs, and Edo's role there was ambiguous. The bakufu oversaw foreign relations as a whole, but just as Matsumae was responsible for its implementation in Ezo, Shimazu of Satsuma was responsible in the Ryūkyūs. And there, Abe knew, Shimazu carried on a valued trade that included tacit dealings with Chinese merchants. Abe chose to recognize Shimazu's customary delegated authority in the Ryūkyūs, extending it to cover the new situation. He instructed the daimyo to handle the matter peacefully, even if that led to French trade in the Ryūkyūs. He insisted, however, that the instructions be kept secret.

As matters worked out, Biddle left peacefully, if unhappily. And Cecille did not insist, so Shimazu made no new arrangements. During the next six years no foreign powers chose to pursue the issue forcefully, so "normalcy" prevailed in foreign affairs. Overseas, most notably in Washington, D.C., politicians and their commercial backers were becoming more and more restive with Japanese refusal to accommodate their wishes, but the problem did not come to a head in Edo until 1853. What it did do in the meantime was generate more heated political discourse and spur attempts to improve coastal defenses.

35. D. C. Greene, "Correspondence between William II of Holland and the Shōgun of Japan, A.D. 1844," *TASJ* 34-4 (1907): 122.
36. Peter Booth Wiley, *Yankees in the Land of the Gods* (New York: Viking, 1990), p. 34.

MILITARY STRENGTHENING AND COASTAL DEFENSE

Since the 1790s Japan's leaders had responded to foreign scares with attempts to strengthen coastal defenses, but most such efforts were seen as temporary deployments. During the 1840s the wish/hope/belief that the foreign threat was transient and could be handled with modest gains in readiness remained strong. However, the increased frequency of incidents and warnings eroded that view, producing more sustained efforts at defense work and a few calls for technological reform, such as that of Takashima Shūhan, or political reform, such as that urged by Nariaki and elaborated by the idiosyncratic scholar Satō Nobuhiro.

By its nature the bakuhan system generated defense work at two levels, that of the han and that of the bakufu. The former could only be local; the latter was hobbled by jurisdictional limitations and political fears. And both suffered from fiscal constraints.

A number of daimyo took steps to strengthen coastal defense. Some efforts occurred in response to bakufu orders; others were owing to local initiative. By the 1840s, daimyo on Kyushu generally were the most interested in new weaponry: they were among the least impoverished, had strong traditions of domanial autonomy, and were nearest to Nagasaki, Dutch learning, and the escalating danger from the south. Satsuma began to strengthen its military capacity from the late 1830s on, and during the 1840s it adopted some of Shūhan's techniques and began purchasing and trying to produce European-style cannon and firearms.

More notable was Saga han, which had standing responsibility for the defense of Nagasaki. As noted in chapter 20, it had been humiliated by the *Phaeton* in 1808 and its daimyo punished for dereliction of duty. During the 1830s, Saga began casting new cannon, and as the prospect grew of a new *Phaeton*-like incident, han leaders took steps to enhance their military capability. They installed more cannon at Nagasaki, improved troop readiness, and in 1850 finished constructing a European-style reverberatory furnace for the casting of heavy cannon. That furnace yielded its first large piece, a cannon capable of lobbing 36-pound shot, in 1853.[37]

A number of other han also rearmed. Much activity was traditional in nature: more training in customary techniques, enhancing coastal defense forces, constructing more artillery emplacements, and casting

37. Chang, *From Prejudice to Tolerance*, pp. 75–76.

more small, bronze cannon. But some involved European-style weaponry and techniques in the manner of Shūhan. In the case of Mito, as noted above, Nariaki sought knowledge of European military methods from the 1830s, and he promoted weapons development as best he could throughout the 1840s. Between 1830 and 1853, he cast a total of 291 cannon, but almost all were of bronze and produced in the traditional manner.

Indeed, in most han the adoption of European-style technology made little progress, often because the attempts to use reverberatory furnaces or other foreign technologies proved too difficult. Two other factors also limited han rearmament: bakufu restraints and fiscal straits.

Even as Edo urged han to rearm, it opposed some of the most promising policies, most notably domanial construction of seaworthy warships, which Edo resisted throughout the 1840s. Finally, in 1850, the bakufu permitted Mito to construct large vessels, but it insisted the work be carried out in cooperation with the finance office, which kept the project under Edo's control. Other daimyo moves to enhance defense capability were also stymied by Edo. When Saga proposed to install a hundred cannon around Nagasaki Bay in 1847, for example, the bakufu vetoed the proposal and took the occasion to require all daimyo to report the casting of any weapon firing shot over 100 *me* (13.25 ounces) in weight.

Military strengthening also suffered from fiscal constraints. Almost no leaders insisted on changes in samurai consumption habits, so few funds became available for redeployment to military purposes. Instead, defense costs were added expenses, and it appears that the contemporary fiscal difficulties of such domains as Himeji, Kawagoe, Mito, Tottori, and Tsushima, and possibly Kii, Ōgaki, and Owari can be partially attributed to the unusual defense burdens they had recently assumed. Edo provided some han with loans and grants of money or land, but the measures were modest and only reduced the resources available to the bakufu itself.

After Abe took personal charge of coastal defense (*kaibō gakari*) in the late summer of 1845, his administration urged han to pursue military strengthening, and by 1850 they were bringing many more men to Edo for training and deployment. By then daimyo were also flooding the bakufu with reports of their energetic enterprises. But much was verbal rearmament, bushels of politically prudent rhetoric enveloping a tiny core of real deeds. On balance that core was thoroughly inadequate to the dangers then looming beyond the horizon.

The bakufu's own record of rearmament was as mixed as that of the daimyo. Tadakuni tinkered with administrative arrangements, trying to improve control of ports under bakufu control, such as Shimoda, Uraga, and Niigata. He and Abe deployed daimyo and devoted the bakufu's own resources to coastal defense, but their efforts were mainly in the Kantō, primarily the approaches to Edo. As the decade advanced, cannon emplacements, troop billets, training areas, and munitions caches were prepared, and scores of small cannon installed and daimyo assigned to man them, but little of the work appears to have produced coastal artillery adequate to its task. In the late 1840s, Abe increased the pressure on shogunal retainers (hatamoto and gokenin), admonishing them to study, train, and get their weapons in shape, but to little apparent effect. Edo cautiously allowed more firearms and cannon practice, but its wish for improved military capacity was always qualified by the fear that such strengthening would enhance the power of some daimyo at bakufu expense.

Slowly and reluctantly the bakufu modified its resistance to European military techniques. In 1848 Abe reauthorized the military tactics that Shūhan had earlier advocated. A year later he ordered one of Shūhan's students to cast a few European-style cannon for the bakufu. And in 1850 he agreed to carefully supervised construction of large warships. To many observers the direction of movement seemed appropriate but the pace did not, and the issue of defense preparation gave rise to political friction that involved not only the usual bakufu officials but also daimyo and, most important, Tokugawa Nariaki, and even the imperial court.

THE POLITICS OF DEFENDING THE REALM

During the decade after Mizuno Tadakuni's resignation, the key figures in Japan's political life were Abe Masahiro and Tokugawa Nariaki, and the issues that dominated their relationship were the growing foreign threat and the condition of Mito. For both men the foreign threat was important because it touched the larger issue of Japan's well-being. Mito was important to Nariaki for obvious reasons; it was important to Abe because Mito was a key prop—or a key threat—to the bakufu, and hence himself.

Nariaki's energetic reform program of the 1830s had generated much resistance within Mito because such policies as changing military systems and relocating city samurai to the hinterland disrupted lives and threatened interests and values. In the manner customary to bakuhan politics, those opposing Nariaki in Mito sought allies in the bakufu, and his persistent and abrasive lobbying at Edo gave them ample candidates. Tadakuni tried to manage him by exiling him to Mito in 1841, but that move only improved his capacity to pursue reform, further aggravating tensions within the han.

The infighting that surrounded the collapse of Tadakuni's reform did not improve Nariaki's standing at Edo, and in 1844 actions by him and his vassals added to bakufu displeasure. A basic policy in shogunal control of daimyo was keeping wives and heirs hostage at Edo, but when Nariaki was exiled to Mito in 1841, his retainers asked that his wife be allowed to join him. The request was rejected out of hand, but in early 1844 they made it again. While bakufu leaders mulled that over, Nariaki had his men put on display in Edo a sampling of Mito military equipment. That implicit rebuke to bakufu defense efforts evidently proved too much. Edo leaders curtly denied the petition regarding his wife and put Abe in charge of an inquiry. He instructed Mito leaders to answer the following questions:

1. We have heard that you are casting guns. In what way are you using them?

2. We hear that your *han* finances are in difficulty. How has this come about? Is it necessary for someone to go into the *han* to scrutinize affairs?

3. What is your intention in the Matsumae affair?

4. Why are you collecting unemployed warriors [ronin]?

5. What is the meaning of the destruction of Buddhist temples?

6. How high are the walls about the Kōdōkan [the new school in Mito castle]? What construction is going on in the Kōdōkan grounds?

7. Why are you promoting repairs of the Tōshōgū?[38]

Rarely had bakufu leaders addressed such damning questions to a daimyo; they hearkened back to those Ieyasu directed to Toyotomi Hideyori in 1614. The implicit queries were clear: Are you preparing to rebel and claim the shogunal title? Will it be necessary to seize the han to rectify affairs?

The questions were largely rhetorical. Even before Mito could answer, the bakufu summoned Nariaki to Edo and took actions commensurate with its suspicions. It ordered him to retire in favor of his twelve-year-old son, Yoshiatsu, and placed him under house arrest in his secondary mansion at Komagome. It put Mito in the hands of a three-

38. Totman, "Political Succession," p. 115.

man regency composed of daimyo from branch han, and with bakufu approval the regents conducted a purge that ousted Fujita Tōko and dozens of Nariaki's other supporters from office. The draconian measures stopped Nariaki's reform. But they silenced him only for a moment, and they enraged his followers and deepened their antipathy for Edo.

When Abe emerged as leader of the bakufu in 1845, he thus found himself allied with Nariaki's enemies at Mito. Within months, however, as he became more involved in defense work, it became apparent that his was the poorer choice of sides, and he began the awkward task of rebuilding and rearranging Edo-Mito relations by rebuilding his own relationship to Nariaki.

It was a difficult task, because Nariaki was uncompromising. When the self-assured, hard-driving, and high-ranking ex-daimyo, who was in his forties, wrote to the cautious, conciliatory, and lower-ranking rōjū, who was in his twenties, the elder saw little need for subservience or restraint. Calling the issues as he saw them, Nariaki began writing Abe from the latter part of 1845, after Abe was placed in charge of coastal defenses. He complained about Mito's leaders, about bakufu disregard of sanke opinion, and about the handling of foreign affairs. He argued that the 1825 uchiharai law should be restored, criticized Abe for allowing castaways to be landed at Uraga, faulted his handling of the King William letter, warned of Dutch perfidy, and reiterated his arguments about building large ships, casting cannon, and strengthening Ezo defenses.[39]

In 1846, Nariaki evidently discovered that Abe had not rejected the French request for Ryūkyūan trade, and he wrote to complain. His criticism of that matter, in which Abe was clearly vulnerable to attack, prodded the young rōjū to begin conciliating the former Mito lord. Abe contended that defenses must be strengthened before the uchiharai policy could be restored but that such an outcome was desirable in principle. It was Abe's first substantive response to Nariaki's letters, and within a few months the latter modified his position enough to fit Abe's suggested sequence. The two thus found a basis for political collaboration in the notion that defense preparation must be pursued so that someday uchiharai could be revived.

One reason Abe wished Nariaki's support was that the imperial court

39. Conrad Totman, "Political Reconciliation in the Tokugawa Bakufu: Abe Masahiro and Tokugawa Nariaki, 1844–1852," in Craig and Shively, eds., *Personality in Japanese History*, pp. 186–92.

was becoming alarmed at the growing foreign presence. About three months after the Biddle and Cecille visits, and one month after Abe wrote Nariaki, the court, prodded by Nariaki, sent a notice to Edo in which it "warned about the repeated arrival of ships, urged military and civil training, stressed the need for coastal defense, and cautioned the bakufu to prevent any stain on the national honor."[40] To quiet courtly fears, Abe instructed the Kyoto deputy (*shoshidai*) to inform the court of the foreign ship situation and to assure it that all was well. Abe's promotion of defense work during the next several years appeased the court, but he realized that having Nariaki in his corner helped. In 1850 he implemented another stratagem for using Mito to cement Edo-Kyoto ties by executing the ceremonial steps through which a young Kyoto woman was adopted by the shogun for subsequent presentation as a bride to the young Mito lord, Yoshiatsu.

Abe also addressed the question of control in Mito. Step by step, he moved to restore Nariaki's influence in the han, hoping in the process to heal the factional divisions and establish closer Mito-Edo ties. In 1849, after Yoshiatsu came of age, Abe dissolved the regency. He criticized members of the ruling faction for abuses of power, gradually released Nariaki's loyalists from confinement, and eventually readmitted them to active political roles. The divisions in the han were so bitter, however, that by 1851 he believed the best he could do was to ease out the ruling faction and allow Nariaki and his supporters to resume control. By the end of 1852, the process was complete. Nariaki was back in power, Yoshiatsu was reluctantly obedient to his will, and Fujita Tōko and others were again staffing the han government. But whereas Edo and Mito had been bitterly at odds a decade earlier, Abe and Nariaki had developed a sufficiently amicable relationship for the latter's considerable reputation among the daimyo to strengthen Abe and the bakufu rather than to weaken them.

How long the honeymoon would last depended mainly on how the foreign threat developed. In the autumn of 1852, the Dutch delivered a report that an American delegate was planning to visit Japan the following year. But the Dutch had warned of British visits in 1842 and again in 1844 and neither had materialized. Evidently the Dutch had cried wolf too often; the report elicited no expression of concern in Edo.

40. Lamberti, "Tokugawa Nariaki," p. 106. The phrasing is Lamberti's.

Breaking Up
and Breaking Out,
1850–1870

Breaking Up the *Bakuhan* System

Breaking Out of the Archipelago

Cultural Trends after 1850

Ecological Trends after 1850

In 1853 Japan's leaders found the rules of political life sharply altered. For decades they had dealt with foreigners who requested that they change their ways, but in 1853 the requests became demands. Not since Khvostov and Davydov engaged in pillaging back in 1807 had Tokugawa leaders faced a direct military threat from abroad. And whereas the two Russians had used force on behalf of one disgruntled diplomat, the American Commodore Matthew C. Perry was authorized and prepared to make war on behalf of his government. This radical escalation in foreign aggressiveness extracted commensurate concessions from Edo and set in motion political, sociocultural, and ecological changes that are still unfolding a century and a half later. During the 1850s and 1860s, the dominating issues were political, but the basic trajectories of broader changes started becoming apparent.

BREAKING UP THE *BAKUHAN* SYSTEM

The political history of the years after 1853 has been told a number of times in English and does not warrant narrative reiteration here.[1] Some interpretive comments about the overall process of political change may

1. A convenient summary may be found in W. G. Beasley, *The Modern History of Japan* (New York: St. Martin's Press, 1981). See Suggestions for Further Reading in English for other titles.

be helpful, however, because that process was crucial to the broader changes that cumulatively marked the end of Japan's period of self-contained historical development.

In hindsight it is obvious that the changed global context doomed the Tokugawa order to collapse. But how and when that would occur and who would be in charge of dismantling the old regime and creating its successor—whether Japanese, foreigner, or no one in particular—was not determined by the mere inevitability of change. At the time, moreover, no one really grasped what lay in store for the imperial realm. Not even the best-informed rangaku scholar was aware of the resources that European governments and the United States could deploy in pursuit of their policies or the ideological and situational elements that sustained their aggressive behavior.

Unsurprisingly, therefore, the most pervasive characteristic of Japan's policy-making and punditry during the midcentury years was underassessment of the threat and its implications. Even Tokugawa Nariaki and the proponents of Mitogaku, who had the keenest appreciation of the danger, believed that if the threat were exploited to revitalize samurai elan and repeal a few restrictions on armaments, Japan could generate enough defensive capacity to preserve the bakuhan system intact.

Within this larger context of overall underestimation of the problem, one can speak of two general political postures that ran through debates from 1853 to 1868. One was an inclusivist posture that sought to rally all political participants in voluntary resistance to the foreigners. The other was an exclusivist viewpoint that said a willful leadership must hammer others into submission as essential prelude to confronting the foreigners. The former posture was dominant through 1857 in Abe Masahiro's bakufu-led response to the first wave of foreign treaties. It disintegrated in 1858 in the face of heightened foreign demands, which sharply escalated policy conflicts in Edo and led to an attempt at bakufu exclusivism directed by the forceful Ii Naosuke. That effort collapsed in early 1860 when assassins, mostly from Mito, gunned and hacked Naosuke to death.

The next four years were marked by confusion and disorder. An inclusivist strategy known as kōbugattai, or "union of court and camp," was pursued by senior figures at court, in Edo, and among the major domains. It was hobbled from the outset, however, by a tension between proponents of bakufu supremacy and daimyo dominance. Senior bakufu officials and Nariaki's son Yoshinobu, who was serving as a

sort of regent to a young shogun, employed the rhetoric of kōbugattai
to draw daimyo and court into active support of Edo, while leaders of
a few great han, Satsuma and Chōshū most notably, invoked it to establish the political predominance of major daimyo. By 1864 these internal tensions were pitting would-be collaborators against one another
so harshly that the kōbugattai effort collapsed amidst bitter recriminations. After that, exclusivism came to prevail, culminating in 1867–68
in a struggle that pitted bakufu leaders against a few key han, while
most daimyo avoided entanglement until "Sat-Chō" success on the battlefield revealed the prudent policy choice.

Although the "court and camp" coalition of high-status figures disintegrated in 1864, it did succeed in riding out a wave of nativist-inspired
sonnō jōi ("revere the emperor; expel the barbarian") rebelliousness
that swept the country during the early 1860s. Edo's acquiescence to
Perry's demands in 1854 had alarmed many samurai, but as long as
Abe and Nariaki maintained some semblance of cooperation and as
long as foreigners made no further demands, the alarm did not lead to
anti-bakufu activism. Abe died, however, and Nariaki became alienated
from Edo leaders. In 1857 the foreigners presented more demands, of
which the most alarming was their insistence on setting up permanent
legations in Edo. The new round of demands coincided with the illness
and death of a childless shogun and transformed a routine question of
shogunal succession into an angry struggle for control of the bakufu
and, through it, control of national policy.

In the outcome, Ii Naosuke seized control and accepted the foreign
demands despite an imperial order to the contrary. He also settled the
shogunal succession to his own satisfaction and punished his domestic
critics, Nariaki most notably but some other major lords as well, for
continuing to protest. These events convinced Mitogaku scholars and
nativists such as Yoshida Shōin of Chōshū that the bakufu as currently
led must be resisted and its policy reversed.[2] In the following months,
that view was sustained by Naosuke's conduct of affairs and by escalating foreign inroads. The most notable inroads were the establishment

---

2. In English, Yoshida Shōin is the best-studied figure of 1850s Japan. A convenient
entrée is David Magarey Earl, *Emperor and Nation in Japan* (Seattle: University of Washington Press, 1964), pt. 2, whose bibliography will lead to older works. A more recent
interpretation of Shōin is chs. 2–4 of Thomas M. Huber, *The Revolutionary Origins of
Modern Japan* (Stanford: Stanford University Press, 1981). For a discursive examination
of Shōin's thought, see ch. 4 of H. D. Harootunian, *Toward Restoration: The Growth of
Political Consciousness in Tokugawa Japan* (Berkeley and Los Angeles: University of
California Press, 1970).

of legations in the vicinity of Edo and the rise of trading activity at the newly created nearby port of Yokohama.

Under these circumstances, nativist ideas that derived from Mitogaku and Hirata Atsutane's kokugaku flourished during the years 1859–64, acquiring the policy rubric *sonnō jōi.* Numerous samurai, Shintō priests, and commoners all across the country, to say nothing of court nobles in Kyoto, became politically active. They were enraged by the seemingly endless foreign demands and by the failure of domestic authorities to reject them. And they were inspired by the teachings of Shōin, who was executed at Naosuke's behest for his part in anti-bakufu plotting.

Highly motivated, the activists pursued a nebulously conceived "imperial restoration" (*ōsei fukkō*). They intended it to subordinate bakufu leaders to the court, repudiate Edo's spineless foreign policies and domestic abuse of emperor and imperial loyalists, invigorate the samurai fighting spirit, drive the barbarians from Japan, and thus restore the pristine virtue of the imperial realm. To attain these goals, they made numerous attacks on high officials and foreigners, lobbied for radical policy change, and planned and attempted a rash of coups d'état. Ironically, however, the most tragic casualty of that rebelliousness was Mito han itself. There, ideologically intense factional feuding deteriorated into the civil war that embroiled bakufu forces in 1864 and culminated in the deaths of some 1,300 people, the crippling of Mitogaku, and the ruination of the domain.

Even as alarmed kōbugattai leaders above were collaborating to control the insurgents below, they were acquiring, through study and a series of military humiliations, an ever-deeper appreciation of what the foreign threat meant to Japan. As a result, whereas the dominant figures before 1858 had believed that the basic structure of the bakuhan system could be kept intact if sufficient military reform and revitalization were carried out, by 1865 key figures in all camps were becoming convinced that only basic structural change could save the realm. An unpleasant corollary followed: somebody's interests must be sacrificed. And not merely the interests, for example, of archers or swordsmen, who already were being forced to acquire unwelcome military skills, or minor servants, who were being fired so that funds could go to military strengthening, or merchants and artisans in one place, who were losing their trade to domestic or foreign competitors in another. What was at stake, the rulers were coming to understand, was the hereditary privilege of their own class and the social structure that assured it.

22. Highway Scene with Samurai at Namamugi in Sagami. Samurai outfitted for workaday service stand on the Tōkaidō at Namamugi village. At this peaceful site on the highway between Edo and Kanagawa in the autumn of 1862, samurai of Satsuma han cut down the English merchant C. L. Richardson for failing to show proper respect toward their lord. Courtesy of the Study and Documentation Centre for Photography, University of Leiden, Collection Bauduin, Neg. No. B3–44.

As awareness spread that basic changes must occur, major groups began organizing to protect their own interests by assuring that they would be in positions to help shape the new arrangements. The major groups in this exclusivistic race to prevail included leaders of the bakufu and key figures in a few of the largest domains, Satsuma and Chōshū most notably. In addition, a few court nobles played key roles, and a number of han leaders tried to forge regional coalitions and federations in the southwest and northeast. During the next three years, these groups maneuvered for position and pursued crash programs of military strengthening. And some even cultivated foreign connections that seemed to offer advantage, the bakufu seeking French help; Satsuma and Chōshū, British.

In this escalating power struggle, the sonnō jōi rhetoric of imperial loyalism that had inspired the earlier rash of self-sacrificing terror and uprisings was used with calculated intent by leaders of all sides to mobilize support and discredit rivals. In 1866 the bakufu was repulsed militarily after trying to punish Chōshū for earlier misdeeds, and fol-

lowing that reversal the erudite but unwarlike Yoshinobu became shogun. He pursued a vigorous program of reform and rearmament, and
at the end of 1867, after another brief stab at kōbugattai-style inclusiv-
ism had petered out, the decisive struggle for supremacy was joined.

When Yoshinobu's armed forces tried to pass through the lines of
Satsuma and Chōshū troops near Kyoto, the latter launched an assault.
Better led, better motivated, and better armed, the Sat-Chō insurgents
prevailed, defeating Yoshinobu's main army in four days of battle. They
then extended their conquest by skillfully allowing the bulk of the fragmented bakuhan elite and their armed forces to join the victors at no
immediate cost while making examples of a few recalcitrant han. The
bakufu's abrupt collapse brought the long-smoldering regional tension
between northeast and southwest to the fore, and the harshest fighting
occurred in Tōhoku, especially at Aizu. There the struggle for supremacy led to fierce military resistance, defeat, brutal punishment, and, in
the outcome, ill will that endured well into the twentieth century.

Just as Ieyasu had obtained an imperial statement sanctioning his
victory at Sekigahara in 1600, so the new conquerors employed an imperial decree to legitimize their seizure of power and suppression of
opposition, a process they characterized as ōsei fukkō. During the next
few years, they consolidated their position under the nominal authority
of the youthful Meiji emperor. They sorted out their membership and
launched a wide array of policies designed to create a strongly centralized regime capable of preserving Japanese independence and their own
supremacy. The core of their strategy was maintenance of a strong military system anchored in a vigorous economy, a policy they identified
by the classic Chinese phrase, *fukoku kyōhei,* "rich country, strong army."
Within a few years reform measures had eliminated daimyo domains,
abolished most of the hereditary privileges of samurai, and established
a unified imperial regime in Tokyo, the former Edo. That government
taxed all of Japan directly and treated all Japanese men as eligible for
military service, thereby guaranteeing itself a level of funding and manpower vastly exceeding that of the defunct bakufu.

The Meiji leaders thus dismantled the old regime and consolidated
the new. In part their survival reflected their political skill. But in part
it reflected the absence of revanchist sentiment: by 1868 no one of consequence had any illusions about the viability of the old bakuhan system, so discontent with the new rulers was fragmented, focused on particular grievances and lacking any broader unifying desire to restore the
"good old days" of Tokugawa hegemony.

The other noteworthy success of those who toppled the old order was that they managed to stay out of foreign clutches. In part that outcome reflects the brevity of the civil war, which ended before either side gave outsiders pretext to interpose themselves forcefully in Japan. In part it reflects the ideology of nativism, which identified alien influence as the ultimate danger with such clarity that participants in the domestic struggle drew back at critical junctures from the temptation to sacrifice autonomy for foreign assistance. And in part it reflects prudence on the part of the new rulers: when anti-bakufu troops attacked some foreigners, threatening to turn them against the new regime, the new rulers responded by harshly punishing the men charged with the attacks. And when foreigners protested the new regime's anti-Christian policies, the new rulers chose to revise those policies rather than defy the foreigners, their earlier sonnō jōi protestations notwithstanding.

In part, finally, Japan escaped foreign clutches because the imperialist powers were distracted by other matters. The Americans were consuming themselves in their civil war; the Russians were recovering from the Crimean War and facing domestic problems; the French were confronted by an expansionist Prussia; Britain had recently faced the Sepoy Mutiny in India. Britain and France then engaged China in renewed warfare and concessions that absorbed more of their Asian military capacity. For those powers, Japan was at the very most a distant and minor consideration, and engagement in these other, more pressing matters reduced even further their interest in turning Japanese disorder to foreign benefit. So the fragile new regime weathered its birthing years and went on to emulate and at times outdo those whom it had successfully held at bay.

BREAKING OUT OF THE ARCHIPELAGO

In the outcome then, Japan's political elite managed to restructure their polity without coming under foreign political domination. And the restructured system preserved the imperial realm's political independence until 1945. In the course of scrapping the bakuhan system, however, that elite changed much more than a mere political structure; they also altered the trajectory of cultural life and launched a basic redefinition of their civilization's ecological foundation and global role.

CULTURAL TRENDS AFTER 1850

In cultural developments, as in political, the most noteworthy trends of the years after 1850 related to Japan's engagement with the outside world. However, the evolution of kokugaku also proved of capital importance, as the political summary has suggested.

In terms of aesthetics and entertainment, the established forms of fiction, poetry, and drama continued to be pursued, with new material on foreigners and treaty ports gradually enriching them. Fascination with things foreign was most evident in painting and wood block prints, where foreigners, their physiognomies, clothing, accessories, ships, and treaty port facilities became popular subjects for representation. Even the great catfish (*namazu*) occasionally took the foreigners into account, as the inscription on one namazu print of 1855 indicates:

> Of late foreign fellows repeatedly visited this country. Even [we namazu] under the ground got annoyed and at the very moment [our] tails were presumably shaking and smashing North America with all might, it turned out to be the surface of Edo! . . . [we] beg your pardon, oh [we] ask you many times to forgive [us]. . . . [3]

In scholarly arenas the impact of the political turmoil after 1853 was pronounced. Mitogaku, as noted above, remained vital during the 1850s but was ravaged by the Mito civil war of 1863–64. Kokugaku, by contrast, flourished as never before.

Kokugaku, which had been an individualistic, unofficial academic activity at the time of Motoori Norinaga, and which acquired a more explicitly political and aggressively ethnic thrust at the hands of Hirata Atsutane, blossomed during the 1850s and 1860s into a widely accepted rationale for individual action in defense of the realm and against the foreign threat. The vision of Japan and its people as the land of the gods proved so effective at winning support across class and domanial boundaries that by the mid 1860s political leaders in all camps were vigorously invoking the rhetoric to enlist followers. And the leaders of the new Meiji regime absorbed it into their official ideology and enmeshed it in the structure, protocol, and policy of the regime, transforming into state dogma what had begun as the personal vision of scholars.

Rangaku, on the other hand, fared poorly during these years, a belated victim of Britain's displacement of the Netherlands as premier global empire-builder. Because Britons and Americans presented the principal threats to Japan in the 1850s, the scholars who had struggled for years to master Dutch found their language skills irrelevant and their knowledge marginal or out of date. For many the task of master-

3. Cornelis Ouwehand, *Namazu-e and Their Themes* (Leiden: E. J. Brill, 1964), p. 20.

ing an entirely new language proved overwhelming, and they fell silent, leaving others to develop the skills required by the times. Linguistic chance thus achieved what surges of anti-rangaku activism had failed to do.

As a result much of Japan's painfully accumulated knowledge of Europe was lost to public service just when it was most desperately needed, and the realm had to produce a new generation of foreign experts on a crash basis. The bakufu promoted study of several European languages, but by 1860 English was becoming the most valued despite counter-blandishments by Dutchmen, Frenchmen, and Russians. In the outcome, the study of English became central to yōgaku, "Western" or "European" learning, the term that displaced rangaku. In the following years, students of yōgaku proliferated and its study advanced with startling speed.

Military matters were the primary focus of yōgaku, with the bakufu and many han encouraging vassals to learn and introduce new techniques of land and sea warfare. As the 1860s advanced, both bakufu and han hired foreigners to provide instruction, and they sent delegations of diplomats and students to Europe and North America to learn and report. By 1867, senior figures at Edo and in the major domains had access to information on the governmental, economic, and social systems of Europe. That knowledge helped persuade them of the bakuhan system's obsolescence and influenced their thinking on how to reconfigure Japan. From about 1870 on, the broader exploration of European philosophy and higher arts commenced in earnest, and the process of grounding Japan's civilization in the global human experience continues today.

ECOLOGICAL TRENDS AFTER 1850

Back in the seventeenth century, Japan's leaders decreed, in effect, that their people must make do with the yield of their archipelago. That policy permitted a century of striking growth but produced during the eighteenth century a painful period of adaptation as people struggled to survive in a realm whose resources were largely tapped. In the process of adaptation, as chapter 13 noted, limited forms of ecological expansion were devised, most notably the exploitation of ancient biomass through the use of ground coal, maritime expansion through formation of a fishing industry, and very limited terrestrial expansion through exploration and trade in the Ezo region. Social and agronomic changes also facilitated more intensive exploitation of the arable and forest land already in use.

After 1860 these processes of expansion all began to accelerate, expedited by the piecemeal introduction of new industrial technology and trade arrangements. The opening of ports to foreign trade created a new market for exports, the most important of which was silk, and silk production expanded as merchants pursued opportunities for gain and the bakufu tapped a new fiscal source. During the 1860s, the bakufu also hired a few foreign technicians to explore for minerals, and bakufu and han began employing foreigners to assist in military strengthening, the creation of new industries, and the development of shipping and railroads, all of which increased the rate of wood, coal, and other resource consumption.

In terms of ancient biomass explicitly, domestic coal mining expanded sharply from the 1860s on, and predominated for a few decades, later being supplemented by Japan's limited reserves of oil and natural gas. Maritime expansion intensified along with fossil fuel exploitation. The adoption of European-style vessels and gear enabled the fishing and whaling industries to grow and extend their extractive activity ever farther afield, moving from one depleted fishery to another as necessary to sustain commerce. Meiji interest in wide-ranging pelagic exploitation was reflected in treaties negotiated with Russia in the 1870s, which were careful to assure Japan the port and transit arrangements necessary for working the seas off eastern Siberia.

Terrestrial expansion followed a more awkward path because it raised more acute intersocietal jurisdictional issues. During the 1860s, bakufu leaders successfully asserted European-style sovereignty over the Bonin and Ryūkyū island chains. And with British help they turned aside a Russian move to seize Tsushima in 1862. They also revived the dormant issue of Ezo but during the 1860s were unable to agree with the Russian authorities on how to carve up the region. The resident people were not consulted, and pending a final diplomatic arrangement, Russian and Japanese explorers and settlers busily staked out claims on Sakhalin and the Kurils. In 1875 the two governments negotiated a settlement that gave all the Kurils to Japan and all of Sakhalin to Russia.[4] Wars of the twentieth century produced changes that benefited the victors, and as of this writing both Sakhalin and the Kurils are under Russian control.

4. George Alexander Lensen, *The Russian Push toward Japan* (Princeton: Princeton University Press, 1959), pp. 443–44.

During the 1860s, while the status of Ezo was still in limbo, bakufu leaders found their attention drawn to Korea. Back in the 1620s–1640s, as noted in chapter 7, Edo had toyed with the idea of deploying forces to Korea to help the Yi and Ming governments fend off Manchu invaders. But nothing came of the thought, and a politically stable, Tsushima-mediated, Korean-Japanese trade relationship was maintained into the nineteenth century. In the mid 1860s, however, Edo again became alarmed at reports of foreign activity in Korea. The intruders this time were European, and after hearing of a Franco-Korean confrontation in early 1867, bakufu leaders decided to despatch an armed mission to Korea "to work for peace."[5] Reports of the scheme dismayed the government in Seoul, and the plan aborted when civil strife engulfed Japan later in the year. During the 1870s, Meiji leaders picked up the issue, and in the following decades policy gradually evolved into an overtly expansionist program that was one expression of a broader strategy of enhancing Japan's resource base through use of politico-military power in the manner of recent European and American empire builders.

From the 1860s Japan thus began moving from the self-sufficient arrangements of the Tokugawa order to an industrial order that saw the resources of the globe as its material base. Like other industrial societies, it used money and muscle as seemed most effective to obtain these resources. In subsequent decades the process was legitimized—and sustained—by an ideological amalgam that employed elements of the domestic kokugaku legacy, Tokugawa Confucian notions of duty and hierarchy, and European ideas of race, social Darwinism, and progress.

One of the most striking changes that accompanied breakup of the early modern order and breakout from the archipelago was the trajectory of population. As noted earlier, the population increase of the early nineteenth century was reversed during the 1830s, but by 1850 the level of the 1820s had been recovered. Population figures for the 1850s and 1860s do not exist, and those of the 1870s are based on different methods of tallying, which makes hazardous guesswork out of attempts to link figures of the 1840s to those of the 1870s and later.[6]

5. Conrad Totman, *The Collapse of the Tokugawa Bakufu, 1862–1868* (Honolulu: University Press of Hawaii, 1980), p. 325.

6. The best treatment of this "demographic transition" is Hayami Akira, "Population Changes," in Marius B. Jansen and Gilbert Rozman, eds., *Japan in Transition from Tokugawa to Meiji* (Princeton: Princeton University Press, 1986), pp. 280–317. Hayami argues that the demographic story from the 1790s onward is best seen as one of linear growth.

The demographic growth of the 1840s probably continued during the 1850s, as Hayami Akira believes, buoyed by the continuation of generally favorable weather and the earlier-cited enhancements of the resource base. The 1860s, however, were a difficult period of irregular weather, political turmoil, armies in motion, and heightened public hardship and turbulence. The foreigners played an ambiguous demographic role. On the one hand, they introduced Asiatic cholera, which raged through the country in the years 1858–61, driving the population downward. On the other hand, some grain imports a few years later may have saved lives, and foreign trade may have created pockets of economic opportunity that translated into more live births. Where these factors left Japan's population at the time of the Restoration is unknown. It is clear, however, that from the 1870s on, it entered a phase of striking growth, which continued into the twentieth century, raising an 1872 population reported at 33,100,000 to some 72,000,000 by 1936 and about 120,000,000 in 1990.

The rapid and sustained population growth since the Restoration is reminiscent of the seventeenth century. But where the older surge was eventually throttled by politically enforced territorial limits, the modern one, linked as it is to the ideology of material progress, has created both a compelling need for extraction of overseas resources and a convenient justification for seeking out and acquiring those resources. In that way, as well as in cultural terms, changes associated with the passing of the early modern order have linked Japan inextricably to the modern fate of global humankind.

Year Periods (*Nengō*), 1570–1868

Period name	Starting date	Period name	Starting date
Genki	1570/4/23	Kanpō	1741/2/27
Tenshō	1573/7/28	Enkyō	1744/2/21
Bunroku	1592/12/8	Kan'en	1748/7/12
Keichō	1596/10/27	Hōreki	1751/10/27
Genna	1615/7/13	Meiwa	1764/6/2
Kan'ei	1624/2/30	An'ei	1772/11/16
Shōhō	1644/12/16	Tenmei	1781/4/2
Keian	1648/2/15	Kansei	1789/1/25
Jōō	1652/9/18	Kyōwa	1801/2/5
Meireki	1655/4/13	Bunka	1804/2/11
Manji	1658/7/23	Bunsei	1818/4/22
Kanbun	1661/4/25	Tenpō	1830/12/10
Enpō	1673/9/21	Kōka	1844/12/2
Tenwa	1681/9/29	Kaei	1848/2/28
Jōkyō	1684/2/21	Ansei	1854/11/27
Genroku	1688/9/30	Man'en	1860/3/18
Hōei	1704/3/13	Bunkyū	1861/2/19
Shōtoku	1711/4/25	Genji	1864/2/20
Kyōhō	1716/6/22	Keiō	1865/4/8
Genbun	1736/4/28	Meiji	1868/9/8

Nengō starting dates are given in year-month-day order.
Source: *Nihonshi nenpyō* (originally a volume of *Nihon rekishi daijiten*) (Tokyo: Kawade Shobō shinsha, 1973).

Dates of Tokugawa Shogun

No.	Name (descent status)	Reign dates	Life dates
1	Ieyasu (founder)	1603/2/12–1605/4/16	1542–1616
2	Hidetada (son)	1605/4/16–1623/7/27	1578–1632
3	Iemitsu (son)	1623/7/27–1651/4/20	1604–1651
4	Ietsuna (son)	1651/8/18–1680/5/8	1641–1680
5	Tsunayoshi (brother)	1680/8/23–1709/1/10	1646–1709
6	Ienobu (nephew)	1709/5/1–1712/10/14	1662–1712
7	Ietsugu (son)	1713/4/2–1716/4/30	1709–1716
8	Yoshimune (near cousin)	1716/8/13–1745/9/25	1684–1751
9	Ieshige (son)	1745/11/2–1760/5/13	1711–1761
10	Ieharu (son)	1760/9/2–1786/9/8	1737–1786
11	Ienari (near cousin)	1787/4/15–1837/4/2	1773–1841
12	Ieyoshi (son)	1837/9/2–1853/6/22	1793–1853
13	Iesada (son)	1853/10/23–1858/7/4	1824–1858
14	Iemochi (distant cousin)	1858/10/25–1866/8/11	1846–1866
15	Yoshinobu (distant cousin)	1866/12/5–1867/12/9	1837–1913

Reign dates in year-month-day order, as given in *Nihonshi nenpyō* (originally a volume of *Nihon rekishi daijiten*) (Tokyo: Kawade Shobō shinsha, 1973). Descent status from entries in *Daijinmei jiten* (Tokyo: Heibonsha, 1957).

APPENDIX C

Early Modern Emperors Mentioned in the Text

Emperor	Formal reign dates	Life dates
Ōgimachi	1557/10/27–1586/11/7	1517–1593
Goyōzei	1586/11/7–1611/3/27	1571–1617
Gomizuno-o	1611/3/27–1629/11/8	1596–1680
Meishō	1629/11/8–1643/10/3	1623–1696
(Gokōmyō)	1643–1654	
(Gosai)	1654–1663	
(Reigen)	1663–1687	
(Higashiyama)	1687–1709	
Nakamikado	1709/6/21–1735/3/21	1701–1737
Sakuramachi	1735/3/21–1747/5/2	1720–1750
Momozono	1747/5/2–1762/7/12	1741–1762
(Gosakuramachi)	1762–1770	
(Gomomozono)	1770–1779	
Kōkaku	1779/11/25–1817/3/22	1771–1840
(Ninkō)	1817–1846	
Kōmei	1846/2/13–1866/12/25	1831–1866
Meiji	1867/1/9–1912/7/30	1852–1912

Formal reign dates in year-month-day order, as given in *Nihonshi nenpyō*. Actual accession dates sometimes varied somewhat. Life dates are from entries in *Daijinmei jiten*. Emperors not mentioned in the text are listed in parentheses. A convenient list of first and last years of emperors and year-periods is to be found in Andrew N. Nelson, *The Modern Reader's Japanese-English Character Dictionary*, rev. ed. (Rutland, Vt.: Charles E. Tuttle, 1966), pp. 1018–22.

Glossary of Japanese Terms

Names of people, places, and year periods are omitted.

Ainu: native people of the Ezo region
Akaezo fūsetsu kō: A study of Red Ainu reports (Kudō Heisuke)
Amaterasu: the sun goddess of Shintō
Azuma kagami: Mirror of the east (anonymous)
Baienjuku: school of Miura Baien in Kyushu
bakufu: shogunal government; military headquarters
bakuhan taisei: political system consisting of bakufu and daimyo domains
bansho wage goyō: bakufu office of translation and documentation
bantō: chief clerk
Bendō: Distinguishing the way (Ogyū Sorai)
beni-e: rose-colored tinting
benizuri-e: rose-and-green prints
Benmei: Distinguishing names (Ogyū Sorai)
biwa: lute
Buke shohatto: Laws for the military households (bakufu)
bu: military arts
buikukyoku: Chōshū han's savings fund
bun: civil or literary arts
bunbu: arts of peace and war
bunjin: literatus
bunjinga: literati art (also called nanga)
bushi: samurai
bushidō: Way of the warrior
chanoyu: tea ceremony
ch'in: Chinese zither

Chishima ibun: Strange tales of the Kurils (Aizawa Seishisai)
Chōja kyō: The millionaire's gospel (anonymous)
chōnin: townsman; merchant class
Chūshingura: see *Kanadehon chūshingura*
daigaku no kami: head of the university; title of Hayashi scholars
Daigaku wakumon: Questions on the Great Learning (Kumazawa Banzan)
daikan: shogunal intendant
daimyō: daimyo; "great name"
Daimyō katagi: Portrait of a daimyo (Matsudaira Sadanobu)
daimyōjin: divine rectifier; savior
Dai Nihon shi: History of Japan (Mito han)
Daizō ichiranshū: Digest of the Tripitaka (Chinese)
dekasegi: working away from home
Dōjimon: Boys' questions (Itō Jinsai)
dōjō: court poets
dōza: copper mint
Edokko: brash Edo townsmen
eejanaika: "Ain't it great!"; raucous celebration
ehon: picture book
Emishi: native people (also called Ezo) of Ezo region
Enryakuji: Tendai monastery on Mount Hiei
Ezo: *see* Emishi
fudai: hereditary servants or vassals
fudoki: geographical works
Fugaku sanjū rokkei: Thirty-six views of Mount Fuji (Katsushika Hokusai)
Fujikō: cult whose worship focused on Mount Fuji
Fujufuse: subsect of Hokke sect of Buddhism
fukoku kyōhei: rich country, strong army
fushin yaku: construction agency
gando gaeshi: kabuki scene-changing device
Gansuidō: Confucian school in eighteenth-century Osaka
gekokujō: those below toppling those above
Genji monogatari: Tale of Genji (Murasaki Shikibu)
gesaku: silly or light works
gimin: righteous man
ginza: silver mint
giri: social duty; obligation
gōgaku: village, local, or branch school
gōkan: bound-together volumes
gokenin: Minamoto vassals in Kamakura period; minor shogunal vassals in
   Edo period
Gomō jigi: The meaning of terms in the Analects and Mencius (Itō Jinsai)
goningumi: five-household mutual-responsibility group
goyōkin: forced loans
gundai: shogunal intendants
gunken: centralized (lit. province-district), as in centralized government (cf.
   hōken)

gunki monogatari: war tales
Gunsho chiyō: Collected works on government (Chinese)
Hachimonji-ya: a Kyoto publisher
Hagakure: Hidden behind leaves (Yamamoto Tsunetomo)
haiga: a style of poem promoted by Yosa Buson
haikai: a type of 17-syllable poem
haikai no renga: comic linked verse
Haisho zanpitsu: Autobiography in exile (Yamaga Sokō)
hama goten: villa of Ieyasu at Shimizu
han: daimyo domain
han satsu: domain paper money
hanamichi: passageway through audience in kabuki theater
Harusame monogatari: Tales of the spring rain (Ueda Akinari)
hashira-e: pillar prints
hatamoto: bannermen; middling vassals of Tokugawa shogun
hatamoto yakko: urban gangs of hatamoto and their menservants
hiden: secret transmission of knowledge
hiiki renchū: fan clubs for kabuki actors
hinoki: Japanese cypress
Hoei mondō: Dialogues on the capture of phantoms (Ōtsuki Gentaku)
Hōjōki: Account of my hut (Kamo no Chōmei)
hōken: decentralized; feudal
Hokke: Lotus or Nichiren sect of Buddhism
Hōkōji: Tendai temple built by Hideyoshi and Hideyori
Honchō bugei shōden: Biographical sketches of military arts in Japan (Hinatsu Shigetaka)
Honchō tsugan: General mirror of Japan (Hayashi Gahō)
hongawara: semi-tubular roofing tile
Horikawa nami no tsuzumi: The drum of the waves of Horikawa (Chikamatsu Monzaemon)
Hōtoku: the teaching of Ninomiya Sontoku
Hyakunin jōrō: A hundred noble ladies (Hanabusa Itchō)
hyakushōdai: peasants' representative
hyōbanki: critical booklet
hyōjōsho: bakufu judicial office
Ibukiya: school of Hirata Atsutane in Edo
igaku no kin: Matsudaira Sadanobu's ban on heterodoxy
ikigami: one who becomes a kami while still alive
ikki: protest; riot
Ikkō: subsect of the Jōdo sect of Buddhism
iriaichi: common land
Ise monogatari: Tales of Ise (anonymous)
ishizuri: stone rubbing
isshugin: a gold-denominated silver coin = 1/16 ryō
itowappu: yarn guild
jamisen: precursor of samisen, which *see*
jidaimono: style of drama; period piece

Jikata hanreioku: an exegesis on practical affairs (Ōishi Hisayoshi)

jikatasho: agronomic writing; farm manual

Jingi kanryō: Head of Shintō affairs at imperial court

Jinnō shōtōki: Records of the true imperial succession (Kitabatake Chikafusa)

jin'ya: headquarters; regional administrative office

jitsugaku: real, useful, or practical learning

Jōdo: Pure Land sect of Buddhism

Jōgan seiyō: The essentials of governance (Chinese)

jōkamachi: castle town

jōruri: text for puppet drama

junkenshi: circuit inspection of daimyo domains

Jurakudai: mansion of Hideyoshi in Kyoto

jusha: Confucian scholar

kabu nakama: chartered trade association

kabuki: drama form of the Tokugawa period

kaibō gakari: charge of coastal defense

Kaihodō: school of Sugeno Kenzan in Edo

Kaikoku heidan: Military talks for a maritime nation (Hayashi Shihei)

Kaitai shinsho: A new book of anatomy (Sugita Genpaku et al)

Kaitokudō: school of Nakai Shūan in Osaka

kakaku: family status

kami: Shintō deity

kami no michi: Way of the gods

kamon: related household

Kamusumeraki no michi: Way of gods and emperors

kan: measure of weight (8.72 lbs; 3.75 kg)

kana zōshi: forerunner of ukiyo zōshi, which *see*

Kanadehon chūshingura: The treasury of loyal retainers (Takeda Izumo II)

Kan'eiji: Tendai temple in Edo

Kangien: school of Hirose Tansō in Kyushu

kanjō bugyō: finance magistrate

kanjō ginmiyaku: comptroller

kanjōsho: finance office

Kannō wakumon: Issues in agronomy (Fujita Yūkoku)

kanpō: holistic Chinese medicine

kanshi: Chinese poetry

kansho: sweet potato

karagokoro: China heart; Sinophilia

kaseiki: the years 1804–29

ken: measure of length: six shaku (approx. two meters)

kibyōshi: yellow-cover books

Kikōben: Some call me disputatious (Aizawa Seishisai)

Kimon: school of Yamazaki Ansai in Kyoto

kinpiramono: puppet plays about the fictitious hero, Sakata Kinpira

kinza: gold mint

kiwari: modular construction

Kiyomizu monogatari: Tale of Kiyomizu (Asayama Irin'an)
kō: communal savings fund
Kōbō Daishi: religious title of priest Kūkai, founder of Shingon
kōbugattai: union of court and camp
Kōdōkan: Mito domain academy
kogaku: ancient learning
kōgi: public affairs
Kogidō: school of Itō Jinsai in Kyoto
Kojiki: Records of ancient matters (Ō no Yasumaro)
Kojikiden: A commentary on the *Kojiki* (Motoori Norinaga)
Kokinshū: Collection of ancient and modern poetry (Ki no Tsurayuki et al.)
Kokka hachiron: Eight theories on Japanese poetry (Kada Arimaro)
kokkeibon: humorous books
koku: measure of volume; 180 liters; approx. five bushels
kokubunji: provincial monastery
kokudaka: putative yield of a field, village, or domain
kokugaku: Japanese learning
kokujin: local man of power ca. sixteenth century
Kokusen'ya kassen: The battles of Coxinga (Chikamatsu Monzaemon)
kokutai: national essence; uniquely Japanese polity
komononari: miscellaneous produce taxes
Konjin: a demonic kami of the Okayama region
Konkōkyō: religious movement attributed to Kawate Bunjirō
Kōrakuen: garden of Mito lord in Edo; daimyo's garden in Okayama
kōsha: school of Shingaku religious organization
Kōshoku ichidai otoko: The life of an amorous man (Ihara Saikaku)
kuge: court noble or nobility
kumi gashira: village group leader; military unit leader
kumiai: private trade organization
kuniyaku bushin: construction service for the domain
kuroshio: Japan current
Kurozumikyō: religious movement attributed to Kurozumi Munetada
kyō: a religious faith or teaching
Kyō warabe: Kyoto's child (a guide to the city) (Nakagawa Kiun)
kyōdōtai: a system of communal, self-sufficient villages
machi: town
machi bugyō: city magistrate
machi yakko: town rowdies
magokoro: a true, pure, or righteous heart
Maitreya: *see* Miroku
Manpukuji: Ōbaku Zen temple in Uji
Man'yō daishoki: A stand-in's chronicle of the *Man'yōshū* (Keichū)
Man'yōshū: Collection of a myriad leaves (Ōtomo no Yakamochi et al.?)
masu: a measure of volume; approx. two liters
matsuri: festival
me: measure of weight (= monme) (375 g; 13.25 oz)
Meirinsha: central college of Shingaku

meishoki: gazetteer
Meiwa *tenma sōdō:*   post-horse rebellion of the Meiwa period
metsuke: bakufu inspector
michiyuki: poetic journey in kabuki play
mikunigokoro: Japanese heart
Miroku: Buddha of the future; Maitreya
miso: edible soybean paste
Mitogaku: teachings of major Mito scholars in the late Tokugawa period
mizu mondai: disputes over water use
mono no aware: the sadness of things; sensibility to beauty
Musashi abumi: The stirrups of Musashi (Asai Ryōi)
muyōsha uchiharai: shell and repel without mercy
myōgakin: license fee; a forced or "thanks" contribution
Nagasaki bugyō: Nagasaki magistrate
Nagasaki kaisho: Nagasaki clearing house for foreign trade accounts
naiyū gaikan: the Confucian epigram, "internal troubles and external catastrophes"
nakagai: jobber
nakama: trade association
namazu: mythical underground catfish; cause of earthquakes
nanban: southern barbarian; European
nanga: southern painting; literati painting (bunjinga)
Naobi no mitama: The rectifying spirit (Motoori Norinaga)
Nanryō nishugin: the Nanryō two-shu silver coin
Nansō satomi hakkenden: Biographies of eight dogs (Takizawa Bakin)
nengō: year period
nengu: grain tax
Nezumi no sōshi: The tale of the mouse (anonymous)
Nihongi: see *Nihon shoki*
Nihon ōdai ichiran: A synopsis of Japanese reigns (Hayashi Gahō)
Nihon shoki: Chronicles of Japan (Prince Toneri et al.)
Nikkō Tōshōgū: Mausoleum of Ieyasu at Nikkō
ninennaku uchiharai: shell and repel without second thought
ningyō jōruri: puppet theater
ninjō: human feelings; affection
ninjōbon: love stories; books about human feelings
Nise Murasaki inaka Genji: The false Murasaki and the rustic Genji (Ryūtei
   Tanehiko)
nishiki-e: fully colored or brocade prints
Nishiyama monogatari: Tale of the western hills (Takebe Ayatari)
nishugin: a gold-denominated silver coin = 1/8 ryō
nō: the medieval nō drama
nōsho: agronomic writings; farm manual
Nozarashi kikō: Exposure in the fields, a travel account (Matsuo Bashō)
nuki mairi: unauthorized pilgrimage
Ōbaku: a sect of Zen Buddhism
odori: dance

odorikomi: "dance-in"; raucous protest
Ōen: school of Ikuta Yorozu in Kashiwazaki
Ofuregaki kanpō shūsei: Kanpō-era compilation of ordinances (bakufu)
Ōgosho: retired shogun
oiemono: dramas about the great households
oie sōdō: disturbances in the great (daimyo) households
okage mairi: pilgrimage
Oku no hosomichi: The narrow road of Oku (Matsuo Bashō)
ōmetsuke: senior inspectors
onna kabuki: women's kabuki
ōsei fukkō: imperial restoration
otetsudai bushin: daimyo-assisted public works
Ōtsu-e: anonymous popular paintings sold around Ōtsu
oyashio: Chishima (Kuril islands) current
rakugo: a comic story; style of oral storytelling
rakuichi: tax-free market
rangaku: Dutch learning
ranpeki: Dutch mania
renga: linked verse
Rikugien: walking garden on the north edge of Edo
Rinzai: a sect of Zen Buddhism
rōjū: senior council; elders
rōnin: masterless samurai
Ryūshi shinron: A new thesis of Ryūshi (Yamagata Daini)
Saga bon: Saga books
Saikaku oridome: Saikaku's last weaving (Ihara Saikaku)
sakoku: closed country
samisen: long-necked, three-string lute
samurai: military man
sangawara: flat roofing tile
sanke: three houses; major Tokugawa cadet houses
sankin kōtai: alternate attendance
Sannō gongen: the fundamental god of life for Heaven, Earth, and Man;
   incarnation of the deity Sannō
sarugaku: musical skit
Seidan: A discussion on government (Ogyū Sorai)
seii taishōgun: barbarian-subduing generalissimo
Seijukan: school of Taki Motonori in Edo
Seiken igen: A last offering for peace (Asami Keisai)
Seikyō yōroku: Essential teachings of the sages (Yamaga Sokō)
Seimeiron: On the rectification of names (Fujita Yūkoku)
Seji kenmonroku: A record of things seen and heard (Buyō Inshi)
Seken munesan'yō: Worldly mental calculations (Ihara Saikaku)
sengoku daimyō: warring-states-type daimyo
Senjikan: school of Asada Gōryū in Osaka
Senshindōjuku: school of Ōshio Heihachirō in Osaka
seppuku: suicide of honor

setchūgaku: eclecticism
sewamono: style of drama; domestic piece
sharebon: pulp fiction; witty books
shijuku: private or proprietary school
Shikidō ōkagami: The great mirror of the art of love (Fujimoto Kizan)
shikishi: poem squares (approx. 25 x 27 cm)
Shingaku: the teachings propounded by Ishida Baigan
Shingon: a sect of Buddhism
shinjū: love suicide
Shinjū ten no Amijima: The love suicides at Amijima (Chikamatsu Monzae-mon)
Shinkokinshū: The new *Kokinshū* (Fujiwara no Teika et al)
shi-nō-kō-shō: samurai-peasant-artisan-merchant
shinpan: Tokugawa-related households
Shinron: New theses (Aizawa Seishisai)
Shintō: Way of the gods
Shirandō: school of Ōtsuki Gentaku in Edo
shōen: chartered corporate estates
Shōheikō: Hayashi school at Shōheizaka in Edo
Shōheizaka gakumonjo: official name of Hayashi school after 1797
Shōkōkan: Mito bureau preparing *Dai Nihon shi*
shomotsu aratame yaku: inspector of books
shōsetsu: *see* yomihon
shoshidai: shogunal deputy (in Kyoto)
shōya: village headman
shuinjō: sailing permit
shūmon aratame: board of religious examiners
shūmon aratamechō: register of religious faith
shunga: spring pictures; erotic art
Shunshoku umegoyomi: Colors of spring: the plum calendar (Tamenaga Shunsui)
sobayōnin: grand chamberlain
Sōbō kigen: A garrulous exegesis (Nakai Chikuzan)
sōdō: disturbance, disorder
Sonezaki shinjū: The love suicides at Sonezaki (Chikamatsu Monzaemon)
sonnō: imperial loyalism
sonnō jōi: revere the emperor; expel the barbarian
Sōtō: a sect of Zen Buddhism
sugi: cryptomeria
Suika Shintō: Shintō interpretation of Yamazaki Ansai
Suitō hiroku: Confidential memoir on social control (Satō Nobuhiro)
sukegō: villages required to provide highway corvée labor
sumi-e: ink-line painting
Sunpuki: The annals of Sunpu (bakufu)
Taiheisaku: A proposal for a great peace (Ogyū Sorai)
tan-e: hand coloring
tashidaka: supplemental stipend

tatami: sedge mat
taue-uta: song for rice planting
tegata: negotiable paper certificate
Tekijuku: school of Ogata Kōan in Osaka
Tenchō mukyūreki: Annals of the eternal court (Hirata Atsutane)
Tendai: a sect of Buddhism
tendō: the Heavenly Way
tengu: long-nosed goblin
tenka: the realm
tennō: the emperor
Tenrikyō: religious movement attributed to Nakayama Miki
terakoya: small local school
Tōdaiji: major Buddhist monastery in Nara
Tōkaidō: highway from Kyoto to Edo via south coast
Tōkaidō gojūsan tsugi: Fifty-three stations of the Tōkaidō (Andō Hiroshige)
Tōkaidōchū hizakurige: By foot along the Tōkaidō (Jippensha Ikku)
tokonoma: decorative alcove
ton'ya: merchant house
toshiyori: elders; senior council
Tōshōgū: *see* Nikkō Tōshōgū
Tōshōgū goikun: Ieyasu's testament (Tenkai?)
Tōto meisho ichiran: Famous views of the eastern capital (Katsushika Hokusai)
tozama: outside daimyo
Tsurezuregusa: Essays in idleness (Yoshida Kenkō)
uchiharai: shell and repel; drive off with cannon fire
uchikowashi: house smashings
Ugetsu monogatari: Tales of moonlight and rain (Ueda Akinari)
uji: lineage group
uki-e: perspective print
ukiyo: floating world
ukiyo-e: floating world art
Ukiyo monogatari: Tales of the floating world (Asai Ryōi)
Ukiyoburo: The bathhouse of the floating world (Shikitei Sanba)
ukiyo zōshi: stories of the floating world
unjō: business fee or tax
urushi-e: lacquered prints
wabicha: poverty tea
wagaku: Japanese studies
Wagaku goyō: specialist in Japanese learning
Wagaku kōdansho: office for compiling historical records (bakufu)
waka: classical 31-syllable Japanese poem
wakadoshiyori: junior councillor
wakashū kabuki: youth's kabuki
wakō: Japanese pirates
Yakubun sentei: Helps for translation (Ogyū Sorai)
yamase: cooling effect of summer polar air over Tōhoku

Yamato-e: classical Japanese style of painting
yōgaku: Western or European learning
yomi: dark world of the dead
yomihon: books for reading; serious fiction (shōsetsu)
yonaoshi: world renewal
yonaoshi daimyōjin: a god of world renewal; savior and rectifier
yoriki: police captain; head of police unit
Yoshida Shintō: a body of Shintō interpretation
Yoshiwara makura: Yoshiwara pillow (anonymous)
yūgei: polite accomplishments
Yuiitsu Shintō: a body of Shintō interpretation
yūkaku: licensed quarters
Zen: a sect of Buddhism
zeni: copper coin

Suggestions for Further Reading in English

These suggestions are intended to guide students to basic works in English, from which they can proceed to other studies that will facilitate fuller exploration of particular topics. Some of those other studies are cited in the footnotes of this book. Others are given in bibliographical works cited here, and yet others can be found in the bibliographies and footnotes of the scholarly studies cited themselves.

INTRODUCTION

The bibliographical guide to works in English that most successfully combines convenience and completeness is John W. Dower, *Japanese History & Culture From Ancient to Modern Times: Seven Basic Bibliographies* (New York: Markus Wiener, 1986). Dower lists both books and articles, arranging them topically within general chronological categories and adding brief annotations after many titles. He also lists other reference works and thus provides a means of pursuing other materials relating to particular topics. Exhaustive listings of new books and articles are provided by the annual *Bibliography of Asian Studies* (Ann Arbor: Association for Asian Studies). Users will discover, however, that as semi-scholarly commentary on current affairs has proliferated during recent decades, the *Bibliography*'s editors have been compelled to multiply their entry categories, with the result that works dealing with topics in early modern Japanese history have become scattered and more difficult to locate.

Of the many reference works on Japanese history, two merit specific note. *The Encyclopedia of Japan,* 7 vols. (Tokyo: Kodansha, 1983), a gold mine of detail, contains numerous entries on the early modern period. The newly issued volumes 4 and 5 of *The Cambridge History of Japan* (Cambridge: Cambridge University Press, 1989–), consist of essays on early modern Japan that are

solid summaries of standard topics and reflect the dominant interpretations of
the preceding three decades.

PART ONE: BACKGROUND

Readings on the background to early modern Japan's history cover diverse topics, which must be treated separately.

CHAPTER ONE: GEOGRAPHY AND CLIMATE

Teikoku's Complete Atlas of Japan (Tokyo: Teikoku-shoin, 1977) is a convenient atlas. Yoshida Takashi, ed., *An Outline of the Geology of Japan,* 3d ed.
(Kawasaki: Chishitsu Chōsajo, 1976) is a concise, technical discussion of geology.
     Translations of eighteen excellent technical essays by Japanese specialists
may be found in Association of Japanese Geographers, eds., *Geography of Japan* (Tokyo: Teikoku-shoin, 1980). Among them are pieces on climate, geology, historical geography, and the geography of contemporary Japan. A valuable discussion of geography as a discipline in the study of early modern Japan
is Kären Wigen, "The Geographic Imagination in Early Modern Japanese History: Retrospect and Prospect," *JAS* 51-1 (February 1992).
     On weather in Japanese history, a number of scholars, most notably H. Ara-
kawa, have written pertinent essays, as indicated in the footnotes.

CHAPTER TWO: THE HUMAN LEGACY

The scholarly literature on Japan before 1568 is extensive but badly imbalanced: a few general accounts, a growing number of fine archaeological studies,
a few works on art history, a comparative wealth of detailed monographs and
translations on elite politics, literature, and religion, and little else. In part this
situation reflects the historical record—scholars have written about what was
most fully documented—but it also reflects scholarly interests. In recent years
this concentration on the activities of the favored few has begun to change, but
the trend is still in its early stages. Only time will make it possible for us to
present with any confidence the fuller-bodied picture of pre-1568 history that
one wishes to see.
     Among general accounts, the most detailed is in volumes 1 and 2 of George
B. Sansom, *A History of Japan,* 3 vols. (Stanford: Stanford University Press,
1963). Chapters 1–5 of Mikiso Hane, *Premodern Japan, A Historical Survey*
(Boulder, Colo.: Westview Press, 1991) offer a readable and factually solid
overview. A general account that treats higher culture felicitously is H. Paul
Varley, *Japanese Culture* (Honolulu: University of Hawaii Press, 1984). A short
account that touches themes found in this chapter is Conrad Totman, *Japan
before Perry* (Berkeley and Los Angeles: University of California Press, 1981).
A valuable source book that has, regrettably, been out of print for several years

is David John Lu, *Sources of Japanese History*, 2 vols. (New York: McGraw-Hill, 1974).

On village life, the best and most provocative study is William Wayne Farris, *Population, Disease, and Land in Early Japan, 645–900* (Cambridge, Mass.: Harvard University Press, 1985). It will be supplemented in future, we may hope, by the work of Kristina Troost, who has recently completed her doctoral study of the development of agriculture and village life during the medieval centuries. Insight into the religious life of villagers can be derived from Ichiro Hori, *Folk Religion in Japan* (Chicago: University of Chicago Press, 1968).

The political legacy has been the focus of nearly all historical studies in English, which Dower lists carefully. For narrative politics, Sansom's first two volumes provide an ample beginning. A solid study of the long-term evolution of political institutions is John W. Hall, *Government and Local Power in Japan, 500–1700* (Princeton: Princeton University Press, 1966). On the long-term evolution of military institutions, see a forthcoming study by William W. Farris. For insight into the political complexities of the centuries just preceding the early modern reconsolidation, consult John Whitney Hall and Toyoda Takeshi, eds., *Japan in the Muromachi Age* (Berkeley and Los Angeles: University of California Press, 1977).

On the religious legacy, scholars have recently produced a number of fine monographic studies. At a more general level, besides Hori's account cited above, there is a reissue of the pioneer 1930 study by Masaharu Anesaki, *History of Japanese Religion* (Rutland, Vt.: Charles E. Tuttle, 1963), and somewhat more recently, Joseph H. Kitagawa, *Religion in Japanese History* (New York: Columbia University Press, 1966).

The commercial legacy is lamentably understudied, but Dower lists a few titles. George Sansom discusses medieval commerce briefly in volume 2 of his *History of Japan*. The old study by Takao Tsuchiya, "An Economic History of Japan," *TASJ*, 2d ser., 15 (1937), contains useful information on developments in technology and material production.

The urban tradition as elite culture is well studied, as reference to Dower indicates. In its sociological dimensions it has been examined in chapters 2–4 of Takeo Yazaki, *Social Change and the City in Japan* (Tokyo: Japan Publications, 1968). Ivan Morris, *The World of the Shining Prince* (Baltimore: Penguin Books, 1969), evokes the ethos of the aristocratic few during the heyday of Heian. Edward G. Seidensticker has prepared a helpful abridged translation of *The Tale of Genji* (New York: Vintage Books, 1990). And the classic compilation, Ryusaku Tsunoda et al., eds., *Sources of the Japanese Tradition* (New York: Columbia University Press, 1958), provides revealing translations of the urban elite's primarily religious intellectual legacy.

CHAPTER THREE: EARLY MODERN JAPAN

The most complete general coverage of early modern Japan is offered by George Sansom's epic trilogy, *A History of Japan*, specifically the last 125 pages of volume 2 and all of volume 3. Although dated in many ways, the pertinent parts of his two older works, *Japan: A Short Cultural History* (New York: Appleton-Century-Crofts, 1943) and *The Western World and Japan* (New York: Knopf, 1951), still merit rereading. For a pleasant but static descriptive treatment of early modern society, see Charles J. Dunn, *Everyday Life in Traditional Japan* (New York: G. P. Putnam's Sons, 1969). A new collection of essays on social and economic history by noted Japanese scholars is Chie Nakane and Shinzaburō Ōishi, eds., *Tokugawa Japan: The Social and Economic Antecedents of Modern Japan* (Tokyo: University of Tokyo Press, 1990).

Two major assemblages of information require mention here because they are too grand for other locations. One is Yosaburo Takekoshi, *Economic Aspects of the History of the Civilization of Japan*, 3 vols. (New York: Macmillan, 1930), a richly detailed but poorly arranged body of data on aspects of material history, primarily for the early modern period. The other is John H. Wigmore, *Law and Justice in Tokugawa Japan: Materials for the History of Japanese Law and Justice under the Tokugawa Shogunate, 1603–1867*, 10 parts (Tokyo: University of Tokyo Press, 1969–), a massive collection of documents and Meiji-era analyses of the Tokugawa judicial system.

PART TWO: THE ERA OF PACIFICATION, 1570–1630

Works on the years 1570–1630 nicely reveal the priorities that foreign scholars bring to the subject. They primarily focus on two topics: politics and the European presence.

A splendid bibliographical source is Bardwell L. Smith, "Japanese Society and Culture in the Momoyama Era: A Bibliographic Essay," in George Elison and Bardwell L. Smith, eds., *Warlords, Artists, and Commoners: Japan in the Sixteenth Century* (Honolulu: University of Hawaii Press, 1981). That essay is so exhaustive and so well organized that further citation of pre-1980 works seems almost frivolous. However, it may be helpful to list a few references, and the reader who wishes a fuller bibliography should turn to the Smith essay.

For general accounts, one may consult the basic texts mentioned previously, notably the last chapters of volume 2 and first chapters of volume 3 of the Sansom trilogy.

The European involvement received its classic treatment in C. R. Boxer, *The Christian Century in Japan* (Berkeley and Los Angeles: University of California Press, 1951). Michael Cooper, comp., *They Came to Japan: An Anthology of European Reports on Japan, 1543–1640* (Berkeley and Los Angeles: University of California Press, 1965), is a skillfully organized collection of observations that European visitors made about Japan during this period. A provocative study of the intellectual interaction of missionary and Japanese is George Elison, *Deus Destroyed: The Image of Christianity in Early Modern Japan* (Cambridge, Mass.: Harvard University Press, 1973). A recent work that examines English activity is Derek Massarella, *A World Elsewhere: Europe's Encounter with Japan in the Sixteenth and Seventeenth Centuries* (New Haven: Yale University Press, 1990).

Political history has been examined in considerable detail. Two recent and valuable works are the set of essays edited by John Whitney Hall, Nagahara Keiji, and Kozo Yamamura, *Japan before Tokugawa: Political Consolidation and Economic Growth, 1500 to 1650* (Princeton: Princeton University Press, 1981), and the interpretive political biography by Mary Elizabeth Berry, *Hideyoshi* (Cambridge, Mass.: Harvard University Press, 1982). One should also consult chapters 10–13 of Hall's *Government and Local Power,* cited above. The fullest study of Nobunaga's policy is Neil McMullin, *Buddhism and the State in Sixteenth-Century Japan* (Princeton: Princeton University Press, 1984). A less scholarly work, but one that provides biographical detail on the Tokugawa founder, is Conrad Totman, *Tokugawa Ieyasu: Shogun* (South San Francisco: Heian International, 1983). A splendid examination of the role of foreign relations in domestic politics of the day is Ronald P. Toby, *State and Diplomacy in Early Modern Japan: Asia in the Development of the Tokugawa Bakufu* (Princeton: Princeton University Press, 1984).

Economic development of these decades has yet to receive book-length treatment, although a substantial portion of Robert LeRoy Innes, *The Door Ajar: Japan's Foreign Trade in the Seventeenth Century,* 2 vols. (Ann Arbor: University Microfilms, 1980), deals with foreign trade of this period. The only essay that focuses on overall domestic economic development is Kozo Yamamura, "Returns on Unification: Economic Growth in Japan, 1550–1650," in Hall et al., *Japan before Tokugawa,* cited above. A recent essay that deserves note because it focuses on a field of inquiry nearly unstudied in English is Nagahara Keiji and Kozo Yamamura, "Shaping the Process of Unification: Technological Progress in Sixteenth- and Seventeenth-Century Japan," *JJS* 14-1 (Winter 1988).

The cultural blossoming of Azuchi-Momoyama, particularly the arts, has attracted considerable attention, notably in the set of essays edited by Elison and Smith, *Warlords, Artists, and Commoners,* cited above, which will guide readers to other works. A handsomely illustrated examination of *nanban* ("southern barbarian") art of the day is Yoshitomo Okamoto, *The Namban Art of Japan* (Tokyo: Weatherhill, 1972).

PART THREE: THE HEYDAY OF THE TOKUGAWA ORDER, 1630–1710

Much of the older scholarship on early modern Japan focuses on the Tokugawa heyday, and political history is, again, the main area of attention. Seventeenth-century higher culture, notably intellectual and literary trends, have also been much studied.

Studies of political history have focused on bakufu and daimyo administration. Several of the latter were reissued as a volume edited by John W. Hall and Marius B. Jansen, *Studies in the Institutional History of Early Modern Japan* (Princeton: Princeton University Press, 1968). *Fudai* daimyo are examined in Harold Bolitho, *Treasures among Men: The Fudai Daimyo in Tokugawa Japan* (New Haven: Yale University Press, 1974). For a general description of the bakufu, see Conrad Totman, *Politics in the Tokugawa Bakufu, 1600–1843* (Cambridge, Mass.: Harvard University Press, 1967; paperback, Berkeley and

Los Angeles: University of California Press, 1988). The 1988 edition contains an updated bibliography of works on early modern political history. The imperial court is examined in Herschel Webb, *The Japanese Imperial Institution in the Tokugawa Period* (New York: Columbia University Press, 1968). A splendid, specialized study is Toshio G. Tsukahira, *Feudal Control in Tokugawa Japan: The Sankin Kōtai System* (Cambridge, Mass.: Harvard University Press, 1966). A recent, specialized essay that deserves citation because it illuminates the mechanics of the land-tax system, upon which the polity depended for fiscal survival, is Philip C. Brown, "The Mismeasure of Land: Land Surveying in the Tokugawa Period," *MN* 42-2 (Summer 1987). Kate Wildman Nakai, *Shogunal Politics: Arai Hakuseki and the Premises of Tokugawa Rule* (Cambridge, Mass.: Harvard University Press, 1988), focuses on the regime at the end of its heyday but provides considerable information on earlier decades.

On the economy, works tend to be thin, probably because, compared to later times, statistical data are scarce and solid analysis is difficult. Takekoshi is the richest source of information on the economy as a whole. A readable and provocative interpretation is Charles David Sheldon, *The Rise of the Merchant Class in Tokugawa Japan, 1600–1868* (Locust Valley, N.Y.: J. J. Augustin, 1958), chapters 1–5 dealing with the seventeenth century. For a different perspective, a valuable and concise essay is E. S. Crawcour, "Changes in Japanese Commerce in the Tokugawa Period," in Hall and Jansen, eds., *Studies,* cited above. Yamamura's "Returns on Unification," in Hall et al., eds, *Japan before Tokugawa,* covers much of the heyday, and Ennis's fine study, *The Door Ajar,* examines international trade. It also contains an invaluable bibliography. Because urban growth was greatest during the seventeenth century, city growth has received some attention. Chapters 5 and 6 of Yazaki's *Social Change and the City* contain useful information. The most felicitous investigation of seventeenth-century urbanization is James L. McClain's handsome *Kanazawa: A Seventeenth-Century Japanese Castle Town* (New Haven: Yale University Press, 1982).

The intellectual life of the century has received considerable attention, as Dower's bibliography indicates. Readers will also find a valuable bibliography in Mary Evelyn Tucker, *Moral and Spiritual Cultivation in Japanese Neo-Confucianism: The Life and Thought of Kaibara Ekken (1630–1714)* (Albany: State University of New York Press, 1989). The most insightful examination of seventeenth-century thought as a whole is Herman Ooms, *Tokugawa Ideology: Early Constructs, 1570–1680* (Princeton: Princeton University Press, 1985). Two collections of essays merit note: Peter Nosco, ed., *Confucianism and Tokugawa Culture* (Princeton: Princeton University Press, 1984), and Wm. Theodore de Bary and Irene Bloom, eds., *Principle and Practicality* (New York: Columbia University Press, 1979). Tsunoda's *Sources,* cited above, offers translations of excerpts from several thinkers.

The creative arts have also been widely treated. Several beautifully illustrated books, such as Hiroshi Mizuo's *Edo Painting: Sōtatsu and Kōrin* (New York: Weatherhill, 1972) and Richard Lane, *Images from the Floating World* (New York: G. P. Putnam's Sons, 1978), examine the works of famous painters and print artists. David Chibbett, *The History of Japanese Printing and Book Illustration* (Tokyo, Kodansha, 1977), provides a valuable overview of his subject.

A new and elegant study of early modern book-making that focuses on prints is Jack Hillier, *The Art of the Japanese Book*, 2 vols. (London: Philip Wilson Ltd. for Sotheby's Publications, 1987). The early chapters of Donald Keene's masterful *World within Walls* (New York: Grove Press, 1976), examine seventeenth-century prose and poetry and provide leads to other studies and translations. Works focusing on *ukiyo* culture are numerous. A delightful introduction to Ihara Saikaku is Ivan Morris, tr., *The Life of an Amorous Woman and Other Stories* (New York: New Directions, 1963). On kabuki, a good scholarly introduction, with leads to other works, is James R. Brandon et al., *Studies in Kabuki: Its Acting, Music, and Historical Context* (Honolulu: University Press of Hawaii, 1978).

Ecological history of the seventeenth century remains largely unexamined. Chapters 3 and 4 of Conrad Totman, *The Green Archipelago: Forestry in Preindustrial Japan* (Berkeley and Los Angeles: University of California Press, 1989), address forest matters. William Kelly, *Water Control in Tokugawa Japan: Irrigation Organization in a Japanese River Basin, 1600–1870*, East Asia Papers, 31 (Ithaca, N.Y.: Cornell University, 1982), describes the growth and operation of an irrigation system in Tōhoku. In addition, the essays by Kozo Yamamura cited above, as well as the early chapters of T. C. Smith's great classic, *The Agrarian Origins of Modern Japan* (Stanford: Stanford University Press, 1959), contain material germane to the topic.

PART FOUR: STRUGGLING TO STAND STILL, 1710–1790

For a long time the eighteenth century was treated as the "dead" middle of the Tokugawa period, the poorly articulated time after the system was established and before its disintegration became pronounced. More recently, scholars have begun to explore this wasteland, but mostly in the realm of intellectual history, leaving many areas to be treated. And much of the investigation treats the century in larger terms of later Tokugawa history as a whole or as a subject for dissection in terms of a pre-environmentalist "modernization" model.

Ecological history of the later Tokugawa period, as the footnotes to chapters 12 and 13 reveal, is little treated in English. A valuable study of epidemic disease is Ann Bowman Jannetta, *Epidemics and Mortality in Early Modern Japan* (Princeton: Princeton University Press, 1987). Fisheries, riverine affairs, and coal use are nearly unexamined; crop failure and famine have received only glancing attention.

Demography has received enough attention to stand as an independent category, thanks largely to the dedicated pioneering work of Hayami Akira. Apart from Hayami's own crucial contributions, a large number of essays have emerged from the pens of such scholars as Laurel Cornell, Griffith Feeney, W. Mark Fruin, Susan B. Hanley, Arne Kalland, Carl Mosk, and T. C. Smith. Two book-length works merit specific citation: Susan B. Hanley and Kozo Yamamura, *Economic and Demographic Change in Preindustrial Japan, 1600–1868* (Princeton: Princeton University Press, 1977), and Thomas C. Smith, *Naka-*

hara: Family Farming and Population in a Japanese Village, 1717–1830 (Stanford: Stanford University Press, 1977).

Rural affairs have received valuable attention. Besides *Agrarian Origins*, cited above, T. C. Smith recently issued a collection of his essays as *Native Sources of Japanese Industrialization, 1750–1920* (Berkeley and Los Angeles: University of California Press, 1988). Mention must be made of a fine new essay by Tsuneo Satō, "Tokugawa Villages and Agriculture," in the abovementioned *Tokugawa Japan*, ed. by Chie Nakane and Shinzaburō Ōishi. On social attitudes and unrest, the pioneering study by Hugh Borton, "Peasant Uprisings in Japan of The Tokugawa Period," *TASJ*, 2d ser., 16 (May 1938): 1–219, has been followed by many fine scholarly essays and book-length studies, which are discussed in the bibliographical essay by Conrad Totman, "Tokugawa Peasants: Win, Lose, or Draw?" *MN* 41-4 (Winter 1986). See, in particular, titles by Herbert P. Bix, William J. Chambliss, William B. Hauser, William Kelly, Irwin Scheiner, Stephen Vlastos, and Anne Walthall.

Politics of the eighteenth century has received spotty treatment. The most remarkable lacunae relate to the shogun Yoshimune and the domains of major daimyo. Kate Nakai's earlier-noted study, *Shogunal Politics*, examines affairs around 1710. John W. Hall, *Tanuma Okitsugu (1719–1788), Forerunner of Modern Japan* (Cambridge, Mass.: Harvard University Press, 1955), and Herman Ooms, *Charismatic Bureaucrat: A Political Biography of Matsudaira Sadanobu, 1758–1829* (Chicago: University of Chicago Press, 1975), examine those two major political figures. Although published studies of eighteenth-century daimyo domains do not exist, a few fine works are currently being written. And there are, as footnotes indicate, a number of valuable essays on monetary affairs, other aspects of the economy, and intellectual life that have relevance to the polity. Kozo Yamamura, *A Study of Samurai Income and Entrepreneurship* (Cambridge, Mass.: Harvard University Press, 1974), deals with the fiscal condition of shogunal vassals.

Educational developments of the later Tokugawa period have been treated in a number of fine works. Three books merit note. Herbert Passin, *Society and Education in Japan* (New York: Teachers College Press, 1965), is mainly concerned with the modern period. R. P. Dore, *Education in Tokugawa Japan* (Berkeley and Los Angeles: University of California Press, 1965), is strongest on domain schools. Richard Rubinger, *Private Academies of Tokugawa Japan* (Princeton: Princeton University Press, 1982), focuses on proprietary schools.

Intellectual activity of the eighteenth century has begun to receive solid attention in both articles and books. Besides the two earlier cited collections of essays edited by Nosco and by de Bary and Bloom, several books merit citation. Robert N. Bellah, *Tokugawa Religion: The Values of Pre-Industrial Japan* (Glencoe, Ill.: Free Press, 1957), a study of Shingaku, and J. R. McEwan, *The Political Writings of Ogyū Sorai* (Cambridge: Cambridge University Press, 1962), are pioneer works that set high standards of scholarly excellence. Olof G. Lidin has written extensively on Ogyū Sorai, as in *Distinguishing the Way* (Tokyo: Sophia University Press, 1970), his annotated translation of Sorai's *Bendō*. Maruyama Masao, *Studies in the Intellectual History of Tokugawa Japan* (Princeton: Princeton University Press, 1974), established an interpretive framework that still shapes scholarly thought. Its influence is evident in Tetsuo Najita, *Japan* (Englewood Cliffs, N.J.: Prentice-Hall, 1974), an interpretation of long-term change in Tokugawa and later thought. Najita's *Visions of Virtue in Tokugawa Japan: The Kaitokudō Merchant Academy of Osaka* (Chicago: University of Chicago Press, 1987), is a careful study of Osaka merchant thought in the later Tokugawa period. Shigeru Matsumoto, *Motoori Norinaga, 1730–1801* (Cambridge, Mass.: Harvard University Press, 1970), offers a thoughtful profile of that scholar, and Peter Nosco, *Remembering Paradise: Nativism and Nostalgia in Eighteenth-Century Japan* (Cambridge, Mass.: Harvard University Press, 1990), is a splendid treatment of key eighteenth-century nativist scholars.

The later *ukiyo* arts and letters are treated in several of the works cited earlier as well as in an array of specialized literary and artistic studies, as footnotes indicate. Keene's *World within Walls* deals with the century extensively, and essays in C. Andrew Gerstle, ed., *18th Century Japan* (Sydney: Allen & Unwin, 1989), explore particular topics.

PART FIVE: THE EROSION OF STABILITY, 1790–1850

The historiography of the early nineteenth century is a very mixed bag. The history of the century's latter half is such a mesmerizing topic that scholars have had little luck in examining earlier decades in terms of their own priorities. Mostly they are treated as prelude to the main event, a tradition reflected in this volume.

Late Tokugawa arts and letters are the topics where scholarship has been least shackled by hindsight. Besides the valuable chapters in Keene's *World within Walls,* a growing number of translations and monographs on literature and art illuminate the age. Calvin L. French, *The Poet-Painters: Buson and his Followers* (Ann Arbor: University of Michigan Museum of Art, 1974), and French's *Shiba Kōkan* (Tokyo: Weatherhill, 1974) provide rich insight into their subjects. As footnotes indicate, a large number of other works by French, Stephen Addiss, James Cahill, Jack Hillier, and others explore facets of this artistic legacy. Two valuable biographies of literary figures are Leon M. Zolbrod, *Takizawa Bakin* (New York: Twayne, 1967), and Robert W. Leutner, *Shikitei Sanba and the Comic Tradition in Edo Fiction* (Cambridge, Mass.: Harvard University Press, 1985). Patricia Fister, *Japanese Women Artists, 1600–1900* (Lawrence: Spencer Museum of Art, University of Kansas, 1988), introduces an impressive array of women poets, painters, and printmakers. And a lovely essay, Edwin McClellan's *Woman in the Crested Kimono* (New Haven: Yale University Press, 1985), offers a rare insight into the life of a cultured woman of the day.

Aspects of popular thought of the nineteenth century have been treated in a number of books and essays. As footnotes indicate, the new religious movements have received attention, as have the pilgrimage and millennialist activities of the age. The two-part essay by Winston Davis, "Pilgrimage and World Renewal," in *History of Religions* 23-2 and 3 (1984), seems particularly helpful.

Dutch learning, or *rangaku,* has long received substantial attention. French's biography of *Shiba Kōkan* sheds light on a major *rangaku* figure. One of the early interpretive essays was Donald Keene, *The Japanese Discovery of Europe, 1720–1830* (Stanford: Stanford University Press, 1969; revised and expanded from a work published in 1952). Three valuable sources of detail on *rangaku* are these: Grant K. Goodman, *Japan: The Dutch Experience* (London: Athlone Press, 1986; revised from a work published in 1967); *MN* 19, combined issue no. 3–4 (1964); *AA,* no. 42 (1982). The two journal issues are collections of specialized essays by Japanese scholars that examine the corpus of works known as *rangaku.*

Scholarly intellectual life became highly politicized during the nineteenth century, as is apparent from studies of the topic. Ooms's earlier-cited study of Matsudaira Sadanobu, *Charismatic Bureaucrat,* together with the *HJAS* essays in which Robert L. Backus examines Sadanobu's policies on scholarship and ideology, show early symptoms of this development. The nativist thought of *Mitogaku* and *kokugaku* is the topic of several studies. A broadly arched pioneer work was David Magarey Earl, *Emperor and Nation in Japan* (Seattle: University of Washington Press, 1964). Also broad in its agenda was H. D. Harootunian, *Toward Restoration: The Growth of Political Consciousness in Tokugawa Japan* (Berkeley and Los Angeles: University of California Press, 1970). *Mitogaku* is central to three valuable works. Richard T. Chang, *From Prejudice to Tolerance* (Tokyo: Sophia University Press, 1970), explores the interplay of established views and new information about the West. Bob Tadashi Wakabayashi, *Anti-Foreignism and Western Learning in Early Modern Japan* (Cambridge, Mass.: Harvard University Press, 1986), examines that issue in the influential essay *Shinron,* by Aizawa Seishisai. J. Victor Koschmann, *The Mito Ideology* (Berkeley and Los Angeles: University of California Press, 1987), treats *Mitogaku* in its domestic context. Nineteenth-century *kokugaku* is the topic of Harootunian's *Things Seen and Unseen* (Chicago: University of Chicago Press, 1988). Finally, a collection of essays that merits note here is Tetsuo Najita and Irwin Scheiner, eds., *Japanese Thought in the Tokugawa Period, 1600–1868* (Chicago: University of Chicago Press, 1978).

Politics of the early nineteenth century are deplorably understudied. A few old essays examine diplomatic incidents and developments. Other political studies look at the period as mere background to the Restoration and subsequent developments. Essays by Marius B. Jansen and Harold Bolitho in volume 5 of *The Cambridge History of Japan* only begin to remedy the situation.

Aspects of foreign relations are examined in several solid works. A pioneer study of relations with Britain is H. Paske-Smith, *Western Barbarians in Japan and Formosa in Tokugawa Days, 1603–1868* (1930; New York: Paragon Book Reprint Corp., 1968). W. G. Beasley, *Great Britain and the Opening of Japan, 1834–1858* (London: Luzac, 1951), is a more scholarly treatment. On the northern regions and Russo-Japanese relations, there are several valuable studies, notably George Alexander Lensen, *The Russian Push toward Japan: Russo-Japanese Relations, 1697–1875* (Princeton: Princeton University Press, 1959), and John J. Stephan, *The Kuril Islands* (London: Oxford University Press, 1974). On U.S.–Japan relations, a new book whose bibliography will guide readers to older works is Peter Booth Wiley, *Yankees in the Land of the Gods* (New York: Viking, 1990).

EPILOGUE

The political process of the 1850s–1860s that led to the Meiji Restoration has received much attention. The first solidly scholarly treatment in English was W. G. Beasley, *Select Documents on Japanese Foreign Policy 1853–1868* (London: Oxford University Press, 1955), which consists of a compact introductory essay and translations of many key documents. Beasley followed that with a major integrative study, *The Meiji Restoration* (Stanford: Stanford University Press, 1972). A series of more specialized works also exists. Albert M. Craig, *Chōshū in the Meiji Restoration* (Cambridge, Mass.: Harvard University Press, 1961); Thomas M. Huber, *The Revolutionary Origins of Modern Japan* (Stanford: Stanford University Press, 1981); Marius B. Jansen, *Sakamoto Ryōma and the Meiji Restoration* (Princeton: Princeton University Press, 1961); Conrad Totman, *The Collapse of the Tokugawa Bakufu, 1862–1868* (Honolulu: University Press of Hawaii, 1980).

The intellectual history of the Restoration is examined in the earlier-cited works of Earl, Harootunian, and Koschmann, and in some of the essays in Tetsuo Najita and J. Victor Koschmann, eds., *Conflict in Modern Japanese History* (Princeton: Princeton University Press, 1982).

Social aspects of these decades are suggested by a few translated works such as Fukuzawa Yukichi, *The Autobiography of Fukuzawa Yukichi*, tr. Eiichi Kiyooka (1899; New York: Columbia University Press, 1966), and Shimazaki Tōson, *Before the Dawn* (Honolulu, University of Hawaii Press, 1988). Diverse topics are treated in the seventeen essays found in Marius B. Jansen and Gilbert Rozman, eds., *Japan in Transition from Tokugawa to Meiji* (Princeton: Princeton University Press, 1986).

Index

1. Birth and death dates are given where known.
2. Consult the Glossary for the meaning of Japanese terms not listed in the Index.
3. To locate schools and literary and art works not listed by title in the Index, consult the Glossary.

Key Terms: guides to other entries (printed in **bold type** in index)

Art	Government	Science
Commerce	Letters	Society
Environment	Primary Production	Theater
Foreign Relations	Religion	

Index 589

and, 321–23; in early Tokugawa, 97–98, 108, 111–12, 115–16, 240; in later Tokugawa, 317–21, 442–43; millennialism, 445–47; new religions, 447–50; pilgrimage, 443–45; Tanuma and, 341, 343, 345–46; Yoshimune and, 294–95, 308, 309, 311, 315. *See also* Corvée labor; Famine; Millennialism; Shimabara rebellion; Uchikowashi
Publishing: later, 198–99, 210–11, 213, 382, 390, 421; pacification and, 87, 94, 96. *See also* Libraries; Literacy; Saga bon
Puppet theater: in Genroku, 210, 217–22; in seventeenth century, 199, 200, in eighteenth century, 382, 385–86
Pusan, 48, 76–77, 142–43, 311

Quaeckernaeck, Jacob, 77

Raffles, Stamford, 498
Rai San'yō (1780–1832), 425
Rakugo, 417, 421
Rakuichi, 72, 157
Rangaku. *See* European learning
Rationing. *See* Sumptuary regulation
Religion. *See* Buddhism; Christianity; Confucianism; Kokugaku; Millenialism; New Religions; Shingaku; Shintō
Renga, 26, 86, 201
Resource depletion: arable land, 248, 294; forest products, 224, 226–29, 246, 261–62, 268, 271, 273, 324–25; precious metals, 141, 143, 146, 147, 224–26, 311. *See also* Fertilizer; Sumptuary regulation
Rezanov, Nikolai, 487–88, 497
Rice, 6. *See also* Agriculture
Ricord, Petr, 491–92
Rikugien, 189, 284
River problems: later rulers and, 337, 343, 481; in seventeenth century, 227, 300; in later Tokugawa, 238–39, 242–43, 269–70; Yoshimune and, 300, 314. *See also* Soil erosion
Rodrigues, João, 9
Rōjū, 107, 131, 342, 518, 532
Rōnin, 37–38; abroad, 54, 74, 113; Akō incident, 222; in mid-seventeenth century, 126–28, 131, 171; later individuals, 302, 337, 363, 414, 415, 466, 517; at Osaka in 1615, 52–53, 55; scholarship and, 161, 163, 164, 349; specific instances of, 165, 171, 217, 283–84. *See also*

Kanadehon chūshingura; Yui Shōsetsu
Rubinger, Richard, 352
Russians: contacts around 1800, 276–78, 454, 482–93, 499, 505; in 1860s, 546, 549; views on, 275–76, 278, 457, 459–60, 497, 510. *See also* Ezo region
Ryōkan (1758–1831), 423
Ryukyus: Europeans and, 498, 501, 533, 549; in Ieyasu's day, 76, 77; Satsuma and, 142–43, 312, 313
Ryūtei Tanehiko (1783–1842), 418–19

Saga bon, 94, 187, 190, 192, 198
Saga domain, 350; in 1840s, 534, 535; and *Phaeton,* 494–96
Saitō Dōsan (?–1556), 24
Sakai Tadakiyo (1623–1681), 131–32
Sakata Tōjūrō (1647–1709), 217, 220
Sakhalin, 460, 488, 489, 490, 549. *See also* Ezo region
Sakoku, 117, 270. *See also* Uchiharai
Sakuma Shōzan (1811–64), 425, 440, 453
Sakura Sōgorō (?–?), 319–20
Sakuramachi (1720–50), 309
Salt production, 229, 271–72
Samisen, 88, 213
Samurai. *See* Bunbu; Bushidō; Daimyo domains; Gokenin; Hatamoto; Political thought; Rōnin; Shogunate
Sangawara, 297–98
Sanke, 118, 458, 521
Sankin kōtai: consequences of, 134, 150, 153, 158, 214, 219; daimyo and, 117, 121, 125, 126, 152, 188; establishment of, 108–11; Kyōhō reform and, 289, 299, 300, 307
Santō Kyōden (1761–1816), 415, 416, 419, 420, 472
Satake Shozan (Yoshiatsu) (1748–85), 409–10
Satō Nobuhiro (Shin'en) (1769–1850), 437, 453–56, 476, 519, 534; influences on, 413, 463–64
Satomura Jōha (1524–1602), 86
Satsuma, xxv, 67, 119; and Europeans, 502, 533, 534; in 1860s, 542, 544–45; and Ryukyus, 77, 142, 533; and sugarcane, 312, 332, 519; Tenpō reform in, 518, 519
Savant, 163–66, 186, 337, 349
Science. *See* Agronomic writings; Astronomy; European learning; Medicine
Seidan, 284, 286, 287